THE ONLY GUIDE CONTAINING OVER 100 PAGES OF THE OFFICIAL *INTERNAL REVENUE MANUAL FOR AUDITORS*, FULLY ANNOTATED BY THE AUTHOR

The Internal Revenue Service's army of auditors, slated to grow by a monumental 40 percent, will soon examine over two million returns each year. Now more than ever before, it is vital that every taxpayer learn how to avoid an audit, or, if the infamous "audit invitation" arrives, how to cope with the IRS.

Audit-Proof Your Tax Return is the first book to offer everything you need to know about developing your own audit-proofing strategy—an ongoing program designed to keep you out of tax trouble before, during, and after an audit!

AUDIT-PROOF YOUR TAX RETURN

JACK WARREN WADE, JR., an IRS Revenue Officer from 1971 to 1979, is the author of the bestselling tax references, *When You Owe the IRS* and *How to Reduce Your Withholding and Increase Your Take-Home Pay*. He is a consultant for the National Taxpayers Union and sits on the board of directors of the National Society of Tax Professionals. He lives in Oakton, Virginia.

Audit-Proof Your Tax Return

Revised and Updated Edition

Jack Warren Wade, Jr.

A PLUME BOOK
NEW AMERICAN LIBRARY
NEW YORK AND SCARBOROUGH, ONTARIO

PUBLISHER'S NOTE

This publication is designed to provide accurate and authoritative information in regard to the subject matter covered. It is sold with the understanding that the publisher is not engaged in rendering legal, accounting or other professional service. If legal advice or other expert assistance is required, the service of a competent professional person should be sought.

Published by arrangement with Macmillan Publishing Company.

PLUME TRADEMARK REG. U.S. PAT. OFF. AND FOREIGN COUNTRIES
REG. TRADEMARK—MARCA REGISTRADA
HECHO EN HARRISONBURG, VA., U.S.A.

SIGNET, SIGNET CLASSIC, MENTOR, ONYX, PLUME, MERIDIAN and NAL BOOKS are published *in the United States* by NAL PENGUIN INC., 1633 Broadway, New York, New York 10019, *in Canada* by The New American Library of Canada Limited, 81 Mack Avenue, Scarborough, Ontario M1L 1M8

Library of Congress Cataloging-in-Publication Data

Wade, Jack Warren.
Audit-proof your tax return.

Rev. ed. of: Audit-proofing your return. c1986.
1. Tax auditing—United States. 2. Tax returns —United States. 3. United States. Internal Revenue Service. I. Wade, Jack Warren. Audit-proofing your return. II. Title.
KF6314.Z9W33 1987 343.7305'2 87-17485
ISBN 0-452-25989-4 347.30352

First Plume Printing, November, 1987

1 2 3 4 5 6 7 8 9

PRINTED IN THE UNITED STATES OF AMERICA

Dedicated to Mom and Dad,
for their love and inspiration

Contents

Preface

In the last six years there has been a proliferation of tax, IRS, and financial planning books written for the savvy consumer who likes to handle his or her own affairs. Before 1980 there were no consumer books on the inner workings of the IRS, due to government restrictions on the release of such information. The tax market consisted solely of tax preparation guides. Now there are books that cover everything from audits and delinquent returns to criminal investigations.

All tax guides offer tax tips along with their preparation instructions, and all books on the IRS offer insight and advice for IRS encounters that occur *after* the return has been filed. While many other books offer *tax-planning advice* applicable before filing, none extensively covers pre-filing audit preparation strategies.

It's important to give consideration to the possibility of a future IRS audit *during the tax year* for these reasons:

1. Financial transactions and arrangements have tax ramifications. Thinking about the IRS helps one to become taxwise and to consider the tax benefits and requirements *during* the transaction.
2. An IRS audit not only examines whether you have complied with the tax rules, it also tests whether you can substantiate your deductions and expenses. What better way is there to prepare for proving your deductions and expenses than by knowing what the IRS will accept as proof and what questions they are going to ask?

This is the first book that offers taxpayers such complete inside information that they can develop an audit-proofing strategy when it's most needed—*during the tax year* before the return is filed.

Obviously many taxpayers are afraid of the IRS, and even more afraid of being audited. Writers have tried to help minimize that fear by exposing how the IRS conducts itself, and providing guidance to taxpayers to deal with various problem situations. But there has always been the missing ingredient: the extent of information a taxpayer needs before he or she ever prepares the return.

This book bridges that gap with the creation of an *audit-proofing strategy*. By following the four single steps outlined here in Part I, you will be prepared to face any IRS challenge. You will learn:

- How the IRS selects returns for audit, and the one most important ingredient in the selection process.
- What the IRS requires for proof to substantiate your deductions.
- What rules of law are most commonly tested during an audit.
- What questions the IRS auditor will ask.
- What books and records *must* be kept.
- How to know if an IRS auditor is "out for blood."
- When you must retain a tax attorney.
- How the IRS suspects fraud.
- How to get the IRS to give you a private letter ruling or special technical advice.
- How to determine if the IRS suspects your tax shelter is abusive.
- What tax scams and shams you should avoid.
- Where you stand on the audit totem pole.

As of this writing the IRS is planning to add an additional 7,500 auditors within the next three years, a monumental 40 percent increase over the present staffing of 17,500 revenue agents and tax auditors. With a 40 percent increase in staffing the IRS will soon be auditing over 2 million taxpayers a year. It's now more important than ever that you be properly prepared to deal with this new enforcement posture, in spite of the proposed tax simplification legislation.

In the first edition of this book, I wrote that there was little doubt that 1986 would bring tax reform. After all, I explained, Congress is a tax code junkie, getting its fix by passing biennial reforms, at least seven between 1975 and 1986. The dust had barely settled on the Deficit Reduction Act of 1984, at the time the country's most massive revision of the tax code since 1954, when the Tax Reform Act of 1986 was passed and signed into law. Most tax practitioners had not even recovered from the 1984 act when the 1986 law made thousands of new changes.

Unless you have been living on a desert island, you now know that tax simplification, one of the foremost goals of the Tax Reform Act of 1986, is an illusion. Excepting the 6 million taxpayers who will not have to file a tax return any longer (except to get a refund), the tax preparation process will become much more difficult for the rest of us. Even the Schedule A will include several new mathematical steps making it just a bit more difficult. Because of "tax simplification," the IRS has had to revise over 200 forms and create 40 new ones!

Your first experience with "tax simplification" arose very early in 1987 when the IRS issued a very complex and difficult W-4 form, a form that everyone in the country was forced to file. This was the first evidence that the Tax Reform Act of 1986 was not true "tax simplification." You were led to believe that the new law simplified things because the rate structure was reduced from 14 brackets to 5. This was the illusion of "tax simplification." With this one maneuver, you were supposed to believe that the new law had created true tax reform.

Yet when the dust had settled, it was clear that only a small portion of the Tax Reform Act of 1986 applied to middle-income taxpayers. Over 80% of the law applied to financial institutions, insurance companies, pensions, foreign tax provisions, tax-exempt bonds, trusts and estates, exempt and nonprofit organizations, etc. For all the intensity and behind-the-scenes machinations, the final result of "tax simplification" was dropping a few deductions, changing a few rules, and putting limits on such deductions as miscellaneous itemized deductions and IRAs.

As I wrote in the first edition, tax simplification is *not* inevitable. In this highly technical and complicated world, we have the ability to complicate our lives to an almost incomprehensible degree. The fact is, there will always be taxes, an IRS, and tax audits. After all, if the system were to really be simplified, how long would it last?

Even in the middle of creating "tax simplification" vis-à-vis the Tax Reform Act of 1986, Congress was planning to expand the audit resources of the IRS. Over a three-year period beginning in 1986 the IRS will hire an additional 7,500 auditors, an increase in excess of 50%. Now that the number of audits is scheduled to soar, there is an even greater need for sound audit-proofing strategies.

Audit-Proof Your Tax Return

Introduction Audit-Proofing and the IRS

Let's begin with a true story:

In December 1979, Revenue Agent Richard Boandl of the Philadelphia District was assigned to examine the 1977 tax return of Thomas Treadway. Agent Boandl subsequently audited the 1978, 1979, and 1980 tax returns of Mr. Treadway.

In February 1982, Agent Boandl came to a final assessment of approximately $247,000 in additional taxes against Mr. Treadway, who did not agree with the assessment. Because Agent Boandl became concerned that Mr. Treadway was selling his property and giving the funds to his companion and good friend, Shirley Ann Lojeski, the revenue agent recommended a jeopardy assessment against Mr. Treadway. An extreme measure, a jeopardy assessment allows the IRS, in certain circumstances, to make an immediate assessment and a demand for payment, and, if necessary, to proceed immediately to collect the tax by whatever means necessary.

Agent Boandl testified in court that he never checked the real estate records, nor did he know what funds Mr. Treadway had actually received from the sale of his property.

Even though it was Mr. Treadway who owed the tax, on or about August 3, 1982 Revenue Officer George Jessup (a revenue officer collects delinquent taxes) filed a tax lien against *Ms. Lojeski* in the amount of $247,000 and seized $24,000 from her bank accounts. Jessup testified that he had no approval from his superior before filing the tax lien. Prior to seizing her property, Jessup gave no notice to Ms. Lojeski.

On September 23, 1982 an IRS appeals officer, after conducting an administrative review, determined that the $247,000 assessment was not reasonable and proceeded to abate the tax. But the tax lien against Ms. Lojeski was not released until November 30, and the seized funds were not returned until January 1983, five months after seizure.

Ms. Lojeski testified that after the IRS filed the lien:

- She was threatened with foreclosure on her farm because she didn't have the money to pay her mortgage.
- She couldn't run her horse business because she didn't have the money to buy feed and other items.
- She lost her health and life insurance policies because she did not have the funds to pay the premiums.
- She was sued by one supplier because she did not have the money to pay the bill.
- She had to borrow money to buy groceries.
- She was humiliated, degraded, and withdrawn.
- She didn't leave the farm because she was ashamed to meet people, and because she was afraid that Jessup would come back to the farm and remove her personal property.
- She could not sell her farm because purchasers were leery of the IRS lien.

The U.S. District Court ruled that the IRS had violated her constitutional rights under the Fourth Amendment prohibition of unreasonable searches and seizures, and under the Fifth Amendment guarantee of due process of law. The court granted damages against Agent Boandl and Officer Jessup in the amount of $67,000. (*U.S. District Court, East. Dist. Pa, C.A. No. 84-3591, 01/23/85*)

The IRS appealed the decision to the Third Circuit Court of Appeals, however, where the IRS argued that Ms. Lojeski had no rights of constitutional protection against what they did to her. The court agreed and ruled that the IRS had not violated her Fourth Amendment rights against *warrantless* seizures for the "simple reason that such actions violated no privacy interest." The court totally ignored the fact that Ms. Lojeski *did not owe any taxes*. The case was not appealed to the Supreme Court.

This is the same case you may have seen on ABC's *Nightline* show on April 14, 1987.

WHO'S AFRAID OF THE IRS?

Most people! They fear the awesome power of the IRS; they are afraid of being audited and dread the consequences. It's a fear that comes legitimately, though. For fear is the main ingredient in making voluntary compliance work, the result of an image-building process cultivated by the IRS for decades.

By now you have probably heard horror stories about IRS agents, from backyard neighborhood gossip to *Parade* magazine articles and "60 Minutes" on TV. You are probably already aware of the IRS's reputation for being tough, uncaring, and bureaucratic. You may even have heard of taxpayers who faced burly, growling auditors with the sympathy of a moon rock and the understanding of a doorstop. If you ever had an encounter or unpleasant dealings with tax agents or officers, you've probably already developed fairly strong feeling about them. If you never had an experience with the IRS, you probably have serious questions and concerns about how tough and demanding they are.

After all, everyone knows what the IRS did to Al Capone, the country's most notorious gangster who could not be touched until the IRS got him. That one legendary act has probably done more for voluntary compliance and the image of the IRS than any other event in its history. Fifty years later, taxpayers still remark that they don't want to tangle with the IRS because of what it did to Al Capone.

One of the more memorable IRS incidents involved Spiro Agnew, former vice president under Richard Nixon. Here was the second highest-ranking government official in the United States government, only a heartbeat away from being president, brought down by the IRS.

And, as if President Nixon didn't have his hands full with Watergate and the Spiro Agnew problems, the IRS had over thirty agents conducting the most exhaustive audit ever performed. They literally raked him over the coals with several hundred thousand dollars in additional taxes.

The most recent media event concerning taxes and politicians involved Geraldine Ferraro, the first woman to run for vice president. Her accountant had not reported her husband's real estate transactions properly, prompting immediate filings of amended returns and payments of over $53,459 in additional taxes. Even major politicians take the IRS seriously.

These events have left their lasting impression on tens of millions of taxpayers who have nothing but the utmost respect and the utmost fear of the IRS. Even though the IRS says it does not know why people comply with the tax laws, it knows it has a good thing going. It wants taxpayers to be afraid. Voluntary compliance, though fragile, is the major support of our tax system. There are those inside the IRS who think it is their mission to make people afraid of them, believing the more people are afraid, the more they'll comply with the tax laws. Events like those in Pennsylvania are designed to project a "firm enforcement image."

IRS auditors won't go out of their way to dispel taxpayers' notions about their image. You will find them courteous and polite, but don't expect them to be friendly. First names are a no-no, and so are lunches and dinner. Bringing flowers with you to the audit will *not* enhance your image. Instead it will cast suspicions upon your motives, and result in a more vigorous audit.

Remember that IRS employees are basically suspicious individuals. They don't trust anyone, not even co-workers, so they could hardly be expected to trust taxpayers, particularly those being audited. Forget all the business techniques you've learned about social communication skills. When you walk into an IRS office, you enter a different world.

THE IRS IN A NUTSHELL

The IRS is a gigantic agency with gigantic powers. Consisting of over 102,000 employees, the IRS is undoubtedly one of the government's largest. It has 7 regions and 63 districts with hundreds of posts of duty all around the country. These are the enforcement people you need to be familiar with:

- *Tax Auditors* conduct the audits that are usually handled in the local IRS office. For the most part, tax auditors only conduct audits of 1040 tax returns and related schedules. Occasionally, they may audit 1040s with uncomplicated Schedule Cs.
- *Revenue Agents* conduct audits of the more complicated 1040s and business returns such as 1040s with Schedule Cs, forms 1065, Partnership Income Tax Return, and 1120, Corporation Income Tax Return. Most audits conducted by revenue agents are done on site at the taxpayer's place of business.
- *Revenue Officers* collect delinquent taxes. You will only need to know more about them if you can't pay your audit assessment.
- *Special Agents* conduct criminal investigations. They sometimes carry guns, and sometimes make arrests. If one reads you your rights, you'll know you're in serious trouble.

Tax auditors and revenue agents belong to IRS's Examination Division. The term "examination" relates to what they are really doing when they are challenging your deductions: They are "examining" the return. The IRS does not use the term "audit," but because they *did* use it at one time, it has stuck and the entire country still uses it. Therefore, we will continue to use it in this book.

The term "tax examiner" is also frequently used by the IRS in its internal publication, the *Internal Revenue Manual* (IRM). Because tax auditors and revenue agents use the same IRM, the term "tax examiner" is used to refer to both categories. We will also use that term throughout the book.

Many taxpayers go into an audit totally unprepared and hope for the best. Some think that if they can impress the auditor that they are nice, law-abiding, decent human beings—not common criminals—then the IRS auditor will mellow, be sympathetic, and politely let them off the hook. Forget it! Tax auditors are nice, decent human beings too, but most importantly, *they pay their taxes*. And they don't think too kindly of others who don't. So right off the bat you have two strikes against you in the sympathy and understanding department:

- First, you're not one of them.
- Second, it's assumed that you haven't done everything right on your tax return, otherwise you wouldn't be there!

In the IRS world there is only one mentality that perseveres: *Us against them*. This attitude permeates the organization, from top to bottom. Indirectly, it will even affect your audit, and your relationship with your auditor. There may be times during the audit ordeal and its aftermath that you will come to believe that these people are unreasonable, that they are unconscionable, and that they do not belong to the "brotherhood of man."

This is all part of the game and part of the process of "promoting voluntary compliance."

So, how do you deal with it, you ask? The answer is, through preparation.

AUDIT-PROOFER'S STRATEGY RULE

A good audit-proofer* prepares *for an audit, and when "invited" to an audit,* plans strategy *beforehand.

If you think about it, this is the same technique that you probably use in every other aspect of your life. Planning and preparation are the key ingredients of any successful endeavor, but if you've never been through an IRS audit before, you need to know what to plan, and what to prepare for.

WHAT IS AUDIT-PROOFING?

The basic concept of this book centers on *audit preparation during the tax year,* not next year when you file your tax return, nor two years later when you get an "invitation" from the IRS to "come down and show us your books." *Audit-proofing means preparing* for the possibility of an audit day by day during the current tax year. You prepare for an IRS audit by knowing what tax law rules the IRS could question, and what documentation it could require to substantiate or verify your current on-going deductions and expenses.

In this book, I differentiate audit-proofing from audit-planning: Audit-planning occurs immediately before an impending audit when you prepare your strategy for appearing at an audit. This means that once you receive an audit "invitation" letter, you take the time to plan your defense against the upcoming attack on your tax return. Audit-planning usually involves a strategy session with your tax preparer or consultant, *when the need arises*. Audit-proofing is an on-going activity year-round, every year.

This distinction is vital to understanding the concept of audit-proofing presented in this book. *To audit-proof your tax return means to prepare during the tax year so that you could later withstand the complete scrutiny of an IRS audit*. The objective of an audit-proofed tax return is a "no-change audit"—or an audit, should one occur, that will result in *no additional taxes*.

Audit-proofing does not mean that you will never be audited. No one could ever guarantee that.

Audit-Proofing and Tax-Saving

Audit-proofing does not mean playing it safe. I am *not* advocating a conservative, meek approach to doing your tax return as a means of audit-proofing it. At no point do I suggest that you not take any deductions because they may increase your chances of being audited. On the contrary, you should take every deduction that you are legally entitled to take, regardless of whether it may increase your chances of being audited. *You should not be afraid of taking legitimate deductions because you are afraid of being audited*. No matter how scary the prospect seems to you, your tax strategy should not be based on fear.

Your taxes represent your hard-earned dollars. What you pay to the IRS comes right out of your pocket. Forget, for a moment, that taxes are withheld from your paycheck, that you almost never see them, except if they are returned to you in the form of a refund check. Think how hard you've worked and slaved to earn your gross earnings. Every dollar in taxes that you pay comes out of those earnings. If you had less taxes to pay, your paycheck would be bigger. Think what *you* could do with the extra money.

The point is saving in taxes converts to saving dollars: Less to Uncle Sam means more to you. As a necessary tool of financial management, *your tax strategy should always be tax reduction*. Everything you do should be tax-efficient or tax-considerate. That means you should consider the tax ramifications of everything you do that involves money. Buying a house? Getting a divorce? Sending your kids to summer camp? Hiring a babysitter? Making trips to the doctor? All these activities have tax ramifications.

For tax purposes, there's a right way and a wrong way, and the *wrong way will cost you extra dollars*.

Audit-proofing your tax return translates into saving tax dollars in several ways:

- First, when you become disciplined about keeping good records, you will probably end up taking deductions for items you never took before simply because you never knew they were deductible.
- Secondly, with proper recordkeeping you will probably end up taking deductions you never *dared* to before simply because you weren't sure you could support them in the event you were audited.
- Thirdly, if you are audited and win, you won't have to pay additional penalties and interest for the back taxes they would otherwise hit you with.

Perhaps the most worthwhile reason to audit-proof your tax return is the peace of mind that ensues, if you are audited, in knowing what the IRS will be looking for, and being properly prepared for them to find it. For many taxpayers, that advantage alone is worth far more than the cost of this book and the little extra time and effort that goes with audit-proofing.

The purpose of this book is to help you prepare to face the IRS by giving you the information you need to do so. There's an old adage on Wall Street that goes: "If only I could have tomorrow's *Wall Street Journal* today." In the same vein, many taxpayers have come out of a gut-wrenching IRS audit thinking: "If only I had known yesterday what they'd be looking for today."

This book gives you today the equivalent of tomorrow's *Wall Street Journal*. Each chapter contains exhibits of information taken directly out of the official *Internal Revenue Manual for Auditors;* plus, Part Three presents the complete auditing guidelines for practically every item on your tax return. This material is invaluable, so read it carefully.

Audit-proofing your tax return involves these 4 steps:

STEP 1. Keeping proper records for an IRS Audit.
STEP 2. Getting correct information from the IRS (and others).
STEP 3. Knowing what the IRS will be looking for.
STEP 4. Avoiding tax scams, shams, and illegal shelters.

By following these four steps you will help yourself be prepared for the possibility of an IRS audit. While no one can prepare themselves for the circumstances that Mr. Treadway and Ms. Lojeski encountered, by audit-proofing your return, you not only save tax dollars but you will also give yourself significant and invaluable peace of mind. That's not to say that you won't be nervous about being audited; you just shouldn't be *terrified* about it any longer. The information given here should ease a lot of your anxieties about what formerly was a mysterious event.

POPULAR MISCONCEPTIONS ABOUT AN IRS AUDIT

Audit Misconception #1: "I just got my refund check, so that means I won't be audited."

Many taxpayers are relieved when they've gotten their refund check, because they assume it means the IRS has checked over their return, everything's okay, and therefore they won't be audited. This is totally wrong. While the IRS now withholds portions of refunds due to the discovery of obviously erroneous deductions (see Chapter 6), the issuance of a refund has *no* bearing on whether you will be audited.

In the absence of a clearly disallowable deduction, refund checks are sent out, while the determination of who will be audited is made much later, after a series of steps involving computer identification and manual selection procedures. Also, the IRS audits less than 1½ percent of all income tax returns, and it would be a hardship to withhold the refunds of about 75 million taxpayers, just because the other 1.2 million may owe additional taxes.

This misconception also assumes that those who are audited always owe additional taxes as a result of the audit. This is almost true, but in 1986 IRS audits resulted in 68,310 taxpayers receiving refunds of ¾ billion dollars.

From the date a tax return is filed, the IRS has three years to audit and assess additional taxes. There is no time limitation on assessment if the return is false or fraudulent or no return was filed. (The IRS has authority to prepare and sign a return if the taxpayer doesn't.)

The IRS likes to audit a tax return as soon as possible after filing, but many audits occur at least two years after filing. There's no way the IRS would hold up refund checks that long. Besides, the Internal Revenue Code requires the IRS to pay interest on refunds within 45 days of filing or within 45 days of the due date, whichever is later. If the IRS had to pay interest on 75 million refund checks, the cost would be enormous and would far exceed (by billions) the interest that is now charged back to taxpayers on the additional taxes that are now due from the audits of the 1½ percent.

Audit Misconception #2: "Each year I file my tax return around April 15th because it reduces my chances of being audited."

This misconception, started a few years ago by another tax author, was based on an erroneous assumption about the IRS's computer system.

During the processing routine all tax returns are scored or rated for audit potential under IRS's top secret computer program called DIF, for Discriminant Function. The higher the DIF score, the greater the potential of bringing in additional taxes under an audit. The IRS strives to audit the higher-scored returns first because of the expectation of getting more revenue for government coffers. DIF scores are developed from an analysis of a series (involving up to 50,000 randomly selected returns) of intensive audits, conducted every few years, called the Taxpayer Compliance Measurement Program (TCMP). In a TCMP audit, the IRS will analyze *every* item on the tax return, including proof of income. (DIF scores therefore reflect correlated averages found on a cross-section of tax returns.)

The assumption behind this misconception is that a cut-off score of 240 may be the high cut-off score in February when fewer returns are filed, but 260 may be the cut-off score in April when more returns are filed. Therefore, if your DIF score is somewhere between 240 and 260, then your chances of being audited are lessened by filing in April when everyone else files.

This misconception is based on a poor understanding of how returns are selected for audit. The selection process does not even begin until after the end of June, over two months past the end of the April 15 filing deadline. The first step occurs when computer-selected returns are arranged in batches by examination class, a method used to categorize returns by the total amount of income reported. All returns are placed into one of 12 classes based on their total positive income (TPI) for individuals or total gross receipts (TGR) for businesses. (See Exhibit 5-3 in Chapter 5 for a breakdown of each TPI and TGR category, the number and percentage of returns audited and the average tax and penalty recommended per return in each category.)

Throughout the year, district IRS offices place orders with the IRS service centers for returns to audit. The service center then pulls those returns that are above a specific DIF cutoff score and sends them to the district office. Districts are required to order returns numerous times over a twelve-month period so that all tax returns, regardless of their filing date, have an equal chance of being delivered to the district for classification, a manual selection procedure performed by revenue agents called classifiers.

Another aspect of the selection system is the actual classification process. The IRS requires that the highest DIF scores within each examination class be pulled and manually screened for audit potential by the classifier. A high DIF score is "any return with a score above the median score delivered for each examination class."

If it appears to the classifier that the tax return is in order or that you have included sufficient substantiating or appropriate documentation with the return, the return will most likely be sent back to the service center without being audited. The classifier relies on his or her experience, judgment, and instincts to analyze the returns to find the ones with the greatest likelihood of change.

The interesting part of this whole process is that *while the classifier receives a high DIF–score return, the various items on the return that resulted in the high DIF score are not identified. Therefore, the classifier must decide what items on the tax return will be questioned during the audit.* More than any other non-DIF factor, the classifier's decision is the most significant variable in the selection process. See Exhibit 0-1 for IRS guidelines to classifiers on how to identify significant issues when selecting returns for audit.

Agents with classification experience have stated that subjective factors frequently enter into the selection process. For example, one classifier selected returns that were sloppily prepared, or ones that had a lot of rounded numbers in the expense columns (for example, $25,000 for travel expenses instead of $24,679). Another agent stated he selected returns that were prepared by certain commercial tax preparers.

The fact is *you cannot influence your DIF score,* and you should not try by fooling around with the expense figures on your return. *But you may be able to influence the classifier's decision and reduce your chances of being audited by following this simple rule that may turn out to be the single most important audit-proofing strategy rule in the entire book:*

AUDIT-PROOFER'S STRATEGY RULE

If you want to reduce your chances of being selected for an audit, you should attach supporting and substantiating documentation to your return.

While attaching documentation to the tax return is *not* commonly done, and frowned on by the IRS, a classifier may not bother with selecting your tax return for audit if the items under question are supported with photocopies of cancelled checks, or legal documents, or other records. You are not required to send supporting and substantiating documentation at the time of filing, but by doing so you can make a constructive contribution to reduce your chances of being audited.

It is not necessary to include supporting documentation on every item, just the ones that you think are unusual enough to be questioned. But if you really want to play it safe, attach a copy of every supporting document you have—but never send an original of any document with your tax return; it could be lost. Don't worry if your tax return is one inch thick—the IRS is used to fat packages. Use a large brown envelope if you have to. Generally it is a safe strategy to *inundate them with paper.*

Audit Misconception #3: "I'll just ignore those letters from the IRS; they can't do anything if they can't find me."

You wanna bet? Letters from the IRS are not to be ignored under any circumstances. If you don't respond to the audit "invitation" letter, the tax auditor may decide to disallow the items under question and assess additional taxes against you anyway.

You may not discover your misconception until it's too late, when the Collection Division starts seizing your bank account or pay check. If you think that you can get some sympathy from the Collection Division, you obviously have not read my other book, *When You Owe the IRS*. You must realize that once the deficiency assessment has been made by the auditor, the tax is payable and collectible like all other taxes. Revenue officers are not auditors. They cannot abate audit assessments.

However, it is not uncommon for a taxpayer to be assessed additional taxes and not know about it. This usually happens when the taxpayer has moved and the examiner hasn't been able to locate him. The tax is assessed anyway, and the burden then falls upon the revenue officer to locate the taxpayer and collect a tax the taxpayer doesn't know anything about. A situation like this calls for a little extra compassion on the part of the revenue officer. Most good revenue officers will temporarily suspend collection in this situation while requesting a reopening of the audit case. But taxpayers have no real legal recourse in this situation and are totally at the mercy of the IRS.

AUDIT-PROOFER'S STRATEGY RULE

If you are being asked to pay additional taxes from an audit assessment you know nothing about, and the revenue officer handling your case is demanding that you pay the tax, you have several options to follow: You can request that the audit be reopened; you can pay in part or in full while at the same time appealing the decision.

- You can request that the audit be reopened so that you can submit substantiating documentation or proof of the items that were disallowed. You can find out what was disallowed by asking the revenue officer to requisition a copy of the tax return and the audit report. *Internal Revenue Manual Section 53(10)4* requires the revenue officer to refer your request to the Examination Division. *In-*

ternal Revenue Manual Section 4023:(10) requires the Examination Division to reopen the case if: you contend you have never received any notification of the audit prior to receiving balance due notices or a collection contact; you have moved since you filed the tax return in question; and/or, you have never had the opportunity to submit the substantiation required.

- You can pay part of the tax and file Form 843, "Claim," for a refund of the portion you paid. While the IRS doesn't have to honor a partial tax payment claim, they will usually reopen a previously examined case in extenuating circumstances.
- You can pay the full amount of tax, and then follow the refund claim route as above. If the IRS denies your refund claim then you have the option of taking it to the Claims Court or a U.S. District Court.

Audit Misconception #4: "I made an error on my tax return, but I'm afraid to amend it because I may be audited."

When an amended return is received at the service center it is associated with the original return and reviewed for completeness, validity, timely filing, and a determination if the issues in the claim involve an audit matter.

The service center will process an adjustment without referral to the Examination Division if the claim involves a mathematical or processing error, the inclusion of a previously omitted item, or similar errors. An evaluation is made of all the documents in the case, and if enough information is available to reasonably accept the claim, or if the claim is not worthy of an audit, it will be accepted. The basic rule is that if the item on the claim would not have been questioned on the original return, it won't be questioned on the claim.

Exceptions involve large dollar claims for refund (based on district policy), previously audited issues, and redeterminations of tax based on an interpretation of the tax law inconsistent with Service policies; it is these situations that may mean an automatic audit of the issues presented on the amended return.

Audit Misconception #5: "So what if I'm audited, I'll just pay them when I can."

Don't count on it. As I have already explained, the Collection Division has no leniency policy for those who have been audited. You'll be expected to pay according to your ability to pay, and the revenue officer determines what your ability is, not you. Remember also that you will have to pay interest on the additional taxes, and penalties if you don't pay in full within ten days of the first notice.

Exhibit 0-1

How Classifiers Identify Significant Issues on Individual Nonbusiness Returns
(*Internal Revenue Manual*, Part IV)

Listed below are suggested guidelines to assist classifiers in identifying significant issues on individual nonbusiness tax returns.

EXEMPTIONS AND ITEMIZED DEDUCTIONS

General

- Important! Look first at overall potential based on the amount of excess itemized deductions above the zero bracket amount.
- Verify that itemized deductions are not claimed elsewhere on the return when the standard deduction has been elected (e.g., personal real estate taxes and mortgage interest deducted on rental schedule).

Exemptions

- Exemptions claimed by the noncustodial parent have proven to have high potential for adjustment.
- When married persons file separately, both taxpayers may not have made the same election for standard, or itemized, deductions. If dependent children are claimed, the other spouse may also be claiming them.

Medical Expenses

- High medical expenses for large families, deceased taxpayers, or older taxpayers are usually not productive to yield more taxes, if the return is audited.

Taxes

- Real Estate Taxes—Consider changes in address (i.e., W-2, 1040, 2119) to verify the claimed deduction.
- Sales Tax—Consider significant amounts above table allowance or nonqualifying items.

Interest Expense

- Interest is generally not productive when questioning all the small items that may be listed or combined.
- Productive issues could come from payments to individuals, and closing costs on real estate transactions.
- Home mortgage interest usually is unproductive.

Contributions

- Check to see if contributions exceed 50 percent of Adjusted Gross Income (AGI).
- Check large donations made to questionable miscellaneous charities.
- Check for payments which may represent tuition.
- Check for large donations of property, other than cash.

Casualty or Theft Losses

- Watch for business assets, valuation methods, and limitations.

Miscellaneous Deductions

- Scrutinize large, unusual, or questionable items.

INCOME

Capital Transactions

- Gains on sales of rental and other depreciable property, where the taxpayer has been using an accelerated method of depreciation or ACRS, should be questioned since the taxpayer may have to report ordinary income.
- Loss on the sale of rental property, recently converted from a personal residence, is usually productive.
- Current-year installment sales and exchanges of property should be carefully scrutinized as taxpayers frequently make errors in computing the recognized gain.
- Check to see if the gain on a sale is large enough to require the alternative minimum tax computation.

Pension and/or Annuity

- Verify if distribution qualifies under the three-year rule.
- Check whether distribution qualifies as a lump-sum distribution.

Rental Properties

- Consider fair rental value.
- If the rental property is located at the same address as the taxpayer's residence, consider whether the allocation is proper between the rental portion and the portion used personally by the taxpayer.
- Repairs may be capital improvements.
- Consider whether the cost of land is included in the basis.
- The rental of vacation/resort homes should be scrutinized.

Sales of Residence

- Check to be sure that the taxpayer purchases a more expensive residence to qualify for deferral of the gain.

Unreported Income

- Is the income sufficient to support the exemptions claimed?
- Installment sale of property but no interest reported.
- Does the taxpayer show interest and real estate tax deductions for two residences but no rental income?
- If a taxpayer lists his/her occupation as waiter, cab driver, porter, beautician, etc., tip income is a productive issue.
- Are there substantial interest expenses with no apparent source of funds to repay the loans?
- Does the taxpayer claim business expenses for an activity that shows no income on the return (i.e., beautician supplies, but no Form 1099 or W-2 for that occupation)?

Copy of Schedule K-1

- Items of self-employment income shown on Schedule K-1 should be matched to Schedule SE to ensure that the amounts are properly included in the self-employment tax computation.

ADJUSTMENTS TO INCOME

Moving Expenses

- Review W-2's for address and other compensation. Also, consider sale of residence.

Employee Business Expenses

- Amounts should be reasonable when compared to the taxpayer's occupation and income level.
- Avoid auto expenses as an issue where the standard mileage computation is used and the mileage shown does not appear excessive.
- Transportation expenses for construction workers, carpenters, etc., who appear to have several different employers at different locations, have not proven to be productive. However, be alert for expenses claimed for travel to a remote job site(s).
- Expenses for clubs, yachts, airplanes, etc., must meet the facilities requirements of IRC 274 and therefore are usually productive issues.

TAXPAYER'S PREVIOUS/SUBSEQUENT YEAR RETURN

Determine whether the previous/subsequent year return should be inspected. If so, you must note the checksheet. Situations where inspection may be warranted are:

- Probable carryover adjustments (i.e., capital loss carryover, substantial depreciation changes).
- Items which, if disallowed in the selected year, may be allowable in the following year.

BUSINESS INDIVIDUAL RETURNS

- Determination of Office/Field Examinations—One of the key contributions to the success or failure of our Examination Program in the business categories is the selection of the proper function to conduct the examination. If we are to meet our Program objectives, it is essential that we input those returns that are most adaptable for office interview to Office Examination and those requiring the skills of a revenue agent to Field Examination. This decision is very important from several aspects:
  1. The planned time of an examination of a business return in Office Examination is about half of that planned for Field Examination. However, substantial issues should not be excluded as identified issues to convert what would be a Revenue Agent assignment, to a Tax Auditor assignment.
  2. Office examinations usually do not involve a visitation to the taxpayer's place of business. Field Examination returns should require a more in-depth knowledge of accounting principles.
- Generally, business returns should be selected for Field Examination when the following conditions occur:
  1. Voluminous records.

2. Complex accounting method.
3. Extensive timeframe required to complete the examination.
4. Advisability of on-site inspection of business.
5. Inventories are substantial and material.
6. Termination of business before the end of a taxable year.
7. Unusual issues that appear to be complex and time consuming to develop. For example:
   a. Nontaxable transfers.
   b. Complex oil or mineral explorations.
   c. Sale of IRC 1231 assets.
   d. Unstated interest (IRC 483).
8. The size of a business is also an indicator of what may be involved when an actual examination is made of the books and records of any particular taxpayer.
9. The businesses listed below would normally not be adaptable to Office Examination:
   a. Contractors.
   b. Manufacturers.
   c. Auto dealers.
   d. Funeral parlors.

- The areas discussed above are meant to operate only as a guide. In addition to considering these items, heavy reliance must be placed on judgment and experience.

Net Profit

- Is the taxpayer engaged in the type of business or profession normally considered to be more profitable than reflected on the return?
- Is the zero bracket amount used with high gross income and low net profit shown on the business schedule? Experience has shown that the incidence of fraud is greater on low business returns when the return reflects large receipts ($100,000 or more), a sizable investment, and the standard deduction is used.
- Does the address, real estate taxes, and/or mortgage interest indicate a higher mode of living than justified by the reported income?
- Does the return reveal large amounts of interest/dividend income not commensurate with current sources of income?

Cost of Goods Sold

- Check for the possibility of withdrawal of items for personal use.
- Is the ending inventory inclusive of all costs, direct and indirect?

Bad Debt Deduction

- Is it a cash business?
- Is it disproportionate for the indicated value of sales?

Depreciation

- Does the schedule contain an adequate description of the asset?
- Are personal assets being depreciated?
- Consider investment credit aspects and sales of property simultaneously with depreciation issues.

Sale of Assets

- Is there a sale of business assets during the year without investment credit or depreciation recapture?
- Is the gain large enough to require the alternative minimum tax computation?

Farm Returns

In the analysis of a Schedule F, you should keep in mind the usual features of a farm return. The farmer may be engaged in a specialized area of dairy cattle, beef cattle, grain, swine, vegetables, poultry, or a multiple of these items. The operation may vary from that of a few acres to several thousand acres. The operator of the farm may own all or a portion of it. Consider whether the farm is an actual business operation or a hobby.

OTHER TAXES

Self-Employment Tax

- All returns should be screened for self-employment tax issues, including returns with Schedule SE attached. Look for income such as director's fees, janitorial services, miscellaneous income, partnership income, etc., which may be subject to self-employment tax.
- Some items of income earned by independent contractors may be reported as wages or other income. Where the income appears to be personal service income, it must be considered for Social Security tax purposes.

Part I AUDIT-PROOFING YOUR RETURN

Step 1 Keeping Proper Records for an IRS Audit

During 1985 "recordkeeping hype" reached new heights. The Tax Reform Act of 1984 required that "contemporaneous" records be maintained to substantiate tax deductions and credits claimed for traveling expenses, entertainment, gifts, and business use of automobiles, other vehicles, and computers. Then the IRS issued regulations that almost everyone in the world opposed. Many taxpayers claimed they would spend more time complying with the law than they would in making a living.

The debate heated up, forcing Congress to repeal the "contemporaneous" provision of the law as though never enacted, and reinstate thc previous standards of recordkeeping. With all the confusion surrounding the debate and the repeal, people are more perplexed than ever about proper recordkeeping.

In a nutshell, nothing has changed since before the Tax Reform Act of 1984. For 1985, the recordkeeping requirement was the same as for 1984, while for 1986 and thereafter there is a slight change.

Internal Revenue Code *Section 6001* still requires every person liable for any tax to keep certain records as required by the IRS. In turn, IRS regulations require that any person required to file an income tax return must keep "such permanent books of account or records, including inventories, as are sufficient to establish the amount of gross income, deductions, credits, or other matters required to be shown by such person in any return."

In addition, Code *Section 7203* relating to willful failure to file also includes willful failure to "keep any records" as a misdemeanor with possible fines up to $25,000, and imprisonment up to one year with costs of prosecution. Focusing on just the records provision, Code *Section 7203* reads in part:

> Any person required under this title . . . or required by this title or by regulations made under authority thereof to . . . keep any records . . . who willfully fails to . . . keep such records . . . at the time or times required by law or regulations, shall, in addition to other penalties provided by law, be guilty of a misdemeanor.

AUDIT-PROOFER'S STRATEGY RULE

You* must *keep adequate records to support your income and your deductions, as required by law. It is* your *loss should you fail to do so.

WHY YOU SHOULD MAINTAIN ADEQUATE RECORDS

Inadequate records are defined as "the lack of records, or records so incomplete that correctness of taxable income cannot be determined." Your taxable income is the amount upon which you compute your tax, *after* subtracting adjustments to income, exemptions, and itemized deductions. In short, anything that has a bearing on your income tax return and affects your tax liability in any way must be available for inspection when requested by the IRS.

You are required to maintain records in sufficient detail to enable you to make a proper income tax return. In order *to determine the correctness of the return,* the IRS has authority to examine those records or any other data which may be relevant or material. The IRS is also authorized to issue a summons compelling *any* person it deems proper to appear with his or her books and records at a reasonable place and time and give testimony, under oath. You are required to maintain records as long as they are material to the administration of the Internal Revenue laws.

Keeping proper records is to your advantage. As discussed later in Step 3, if you know what items of proof you need to substantiate your deductions, you'll be better prepared to face the IRS in the event of a challenge. Saving taxes is saving your dollars. Other considerations in proper recordkeeping include:

- Inadequate or irregular recordkeeping is a "badge of fraud" (see Chapter 7). It can immediately arouse the suspicion of the tax examiner who may be compelled to probe deeper into your finances in anticipation of discovering unreported sources of income. Such a finding could turn into a criminal investigation leading to prosecution, and possibly jail.
- The IRS examiner could assess a negligence penalty of an additional 5 percent of the underreported tax (see Chapter 7). A Congressional Committee report indicates Congress is concerned that negligence and fraud penalties (also see Chapter 7) have not been applied by the IRS or the courts in a substantial number of instances where their application would be fully justified. The Committee report emphasizes that negligence and fraud penalties are appropriate if a taxpayer claims tax benefits that cannot be supported by the substantiation requirement of Code *Section 274(d)* (this is explained later).
- Regarding *any* item on your tax return, *the burden is on you* to prove its accuracy in any audit. The burden of proof only shifts to the government in fraud cases. If you cannot meet the burden of proof for any deduction, the IRS may disallow it in its entirety, especially if supporting documentation or collateral evidence is not available.
- Inadequate recordkeeping also puts a burden on your professional income tax preparer, who is also subject to penalties from the IRS. An income tax return preparer may be subject to a civil liability for understating your tax liability resulting from negligence or an intentional disregard of rules and regulations. Because the IRS has been clamping down hard on preparers, you may not even be able to find one to do your tax return if your books and records are disorganized.
- Courts have ruled that failure to keep accurate books and records may be taken into consideration in determining whether you have intended to evade or defeat payment of the tax, a criminal offense under Code *Section 7201* (see Chapter 7).
- The concept of audit-proofing requires that you keep good books and records. Step 3 in the audit-proofing process involves knowing what the IRS will be looking for. The first aspect of that step is knowing what proof is necessary to support each deduction and making sure that it is available should the IRS want to see it. You cannot audit-proof your tax return without keeping good books and records of income and expenses supported by documentary evidence.

WHAT RECORDS ARE NECESSARY?

IRS regulations state that records required to be maintained by the IRS must be accurate, but no particular form is required. However, other IRS guidelines specify the following:

- Taxpayers whose only income is from salaries, wages, or similar compensation for personal services rendered are required by the IRS to be prepared to show how each item of income and expenses on the return was computed. Therefore, the only records you need to keep are records to support your income and deductions. See Step 3 for a listing of types of proof the IRS will allow to substantiate your deductions.
- Taxpayers who are in business or self-employed must keep primary and secondary records. Primary records are those documents upon which individual transactions of buying and selling merchandise, supplies, services, and business assets are recorded. Examples are: invoices, vouchers, bills, receipts, tapes, detailed inventory lists, canceled checks, duplicate deposit slips, bank statements, etc. Secondary records are the permanent books, worksheets, tallies, etc., which list or summarize the primary records into classifications of income or expenses. These records may consist of a simple book or record, a simple set of books, or a complicated set of records in which numerous analyses, consolidations, or summarizations are made to achieve the final product.

AUDIT-PROOFER'S STRATEGY RULE

For all taxpayers there are at least three aspects to proper recordkeeping that are necessary to sustain a deduction: (1) You must know the tax rules. (2) You must keep adequate records of your deductible expenses. (3) You must keep proofs (receipts, cancelled checks) of your expenses.

1. *You need to know the rules* under which an expense is deductible or income is reportable. Knowing the rules helps you to become tax-wise, thereby translating into saving tax dollars. By knowing the rules, you focus your time and energies on those things that are important, or those expenses that are tax deductible. For example, if you know that your aerobic exercise program is not deductible, you won't waste your time keeping track of the expense and the receipt.

2. *You need to record your tax deductible expenses,* or keep track of them in some way. This can be done by buying a tax recordkeeping book, or by setting up a simple system you design yourself. For example, if you use your checking account for *all* your disbursements and income, you already have a means of keeping track. All you have to do next is to mark your check register in some way to indicate deductible expenses; you could circle the check number, or underline the payee in red. Just by keeping track of your tax deductible expenditures, you will help yourself immensely in preparing your tax return.
3. *You need to maintain proof* of your expense. A very simple way to maintain proof is to set up a file box with jacket folders for the appropriate receipts and documents. A minimal attempt could be made just by keeping receipts in a shoe box. But keeping receipts and documents is just part of the job. You should also be able to locate the right receipt with the right cancelled check, and provide an explanation of what the expense was for. For example, a receipt and a cancelled check paid to the Girl Scouts might not be sufficient to substantiate a charitable contribution. The expense must be able to meet the rules, or the IRS may disallow it if your proof doesn't support the rules. In this example, the IRS may suspect you purchased Girl Scout cookies (not deductible in full; only the excess value over their fair market value is deductible), paid to send your daughter to a weekend camp, or made a purchase of supplies for your Girl Scout daughter.

   It's also important you know what proof is required to be kept. You will find that information in Step 3.

A good recordkeeping system will bridge all three aspects so that you'll be readily prepared to support any item on your tax return the IRS may question.

TRAVEL AND ENTERTAINMENT EXPENSE RECORDS

There is one area that the IRS is very strict with: travel and entertainment. It is very common for taxpayers to attempt to write off personal expenses as business expenses in this category. Even though Congress made *substantiation and recordkeeping requirements* for travel and entertainment in 1962, it is still a problem area for most taxpayers.

Whether you are self-employed, or work for someone else, you may have business expenses related to travel away from home, and entertainment. If so, you need to read this section. Tax examiners love to challenge travel and entertainment expenses because they are "easy pickings," and often result in additional taxes. When you read the rules, you'll understand why.

In 1962 Congress adopted special rules under Code *Section 274(d)* requiring taxpayers to substantiate their deductions for overnight traveling expenses, entertainment, and gifts, by providing either *adequate records* or by *sufficient evidence,* as corroboration of the taxpayer's own statement. Congress established five elements of information that were required to support the deduction.

In 1984 Congress made changes in this area that caused a groundswell of opposition. They eliminated the sufficient evidence test, required that adequate records be "contemporaneous," and expanded the rules to cover local travel of passenger automobiles, other transportation vehicles, computers, property related to entertainment, amusement, or recreation, and any other type of property the IRS wanted to apply the rules to (all these were known as *Section 280F* property).

Congress reacted to the subsequent flood of complaints by repealing the "contemporaneous" requirement and restoring the sufficient evidence test. The requirement to include *Section 280F* property in the *Section 274(d)* substantiation requirements was postponed until 1986. In addition, Congress specifically prohibited the IRS from requiring you to keep a daily contemporaneous log of your automobile use for local travel. An exception from the substantiation requirement of *Section 274(d)* was also made for minimal personal use of business vehicles.

Code *Section 274(d)* now requires you to substantiate your deductions or tax credits in connection with the following business-related expenditures:

- Local travel, computer usage and listed property under Section 280F;
- Traveling expenses, including meals and lodging, while away from home;
- Cost of business meals of $25 or more, entertainment, amusement, or recreation activities or property, or the use of facilities; and
- Gifts.

Deductions for the above expenses will not be allowed unless you can provide either *adequate records* or *sufficient evidence* to corroborate your own statement with the following five elements:

1. The amount of the expense,
2. The time and place of the travel, business meal, entertainment, or amusement, or use of such facility,
3. The business purpose of the expense,
4. The business relationship to you of the persons you entertained, used the facility, or received the gift,
5. The date and description of the gift.

It's important to note that these elements do not stand alone. You must first establish that the expense qualifies as a deduction even before the substantiation requirements of *Section 274(d)* become applicable. Deductions are not allowed for approximations, or estimates; or for expenses for lavish or extravagant entertainment.

WHAT ARE ADEQUATE RECORDS OR SUFFICIENT EVIDENCE?

IRS regulations are quite specific and put the burden squarely on you to maintain adequate records which may take the following forms: account books, diaries, logs, trip sheets, expense reports, statements of witnesses or similar specific records, that are "made at or near the time of the expenditure." These records must be supported by *sufficient documentary evidence* which together constitute clear proof of each element of an expenditure for travel, entertainment, and gifts. Without adequate substantiation of expenses, travel and entertainment expenses may be disallowed in their entirety. Whereas the IRS may allow a reasonable amount for other types of unsubstantiated deductions, they are prohibited from doing so with travel and entertainment expenses.

During the debate the House and Senate wrestled with this issue quite a bit. The House Ways and Means Committee attempted to impose an alternate test of "sufficient *written* evidence corroborating the taxpayer's own statement." When the House and Senate versions went to conference to resolve their differences, the written test requirement was removed, but the Committee Report states:

> Oral evidence, such as oral testimony from a disinterested, unrelated party describing the taxpayer's activities, may be of sufficient probative value that it should not be automatically excluded from consideration under *Section 274(d)*.

The Committee report further points out that:

> Different types of evidence have different degrees of probative value. The conferees believe that oral evidence alone has considerably less probative value than written evidence. In addition, the conferees believe that the probative value of written evidence is greater the closer in time it relates to the expenditure. Thus, written evidence arising at or near the time of the expenditure, absent unusual circumstances, has much more probative value than evidence created later, such as written evidence first prepared for audit or court.

This means that Congress didn't have the nerve to require you to maintain written "contemporaneous" records, but they want you to know that it is in your best interests to keep good written records made "the closer in time it relates to the expenditure." (Sounds a bit like the definition of "contemporaneous" doesn't it?)

The Committee Report points out that they "specifically approve the types of substantiation that were required under prior law, and consider the long-standing Treasury regulations on recordkeeping . . . to reflect accurately their intent as to the substantiation that taxpayers are required to maintain."

IRS REGULATIONS ON ADEQUATE RECORDS FOR TRAVEL AND ENTERTAINMENT EXPENSES

IRS regulations require you to include a written statement of the business purpose of an expense unless it is evident from the surrounding facts and circumstances. Documentary evidence, such as receipts, paid bills, or similar evidence sufficient to support an expenditure is required for:

- Any expenditure for lodging while away from home, and
- Any other expenditure of $25 or more, except for transportation charges when documentary evidence is not available.

Documentary evidence is considered adequate to support an expenditure if it establishes the amount, date, place, and the essential character of the expenditure. For example, a hotel receipt is sufficient to support business travel expenditures if it contains the following: name and location of the hotel, date, and separate amounts for such charges as lodging, meals, and telephone. A restaurant receipt is sufficient to support a business meal expenditure if it contains the following: name and location of the restaurant, the date and amount of the expenditure, and indications of charges made for items other than meals and beverages.

IRS regulations further state that "It is not necessary to record information in an account book, diary, log, statement of expense, trip sheet, or similar record which duplicates information reflected on a receipt so long as the account book, etc., and receipt complement each other in an orderly manner."

Important: In some cases, a document may not be sufficient to support more than one (or part of one) element of an expenditure. Thus, a cancelled check, together with a bill or receipt from the payee would ordinarily establish the element of cost. In contrast, a cancelled check alone would not be sufficient without other evidence showing that the check was used for a certain business purpose.

The IRS may still allow a deduction, even though all elements of a particular expenditure have not been substantiated, as long as you have *substantially complied* with the "adequate records" requirement. The regulations do not define substantial compliance but the *Internal Revenue Manual* states that it depends upon the circumstances and whether or not you have made a good faith effort to comply with the requirements. Tax auditors are told to consider the following factors when determining if there has been substantial compliance:

- The number and type of expenditures involved.
- The number of missing elements.
- What documentation is missing.
- Reasons why the element was not properly substantiated.
- Availability of other information to substantiate the expenditure.

If you fail to show the IRS that you have substantially complied with the "adequate records" requirement with respect to an element of an expenditure, then you must establish such element:

- By your own written or oral statement, containing detailed, specific information about the element; *and,*
- By other corroborative evidence sufficient to establish such element.

If the unsubstantiated element is the description of a gift, or the cost, time, place, or date of an expenditure, the corroborative evidence must be "direct evidence," such as a written or oral statement from persons entertained or other witnesses who can set forth detailed information about the element. If this is not available, the corroborative evidence must be documentary evidence.

If you have failed to substantiate either your business relationship to the persons you've entertained, or the purpose of a business expenditure, the corroborative evidence can be circumstantial evidence.

In the event you have lost your records through circumstances beyond your control, such as destruction by fire, flood, earthquake, or other casualty, you have the right to substantiate your deduction by a reasonable reconstruction of your records.

SPECIAL SUBSTANTIATION RULES FOR 1986

For 1985 the substantiation requirements of Code *Section 274(d)* only apply to travel while away from home, entertainment, recreation or amusement expenses, and gifts. They do not apply to local travel expenses, computers used for business purposes, and other listed property known as *Section*

Exhibit 1–X

SUBSTANTIATING BUSINESS-RELATED EXPENSES AS REQUIRED BY INTERNAL REVENUE CODE SECTION 274(d)

Elements to Be Substantiated	*For Travel Expenses Away From Home*	*For Entertainment Expenses and Business Meals (Limited to 80%)*	*For Gift Expenses*	*For Listed Property as Defined In Section 280F(d)(4)*
AMOUNT	Amount of each separate expense for transportation, lodging, and meals. Incidental expenses may be totaled in reasonable categories, such as gas and oil, taxis, daily meals for traveler, etc.	Amount of each separate expense. Incidental expenses, such as taxis, telephones, etc., may be totaled on a daily basis.	Cost of gift.	(a) Expenditures. The amount of each separate expenditure with respect to an item of listed property, such as the cost of acquisition, the cost of capital improvements, lease payments, the cost of maintenance and repairs, or other expenditures; and, (b) Uses. The amount of each business/investment use based on the appropriate measure (e.g., mileage for automobile use) and the total use of the listed property for the taxable period.
TIME	Date you left and returned for each trip, and number of days away from home spent on business.	Date of entertainment or use of a facility for entertainment. For entertainment directly before or after a business discussion, the time spent discussing business.	Date of gift.	Date of the expenditure or use with respect to listed property.

PLACE	Name of city or other designation.	Name and address or designation of place of entertainment, or place of use of a facility for entertainment. Type of entertainment if not otherwise apparent. Place where business discussion was held if entertainment is directly before or after a business discussion.	Not applicable.	Not applicable.
DESCRIPTION	Not applicable.	Not applicable.	Description of gift.	Not applicable.
BUSINESS PURPOSE—A written statement is generally required.	Business reason for travel or nature of business benefit gained or expected to be gained.	Business reason or nature of business benefit gained or expected to be gained. Nature of business discussion or activity.	Business reason for making the gift or nature of business benefit gained or expected to be gained.	The business purpose for an expenditure or use with respect to any listed property.
BUSINESS RELATIONSHIP	Not applicable.	Occupations or other information—such as names or other designations—about persons entertained that shows their business relationship to you. If all people entertained did not take part in business discussion, identify those who did.	Occupation or other information—such as name or other designation—about recipient that shows business relationship to you.	Not applicable.

280F property. Instead, tax deductions and credits for local travel and *Section 280F* property are subject to the general substantiation requirements applicable to all other business expenditures.

However, beginning in 1986, *Section 280F* property now falls within the *Section 274(d)* substantiation requirements, except for minimal personal use of business vehicles which still must be justified under Code *Section 162* relating to business expenses or Code *Section 212* relating to income-producing expenses.

The Committee Report states "the conferees intend that the principles of these regulations fully apply to deductions and credits claimed for local travel and the use of other listed property under *Section 274(d),*" but that "these principles will need to be carefully applied." This is because expenses for local travel or the use of computers commonly do not involve receipts, and may occur more frequently than expenses for overnight travel.

The IRS has issued regulations specifying how such recordkeeping is to be required, and what documentation is required for local travel (these regulations were issued on November 1, 1985). Taxpayers are *not* required to maintain trip-by-trip logs and records encompassing each element of the substantiation standards of *Section 274(d)* to justify a deduction or credit. Instead, taxpayers may substantiate their automobile business use with a journal in which each element of business use during the week is recorded at the end of the week. Also, if the business use follows a consistent pattern, detailed records are not necessary. Instead, you can maintain adequate records for portions of the taxable year that are representative of the business use for the entire year and employ those percentages extrapolated for the whole year.

Congress wants to ensure that you only claim those deductions and credits to which you are entitled without being unduly burdened by unnecessarily complex recordkeeping requirements. Yet Congress also believes that you should provide sufficient information on your tax return so that the IRS can make a preliminary evaluation of the "appropriateness" of your deductions or credits claimed for the business use of an automobile. Previously, this was difficult to do unless you were audited.

Congress has now directed the IRS to obtain certain information from you directly from your tax return. Starting with the 1985 tax year, on returns due April 15, 1986, the IRS began asking you to provide this information about your use of a business automobile:

- Total mileage driven during the year, divided into separate categories for business, commuting, and personal use.
- The percentages of business use and personal use.
- Whether you had the personal use of other vehicles.

- Whether you were able to use the vehicle during after-work hours.
- Whether you have adequate records or sufficient evidence to support the business use claimed on the return.

In the case of other *Section 280F* property subject to *Section 274(d)* rules, such as yachts, computers, and airplanes, the IRS will ask you the percentage of business use, and whether you have evidence to support the business use. For computers, the IRS is *not required* to ask you what percentage of the year your computer was located at your home, as was originally planned by the House version.

RECORDKEEPING BY EMPLOYEES

IRS regulations also provide rules for the reporting of information on tax returns and the recordkeeping substantiation requirements of those who incur *ordinary and necessary* business expenses as an employee. The term "ordinary and necessary business expenses" means only those expenses which are a normal and regular part of the conduct of your business and are *directly attributable* to such business. The term does not include nondeductible personal, living, or family expenses.

Employees who pay for ordinary and necessary business expenses themselves are usually reimbursed by their employers. The general rule is that an employee who makes an adequate accounting to his employer is not required to substantiate that expense account information to the IRS, except if there is an excess of reimbursement over expenses, or if certain other situations exist, as discussed below.

Employees who are *not* required to make an adequate accounting to their employers must substantiate their expenses to the IRS. IRS regulation 1.274-5(e)(4) states:

> An adequate accounting means the submission to the employer of an account book, diary, log, statement of expenses, trip sheet, or similar record maintained by the employee in which the information as to each element of an expenditure . . . is recorded at or near the time of the expenditure or use, together with supporting documentary evidence . . . An adequate accounting requires that the employee account for all amounts received from his employer during the taxable year as advances, reimbursements, or allowances . . . for travel, entertainment, gifts, and the use of listed property.

Although the IRS can require any taxpayer to substantiate any pertinent information concerning expense accounts, you will not be called upon to substantiate your expense account information *unless* you fall within one of the following categories:

- You are not required to account to your employer, or you do not make such an accounting.
- Your expenses exceed the total amounts reimbursed or advanced to you, and you claim a deduction on your tax return for the excess.
- You are related to your employer within the meaning of Code *Section 267(b)* (such as family members, individuals who own more than 50 percent of the stock in their corporation). Or,
- The IRS has determined that the accounting procedures used by your employer for the reporting and substantiation of expenses by employees are not adequate.

IRS regulations include a note that says:

> It is to the advantage of taxpayers who may be called upon to substantiate expense account information to maintain as adequate and detailed records of travel, transportation, entertainment, and similar business expenses as practical since the burden of proof is upon the taxpayer to show that such expenses were not only paid or incurred but also that they constitute ordinary and necessary business expenses.

The regulations even contain suggestions that an employee prepare a daily diary or record of expenditures, "maintained in sufficient detail to enable him to readily identify the amount and nature of any expenditure, and the preservation of supporting documents, especially in connection with large or exceptional expenditures." The IRS recognizes that it is often difficult to do this and they are willing to give a little: "Detailed records of small expenditures incurred in traveling or for transportation, as, for example, tips, will not be required." (Aren't they understanding?)

To put this in perspective read the following rules keeping this basic fact in mind: Whenever you take a deduction on your tax return for an ordinary and necessary business expense as an employee, *you must maintain such records and supporting evidence as will substantiate each element of an expenditure* as required by Code *Section 274(d)*. These rules apply to employees who are not outside salespeople.

Rule #1: You need not report on your tax return any expenses for travel, local transportation, and entertainment, paid or incurred by you solely for the benefit of your employer *if you account* to your employer, and such expenses are either charges to your employer, or you are reimbursed or advanced in full an amount *equal* to the expenses. In this situation the reimbursement is not reported on your return either. However, if your reimbursements equal your expenses, and you do *not* account to your employer, you must attach a completed IRS Form 2106, "Employee Business Expense," to your tax return.

Rule #2: You must report as income on your tax return any amount of reimbursement or advance paid you by your employer in *excess* of the ordinary and necessary business expenses paid or incurred by you.

- You do not have to file Form 2106 (or a similar statement) if you accounted to your employer, and your employer does not include the total reimbursements on your Form W-2. Instead you will report the excess as income on line 7 of your Form 1040.
- You must file Form 2106 (or a similar statement) if your employer includes the total reimbursement on your Form W-2, regardless of whether you account to your employer.
- You must file Form 2106 (or a similar statement) if your employer does not include reimbursements on your Form W-2 and you do not account to your employer.

Rule #3: If your ordinary and necessary business expenses exceed the amount reimbursed or advanced to you by your employer, you are allowed to deduct the excess payment on your tax return. To secure a deduction for such excess payment, you must submit IRS Form 2106, "Employee Business Expenses," with your tax return. If you decide *not* to take a deduction for the excess, you do not need to file Form 2106.

Rule #4: If you are not required to account to your employer for your ordinary and necessary business expenses, and therefore are not reimbursed for such expense, you can take a deduction on your tax return by filing IRS Form 2106 with your tax return.

Rule #5: If you do not claim from your employer a reimbursement to which you are entitled, you may not claim a deduction for the expenses to which that reimbursement applies.

If you are *not* an outside salesperson you can only use Form 2106 for:

- Reimbursed or unreimbursed transportation expenses, car expenses, travel away from home, and
- Other expenses that are reimbursed. Other expenses that are *not* reimbursed are reported on Schedule A.

If you *are* an outside salesperson you use Form 2106 for all your reimbursed or unreimbursed business expenses.

Exhibit 1-1

Recordkeeping for Individuals
(IRS Publication 552)

INTRODUCTION

You must keep records that will enable you to prepare a correct tax return. These records will help you prepare your income tax return so that you will pay only your proper tax. If you keep a record of your expenses during the year, you may find that you can reduce your income tax by itemizing your deductible expenses. Your deductible expenses may include a part of your medical and dental bills, interest payments, contributions, taxes, and certain other expenses. You must have a record of the amounts you spent to deduct them.

Good records will help you if the Internal Revenue Service selects your tax return for examination. Usually, an examination occurs one to three years after a return is filed. If you have kept good records, you should be able to clear up questionable items and arrive at the correct tax with a minimum of effort. If you have not kept good records, you may have to spend time getting statements and receipts from various sources. Also, you may have to pay more tax because you cannot prove your deductible expenses or because you cannot prove the basis you used in figuring your gain or loss on the sale of property.

Use this information to help you decide what records you should keep and how long to keep them. IRS Publication 583, Information for Business Taxpayers, has a discussion of business records.

If you have questions about the tax treatment of income, expenses, or other items, see the list of publications at the end of Chapter 2.

Read the instructions that come with your tax forms each year to see if changes in the law affect you.

RECORDS YOU SHOULD KEEP

The law does not require that you keep any particular kind of records. However, you should keep all sales slips, invoices, receipts, cancelled checks, stock brokerage statements, forms W-2, W-2P, and 1099, and other documents that prove the amounts you show on your return as income, deductions, and credits. Your records must be kept available for inspection by the Internal Revenue Service in a manner that will enable the Service to determine your proper tax.

Copies of Tax Returns

You should keep copies of your tax returns as part of your tax records. They may help you prepare future tax returns, and they are necessary if you file an amended return. Copies of your returns, and your other records, may be helpful to either your survivor, or the executor or administrator of your estate, or both.

If necessary, you may request a copy of a return by sending a Form 4506, Request for Copy of Tax Form, to the Internal Revenue Service Center where you filed the return. The charge for a copy of a return is $5 and must be paid with Form 4506. Prepare a separate Form 4506 for each return you request, and allow a minimum of several months for receipt of the copy or copies. You should be able to get copies of your returns for at least 6 years.

Employee Expenses

If you have travel, entertainment, and gift expenses related to your job, see IRS Publication 463, Travel, Entertainment, and Gift Expenses, for a discussion of the records you need to keep. [See also sections 547 and 5(10)(16) in Chapter 8.]

Reporting Earnings for Self-Employment Social Security Tax

The Social Security benefits paid to you for disability or retirement, or to your family if you die, depend on your reporting accurately your earnings from self-employment. Therefore, keep accurate records of your business income and expenses (see IRS Publication 583).

Capital Gains and Losses

You may be able to report the sale of an asset as a capital gain or loss. To do this, your records must show when and how an asset was acquired, how the asset was used, and when and how it was disposed of. Records must also show your cost or other basis, the gross selling price, and the expenses of sale. You also may be allowed to postpone paying tax on certain gains.

For more information on capital gains and losses, see Publications 544, Sales and Other Dispositions of Assets, and 550, Investment Income and Expenses.

Basis of Property

You should keep records that show the basis of property you own.

- **Your home.** If you own a home, you must keep records on the property to show your purchase price, your purchase expenses, your cost of improvements, and any other adjustments to basis, such as for depreciation and casualty losses.

  The records you keep on your home should include information on a house you sold and replaced with your current house if you postponed tax on the gain on the sale of the former house. The basis of your current house is affected by the postponed gain. See IRS Publication 523, Tax Information on Selling Your Home.

- **Reinvested dividends.** If dividends on stock you own are reinvested, that is, the company buys additional whole or fractional shares for you with the dividends, you should keep records to show the amount of all the reinvested dividends.
- **Basis of property received as a gift.** Sometimes you can increase the basis of property received as a gift if your records show your basis, the donor's basis, the fair market value of the property on the date of the gift, and any gift tax paid. This is explained in IRS Publication 551, Basis of Assets.

Performing Services for a Charitable Organization

If you perform services without pay for a charitable organization, you should keep records of the out-of-pocket expenses you pay to perform the services. For information about these expenses, see IRS Publication 526, Charitable Contributions.

Pay Statements

If you receive pay statements, each pay day or less often, keep them together for a record of deductible expenses that are withheld from your paycheck.

Divorce Decree

If you take a deduction for alimony payments, keep your cancelled checks as well as a copy of the divorce, separate maintenance, or support decree, or written separation agreement. See IRS Publication 504, Tax Information for Divorced or Separated Individuals.

Miscellaneous Expenses

The following are suggested types of receipts you should keep for specific expenses—

- **Medical and dental expenses.** Keep bills along with the cancelled check to show when the expense was paid. If you pay by cash, most providers of medical and dental services will give you a signed receipt. You can keep a log to record mileage, taxi, or bus fares for medical transportation. If your employer withholds amounts from your wages for medical insurance, keep your payroll statements to establish the premiums you paid through withholding.
- **Taxes.** Form W-2 shows the state income tax withheld from your wages. If you made estimated state income tax payments, keep your cancelled checks and a copy of the state estimated tax return. Your prior-year state return shows any additional state tax paid, or any refund received, in the current year. Keep cancelled checks and statements or other documents for your real estate and personal property taxes paid.

- **Interest.** Keep statements, notes, and cancelled checks to prove your interest payments on loans, a mortgage, and credit cards.
- **Contributions.** The kinds of records you must keep for each contribution depend on whether you contribute cash or noncash property.
  1. *Cash.* If you contribute cash, you must keep one of the following for each contribution: (1) a cancelled check; (2) a receipt from the charity showing its name and the amount and date of the contribution; or (3) in the absence of a check or receipt, other reliable written records, which are reasonable under the circumstances, showing the name of the charity and the amount and date of the contribution.
  2. *Property.* If you contribute property, you must keep for each contribution a receipt from the charity showing: (1) the name of the charity; (2) the date of donation and location of the property; and (3) a description of the property in detail reasonably sufficient in view of the property and under the circumstances.

     A receipt is not required if it is not practical to get one (for example, when depositing property at an unattended drop site). In all cases you must keep certain records, which are listed in Publication 561, Determining the Value of Donated Property. You must keep additional records if you claim a deduction of more than $500 for an item of property. If you are claiming a deduction for noncash contributions totalling more than $500, you must file Form 8283, Noncash Charitable Contributions. Special substantiation requirements apply when an item, or a number of similar items together, are valued at more than $5,000. For details, see Pub. 561.
- **Union dues.** If union dues are withheld from your wages, keep your pay statements to show the amount. If you pay by cash or check, keep the receipts and cancelled checks.

How to Keep Records

It may be helpful to write down your ordinary expenses that may be deductible. How often you record these expenses is up to you.

Income Statements

You should also keep your income statements. These include Form W-2 for your wages and Forms 1099 for interest and dividends.

Your Checkbook

Your checkbook can be a basic source for keeping a record of your deductible expenses. If your checkbook has enough space, record sufficient information at the time you write a check so you can determine, when preparing your return, if the amount is a deductible expense. Cancelled checks alone are not always adequate evidence that an amount is deductible. You should keep receipts, sales slips, and any other documents that establish the deductibility of an amount.

You may keep receipts in any manner that best suits you as long as you can adequately document each deduction you take. One method is to use an envelope for each type of deductible expense. For example, you may keep all medical and dental receipts in one envelope and all tax statements in another envelope. Other envelopes you may need are for interest, contributions, and miscellaneous deductions.

If you pay a lot of expenses with cash, make it a habit to ask for a dated and, if appropriate, signed receipt if the expense may be deductible.

How Long You Should Keep Records

Generally, your records must be kept as long as they are important for any federal tax law. Records that support an item of income or a deduction on your return should be kept at least until the period of limitation expires for that return. Usually this is 3 years from the date the return was due or filed, or 2 years from the date the tax was paid, whichever is later. If an amount of income that should have been reported was not reported, and it is more than 25 percent of the income shown on the return, the period of limitation does not expire until 6 years after the return was filed. There is no period of limitation when a return is false or fraudulent, or when no return is filed.

Sometimes you should keep your records longer than the period of limitations. For example, if you want to use income averaging to figure your tax, you must show your taxable income for the 3 previous years. The taxable income figures can be obtained from copies of your tax returns. Records verifying the basis of property you own should also be kept until you are sure that they are no longer needed.

Sometimes new laws give tax benefits to taxpayers who can prove from their records of previous years that they are entitled to such benefits.

Exhibit 1-2

IRS Record Retention Guide for Income Taxes

Persons Subject to Income Tax

(a) *General.* Except as provided in paragraph (b), any person subject to tax, or any person required to file a return of information with respect to income shall keep such permanent books or records, including inventories, as are sufficient to establish the amount of gross income, deductions, credits, or other matters required to be shown by such person in any return or such tax or information.

(b) *Farmers and wage-earners.* Individuals deriving gross income from the business of farming, and individuals whose gross income includes salaries, wages, or similar compensation for personal services rendered, are required to keep such records as will enable the district director to determine the correct amount of income subject to the tax, but it is not necessary that these individuals keep the books of account or records required by paragraph (a).

(c) *Exempt organizations.* In addition to the books and records required by paragraph (a) with respect to the tax imposed on unrelated business income, every organization exempt from tax under section 501(a) of the Code shall keep such permanent books of account or records, including inventories, as are sufficient to show specifically the items of gross income, receipts and disbursements, and other required information.

(d) *Notice by District Director requiring returns, statements, or the keeping of records.* The District Director may require any person, by notice served upon them, to make such returns, render such statements, or keep such specific records as will enable the District Director to determine whether or not such person is liable for tax under subtitle A of the Code, including qualified State individual income taxes, which are treated pursuant to section 6361(a) of the Code as if they were imposed by chapter 1 of subtitle A.

Retention Period

The period for which records should be kept varies from a few years to a length of time that may cover more than one taxpayer's lifetime. The general requirement as stated in 26 CFR 1.6001-1 is that records must be kept "so long as the contents thereof may become material in the administration of any internal revenue law." Some books and records of a business may be "material" for tax purposes so long as the business remains in existence, and there may be reasons other than the Federal tax consequences to the individual taxpayer for retaining certain records for an indefinite period. However, the general requirements can be more precisely stated in terms of (1) records of property subject to gain or loss treatment, and (2) records supporting items of income deductions and credits.

- *Records of property* for which a basis must be determined to compute gain or loss upon disposition (and depreciation, amortization, or depletion allowed or allowable) must be retained until a taxable disposition is made. Thus, if property is given a substitute basis, i.e., the basis it had in the hands of the prior owner adjusted as required by the Code or regulations, all records pertaining to that property must be retained. After a taxable disposition, the record retention rules explained below will generally apply.

- *Records of income, deductions, and credits* (including gains and losses) appearing on a return should be kept, at a minimum, until the statute of limitations for the return expires. The general rule is that the amount of any tax imposed by the Internal Revenue Code shall be assessed within 3 years after the return was filed; and a claim for refund or credit must be filed within three years from the date of filing the return or 2 years after payment, whichever is later. However, there are many exceptions. For example, a 6-year period of limitation applies for assessment if there has been a substantial omission of income, and a 7-year period applies for filing a claim for credit or refund relating to bad debts or losses on securities. The period of limitations may be extended by mutual agreement for any length of time, and no statutory period applies if fraud is established or if no return was filed.

Failure to retain records for a sufficient length of time could result, for example, in the assessment of additional tax because of disallowance of deductions or a downward adjustment of basis used in determining gain or loss on the disposition of property.

The following record requirements have not been assigned a specific record retention period and the general "materiality" rule applies:

Residential energy credit—To maintain records that clearly identify the energy-conserving components and renewable energy source property with respect to which a residential energy credit is claimed, and substantiate their cost to the taxpayer, any labor costs properly allocable to them paid for by the taxpayer, and the method used for allocating such labor costs.

Persons subject to a minimum tax on items of tax preference—(a) *General.* To maintain permanent records of all the facts necessary to determine the amounts expended and adjustments made to property acquired and held for investment, and to maintain permanent records necessary to verify the exercise of a qualified stock option. To maintain records of the amount of debts written off and the amount of the loans outstanding with regard to the reserve for losses on bad debts of financial institutions for the taxable year and the 5 preceding taxable years or such shorter or longer period as appropriate.
(b) *Net operating losses.* To maintain permanent records of all the facts necessary for the first taxable year and each succeeding year in which there is a net operating loss or a net operating loss carryover, including the amount of net operating loss in each taxable year in which tax preference items exceed the minimum tax exemption, the amount of items for each such taxable year, the amount net operating loss reduces taxable income in any taxable year, and the amount net operating loss is reduced in any taxable year.

Persons not totally blind claiming the additional exemption for blindness—To retain a copy of the certified opinion of the examining physician skilled in the diseases of the eye that there is no reasonable probability that his visual acuity will ever improve beyond the minimum standards described in section 1.151-1(d)(3) of the regulations.

Persons paying travel or other business expenses incurred as an employee in connection with the performance of his services—To maintain adequate and detailed records of ordinary and necessary travel, transportation, entertainment, and other similar business expenses, including identification of amount and nature of expenditures, and to keep supporting documents, especially in connection with large or exceptional expenditures.

Persons claiming allowance for depreciation of property used in trade or business or property held for the production of income—To keep records and accounts with respect to basis of property, depreciation rates, reserves, salvage, retirements, adjustments, elections, property excluded from elections, cost of repair, maintenance or improvement of property, agreements with respect to estimated useful life, rates of salvage, and other factors.

Persons claiming depreciation with respect to residential rental property—To maintain a record of the gross rental income derived from a building, and the portion thereof which constitutes gross rental income from dwelling units, in addition to records required under section 1.167(a)-7(c) with respect to property in a depreciation account.

Persons claiming depreciation of expenditures to rehabilitate low-income rental housing—To maintain detailed records which permit specific identification of the rehabilitation expenditures that are permitted to be allocated to individual dwelling units under the allocation rules and income certifications that must be obtained from tenants who propose to live in rehabilitated dwelling units after the close of the certification year.

Persons claiming a deduction for amounts expended in maintaining certain students as a member of household—To keep adequate records of amounts actually paid in maintaining a student as a member of the household. For certain items, such as food, a record of amounts spent for all members of the household, with an equal portion thereof allocated to each member, will be acceptable.

Persons electing additional first-year depreciation allowance for section 179 property—To maintain records which permit specific identification of each piece of "section 179 property" and reflect how and from whom such property was acquired.

Election to deduct expenditures for removing architectural and transportation barriers to the handicapped and elderly—To retain records and documentation, including architectural plans and blueprints, contracts, and building permits, of all facts necessary to determine the amount of any deduction to which the taxpayer is entitled by reason of the election, as well as any adjustment to basis made for expenditures in excess of the amount deductible.

Persons receiving any class of exempt income or holding property or engaging in activities the income from which is exempt—To keep records of expenses otherwise allowable as deductions which are directly allocable to any class or classes of exempt income and amounts of items or parts of items allocated to each class.

Taxpayer substantiation of expenses for travel, entertainment, and gifts related to active conduct of trade or business—A taxpayer must substantiate each element of an expenditure by adequate records or sufficient evidence corroborating his own statements.

Persons required to seek the approval of the Commissioner in order to change their annual accounting period—To keep adequate and accurate records of their taxable income for the short period involved in the change and for the fiscal year proposed.

Persons selling by the installment method—(a) *Installment method.* In adopting the installment method of accounting the seller must maintain such records as are necessary to clearly reflect income. A dealer who desires to compute income by the installment method shall maintain accounting records in such a manner as to enable an accurate computation to be made by such method.
(b) *Revolving credit plan.* To maintain records in sufficient detail to show the method of computing and applying the probability sample.

Persons permitted or required to use the LIFO method of inventory valuation—(a) *General.* To maintain such supplemental and detailed inventory records as will enable the District Director to verify the inventory computations.
(b) *Dollar-value method.* To maintain adequate records to support the appropriateness, accuracy, and reliability of the index or link-chain method.

Controlled entities arm's-length charges—To maintain adequate books and records to permit verification of costs or deductions when a factor in determining the arm's-length charge for services rendered to other members of a controlled group.

Persons claiming an allowance for depletion and depreciation of mineral property, oil and gas wells, and other natural deposits—To keep a separate account in which shall be accurately recorded the cost or other basis of such property together with subsequent allowable capital additions to each account and all other required adjustments; and to assemble, segregate, and have readily available, at his principal place of business, all the supporting data which is used in compiling certain summary statements required to be attached to returns and such other records as indicated in the sections cited.

Persons claiming an allowance for depletion of timber property—To keep accurate ledger accounts in which shall be recorded the cost or other basis of the property and land, together with subsequent allowable capital additions in each account and all other adjustments. In such accounts there shall be set up separately the quantity of timber, the quantity of land, and the quantity of other resources, if any, and a proper part of the total cost or value shall be allocated to each after proper provision for immature timber growth. The timber accounts shall be credited each year with the amounts of the charges to the depletion accounts or the amount of the charges to the depletion accounts shall be credited to depletion reserves accounts.

Persons claiming credit for taxes paid or accrued to foreign countries and possessions of the United States—To keep readily available for comparison on request the original receipt for each such tax payment, or the original return on which each such accrued tax was based, a duplicate original, or a duly certified or authenticated copy, in case only a sworn copy of a receipt or return is submitted.

Executors or other legal representatives of decedents, fiduciaries of trusts under wills, life tenants and other persons to whom a uniform basis with respect to property transmitted at death is applicable—To make and maintain records showing in detail all deductions, distributions, or other items for which adjustment to basis is required to be made.

Persons making or receiving gifts of property acquired by gift after December 31, 1920—To preserve and keep accessible a record of the facts necessary to determine the cost of the property, its fair market value as of the date of the gift and, if pertinent, its fair market value as of March 1, 1913, to insure a fair and adequate determination of the proper basis.

Corporations and shareholders with respect to the substantiation of ordinary loss deductions on small business corporation stock—(a) *Corporations.* The plan to issue stock which qualifies under section 1244 of the Internal Revenue Code must appear upon the records of the corporation. In addition, in order to substantiate an ordinary loss deduction claimed by its shareholders, the corporation should maintain records as indicated in section cited.

(b) *Shareholders.* Any person who claims a deduction for an ordinary loss on stock under section 1244 of the Code shall file with his income tax return for the year in which a deduction for the loss is claimed a statement setting forth information indicated in section cited. In addition, a person who owns "section 1244 stock" in a corporation shall maintain records sufficient to distinguish such stock from any other stock he may own in the corporation.

Guidelines for Recordkeeping for Taxpayers with Wagering Winnings and Losses

An accurate diary or similar record regularly maintained by the taxpayer, supplemented by verifiable documentation, will usually be acceptable evidence for substantiation of wagering winnings and losses. In general, the diary should contain at least the following information:

- Date and type of specific wager or waging activity;
- Name of gambling establishment;
- Address or location of gambling establishment;
- Name(s) of other person(s) (if any) present with taxpayer at gambling establishment; and
- Amount(s) won or lost.

Verifiable documentation for gambling transactions includes but is not limited to Forms W-2G; Forms 5754, Statement by Person Receiving Gambling Winnings; wagering tickets, cancelled checks, credit records, bank withdrawals, and statements of actual winnings or payment slips provided to the taxpayer by the gambling establishment.

Where possible, the diary and available documentation generated with the placement and settlement of a wager should be further supported by other documentation of the taxpayer's wagering activity or visit to a gambling establishment. Such documentation includes, but is not limited to, hotel bills, airline tickets, gasoline credit cards, cancelled checks, credit records, bank deposits, and bank withdrawals.

Additional supporting evidence could also include affidavits or testimony from responsible gambling officials regarding wagering activity.

The Service is required to report to the Congress by 1979 on the issue of whether casino winnings should be subject to withholding. In the absence of legislation requiring withholding on casino winnings, the instructions for preparing Form 5754 will not be applicable to winnings from keno, bingo, or slot machines. However, all other items of documentation to verify gambling losses from casino winnings are applicable.

With regard to specific wagering transactions, winnings and losses may be further supported by the following items:

- Keno—Copies of keno tickets purchased by the taxpayer and validated by the gambling establishment, copies of the taxpayer's casino credit records, and copies of the taxpayer's casino check-cashing records.
- Slot Machines—A record of all winnings by date and time that the machine was played. (In Nevada, the machine number is the number required by the State Gaming Commission and may or may not be displayed in a prominent place on the machine. If not displayed on the machine, the number may be requested from the casino operator.)
- Table Games: Twenty One (Blackjack), Craps, Poker, Baccarat, Roulette, Wheel of Fortune, etc.—The number of the table at which the taxpayer was playing. Casino credit card data indicating whether the credit was issued in the pit or at the cashier's cage.
- Bingo—A record of the number of games played, cost of tickets purchased, and amounts collected on winning tickets. Supplemental records include any receipts from the casino, parlor, etc.
- Racing: Horse, Harness, Dog, etc.—A record of the races, entries, amounts of wagers, and amounts collected on winning tickets and amounts lost on losing tickets. Supplemental records include unredeemed tickets and payment records from the racetrack.
- Lotteries—A record of ticket purchases, dates, winnings, and losses. Supplemental records include unredeemed tickets, payment slips, and winnings statement.

The recordkeeping suggestions set forth above are intended as general guidelines to assist taxpayers in establishing their reportable gambling gains and deductible gambling losses. While following these will enable most taxpayers to meet their obligations under the Internal Revenue Code, these guidelines cannot be all-inclusive and the tax liability of each depends on the facts and circumstances of particular situations.

Step 2 Getting Correct Information From the IRS (And Others)

A good audit-proofer knows the tax laws are complicated; there are too many rules; and that the average person cannot possibly spend the time to become an expert. But you want to do the best you can to figure your taxes at a minimum level and your refund at a maximum amount without taking unnecessary risks. This means taking every deduction that can be taken according to tax law.

AUDIT-PROOFER'S STRATEGY RULE

Use the IRS's vast array of information services to keep informed and on top of the tax laws. In other words, use the IRS to beat the IRS.

"Tax law" is really a generic term that has many references that all originate with the Internal Revenue Code. The "Code," as it is called by tax practitioners and IRS employees, is literally thousands of pages long and contains some of the world's most confusing and ambiguous language. It is also the bedrock or the central document upon which "tax law" evolves. In the tax field the Code is the "tax law." But in a generic sense, the term encompasses the whole body of legislative, judicial, and executory rule-making.

Tax law also includes such IRS-issued peripheral items as information letters, regulations, revenue rulings, revenue procedures, private letter rulings, delegation orders, written determinations, closing agreements, and technical advice memorandums. But it doesn't stop there. We also have tax conventions, executive orders, treasury decisions, treasury department orders, statements of procedural rules, and GCMs, or General Counsel Memorandums. Then there are "memorandum decisions" and "regular decisions" of the Tax Court.

To make it even worse we also have opinions by district courts, Claims Courts, Courts of Appeals, and the Supreme Court, with an occasional opinion from the Comptroller General. To confuse things even more, the IRS announces whether or not it will follow the court cases by *acquiescence* or *nonacquiescence*.

Even tax lingo becomes part of the tax law. For example, sometimes the IRS will change revenue rulings by *clarifying* them, but if that doesn't do the trick, then they are *amplified*. If things get too confusing, the rulings are *distinguished,* but the IRS always reserves the right to *modify* them. If a revenue ruling gets really "hairy," it can be *revoked, superseded,* or *obsoleted,* not to mention *supplemented,* or *suspended*. All in a day's work at the IRS in Washington, D.C.

Now you know, kind of, what tax law is.

WHERE TO GO FOR ANSWERS

It's nice to know what tax law is, but that won't save you any dollars on your taxes. The real question is, "Where do you go to find *the answer* to your questions?" The IRS? The Tax Court? A tax attorney? A CPA? Your local Enrolled Agent? A public accountant? The big tax prep (IRS talk for preparation) chain? Your local newspaper? The library? Your Congressman? The President? Sylvia Porter? Jane Fonda? Dr. Ruth?

A logical first step would be a tax practitioner. Almost 50 percent of all taxpayers pay someone to prepare their tax returns. But few taxpayers fully use their tax practitioners to help them understand the tax ramifications of other aspects of their financial life. A good audit-proofing strategy demands that you think "taxes" on all aspects of your financial life. Think of the tax ramifications of everything you do, because taxes are dollars, and dollars can be saved.

Too many taxpayers never bother to think "taxes" until it's time to prepare their tax return, when they start thinking "refund." Then it's too late to be considering tax reduction strategies for a year that's gone by. Just about anyone who files a Form 1040 with supplemental schedules other than Schedules A and B could benefit from at least one *tax reduction consultation* with a knowledgeable tax consultant. The fee for at least one hour a year is a necessary expense you should plan for. Remember, it's tax deductible too.

AUDIT-PROOFER'S STRATEGY RULE

Find yourself a good tax consultant who's available year-round to give you guidance on legal tax-reduction or tax-avoidance strategies. **Before** ***you enter into any financial situation or arrangement, call your tax consultant and ask for advice on its tax ramification. This will help you to structure the situation to your best financial benefit, and save tax dollars. The following April 15th may be too late.***

Learning to rely on the advice of a tax consultant year-round is good discipline. It will reinforce the concept of thinking audit-proofing at the same time.

Many taxpayers reading this would still rather do their own tax return, and find answers themselves to their uncomplicated, but moderately difficult, questions. Many people feel this way, not necessarily because they don't want to spend the money for tax consultation services, but because they don't think their financial affairs are so complicated that they can't handle it themselves.

And you're probably one of those who think that way, otherwise you wouldn't be reading this. Bravo for you! The more you learn about taxes and proper tax reduction strategies, the more confident you will be to face other tax challenges. And the more you think about facing an IRS auditor for instance, the more you're going to think *audit-proofing*.

AUDIT-PROOFER'S STRATEGY RULE

A good audit-proofer is **taxwise:** ***he or she not only arranges financial affairs to be*** **tax-efficient,** ***but also takes steps to protect and preserve his or her tax efficiency by preparing early to beat an IRS audit. No one knows how many billions of dollars taxpayers have had to pay in additional taxes because they didn't think audit-proof at the right time, and didn't retain the necessary information or documentation. A good audit-proofer is always looking ahead and is*** **taxwise during the year,** ***not after the year.***

If you're *not* going to rely on a tax consultant for your total tax strategy and to answer all your tax questions, you need to know where to go and where to look, before the fact.

The Tax Code—Stay Away!

The absolute last place in the world you want to look for an answer to a tax question is the Code. It's the biggest mess of mind-boggling, obfuscating, mumbo jumbo you've ever read. You'd probably have an easier time trying to understand Shakespeare in Elizabethan English.

The Code is the birthplace of such things as ACRS, ESOPS, zero bracket amounts, cafeteria plans, collapsible corporations, golden parachute payments, DISCs, carryover, carrybacks, rollovers, mixed straddles, LIFO, FIFO, depletion, amortization, involuntary conversions, GSOCs, DECs, IRAs, SEPs, lump-sum distributions, and VEBAs.

It is also the embodiment of such famous legalisms as "notwithstanding the above," "except as otherwise provided," "subject to such terms and conditions as may be provided," "the secretary shall prescribe," "in the case of," "in the manner provided by" . . .

The Code is used only by tax attorneys during court cases, by tax practitioners who like to show off, and by authors of tax books and articles who like to give their pronouncements an air of legitimacy and authority. For anyone else, the Code is *not* the place to go for research.

The IRS—Watch Your Step

In your quest for an answer to a tax question, the first place to check for information is, obviously, the IRS. But you have to be careful how you go about that. You have the option of picking up the phone and calling them, or you can go to them at your local IRS office. If you phone in, you can ask your question of whomever answers the phone, you can listen to a prerecorded cassette tape, or you can request published material to be sent to you. If you go to the office (you are then a "walk-in" in IRS lingo) you won't be able to listen to a prerecorded tape, but you may find someone who will answer your question, and you should be able to pick up a booklet on the tax law related to your question.

The person you'll be talking to will be either a Taxpayer Service Representative (TSR) or a Taxpayer Service Specialist (TSS) in the Taxpayer Service Division. These people are IRS's front-line information sources. Usually a TSR will help you, but if he or she can't, then you'll be referred to a TSS.

There are many aspects to IRS's Information and Assistance Program; consult Exhibit 2-1 for a complete list of ways in which they can help you. Note particularly the Taxpayer Education Programs, which can help you in two ways: They not only provide an opportunity for assistance, but they also provide an opportunity for learning about taxes. These free programs are a good way to start learning the basics of tax law.

The IRS says the Taxpayer Service Division responded to 37.9 million telephone calls, and helped 8.1 million walk-ins in 1986. Approximately 65% of these occurred in the 16-week period from January 1 through April 26th. The IRS says their people respond with an accuracy rate of 93 percent.

There are several things you need to know about this accuracy rate. First, because the IRS hires seasonal assistors for the filing season who are relatively inexperienced, temporary employees, their accuracy rate will be lower at the beginning of the season. But after answering thousands of questions eight hours a day for a couple of months, their accuracy rate increases as they become more familiar with the nuances of the law. Therefore, if you've got a moderately difficult question, you should be somewhat suspicious of any answer you get during the first couple of months. After the middle of March, the reliability rate improves significantly.

Secondly, the IRS accuracy figures are misleading because they are skewed. About half of the telephone questions are rather innocuous and mundane. The IRS refers to them as the "10 most frequently asked questions." They include: "Where do I send my tax return?" "How long will it take for me to get my refund?" "Can I staple my W-2 to my form?" With those kinds of questions, anyone can have a 93 percent accuracy rate!

If the IRS were to publish accuracy rates according to degree of difficulty of the question, you would probably find that the error rate goes up with increasing level of difficulty. The more difficult your question, the less likely you'll get a correct answer. This has been proven many times by magazine and newspaper reporters who call numerous IRS offices with moderately difficult questions only to get variously different answers.

AUDIT-PROOFER'S STRATEGY RULE

Don't rely solely on oral advice from the IRS. Oral advice is only advisory; the IRS will* not *stand behind it, and it is not sustainable in any subsequent challenge by an IRS Auditor.

The reasons are obvious: First, unless you tape the conversation, you could never prove what was actually said. Second, there is the communication factor; in any conversation, what is spoken by one person may be easily misperceived by the other, particularly if either party consciously or otherwise, makes inherent assumptions in the conversation. Third, the IRS is a word factory, and spoken words cannot be traced. Tax law is written law. The only advice the IRS stands on is published advice.

AUDIT-PROOFER'S STRATEGY RULE

Always ***support your position with*** **written** ***instructions from the IRS. Whenever you call or visit the IRS,*** **always** ***ask for a publication related to the topic of your question, so that you can do your own research. Do this even if you feel confident that you've gotten a concise and accurate answer from Taxpayer Service.***

IRS Policy Statement P-1-157 states, "Taxpayers will assume that they can rely on the accuracy of all official publications." The IRS has a number of publications you can order, from the 184-page Publication 17, "Your Federal Income Tax," to over 90 other publications on specialized topics in the 500 and 900 numerical series. Exhibit 2-2 has a complete listing of all these publications and the type of information in each.

A note of caution is in order here. You should understand that IRS publications are good for conducting research, because they reflect the tax law that will be used by IRS auditors, but *they are not good for tax tips*. The IRS publications do not offer tax savings tips or tax avoidance strategies. They do not offer guidance on how to structure your financial affairs for maximum tax benefit. *They are not written to save you tax dollars*. They are written to reflect the views and positions of the IRS. They will not, for example, even tell you of the different Circuit Court interpretations that may benefit you.

AUDIT-PROOFER'S STRATEGY RULE

You must rely on a number of resources to find tax laws that will benefit you without unnecessary risk. This means using commercial reference materials published by others outside of the IRS.

There are a number of good commercial tax preparation guides available, and it might be to your benefit to buy several each tax season. Each one has its own strengths and weaknesses, so you need to try several before you find the two or three that you think are right for you. In the absence of your own personal tax consultant, you need reference materials to give you tax guidance with your financial affairs.

Make sure that the prep guide you are using is published by a recognized authority and by a leading publishing house. An off-the-wall local edition published by a small press may not be as accurate as what you are looking for.

Also, stay away from books that'll get you in trouble, even if they are carried by a major bookstore chain. These are books that tell you by some twisted illogical reasoning that you don't have to file a tax return because either the tax laws or the IRS is unconstitutional. Remember that bookstore owners don't necessarily read what they sell, and just because it's a published manuscript doesn't mean it has a legitimate premise.

Additional IRS Resources

In your research you may have to consult IRS regulations ("regs") which can be found in some major libraries. Issued by the IRS, regulations implement the Tax Code. The regs are not only published by the government, but also by several major loose-leaf tax reporting services. Another place to check is your local IRS office. Most likely, there will be a set there that you can use.

While at the IRS, you can also ask for information relating to revenue rulings or revenue procedures that may pertain to your research. These are guidelines published in the *Internal Revenue Bulletin,* the official publication of the IRS. See Exhibit 2-4 for a complete explanation of revenue rulings, revenue procedures, and the *Internal Revenue Bulletin* (the IRB).

There are other ways very few taxpayers know about in which you can use the IRS in setting up your audit-proofing strategy. For example, you can get personalized help in the following situations:

- You are about to enter into an unusual financial arrangement, but you want to know what the tax ramifications are before you sign the contracts.
- You have already entered into an unusual financial arrangement, but you want to know how to treat it on your tax return before you file.
- You are in the midst of being audited and your IRS auditor proposes treating your unusual financial arrangement in a way that will result in a higher tax bill than you believe is justified.
- You want to find out how the IRS treated other taxpayers in similar circumstances.

Usually, the taxpayers who avail themselves of the opportunity to use the IRS help in these situations are those who can afford to have a tax practitioner pursue it for them. Even if you want to prepare your own tax return, or do your own research, these are situations in which it may be in your best interests to pay a practitioner to obtain the right information. Whether you do it yourself or not, it is important that you at least know that these tools are available to you.

AUDIT-PROOFER'S STRATEGY RULE

- ***If you want to know what the tax ramifications of a particular financial transaction would be, you can request a* private letter ruling. *See Exhibit 2-6 on the following pages.***
- ***If you have already participated in a financial transaction and you want to know how it is to be handled on your tax return, you can request a* written determination. *See Exhibit 2-6 on the following pages.***
- ***If you are in the midst of an audit, and you don't believe that the auditor is treating your unusual financial transaction properly, then you can request* technical advice *from the National Office in Washington, D.C. See Exhibit 2-5 on pages 76–78.***
- ***If you want to know how the IRS has treated other taxpayers in similar situations, you can review censored versions of private letter rulings and written determinations previously issued by the IRS. You need to either check with a subscriber to a loose-leaf reporting service that publishes those rulings and determinations (some tax practitioners carry them), or with an IRS Freedom of Information Reading Room located either in Washington, D.C. or in one of the regional headquarters offices.***

RECOMMENDED TAX PREPARATION GUIDES

Although not intended to be all-inclusive, the following is a list of commercially published tax preparation guides that you may find helpful when preparing your own tax return.

1. *H & R Block Income Tax Workbook* by H & R Block (Macmillan Publishing Company)
2. *J. K. Lasser's Your Income Tax* by J. K. Lasser Tax Institute (Simon & Schuster)
3. *Miller's Personal Income Tax Guide* by Martin Miller, CPA, L. Harold Levinson, JD, CPA, and Laura P. Stephenson, JD (Harcourt Brace Jovanovich)
4. *Pay Less Tax Legally* by Barry R. Steiner, CPA (New American Library)

5. *The Arthur Young Tax Guide* by Arthur Young & Co. (Ballantine Books)
6. *Everyone's Income Tax Guide* by S. Jay Lasser, CPA (Hilltop Publications)
7. *Sylvia Porter's Income Tax Book* by Sylvia Porter (Avon Books)
8. *Cut Your Own Taxes and Save* by Robert Metz and Sidney Kess (World Almanac Publications)

RECOMMENDED NEWSLETTERS ON TAX-SAVING STRATEGIES

Although not intended to be all-inclusive, the following is a list of commercially prepared newsletters on taxes. These newsletters commonly cover numerous tax-saving strategies that you may find helpful. You must write to the publisher for current subscription rates.

1. *Tax Savings Report* by National Taxpayer's Union, 325 Pennsylvania Ave., S.E., Washington, D.C. 20003.
2. *Tax Angles* by American Tax Institute, Inc., Tower Suite, 870 Seventh Avenue, New York, NY 10019.
3. *Tax Hotline* by Boardroom Reports, Inc., 330 W. 42 St., New York, NY 10036.
4. *Tax Avoidance Digest* by Euler Enterprises, Inc., Penthouse 11, 4853 Cordell Ave., Bethesda, MD 20814.
5. *Monthly Tax Service*, exclusively for subscribers of J. K. Lasser's *Your Income Tax*, by Simon & Schuster, Inc., Simon & Schuster Bldg., 1230 Avenue of the Americas, New York, NY 10020.
6. *The Kiplinger Tax Letter* by The Kiplinger Washington Editors, 1729 H. St. N.W., Washington, D.C. 20006.

Exhibit 2-1

IRS Information and Assistance

(IRS Publication 910)

Most taxpayers should be able to meet the requirements of the tax laws by using information such as tax package instructions, publications, taxpayer education, education programs, films, and library programs. If further information and assistance are needed, services are available as indicated in the following paragraphs.

Toll-free telephone and walk-in assistance is available to answer questions on taxpayer accounts, IRS procedures, or technical inquiries as defined below.

An Account Inquiry is any inquiry that:

- Results from:
  1. a notice or bill, or
  2. correspondence related to the processing of a return, or taxpayer's account;
- Requests information on the status of a tax account, processing of a tax return, or refund due; and/or
- Requires research in IRS tax accounting records to resolve.

A Procedural Inquiry is any inquiry that:

- Requests advice, information, or action that only IRS can provide/perform (that is, Freedom of Information requests, Federal Tax Deposit requests, Form W-2 inquiries);
- Requests information about the operating procedures of IRS (that is, Collection, Examination, Criminal Investigation, Alien Clearance);
- Requests information on IRS programs or IRS-sponsored programs (that is, office hours, locations, Volunteer Income Tax Assistance, Tax Counseling for the Elderly); and/or
- Results from IRS-generated correspondence not related to the processing of a tax return (for example, Examination appointment).

A Technical Inquiry is any inquiry that:

- Requests an explanation of tax law not related to a notice, bill, or correspondence; and/or
- Requests an interpretation/service position on current or proposed tax law.

Telephone Service

Toll-free telephone assistance is available in all 50 states as well as the District of Columbia, Puerto Rico, and the Virgin Islands. Under this system you pay only local charges, with no long-distance charge for your call. Through the toll-free system you may obtain assistance on account-related, procedural, or technical questions. (Please see the above paragraphs for a definition of these types of questions.)

To measure courteous responses and accurate information, an IRS employee will occasionally listen in on telephone calls. No record will be made of your name, address, or Social Security number except where a follow-up telephone call must be made.

During periods of peak demand for telephone assistance you may encounter busy signals when trying to call. Generally, demand is lower early in the morning and later in the week, so you may want to call at those times.

Tele-Tax

The IRS provides a telephone service called Tele-Tax. This service has Recorded Tax Information tapes on about 150 topics covering such areas as filing requirements, dependents, itemized deductions, and tax credits. Recorded Tax Information is available 24 hours a day, 7 days a week to taxpayers using a pushbutton (tone signaling) phone. It is also available during normal business hours to taxpayers using a rotary (dial) or pushbutton (pulse dial) phone.

Tele-Tax includes Automated Refund Information. If it has been ten weeks since you mailed your tax return, the IRS will be able to check the status of your refund. Automated Refund Information is not available between January 1st and March 15th.

Depending on where you live, calling Tele-Tax may be a long-distance call for you. A complete list of the telephone numbers is available in IRS Publication 910. See Exhibit 2-3 for a complete listing of what topics are available on the tapes.

Telephone Service for Deaf Taxpayers

Toll-free telephone assistance for deaf taxpayers is available for those who have access to TV/Telephone-TTY equipment. The hours of operation of this service are 8:00 a.m. to 6:45 p.m. (Eastern Standard Time) for January through April, and 8:00 a.m. to 4:30 p.m. for May through December. Residents of Indiana may call 1-800-382-4059. Residents elsewhere in the U.S., including Alaska, Hawaii, Puerto Rico, and the Virgin Islands may call 1-800-428-4732.

Information for the Blind

Braille materials are available at Regional Libraries for the Blind and Physically Handicapped in conjunction with the Library of Congress. These materials include Publications 17 and 334, forms 1040, 1040A, and 1040EZ and Schedules A and B, W, and instructions.

Walk-In Service

While the Internal Revenue Service will not prepare your tax return for you, assistors are available in most IRS offices throughout the country to help you prepare your own tax return. You will be expected to help yourself to the maximum extent possible. However, the IRS will provide some assistance and at the same time teach you how to research and prepare your own tax return. An assistor will "walk-through" a return with you and a number of other taxpayers in a group setting.

If you have a question that does not involve any return preparation, a walk-up counter may be available to help minimize waiting time.

If you wish assistance with your tax return, you should take with you your tax package, your W-2 and 1099 forms, and any other information (such as a copy of last year's return) that will be necessary for preparing your return.

Taxpayer Information Publications

Tax information helpful in understanding your tax responsibilities may be found in the publications listed on pages 63–68. You may order these free publications and forms from the IRS Forms Distribution Center for your state. Addresses for the Forms Distribution Centers along with an order blank can be found on the last page of Publication 910. You may find it convenient to obtain copies of many forms and schedules at public libraries, which have been furnished reproducible copies. A reference set of Taxpayer Information Publications is also available at some libraries.

Computer Tax Database

The IRS has prepared a database of tax information that is available through several commercial information retrieval (videotex) services. These services are accessible on a subscription basis by computer terminals that are equipped with modems.

The database consists of selected Taxpayer Information Publications, answers to the most commonly asked tax-related questions, and other items that are prepared for information retrieval. The database covers many topics that can be used in preparing Federal tax returns and as a reference source for year-round tax planning.

Problem Resolution Program (PRP)

The Problem Resolution Program (PRP) is for taxpayers who have been unable to resolve their problems through normal Internal Revenue Service channels. Someone with a tax problem should first contact IRS taxpayer assistance, or in the case of a letter or notice from the IRS, call the number provided. Generally, questions are answered and problems solved right then—but not always. That's when PRP steps in. Each of the IRS's 63 district offices has a PRP office whose specialty is assisting taxpayers who previously contacted the IRS with their tax problems but could not get them resolved. People in the PRP office have the authority to cut through the red tape and handle problems promptly. The taxpayer generally deals with one person and is kept informed of the case's progress. Taxpayers can contact PRP by calling the IRS assistance number listed in Pub. 910 or writing to their local Internal Revenue Service District Director and asking for Problem Resolution assistance. While PRP offices do everything they can to help taxpayers, there are some things they cannot do. Appeals of decisions made in tax examinations, Freedom of Information Act requests, Privacy Act inquiries, and complaints about hiring practices are all outside of PRP's authority.

Taxpayer Education Programs

The Internatal Revenue Service has a number of programs designed to educate the public about our nation's voluntary compliance tax system and each citizen's share in it so that the system works as smoothly as possible. The more that citizens understand their role in this tax system, the better they will be able to carry out their responsibilities with a minimum of intrusion in their lives by the government. All of these taxpayer education programs offer opportunity for citizen involvement through service as volunteers.

Understanding Taxes

This is a tax education program that begins in the schools, where young people are taught about their tax rights and responsibilities under our voluntary compliance tax system. They also learn how to fill out basic tax returns. Since many of them already are working, often at their first jobs, this learning has immediate practical value. They also learn about the history of taxes and current issues in taxation, such as tax reform. All materials teachers need are available free of charge, including a six-part film series, "Tax Whys: Understanding Taxes." These films are produced in cooperation with the states. Workshops are conducted during the year to help prepare teachers for course instruction.

Small Business Workshops

These workshops help people start small businesses by providing them with the information they need to carry out their tax responsibilities, including tax withholding, making correct and timely tax deposits, and filing a business return. Some sessions focus on the needs of the self-employed, minority entrepreneurs, and specialized business groups.

Volunteer Income Tax Assistance

The Volunteer Income Tax Assistance program (VITA) provides free tax assistance to lower income, elderly, non-English-speaking and handicapped people, and also to members of the military. Generally those who receive these services can't afford professional tax assistance. After completing IRS training, volunteers provide free help at special locations.

Tax Counseling for the Elderly

Tax Counseling for the Elderly (TCE) provides free tax assistance to people 60 or older, especially those who are disabled or have other special needs. Non-profit organizations under cooperative agreements with the IRS provide local assistance.

Both VITA and TCE sites usually are located in neighborhood centers, libraries, churches, and other places in the community.

Student Tax Clinics

Another program, Student Tax Clinic, uses volunteer law and graduate accounting students who have received permission from the Treasury Department to represent taxpayers before the IRS. They provide free assistance to taxpayers during IRS examination and appeals proceedings.

Community Outreach Tax Assistance

This is a year-round program of assistance to groups who need help understanding the tax laws, especially as they apply to members of their profession or group, such as teaching or business or farming. Seminars are conducted at times and locations in the community that are convenient for members of the group.

For all of these programs, contact your local IRS office for more information and locations of sites or presentations in your areas.

Taxpayer Information Program

The Taxpayer Information Program is designed to give taxpayers the information they need to understand their rights and comply with their responsibilities under the tax laws.

To reach the greatest number of taxpayers, the Taxpayer Information Program provides print and audio-visual public service materials directly to the public, and to the news media for dissemination to the public. In cooperation with the public television stations IRS also produces programs for broadcast which take taxpayers step-by-step through Forms 1040A and 1040EZ, and highlight Form 1040 and Schedules A and B.

The IRS provides local libraries with audio cassettes and videocassettes, for loan to the public, on how to fill out Forms 1040EZ, 1040A, 1040, and Schedules A and B. These tax tapes contain simple, step-by-step instructions through the forms, tax tips, and special rules for the military.

IRS-produced films and videotapes are available for loan directly from the IRS, without charge, to groups or interested organizations. To order the film of your choice, call your local office and ask for the Public Affairs Officer.

- **How to Fill Out Your Tax Return**—A line-by-line guide on how to fill out Forms 1040EZ, 1040A, 1040, and Schedules A and B. It explains how to choose the right tax return and discusses filing status, deductions, tax law changes, tax credits, and tax computations as well as other topics pertaining to your tax returns. (60 mins. ¾", ½" Beta and VHS. Updated versions available by January of each year.)
- **Why Us, the Lakens?**—This film, narrated by Lyle Waggoner, highlights taxpayers' rights during a tax audit and their Appeal rights. It follows Jeff and Kathy Laken, whose tax return has been selected for an IRS audit. Unhappy with the audit finding, the Lakens appeal and the viewer learns not only how the audit procedure works but the appeals system as well. (28 mins. 16mm film and ¾" videocassettes.)
- **A Trip Down the Pipline**—The 14-minute film, narrated by Terry Carter, who appeared in such popular TV programs as *Battlestar Galactica* and *McCloud*, shows how a tax return is processed at an IRS Service Center. The film depicts the various steps that occur in the processing cycle, or along the pipeline. (14 mins. 16mm film.)
- **A Vital Service**—People helping people with their federal taxes is what "A Vital Service" is all about. It aims at enlisting groups and organizations into the Volunteer Income Tax Assistance (VITA) Program in which IRS trains volunteers to help the low-income, elderly, non-English speaking, and the handicapped with their tax forms. (9½ mins. 16mm film and ¾" videocassettes.)
- **Helping to Recover**—Focuses on how to claim disaster, casualty, and theft losses. (13 mins. ¾" videocassette.)
- **Hey, We're in Business**—A couple just starting their own restaurant business—and encountering the related tax problems—are the focus of this dramatized presentation. Jim Backus, David Hedison, Pat Crowley, and Nehemiah Persoff form the cast of this production about good recordkeeping, tax deadlines, and free IRS assistance to business persons. (27½ mins. 16mm film. English and Spanish.)

Exhibit 2-2

Taxpayer Information Publications
(IRS Publication 910)

The Internal Revenue Service publishes many free pamphlets to help you with your taxes. These publications are listed here, generally in numerical order. The list describes the ones used most often and indicates the main related forms and schedules. A form or schedule listed appears as a filled-in example in the publication.

The four publications listed first give general information about tax for individuals, small businesses, farming, and the fishing industry. You may want to order one of these publications, and then, if you need detailed information on any subject, order the specific publication about it. The fifth publication listed here (#553) highlights tax changes since last year.

#17: Your Federal Income Tax

This publication can help you prepare your own return. It takes you through the return and explains the tax laws that cover salaries and wages, interest and dividends, itemized deductions, rental income, gains and losses, and adjustments to income (such as alimony, moving expenses, employee business expenses, and the deduction for a married couple when both work).

Examples illustrate typical situations. Filled-in forms and schedules show how to report income and deductions.

The Tax Table, Tax Rate Schedules, sales tax tables and earned income credit tables are not included in this publication. They are in the instructions for Form 1040. The Tax Table and earned income credit table are also in the instructions for Forms 1040A and 1040EZ.

Includes: Forms 1040, 1040A, 1040EZ, Schedules A, B, D, E, R, SE, Forms 2106, 2119, 2441, 3903.

#334: Tax Guide for Small Business

This book explains some federal tax laws that apply to businesses. It describes the four major forms of business organizations—sole proprietorship, partnership, corporations, and S corporation—and explains the tax responsibilities of each.

This publication is divided into eight parts. The first part contains general information on business organization and accounting practices. Part II discusses the tax aspects of accounting for the assets used in a business.

Parts III and IV explain how to figure your business income for tax purposes. They describe the kinds of income you must report and the different types of business deductions you can take.

Part V discusses the rules that apply when you sell or exchange business assets or investment property. It includes chapters on the treatment of capital gains and losses, and on involuntary conversions, such as theft and casualty losses. The chapters in Part VI bring together some specific tax considerations for each of the four major forms of business organizations.

Part VII looks at some of the credits that can reduce your income tax, and some of the other taxes you may have to pay in addition to income tax. The last part shows how to fill out the main income tax forms businesses use.

Includes: Schedule C (Form 1040), Forms 1065, 1120, 1120-A, 1120S, Schedule K-1 (Form 1065), Forms 4562 and 4797.

#225: Farmer's Tax Guide

This publication explains how the federal tax laws apply to farming. It gives examples of typical farming situations and discusses the kinds of farm income you must report and the different deductions you can take.

Includes: Form 1040, Schedule F (Form 1040), Schedule A, D, SE (Form 1040), Forms 3468, 4136, 4255, 4562, 4684, 4797, and 6251.

#595: Tax Guide for Commercial Fishermen

This publication will familiarize you with the federal tax laws as they apply to the fishing business. It is intended for sole proprietors who use Schedule C (Form 1040) to report profit or loss from fishing. This guide does not cover corporations or partnerships.

The publication's 16 chapters each give tax information about a different aspect of the fishing business. The last chapter gives an example of a fisherman's record-keeping system and sample tax forms.

Includes: Schedule C (Form 1040), 1099-MISC, 4562, and 4797.

#553: Highlights of Tax Changes (issued annually)

This publication discusses the more important changes in the tax rules brought about by recent legislation, rulings, and administrative decisions. It does not discuss all new tax rules or detail all changes. It highlights the important recent changes that taxpayers should know about when filing their tax forms and when planning for the current tax year.

#15: Circular E, Employer's Tax Guide

Every employer automatically receives an annual revision of this publication and every person who applies for an employer identification number also receives a copy.

Includes: Forms 940, 941, and 941E.

All Other Free IRS Publications

#51: Circular A, Agricultural Employer's Tax Guide—Form 943

#54: Tax guide for U.S. Citizens and Resident Aliens Abroad—Forms 2555, 1116, and 1040, Schedule SE (Form 1040)

#80: Circular SS, Federal Tax Guide for Employers in the Virgin Islands, Guam, and American Samoa—Forms 940, 941 SS and 943

#179: Circular PR, *Guia Contributiva Federal Para Patronos Puertorriquenos* (Federal Tax Guide for Employers in Puerto Rico)—Forms W-3PR, 940PR, 941PR, 942PR, and 943PR

#349: Federal Highway Use Tax on Heavy Vehicles—Form 2290

#378: Fuel Tax Credits—Forms 4136 and 6478

#448: Federal Estate and Gift Taxes—Forms 706 and 709

#463: Travel, Entertainment, and Gift Expenses—Form 2106

#501: Exemptions—Form 2120

#502: Medical and Dental Expenses—Schedule A (Form 1040)

#503: Child and Dependent Care Credit, and Employment Taxes for Household Employers—Forms W-2, W-3, 940, 942, Schedule 1 (Form 1040A), and 2441

#504: Tax Information for Divorced or Separated Individuals

#505: Tax Withholding and Estimated Tax—Forms W-4, W-4P, W-5, W-4S, 1040-ES, 2210, and 2210F

#508: Educational Expenses—Form 2106

#509: Tax Calendars for Current Tax Year

#510: Excise Taxes for Current Tax Year—Form 720

#513: Tax Information for Visitors to the United States—Forms 1040C, 1040NR, 2063, and 1040-ES(FOD)

#514: Foreign Tax Credit for U.S. Citizens and Resident Aliens—Form 1116

#515: Withholding of Tax on Nonresident Aliens and Foreign Corporations—Forms 1042 and 1042S

#516: Tax Information for U.S. Government Civilian Employees Stationed Abroad

#517: Social Security for Members of the Clergy and Religious Workers—Form 2106, Form 4361, Form 1040, Schedule SE (Form 1040), and Schedule C (Form 1040)

#518: Foreign Workers, Scholars, and Exchange Visitors—Forms 1040NR and 2063

#519: U.S. Tax Guide for Aliens—Forms 1040, 1040C, 1040NR, 2063, and Schedule A (Form 1040)

#520: Scholarships and Fellowships

#521: Moving Expenses—Forms 3903, 3903F, and 4782

#523: Tax Information on Selling Your Home—Form 2119

#524: Credit for the Elderly and the Permanently and Totally Disabled—Schedule R (Form 1040)

#525: Taxable and Nontaxable Income

#526: Charitable Contributions

#527: Rental Property—Schedule E (Form 1040), Forms 4562 and 4797

#529: Miscellaneous Deductions—Schedule A (Form 1040)

#530: Tax Information for Owners of Homes, Condominiums, and Cooperative Apartments

#531: Reporting Income from Tips—Forms 4070 and 4070A

#533: Self-Employment Tax—Schedule SE (Form 1040)

#534: Depreciation—Form 4562

#535: Business Expenses

#536: Net Operating Losses and the At-Risk Limits

#537: Installment Sales—Form 6252

#538: Accounting Periods and Methods—Forms 1128 and 3115

#539: Employment Taxes and Information Return Requirements—Employees Defined, Income Tax Withholding, Social Security Taxes (FICA), Federal Unemployment Tax (FUTA), Reporting and Allocating Tips, Information Returns—Forms 940 and 941

#541: Tax Information on Partnerships—Forms 1065, 4797, and Schedules D, K, and K-1 (Form 1065)

#542: Tax Information on Corporations—Form 1120 and 1120-A

#544: Sales and Other Dispositions of Assets—Schedule D (Form 1040) and Form 4797

#545: Interest Expense—Schedule A (Form 1040)

#547: Nonbusiness Disasters, Casualties, and Thefts—Form 4684

#548: Deduction for Bad Debts

#549: Condemnations and Business Casualties and Thefts—Forms 4797 and 4864

#550: Investment Income and Expenses—Schedules B and D (Form 1040)

#551: Basis of Assets

#552: Recordkeeping for Individuals and a List of Tax Publications

#553: Highlights of Current Year Tax Changes

#554: Tax Benefits for Older Americans—Schedules B, D, and R (Form 1040), Forms 1040 and 2119

#555: Community Property and the Federal Income Tax

#556: Examination of Returns, Appeal Rights, and Claims for Refund—Forms 1040X and 1120X

#556S: *Revision de las Declaraciones de Impuesto, Derecho de Apelacion y Reclamaciones de Reembolsos* (Examination of Returns, Appeal Rights, and Claims for Refund)—Forms 1040X and 1120X

#557: Tax-Exempt Status for Your Organization—Forms 1023 and 1024

#559: Tax Information for Survivors, Executors, and Administrators—Form 1040, Schedules A, B, E (Form 1040), Form 1041, Schedule D (Form 1041), and Form 4562

#560: Self-Employed Retirement Plans

#561: Determining the Value of Donated Property

#564: Mutual Fund Distributions—Form 1040, Schedule B(Form 1040), and Form 1099-DIV

#567: U.S. Civil Service Retirement and Disability—Form 1040

#570: Tax Guide for U.S. Citizens Employed in U.S. Possessions—Forms 4563 and 5074

#571: Tax-Sheltered Annuity Programs for Employees of Public

Schools and Certain Tax-Exempt Organizations—Form 5330

#572: Investment Credit—Forms 3468, 3800, and 4255

#575: Pension and Annuity Income—Forms 1040, 1099-R, and 4972

#578: Tax Information for Private Foundations and Foundation Managers—Form 990PF

#579S: *Como preparar la declaracion de impuesto federal* (How to Prepare the Federal Income Tax Return)—Forms 1040, 1040A, 1040EZ, 1040NR, 1040X, Schedules A, B, and W (Form 1040), Forms 2441 and W-2.

#583: Information for Business Taxpayers—Business Taxes, Identification Numbers, Recordkeeping—Schedule C (Form 1040), Form 4562

#584: Nonbusiness Disaster, Casualty, and Theft Loss Workbook

#585: Voluntary Tax Methods to Help Finance Political Campaigns

#586A: The Collection Process (Income Tax Accounts)

#586S: *Proceso de cobro (Deudas del impuesto sobre ingreso)* (The Collection Process (Income Tax Accounts))

#587: Business Use of Your Home—Schedule C (Form 1040) and Form 4562

#588: Tax Information For Homeowners Associations—Form 1120-H

#589: Tax Information on S Corporations—Form 1120S and Schedule K-1(Form 1120S)

#590: Individual Retirement Arrangements (IRAs)—Forms 1040 and 5329

#593: Income Tax Benefits for U.S. Citizens Who Go Overseas

#594: The Collection Process (Employment Tax Accounts)

#595: Tax Guide for Commercial Fishermen

#596: Earned Income Credit—Forms W-5, 1040, and 1040A

#597: Information on the United States–Canada Income Tax Treaty

#598: Tax on Unrelated Business Income of Exempt Organizations—Form 990-T

#686: Certification for Reduced Tax Rates in Tax Treaty Countries

#721: Comprehensive Tax Guide to U.S. Civil Service Retirement Benefits—Form 1040

#794: Favorable Determination Letter

#850: English-Spanish Glossary of Words and Phrases Used in Publications Issued by the Internal Revenue Service

#901: U.S. Tax Treaties

#904: Interrelated Computations for Estate and Gift Taxes—Forms 706 and 709

#905: Tax Information on Unemployment Compensation

#906: Jobs and Research Credits—Forms 5884 and 6765

#907: Tax Information for Handicapped and Disabled Individuals—Schedule A (Form 1040), Form 2441

#908: Bankruptcy—Forms 1040, 1041, 1120

#909: Alternative Minimum Tax—Forms 1116 and 6251

#911: Tax Information for Direct Sellers—Schedules C and SE (Form 1040), and Form 4562

#915: Tax Information on Social

Security Benefits (and Tier 1 Railroad Retirement Benefits)—Forms SSA-1099 and RRB-1099, Social Security Benefits Worksheet, Notice 703, Forms SSA-10425 and RRB-10425

#916: Information Returns—Forms 1099 Series, W-2G, 1098, 5498, 8300, 8308, 8362

#917: Business Use of a Car—Form 2106

#919: Is My Withholding Correct?—Form W-4

#920: Explanation of the Tax Reform Act of 1986 for Individuals (Also includes IRS Pub. 928, "Are You Having Enough Tax Withheld?," reprinted at the end.)

#921: Explanation of the Tax Reform Act of 1986 for Business.

#928: Are You Having Enough Tax Withheld?—Form W-4.

#1004: Identification Numbers Under ERISA

#1048: Filing Requirements for Employee Benefit Plans—Forms 5500, 5500-C, and 5500-R

#1212: List of Original Issue Discount Instruments—Schedule B (Form 104) and Forms 1099-OID and 1099-INT

#1244: Employee's Daily Record of Tips (Form 4070-A) and Employee's Report of Tips to Employer (Form 4070)—Forms 4070 and 4070-A

Exhibit 2-3

Tele-Tax Subjects and Audio Tape Numbers
(IRS Publication 910)

IRS Procedures and Services

Audio Tape Number	Subject
100	IRS help available—Volunteer tax assistance programs, toll-free telephone, walk-in assistance, and outreach program
101	Tax assistance for handicapped individuals and the deaf
102	Small business tax workshops—Tax help for the new business person
103	Problem Resolution Program—Special help for problem situations
104	Public libraries—Tax information tapes and reproducible tax forms
105	Examination procedures and how to prepare for an audit
106	The collection process
107	Tax fraud—How to report
108	Special enrollment examination to practice before IRS
109	Organizations—How to apply for exempt status

Filing Requirements, Filing Status, Exemptions

Audio Tape Number	Subject
110	Who must file?
111	Which Form—1040, 1040A, or 1040EZ?
112	When, where, and how to file
113	Filing requirements for a dependent child
114	Filing as single
115	Filing joint or separate
116	Filing as head of household
117	Filing as qualifying widow/widower
118	Filing status for separated individuals
119	Exemptions for age and blindness
120	Dependent—Who can be claimed?
121	Dependent Child—Divorced or separated parents
122	Dependent—Items to include in determining support
126	Estimated tax
127	Amended returns
128	Decedents

Types of Income

Audio Tape Number	Subject
130	Wages and salaries
131	Tips
132	Interest received
133	Dividends and dividend exclusion
134	Refund of state and local taxes
135	Alimony received
136	Business income
137	Sole proprietorship income
138	Capital gains and losses
139	Pensions and annuities
140	Pensions—The general rule
141	Lump-sum distributions—Profit sharing plans
143	Rental income and expenses
200	Renting vacation property/Renting to Relatives
201	Royalties
202	Farming and fishing income
203	Earnings for clergy members
204	Unemployment compensation
205	Gambling income and expenses
206	Bartering income
207	Scholarships, fellowships, and grants
208	Nontaxable income
209	Social Security and Tier 1 railroad retirement taxability
210	Social Security Benefit Statement—Form SSA-1099

Adjustments to Income

Audio Tape Number	Subject
211	Charitable contributions deduction for those who do not itemize
212	Deduction for married couples when both work
213	Moving expenses
214	Employee business expenses
215	Business use of car
216	Business travel expenses
217	Business entertainment expenses
218	Individual retirement accounts (IRAs)
219	Alimony paid
225	Bad debt deduction
226	Tax shelters

Itemized Deductions

Audio Tape Number	Subject
227	Should I itemize?
228	Medical and dental expenses
229	Medical insurance
231	Taxes
233	Interest expense
234	Contributions
235	Casualty losses

236	Miscellaneous expenses
237	Office-in-the-home expenses
238	Educational expenses

Tax Computation

Audio Tape Number	Subject
240	Tax table and Tax rate schedules
243	Tax and credits figured by IRS
300	Self-employment tax
301	Ten-year averaging for lump-sum distributions
303	Alternative minimum tax
304	Gift tax
305	Estate tax

Tax Credits

Audio Tape Number	Subject
306	Child care credit
307	Earned income credit
308	Residential energy credit
309	Credit for the elderly and the permanently and totally disabled
310	Tax credit for contributions to candidates for public office
311	Investment credit
312	Qualified royalty owners exemption (windfall profit tax)

General Information

Audio Tape Number	Subject
314	Substitute Tax Forms
315	Highlights of Current Year tax changes
316	Refunds—How long they should take
317	Copy of your tax return—How to get one
318	Forms/Publications—How to order
319	Tax shelter registration
320	Extensions for time to file your tax return
325	Form W-2—What to do if not received
326	Highlights of the Tax Reform Act
327	IRS notices and bills/ Penalty and interest charges
328	Tax benefits for low-income Americans
329	Penalty for underpayment of estimated tax—Form 2210
330	Recordkeeping
331	How to choose a tax preparer
332	Audit appeal rights
333	Failure to pay child/ spousal support
335	Withholding on interest and dividends
336	Highway use tax
337	Checklist/common errors when preparing your tax return
338	Withholding on pension and annuities
339	Your tax form is overdue—Let us hear from

	you
340	Second request for information about your tax form
341	Notice of intent to levy
342	Notice of underreported income—CP 2000

Basis of Assets, Depreciation, Sale of Assets

Audio Tape Number	Subject
343	Sale of personal residence—General
344	Sale of personal residence—How to report gain
400	Sale of personal residence—Exclusion of gain, age 55 and over
401	Basis of Assets
402	Depreciation—General
403	Depreciation—Accelerated cost recovery system
404	Installment sales

Employer Tax Information

Audio Tape Number	Subject
406	Social Security withholding rates
407	Form W-2—Where, when, and how to file
408	Form W-4—Employee's Withholding Allowance Certificate
409	Federal tax deposits—General
410	Employer identification number—How to apply
411	Paying taxes on your employees
412	Form 942—Employer's Quarterly Tax Return for Household Employees
413	Form 941—Deposit requirements
414	Form 941—Employer's Quarterly Federal Tax Return
415	Form 940—Deposit requirements
416	Form 940—Employer's Annual Federal Unemployment Tax Return
417	Targeted jobs credit
418	Tips—Withholding and reporting

Tax Information for Aliens and U.S. Citizens Living Abroad

Audio Tape Number	Subject
420	Resident and nonresident aliens
425	Dual status alien
426	Alien tax clearance
428	Foreign earned income exclusion—General
429	Foreign earned income exclusion—Who qualifies?
430	Foreign earned income exclusion—What income qualifies?
431	Foreign tax credit

Exhibit 2-4

General Information About Regulations, Revenue Rulings, and Revenue Procedures
(*Internal Revenue Manual*)

REGULATIONS

Regulations are the IRS Commissioner's rules, approved by the Secretary of the Treasury or the Secretary's delegate, for the application and administration of the Internal Revenue laws. The purpose of regulations is to provide taxpayers, their representatives, and Service personnel with rules of general application so they may clearly understand the taxpayer's rights and duties under the law.

Regulations are promulgated by publication in the *Federal Register,* and usually are published in the weekly *Internal Revenue Bulletin* (IRB) and semiannual *Cumulative Bulletin.* All persons concerned are, by reason of publication of regulations in the *Federal Register*, given notice of the official rules of the Department of the Treasury for the administration, application, and enforcement of the Internal Revenue laws.

In some cases the law requires that regulations be issued with respect to specific matters; in all other cases regulations are authorized by law to supply such detail concerning the administration of the provision of law and its interpretation as is appropriate to carry out the statutory enactment. So long as the regulations of the Commissioner, approved by the Secretary of the Treasury or the Secretary's delegate, remain in effect, they must be observed by all members of the department.

REVENUE RULINGS AND REVENUE PROCEDURES

A *revenue ruling* is an official interpretation by the Service that has been published in the *Internal Revenue Bulletin*. Revenue rulings are issued only by the national office and are published for the information and guidance of taxpayers, Internal Revenue Service officials, and others concerned.

A *revenue procedure* is an official statement of a procedure published in the IRB that either affects the rights or duties of taxpayers or other members of the public under that Internal Revenue Code, related statutes, tax treaties, and regulations, or, although not necessarily affecting the rights and duties of the public, should be a matter of public knowledge.

Revenue procedures usually reflect the contents of internal management documents, but, where appropriate, they also are published to announce practices and procedures for guidance of the public. It is Service practice to publish as much of the internal management document or communication as is necessary for an understanding of the procedure. Revenue procedures also may be based on internal management documents that should be a matter of public knowledge even though not necessarily affecting the rights and duties of the public.

Revenue rulings and revenue procedures are alike in that both are issued only by the National Office and both are published in the IRB for the information and guidance of taxpayers, Internal Revenue personnel, and others concerned. However, one numerical series is used for revenue rulings and another is used for revenue procedures; and whether an item will be published as a revenue ruling or revenue procedure depends on its content.

A revenue ruling tells what to do, whereas a revenue procedure tells how to do it. For example, a revenue ruling holds that taxpayers may deduct certain automobile expenses, and a revenue procedure provides that taxpayers entitled to deduct automobile expenses may compute them by applying certain mileage rates in lieu of determining actual operating expenses.

The revenue ruling series is used for statements of Service position or interpretation of law with respect to a particular tax issue, whereas the revenue procedure series is used for statements of general procedure or instructional information.

Other principal sources of issues to be published in revenue rulings are:

- Announcements of acquiescence or nonacquiescence in Tax Court decisions.
- Decisions of other Federal courts that are contrary to Service position.
- Interpretations of substantive tax law made by the Chief Counsel's office and referred to the Assistant Commissioner (Technical) for possible publication.

Other principal sources of matters to be published in revenue procedures are:

- Internal management documents that impose a duty or obligation on taxpayers.
- Internal management documents setting forth Service practices and procedures that affect taxpayers' rights in dealing with the Service.
- Asset guideline classes, lives and depreciation periods and ranges established by the Treasury and forwarded to the Service for publication in the IRB pursuant to section 1.167-(a)(11) of the Income Tax Regulations.

Effect of Published Revenue Rulings

Revenue rulings (other than those relating to the qualification of pension, annuity, profit-sharing, stock bonus, and bond purchase plans) apply retroactively unless the revenue ruling includes a specific statement indicating, under the authority of IRC 7805(b), the extent to which it is to be applied without retroactive effect. Where revenue rulings revoke or modify rulings previously published in the IRB, the authority of IRC 7805(b) ordinarily is invoked to provide that the new rulings will not be applied retroactively to the extent that the new rulings have adverse tax consequences to taxpayers. IRC 7805(b) provides that the Secretary of the Treasury or the Secretary's delegate may prescribe the extent to which any ruling is to be applied without retroactive effect.

Revenue rulings *published* in the IRB *do not* have the force and effect of Treasury Department Regulations (including Treasury Decisions), but are published to provide precedents to be used in the disposition of other cases, and may be cited and relied upon for that purpose. No *unpublished* ruling or decision will be relied on, used, or cited, by any officer or employee of the Service as a precedent in the disposition of other cases.

Taxpayers generally may rely upon revenue rulings published in the IRB in determining the tax treatment of their own transactions and need not request specific rulings applying the principles of a published revenue ruling to the facts of their particular cases. However, since each revenue ruling represents the conclusion of the Service as to the application of the law to the entire state of facts involved, taxpayers, Service personnel, and others concerned are cautioned against reaching the same conclusion in other cases unless the facts and circumstances are substantially the same. They should consider the effect of subsequent legislation, regulations, court decisions, and revenue rulings.

INTERNAL REVENUE BULLETIN AND CUMULATIVE BULLETIN

The *Internal Revenue Bulletin* is the official publication of the Internal Revenue Service for announcing rulings and procedures of the Service and for publishing Treasury Decisions, Executive Orders, tax conventions, legislation, certain court decisions, and other items of general interest.

It is the policy of the Service (P-(11)-68) to publish revenue rulings and revenue procedures in the *Bulletin* to promote correct and uniform application of the tax laws by Service employees and to assist taxpayers in attaining maximum voluntary compliance by informing Service personnel and the public of National Office interpretations of internal revenue laws, related statutes, treaties, regulations, and statements of Service procedures affecting the rights and duties of taxpayers.

The *Bulletin* is published weekly and may be obtained by the public from the Superintendent of Documents on a subscription basis or by single copy purchase. *Bulletin* contents of a permanent nature are consolidated semiannually into *Cumulative Bulletins*, which are sold on a single-copy basis.

Announcements of Acquiescence or Nonacquiescence

The Internal Revenue Service announces in the *Internal Revenue Bulletin* at the earliest practicable date the determination of the Commissioner to acquiesce or not acquiesce in a decision of the United States Tax Court that disallows a deficiency in tax set by the Commissioner. Acquiescence or nonacquiescence in a decision of the Tax Court relates only to the issue or issues decided adversely to the IRS. No announcements are made in the *Bulletin* with respect to memorandum opinions of the Tax Court. In a nutshell, when the Commissioner acquiesces in a Tax Court decision, it means the IRS will follow the court's guidelines in closely similar cases. Nonacquiescence means that the IRS will *not* follow the guidelines in closely similar cases—which would require a determined taxpayer to take the IRS back to Tax Court to try to win a similar victory.

Decisions in which the Commissioner acquiesces or nonacquiesces are announced in listings published periodically in the weekly *Bulletin*.. The lists published during January through June each year are consolidated in a list published in the first weekly *Bulletin* in July and in the *Cumulative Bulletin* for January through June. A consolidated list for each calendar year is published in the first weekly *Bulletin* for the following January and in the *Cumulative Bulletin* for the last half of the year in which the various lists were published.

Exhibit 2-5

Technical Advice
(*Internal Revenue Manual*)

DEFINITION

Technical advice is furnished as a means of assisting Service personnel in closing cases and establishing and maintaining uniformity in the treatment of issues. Technical advice is issued to District Directors, the Director of International Operations, and Chiefs, Appeals Offices.

"Technical advice" means advice or guidance furnished by the National Office upon request of a District or an Appeals Office in response to any technical or procedural question that develops during any stage of any proceeding on the interpretation and proper application of tax law, tax treaties, regulations, revenue rulings, or other precedents published by the National Office to a specific set of facts involved in:

- The examination of a specific taxpayer's return or consideration of a taxpayer's claim for refund or credit;
- The proposed revocation or modification of a ruling to a taxpayer;
- Consideration of a nondocketed case in an Appeals office;
- A proposed revocation of tax-exempt status under IRC 521;
- Consideration of a taxpayer's application to enter into an agreement as to useful life, method and rate of depreciation of business property provided by IRC 167(d); or
- An examination to determine whether obligations issued are described in IRC 103(a).

REQUESTING TECHNICAL ADVICE

Technical advice may be requested by a District Director on any technical or procedural question that develops during the examination of a taxpayer's return, or consideration of a claim for refund or credit filed by a taxpayer. Technical advice may also be requested by an Appeals Office in the processing and consideration of a nondocketed case. IRS field offices are encouraged to request technical advice at the earliest possible stage of the proceedings on any technical or procedural question that cannot be resolved on the basis of law, regulations, or a clearly applicable revenue ruling or other precedent published by the National Office. Technical advice should be requested in every case in which any of the following conditions exist:

- The law and regulations are not clear as to their application to the issue being considered and there is no published precedent for determining the proper treatment of the issue;
- There is reason to believe that a lack of uniformity in the disposition of the issue exists;
- A doubtful or contentious issue is involved in a number of cases;
- The issue is so unusual or complex as to warrant consideration by the National Office; or
- The District Director or Appeals Office believes that securing technical advice from the National Office would be in the best interest of the Service.

During the course of an examination or a conference in a District or Appeals Office, a taxpayer or representative may request that an issue be referred to the National Office for technical advice on the grounds that a lack of uniformity exists as to the disposition of the issue, or that the issue is so unusual or complex as to warrant consideration by the National Office.

While taxpayers are encouraged to make *written* requests setting forth the facts, law, and arguments with respect to the issue, and reasons for requesting National Office advice, a taxpayer may make the request orally.

The taxpayer may submit a statement explaining the taxpayer's position on the issues and citing precedents that the taxpayer believes will bear on the case.

At the time the taxpayer is informed that the matter is being referred to the National Office the taxpayer will also be informed of the right to a conference in the National Office in the event an adverse decision is indicated, and will be asked to indicate whether such a conference is desired.

It is the general practice of the Service to furnish copies of the technical advice memorandum to taxpayers upon request, after they have been adopted by the District Director or Chief, Appeals Office.

EFFECT OF TECHNICAL ADVICE

A technical advice memorandum represents an expression of the views of the Service as to the application of tax law, tax treaties, regulations, revenue rulings, or other precedents published by the National Office to the facts of a specific case, and is issued primarily as a means of assisting District Offices in the examination and closing of a specific case. A technical advice memorandum also may be issued as a means of assisting an Appeals office in the processing and closing of a nondocketed case.

Except in rare or unusual circumstances, a holding in a technical advice memorandum that is favorable to the taxpayer is applied retroactively.

Moreover, since technical advice usually is issued only on closed transactions, a holding in such a technical advice memorandum that is adverse to the taxpayer also is applied retroactively unless the Assistant Commissioner (Technical) exercises the discretionary authority under IRC 7805 (b) to limit the retroactive effect of the holding.

Exhibit 2-6

Rulings, Determination Letters, Information Letters, and Closing Agreements

(*Internal Revenue Manual*)

DEFINITIONS

Ruling

A "ruling" is a written statement issued to a taxpayer or authorized representative by the National Office that interprets and applies the tax laws to a specific set of facts. Rulings are issued only by the National Office. The National Office issues rulings on prospective transactions and on completed transactions before the return is filed for those transactions.

Determination Letter

A "determination letter" is a written statement issued by a District Director, a director of an Internal Revenue Service Center, or the director of the Foreign Operations District, in response to a written inquiry by an individual or an organization that applies to the particular facts involved, the principles and precedents previously announced by the National Office. A determination letter is issued only where a determination can be made on the basis of clearly established rules as set forth in the statute, Treasury Decision or regulation, or in a ruling, opinion or court decision published in the *Internal Revenue Bulletin.* Where such a determination cannot be made, such as where the question presented involves a novel issue or the matter is excluded from the jurisdiction of a District Director by the provisions of the *Internal Revenue Manual*, a determination letter will not be issued.

Information Letter

An "information letter" is a written statement issued either by the National Office or by a District Director that does no more than call attention to a well-established interpretation or principle of tax law, without applying it to a specific set of facts. An information letter may be issued when the nature of the request from the individual or the organization suggests that it is seeking general information, and it is believed that such general information will assist the individual or organization.

Closing Agreement

A "closing agreement," as the term is used here is an agreement between the IRS and a taxpayer with respect to a specific issue or issues entered into pursuant to the authority contained in IRC 7121. Such a closing agreement is entered into only in the National Office and is based on a ruling that has been signed by the Commissioner or the Commissioner's delegate in which it is indicated that a closing agreement will be entered into on the basis of the holding of a ruling letter. Closing agreements are final and conclusive except upon a showing of fraud, malfeasance, or misrepresentation of material fact. They may be entered into where it is advantageous to have the matter permanently and conclusively closed, or where a taxpayer can show good and sufficient reasons for an agreement and the Government will sustain no disadvantage by its consummation.

In income and gift tax matters, District Directors issue determination letters in response to taxpayers' written requests submitted to their offices involving *completed transactions* affecting returns that will be under their examination jurisdiction, but only if the answer to the question presented is covered specifically by statute, regulation, or specifically by a ruling, opinion, or court decision published in the *Internal Revenue Bulletin*. A determination letter will *not* usually be issued with respect to a question that involves a return *to be filed* by the taxpayer if the identical question is involved in a return or returns already filed by the taxpayer. District Directors will not issue determination letters as to the tax consequences of prospective or proposed transactions, except as provided below.

In appropriate cases, taxpayers may be required to enter into a closing agreement as a condition to the issuance of a ruling. Where, in a single case, closing agreements are requested on behalf of each of a number of taxpayers, such agreements are not entered into if the number of such taxpayers exceeds 25. However, in a case where the issue and holding are identical as to all of the taxpayers and the number of taxpayers is in excess of 25, a "mass closing agreement" will be entered into with the taxpayer who is authorized by the others to represent the entire group.

Discretionary Authority to Issue Rulings or Determination Letters

Except as provided in the paragraph below, the Service has discretionary authority to issue rulings or determination letters, or to enter into closing agreements. That discretion is exercised in the light of all relevant circumstances, including the business or other reasons motivating the transaction, and with a view to issuing such definite holdings only to the extent consistent with a wise administration of the revenue system. However, the National Office and District Directors may, when it is deemed appropriate and in the best interest of the Service, issue information letters calling attention to well-established principles of tax law.

The National Office will issue rulings in all cases on prospective or future transactions when the law or regulations require a determination of the effect of a proposed transaction for tax purposes.

Generally, the Service does not issue rulings dealing with a particular area that is under extensive study or review, except that where the Service has a clearly established position it will ordinarily continue to rule in accordance with that position until it has adopted a new or changed position.

Rulings will be made on provisions of the Code under which regulations have not been issued if the question raised is clearly covered by the Code. If the answer is not entirely free from doubt, but is reasonably certain, a ruling will be made only after it is established that a business emergency requires a ruling or that unusual hardship will result from failure to obtain a ruling. No ruling will be issued if doubt as to the interpretation of the law governing the question cannot be reasonably resolved before the issuance of regulations.

If the request from the taxpayer or the taxpayer's representative meets all the requirements of a request for a ruling or determination letter, it will be acted upon as such a request even though the taxpayer or representative does not specifically ask for a "ruling" or "determination".

Questions on Which No Rulings or Determination Letters Will Be Issued

There are certain areas where, because of the inherently factual nature of the problem involved, or for other reasons, the Service will not issue, or ordinarily will not issue, advance rulings or determination letters. A list of these areas is set forth in a revenue procedure published annually in the first quarter of the calendar year. When there are additions to and deletions from this "no-rule" revenue procedure, they are announced in revenue procedures published during the year.

For example, a favorable ruling or determination letter is not issued on:

- The tax consequences of schemes, devices, and maneuvers that have as their *principal* purpose the avoidance or reduction of Federal taxes.
- Alternative plans of proposed transactions or on hypothetical situations.
- A matter upon which a court decision adverse to the Government has been handed down and the question of following the decision or litigating further has not yet been resolved.

The National Office issues rulings on issues arising under the provisions of the Internal Revenue Code and related statutes, and the regulations thereunder, that relate primarily to the time, place, manner, and procedures prescribed for reporting and paying taxes; assessing and collecting taxes (including interest and penalties); abating, crediting, or refunding over-assessments or overpayments of tax; and filing information returns.

Rulings ordinarily will not be issued to taxpayers if at the time the request for a ruling is submitted, the identical issue is involved in a return of the taxpayer for a prior period and that issue is under consideration by a District Director, the Director of a service center, or an Appeals office, or has been considered by those offices, and the statutory period of limitation on assessment or refund of tax has not expired or a closing agreement has not been entered into.

If a return involving an issue for a particular year is filed while a request for a ruling on that issue is pending, the National Office will issue the ruling unless an examination of the issue for which a ruling is requested or an examination of the identical issue on a prior year's return has been initiated by a District Director or a Director of a service center. Even in the event that consideration is initiated, the National Office ordinarily will issue the ruling if the District Director or the director of a service center agrees, by memorandum, to permit the issuance of the ruling.

EFFECT OF RULINGS AND DETERMINATION, OPINION, OR INFORMATION LETTERS

Generally, no statement by any official of the Service, other than a closing agreement under IRC 7121, is final and conclusive upon the Service. Thus, a ruling, except to the extent incorporated in a closing agreement, may be revoked or modified at any time under appropriate circumstances.

Except to the extent incorporated in a closing agreement, a ruling found to be in error or not in accord with the current views of the Service may be modified or revoked. Modification or revocation of a ruling may be effected by:

1. A notice to the taxpayer to whom the ruling was issued;
2. Enactment of legislation or ratification of a tax treaty;
3. A decision of the United States Supreme Court;
4. Issuance of temporary or final regulations; or
5. Issuance of a revenue ruling, a revenue procedure, or other statement published in the *Internal Revenue Bulletin.* Consistent with these provisions, if a ruling relates to a continuing action or a series of actions, the ruling will ordinarily be applied until any one of the actions described above has taken place, or until specifically withdrawn.

Except in rare or unusual circumstances, a ruling that revokes or modifies a prior ruling will not be applied retroactively with respect to the taxpayer to whom the ruling was originally issued or to a taxpayer whose tax liability was directly involved in such ruling if:

- There has been no misstatement or omission of material facts;
- The facts subsequently developed are not materially different from the facts on which the ruling was based;
- There has been no change in the applicable law;
- The ruling was originally issued with respect to a prospective or proposed transaction; and
- The taxpayer directly involved in the ruling acted in good faith in reliance upon the ruling and the retroactive application of the new ruling would be to the taxpayer's detriment.

A ruling issued to a taxpayer with respect to a particular transaction represents a holding of the Service on that transaction only. A taxpayer may not rely on a ruling issued to another taxpayer.

Determination Letters

A determination letter issued by a District Director will be given the same effect upon examination of the return of the taxpayer to whom the determination letter was issued as is described previously in the case of a ruling issued to a taxpayer.

Information Letters

An information letter issued by the National Office or by a District Director is advisory only.

Oral Advice to Taxpayers

The Service does not issue rulings or determination letters upon oral requests. Oral advice is advisory only and the IRS is not bound to recognize it in the examination of a taxpayer's return.

Officials to Whom Requests for Rulings, Determination Letters, and Closing Agreements Are to Be Submitted

Technical personnel will provide taxpayers and their representatives with information on whether the IRS will rule on a particular issue. They will also answer questions on procedural matters relating to the filing of a ruling request, including the correct preparation procedures announced in the first Revenue Procedure of each year.

Requests with respect to matters on which a ruling is desired or on which a closing agreement is desired should be addressed to the Internal Revenue Service, Associate Chief Counsel (Technical), Attention: CC:IND:S:3:3, Room 6545, 1111 Constitution Avenue, N.W., Washington, D.C. 20224.

Requests with respect to matters on which a determination letter from a District Director is desired should be addressed to the District Director who has or will have examination jurisdiction of your return.

Step 3 Knowing What The IRS Will Be Looking For

The second question (the first being: "Why me?") everyone asks after they open the IRS envelope and read the "audit invitation" is: "What are they going to be looking for?" There's not a tax practitioner in this country who hasn't heard that question dozens of times.

The problem with that question is that it's often asked too late; that is, too late to be any help in preparing the tax return, and sometimes too late for the preparation of the audit. Even though an audit-proofer understands that his chances of being audited are slim, he or she still wants to prepare for that possibility.

AUDIT-PROOFER'S STRATEGY RULE

Audit-proofing your tax return means knowing what the IRS will be looking for long before your tax return is prepared, and beating the auditor to the punch.

Tax examiners are impressed when they encounter taxpayers who are not only versed on the finer points of the tax law, but who are also totally prepared with all the substantiating documents to back up their deductions and expenses. A tax examiner impressed with your cooperation and preparedness may be less inclined to probe deeper to find something wrong, if he sees that you are very much on top of everything. Tax examiners develop gut instincts and feelings about the taxpayer very early in the examination. Sometimes it's almost psychic the way that they perceive their subjects.

AUDIT-PROOFER'S STRATEGY RULE

Your objective should be to impress the tax examiner. Begin during the tax year with your recordkeeping program, as discussed in Step 1.

If you have developed a system of records, or at least a document retention program (Step 1), and if you have done your best to obtain the correct information (Step 2), then you will be prepared for the third step in audit-proofing your tax returns: *Knowing what the IRS will be looking for in the event you are audited.*

Knowing what the IRS will be looking for involves two aspects:

- Knowing what documents are necessary to substantiate your expenses and deductions; and
- Knowing what points of law they will be checking.

THE FIRST ASPECT: CORRECT DOCUMENTATION

It's not too difficult to save every scrap of paper or receipt, but it's a whole different thing to save the *correct* documentation that will justify your deductions and expenses. *The correct documentation is what the IRS says is correct!* And what the IRS says is correct is, for the most part, what you are going to need when you are audited.

The IRS has never published the list of proof taxpayers need to substantiate their deductions. Unless a taxpayer got an audit invitation letter, with a notice requesting the correct documentation, he never knew what to expect. Even most tax practitioners have had to rely on their experience with the IRS to advise their clients what documentation was needed. And until now, no one has ever published the complete list of proof demanded by the IRS.

Turn to Exhibit 3-1. This exhibit is a compilation of the documentation that the IRS requests whenever it is challenging particular items on the tax return. Study this exhibit carefully! It will tell you what to save *now* so that *next year,* when you prepare *this year's* tax return you will have all the proof you need.

Realize how valuable this information can be to you. By thinking audit-proofing in all your financial transactions, and knowing what documents must be saved, you are well on your way to cutting your tax liability in ways you never dared to before, especially if you were afraid to take a deduction for expense items you weren't sure you could prove.

Ask yourself these questions. Have you been:

- Saving your itemized receipts for drugs and medicine that you got from your pharmacist, or have you been expecting your cancelled checks to be sufficient?
- Claiming an exemption for a dependent who does not live with you, but haven't been saving receipts to verify amounts you spent for the dependent's support?
- Making cash contributions to qualified charitable organizations and neglecting to obtain receipts?
- Making trips to your doctor, but failing to keep a log of the mileage?
- Given a statement from your employer that your expenses for uniforms, equipment, and/or tools were required? Have you been saving receipts for such expenditures?
- Retaining copies of expense vouchers for employee business expenses you claim from your employer?
- Making records and retaining receipts related to your entertainment expenses that show such information as the names and business relationships of the persons entertained, purpose of the entertainment, place where the entertainment took place, dates, amounts, etc.?

The fact is most people don't keep this information because, until they are audited, they don't know it's required. Without the proper supporting documentation, or receipts, the IRS will disallow the deductions, resulting in a bill for more tax. More taxes translates into *out-of-pocket dollars.*

AUDIT-PROOFER'S STRATEGY RULES

- **Use Exhibit 3-1 as a checklist.** ***Make a New Year's resolution to think audit-proofing and make it a habit to save, save,*** **save receipts,** ***or any other required documentation.***
- **As you go through the checklist, pay particular attention to the categories that pertain to your situation.** ***If you have*** **not** ***been collecting the essential information, make a commitment to yourself to begin.***
- **Refer to this exhibit often.** ***Put a notation in your appointment calendar, right now, on the first Monday of each month to: Read IRS proofsheet in audit-proofing book. By rereading this section every month you will begin to consider the tax ramifications of all your financial affairs*** **during the year,** ***rather than just on April 15th, when it's too late.***

THE SECOND ASPECT: CORRECT INFORMATION

The second aspect to the question, "What will the IRS be looking for," relates to **rules of law.** First you must acknowledge that the Tax Code is thousands of pages long; that the IRS instructions contain millions of words; and, that there are hundreds of thousands of court cases yielding numerous esoteric interpretations for even the most specific and obscure circumstance.

With such a vast universe of laws, rules, regulations, procedures, and court cases, the question is: How does the IRS know where to draw the line? How deeply will they probe to make sure you've applied the law correctly? How do they know what's important enough to look for, and what's not?

Add to that the basic insecurity *every* taxpayer experiences wondering whether he or she has met all the tests from the laws, rules, regulations, procedures, and court cases. This insecurity is a basic part of every taxpayer's fear of being audited. Sometimes taxpayers aren't even sure of what it is they do know, so they can hardly be aware of what it is they don't know. And with all the civil and criminal penalties that the IRS can throw at taxpayers for not preparing their tax return correctly, it's no wonder that most taxpayers are afraid of being audited.

One Solution

With the help of an obscure portion of the *Internal Revenue Manual* for auditors, I have prepared a "Checklist of What Rules and Information the IRS Will Be Verifying" in Exhibit 3-2. This checklist is a comprehensive listing of the basic rules of law and other information the IRS expects its tax examiners to check for. It has been edited so that you can use it as you prepare your tax return to see how you will do under the scrutiny of an IRS tax audit.

The checklist is not meant to be the "end-all" perfect solution to a complete 100 percent accurate tax return. But the IRS knows from experience that they don't have to test every law, rule, regulation, procedure, or court case to discover errors on tax returns. They don't have to try and trip up taxpayers on unknown exceptions or qualifying circumstances; there are enough errors made on the basic rules alone to make it worthwhile, at least initially, to only look for the basics.

AUDIT-PROOFER'S STRATEGY RULE

Use the checklist in Exhibit 3-2 after you've prepared your return but before you send it in to the IRS. ***Use it to determine if you have violated any of the basic items of information or rules of law.***

If you prepare your own tax return, you are well aware how easy it is to misread a rule from an IRS publication, or how easy it is to accidentally overlook something, or how easy it is to miss something because of a change in the tax laws. This checklist will help you to avoid those problems.

For example, suppose you deducted your membership dues to a country club as a business expense because your social contacts there sometimes lead to business deals and you frequently discuss business with your golf partners. Perhaps you were told by one of your associates that this was a legitimate deduction. By using the checklist you not only discover that your membership dues are not deductible because you don't use the club more than 50 percent for business purposes, but that this deduction is one of the basic items that the IRS will be looking for. As an audit-proofer you decide to delete the deduction.

By using the checklist to eliminate proven problem areas, you will create a tax return that not only will pass initial scrutiny, but will also impress the tax examiner with the thoroughness of your preparation. An examiner who finds nothing with his initial tests and basic questions, may feel that he is wasting his time by looking for other errors. If you have other potentially troublesome items on your return, that are not on the checklist, but which may be "gray areas" that involve a subjective interpretation of the tax law, you decrease your chances of having the tax examiner find them if you can impress your tax examiner that you know the basics.

AUDIT-PROOFER'S STRATEGY RULE

Use the checklist this year if you have been called in for an audit, to find your problem areas or weaknesses before the tax examiner does.

If you can see, beforehand, that you are going to have a problem with something, then you can *focus your energies* more constructively on dealing with the problem rather than spending your time in *worrying* about the audit.

For example, suppose you are a computer programmer and your employer asked you to take a college course in computer architecture, which you subsequently did and paid for yourself. Afterward you are notified by the IRS that your deduction is under question. You review the requirements for deducting educational expenses and discover that the expense must have been ordinary and necessary, and required as a condition of your employment. Now you know that you are going to need a statement from your employer substantiating that he *required* you to take the course as a condition of your employment.

Also, by knowing the basic errors you have made, later you will be able to explain them in a way that may convince the tax examiner not to assess you additional penalties for your errors. Be careful, though, not to give anything away to the tax examiner. If you come right out and show the examiner what errors you made, he may become suspicious and think you are trying to throw him off track from finding something even bigger. He may even think that if you're dumb enough to confess your sins to him, then you may be dumb enough to try and pull something bigger.

SPECIAL IRS AUDIT TARGETS YOU SHOULD KNOW ABOUT

The IRS Audit (or Examination) Division faces continuing increases in its workload each year as the number of returns filed grows, new and more difficult schemes are used to avoid taxes, and tax laws become more complex. IRS resources have not kept pace with the growing filing population and audit coverage has declined in the last 10 years from 2.4 percent to 1.31 percent of individual income tax returns. The audit activity is IRS's biggest tool for promoting voluntary compliance; it employs approximately one third of all of IRS's resources. Program priorities are provided for guidance in determining the application of resources and input of returns. These priorities represent national goals for the utilization of Examination resources and should be followed in the sequence followed below:

1. Returns involving Taxpayer Compliance Measurement Program (TCMP) audits and nationally directed compliance studies, such as unreported tips income study.
2. Returns identified as abusive tax shelters. (See Chapter 7.) Sufficient resources will be allocated so districts can timely investigate *each* abusive tax shelter package referred by the service centers.
3. Returns in need of examination which represent a national commitment to specific areas of abuse: tax protestors, tax havens, foreign tax credit manipulations, abusive W-4, unreported income projects, and returns with potential unreported income shown or foreign information documents.

4. Special Noncompliance Projects: to identify and examine U.S. persons who may be using foreign entities to evade U.S. taxes by concealing income and/or creating false deductions.
5. Schedule C and Revenue Initiatives: to identify noncompliant taxpayers by making in-depth probes for unreported income, and to audit corporate returns in asset class $100 million and over.
6. Information Returns Program cases. (See Chapter 6.)
7. Locally initiated projects, such as the Unreported Income Program, involving areas of high non-compliance.

Areas of Emphasis

The following programs represent areas that are to receive special emphasis from the IRS this year:

- Fraud: identify and develop cases with fraud potential by emphasizing efforts against organized crime and high-level drug traffickers, using multiple year examinations, and probing for unreported income.
- Payer compliance: ensure employers are submitting W-4s, identifying tax protestors, aggressively asserting civil penalties, ensuring informational returns such as W-2s and 1099s are provided to taxpayers.
- Computer-Assisted Audit Activity: emphasize the identification of all ADP records, especially those created and retained on data base systems—using specialists to emphasize proper recordkeeping—aggressively pursue civil penalties where taxpayers have failed to retain machine-sensible records—maximize use of computers in audits.
- Resolution of cases: to obtain a greater number of agreements to tax determinations.
- Identifying instances of misconduct by *return preparers* and aggressively asserting the appropriate penalties under the Return Preparers Program.
- Encouraging taxpayer compliance with the audit process.

Service Center Targets

- Abusive Tax Shelter Detection Teams are established in each service center to identify potentially abusive tax shelter schemes.
- Special emphasis to detection of fraud cases.
- Tax Protestors—to identify and examine protest scheme returns—the National Illegal Tax Protestor Data Base will be implemented to stop issuance of improper refunds and for identifying new schemes.
- Information Returns Program (IRP). (See Chapter 6.)
- Examination Initiatives:

1. The Partnership/Investor Control System (PICS) implemented to control investor returns related to TEFRA partnership/S corporation examinations.
2. TIP Income Allocations—a matching program for tax year 1983 returns to discover employees who have underreported tip income.
3. Examination of investors who have received Pre-filing Notification and Pre-refund Letters due to potentially abusive tax shelter.

- Future Examination Initiatives:

1. Individual Retirement Arrangements—a matching program similar to IRP is being developed to verify that an IRA exists, and that IRA deductions claimed by taxpayers are not overstated. Verification of rollover amounts and excess contributions will be built into the program.
2. Expansion of IRP matching to include bartering transactions, stock and securities sales, and tip reporting.
3. Matching state and local income tax refunds.

Special Projects

1. *Direct Sellers of Home Products Study*

Direct sellers of home products are individuals who sell consumer products to others on a person-to-person basis, usually working out of their own home. They may sell door to door, through a sales party plan, or by appointment in someone else's home. Or they may find their customers among their co-workers, friends, relatives, or neighbors.

Subject to certain limitations and substantiation requirements, ordinary and necessary expenses incurred by an individual in carrying on a trade or business are deductible for income tax purposes (Code *Section 162*). The determination of whether an expense is ordinary and necessary to the operation of a business is a factual question.

Except for certain expenses allowed as itemized deductions, an individual's *personal,* living, or family expenditures are not deductible (Code *Section 262*). Certain expenditures which otherwise would be treated as personal living expenses, such as expenditures for meals, lodging, travel, or entertainment, may be deductible when incurred in a business or investment activity.

If the expenses from a business exceed the taxpayer's income from the business for the year, the net business loss may be used to offset income from other sources, such as employee wages received by the taxpayer.

This study will address the issues of taxpayers who claim a business loss from direct selling activities on their Schedule C and use such loss to offset other types of income thereby reducing their tax liability. It will be determined if expenses claimed are ordinary and necessary for carrying on the business and if income is properly reported.

The objectives of this study are:

- To determine compliance levels of taxpayers claiming a loss from direct selling activities;
- To evaluate the feasibility, practicality, costs, and revenues of a continuing compliance program in this area;
- To develop a profile that can be used to supplement current selection methods if necessary;
- To determine the need for legislative proposals to enhance voluntary compliance.

Even though this study has been completed, it was designed to produce a "supplemental return selection system." That means that very soon that IRS will be targeting direct sellers on a nationwide basis.

Direct sellers should note that the line items on their return that will be scrutinized the closest are:

- Cost of goods sold.
- Car and truck expenses.
- Travel and Entertainment.
- Other Expenses.
- Office-in-the-home expense.

2. *Unreported Income DIF Scoring*

   A selection system has been implemented to score returns with a high potential for unreported income.

3. *Lifetime Exclusion of Gain or Sale of Residence (LTEX)*

   This program identifies taxpayers who have claimed the lifetime exclusion of gain on sale of their personal residence, determines that the exclusion is properly claimed, and corrects returns claiming the exclusion which appears to be unallowable.

   Code *Section 121* now allows taxpayers age 55 and over to elect a lifetime exclusion up to $125,000 of the gain on the sale or exchange of their residence. ($62,500 if married filing separately.) The taxpayer must have owned and used the principal residence for a period of three or more years during the five years preceding the sale.

   Because the law allows a taxpayer to make this election only once in a lifetime, the IRS will track these elections until the taxpayer's death.

The law further stipulates that a taxpayer is not eligible for the election if the spouse previously elected the exclusion in another sale or exchange. In the case of a jointly filed return with an election present, the account will be tracked for the lifetime of both spouses regardless of taxpayers' subsequent marital status.

4. *Questionable Form W-4 Program*

   Employers are required to submit to the IRS any W-4 submitted to them that claims more than 14 withholding allowances, or claims exemption from withholding even though the employee is earning more than $200 a week.

   The IRS reviews the W-4s for accuracy. If not accurate, the employee and the employer are notified and the employee is prohibited from claiming more allowances than the IRS allows.

Exhibit 3-1

Proof You Will Need to Substantiate Your Deductions
(*Internal Revenue Manual*)

Alimony Payments

- Copy of divorce decree, separate maintenance decree, or other instrument which specified the basis for alimony payments.
- Current name, address, and Social Security number of divorced or separated spouse.
- Cancelled checks or receipts to verify payments you made. If alimony payments are not made directly by you, you may need documents showing the source. For example, insurance policy, endowment or annuity contract, etc.

Bad Debts

- Verification of the debt such as a note or contract that would establish a debtor-creditor relationship.
- Full name and last known address of the debtor.
- Evidence of your efforts to collect the debt.
- Evidence of uncollectibility of the debt in the year claimed.

Business Use of Home

- Statement from your employer if you are required to provide an office in your home or elsewhere.
- Cancelled checks or receipts verifying expenses incurred.
- Verification of percentage of square footage of home used for business to total square footage of home.

Business vs. Nonbusiness Activity

- Copies of tax returns for the 4 preceding years (6 years if the activity involves horses) if you were engaged in the activity during those periods.
- If this is your first year for the activity, be prepared to discuss:
  1. Manner in which you carry on the activity;
  2. Expertise of you or your consultants;
  3. Expectations of the anticipated increase in value of business assets;
  4. Success in carrying on other activities;
  5. Elements of personal pleasure or recreation involved in carrying on the activity.

Car and Truck Expenses—Schedule C or F

- Repair receipts, inspection slips, or any other records to show total mileage driven for the year.
- Log books and other records verifying the business mileage claimed.
- If you did not keep a log or other formal record of your business mileage, reconstruct the business use of the vehicle. This information should include current mileage reading on the vehicle used for business purposes, mileage reading on the vehicle when you acquired it, mileage reading for January 1 and December 31, and mileage distance between your residence and your business location. Also an appointment book or calendar of your business activities during the year, if you kept one.
- If you claimed actual expenses, you may have to provide paid bills, invoices, and cancelled checks for automobile expenses you incurred during the year. These include gas, oil, tires, repairs, insurance, interest, tags, and taxes.

Casualty Losses

- Insured Property: A copy of insurance report showing date and nature of loss or damage claimed, amount of damages claimed on insurance, amount of coverage carried and the date and amount of claim paid by insurance (or amount of claim pending);

- Uninsured Property: Any fire or police department reports on fire losses, theft losses, or losses from accidents.
- Photographs showing extent of loss, if available.
- Appraisal from a qualified estimator or adjustor showing fair market value of the property before and after the casualty; or an estimate of the damages.
- Cost or other basis of property and date acquired.
- Verification of actual cost of repairs.

Commissions or Contract Labor

- Copies of Forms 1099 for commissions paid.
- If Forms 1099 were not issued to individuals who were paid commissions, provide the names, addresses, and Social Security numbers of the recipients.
- Provide cancelled checks or other records to verify the amount paid to each individual.

Contributions

- Cancelled checks and receipts for contributions to church or charitable organizations.
- If the contribution was other than money, show: (a) name and address of the charitable organization; (b) items contributed; (c) appraisal of the fair market value of each item on the contribution date; (d) original cost.
- If you reported expenses for attending a church convention or similar activity, furnish a statement showing you were an official representative of your church.

Cost of Livestock or Other Items Bought for Resale

- Physical inventory sheets for both beginning and ending inventory for the year and copies of Federal tax returns for the year before and the year after the tax return year.
- Cancelled checks, receipts, and purchase journal or summaries for goods purchased for resale.
- Information or computation concerning cost of inventory items that were withdrawn for personal use.

Cost of Goods Sold

- Physical inventory sheets for both beginning and ending inventory and copies of Federal tax returns for the year.
- Cancelled checks, receipts, and purchase journal or summaries for goods purchased for resale.

- Information or computation concerning cost of inventory items that were withdrawn for personal use.

Credit for Child or Dependent Care Expenses

- If you are a divorced or separated parent, you will need a copy of the divorce decree or separation agreement, dates you had custody of the child and dates the other parent had custody of the child.
- If you paid for care of a disabled dependent, you will need a doctor's statement showing the dependent was physically or mentally unable to care for self.
- Names and addresses of persons or organizations you paid for child care or for care of a disabled dependent. Copies of cancelled checks and receipts verifying costs.
- If you do not have cancelled checks, obtain statement from the person or organization showing name, address, period of care, and amount paid.

Depletion

- Evidence of consideration paid and document showing legal description of the property, kind of interest (that is, working interest or royalty), and date of acquisition. If property was inherited, copy of estate tax return or state inheritance tax return showing value of the property.
- Mineral purchaser's monthly statement showing amount paid you and number of barrels of oil or thousand cubic feet of gas purchased. These statements should be for the months included in the income tax return.
- If you claimed cost depletion, you will need evidence to show any increase in cost (above acquisition cost shown above), records of previous depletion claimed, and supporting evidence for figuring the depletion as claimed.

Depreciation of Rental Property

- Evidence to verify ownership of property, date property acquired, cost or other basis showing amount allocated to land and to the building, cost of improvement, and additions to property.

Depreciation—Schedule C or F

- Purchase invoices and receipts for assets acquired.
- Your computation of how the depreciable basis was figured if different from the cost of the assets.
- If you have depreciable assets that are used for personal and busi-

ness purposes, provide records, log books, etc., showing total, business, and personal use.

- Records, invoices, and receipts for depreciable assets sold or otherwise disposed of during the year.

Education Expenses

- Documents (transcripts, course description, catalog, etc.) showing period of enrollment in educational institution, principal subjects studied, and description of educational activity.
- Cancelled checks and receipts to verify amount you spent for tuition and books, meals and lodging while away from home overnight for educational purposes, travel and transportation, and other educational expenses.
- Statement from your employer explaining whether the education was necessary for you to keep your employment, salary, or status, how the education helped maintain or improve skills needed in your employment, and how much education expense reimbursement you received, showing this by kinds of expense.
- Complete information about any scholarship or fellowship grant, including amount, you received during the year.
- Teachers Only: A statement showing the kind of teacher's certificate under which you taught, date certificate was issued, and a list of subjects taught.

Employee Business Expenses

- Statement from your employer showing employer's reimbursement policy, amount and kind of expense reimbursed, charged, or provided, specific expenses not covered by reimbursement policy, territory assigned to you, dates and locations of temporary jobs, and brief outline of your duties.
- Copies of expense vouchers submitted to your employer.
- Logs, diaries, or other records of expenses not reimbursed by your employer.

Energy Credit

- Cancelled checks and receipts verifying the cost and items for which credit was claimed.
- Copies of prior year Federal tax returns on which energy credit was claimed.
- For home energy conservation costs, records showing when the home was substantially completed.

Entertainment and Gifts

- Records and receipts for entertainment expenses you claimed. These records must show the names and business relationship of the persons entertained, purpose of the entertainment, place where the entertainment took place, date of the entertainment, and the amount of the expenditure.
- If you claimed expenses maintaining an entertainment facility you may have to provide records showing total use and business use of the facility, and expenses incurred, in addition to the information requested above.
- If you claimed expenses for business gifts, provide records and receipts showing cost of the gifts, persons to whom the gifts were made, and their business relationship.

Exemptions for Age and Blindness

- If you claimed an exemption because you are 65 or older:
  1. A copy of your birth certificate, Social Security documents, or employment record showing your age. If a joint return was filed and both husband and wife were 65 or older, include the necessary record for each.
- If you claimed an exemption because of blindness:
  1. If completely blind, your statement to that effect;
  2. If partially blind, a statement from a qualified physician or a registered optometrist indicating that: (1) you cannot see better than 20/200 in the better eye with glasses, or (2) that your field of vision is not more than 20 degrees.
- If a joint return was filed, and both husband and wife qualified for the exemption for blindness, you may need a statement for each.

Exemptions for Other Dependents

- A computation of the total cost of the dependent's support including the amount of income or other funds received by or for the dependent (show how these funds were used), and the amount contributed to household expenses by each person living in the household with the dependent.
- If other persons or agencies contributed to the dependent's support, furnish the name, address, and phone number of each contributing person or agency and a statement from the person or agency that provided aid, showing the amount provided.
- If the dependent did not live with you, provide cancelled checks and receipts to verify amount you spent for the dependent's support. If possible, be able to provide a signed statement from each person the

dependent lived with, confirming that that person did not claim an exemption for the dependent and that you furnished more than half of the dependent's total support.

- If you were divorced or legally separated from the dependent's other parent, you may have to provide a copy of your divorce decree, your separate maintenance decree, and any written agreement showing which parent will claim the dependency exemption.

Exemptions for Your Children Who Live With You

- School, medical, or other records to determine dependent's place of residence.
- A record of income or other funds received by or for the dependent, including but not limited to social assistance, Social Security, V.A. benefits, and child support. Show how these funds were used.
- A record of the amounts contributed to household expenses by each person living in the household with the dependent.
- A record of the funds spent for the dependent's support from all sources.
- If you were divorced or legally separated from the dependent's other parent, you may have to provide a copy of your divorce decree or separate maintenance decree, and any written agreement showing which parent will claim the dependency exemption.

Filing Status—Head of Household

- Copy of divorce decree or separation agreement, if you were divorced or legally separated.
- Cancelled checks and receipts for the qualifying relative's household expenses (taxes, interest, rent, utilities, repairs, insurance, and food).
- School records, driver's license, statement from qualifying relative, etc., to verify his or her place of residence.
- Amounts other persons contributed for household expenses.

Filing Status

- If on your return you checked "married filing separately," you may need a copy of your spouse's Federal income tax return for the same year. If you cannot get a copy of the return, you will need to furnish your spouse's full name, current address, and Social Security number.

Gambling Losses

- Furnish a log or diary showing place, date, and amount of winnings and losses. This information should include tickets and programs.

Gas, Fuel, and Oil—Schedule F

- Cancelled checks and receipts for gas, fuel, and oil expense you claimed.
- If you claimed a gasoline tax credit, you will need documentation that the amount of credit was reported as income on your Schedule F.

Income

- Verification of income received from the following sources:
  1. Wages, salaries, tips, fees, etc. (copies of W-2's).
  2. Interest, dividends, unemployment compensation, etc. (copies of 1099's).
  3. Pensions, annuities, royalties, estates, trusts, nonemployee compensation, etc.
  4. Alimony received (copy of divorce decree or separation agreement).
  5. Bond interest, commissions, tips, winnings, prizes, awards, schedule K-1's, scholarships, grants, disability income, property or goods received for services, and any other income.

Income Averaging

- To verify base period income, you will need copies of your tax return for the base period years. If you amended your return or if the Internal Revenue Service adjusted it for any of these years, you will also need a copy of the amended return or the change notice or examination report.

Individual Retirement Account

- Copy of the document(s) which establish your Individual Retirement Account (IRA) and cancelled checks showing all contributions to the IRA for the year under examination. Bring a copy of the statement provided by the trustee or custodian of your IRA which shows receipts, disbursements, and accumulated assets.
- If there were any rollover contributions to your IRA from a qualified pension or profit-sharing plan or from another IRA, please bring documents showing the source of such rollover.

Insurance Expenses—Schedule C or F

- All insurance policies for which you deducted premiums paid.
- Cancelled checks, bills, or invoices for insurance expense paid or owed.

Intangible Drilling Costs and Dry Hole Cost

- Document (deed, letter agreement, partnership agreement, etc.) showing date of acquisition, description of property, interest owned in property, consideration paid, and obligations assumed.
- Copy of drilling contract, drilling progress reports, billing statements, cancelled checks, and well completion or abandonment report.

Interest on Business Indebtedness—Schedule C or F

- Copies of loans, payment information, and interest statements on loans in effect during the year.

Interest Expenses

- Receipts or statements from creditors showing amounts of interest paid and names of payees.
- Payment books on installment purchases or contract on purchase, and cancelled checks, receipts, or other evidence of payments made on the contract.
- Land contract for interest and mortgage receipts.
- Statement from bank or savings and loan to show amount of interest forfeited.

Investment Credit

- Provide purchase invoices for depreciable assets acquired on which the credit was claimed.
- Provide explanation of the property's use and the date placed in service.
- If the current year investment credit is carried back to prior years or forward to subsequent years, you will need copies of your tax returns for those years.

Job-Hunting Expenses

- Furnish a log or diary showing job-hunting activity, and cancelled checks or receipts showing expenses paid for this activity.
- If you were reimbursed for any of these expenses, please provide a statement from your employer showing amount of reimbursement.
- Cancelled checks or receipts showing amount of payments to employment agencies.

Keogh Retirement Plan

- Copy of the documents which established your Keogh Plan, cancelled checks showing all contributions to the plan for the year.
- A list of all bona fide employees who have at least 3 years of service.

Labor Hired—Schedule F

- Employment tax returns (Forms 940 and 943) filed to support your deduction for salaries and wages paid to your employees.
- Copies of Forms W-4 for all your employees.
- Copies of Forms W-2 for employees who were paid salaries or wages.

Legal, Tax Investment Counsel Fees

- Cancelled checks, receipts, or statements showing amount of payment and purpose of expense.

Machine Hire or Contract Labor—Schedule F

- Copies of all Forms 1099 for machine hire expenses paid.
- If Forms 1099 were not issued to individuals who were paid for machine work, provide the names, addresses, and Social Security numbers of the recipients.
- Provide cancelled checks or other records verifying the amount paid to each individual.

Meals and Lodging Expenses

- Verification of the number of days away from home overnight for business purposes.
- Receipts or records for meals.
- Receipts for lodging.

Medical and Dental Expenses

- Insurance policies on which you deducted the cost of premiums paid. Include your records for payment of these premiums.
- Itemized receipts for drugs and medicine showing the person for whom the drugs and medicine were purchased. Cancelled checks alone are not acceptable.
- Cancelled checks, receipts, or statements for all medical and dental expenses showing the person for whom each expense was incurred.

- Statement from insurance company showing any expense reimbursed or paid directly by it.
- Statement to show cost and medical requirement for special equipment or education expense.

Miscellaneous

You will need your records, including cancelled checks, receipts, explanations, etc., as appropriate, for the following items to be covered during the examination of your return:

- Supplies—Schedule C or F.
- Utilities and Telephone Expenses.
- Dues and Publications—Schedule C or F.
- Legal and Professional—Schedule C or F.
- Fertilizer, Lime, Chemicals—Schedule F.
- Veterinary Fees, Medicine Expenses.
- Advertising Expenses.
- Land Clearing and Conservation Expenses.
- Feed, Seed, Plants Purchased.
- Earned Income Credit.
- Self-Employment Tax.
- Credit for Political Contribution.

Moving Expenses

- Cancelled checks and receipts verifying amount of moving expenses you paid.
- Names and relationships to you of members of your household who moved with you.
- Computations showing number of miles by direct route from your *old* residence to your *new* place of employment and to your *old* place of employment.
- Name and address of each employer you had since you moved to new place of employment and period of time you were employed by each.
- Statement from your employer of the allowance or reimbursement paid you for moving expenses showing amounts by kinds of expense, such as plane or train fares, meals and lodging, automobile expense, transportation of household and personal property.
- Closing statements on purchase and sale of personal residence. Copies of lease agreement where applicable.

Pension or Annuity Income

- Furnish records of the amount received for the year and what part is excludable.

Pension or Profit Sharing Plans—Schedule C or F

- Cancelled checks and other documents verifying contributions to the plan for the year.
- Copy of Form 5500-C or 5500-R, whichever is appropriate.

Real Estate and Personal Property Taxes

- Verification of legal ownership of the property.
- Cancelled checks and receipts for taxes paid; for example, statement from mortgage company.
- If you sold or purchased real property, a copy of the settlement statement.
- Identification of any special assessments deducted as taxes, and an explanation of their purpose.

Rent on Farm, Pasture

- Copies of leases or rental agreements, cancelled checks, and statements for rent paid or owed during the year.

Rent on Business Property—Schedule C or F

- Copies of leases or rental agreements, cancelled checks, and statements for rent paid or owed during the year.

Rental—Vacation Home

- If you own and rent a home or other dwelling unit that you also use as a residence in the tax year, supply the following:
    1. A diary reflecting the number of days for personal use and the number of days for business use.
    2. Records to verify rental income and rental expenses as well as depreciation claimed.

Rental Income and Expenses

- Records showing total of rent you received.
- Cancelled checks and receipts to verify all expenses claimed.
- If any units were occupied rent free or below rental value during the year, an explanation of the reason.
- If the unit was used for personal reason, show the total number of days rented and number of days used for personal purposes.
- Evidence to verify ownership of property, date property was acquired, cost or other basis showing amount allocated to land and to buildings,

cost of improvements and additions to property. Include escrow papers and property tax bill for the year of purchase.
- If property was converted from a personal residence to rental property, show date converted, and appraisal of fair market value when converted.

Repairs—Schedule C or F

- Cancelled checks, receipts, and invoices for repairs.
- For large repairs, description of the nature of the repair.

Salary and Wages—Schedule C

- All four quarterly employment tax returns (Forms 940 and 941) filed to support your deduction for salaries and wages paid to your employees.
- Copies of Forms W-4 for all your employees.
- Copies of Forms W-2 for employees who were paid salaries or wages.

Sale of Personal Residence

- Closing statements for sales of the residence and for cost of this residence when purchased.
- Cancelled checks and receipts for improvements made to the residence sold.
- Cancelled checks and receipts for fixing-up expenses incurred within 90 days of selling your residence (these expenses must have been paid within 30 days after the sale).
- If you replaced the residence that was sold, provide the closing statement on purchase of the new residence.
- If any part of your residence was used for business use prior to the sale, you should have a copy of your income tax return for the last year the home was used for business before the sale.

Sales of Property Other Than Stock

- Closing statements on purchase of property.
- Verification of capital improvements to property (receipts, bills, contracts).
- You will need records showing terms and expenses of sale, and copy of closing or settlement sheet.
- If sale involved rental or business property, you should have copies of your income tax returns for the 2 years before the year of sale.

- If you reported gain or loss from repossession you should have a copy of your income tax return for the year of the original sale, all contracts or legal documents involved, and verification of repossession costs.

Sales Taxes

- Receipts for sales taxes paid on a car, motorcycle, motor home, truck, boat, airplane, home (including mobile or prefabricated), or building materials you bought to build a new home.
- If you used actual receipts to compute your sales tax, you will need verification of all purchases on which sales tax was paid.

Schedule C (or F)—General

- All books, journals, ledgers, and workpapers used in preparing your return.
- All bank statements and cancelled checks (both business and personal) for the 14-month period from December through January of the following tax year.
- Records of all savings and invested funds for the year.
- Records of all business and personal loan activity (proceeds and payments).
- Purchase invoices or closing statements covering acquisition and disposition of capital items (business and personal). This includes real estate, automobiles, machinery, and equipment.
- Information on any nontaxable income received, including but not limited to Social Security benefits, gifts, and inheritances.
- Copies of your four most recent Forms 941 and related W-4's.

Scholarship or Fellowship Grant

- A statement from the grantor of your scholarship or grant showing the following:
    1. Funds from which grant was paid.
    2. Amount of grant and period covered.
    3. Requirements of grant including any present, past, or future obligations or services. (Are all candidates for the degree you're working toward required to perform these services?)
    4. Fringe benefits you derived (medical insurance, awards, bonuses, etc.).
    5. Benefits derived by grantor.
    6. Selection criteria for recipients.
- Current transcript of credits for degree.

- University bulletin outlining degree requirements.
- A copy of the official instrument establishing the scholarship or fellowship program.

State and Local Income Taxes

- Copies of state and local income tax returns for any of the 3 previous years.
- Copy of Federal income tax return for any of the 3 previous years.
- Cancelled checks and receipts showing taxes paid.

State Income Tax Refund

- Furnish a copy of your Federal income tax return for any of the 3 previous years.
- Furnish a copy of your state income tax return for any of the 3 previous years.

Stock Sales

- Brokerage vouchers establishing the purchase price, sales price, and dates of transactions.
- If you sold securities on which you had a return of capital you will need records showing the nontaxable distributions received during the holding period.
- If you claim worthless securities, you will need verification of dissolution or liquidation and liquidation distribution.

Travel—Employee Business Expenses

- Furnish a log or diary for travel costs incurred while away from home on business. This information should include transportation tickets, receipts, and cancelled checks, etc.

Travel and Entertainment Expenses

- A log or diary for travel costs incurred while away from home on business. This information should include transportation tickets, receipts, and cancelled checks.
- Records and receipts for entertainment expenses you claimed. These records must show the names and business relationship of the person(s) entertained, purpose of the entertainment, place where the entertainment took place, date of the entertainment, and amount of the expenditure.

- If you claimed expenses for maintaining an entertainment facility, provide records showing the total use and business use of the facility, and expenses incurred, in addition to the information required above.
- If you claimed expenses for business gifts, provide records and receipts showing cost of the gifts, persons to whom the business gifts were made, and their business relationship.

Travel Expenses—Miscellaneous Deductions

- Furnish a log or diary for travel costs incurred while away from home on business. This information should include transportation tickets, receipts, and cancelled checks, etc.

Uniforms, Equipment, and Tools

- Explanation of how expense related to your employment including a description of the uniform.
- Statement from your employer that the expense was required, reimbursement policy, and amount reimbursed or allowance paid.
- Cancelled checks and receipts verifying the expense.

Exhibit 3-2

Checklist of What Rules and Information the IRS Will Be Verifying

(*Derived from the IRS Auditor's Manual*)

REPORTABLE INCOME

Earned Income—You have reported on your tax return:

- All compensation you received for services, including fees, commissions, tips, gratuities, and similar items.
- All your business gross receipts.
- Your gross wages that agree with the amounts shown on your Forms W-2.
- Any supplemental compensation and bonuses.
- All income that has been constructively received. (Income is constructively received when it is credited to your account, or unconditionally set apart for you so that you may draw upon it at any time.)

Nontaxable Income—You have reported on your tax return:

- No amounts you have received for child support because they are not taxable.
- Only your wages and those of your spouse if you have filed a joint return. (You do not include the wages of any other individual on your tax return.)

Other Income—You have reported on your tax return:

- Any income in any form other than cash at its fair market value.
- A refund of any part of your state income tax that you deducted in prior years, and which reduced your Federal income tax in those years, provided this was the year you received the refund.
- The recovery of a bad debt that you deducted in prior years, and which reduced your Federal income tax in those years, provided this was the year you recovered the debt.
- The amount of your debt if this was the year in which it was forgiven.
- Amounts shown on your Forms W-2, W-2G, 1099 series, etc.
- Any payments you received from your employer during periods of unemployment under a collective bargaining agreement that guaranteed you full pay during the year.
- Strike and lockout benefits paid by the union from union dues, including both cash and fair market value of any goods you received.
- Supplemental unemployment benefit payments you received from a company-financed supplemental unemployment benefit fund.
- The right to a credit for goods and services offered for exchange in a barter operation when you received that right.
- The retirement of bonds issued with "original issue discount."
- Any profit from the sale of state or municipal securities.
- Life insurance proceeds payable by reason of death of the insured and received by you as beneficiary in installments, when any part of the installment payments in effect represented interest on the insurance proceeds in excess of the $1,000 a year exclusion.
- Any amounts realized by you on foreclosure of a mortgage to the extent that the mortgage indebtedness exceeded the adjusted basis.
- Any consideration received for a covenant not to complete.
- A note in payment for services you received, if you are on the cash basis of accounting and this is the year you received the note.
- The amount you received as a payment from your individual retirement account if you received the payment before you reached age 59½ or became disabled. Your tax was also increased by 10 percent of this premature distribution.

- A sale or exchange of assets unless a nontaxable exchange was made under Section 1031 of the Internal Revenue Code. To qualify, the transaction must have been an exchange rather than a sale of qualified property exchanged solely for property of like kind.
- The gain you realized if the property you exchanged was not held for use in a trade or business or for investment. (The transaction does not meet the requirements of a like/kind exchange.)
- The gain you realized on an exchange if you received nonqualified property (BOOT) in addition to qualified property.
- The excess that is treated as BOOT if you were relieved of more liabilities than you assumed in the exchange.
- Your unemployment compensation that is either fully or partly taxable because of other adjustments to your income or filing status.
- One-half of the unemployment compensation you received if you are married filing a separate return and you did not live with your spouse at any time during the year.

Reimbursement and Allowances—You have reported on your tax return:

- Any part of reimbursements and allowances received from your employer for moving expenses that exceeded your actual expenses.
- The reimbursements and allowances you received from your employer for employee business expenses that are required to be reported.
- The reimbursements and allowances you received from your employer for personal expenses.
- Cash allowances received from your employer for meals or lodging.
- The value of meals unless the meals were furnished: (a) on your employer's business premises, and (b) for your employer's convenience.
- The value of lodging unless the lodging was furnished: (a) on your employer's business premises, (b) for your employer's convenience, and (c) on your employer's business premises as a condition of employment.
- All moving expense reimbursements for the year in which they were received.
- Reimbursements from your employer if your employer paid your moving expenses back to the United States from overseas and you continued to work for him/her, because the reimbursements are considered as income from sources within the United States.
- Foreign taxes paid by your employer on your behalf.

Rental Income—You have reported on your tax return:

- All rental income.
- Advance rent in the year received, regardless of the period covered or the accounting method used.
- Payment received for cancellation of a lease in the year received.
- Security deposits that were not refundable because they constitute rent paid in advance and are taxable income in the year of receipt.
- Forfeited security deposits.
- Improvements made by a lessee, intended as rent, which became the property of the lessor on termination of the lease.
- Improvements to property made by a lessee in lieu of rent because they are treated as rent in the year they are made.
- As rent in the year a lease is terminated, the value of buildings constructed or improvements made by a lessee that represent a full or partial liquidation of a lease rental.
- Your expenses limited to your rental income if a vacation home or other dwelling unit was used by you, your relatives, or your friends for more than the larger of 14 days or 10 percent of the number of days the unit was rented at fair rental.

Unearned Income—You have reported on your tax return:

- Alimony or separate maintenance payments you received.
- Funds you embezzled.
- Your total gambling winnings.
- Prizes and awards you won.
- All interest income you received unless specifically exempted by law.
- The pension you received.
- The annuity you received.
- The corporate funds you received as dividend income.
- Your dividend income as reflected by the amounts shown on your Form 1099-DIV.
- All capital gain dividends you received during the year, less the applicable percentage of exclusion.
- Your interest income as shown on your Form 1099-INT.
- Any profit from the sale of state or municipal securities.
- Interest income you received on state/municipal securities that were on open account indebtedness and there was no written agreement to pay the interest.
- Any distribution you received out of earnings and profits of the distributing corporation, because it is taxable as a dividend.

EXCLUDABLE INCOME

Discharged Student Loans—You have **not** *reported on your tax return:*

- A student loan forgiven before January 1, 1983, that was furnished by the Government, or by the school board under an agreement with the Government (Federal, state, or local). (If your loan was furnished by an organization other than a Government agency, the amount forgiven is not excludable from income.)

Dividend Exclusion (Not available after the 1986 tax year.)

- You did not use the dividend exclusion to offset dividends that do not qualify for the exclusion.
- You did not use the dividend exclusion to offset interest income.
- You did not use the dividend exclusion to offset "dividends" on deposit in credit unions as these amounts are reported as interest.
- You have reported all dividends you received from foreign corporations.

Scholarships and Fellowships (New rules apply after August 16, 1986.)

- If you are not a candidate for a degree, the period for which you have excluded amounts you received as scholarships or fellowship grants has been limited to 36 months during your lifetime. (The 36 months need not be consecutive.)
- You have not excluded from income payments that represent compensation for past, present, or future services.
- You have not excluded from income a scholarship or fellowship grant that was paid by your employer.
- You have not excluded from income amounts you received that cannot be established as either a scholarship or fellowship grant.
- If you are not a candidate for a degree, your exclusion for payments received under a grant has been limited to $300 times the number of months that you received payments during the tax year.
- You have not excluded from income any amounts you received for study and training if it was actually compensation for services you performed primarily for the grantor's benefit.
- If a university or other organization contracts with a government agency or private organization to perform a research project for a consideration, that consideration is compensation for service, regardless of whether it is designated as a payment or a grant. If the

contracting organization employs researchers to fulfill the contract, payment to them is compensation for services rendered. If you were employed to help the institution fulfill a research contract, its payment to you is taxable compensation for services rendered, and you have reported such payment on your tax return.

DEDUCTIONS AND EXPENSES

Alimony (New rules apply for agreements made after 1986.)

- Premiums paid on your life insurance policy were not deducted as alimony unless the policy was owned by your spouse or former spouse, who was also the beneficiary.
- (Before 1985 only.) Unless the periodic payments to your spouse were made as a result of a written separation agreement, they were not deducted as alimony.
- Payments made for child support were not deducted as alimony.
- If you made a periodic payment for both alimony and child support that was less than the amount called for in the decree, you first applied the payments to child support and only then deducted any remaining amount as alimony.
- Delinquent payments for child support made under a divorce decree are considered reimbursements to your former spouse for child support furnished during periods when payments were in arrears. These reimbursements were not deducted.
- No alimony deduction was made for any amount paid in excess of the amount specified in the decree or agreement.
- Lump-sum cash or property settlements were not deducted as alimony.
- (Before 1985 only.) If you were not required to make the payments for more than 10 years, and there were no contingencies, the payments were not considered periodic payments and were not deducted as alimony.
- If the alimony was not paid during the taxable year, it was deducted.
- The amount of your alimony deduction can be verified as paid.

Bad Debts

- Since *nonbusiness* bad debts must be treated as short-term capital losses, your deductible loss was limited to $3,000.
- Loans which you made to relatives or friends and later forgave were not deducted as bad debts, because they are considered to be gifts.
- If you use the specific charge-off method for your bad debt deduction,

only debts which became worthless during the taxable year were deducted.

- You only deducted bad debts that became worthless during the taxable year.
- You can show that all reasonable steps were taken to collect the debt.
- You can establish that the amount shown was a bad debt arising from a true debtor-creditor relationship based upon a valid and legally enforceable obligation.
- You did not deduct a nonbusiness bad debt that was partially worthless, in the current year. (No deduction is available for partial worthlessness of nonbusiness bad debts.)
- You can show there was a valid enforceable obligation to pay a fixed or determinable sum of money.
- If you are a cash-basis taxpayer you only claimed a bad debt deduction from sales, professional services rendered, rents, interest, and similar items if such items were included in gross income on the return for which the deduction is claimed, or included in gross income for a previous year.

Capital Gains and Losses (Different treatment beginning 1987.)

- If you and your spouse filed separate returns, your deduction for net capital losses was limited to $1,500.
- For capital assets acquired after June 22, 1984, if you held property for 6 months or less, the gain (or loss) was reported as a short-term capital gain (or loss).

Casualty and Theft Losses

- Your casualty loss was reported as the lesser of: (a) the decrease in the fair market value of the property as a result of the casualty, or (b) the adjusted basis of the property.
- Your casualty was the complete or partial destruction or loss of property resulting from an event that was: (a) identifiable, (b) damaging to property, and (c) sudden, unexpected, or unusual in nature.
- Your casualty loss was deducted only in the taxable year in which the casualty occurred.
- If the trees, shrubs, etc., on your property were damaged or destroyed by disease instead of by a casualty, you did not deduct their value as a casualty loss.
- The cost of repairing termite or moth damage was not deducted as a casualty loss.
- Normal progressive deterioration was not deducted as a casualty loss.
- Expenses indirectly connected with a casualty, such as the cost of

care for personal injuries, fuel, moving, or rental of temporary quarters, were not deducted as casualty losses.

- Insurance proceeds or any other recovery received, or expected to be received, reduced your casualty or theft loss deduction.
- You did not deduct the casualty or theft loss of damaged, destroyed, or stolen property you did not own.
- Your theft loss was deducted in the tax year in which the theft loss was discovered.
- You can establish the amount of the decrease in either the fair market value of your property or your adjusted basis in the property as a result of the casualty.
- You can furnish evidence that the item was stolen rather than lost.
- Insurance proceeds or any other recovery you received reduced your casualty or theft loss deduction. If you chose not to file a claim for reimbursement with your insurance company, your loss was not deducted to the extent that reimbursement could have been received.
- (For tax years beginning after 1986) For a loss covered by insurance, you have evidence proving that you did file a claim for that loss with your insurance company.

Contributions

- Your reported contribution was made to a qualified organization.
- You did not deduct the value of time or services donated to charitable causes.
- Contributions made directly to a foreign organization were not deducted.
- Amounts paid for raffle tickets, to play bingo, or to engage in other games of chance were not deducted as contributions.
- Contributions made for the benefit of a specified individual were not deducted.
- Membership dues paid to country clubs and other social organizations were not deducted.
- Personal tuition expenses were not deducted.
- The contribution deduction of property to a qualifying organization was measured by the fair market value of that property at the time the gift was made.
- If the contributions were not made during the tax year, they were not deducted.
- Your deduction for car expenses related to charitable contributions was either at the standard rate of 9 cents a mile for tax years beginning after December 31, 1979, but before 1985 (in 1985, the amount was raised to 12 cents per mile); or
- You reported car expenses only to the extent that they represented out-of-pocket expenditures for such items as gas, oil, and parking

fees. (Depreciation, insurance, and the pro rata portion of general repairs and maintenance expenses were not deducted.)

- You can substantiate each reported contribution. If you cannot substantiate all contributions reported, your deduction was limited to the amount verified or determined reasonable based on all available information.
- Your charitable contributions conform with the percentage limitations.
- Your deduction for charitable contributions in the form of clothing and personal and household goods was limited to the fair market value of these items at the time of donating. (Since these items, particularly clothing, have very little resale value, your deduction reflects a reasonable amount.)

Educational Expense

- You can establish that education expenses were incurred to maintain or improve skills required in your employment, or they were required by your employer, law, or regulations for keeping your salary, status, or job.
- If these expenses were incurred to meet the minimum educational requirements for qualifications in your employment, they were not deducted.
- If courses you took are part of a program of study that may lead to qualifying you for a new trade or business, the expenses were not deducted.
- Educational expenses incurred before re-entering your trade or profession were not deducted.
- Educational expenses incurred while you were not employed, or not actively engaged in a trade or business, were not deducted.
- Educational expenses incurred for a dependent were not deducted.
- Educational expenses incurred for personal reasons were not deducted.
- To be allowed a deduction for educational expenses, you can furnish information to establish: (a) payment was actually made during the taxable year, and (b) the expense was ordinary and necessary to your employment.

Entertainment

- You can establish that a business benefit could reasonably be expected as the result of incurring entertainment expenses.
- Club dues or fees paid for the use of a facility were not deducted unless the facility was used more than 50 percent of the time for business purposes.
- To be allowed a deduction for entertainment expenses, you can fur-

nish information to establish that: (a) payment was actually made during the taxable year, and (b) the expense was ordinary and necessary to your business or profession.

- To be allowed a deduction for entertainment expenses, you have maintained adequate records to establish:
  1. Amount of each expenditure,
  2. Date the entertainment took place,
  3. Location of the entertainment,
  4. Business purpose for the entertainment, and
  5. Business relationship to you of the person entertained.
- You did not deduct the cost of entertainment allocable to your spouse or to the spouse of a business customer unless you can show that you had a clear business purpose rather than a personal or social purpose in incurring such expenses.

Exemptions

- If you were divorced or legally separated at the end of the tax year, you did not claim your former spouse as an exemption.
- If you filed a separate return and your spouse had gross income, you did not claim your spouse as an exemption.
- If you filed a separate return and your spouse was another taxpayer's dependent, you did not claim your spouse as an exemption.
- You did not claim your deceased spouse as an exemption after the year of death.
- You have provided more than 50 percent of the person's total support.
- The person did not have gross income of $1,900 or more, in 1987.
- The person did not file a joint return, except to solely receive a refund.
- An unrelated person was a member of your household for the entire tax year.
- The relationship between you and this person was not in violation of local law.
- The person was either a U.S. citizen or national, or a resident of the United States, Canada, or Mexico.
- If you contributed less than one-half of the person's total support, you have submitted a Form 2120, Multiple Support Declaration, for each other person who contributed more than 10 percent of the person's support.
- Contributions by a member of a household apply first to the payment of his/her own share of the expenses, and then any excess which cannot be traced to a certain member is considered to apply *pro rata* to the expenses of all who did not provide their own full support. Under this method of distribution, you can establish that you furnished more than one-half of the cost of the support for the dependent you claimed.

- Even though your child is a student, you must still meet the support test. Any amount spent from the dependent's own funds, including his/her wages, on such things as clothing, education, medical and dental care, recreation, transportation, entertainment, and similar items, must be added to the dependent's total cost of support in determining whether you furnished more than one-half of the support. You can establish that you furnished more than one-half such support for this individual.
- If you are divorced and your former spouse has remarried, the contribution of the divorced parent's new spouse to the support of your child is considered part of the divorced parent's contribution. If the combined contribution of both your former spouse and his/her new spouse is more than 50 percent of the total cost of support for the dependent(s), you have not claimed the exemption(s).
- To determine whether you contributed more than one-half of the cost of the dependent's support, it is necessary to know the total cost. You can show the total cost of support provided from all sources.
- Tax-free income (such as Social Security benefits, pensions, and state welfare benefit payments received by a claimed dependent) is part of support unless established otherwise. You did not claim an exemption if the benefits received represent more than one-half of the dependent's support.
- (Before 1985 only) For tax years beginning after October 4, 1976, under special rules for divorced or legally separated parents, you are allowed an exemption for your child (or children) only if you can meet these requirements:
  1. You contributed $1,200 or more for each child's support; and
  2. The other parent cannot clearly establish the provision of more support than you contributed.
- For tax years beginning after October 4, 1976, under special rules for divorced or legally separated parents, one of the parents may be entitled to a dependency exemption for a child if:
  1. Together they furnish more than one-half of the child's support for the calendar year; and
  2. The child was in the custody of either or both of them for more than one-half of the calendar year.

When these conditions are met, the parent who had custody of the child for the greater part of the calendar year is entitled to the exemption unless the other parent:

- Contributed at least $600 toward the child's support during the calendar year, and the decree of divorce, separate maintenance, or written agreement between the parents specifies that the noncustodial parent is entitled to the exemption; or the custodial parent signs a statement releasing the claim for exemption (Form 8332); or
- (Before 1985 only) Contributed $1,200 or more toward the support of

each child (or $1,200 toward the support of the child if more than one) during the calendar year, and the parent who has custody does not clearly establish the provision of a greater share of the child's support.

You can meet these requirements or show that you furnished more than one-half of your child's support for the calendar year.

Gifts

- Business gifts deductions do not exceed $25 to any one individual.

Insurance

- House and household insurance premiums on your personal residence were not deducted.
- If you used the standard mileage rate to compute your automobile expense deduction, you did not deduct your automobile insurance expense.
- You did not deduct automobile insurance expense for the amount attributable to personal use.
- Premiums paid on life insurance policies were not deducted.
- Deductions and/or payments for credit liability insurance or insurance guaranteeing lines of credit were not deducted.

Interest Expense (Limited beginning in 1987.)

- You were legally liable for the debt of any interest expense you claimed.
- Points you paid as a borrower as compensation for specific services that the lender performed in connection with your account were not deducted as interest.
- Points paid as a seller were not deducted as interest.
- You did not deduct interest paid on a loan used to purchase or hold tax-exempt securities.
- You did not deduct interest paid on a loan used to purchase or hold a: (a) single premium annuity contract purchased after March 1, 1954, (b) single premium endowment contract, or (c) single premium life insurance policy.
- Tax penalties were not deducted as interest.
- If you are an accrual-basis taxpayer, you deducted your interest expense ratably over the period for which it accrued.
- Escrow fees paid in connection with the purchase or refinancing of your home were not deducted. (Instead these fees were added to the cost.)

- If you use the cash method of accounting and the interest expense was not *paid* during the taxable year, it was not deducted.
- If you use the accrual method of accounting and the interest expense was not *incurred* during the taxable year, no deduction was made.
- You can furnish acceptable documentary evidence, such as statements from banks, finance companies, etc., to verify the interest paid during the year.
- If you have an outstanding loan that was not taken out for purposes of personal need or to conduct a trade or business, and you simultaneously own tax-exempt securities, there is a presumption that the purpose of the loan was to carry the tax-exempt holdings. Unless you can provide evidence of your motives for incurring the indebtedness, your interest expense was not deducted.
- The deduction shown on your return as interest was for interest on a *bona fide* debt.
- Only conventional mortgage points on a personal residence were deducted as interest. Loan origination fees and refinancing points were added to the basis of the property.

Legal Expenses

- Legal expenses incurred for defense of title to property were not deducted.
- Legal expenses incurred for the purpose of getting a divorce are personal expenses and were not deducted.
- Legal expenses incurred in connection with influencing the public at large were not deducted.
- Legal expenses incurred in connection with the purchase and sale of a personal residence were not deducted.
- Legal expenses incurred in construction of business buildings were not deducted but were capitalized.
- Legal expenses allocable to tax-exempt income were not deducted.
- Legal expenses incurred in the preparation of a will were not deducted.

Losses

- For an activity that is not engaged in for profit, the income from it is includible on your return. From this income, you have deducted the following expenses in the order shown:
  1. Interest, taxes, and other deductible items without regard to the profitability of the activity;
  2. Operating expenses, except those in item (3) below (to the extent gross income from the activity exceeds deductions allowable under (1) above); and

3. Depreciation and other basis adjustment items to the extent gross income from the activity exceeds deductions allowable under (1) and (2), above.

- If the property sold was not used in a trade or business or held as income producing property, the loss on the sale was not deducted.
- If the loss was incurred on the sale or exchange of property between members of the same family, it was not deducted.
- If the loss was incurred on sale or exchange of property between yourself and a corporation in which you are considered the owner of more than 50 percent of the value of the outstanding stock, it was not deducted.
- A loss on the sale or exchange of your residence was not deducted.
- Losses from wash sales were not deducted.
- Your deduction for gambling losses do not exceed the amount of your gambling winnings.
- Renting a personal residence temporarily prior to its sale does not convert it to business property. If the loss resulted from the sale of a personal residence, it was not claimed.
- For a farm loss to be allowable, you must show you intended to make a profit from your farming operations. This intent can be supported by actions that show that you entered into and operated your farming business in good faith for the purpose of making a profit.
- The excess of your Section 1244 loss over the aggregate limit of $100,000 for a joint return was treated as a loss from the sale or exchange of a capital asset.
- For property rented to a friend, relative, or other parties for less than its fair rental value, expenses attributable to the rental were deducted only to the extent of the income received and only as itemized deductions on Schedule A. You did not deduct a loss from that rental.

Medical and Dental

- Only the amount of medical expenses that exceeds the applicable percentage of your adjusted gross income was deducted.
- Premiums paid for life insurance policies were not deducted as medical expenses.
- Premiums paid for policies which reimbursed you for loss of earnings or for the accidental loss of life, limb, sight, etc., were not deducted as medical expenses.
- Premiums paid for policies that guaranteed a specified amount each day, week, or month in the event of hospitalization were not deducted as medical expenses.
- Your medical expense deduction was reduced by the reimbursements you actually received.
- If the medical expense was not paid for yourself, your spouse, or your

qualified dependent, the amount was not deducted as a medical expense.

- Payments for personal analysis required as part of your training were not deducted as medical expenses.
- Payments for cosmetics, toiletries, toothpaste, and like items were not deducted as medical expenses.
- Payments for items that are not generally accepted as medicine or drugs were not deducted as medical expenses. (Beginning in 1984, they are deductible only if obtainable by prescription or for insulin.)
- If your travel to another city for necessary medical treatment was a personal choice for nonmedical reasons, the travel expense was not deducted.
- A trip taken to change environment or generally improve health was not deducted as a medical expense, even when the trip was made on the advice of a physician.
- Only the costs of permanent improvements made to property for medical reasons that were more than the increase in the fair market value of the property were deducted.
- Payments to household help were not deducted as a medical expense, even when you were physically unable to perform those duties.
- Funeral and burial expenses were not deducted.
- If the medical expenses were not paid during the year, they were not deducted.
- Since many nondeductible items can be bought at drug stores, cancelled checks alone are not considered adequate verification of payment for drugs and medicines reported on your return. You have adequate proof supporting the expenditures.
- The cost of transportation to and from work, even if your condition requires an extraordinary mode of transportation, does not qualify as a medical expense. It is a personal expense and was not deducted.
- You did not deduct medical expenses paid by your dependent.
- Automobile expenses were claimed either for out-of-pocket expenditures for such items as gas, oil, and parking fees, or in the absence of evidence of actual expenses incurred, you substituted a standard rate of 9 cents a mile.
- You can furnish acceptable documentary evidence, such as statements from doctors or hospitals, cancelled checks, receipts, etc., to verify medical expenses paid during the year.

Moving Expense

- You reduced your moving expense deduction by the amount you received as a reimbursement.
- If you were not a full-time employee in the general location of your new

principal place of work for at least 39 weeks during the 12-month period immediately following your arrival, you did not deduct those moving expenses.

- If the move did not take place within 1 year from the date you first reported for the new job, you did not deduct those moving expenses unless you can show that circumstances existed that prevented the move within that time.
- Since a servant, governess, chauffeur, nurse, valet, or personal attendant is not a member of your household, the moving expense for that individual was not deducted.
- Your deduction for the cost of meals and lodging while you were occupying temporary quarters at a new work location was limited to any period of 30 consecutive days after you obtained work.
- The deduction for pre-move house-hunting and temporary living expenses at the new business location was limited to $750 if you reported it on a separate return and $1,500 on a joint return. These expenses, *plus* the expenses of selling or buying a home, were not more than $1,500 on a separate return or $3,000 on a joint return.
- You qualify for a moving expense deduction because the distance between your new business location and your former residence is at least 35 miles farther than the distance between your former business location and your former residence.
- You did not claim a moving expense deduction if you were not self-employed on a *full-time* basis for at least 78 weeks during the 24 months following the move (of which 39 weeks must be in the first 12 months).
- You figured your allowable deduction for car expenses related to moving either at the standard rate of 9 cents a mile, or by actual expenses.
- Your costs for storing and insuring household goods and personal effects were deducted as in-transit expenses because they were incurred within any period of 30 days in a row after the day the goods and effects were moved from your former home and before delivery to your new home.
- The deduction for temporary living expenses for your move outside the United States was limited to 90 days in a row after you obtained employment.
- The deduction for pre-move house-hunting trips and temporary living expenses for your move to a new place of work *outside* the United States was limited to $4,500 ($2,250 on separate returns). These expenses, plus the expenses of selling or buying a home were not more than $6,000 ($3,000 on separate returns).
- Any part of reimbursements and allowances received from your employer for moving expenses that exceeded your actual expenses was included in income.

Office in the Home

- If the business use of a part of your home was for your work as an employee, the use was for the convenience of your employer.
- You did not deduct any expense for the *personal* part of your home as an office-in-the-home expense.
- You did not deduct any expenditures for personal items such as lawn care and landscaping as an office-in-the-home expense.
- You did not deduct any repairs made to the personal portion of your residence as an office-in-the-home expense.
- You claimed a deduction for office-in-the-home expense but you can establish that your employer required you to provide that space for the purpose used. (Voluntary, occasional, or incidental use of part of your home in connection with your employment does not entitle you to a business deduction for the expenses incurred.)
- The part of your home used for business was used regularly and exclusively for that purpose.
- If a portion of your personal residence was used as an office-in-the-home, you did not defer tax on the gain on the sale of your personal residence on the business portion when you purchased another residence.
- (Beginning in 1987) Your total deduction for business use of your home was not more than the gross income received from the business use of your home *minus* the sum of:
  1. The business percentage of your mortgage interest and real estate tax deductions; and
  2. Your business expenses other than those related to the business use of your home.

Taxes

- You did not deduct federal income taxes withheld, Federal excise taxes, withheld Federal Social Security taxes, regulatory license fees or water taxes.
- You cannot prove your actual sales tax expenses, so you deducted an amount based on the State Sales Tax Table for your income bracket and family size (only for the tax years prior to 1987).
- The Federal portion of gasoline tax was not deducted.
- Special assessments were added to the cost of the property and were not deducted.
- If you sold or bought a house, the real estate taxes were apportioned between the buyer and the seller according to the number of days in the real property tax year that each held the property.
- You did not deduct taxes on property unless you own the property.

- You did not deduct state income taxes on income (except interest) which is exempt or excludable for Federal income tax purposes.
- If your taxes were not paid during the taxable year, they were not deducted.
- If you used the State Sales Tax Tables, in addition to the amount shown in the tables, you only deducted the sales tax you paid on the following items: automobiles, boats, airplanes, mobile homes, and materials purchased to build a new home where the materials were billed to you (only for the tax years prior to 1987).
- In taking a deduction for sales tax, you used either the sales tax table for your income bracket and size of family, or the sales tax actually paid, but not both (only for the tax years prior to 1987).

Travel and Transportation

- If you used the standard rate in figuring your car expenses for business purposes, depreciation and out-of-pocket expenses for this travel were not deducted.
- You figured your allowable deduction for car expenses for business purposes at the standard rate of 2.5 cents a mile for the first 15,000 miles (21 cents before 1987) and 11 cents for each additional mile.
- Your allowable car expense deduction was limited to the total expense times the percentage of the total miles driven for business purposes.
- If your employer did not require you to incur these travel or transportation expenses they were not deducted.
- If the travel expenses you claimed were incurred on interim trips home while on temporary assignment, the amounts you spent in excess of what you would have paid for room and board at your temporary assignment are personal expenses and, therefore, not deducted.
- The cost of commuting between your residence and any business location within the area of your principal place of employment was not deducted.
- The cost of traveling to and from your principal place of employment was not deducted.
- Travel expenses incurred while you were *not* away from your tax home were not deducted.
- If you failed to claim from your employer a reimbursement to which you are entitled for travel and transportation expense, you did not claim a deduction for these expenses (prior to 1986).
- No deduction is allowed for any expenditure for business travel away from home (including meals and lodging) unless you keep adequate records and documentary evidence to substantiate this expense. To meet the records requirement, you can show that you have maintained the following:
  1. An account book, diary, or statement of expenses, with entries

made at or near the time of each necessary business expense. You must show the amount spent, the time and place of travel, and the purpose of the business. (Estimates do not qualify as substantiation of these expenses.)

2. Available documentary evidence that will identify the expense, such as receipts, paid bills, or cancelled checks.

- Although "home" ordinarily means the place where you and your family live, your tax home is the entire city or general area in which your principal place of business, employment station, or post of duty is located. If your expenses were incurred at your tax home, they were not deducted as away-from-home expenses.
- The cost of your meals while not away from your principal place of employment overnight on business travel was a personal expense, regardless of the hours or other inconveniences. Therefore, the expense for such meals was not deducted.
- If you moved from job to job, maintaining no fixed place of abode or business locality, each place where you worked became your principal place of business and your tax home. Therefore, you did not deduct your expenses for travel, meals, and lodging.
- If your job at the new location was expected to last for an indefinite period (that is, if its end could not be foreseen within a fixed and reasonably short period), that location then became your new tax home. Therefore, you did not deduct the expenses of travel, meals, and lodging while there, and any reimbursement or per diem you received was included in income.
- A deduction for travel and transportation is allowable only for your own expenses. The part of the expense allocable to other members of your family was not deducted.
- That part of expenses attributable to travel, meals, and lodging for your spouse was not deducted, if you cannot prove a bona fide business purpose for your spouse's accompanying you on the business trip or business convention.
- You can show that your attending a convention benefited or advanced the interests of your business or your own work as distinguished from the business or work of another.

Work Clothes

- If your work clothes are adaptable to general use, the cost of caring for them was not deducted.
- You claimed a deduction for work clothes, because you can furnish information to prove: (a) payment was actually made during the tax year, (b) the clothes were ordinary and necessary to your business or profession, and (c) the clothes were not adaptable to general use.

Miscellaneous Expenses

- You did not deduct personal living or family expenses, other than those specifically provided for by law.
- The value of your time and labor was not deducted.
- Special assessments that did not increase the value of your property were deducted only if they were imposed by a political subdivision.
- You did not claim a deduction for your contributions to a retirement and disability fund. The amount of your pay withheld and contributed to a retirement and disability fund was included in your income in the year in which it was withheld and was not deducted.
- Regarding expenses incurred in the sale or purchase of your home, you did not deduct personal living or family expenses, other than those specifically provided for by law. (Closing costs are nondeductible capital expenditures. The amount paid to purchase a home should be added to the basis. The amount paid to sell a home should be added to the selling expense.)
- Adoption expenses were qualified adoption expenses for a child with special needs (repealed for tax years after 1986).
- Expenses incurred in establishing your business before the time your business began were capitalized rather than deducted in the year incurred.
- Although there is no taxable gain, you reported the sale of your personal residence in the year it was sold. (See Form 2119.)
- Legal expenses were not deductible if they were for the *purchase* of property held for the production of income or used in a trade or business. (Instead, these costs were capitalized by adding them to your basis in the asset.)

TAX CREDITS

Child and Dependent Care Credit

- Your expenses for the care of a qualifying individual were necessary to enable you (husband and wife, if joint return) to be gainfully employed.
- Your expenses for the care of a qualifying individual were deducted because you furnished over half the cost of maintaining a home which was your principal residence as well as the principal residence of the qualifying individual.
- Your employment-related expenses were incurred for the care of one or more of the following qualifying persons: (a) your dependent under

age 15, for whom you are entitled to a personal exemption; (b) your dependent who is physically or mentally incapable of self-care; or (c) your spouse who is physically or mentally incapable of self-care.

- Payments made to *your dependent* or to *your child,* were not deducted as child and dependent care expenses.
- Expenses for education in the first grade or higher were not deducted as child care expenses.
- Payments for the services of a chauffeur or gardener were not deducted as child and dependent care expenses.
- For tax years beginning after December 31, 1981, the maximum expense deducted for the care of your qualifying person(s) was:
  1. $2,400 for the year for one dependent; or
  2. $4,800 for the year for two or more dependents.
- You can establish that the amount shown was paid for the care of a qualifying individual.
- Transportation costs for the child between your household and the care location were not included in figuring the credit for child care expenses.
- If you are a married person filing a separate return, you did not claim the child care credit unless you met the following qualifications:
  1. Your home must have been the home of a qualifying person for more than half the tax year; and
  2. You must have paid more than half the cost of keeping up your home for the tax year; and
  3. Your spouse must not have lived in the home for the last 6 months of the tax year.

Political Contribution Credit (Repealed for tax years after 1986.)

- To qualify for the credit your contributions were made to the following individuals and organizations:
  1. A candidate for Federal, state or local elective office in a primary, general, or special election;
  2. An organization or committee organized exclusively to support one or more candidates for Federal, state, or local elective office; or
  3. A national, state, or local committee of a national political party. The cost of raffle, lottery or similar tickets to raise campaign funds were not claimed for the credit.
- You did not deduct more than $50 when you filed a separate return, or $100 when you filed a joint return.
- Non-cash political contributions were not deducted as a political contribution credit.

Energy Credit (Repealed for tax years after 1985.)

- You can establish that you purchased or installed qualifying energy conservation or renewable energy source items.
- The energy saving items that you installed were new and were expected to last at least 3 years.
- Your renewable energy source equipment was installed for use with your principal residence.
- Your renewable energy source property was new and was expected to last at least 5 years.
- Your furnace replacement burner qualified for an energy credit because the burner replaced an existing burner. (It does not qualify if it is acquired as a component of, or for use in, a new furnace or boiler. (Internal Revenue Regulation 1.44c-2(d)(4)(i))

TAX COMPUTATIONS

- You itemized your deductions, even if your itemized deductions totaled less than your standard deduction or zero bracket amount, because:
  1. You were being claimed as a dependent on your parent's return, have unearned income of more than the value of the personal exemption, and your earned income was less than your standard deduction or zero bracket amount; or
  2. You are married filing a separate return and your spouse itemized deductions; or
  3. You are a U.S. citizen excluding income from sources in U.S. possessions; or
  4. You had dual status as a non-resident alien for part of the year and you were a resident or citizen of the U.S. for the remainder of the year.
- If your spouse itemized deductions on his/her separate return, you also itemized your deductions. If your allowable itemized deductions were less than the zero bracket amount, you added the unused zero bracket amount to your adjusted gross income and recomputed your tax accordingly.

Step 4

Avoiding Tax Scams, Shams, and Illegal Shelters

Everywhere you look there are advertisements promoting books, seminars, and plans for reducing taxes. Some shout: "Pay no taxes, now and forever." Others claim to show: "How to make a fortune and pay zero tax," or "How you too can live like a millionaire and pay no tax."

The idea of saving money on income taxes appeals to everyone. Even the Supreme Court gave the idea respectability when Justice Learned Hand said: "There is nothing sinister in arranging one's affairs as to keep taxes low as possible."

In 1935, Justice Sutherland wrote:

> The legal right of a taxpayer to decrease the amount of what otherwise would be his taxes, or altogether avoid them, by means which the law permits, cannot be doubted.

You may wonder, "What does the law permit?" Some people would say that the law permits whatever *they* say it permits. Some people only believe what *they* want to believe. Yet others are easily convinced that anything is permissible.

The solidity of the Internal Revenue Code isn't even debatable. The massive document is so riddled with loopholes which benefit the special interests, that people readily fall for any scam, sham, shelter, or illegal advice that purports to be legitimate. The average taxpayer is defenseless against the claims of promoters and fancy advertisements promising to bail them out of their ever increasing tax bracket. Even though the IRS has taken positions on a vast number of tax shelters and tax-protester schemes, and has litigated the issues hundreds of times, many illegitimate shelters and schemes are still promoted around the country with alarming success.

So what is a taxpayer supposed to do when he wants to determine if a tax shelter is legitimate? Not only are tax practitioners in disagreement, but IRS employees themselves are little help. The libraries may be full of articles and books on the subject, but the average taxpayer does not have the time and knowledge necessary to conduct the research to make a proper decision. And, in spite of the fact that the IRS has issued rulings and regulations on just about every tax shelter being promoted today, few promoters inform their victims of what IRS's position is, or even if the courts have ruled in favor of the IRS.

Many taxpayers are fooled by financial schemes that allegedly take advantage of loopholes in the law. Taxpayers are unaware of IRS's right to declare these actions a "sham". If the IRS believes that the taxpayer's actions were not legitimately motivated, but were contrived for the sole purpose of tax avoidance, then the transaction could be considered a "sham" and set aside by the IRS.

Be aware that the difference between tax avoidance and tax evasion can be a fine line, distinguished mainly by the motives and the knowledge of the taxpayers. The IRS monitors compliance of taxpayers involved in numerous tax shelters by automatically auditing the returns of those claiming the shelters. To a naive person who unwittingly believes the promises of the shelter promoters and follows their advice, the subsequent IRS audit can be a trying experience.

This chapter will expose the most flagrant and publicly advertised shelters and tax-avoidance devices that IRS feels are tax evasion traps so you won't be taken in. I will discuss each device by explaining what the issues are that the promoters are selling, and what IRS's position is.

TAX SCAMS AND SHAMS

In the last few years taxpayers have been bombarded by promotions of various shady schemes and tactics that challenge the power structure of the government. Even though some are alleged to be tax-avoidance maneuvers, they are really tax-evasion acts that could result in the imposition of heavy civil and criminal penalties.

There are now so many of these patently illegal schemes that the IRS has grouped them into the category of tax-protester activity, even though some schemes are purported to be "tax shelters." The IRS defines a tax protester as, "a person who employs one or more illegal schemes that offset the payment of taxes."

These protesters attempt to undermine the tax system by using various schemes that lead to the evasion of taxes. The "illegal tax-protest movement" is a general term describing several areas of noncompliance in which a growing number of individuals and groups are using illegal methods to protest the tax laws.

The illegal tax-protest movement began in the early 1920s. Until a few years ago, the movement was centered mainly in the western and southwestern parts of the country, and was viewed by IRS as a local compliance problem. The movement consisted of a few individuals who disputed the constitutionality of taxes and who practiced and promoted illegal schemes. The schemes were simple and straightforward—individuals refused to file tax returns, or would file returns but report no income.

The movement grew in the late 1960s, when protest returns were filed by individuals who belonged to geographically isolated groups who protested: (1) the Government's right to tax individual income, (2) the taxability of paper money versus gold or silver, and/or (3) the unwarranted growth of Government. Their protest scheme involved filing blank form 1040 tax returns while citing the Fifth Amendment or monetary arguments. These arguments have long been denied by the courts.

In recent years, the movement has continued to grow and spread across the country as protesters make speeches and offer seminars, often misrepresenting the tax laws. According to the IRS, the movement became more attractive as our Nation's economic conditions worsened. Today people from all walks of life are involved, and the schemes are more sophisticated.

As of September 30, 1986 the IRS had 22,211 protest-type tax returns under examination and had closed another 20,725 cases during the year.

The IRS says these individuals and groups who are attempting to disrupt the effective administration of taxes "present a potential threat to our voluntary compliance system," some by advocating and using violence against IRS employees. The Government acknowledges that all citizens have the right to criticize the tax system and Government policies related to it, as well as to join groups which express such criticisms. But as IRS Commissioner Roscoe Egger once pointed out: "Once an individual moves from expressing dissatisfaction to actually employing schemes with the intention of evading taxes, the Service has an obligation to become involved in order to protect the Government's revenue base and to preserve the tax system."

The basic element in any illegal tax protester scheme is a challenge to the Government's authority to levy and collect taxes. A common characteristic of tax-protest rhetoric is the misleading appeal to patriotism and righteous indignation. Because everyone knows the American Revolution started with a protest against taxes, these appeals to patriotism lead many tax-protest followers into believing that what they are doing is as "American" as apple pie and motherhood. However, illegal tax-protest activities are not really the American way because taxpayers do have *legal* ways to protest the Government's tax policies. Legal tax protesters seek to change the tax laws through legislation, while continuing to pay their taxes in accordance with existing laws. They legally and peacefully exercise their right to petition the Government. California's "Proposition 13" movement is an example of a legal tax protest movement.

Perhaps the most visible legal challengers of our tax code are the high-powered tax-law lobbyists on Capitol Hill. There are virtually thousands of lobbyists trying to influence the writing of the tax code in innumerable and sometimes mysterious ways that could possibly save their clients millions of tax dollars. (Sometimes, lobbyists even write sections of the Tax Code.)

While no one can deny that there are flaws in our tax system, our country is founded upon a respect for law where changes are made *through the law,* not by subverting the law. The irony is that many tax protesters have a "quasi-legal" approach; that is, they initially try to openly subvert the system with an illegal scheme or clearly meritless constitutional attack, but then use the court system, a constitutional and legal approach, to try and prove their point. Using the courts to fight the system and change the laws is an acknowledgment that our system works.

The question then arises, If these tax protesters go so far as to recognize the power of the courts by using the courts for their appeals, then why don't they recognize the previous rulings of the courts in denying the legitimacy of their claims?

Some tax protesters are truly gullible individuals who have been victimized by fast-talking promoters into believing that we have a system of rule without a system of law. For example, many taxpayers have never even heard of the Tax Code and are misled by promoters into believing that the existence of the IRS and our tax system is based either on some arbitrary, authoritarian government fiat or some type of historical accident. Typical arguments making the circuits now are that "wages are not income" because some law in the early 1900s did not tax wages, or that income tax withholding is not legal because the Victory War Tax of 1943, which introduced withholding, has been repealed.

Even though the *mechanics* of how our tax system works may be a mystery to many, the *existence* of our system should not be. It's difficult to comprehend how anyone could think there is no basic legal foundation to our tax system. A visit to any practitioner's tax law library should be sufficient evidence to the contrary, that every mechanism in our tax system has roots embedded in the tax code. Those who believe otherwise are perfect candidates for buying portions of the Brooklyn Bridge. The fact is that most illegal tax protesters are just using these schemes as an excuse not to pay, and their appeals through the courts are nothing more than delaying tactics to forestall paying what they know they owe.

If there should be any outrageous indignation, it should come from the hundred million taxpayers who *do* pay their taxes, and from the 76 million who *overpay* their taxes every year. The Government, as a matter of equity, owes it to the complying millions to ferret out these subversive activists.

Those who are foolish enough to believe that there will be no day of reckoning down the road have no understanding of the awesome powers of the IRS. After the courts have summarily disposed of the tax protester cases, the unpaid taxes will be assessed, and will have to be paid. The Collection Division of the IRS has no special leniency policy for tax protesters; they will not hesitate to use the strongest seizure powers of any governmental authority in the United States. For a good explanation of IRS's seizure powers, read my book, *When You Owe the IRS*.

AUDIT-PROOFER'S STRATEGY RULE

Avoid any type of tax scam or sham that challenges the legality or constitutionality of the tax system. This is not to say that you shouldn't challenge any particular provision of the tax code or any specific action of the IRS when you feel you have a legitimate argument. But, you must avoid any of the spurious arguments associated with the tax-protest movement and which have already been defeated numerous times.

IRS Actions Against Illegal Tax Protesters

The IRS says, "The service centers are identifying more protest returns during processing, and examiners are asserting civil penalties . . . against tax protesters who file frivolous returns." The IRS asserted a $500 penalty against 2,343 taxpayers last year for filing frivolous tax returns.

The frivolous-return penalty allowed by Code *Section 6702* can be immediately imposed upon any taxpayer who files a purported return that fails to contain information from which a correct tax liability can be determined, or contains information that the self-assessment is substantially incorrect, *and* the filing of the return is either due to a frivolous position or a desire to delay or impede the administration of the Federal income tax laws.

The penalty is intended to attack a great variety of tax-protest activities, including:

- Returns that are not complete enough to be processed.
- Returns that refer to spurious constitutional arguments instead of being completed.
- Returns that clearly present inconsistent information.
- Returns that made deductions for "war taxes" or for the government not being "on the gold standard."
- Returns that deliberately use incorrect tax tables.

Unlike other penalties, the frivolous return penalty is not based on any amount of unpaid tax, and can be assessed immediately by the IRS upon filing of the return, with no requirement of an advance notice. Because Congress imposed this penalty to halt the increase of protester returns, the processing of which "delays and impedes the administration of the internal revenue laws," a taxpayer who submits multiple frivolous returns will be subject to *multiple* frivolous penalties.

The Criminal Investigations Division investigates violations of federal tax laws and related offenses. In 1986, about 15 percent of their general enforcement program resources were devoted to illegal tax protesters and fraudulent tax shelters.

The program effort on illegal tax protesters concentrated on the investigation of leaders and promoters of major protest groups and schemes with significant numbers of participants. One investigation resulted in a 19-count indictment of nine leaders of a major mail-order ministry scheme. They were charged with evading the payment of taxes on about $10 million of income received from the sale of mail-order ministry charters. Approximately 1,000 taxpayers who bought those charters and took improper tax deductions for "contributions" to their own churches will have to pay millions of dollars in back taxes and penalties.

Tax Court Actions Against Illegal Tax Protesters

Even though the Government hasn't released any statistics, it is clear from the volume of Tax Court opinions being issued, that a large percentage of docketed cases also pertain to tax-protester appeals. The Tax Court frequently issues summary opinions on these cases against the protester-taxpayers in very short statements denouncing their arguments as "frivolous and without merit." Under Code *Section 6673* the Tax Court is also awarding damages *to the government* up to $5,000 against taxpayers pursuing these ridiculous claims. The award is made, "Whenever it appears to the Tax Court that proceedings before it have been instituted or maintained by the taxpayer primarily for delay or that the taxpayer's position in such proceedings is frivolous or groundless."

COMMON TAX PROTEST SCHEMES

Constitutional Basis Schemes

The constitutional scheme is one of the oldest and most frequently used protest approaches.

Generally, these protesters make the false claim that any payment of tax or providing of tax-return information violates their constitutional rights. In lieu of the information required on Form 1040/1040A, the protester either writes "-0-," "none," or "object"; or cites the Fourth, Fifth, or Sixteenth Amendment to justify his or her refusal. This is commonly referred to as a Porth/Daly return. In some cases, these returns are so incomplete that the IRS treats them as non-filer cases.

For example, protesters may claim they are providing no income information because it would violate their Fifth Amendment right against self-incrimination. The Supreme Court held as early as 1927, however, that a taxpayer could not refuse to file a Federal income tax return on the basis of Fifth Amendment protection. Similarly, protesters mistakenly assert that the internal revenue laws constitute an illegal seizure of property in violation of the due process clause of the Fifth Amendment. The courts have also denied this ridiculous claim, stating that, "It is now well settled that the income tax laws are not unconstitutional under the due process clause of the Fifth Amendment."

A Legal Evaluation of the Constitutional Scheme

First Amendment Contention: The taxpayer refuses to pay income taxes, in whole or in part, on religious or moral grounds, incorrectly contending that to do so would violate First Amendment rights. Federal courts have held in numerous cases that there is no constitutional right to refuse to pay income taxes, in whole or in part on religious or moral grounds, or because the funds are used for government programs opposed by the taxpayer. The fact that some persons may object, on religious grounds, to some of the things that the government does is not a basis upon which to claim a constitutional right to avoid taxation.

Fifth Amendment: The taxpayer claims that the filing of an income tax return violates the Fifth Amendment right against self-incrimination, and that he is entitled to secure a ruling on the incriminating possibility of each item on the return. There is no constitutional right to refuse to file an income tax return because of the Fifth Amendment (*United States v. Sullivan,* 274 U.S. 259 (1927)). In *Sullivan*, the court upheld a conviction for failure to make a return. It held the Fifth Amendment generally does not authorize one to refuse to state their amount of income. (However, some recent cases indicate that taxpayers earning illegal income may be entitled to claim the Fifth Amendment privilege as to the *amount* of income. See *United States v. Barnes,* 604 F.2d 121, 147 (2d Cir. 1979), cert. denied, 446 U.S. 807 (1980); *United States v. Carlson* 617 F. 2d 518 (9th Cir. 1980)).

Fifth Amendment—Due Process: Protesters falsely assert that various provisions of the Internal Revenue laws violate the due process clause of the Fifth Amendment. Generally they claim that the graduated income tax scale and the fact that certain deductions or benefits allowed by the Internal Revenue Code are not available to some people denies them their Constitutional rights. The protesters also assert that some of the statutory collection procedures violate the due process clause. *Brushaber v. Union Pac. RR Co.,* 240 U.S. 1 (1916) held that due process was not denied by discriminating between classes or by having a progressively graduated income tax scale. *United States v. Keig,* 334 F. 2d 823 (7th Cir. 1964) held that progressive rates are constitutional. Further, in *Swallow v. United States,* 325 F. 2d 97 (10th Cir. 1963), cert. denied, 377 U.S. 951 (1964), the court held, "It is now well settled that the income tax laws are not unconstitutional under the due process clause of the Fifth Amendment."

Unconstitutionality of the Federal Reserve System: Protesters contend that the Federal Reserve System is unconstitutional; therefore, the Code is unconstitutional to the extent it taxes income represented by notes or checks which do not contain or are not redeemable in gold or silver. This argument has been consistently rejected by the courts as frivolous. In *Hatfield v. Commissioner,* 68 T.C. 895 (1977), the Court uniformly held that Federal Reserve Notes constitute legal tender, "Money," which must be reported on a taxpayer's accounting.

Thirteenth Amendment: Protesters make the ridiculous assertion that the bookkeeping, records maintenance, and employer withholding requirements are in reality "involuntary servitude" and, therefore, unconstitutional. This ludicrous argument was rejected in *Porth v. Brodrick*, 214 F. 2d 925 (10th Cir. 1954), and is completely without merit.

Tax Court is Unconstitutional: Protesters contend that the Tax Court is illegally constituted, and there is a denial of a jury in tax litigation. Obviously, the Tax Court is a court of record under Article 1, Section 8 of the Constitution. The protester intentionally disregards our right to litigate a tax refund suit before a jury. Numerous decisions have sustained the constitutionality of the Tax Court of the United States in the exercise of the jurisdiction conferred upon it by Congress.

Sixteenth Amendment: Protesters claim that the tax laws are unconstitutional because the Sixteenth Amendment was not properly ratified. They claim that since the State of Ohio was not properly a state at the time of the ratification of the Sixteenth Amendment, the Amendment is not valid and, therefore, the income tax law is unconstitutional. This allegation is overcome by looking at the history of the Sixteenth Amendment. It was ratified by forty states, including Ohio, and a proclamation issued in 1913. Shortly thereafter, two other states also ratified it. Under Article V of the Constitution, only three-fourths of the states were needed to ratify this Amendment so there were enough states (without Ohio) to complete the number needed for ratification. Every case in which this issue has been presented has been decided against the taxpayer.

Warning:

The IRS *and* the courts are losing patience with taxpayers who persist in these spurious assertions. The IRS is stepping up assessments of penalties and so are the courts.

Case Citations—Constitutional Schemes

First Amendment:

1. *Autenrieth v. Cullen*, 69-2 USTC, 9724

Fifth Amendment:

- Incrimination:
  1. *United States v. Sullivan*, 1 USTC, 236
  2. *United States v. Daly*, 68-2 USTC, 9617
  3. *Neff*, 80-1 USTC, 9397
  4. *Carlson*, 80-1 USTC, 9299
  5. *Moore*, 79-2 USTC, 9676
  6. *Garner v. U.S.*, 76-1 USTC, 9301

- Due Process:
  1. *Brushaber v. Union Pac RR Co.*, USTC, 4
  2. *United States v. Keig*, 64-2 USTC, 9563
  3. *Swallow v. United States*, 64-1 USTC, 9117

Thirteenth Amendment:

1. *Porth v. Brodrick*, 54-2 USTC, 9552
2. *American Friends Service Com.*, Sup. Ct., 74-2 USTC, 9774

Sixteenth Amendment:

1. See *Brushaber* above.
2. *Baker, Richard M. T. C.*, Memo 1978-60

Federal Reserve System:

1. *Edward A. Cupp,* 65 TC, 68
2. *U.S. v. Wangrud*, 76-1 USTC, 9358
3. *Hatfield v. Comm.*, 68 TC, 895 (1977)

Tax Court:

1. *Nash Miami Motors, Inc. v. Comm.*, 66-1 USTC, 9354
2. *Hartman v. Switzer*, 74-1 USTC, 9478

Valid Return:

- "Jurat" Omitted:
  1. *Dixon v. Comm.*, 28 TC 338
  2. *Ellison v. Comm.*, 35 TC 1261
  3. *Vaira v. Comm.*, 52 TCM 986
  4. *Lucas v. Pilliod Lumber,* 2 USTC 521
  5. *Moore,* 80-2 USTC, 9627
  6. *Cupp.* See "Federal Reserve System" above.

- Zeros:
  1. *Morris R. Smith,* 80-2 USTC, 9476
  2. *Robert M. Long,* 80-2 USTC, 9627

- Sufficiency of Information:
  1. *Porth*, 70-1 USTC, 9329
  2. *Hatfield*. See "Federal Reserve System" above.
  3. *Daly,* 73-2 USTC, 9574
  4. *Cupp.* See "Federal Reserve System."

Church Related Schemes

A number of dishonest opportunists are involved in the sale of minister's credentials and church charters through mail order. These schemes, which claim to reduce an individual's income taxes, are perhaps the fastest growing area of protest schemes.

The alleged church scheme has two variations. Under the first, an individual purchases fake ministerial credentials and perhaps a church charter. The tax evader then forms a front organization, or becomes a branch of another organization, claiming to establish a tax-exempt church. In most cases, the person's residence houses the "church," and his or her family is the "congregation." The tax protester then contributes up to 50 percent of his or her income—the maximum allowable—to the alleged church and claims it as a Form 1040 deduction, substantially reducing taxes. Of course, the church's revenue is actually used to pay the person's living expenses.

Under the second variation, the tax protester allegedly takes a vow of poverty, pledging to obey the orders of the church. The alleged "orders" actually do no more than "require" a person to retain his or her current job and continue his or her present life-style. While the protester may file a Form 1040 claiming income, he or she then takes an adjustment against gross income for an equal amount. This unreasonable adjustment eliminates any tax liability. Some protesters show no financial data, claiming that they are not required to pay taxes as ministers under a vow of poverty.

Under the law, a "vow of poverty" is characterized in *Order of St. Benedict of New Jersey v. Steinhauser,* 214 U.S. 640 (1914), as a legally enforceable agreement between a religious order and a member of the order to the effect that the gains and acquisitions of the member become the common property of the order. In turn, the order, at least implicitly, agrees to supply the individual with the necessities of life. Most taxpayers who file vow of poverty returns are sincere in their religious convictions, and are not motivated by tax avoidance.

A Legal Evaluation of Alleged Church Schemes

Assignment of Income: It is a basic principle of Federal income tax law that an assignment or similar transfer of compensation for personal services to another individual or entity is ineffectual to relieve the taxpayer of Federal Income tax liability on such compensation, regardless of the motivation behind the transfer. (See *Lucas v. Earl, Helvering v. Horst,* and *Helvering v. Eubank.*)

Any taxpayer, even a member of the clergy, who performs services in an individual capacity is taxed on the income from those services. Therefore, the assignment of income issue in any vow of poverty case depends upon whether the taxpayer is performing services as an *agent* of the church or as a *principal*. If the taxpayer receives income as an agent of the church, that income is deemed to belong to the church and the taxpayer is not taxed on it. If the taxpayer is not an agent, the income is taxed to him or her.

For a minister to be performing services as an agent, the minister is required by the church to perform those services for, or on behalf of, the church. Most importantly, it means that the services are the type that are ordinarily the duties of church members. (See Revenue Rulings 76-323, 77-290, and 78-229.)

Requirements for Deductibility of Contributions: IRC 170(c) defines a charitable contribution, and establishes three important requirements for deductibility:

- The contribution must be a true "gift";
- The gift must be made to an organization that is organized and operated exclusively for religious or charitable purposes; and,
- No part of the net earnings of the organization can inure (accrue) to the benefit of any private shareholder or individual.

Gift (Quid Pro Quo): A gift for the purpose of IRC 170 is a voluntary transfer of money or property that is made with no expectation of receiving a commensurate financial benefit in return.

Revenue Ruling 78-232 states that if the donor can reasonably expect by making the transfer to obtain sufficiently substantial benefits to provide a *quid pro quo* for it, then no deduction under IRC 170 is allowable. *Quid pro quo,* therefore, is the test applied when determining if a gift has been made. It means something given or received in exchange for something else.

If the taxpayer-minister controls the church bank account(s), and causes personal expenses to be paid directly or indirectly to himself or herself, it can be said that he or she received or expected to receive financial benefits in return and that a *quid pro quo* exists. Protesters using the church scheme will generally attempt to have the alleged church pay for lodging, food, automobile, medical, education, or other personal expenses. (See Rev. Rul. 78-232.)

Organized and Operated Exclusively for Religious Purposes: A church need not formally request and receive exempt status from the IRS to be considered exempt. However, for a contribution to be deductible, the burden of proof is on the taxpayer to show that the church is organized and operated for religious purposes. In this regard, Regs. 1.170A-1(a)(2)(iii) states that, "Any deduction for a charitable contribution must be substantiated, when required by the District Director, by a statement from the [church] indicating whether the [church] is a domestic organization, the name and address of the contributor, the amount of the contribution, the date of actual receipt of the contribution, and such other information as the District Director may deem necessary.

Inurement: The term "inurement" relates to the requirement in IRC 170(c)(2) that no part of the church's net earnings may inure to the benefit of any private shareholder or individual. Developing the inurement issue is almost identical to the *quid pro quo* issue, in that if the church has paid personal expenses of the taxpayer, then inurement exists. The difference is that inurement applies in determining if a contribution has been made to a qualified organization under IRC 170(c). That is, if the organization uses the contribution to pay a "dividend" to its members, the organization is not a qualified donee and no deduction is allowed under IRC 170 (a)(1). (See Rev. Rul. 78-232.)

Case Citations—Church Schemes

Charitable Contribution Deduction—In General:
IRC 170(a)
IRC 170(c)

Substantiation Requirements:
Regulation 1.170(A)(2)

Vows of Poverty—Assignment of Income:
Rev. Rul. 80-332, 1980-2 C.B. 34 (C.B. = *Cumulative Bulletin*)
Rev. Rul. 79-132, 1979 C.B.
Rev. Rul. 78-229, 1978-1 C.B. 305
Rev. Rul. 77-436, 1977-2 C.B. 25
Rev. Rul. 77-290, 1977-33 C.B. 11
Rev. Rul. 76-341, 1976-2 C.B. 307
Rev. Rul. 76-323, 1976-2 C.B. 18
Rev. Rul. 68-123, 1968-1 C.B. 1

Lucas v. Earl, 281 U.S. 111 (1930)
Helvering v. Horst, 311 U.S. 112 (1940), 1940-2, C.B. 206
Helvering v. Eubank, 311 U.S. 112 (1940), 1940-2, C.B. 209
Kelly v. Comm., 62 T.C. 131 (1974)
National Carbine Corp. v. Comm., 336 U.S. 422 (1949)

Organized and Operated Exclusively for Religious Purposes:
Brown v. Comm., T.C.M. 1980-553
Abney v. Comm., T.C.M. 1980-27 (1980)
Dusch v. Comm., T.C.M. 1980-4
Walker v. Comm., T.C.M. 1978-493
Heller v. Comm., T.C.M. 1978-149
Western Catholic Church v. Comm., 73 T.C. No. 19 (Oct. 31, 1979)
Oaknoll v. Comm., 69 T.C. 770 (1978)
Clippenger v. Comm., T.C.M. 1978-107

General Conference of the Free Church of America v. Comm., 71 T.C. 920 (1979)
Rev. Rul. 81-94, 1981 C.B. 15

Inurement:
IRC 170(c)(2)(c)
Rev. Rul. 78-232, 1978-1 C.B. 69
Rev. Rul. 69-266, 1969-1 C.B. 151
Abney v. Comm., T.C.M. 1980-27 (1980)
Beth El Ministries v. U.S., 44 AFTR 2nd 5190
Martinsville Ministries v. U.S., 45 AFTR 2nd 80-578 (D.D.C. 1979)
Clippenger v. Comm., T.C.M. 1978-107
Walker v. Comm., T.C.M. 1978-493
Heller v. Comm., T.C.M. 1978-149

Family Estate Trust Schemes

A family estate trust is another questionable vehicle used by tax protesters to avoid or substantially reduce personal income taxes. *The Service has published several rulings adverse to these schemes and the courts have repeatedly upheld the Service's position.*

Under this scheme, an individual assigns all real and personal property, and income from current employment to the trust. In exchange, the creator of the trust receives "compensation" as an officer, trustee, or director, as well as certain "fringe benefits," such as "pension rights," "tax-free use of a residence," and "educational endowments" for children.

Once the taxpayer's income is transferred to the trust, the trust is allegedly taxed only on undistributed net income. Promoters claim that substantially all living expenses of the taxpayer and his or her family may be deducted on the trust's fiduciary income tax return as business expenses, and that the balance might then be distributed to the taxpayer's family or to a separate "non-profit" educational trust, leaving little or no taxable income.

How the Scheme Operates

Typically, the taxpayer attends a family estate trust scheme promotional meeting in which a salesperson explains the purported tax advantages of creating a family estate trust. The sales promotion emphasizes the savings of income taxes, probate fees, and estate and gift taxes. The promoter is paid a fee which may include an amount based on a percentage of the individual's annual gross income and net worth. In return, the taxpayer receives an "educational package" consisting of a *pro forma* trust and indenture containing a copyright seal (often entitled "Declaration of Trust of this Pure Trust"). Included are instructions on how to create and manage the trust, and how to file individual and fiduciary income tax returns for the desired tax result. The package also contains extensive legal opinions on the validity of the family estate trust, and, sometimes, contains guarantees for free legal representation before the IRS.

The specific language and general design of the trust instrument rarely differs from one family estate trust to another. (For an outline of the relevant terms of the "family estate" trust, see *Horvat v. Commissioner,* TCM 1977-104.) The trust instrument generally contains the following characteristics:

- The alleged purpose of the trust is stated in moral terms, such as patriotic, or promotion, of the general welfare. The trust purpose may contain the grantor's constitutional rights or religious beliefs.
- The term of the trust is generally 20 or 25 years. However, the instrument may call for termination at an earlier date by unanimous vote of the trustees who will then distribute the remaining assets to the beneficiaries in proportion to their shares of beneficial interest (see below).
- The trustees generally have sole discretion to distribute income and corpus, but the grantor retains substantial control.
- The trust usually bears the name of its creator and is generally fashioned "John Doe Family Estate (A Trust)."
- The complete trust instrument is signed in the presence of a notary public and may be recorded in a local court of records. Neither procedure is required to establish legal validity. However, the procedure is stressed by promoters as being vital to proper establishment of the trust, apparently to create an atmosphere of legality.

The spouses and a third party are generally named as co-trustees in the original trust instrument. Within a few days of the trust's creation, the third party resigns as co-trustee, leaving the husband and wife as co-trustees. The third party is usually a close relative, such as a sister, brother, or a close personal friend. The third party may also have created a family estate trust scheme.

The taxpayer is named "executive manager," the spouse "executive secretary," and the third-party "treasurer." These terms are generally foreign to the operations of *inter vivos* trusts. After the third party resigns, the spouse may become "secretary/treasurer."

The taxpayer will then transfer personal assets, and possibly business assets, to the trust. Personal assets may consist of the personal residence, automobiles, household furnishings, bank accounts, and securities. Business assets may include lifetime services, inventory, and/or depreciable property. The transfer of real property is generally recorded in the local court of records. Income subsequently earned on the transferred assets is sometimes paid directly to the trust rather than to the individual.

Although personal or business liabilities are allegedly transferred to the trust, there is normally no evidence that they are so transferred. Nonetheless, substantially all personal and business expenses of the grantor and the grantor's family are paid out of "trust funds" and deducted on the fiduciary income tax return.

An essential element of the scheme is the anticipatory assignment of wages, salaries, bonuses, commissions, and income from personal service contracts purported to exist between the trust and the individual's employer. When the individual is the sole stockholder, or a substantial stockholder in a corporation, such a contract may exist. At the direction of the taxpayer/stockholder, earned income will be paid directly to the trust without withholding of Federal, state, and local income taxes, and FICA. In most cases, however, the employee does not have control over the employing company. The employer usually will not be notified of the existence of the trust and will continue to make payments directly to the employee.

In exchange for transferring assets, liabilities, and the "lifetime services," to the trust, the grantor receives units of beneficial interest, represented by printed forms similar to stock certificates. The grantor may then distribute the shares among the grantor's spouse, children, third-party co-trustee, and/or to himself or herself. For example, if there are three children, 100 units of beneficial interest may be distributed in the following manner, 25 units each to the grantor and the grantor's spouse, 20 units to the third party, and 10 to each of the children. Normally, all units of beneficial interest are held by the grantor and/or his family.

A Legal Evaluation of Family Estate Trust Schemes

Assignment of Income:

- *Lifetime Services*—All income, from whatever source derived, is taxed to the person who earns it unless specifically excluded by law. Gross income includes income realized in any form, whether in money, property, or services. (See *Commissioner v. Culbertson,* 337 U.S. 733, 739-740 (1949), 1949-2 C.B. 5; Rev. Rul. 75-257, 1975-2 C.B. 251.)
- *Withholding and FICA*—The grantor, and not the trust, is the employee subject to withholding under IRC 3402(a) and to FICA under IRC 3121 (a), regardless of any payments made directly or indirectly

to a trust under a "lifetime services" contract. (See Rev. Rul. 80-321, IRB 1980-48, 6.)

Grantor Type Trust: For Federal income tax purposes, the grantor is considered the owner of all "family estate" trust income and corpus under IRC 674, 676, or 677, or a combination of these sections as the case may be. *Sham Transaction:* As an alternative to attacking a "family estate" trust with the "assignment of income" and "grantor trust" arguments, the sham-transaction theory may be used. The sham theory is most appropriate where the trust funds are being used to pay the grantor's personal living expenses, the grantor exercises dominion and control over the trust assets as if they were the grantor's own assets, the grantor borrows from the trust without adequate security, and the trust does not maintain a checking account of its own. Under these circumstances, trust income is property attributable to the grantor. (See, generally, *Paster v. Commissioner,* T.C.M. 1961-240; *Jones v. Page,* 102 F. 2d 144, cert. denied, 308 U.S. 562 (1939).)

Corporation Trusts:

- In the case of a transfer of business property to a trust, the IRS will consider Revenue Ruling 75-258. This ruling concluded that the family estate trust, based on the provisions contained in the trust instrument, possessed more corporate than noncorporate characteristics.
- When raising this issue, the IRS may also include the alternative position shifting the income to the grantor's return(s) under the assignment of income principle discussed earlier.
  Warning: The *Internal Revenue Manual* advises all examiners to, "Consider the negligence penalty on all family estate trust cases." This will mean an additional 5 percent penalty plus an additional 50 percent of the interest tacked onto your bill.

Foreign Trust Organization Schemes

Some tax advisors have been promoting abusive foreign trust, or double trust, organization schemes. These schemes are attempts by promoters to reap substantial profits from uninformed taxpayers or from illegal tax protesters willing to gamble that these schemes will not be challenged by the IRS. Generally, the schemes involve at least two foreign trusts and sometimes one or more domestic trusts which enter into sham transactions designed solely as tax-avoidance arrangements. Some taxpayers who use the foreign trust schemes have been coached by promoters to use tax-protester tactics to frustrate, intimidate, or confuse examiners in conducting their examinations.

How the Scheme Works

The scheme is established when an agent, who is named as the creator/grantor, creates a trust in a foreign country, naming the taxpayer as trustee. The trust is usually established in a country that has no tax treaty agreement with the U.S. government for the exchange of information.

The taxpayer then transfers his assets and income-producing property to the trust. The agent then creates a second trust in the same foreign country, naming the first trust as the trustee of the second trust. The taxpayer and both trusts then enter into sham transactions with each other, conceived only for tax purposes.

These schemes sometimes use overseas bank accounts, and may include both domestic and foreign counterfeit trusts.

Example: A doctor establishes a domestic trust to which is transferred the assets of the protester's medical practice. The promoter had created three foreign trusts for the protester: FTO #1, FTO #2, and FTO #3. FTO #1 serves as sole trustee for FTO #2 and FTO #3.

The protester conducts his or her medical practice during the year using the bank accounts of the domestic trust to receive income and to pay expenses. At the end of the year, the trust has a $125,000 profit. The protester directs the trust to pay FTO #2 $125,000 as a management fee. The domestic trust files Form 1041, U.S. Fiduciary Income Tax Return, showing no profit or loss. FTO #1, as trustee for FTO #2, directs FTO #2 to pay a $125,000 management fee to FTO #3. FTO #2 files a Form 1040NR, showing the $125,000 in income and $125,000 in expenses. FTO #3 now has $125,000 in cash. FTO #3 is not required to file a Federal income tax return since it does not conduct business in the United States. FTO #1, as sole trustee of FTO #3, directs FTO #3 to pay the protester the $125,000 as a gift or a loan. The protester claims that since this is a gift or a loan, it is not required to be reported as income.

A Legal Evaluation of Foreign Trust Schemes

The tax advisors who promote these schemes have gone to great lengths to give them the appearance of legitimacy. The protesters may feel they have found a means of legally avoiding their tax liability. Listed below is a brief explanation of three primary approaches that will be used by IRS examiners to defeat these schemes.

- *Substance v. Form*
  1. The courts have long recognized and applied the general principle that the substance, not the form, of the transaction controls the tax consequences. See *Gregory v. Helvering,* 293 U.S. 465 (1935).
  2. When a series of transactions, taken as a whole, show that the transactions themselves are shams, or that the transactions have no substance, utility, or purpose apart from tax considerations, the courts will refuse to allow the sought-after tax benefits of these transactions. See *Goldstein v. Commissioner,* 364 F. 2d 734 (2nd Cir. 1966); *Goldstein v. Commissioner,* 267 F. 2d 127 (1st Cir. 1959).

- *Sham Theory*—Rev. Rul. 80-74, 1980-1 C.B. 137, "Foreign Tax Haven Double Trust," sets forth an example of a foreign tax haven double trust in which two foreign trusts were created to accomplish the "tax benefits" similar to those described earlier. It holds that the creation of both trusts will be considered a sham, and that the substance of the transaction will control. See *Knetsch v. United States,* 364 U.S. 361 (1960); *Higgin v. Smith,* 308 U.S. 473 (1940); *National Lead Co.,* 336 F. 2d 134 (2nd Cir. 1964); *Lynch* 273 F 2d 867 (2nd Cir. 1959).
- *Assignment of Income*—Income will be taxed to the one who earns it or otherwise creates the right to receive it and to enjoy the benefit of it when paid. See *Lucas v. Earl,* 281 U.S. 111 (1930); and Rev. Rul. 75-257, 1975-2 C.B. 251.

  Warning: The IRS states that because of the great latitude and flexibility in the way a trust may be operated, alternative approaches may have to be used. There are at least six other approaches listed in the *Internal Revenue Manual*. The IRS has many weapons to fight these schemes, and it is not likely that you could persevere in the event of an IRS challenge.

Miscellaneous Wild Schemes

False W-4 Scheme

Since 1974, the filing of a false Form W-4, Employee's Withholding Allowance Certificate, has become more common and is often used by illegal protesters in conjunction with another scheme.

Under the false W-4 scheme, an employee claims excessive withholding allowances or complete exemption from withholding so that little or no

Federal income taxes are withheld by the employer. Later, the employee may either underreport income, refuse to pay the difference between taxes withheld and due, or not file a return at all, thus creating a collection problem for IRS.

This scheme usually starts with a few employees and expands as others learn that their counterparts take home more money for the same work. For example, in 1981 about 3,500 General Motors autoworkers in Flint, Michigan, primarily at the urging of two leaders, filed questionable form W-4s. The scheme has even been used by Federal employees and municipal employees, such as policemen and sanitation workers.

Under IRS procedures now in effect, employers are required to send to IRS every W-4 that claims in excess of 10 allowances. The IRS corresponds with taxpayers to determine if they are, in fact, entitled to claim that many allowances.

In 1986 the IRS adjusted 212,000 forms W-4 of employees who underestimated their withholding by claiming too many allowances. The $500 civil penalty for filing false wage withholding information was levied on over 45,000 taxpayers (over 100,000 taxpayers were fined in 1984).

Fair Market Value Scheme

The fair market value scheme, which is seldom used, involves taking a deduction for the declining value of the dollar, thus substantially reducing taxes. Gross income is listed on the face of the return and there is a large adjustment to income which makes the adjusted gross income small enough for the zero bracket amount to eliminate taxable income. The adjustment to gross income is on Schedule D, Schedule of Capital Gains and Losses, or Form 2106, Statement of Employee Business Expenses, for Form 1040. The tax court has upheld IRS's position that such a deduction is neither provided for nor authorized by the Internal Revenue Code or regulations.

Gold/Silver Standard Scheme

Under the gold/silver standard scheme, which is also seldom used, protesters argue that Federal Reserve Notes do not constitute income because they are not redeemable in gold and silver. They further argue that Federal Reserve Notes are not legal tender. In most cases, the protester will file a blank return with supporting arguments attached. These arguments have been consistently rejected by the courts as being frivolous and without merit.

Protest Adjustment and Nonpayment Protest Schemes

The protest adjustment scheme involves the use of an unallowable deduction, adjustment, or credit based on philosophical objections to the use of tax money for certain Government programs, such as defense or foreign aid.

The nonpayment protest scheme involves correctly computing the tax, but refusing to pay the balance due on the basis of philosophical objections.

Federal courts have held in numerous cases involving these schemes that there is no constitutional right to refuse paying income taxes because the funds might be used for Government programs that the taxpayer opposes.

Forms 843 and Amended Returns—Some individuals are filing Form 843 Claims and/or Amended Form 1040(1040X) returns to obtain a total refund on all taxes paid in prior years, even though returns have not yet been filed for the prior years.

Blank Form 1040/1040A—These generally fall into two categories. In one category the individual files a return with only a name and address, and possibly signature, and Form(s) W-2 is attached. This scheme is usually verified upon correspondence with the taxpayer. In the second category, the individual files a return similar to the Porth-type return. In both instances the return may or may not list marital status and/or exemptions.

Other Tax Protester Schemes—Many variations of the above schemes exist. They generally involve frivolous constitutional arguments or sham transactions in continually changing forms. Some examples of these schemes are:

- *"Wages Are Not Income" or Nontaxable Receipts*—These schemes involve various deductions, usually equivalent to the amount of W-4 or 1099 income, based on arguments that wages are not profits or not income and, therefore, not taxable. These deductions have appeared on Schedule C as the total of business expenses, cost of goods sold, or as wage expense. The *Eisner v. Macomber* return is a "Wages Are Not Income"-scheme variation.
- *Eisner v. Macomber*—A document which looks almost identical to page 1 of Form 1040, but line items are altered to reflect *Eisner v. Macomber* and/or other similar court citations to deduct large amounts from income.
- *Factor Discount*—Involves claiming a loss on Form 1040 created by discounting a wage earner's paycheck with a foreign trust financial organization pursuant to a life-services contract. The amount of loss claimed is for the net amount from the face value of the paycheck less a nominal fee. Simultaneously with the discounting, the life-services contract is purchased by a second foreign trust financial organization. These sham transactions disguise what is nothing more than an assignment of income. This scheme is distinguishable from the Multiple Foreign Trust Organization scheme in that the wage earner does not create any foreign trusts.

TAX SHELTERS

What Is A Tax Shelter?

A tax shelter is a method, transaction, or investment that yields tax benefits to the investor. The Internal Revenue Code is deliberately structured to allow us to take advantage of legitimate tax shelters to ensure certain social and economic benefits intended by Congress. In these cases Congress has concluded that the resulting loss of revenue is an acceptable side effect of a special tax provision specifically designed to encourage certain kinds of investments. Therefore, tax shelters are not necessarily abhorrent financial practices. In fact, the residence you own is a form of tax shelter since your mortgage interest expense and real estate taxes are deductible items that offset your otherwise taxable income.

The vast majority of tax shelters are in full compliance with the tax laws, but an increasing number of them have crossed the bounds into being "abusive tax shelters". These are cases where the revenue loss to the government produces little or no tax benefit to society.

In order to understand why Congress deliberately allows tax shelters, keep in mind that the country's economy requires the commitment of huge sums of money, often over long periods of time, for leasing; drilling for gas and oil; mining; farming; building tankers, and constructing apartment buildings, shopping centers, and office buildings. This combination of time and money lends itself to operations which result in tax avoidance, both proper and improper. Participants use different investment vehicles to pool their financial resources and accumulate financial benefits. These vehicles differ not only in form but in right of control, participation in management, personal liability, flexibility, and a vast array of elements involved in carrying out their operations or functions. It is because of the many different variations available for structuring financial and tax arrangements that most tax shelters are created.

Even though the Tax Reform Act of 1986 made many tax shelters undesirable to many investors, they are not yet dead, and taxpayers still need to know how to avoid an abusive tax shelter.

Characteristics of a Tax Shelter

Many tax shelters are business ventures in which accounting losses far exceed the accounting income. These losses are used to offset the taxpayer's income from other sources.

Usually, a tax shelter also provides large deductions in its early years although the taxpayer may not have invested significant amounts of capital up front. For example, a taxpayer might purchase a rental property with a low down payment and offset his rental income with deductions for interest, taxes, and the maximum allowable depreciation.

Generally, losses are generated in the first years of existence and passed through to investors, who sometimes achieve a complete return of their original investment through tax savings in the first two or three years. But the existence of a loss does not always indicate a tax shelter. A loss may also occur as a result of business operations or from an unusual event such as a casualty loss. The key element which distinguishes a tax shelter loss from a true business loss is the *substance* of the event which gave rise to the loss.

There are many methods by which taxpayers shelter their losses, but these three characteristics are usually found in tax shelters, either separately or in combination:

- Taxes are deferred to later years.
- Ordinary gains (100 percent taxable) are converted to capital gains (only 40 percent taxable), or capital losses (only 50 percent deductible), are converted to ordinary losses (100 percent deductible); in both cases producing a lower tax liability (valid until 1987).
- Leverage is obtained through various financing arrangements.

Deferral means the postponement of income taxes. In general, a significant portion of the tax shelter investor's return is derived from "pass-through" deductions used to offset ordinary income from other sources—thus creating significant tax benefits. The tax shelter allows the taxpayer to postpone or even avoid payment of taxes. The deferral of taxes is the equivalent of an interest-free loan from the Government, the economic benefits of which can be significant.

An example of deferral is an IRA, your Individual Retirement Arrangement. The tax on your current year's income that has been placed in an IRA is deferred until you withdraw the funds at retirement, when your annual income and tax bracket should be lower.

Deferral also occurs when excessive deductions are taken in the early years of a tax shelter, a practice the IRS calls "front end loading." Examples of *illegal* front end loading practices are:

- Deducting capital items by classifying them as advisory fees, management fees, or interest.
- Deducting prepaid interest.
- Not including prepaid income.
- Deducting excessive depreciation, amortization, or depletion by using the wrong method, too short a useful life; and/or too large a basis.

Conversion means converting ordinary income items into capital gains or converting capital losses into ordinary losses to reduce taxable income (no longer a characteristic after 1986). Conversions may involve buying a commercial real estate building to obtain a current tax deduction (for example, from a net operating loss on the rental income) against other ordinary income, only to sell it at a later date for a long-term capital gain, which is taxed at a more favorable rate. For example:

Arnold C. purchased a rental building on January 1, 1984 for $1 million. Mr. C. borrowed the entire amount which was to be repaid over 10 years at 10 percent interest. No principal was paid the first year. Mr. C. reported the following items on his Schedule E for 1984:

Rental income		$150,000
Minus: Interest Paid	$100,000	
ACRS S/L Depreciation	66,667	
Other operating expenses	83,333	
Net expenses		−$250,000
Ordinary loss for 1984		($100,000)

On January 5, 1985 Mr. C. sold the rental property for the amount of the unpaid mortgage on the property, which happened to be the same $1 million he paid for it.

Selling price		$1,000,000
Minus Adjusted Basis:		
Cost	$1,000,000	
Minus: ACRS S/L	66,667	−933,333
Long-term capital gain		66,667
Minus: Capital gain deduction		
(per Internal Revenue Code 1202) (60% of $66,667)		−40,000
Taxable gain for 1985		$26,667

Ordinary loss of 1984	($100,000)
Taxable gain for 1985	+ 26,667
Net effect of conversion	($ 73,333)

This two year tax avoidance maneuver resulted in a net $73,333 loss, due mostly to the ACRS depreciation assistance. Basically, for no money down and little risk, Mr. C. received a $73,333 tax deduction which would have been used to offset other taxable income. (Do you ever wonder why the rich get richer?)

Leverage is the ratio of borrowed funds to the amount of at-risk capital invested in an activity or business venture.

The ideal leverage situation for the investor is one in which he enters into a transaction with no down payment whatsoever, buying the property completely on credit. In this situation the taxpayer has *no* at-risk capital and his or her leverage is 100 to 0. Typically, one of the selling points used by financial advisors to draw investors into a tax shelter scheme is the leverage. The best situation exists when the taxpayer finances his or her investment through a *nonrecourse loan*. A nonrecourse loan is any borrowing structured so that the borrower has no personal liability and the lender only looks to the specific assets pledged as security in the event of default on the loan. Simply, what makes nonrecourse financing attractive is that in the event that the taxpayer's investment does not result in enough proceeds to pay the note, the taxpayer is *not* held personally liable to repay the loan balance.

The use of capital through borrowing is the primary attraction of many shelters. At one time, nonrecourse loans enabled high-income investors to deduct losses far greater than the amount personally risked in the investment. An example: purchase agreements that contained a clause stating that the loan would be paid off *only* from the distribution proceeds or from the eventual sale of the purchased asset. If this clause was in the loan agreement, the loan was a nonrecourse loan and the investor was not personally liable for repayment of the loan, even if the asset produced no income.

Now, under IRC *Section 465* (effective after December 31, 1975), a taxpayer's loss is limited to the amount that he has "at risk" and could actually lose from an activity. This prevents a tax loss from exceeding the taxpayer's economic risks. (For more information regarding the "at-risk" rules, see IRS Pub. 536.)

IDENTIFYING AN ABUSIVE TAX SHELTER

The IRS says **abusive tax shelters** are "marketing schemes that involve artificial transactions with little or no economic reality. They often make use of unrealistic allocations, inflated appraisals, losses in connection with nonrecourse loans, mismatching of income and deductions, financing techniques which do not conform to standard commercial business practices, or the mischaracterization of the substance of the transaction. Despite appearances to the contrary, the taxpayer generally risks little. Abusive tax shelters commonly involve package deals that are designed from the start to generate losses, deductions, or credits far in excess of present or future investment, or that promise investors at the start future inflated appraisals to enable them, for example, to reap charitable contribution deductions based on those appraisals. They are commonly marketed in terms of the ratio of tax deductions allegedly available to each dollar invested. This ratio (or "write-off") is frequently said to be several times greater than one to one."

The IRS has also issued the following as a checklist for determining whether a particular offering is an abusive tax shelter. These questions will help to provide a clue as to the abusive nature of the plan:

- Do the benefits far outweigh the economic benefits?
- Is this a transaction you would seriously consider, apart from the tax benefits, if you hoped to make a profit?
- Do shelter assets really exist and, if so, are they insured for less than their purchase price?
- Is there a nontax justification for the way profits and losses are allocated to partners?
- Do the facts and supporting documents make economic sense? In that connection, are there sales and resales of the tax shelter property at ever increasing prices?
- Does the investment plan involve a gimmick, device, or sham to hide the economic reality of the transaction?
- Does the promoter offer to backdate documents after the close of the year and are you instructed to backdate checks covering your investment?
- Is your debt a real debt or are you assured by the promoter that you will never have to pay it?
- Does the transaction involve laundering United States–source income through foreign corporations incorporated in a tax haven and owned by the United States shareholders?

Determining Economic Reality

In recent years, many tax shelters have been formed solely for tax advantages. Investors enter into the venture with little or no promise of a gain, aside from the anticipated tax benefits. The rate of return on investment for an abusive tax shelter is much lower than for other types of investments. The investor is willing to accept this low return because the reduction in taxes which otherwise would be paid is the equivalent of a profit. While the Code allows deductions for losses arising from transactions entered into for profit, *losses are not allowed for transactions entered into for loss, since these are losses for tax avoidance*.

Benz v. Commissioner, 63 T.C. 375, 384 (1974):

> While losses often occur during the formative years of a business . . . the goal must be to realize a profit on the entire operation, which presupposes not only future net earnings but also sufficient net earnings to recoup the losses which have meanwhile been sustained in the intervening years.

The structuring of abusive tax shelters is often highly sophisticated, requiring a broad analysis of intricate interrelationships. From an IRS point of view, the basic question is: "What criteria can be used in determining if a shelter was structured primarily for tax avoidance, that is, how can we recognize a transaction that lacks economic reality?" *From an economic point of view, the key to this determination is a computation that compares the* **present value** *of all future income with the present value of all the investments and associated costs of the shelter.*

Present Value: The discounted value of an income stream if obtained by investing money at the current investment rate rather than in the activity. The present value is the amount of investment required to generate the expected income. This computation compares the amounts invested with the income received or to be received, in terms of current dollars not considering any distortion caused by inflation.

If the present value of all future income is less than the present value of the money invested, the tax shelter may be abusive. In an abusive tax shelter, the primary gain is the tax advantage.

In extreme cases in which economic reality is lacking, the issue often is relatively easy to pinpoint. However, the entire tax shelter area is one of continuing complexity and evolvement, making it difficult to determine the degree of economic reality present in the transactions. In any transaction, though, the IRS will try to answer these three questions:

- Does the price of the asset, together with its related elements, bear a relationship to fair market value?
- Does the transaction provide any true equity build up, thus creating a value to forfeit upon possible termination?
- Does the transaction transfer the burdens and benefits of ownership?

For example:

Roger P. entered into a tax shelter scheme in which he purchased 10 head of cattle for $3,000 each, paying cash of $3,000 and giving a note of $27,000. The current market price for live cattle is $1,600 per head.

The validity of the transaction is questionable as the purchase price exceeds the fair market value. Therefore, the IRS wants to know: Is the note valid?

Assume further that the note is a nonrecourse note. The terms of the agreement state that the note will be paid off through the sale of the cattle. Mr. P. has nothing more to pay in. Thus, he has no real equity build up. He can walk away from the scheme leaving only his $3,000 initial investment. This initial investment, however, would have been recovered through tax write-offs, thus leaving him with no economic losses at all.

Assume further that Mr. P. is protected from losses by a guarantee that any of the cattle that die or become ill will be replaced, so that their full fair market value will be received upon sale. In this case, it is indicated that Mr. P. does not really have the burdens and benefits of ownership. It is not likely he will receive any profits from the sale because the FMV of the purchase is excessive. He will not incur any economic losses.

Overvaluation of the tax shelter product is perhaps now the biggest fraud perpetrated on the government by abusive tax shelters. A sales price totally unrelated to the fair market value of the item being questioned is a major sign of an abusive tax shelter. By purchasing an asset at an inflated value the taxpayer attempts to claim larger deductions for such items as depreciation, interest expenses, and the investment credit. It is usually the deductions of these items that makes the tax shelter program attractive to the taxpayer in the first place.

Overvaluation is typically accomplished through self-serving appraisals. Very often, in charitable contributions schemes, the donee will accept the donor's valuation of the gift (such as a work of art) and have no real knowledge of the item's worth. The IRS is most likely going to rule out as worthless a letter from the donee to the donor valuing the gift.

AUDIT-PROOFER'S STRATEGY RULE

Be aware of the **potential abuse indicators** ***which IRS examiners are instructed to watch for before you enter into any tax shelter.***

Tax examiners are taught to investigate the following situations for possible abusive financial maneuvers:

- Investments made late in the tax year indicate there may be deductions for prepaid expenses that are not allowable.
- A very large portion of the investment made in the first year indicates the transaction may have been entered into for tax purposes rather than economic motivation.

- A loss exceeding a taxpayer's investment indicates the possibility of a nonrecourse note.
- If the burdens and benefits of ownership have not passed to the taxpayer, the parties have not intended for ownership of the property to pass at the time of the alleged sale.
- A sales price that does not relate comparably to the fair market value of the property indicates the value of the property has been overstated.
- If the estimated present value of all future income does not compare favorably with the present value of all the investment and associated costs of the shelter the economic reality of the investment may be questionable.

IRS Tax Shelter Targets

Although tax shelters involve a wide variety of businesses, according to the IRS abusive tax shelters are frequently found in the following areas.

Real Estate: This industry requires the commitment of large sums of capital over a long period of time for the construction of apartment buildings, shopping centers, office buildings, and other structures. Many real estate ventures are profit oriented with tax benefits only a secondary consideration. The IRS will challenge those operations which are not based on providing true economic benefits. Some expenses which may indicate an abusive tax shelter are current deductions for construction period expenses and rapid write-offs of depreciation. Nonrecourse financing is used to provide the needed capital.

Oil and Gas: Oil and gas drilling shelters provide tax benefits through the deduction of intangible drilling costs. These costs may actually represent prepaid expenses when little or no actual drilling is done in the year of payment. Also, deductible expenses paid to related contractors may be inflated.

Farms: Farm tax provisions are intended to benefit the legitimate farmer. Some of these provisions are misused by taxpayers who enter into farming transactions mainly for the tax advantages. One such provision allows the use of the cash method even though inventories are material income-producing items. Another provision allows prepaid feed and herd management fee deductions in the year paid. If these expenses are paid and deducted late in the year, and the goods or services are to be delivered at a later time, the transaction may lack substance and be an abusive shelter.

Motion Pictures: Motion picture and videotape shelters use a combination of leveraging and inflated purchase prices to generate tax benefits. A film is purchased at an inflated price. The cash downpayment usually represents the true value of the film. The balance of the purchase price is financed by a nonrecourse loan, repayment of which is often contingent on the earnings of the film. Depreciation and investment credit are then based on the inflated price. The seller of the film reports income on the installment method, so the only gain reported is based on the cash downpayment. If no actual profit is likely to result from the venture, it is an abusive tax shelter.

The following list of other tax shelter targets was found in the *Internal Revenue Manual:*

- TV Video Tapes.
- Commodities.
- Master Recordings.
- Leasing.
- Books.
- Cable TV.
- T-Bill (other Federal instruments) Futures/Options.
- Contributions.
- Foreign Trusts.
- Mining (all kinds).
- Patents.
- Lithographs.
- Research and Development.

IRS's TAX SHELTER PROGRAM

The Tax Equity and Fiscal Responsibility Act of 1982 (TEFRA) gave the IRS two new tools to combat abusive tax shelters; injunctions to stop promoters from selling abusive shelters, and the imposition of civil penalties against promoters for making false statements about the tax benefits of the plan or for making gross overstatements regarding the value of the property related to the shelter. The Deficit Reduction Act of 1984 gave the IRS additional tools, such as increased penalties, registration procedures, and certain recordkeeping requirements.

In effect, the IRS has declared war on tax shelters. As of September 30, 1986, there were 426,634 tax returns with tax shelter issues in the examination process. In 1986 the IRS closed 171,354 examination cases by recommending an additional $3.7 *billion* in taxes.

The purpose of IRS's Tax Shelter Program is to identify, examine, and investigate those taxpayers "utilizing improper or extreme interpretations of the law or of the facts to secure for investors substantial tax benefits which are clearly disproportionate to the economic reality of the transaction."

Tax shelter coordinators and committees have been established in every region and in every district in the IRS to gather information on tax shelter promotions and to implement and manage the provisions of the program. All managers in local IRS offices have been instructed to promptly forward all prospectuses, advertisements, and any other pertinent information regarding any *potential tax shelter* that should be included in the program. All tax examiners are on the alert for indications of fraud while examining tax shelter issue returns. (See Chapter 7 for indications of fraud.)

The IRS has already sent out tens of thousands of pre-filing notification letters to investors in dozens of abusive shelter projects advising them that their returns will be examined if they claim such benefits. In addition, the IRS is withholding portions of refunds that can be attributed to tax shelters.

The objectives of the Tax Shelter Program are:

- To stop the marketing of abusive tax shelters.
- To prevent future promotional activity of abusive tax shelter schemes.
- To deter other promoters.
- To penalize the promoters of abusive tax shelters.
- To encourage investors to file correct tax returns.
- To discourage future investments in abusive tax shelters.

The "Front End Approach"

Tax shelter schemes use partnership, individual, fiduciary, and other tax return formats, and frequently involve large numbers of related entities throughout the U.S. and other countries. The impact of these schemes has clearly created major administrative problems for the IRS in identifying, controlling, coordinating, and resolving the examination of related returns. The Tax Shelter Program is designed to overcome that.

In the past the IRS has used an "after-the-fact" approach in identifying, selecting, and examining returns involving tax shelters suspected of using improper or implausible interpretations of the law or the facts. Now the Tax Shelter Program has been created to handle the problem with a "front end" approach, in the hope of preventing investors, before filing, from claiming substantial tax benefits which are clearly disproportionate to the economic reality of their transaction.

The "front end" approach includes these tools:

- Tax Code *Section 6700* provides for a civil penalty against persons who promote abusive tax shelters, equal to the greater of $1,000 or 20 percent of the gross income derived from the promotion of the activity. The penalty applies if a person makes a statement concerning a tax benefit he knows was false or fraudulent, or makes a gross valuation overstatement. This is a statement that places the value of property or services, that is directly related to the amount of any income tax deduction or credit, in excess of 200 percent of the property's correct value. This penalty may only be waived if the valuation was made in good faith and with a reasonable basis.
- Code *Section 7408* permits the IRS to obtain an injunction to enjoin any person from further engaging in such shelter activity.
- A tax shelter organizer is now required by Code *Section 6111* to register the shelter with the IRS. This registration number must appear on any tax return which reports a deduction, loss, credit, or other tax benefit associated with that tax shelter. The registration number must also be conveyed when an interest in a registered tax shelter is sold or transferred. (You should be aware that IRS regulations clearly note that tax shelter registration is in no way an indication that the IRS has reviewed, examined, or approved the tax shelter.)
- Any person who organizes or sells an interest in a potentially abusive shelter is required to maintain a list identifying each person who was sold an interest. This list must be made available to the IRS upon request and must be retained for seven years. A "potentially abusive shelter" is one that is required to be registered, or one that has otherwise been determined by IRS regulations as having a potential for tax avoidance or evasion.
- Pre-filing Notification Letters will be sent to investors stating that the IRS believes the purported tax benefits are not allowable, and what the possible consequences may be if the investor/taxpayer claims such tax benefits on his tax return. If the notification letter is received after the tax return has been filed, the taxpayer may submit an amended tax return.
- Referred to as the "substantial understatement penalty," an additional penalty of 25 percent of the understated tax reported on the return may be assessed by the IRS under the authority of Code *Section 6661* if the understatement exceeds the greater of 10 percent of the tax required to be shown on the return, or $5,000. This penalty can only be avoided on tax shelter matters if there was substantial authority for the position taken on the return, *and* the taxpayer reasonably believed that his position was more likely than not to be the proper tax treatment.

- Where there was an underpayment of tax of at least $1,000 due to an overstatement of property valuation, the IRS may assert an additional penalty by authority of Code *Section 6659*. A valuation overstatement occurs when the claimed value of the property is at least 150 percent of the correct value or adjusted basis. In the case of a valuation overstatement of property related to a charitable contribution deduction, the penalty is an additional 30 percent of the tax. In all other situations the penalty ranges from 10 percent to 30 percent of the underreported tax depending upon the ratio of claimed valuation to the correct valuation.
- Beginning in 1985, if the value of the property you donate to a charitable organization exceeds $5,000 (or $10,000 for privately traded stocks), you must get a written "qualified" appraisal of the property's fair market value and attach an appraisal summary to your income tax return. A "qualified" appraisal is one not done by the taxpayer, a party to the transaction in which the taxpayer acquired the property, the donee, or an employee or related party of any of the preceding persons listed.
- If you are audited by the IRS and the IRS proposes over $1,000 in additional tax as a result of your "tax-motivated transaction," you not only may be subject to negligence or civil fraud penalties, but you will have to pay a higher interest rate on the deficiency equal to 120 percent of IRS's underpayment rate.

A tax-motivated transaction is one that includes:

1. Any valuation overstatement of 150 percent or more;
2. Any activity with respect to which a loss or investment credit is disallowed by reason of the at-risk rules;
3. Tax straddles; or
4. Use of any accounting method prescribed by regulations as potentially resulting in a substantial distortion of income.
5. Any sham or fraudulent transaction.

IRS Selection Criteria for Program Enforcement

Returns with tax shelters features that are caught during the processing cycles will be classified in the Service Center by personnel who have sufficient training or experience to determine if the return should be included in the program. Though not inclusive, the following criteria is being used, when the return shows:

- A large net loss.
- Low gross income.

- Large amounts of investment credit.
- Is a first year return, or a final return.
- A *Section 761(a)* election to be excluded from the partnership provisions of the tax code.
- The business is really a nonoperating entity.
- The taxpayer is a passive investor.
- Nonrecourse or not-at-risk questions are not answered or answered affirmatively.
- The activity engaged in has already been identified as a tax shelter area.
- A negative capital account for a partnership not involved in real estate.

The IRS not only maintains complete computerized records of all tax shelter investor returns, but also of all promoters they are aware of. The IRS also has discovery procedures and examination techniques for those tax shelters sold by some promoters in which investors are instructed to claim deductions directly on their tax returns, rather than as a flow-through loss from another entity. If necessary, the IRS will not hesitate to use their summons powers to obtain names of investors from promoters.

The promoter penalty under Code *Section 6700* is broad in scope. Almost anyone connected with a tax shelter could be subject to the penalty, including organizers, sales people, appraisers, accountants, attorneys, and persons "who are in active concert with them."

The following criteria may be considered by the IRS in targeting appropriate shelter promoters and their schemes:

- *Past History of the Promoter:* The prior promotion of abusive shelters raises the possibility that the current offering may be abusive.
- *Type of Shelter:* Asset sale or lease, charitable contribution, research and development, mining, family trust/protester, time share, etc., are some examples of potentially abusive tax shelters. The type of shelter ordinarily indicates the degree of difficulty and time necessary to conduct an examination.
- *Size of Promotion:* The potential number of investors and potential revenue loss must justify pre-filing action and resources required to develop the case.
- *National Impact:* To the extent that handling a promotion with "upfront" actions will have a favorable impact, resources will most likely be concentrated on National shelters/promoters. District IRS personnel are advised not to overestimate the weight of this factor since abusive tax shelters may surface at the local level and these must be considered for compliance impact.

- *Issues Involved:* Asset overvaluation (see IRC 6700(b)), false or fraudulent statements (see IRC 6700(a)(2)(A)), or aberrational use of a technical position(s) are indicators of a potential IRC 6700 case.

TAX COURT RESPONSE

Approximately one-third of the Tax Court's total pending caseload relates to abusive tax shelters. These cases represent over $1 billion in proposed tax assessments. The Tax Court is concerned about the proliferation of tax shelters and has taken a tough stand by consistently denying claimed tax deductions that are based on nothing more than illusory obligations, paper transactions, and fraudulent schemes with no economic substance.

The IRS has prevailed in every Tax Court case involving tax shelters, including every kind of scheme, from movies, cattle, commodities, and charitable contributions, to computer leasing, master recordings, real estate, oil and gas.

In many instances IRS attorneys don't even have to try the case. The court will dispose of them by motions alone. In the majority of opinions, the Tax Court has denied virtually all of the claimed deductions, denying the taxpayers even the recovery of their full out-of-pocket or cash expenditures. The Tax Court has made it very clear that even out-of-pocket costs will not be allowed when the shelter transaction lacks economic substance.

SHOULD YOU INVEST?

Any taxpayer who naively believes a tax shelter promoter's claim that an abusive investment can be shielded from intense IRS scrutiny is living in a dreamworld. Even though it has taken the IRS many years and several legislative packages to deal with the skyrocketing problem of abusive tax shelters, they are now in a position to deal with it very effectively, and very quickly.

If you're worried that a tax shelter may result in your return being audited by the IRS, consider this fact—The only tax shelters that *must be registered* with the IRS are those: (1) in which a person could reasonably infer that the tax shelter ratio (the aggregate amount of deductions plus 350 percent of the tax credits that are represented as potentially allowable to an investor) for any investor may be greater than 2 to 1 as of the close of any of the first 5 years ending after the date on which the investment is offered for sale; and, (2) the investment is subject to a Federal or state securities regulatory scheme, or the shelter's total amount that may be offered for sale exceeds $250,000 and five or more investors will be involved.

The IRS Commissioner has stated, though, that the regulations were broadly written on purpose to create a registration program that included perfectly acceptable shelters along with the abusive ones. This was done to enable the IRS to monitor *all* tax shelters.

However, in order for you to effectively gauge the potential consequences of your investment in an abusive tax shelter, read the IRS example in Exhibit 4-1.

Before investing in any tax shelter:

1. Read and understand the prospectus.
2. Determine if the investment program is required to be registered with the state, the IRS, or other Federal agencies such as the SEC. Obtain proof from the promoter that the registration requirements have been met.
3. Ask yourself: Does the deal seem too good to be true? Try to determine if the investment has economic reality, by computing the present value of all future income to the present value of all the investments and associated costs of the shelter.
   - Does the price of the underlying asset, together with its related elements, bear a relationship to fair market value? Is the property appraised by a "qualified" appraiser?
   - Does the transaction provide for a true equity build up, or is your initial investment the sum total of your involvement? Are there valid at-risk amounts, or does your "loss" involve nonrecourse financing? Are there *unwritten* understandings of the parties involved that must occur before the "loss" is obtained?
   - Does the transaction transfer the burdens and benefits of ownership, or are there cash loss protections built in that negate your loss or risk? Are there documents of ownership or has title to property actually changed hands? Are false statements or documents being used?
   - Does the shelter appear to be an IRS target for examination? If so, could you withstand the intensive scrutiny of an IRS audit? Are you financially prepared to battle the IRS, or to pay the possible consequences?
   - Does the shelter promoter appear to be legitimate? What is his track record? Does he offer a qualified tax opinion? What is the track record of the individual or firm giving the opinion?

4. Have the prospectus checked out by a qualified practitioner such as a tax attorney or a CPA skilled in tax shelter analysis. The best approach is to have a CPA check out the accounting methodology used by the investment company, and a tax attorney to check for tax law conformities and/

or irregularities. The costs of these checks will be well worth it, particularly if they save you thousands of dollars in IRS penalties.

5. If questions still remain, have your tax adviser send the prospectus to the IRS for an opinion of its worthiness.

Exhibit 4-1

IRS Example of Abusive Tax Shelter Consequences

Penalties

Investing in an abusive tax shelter may be an expensive proposition when you consider all of the consequences. First, the promoter generally charges a substantial fee. If your return is examined by the Internal Revenue Service and a tax deficiency is determined, you will be faced with payment of the tax, interest on the underpayment, possibly a 5 percent negligence penalty, and a penalty equal to 50 percent of the interest attributable to negligence or a 75 percent civil fraud penalty. The penalty for overvaluation of property may also be applied, Furthermore, a penalty of 25 percent will be imposed on any substantial understatement of tax (if the understatement exceeds the greater of 10 percent of the correct tax or $5,000). This penalty will not be imposed on any portion of the substantial understatement on which a penalty is imposed for overvaluation of property. Also, the penalty for failure to make the proper estimated tax payments may apply. In addition, if a deficiency is assessed, and is not paid within 10 days of the demand for it, an investor may be penalized with up to a 25 percent addition to tax.

Example

Assume that in 1985 a tax shelter promoter sold to individuals tangible personal property that was 5-year recovery property for purposes of the accelerated cost recovery system (ACRS). An individual purchased the property by making a $10,000 cash down payment and signing a note for the $90,000 balance of the purchase price. The note appeared to be a recourse obligation because, for some period of time, the individual was supposedly personally liable for its payment. However, the note was in reality a nonrecourse obligation, under which the individual was never personally liable for payment.

The promoter claimed that the purchaser would be able to claim an investment tax credit of $10,000, which was 10 percent of the stated purchase price of $100,000. The promoter also claimed that in the first year the purchaser would be able to claim a depreciation deduction of $14,250 [15 percent of $95,000 ($100,000 minus 50 percent of $10,000)].

Assume that a taxpayer in the 50 percent federal income tax bracket purchased the property from the promoter and claimed the depreciation deduction and the investment tax credit as stated above. The taxpayer supposedly saved $17,125 in Federal income tax (the $10,000 investment tax credit plus 50 percent of the $14,250 depreciation deduction).

However, upon examination of the taxpayer's return by the Internal Revenue Service, it was determined that the actual value of the property was really only $10,000. Thus, the depreciation deduction was recomputed to be only $1,425, and the investment tax credit was recomputed to be only $1,000. The taxpayer, therefore, owed an additional $15,413 of tax: $6,413 from the $12,825 reduction in the depreciation deduction and $9,000 from the reduction of the investment tax credit.

The determination that additional tax resulted from the adjustments to the return was only the beginning. The taxpayer claimed the deduction and credit with respect to the property based on a value that exceeded 250 percent of the proper value. Therefore, the taxpayer was subject to the penalty for overvaluation of property in the amount of 30 percent of the underpayment of tax attributable to the overvaluation. The penalty was $4,624 (30 percent of $15,413).

The taxpayer also owed interest on the $15,413 of additional tax from the date the taxpayer's income tax return was required to be filed until the date the taxpayer paid the additional tax and penalty. Thus, by the time the return was examined and the taxpayer paid the additional tax, a substantial amount of interest was also due.

The promoter represented that the investor would save $17,125 in Federal taxes for the first year for a $10,000 cash investment. However, the promotion actually cost the taxpayer not less than $15,413 in additional taxes resulting from adjustments to items on the return, $4,624 in an overvaluation penalty, and a substantial amount of interest. Thus, for reporting the $10,000 "investment" on his or her tax return as the promoter instructed, the taxpayer acquired more than $20,000 in tax liabilities.

In addition, it was likely that the taxpayer would not be able to show that the activity was engaged in for profit. Alternatively, the facts may have indicated that the taxpayer never purchased the property. In either case, the taxpayer would be denied all the claimed deductions and owe additional amounts of tax and interest. As noted earlier, various other penalties would also apply.

Part II WHEN YOU ARE AUDITED

Chapter 5 Fighting and Surviving an IRS Audit

To the average taxpayer, there is nothing more terrifying than an IRS invitation to come in for a friendly audit—some people would rather have their legs broken. The truth is that an audit need not be the frustrating, intimidating ordeal most people expect it to be. The key to ending audit anxiety is audit-proofing and audit-planning. Earlier we defined audit-proofing as the four-step process that occurs during the tax year. Audit-planning is the strategy session that occurs immediately before the actual audit.

If you follow the audit-proofing strategy program, you will be sufficiently prepared to defend yourself against an IRS challenge of any of the items on your tax return. Audit-planning will help relieve some tension because you will know where you stand.

WHERE DO YOU STAND?

Exhibit 5-1 is a chart of preliminary estimates of average deductions taken by taxpayers on income tax returns from 1983. By reviewing this chart you can determine how your deductions differ from the average, thereby helping you to gauge your chances of being audited.

Nobody outside of the IRS knows the DIF formula for rating tax returns

Preliminary 1985 Estimates of Average Deductions

AGI	TOTAL ITEMIZED DEDUCTIONS	MEDICAL	TAXES	INTEREST	CONTRIBUTIONS	MISCELLANEOUS
$20–25,000	$ 6,533	$1,713	$ 1,830	$ 3,221	$ 809	$ 463
25–30,000	7,154	1,379	2,133	3,591	800	562
30–40,000	8,293	1,639	2,696	4,121	891	601
40–50,000	10,356	1,727	3,483	5,234	1,105	699
50–75,000	13,715	2,799	4,750	6,730	1,575	885
75–100,000	20,277	5,550	6,942	10,038	2,538	1,382
100–200,000	30,857	8,500	11,034	14,419	4,237	2,358

for audit potential. However, you could correctly assume that the formula is designed to identify tax returns with deductions outside of the norm.

This chart is *not* provided to influence you to file your tax return using average deductions. Instead, you should use it as a guide to supplement your audit-proofing program. If your deductions are lower than average, you can almost bet the IRS won't question it. If your deductions are higher than average, the probability of a challenge increases proportionately the higher the deduction goes.

Although the IRS may outline the items they want to audit in their invitation letter, they can ask you to substantiate other items on your return. Be prepared to substantiate any items that are noticeably above the average.

Keep in mind that these figures are preliminary estimates for the 1985 tax year. For the 1987 tax year, the figures are already two years old. Allow for the possibility that the average deductions for 1987 may be slightly different depending on the changes in the tax laws that have occurred since then. (Remember the 1,000+ page Deficit Reduction Act of 1984?) For example, in 1983 you determined your medical deduction by first computing all your expenses for medicine and drugs that exceeded 1 percent of your adjusted gross income. But in 1984 you first determined your medical deduction by totalling your prescription medicine, drugs, and insulin without regard to the 1 percent cap. In both years that first computation had to be added to your other medical and dental expenses and then reduced by 5 percent of your adjusted gross income to determine your medical expense deduction.

You should also be aware that although the IRS's audit coverage has declined over the past 12 years, a recent decision to increase the size of the tax examination staff will almost certainly increase your chances of being audited beginning in 1987. Exhibit 5-2 shows the declining audit coverage over the past 12 years. Notice that audit coverage of income, estate, and gift tax returns has declined by half, from 2.4 percent in 1974 to 1.10 percent in 1986. Notice also that the rate of decline has been constant over the past five years.

The IRS is not dumb. They know their audit coverage has declined, but until now the IRS has not been able to convince the Office of Management and Budget to increase their staff. And yet, while the audit coverage has declined, the amount of revenue produced per tax examiner has increased dramatically. Notice that total individual income tax recommended has increased from $1.2 billion in 1974 to $5.7 billion in 1986, an increase of 375 percent. This increase really is impressive when you see that gross individual income tax collections increased from $142.9 billion in 1974 to $416.6 billion in 1986, or an increase of 190 percent. The average tax liability increased from $1,717 in 1974 to $4,068 in 1986, a comparable increase of 137 percent. Tax audit and revenue agent staffing took a slight

Exhibit 5-2

Examination Coverage

	1974	1981	1983	1985	1986
Examinations:	2,188,000	1,930,292	1,676,023	1,458,747	1,292.408
Revenue Agents	689,000	557,084	518,927	519,293	495,672
Tax Auditors	1,499,000	1,211,690	1,006,579	814,213	733,560
Service Center—CORR	80,200	161,518	150,517	125,241	63,176
Percentage Coverage I,E,&G*	2.4%	1.84%	1.56%	1.34%	1.13%
Total Tax Recommended	$5.9 billion	$10.5 billion	$13.7 billion	$17.1 billion	$19.1 billion
Individual Income Tax Recommended	$1.2 billion	$ 2.6 billion	$ 3.9 billion	$ 4.9 billion	$ 5.7 billion
IRP Discrepancies	N/A	1.2 million	2.9 million	3.6 million	3.2 million
IRP Failure to File	N/A	1.6 million	2.6 million	3.0 million	3.3 million
Service Center Corrections	714,000	814,023	930,215	558,876	584,028

*I,E & G = Income, Estate, and Gift Taxes

decrease during this period from 19,926 to 16,911, a 15 percent reduction. The IRS attributes this increase in productivity to the enhancement of their DIF formula, enabling them to better select those tax returns with the best audit potential.

This decline in audit coverage may not continue. Beginning with fiscal year 1985, the IRS was given the authority to begin hiring up to 7,500 new tax auditors and revenue agents, an increase of 44 percent. The plan is to hire 2,500 new tax examiners each year for three years. Obviously, it will take time to train these new recruits, but you can expect more comprehensive audit coverage to have begun in 1987.

Another aspect to knowing where you stand is to know your audit coverage by income, or gross receipts category. Because of the budget deficit, the IRS has shifted its focus to audits that will bring in more bucks. For example, in 1986 the IRS audited 75 percent of the 9,000 corporations with assets over $100 million, bringing in $8.7 *billion* in additional assessments. The average tax and penalty *per return* averaged $1.3 *million*.

Look at the chart on Exhibit 5-3. Find your Total Positive Income (TPI) or Total Gross Receipts (TGR) category. Go across and locate your percentage of audit coverage. Next look at the average tax and penalty per return. This is the scary part. It shows you approximately how much additional tax dollars the tax examiner is going to be aiming for if you are audited. The final category, no-change percentage, is your objective.

THE AUDIT LOTTERY

Most taxpayers worry about being audited because they are afraid of the consequences—a natural fear. They are afraid that if the IRS finds they have cheated a little (or a lot in some cases), they will be socked with an enormous penalty and a jail term. The average law-abiding, middle-income taxpayer is scared to death the first time he or she gets an audit notice.

Despite what first-timers believe, the end result of an audit is usually an additional assessment plus penalties and interest. Only a tiny handful of audits result in a suspicion of fraud, a criminal investigation and prosecution. You are more likely to get cancer than you are to go to jail because of an audit. But just the idea of having a government agent go through your financial affairs is enough to terrify most people. The prospect of the IRS assessing additional taxes that one may not be able to pay is sufficiently upsetting to prevent most taxpayers from playing the "audit lottery."

The "audit lottery" is a term coined by the media to describe the game some taxpayers play to beat the IRS. They deliberately falsify deductions, underreport income, or claim deductions they know are not allowable, figuring that they can save money each year they are not audited or caught.

1986 Audit Results

				Average Tax and Penalty Recommended Per Return			No-Change Percentage	
	Returns Filed (CY 1985)	Total Returns Audited	Percent of Audit Coverage	Revenue Agents	Tax Auditors	Service Centers	Revenue Agents	Tax Auditors
INDIVIDUAL TOTAL	99,529,000	1,090,949	1.10	$14,052	$1,945	$ 862	9	14
1040A, TPI under $10,000	20,353,200	60,098	0.30	13,933	1,195	1,519	9	11
Non1040A, TPI under $10,000	9,905,400	36,995	0.37	5,523	999	1,358	14	16
TPI $10,000–$25,000, simple	20,903,400	101,201	0.48	3,611	916	561	10	12
TPI $10,000–$25,000, complex	10,089,700	126,792	1.26	4,032	853	452	11	12
TPI $25,000–$50,000	23,810,500	389,996	1.64	4,643	1,097	697	9	14
TPI $50,000 and over	8,507,100	238,765	2.81	20,316	5,760	1,476	8	18
Schedule C—TGR under $25,000	1,868,300	24,939	1.33	4,946	1,460	640	11	14
Schedule C—TGR $25,000–$100,000	2,023,600	45,385	2.24	8,693	2,554	1,087	8	14
Schedule C—TGR $100,000 and over	1,117,000	52,303	4.68	24,708	7,043	1,747	10	17
Schedule F—TGR under $25,000	261,500	2,468	0.94	6,158	613	254	11	25
Schedule F—TGR $25,000–$100,000	453,500	5,151	1.14	6,226	1,017	270	11	22
Schedule F—TGR $100,000 and over	235,800	6,856	2.91	26,719	3,180	704	12	23

TPI = Total Positive Income
TGR = Total Gross Receipts

It's a form of roulette in which they bet against the odds, and "dare" the IRS to catch them. For example, these foolhardy lottery players assume that if their chances of being audited are 1 in 76 (a 1.31 percent audit rate), they can expect to face the IRS only once in a lifetime. By playing the audit lottery these taxpayers reason that the taxes they save by cheating the IRS will more than make up for the additional penalties and interest the IRS will assess if they're caught.

Of course, this can turn into a real tragedy if the IRS suspects they have "willfully" underreported their taxes. Even though the IRS only recommends criminal prosecution in less than 3,000 cases a year, this low statistic won't mean much if you're one of the 3,000.

Typically, the IRS prosecutes in cases where the errant taxpayer's wealth or standing in the community will generate good publicity for the voluntary compliance program. If there is a pattern of evasion coupled with substantial amounts of liabilities, the IRS will pursue the case with extreme vigor. These are the factors that are apt to enhance a case's jury appeal, the main unwritten ingredient to prosecuting any tax evasion case. (See Chapter 7 for an explanation of how an audit can turn into a fraud investigation.)

The audit lottery players know the odds are on their side and they exploit them, sometimes for years—until they get caught.

AUDIT-PROOFER'S STRATEGY RULE

By definition an audit-proofer does not play the "audit lottery." Even though the odds are on the side of the audit lottery player, the consequences aren't.

CONSEQUENCES OF AN AUDIT

Besides the additional tax you may have to pay, the IRS can hit you with a number of penalties, plus interest on the underreported tax computed back to the due date of the return and compounded daily.

- *Failure to Pay Penalty*—Once the audit has been terminated and you've received a bill to pay the deficiency, you will have 10 days to pay. If you have not paid by the 11th day, the IRS will begin charging this penalty at ½ of 1 percent per month for each month and fraction of a month the tax remains unpaid. If your liability becomes delinquent, the penalty increases to 1 percent a month.
- *Delinquency Penalty*—If your tax return was not filed on time you probably won't be assessed a delinquency penalty if you received a

refund or had no tax liability. However, if you are audited you will be assessed a penalty equal to 5 percent per month of the underreported tax, not to exceed 25 percent. Once assessed, interest will accrue on this penalty.

- *Negligence Penalty* (see Chapter 7 for a full explanation of the circumstances under which this penalty is asserted)—This penalty arises when there has been negligence or an intentional disregard of published rulings and regulations, such as when you have failed to keep proper records of business expenses. It is computed at 5 percent of the underreported tax plus an additional penalty equal to 50 percent of the interest due on the deficiency attributed to negligence.
- *Civil Fraud Penalty* (see Chapter 7 for a full explanation of the circumstances under which this penalty is asserted)—This penalty arises when there is clear and convincing evidence to prove fraud. It is computed at 75 percent of the entire underpayment of the tax, plus an additional penalty equal to 50 percent of the interest due on the deficiency.
- *Substantial Understatement Penalty*—For individual income taxpayers a substantial understatement exists if the amount of underreported tax exceeds the greater of: 10 percent of the total tax required to be shown on the return, or $5,000. The penalty is 25 percent of the amount of the underreported tax. Once assessed, interest will accrue on this penalty.
- *Abusive Tax Shelter Promoter Penalty* (see Step 4 for a full explanation)—The penalty is the greater of $1,000 or 20 percent of the gross income derived from the activity. The IRS can assess this penalty on the amount of income *to be* derived from the sale of the abusive tax shelter, rather than the money actually collected from sales of the shelters.
- *Aiding and Abetting Penalty*—If you are directly involved in aiding or assisting in the preparation or presentation of a false or fraudulent document connected with any tax matter that results in an understatement of tax you will be subject to this penalty. The penalty is $1,000, unless the document relates to a corporation, in which case the penalty is $10,000.
- *Frivolous Return Penalty* (see Step 4 for a complete explanation)—This is a $500 civil penalty against individuals who file frivolous income tax returns or *amended* income tax returns.
- *Overvaluation of Property Penalty* (see Step 4 for a complete explanation)—Primarily related to abusive tax shelters, this penalty arises if the underreported tax exceeds $1,000 and the overvaluation is at least 150 percent of the adjusted value. The penalty ranges from 10 percent to 30 percent, depending on the degree of overvaluation

between 150 percent and over 250 percent. Once assessed, interest will accrue on this penalty.

- *Increased interest for "tax motivated transactions"* (see Step 4 for a full explanation)—This penalty arises on substantial underpayments exceeding $1,000 attributable to a tax motivated transaction and is computed at 120 percent of the otherwise applicable interest rate.

THE AUDIT PROCESS

Basically there are three different kinds of IRS audits: field audit, office audit, and audit by mail. A field audit is handled by a revenue agent who primarily audits complex and sophisticated 1040s, and all kinds of business income tax returns. It's called a field audit because the revenue agent usually goes outside the office to conduct the audit at the taxpayer's place of business. An office audit is conducted by a tax auditor who primarily audits less complex 1040s. Taxpayers are asked to come into the local IRS office to meet with the auditor and bring their substantiating proof with them. An audit by mail is a simple audit conducted from the service center. Chapter 6 covers the different types of programs the service centers use to audit tax returns by mail.

On the following pages is an explanation of the audit process as presented in IRS Publication 556, *Examination of Returns, Appeal Rights, and Claims for Refund.*

Exhibit 5-4

Examination of Returns

Why Returns Are Selected for Examination

Tax returns are examined to verify the correctness of income, exemptions, credits, or deductions reported on the returns. A computer program called the Discriminant Function System (DIF) selects most of the returns that are examined. Under this program, selected entries on a return are evaluated and the return is given a score. Returns are then screened by Internal Revenue Service personnel. Those returns that have the highest probability of error are selected for examination.

Returns may also be selected under the Taxpayer Compliance Measurement Program (TCMP). TCMP is a random selection system to determine the correct tax liability. The results of examinations in this program are used to measure and evaluate taxpayer compliance characteristics. Information obtained from TCMP is also used to update and improve DIF.

Other returns are selected by such methods as examining claims for credit or refund of previously paid taxes and matching information documents (Forms W-2 and 1099).

An examination of a taxpayer's return does not suggest a suspicion of dishonesty or criminal liability. It may not even result in more tax. Many cases are closed without change in reported tax liability and in many others taxpayers receive refunds.

Confidentiality of Tax Matters

You have the right to have your tax case kept confidential. Under the law, the Internal Revenue Service must protect the privacy of your tax information. However, if a lien or a lawsuit is filed, certain aspects of your tax case will become public knowledge.

The Internal Revenue Service has exchange agreements with state tax agencies under which information about any increase or decrease in tax liability on your state or Federal return is shared with the other agency. If a federal tax return you have filed is changed, either by filing an amended return or as a result of being examined, it may affect your state income tax liability. It may be to your advantage to file an amended state tax return. Contact your state tax agency for more information. Similarly, any change on your state income tax return may affect your federal return.

If Your Return Is Examined

The examination may be conducted by correspondence, or it may take place in your home or place of business, an Internal Revenue office, or the office of your attorney or accountant. The place and method of examination are determined by the Internal Revenue Service. If the place or method is not convenient for you, the examiner will try to work out something more suitable.

Whatever method of examination is used, you may act on your own behalf or you may have someone represent you or accompany you. If you filed a joint return, either you or your spouse, or both, may meet with us. An attorney, a certified public accountant, a person enrolled to practice before the Internal Revenue Service, or the person who prepared the return and signed it as the preparer may represent or accompany you.

You must furnish your representative with written authorization. You may make the authorization on Form 2848, *Power of Attorney and Declaration of Representative,* or on Form 2848-D, *Tax Information Authorization and Declaration of Representative,* or on any other properly written authorization.

Transfers to Another District

As a general rule, your tax return is examined in the Internal Revenue Service District where you live. However, if the examination of your return can be completed more quickly and conveniently in another district, such as when your books and records are located there, you may request that the case be transferred to that district.

The Examination

The examination usually begins when you are notified by the Service that your return has been selected for examination. You will also be notified of the method of examination and the records you will need to assemble to clarify or support items reported on your return. If you have gathered your records before the examination, you will be able to clear up questionable items and arrive at the correct tax liability with the least effort.

When the examination is completed, the examiner will explain to you, or your authorized representative, any proposed change in your tax liability and the reasons for the change. It is important that you understand the reasons for any proposed change. In some instances, the official position taken by the Internal Revenue Service may differ from certain court decisions. Although the Service follows Supreme Court decisions, it is not required to follow lower court decisions for other taxpayers with the same issue. The Service can lose an issue in a lower court and still continue to apply its interpretation of the law to other cases involving similar issues.

Please do not hesitate to ask about anything that is not clear to you. Most taxpayers agree to changes proposed by examiners, and the examinations are closed at this level. If you do not agree, you may appeal any proposed change.

Repetitive Examinations

The Internal Revenue Service tries to avoid repetitive examinations of the same items, but this occasionally happens. If your tax return was examined for the same items in either of the 2 previous years and the examination resulted in no change to your tax liability, please contact the person whose name and telephone number are shown in the heading of the letter you received as soon as possible. The examination of your return will then be suspended pending a review of the files to determine whether it should proceed. However, if your return was selected for examination as part of the random sample for TCMP, discussed earlier, the examination will not be suspended.

Problem Resolution Office

The Internal Revenue Service has a Problem Resolution Program for taxpayers who have been unable to resolve their problems with the Internal Revenue Service. If you have a tax problem you have been unable to resolve through normal channels, write to your local Internal Revenue Service District Director or call your local Internal Revenue Service office and ask for Problem Resolution assistance. The Problem Resolution Office will take responsibility for your problem and insure that it receives proper attention. Although this office cannot change the tax law or technical decisions, it can frequently clear up misunderstandings that resulted from previous contacts.

If You Agree

If you agree with the findings of the examiner, you will be asked to sign an agreement form. By signing the form, you indicate you agree to the changes made to your return.

If you owe any additional tax, you may pay it when you sign the agreement. If you pay when you sign the agreement, interest is charged on the additional tax from the due date of your return to the date you pay.

If you do not pay the additional tax when you sign the agreement, you will receive a bill for the additional tax. Interest is charged on the additional tax from the due date of your return to the billing date. However, you will not be billed for more than 30 days interest from the date you sign the agreement. No further interest or penalties will be charged if you pay the amount you owe within 10 days after the billing date.

If the examination results in a refund, the Internal Revenue Service can refund your money more promptly if you sign the agreement form. You will receive interest at the applicable rate on the amount of the refund.

If You Do Not Agree

If you do not agree with the changes proposed by the examiner, the examiner will explain your appeal rights. This includes your right to request an immediate meeting with a supervisor to explain your position if your examination takes place in an Internal Revenue office. If agreement is reached, your case will be closed.

If agreement is not reached at this meeting, or if the examination takes place outside of an Internal Revenue office, you will be sent:

- A letter notifying you of your right to appeal the proposed adjustments within 30 days;
- A copy of the examination report explaining the proposed adjustments;

- An agreement or waiver form; and
- A copy of Publication 5, *Appeal Rights and Preparation of Protests for Unagreed Cases.*

If after receiving the examination report you decide to agree with the examiner's findings, sign the agreement or waiver form and return the form to the examiner. You may pay any additional amount you owe without waiting for a bill. Make your check or money order payable to the *Internal Revenue Service.* Include interest on the additional tax at the applicable rate from the due date of the return to the date of payment.

In the case of penalties and additions to tax for failure to file, for making valuation overstatements, for making valuation understatement on estate and gift tax returns, and for substantial understatement of tax liability, interest is imposed for the period beginning on the date the tax return, for which the penalty or addition is imposed, is required to be filed (including extensions) and ending on the date of payment of the penalty or addition to tax. This does not apply to penalties and additions to tax for which notice and demand was made before July 18, 1984.

On other penalties and additions to tax, interest is imposed only if the penalty or addition to tax is not paid within 10 days after notice and demand and then only for the period from the date of notice and demand to the date of payment.

Include your social security number, the tax year, and the tax form number on your check or money order. Please do not send cash through the mail.

If after receiving the examination report you decide not to agree with the examiner's findings, we urge you to first appeal your case within the Service before you go to court.

How to Stop Interest from Accruing

If you think that at the end of the examination the Internal Revenue Service will find you owe additional tax, you may want to stop the further accrual of interest on the amount you owe. You can do this by remitting money to the Service to cover all or part of the anticipated deficiency. Interest will stop accruing on any part of the deficiency you cover when the Service receives your remittance.

Your remittance may be made either as a deposit in the nature of a cash bond (deposit) or as a payment of tax. Both types of remittance stop any further accrual of interest. However, the making of a deposit or payment of tax will stop the running of interest on only the amount actually remitted. Because of the compounding rules interest will continue to accrue on accrued interest even though the underlying tax has been paid. If you wish to stop the running of interest on both tax and interest, you should make a remittance for both the tax and interest that has accrued as of the date of remittance. Deposits differ from payments in two ways:

- You can request to have all or part of your deposit returned to you at any time. You do not have to file a claim for a refund, but if a deficiency is later assessed for that period and type of tax and the deposit has been returned at your request, you will not receive credit in figuring the interest for the period in which the funds were on deposit. However, a deposit will not be returned to you once a tax liability has been assessed. The deposit also will not be returned to you if the Service determines that returning it will jeopardize collection of a possible deficiency, or that it should be applied against another tax liability.
- Deposits do not earn interest. No interest will be included when a deposit is returned to you.

Payment or Deposit

If you remit money before a notice of deficiency is mailed, you can ask the Service to treat it as a deposit. You must make your request in writing. If you do not request it to be a deposit and the following conditions apply, it will be considered a payment:

- You make the remittance in response to a proposed liability—for example, after the examiner's report is issued, and
- The remittance is large enough to oover the proposed liability. (A partial remittance will be treated as a payment only if you designate the part of the proposed liability you intend to satisfy.)

If the remittance equals or exceeds the proposed liability, no notice of deficiency will be mailed. You, therefore, will not have the right to take your case to the Tax Court. See *Tax Court*, later.

If you remit money to the Service after a notice of deficiency is mailed, unless you give written instructions, the remittance will be considered a payment of tax. Such a remittance made after the mailing of a notice of deficiency will not deprive the Tax Court of jurisdiction over the deficiency.

A remittance that is specifically designated by you in writing as a "deposit in the nature of a cash bond," will be treated as such by the Service if it is made after the mailing of a notice of deficiency but before the expiration of the 90-day or 150-day period for filing a petition with the Tax Court for a redetermination of the deficiency, or, if a petition is filed, before the decision of the Tax Court is final.

Using a Deposit to Pay the Tax

If at the end of the examination you agree with the findings of the examiner, your deposit will be applied against the amount you owe. A notice of deficiency will not be mailed to you and you will not have the right to take your case to the Tax Court.

Upon completion of the examination, if you do not agree to the full amount of the deficiency, the Service will mail you a notice of deficiency. Your deposit will be applied against the amount of the proposed deficiency after the mailing of the notice of deficiency, unless you make a new request in writing that your remittance continue to be treated as a deposit before the expiration of the 90-day or 150-day period. You will still have the right to take your case to the Tax Court. See *If You Do Not Agree,* discussed earlier.

ANSWERS TO YOUR QUESTIONS ON THE AUDIT INTERVIEW

Q. "I've received notice to come down to the local IRS office and bring some documentation to support my deductions. Frankly, I don't feel like going. They can't do anything to me if I don't cooperate. Right?"
A. Wrong! An Internal Revenue audit is a lawful examination of your

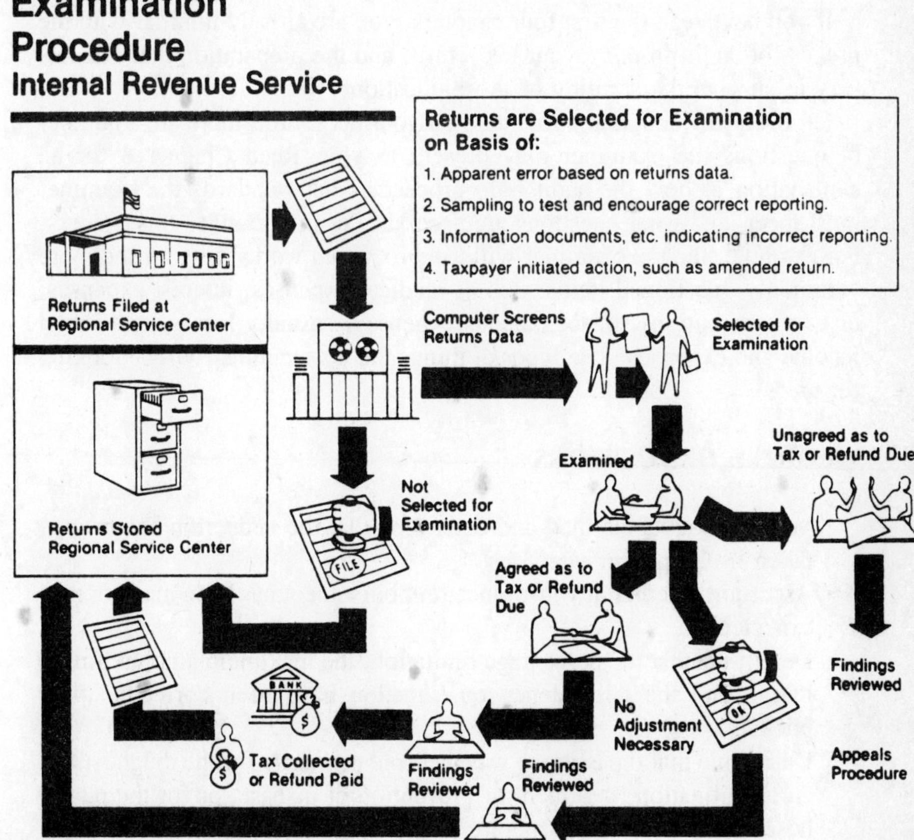

books and records allowed by Code *Section 7602*. If you don't show up at the audit to plead your case, the IRS will go ahead without you. Because the audit is a civil procedure and not a criminal one, the tax system is designed in IRS's favor; that is, the burden of proof falls on your shoulders and not the IRS. If you are not there to substantiate the items in question to their satisfaction they will disallow them and propose to assess you for the corresponding additional taxes. Plus the IRS always has the option of issuing a summons to force you to bring in your books and records. So don't try to be a wise guy. Cooperate as much as you can.

Q. "What happens during an audit?"
A. It's very simple. You will be asked to prove certain deductions on your tax return. There are two basic questions the examiner will be asking:

- Is the deduction allowable under the rules?
- Is there sufficient proof to substantiate the deduction?

If you have read the first four chapters, you are already familiar with the process of audit-proofing your tax return, and the preparation that's necessary to survive the scrutiny of those questions.

For every deduction and line item on your tax return, there are a number of questions the examiner may present to you. Read Chapter 8 for an explanation of how the audit is to proceed, what standards the examiner must meet, and what questions are necessary or important to this process. For example, the tax examiner will use *pro forma* worksheets for the more commonly questioned items such as medical expenses, interest expenses, taxes, contributions, miscellaneous expenses, casualty losses, and rental income and expenses. The types of things the tax examiner will be looking for are:

MEDICAL DEDUCTIONS

- Verify amounts claimed and determine that the deduction has been taken in the proper year.
- Ascertain whether any insurance reimbursement has been made or is expected.
- Determine that the percentage limitation, the maximum amount limitation and the dependency qualification have been correctly applied.
- Determine that the expense was incurred primarily for the diagnosis, cure, mitigation, treatment or prevention of disease, or for the purpose of affecting any structure of the body.

INTEREST DEDUCTIONS

- Verify amounts claimed and determine that the deduction has been taken in the proper year.
- Ascertain whether interest payments are made on a valid, existing debt owed by the taxpayer.
- Interest paid as a guarantor does not constitute an interest deduction.
- Verify that loans from related individuals are valid and that they are not gifts.
- Check for double deductions, i.e., itemized deductions and rental expenses.
- Look at the instruments of debt verification, i.e., mortgage statements, loan contracts, cancelled checks, credit card statements.
- Brokerage accounts, interest expense on margin accounts.
- Amounts paid by purchaser in connection with the occupancy of home prior to the date of enforceable liability on the mortgage may be rent payments.

DEDUCTION OF TAXES

- Verify amounts claimed and determine that the deduction has been taken in the proper year.
- Determine whether the tax is of the type deductible in accordance with the rules and regulations.
- Ascertain that no foreign income taxes have been claimed as a deduction where election has been made to claim the foreign tax credit.
- Verify that the taxpayer has not claimed duplicate deductions for taxes, i.e., itemized deductions and rental expense.
- Verify that any proration of current real estate taxes in the year of purchase or sale is correct.

DEDUCTION OF CONTRIBUTIONS

- Verify amounts claimed and determine that the deduction is claimed in the proper year.
- Determine whether the payments were made to qualified organizations.
- Determine that percentage limitation is correctly computed, has not been exceeded, and that any contribution carryover is correct.
- Determine if contributions claimed are nondeductible personal expenses and ascertain if donor received benefits or consideration in return for contributions.

- In a case where property is contributed ascertain: type of property, cost and fair market value at time of gift, and whether donor retains any control over property.
- Some noncash contributions have the potential of being a tax shelter scheme, for example: gemstones, books, artwork.

MISCELLANEOUS DEDUCTIONS

- Verify amounts claimed and determine that the deduction is claimed in the proper year.
- Ascertain whether any reimbursement has been received.
- If the miscellaneous expense claimed is an education expense:
  1. Determine if the expenses were primarily incurred for the purpose of maintaining or improving skills or meeting express requirements for retention of status. If so, does it qualify:
     a. For a new trade or business?
     b. Meet minimal education requirements?
  2. If the education expenses involve overseas travel, the tour folio, registration receipt, and transcript of studies from the overseas educational institution should be reviewed.

CASUALTY LOSS DEDUCTIONS

- Ascertain that a loss has actually occurred.
- Determine that the taxpayer is the owner.
- Be alert to the possibility that cash stolen may not have been included in income.
- If personal residence is involved in the loss deduction, ensure that the basis of the property has been reduced for all gains previously unrecognized.
- Determine that the amount claimed is equal to the difference in value before and after the loss.
- Check for insurance proceeds.

DEDUCTION OF RENTAL INCOME & EXPENSES

- Verify that net loss from rentals is not due to the property having been rented to a relative or friend at less than fair rental value.
- If a vacation home, determine if allocations for personal use are required.
- Verify that depreciable capital expenditures have not been deducted as an expense.

- Verify that land value has been accounted for in determining depreciable basis of property.

Q. "I've never been audited before. Should I take a lawyer with me?"
A. It depends on how much protection you need, and the answer to a series of introspective questions only you can answer. A lawyer may not necessarily be the solution. You may only need a *representative* to go with you. This could be the person who prepared your tax return, or someone who is qualified to practice before the IRS such as an attorney, CPA, or an Enrolled Agent. Enrolled Agents are practitioners enrolled, or licensed, by the IRS to practice before the IRS.

You must first decide if you need someone simply to explain how your return was prepared, or someone to represent your interests, or someone who could protect you in the event of fraud. If you prepared your own tax return you may be able to represent yourself, at least at an initial interview in an office audit situation, if all that is required is that you bring documentation to substantiate your deductions and the documentation is readily available. It also depends on the complexity of the issues being challenged. If the tax rules under question are fairly simple, and documentation is readily available, you may not need to pay someone to go with you.

However, if your tax return was prepared by someone else, you should at least ask that person to go with you to the initial interview. If that person is *not* going to represent you at appeals, or negotiate on your behalf in your absence, it is not necessary for him or her to be an attorney, CPA, or Enrolled Agent. The IRS allows any tax return preparer to accompany a taxpayer to an audit interview as a witness to explain how the tax return was prepared.

In some cases, it may be advisable for you to obtain an attorney, CPA, or Enrolled Agent to represent you at the audit. This person could be invaluable in helping you through the rough parts, by more eloquently pleading your case with the examiner, and by generally protecting your interest in ways you could not without the necessary experience.

If you are only worried or nervous about being audited, and your conscience is reasonably clear, consider taking a representative as long as it's economical to do so. You can determine this by estimating the amount of additional tax you would owe if all the deductions they are questioning were disallowed and compare that to the cost of hiring the representative to attend the initial interview. For example, if the IRS only wants to question your mortgage interest and real estate tax expense, and you can easily support these deductions by providing the necessary documents, it may not be necessary to have someone go with you. Yet if they are questioning your travel and entertainment expenses, and you believe you may have problems in substantiating every penny you claimed, it may pay for you to spend a couple of hundred dollars to save a couple of thousand. Only you can decide what your risk is and if the expense is necessary. In any event it wouldn't hurt to call around and find out what representation will cost you.

If you are scared out of your wits, by all means take a *qualified and experienced* representative with you. The more qualified and experienced the representative is, the more it will cost you. The peace of mind of having a top-flight representative along may be worth it. Don't hesitate to ask anyone you contact about their credentials, education, background, and experience.

If you've cheated a little, you're not going to be happy unless you take a representative with you. If you cheated a lot, you should read Chapter 7, which covers the situation you are most worried about. If your fears are not assuaged by what you learn in Chapter 7, you may want to hire a *tax attorney* to go with you.

In any event, you may be able to have your representative appear on your behalf without you. You can do this by signing a Form 2848, Power of Attorney (see Exhibit 5-6). You can sign a Power of Attorney over to anyone under IRS's limited enrollment regulations. But if that person "practices" before the IRS, he or she will have to be an attorney, CPA, or Enrolled Agent.

Some tax examiners get a little "antsy" when a representative comes in with a power of attorney and without the taxpayer. Unless the representative is also the preparer, the representative may not be able to answer all the examiner's questions. If the tax examiner insists on your presence, your representative may want the examiner to serve a summons *requiring* your presence before he advises you to appear. Don't be afraid of a summons, but if one is served, you will have to comply or the IRS will take you to court to compel your compliance.

Q. "How do I know the examiner isn't out for blood?"
A. You don't, because you don't know if the audit was precipitated by an informant "squealing" on you, or if your return was routinely selected under IRS's DIF system. There probably isn't any way you could find out for sure, because even if you asked the examiner, he will merely respond that your return was selected under IRS's selection procedures, giving you no clue either way. Unless you have good reason to suspect otherwise, don't be paranoid about your audit. Over a million taxpayers a year are routinely audited. That you were selected is probably nothing more than the "luck of the draw."

Unless you make enemies easily, the source of the IRS's information is probably not going to be a concern for you. The IRS gets lots of informant information, but most of it is handled according to routine procedure. The IRS must still meet the same standards of proof for a criminal case re-

Form **2848**
(Rev. October 1983)
Department of the Treasury
Internal Revenue Service

Power of Attorney and Declaration of Representative

▶ **See separate instructions**

OMB No. 1545-0150

PART I.— Power of Attorney

Taxpayer(s) name, identifying number, and address including ZIP code (Please type or print)

For IRS Use Only		
File So.		
Level		
Receipt		
Powers		
Blind T.		
Action		
Ret.Ind.		

hereby appoints (name(s), CAF number(s), address(es), including ZIP code(s), and telephone number(s) of individual(s)) *

as attorney(s)-in-fact to represent the taxpayer(s) before any office of the Internal Revenue Service for the following tax matter(s) (specify the type(s) of tax and year(s) or period(s) (date of death if estate tax)):

Type of tax (Individual, corporate, etc.)	Federal tax form number (1040, 1120, etc.)	Year(s) or period(s) (Date of death if estate tax)

The attorney(s)-in-fact (or either of them) are authorized, subject to revocation, to receive confidential information and to perform any and all acts that the principal(s) can perform with respect to the above specified tax matters (excluding the power to receive refund checks, and the power to sign the return (see regulations section 1.6012-1(a)(5), Returns made by agents), unless specifically granted below).

Send copies of notices and other written communications addressed to the taxpayer(s) in proceedings involving the above tax matters to:

1 ☐ the appointee first named above, or
2 ☐ (names of not more than two of the above named appointees) ....

Initial here ▶ .... if you are granting the power to receive, but not to endorse or cash, refund checks for the above tax matters to:

3 ☐ the appointee first named above, or
4 ☐ (name of one of the above designated appointees) ▶ ....

This power of attorney revokes all earlier powers of attorney and tax information authorizations on file with the Internal Revenue Service for the same tax matters and years or periods covered by this power of attorney, except the following:

....

(Specify to whom granted, date, and address including ZIP code, or refer to attached copies of earlier powers and authorizations.)

Signature of or for taxpayer(s)

(If signed by a corporate officer, partner, or fiduciary on behalf of the taxpayer, I certify that I have the authority to execute this power of attorney on behalf of the taxpayer.)

.... (Signature) .... (Title, if applicable) .... (Date)

(Also type or print your name below if signing for a taxpayer who is not an individual.)

.... (Signature) .... (Title, if applicable) .... (Date)

* You may authorize an organization, firm, or partnership to receive confidential information, but your representative must be an individual who must complete Part II.

For Privacy Act and Paperwork Reduction Act Notice, see page 1 of the Instructions. Form **2848** (Rev. 10-83)

Form 2848 (Rev. 10-83) Page **2**

If the power of attorney is granted to a person other than an attorney, certified public accountant, enrolled agent, or enrolled actuary, the taxpayer(s) signature must be witnessed or notarized below. (The representative must complete Part II. Only representatives listed there are recognized to practice before the Internal Revenue Service.)

The person(s) signing as or for the taxpayer(s): (Check and complete one.)

☐ is/are known to and signed in the presence of the two disinterested witnesses whose signatures appear here:

-- (Signature of Witness) ---------------- (Date)

-- (Signature of Witness) ---------------- (Date)

☐ appeared this day before a notary public and acknowledged this power of attorney as a voluntary act and deed.

Witness: -- (Signature of Notary) ---------------- (Date) NOTARIAL SEAL (if required by State law)

PART II.—Declaration of Representative

I declare that I am not currently under suspension or disbarment from practice before the Internal Revenue Service, that I am aware of Treasury Department Circular No. 230 as amended (31 C.F.R. Part 10), Regulations governing the practice of attorneys, certified public accountants, enrolled agents, enrolled actuaries, and others, and that I am one of the following:

1 a member in good standing of the bar of the highest court of the jurisdiction indicated below;
2 duly qualified to practice as a certified public accountant in the jurisdiction indicated below;
3 enrolled as an agent prusuant to the requirements of Treasury Department Circular No. 230;
4 a bona fide officer of the taxpayer organization;
5 a full-time employee of the taxpayer;
6 a member of the taxpayer's immediate family (spouse, parent, child, brother or sister);
7 a fiduciary for the taxpayer;
8 an enrolled actuary (the authority of an enrolled actuary to practice before the Service is limited by section 10.3(d)(1) of Treasury Department Circular No. 230);
9 Commissioner's special authorization (see instructions for Part II, item 9) --;

and that I am authorized to represent the taxpayer identified in Part I for the tax matters there specified.

Designation (insert appropriate number from above list)	Jurisdiction (State, etc.) or Enrollment Card Number	Signature	Date

(278)

gardless of the information source. However, if the informant is willing to testify against you in court, and if the informant has evidence indicating your willful tax evasion the situation changes radically. It sure makes a great case for keeping your friends, neighbors, co-workers, and *spouses* happy, doesn't it?

Every audit begins with a scope, or a plan of what items will be questioned. Unless you are one of the 50,000 unlucky souls selected for a Taxpayer Compliance Measurement Program (TCMP) audit, where every single line on the tax return has to be substantiated, you will be notified what particular deductions you will need to prove. You should begin to be concerned if the scope of the audit is expanded. The IRS is now on a big kick to try and uncover unreported sources of taxable income. So don't be surprised if you are asked to support your income figures and your deductions.

To determine when the IRS is examining for something outside their originally planned scope, read Chapter 9, IRS's instructions to examiners on how to conduct an in-depth examination. The IRS says, "Where a regular or normal tax examination ends, an in-depth examination should begin." An in-depth audit is a thorough examination designed to determine if you have complied with all the Internal Revenue laws. Learn how the IRS conducts an in-depth examination from Chapter 9. If the IRS uses any of those techniques during the audit, then they may be "out for blood."

Q. "How should I behave during the audit?"
A. Civilly, no more and no less. Expect a cordial, but polite business relationship. All IRS employees are trained to treat taxpayers with respect and to expect respect in return.

While you should always behave in a businesslike manner, don't be afraid to be somewhat friendly. The obvious rule is to stick to small talk about nontax matters, such as sports and the weather, but avoid such topics as politics, religion, government waste, the President or Vice-President (or the President's or Vice-President's tax return), the Pentagon, double-dipping government employees, problems with Social Security financing, or the budget deficit.

Make your small talk as innocuous, and as inoffensive as you can possibly make it. Every tax examiner has already heard every excuse, every rationalization, and every taxpayer gripe about the government that has ever been sounded. Tax examiners are not responsible for spending the government's money, the nation's social problems, Pentagon waste, or useless government programs. They only play a small part in the overall scheme of things and they get tired of being the government's front-line whipping post for every aggrieved taxpayer. So don't try to alienate your tax examiner by playing the role of a victim of governmental oppression.

You should also be aware of how you dress for the audit. Avoid overdressing for your economic status. While dressing for success is important in the business world, remember that the audit is not a job interview. On the other hand, you probably should avoid intentionally underdressing. Keep in mind that the examiner knows all the tricks.

Another commonsense rule to follow is never *volunteer* any information. Always plan ahead of the audit what you are going to say, and what you are going to present to the tax examiner for proof. This is the necessary audit-planning strategy session you learned about earlier. Always have an audit-planning session with your representative *before* the audit. Your representative will provide you with more suggestions on how to handle yourself.

The most important guideline is to *be credible* and *be prepared*. Read the *Internal Revenue Manual* instructions in Chapter 8 and know every question the tax examiner will ask you about the questionable deductions you must prove. Rehearse beforehand your answers to each question. Use Chapter 8 thoroughly in your planning session with your representative. By just having this information beforehand, *you will be in control of the audit interview, not the tax examiner.*

It's not necessary to do battle with the tax examiner during the audit unless you are provoked. Don't be contentious, arrogant, or intractable. Remember, if you feel you are not being given a proper hearing you have the right to appeal the examiner's deficiency proposal through other channels and even to Tax Court.

On the other hand, don't let an overpowering tax examiner bully you into agreeing to a deficiency you don't believe in. If you succumb to an overly aggressive tax examiner you have no one to blame but yourself. Sometimes inexperienced tax examiner trainees tend to be a little cocky, and a bit overbearing because they have not yet learned how to handle themselves in an adversary relationship. Be careful and on alert for that kind of a situation.

Remember also that you have other options available to you:

1. You can request the tax examiner's group manager to review your case. The group manager can "reeducate" your tax examiner to behave more professionally, or to apply the law according to IRS regulations and policy. He can also transfer the case to another examiner if a personality conflict is adversely affecting the way in which the case is being handled.
2. If you don't believe that the law is being properly applied to the circumstances in your case you can ask the tax examiner to request technical advice from the National Office. The instructions for requesting technical advice are in Step 2.

Q. "What should I do if I can't prove everything but I want to 'make a deal' with the tax examiner?"
A. First, let's get something straight here. One does *not* "make a deal;" one negotiates and compromises. The nature of the audit process itself requires a certain amount of give and take between you and the tax examiner. Not every situation in life is fully anticipated by the Internal Revenue Code or IRS regulations; and not every rule is set in stone; some can be bent a little, or even broken.

In any audit situation you have one advantage over the tax examiner that you probably never thought about: The element of time. Tax examiners are under pressure to be productive. They can't be productive if they spend too much time on any one case. The master plan drawn up by their superiors requires them to audit a specified number of tax returns during the fiscal year. With this specified number of audits comes the expectation of a certain amount of revenue.

Your tax examiner is aware of the time constraints, and unless he or she is inclined to make an example out of you, or to demonstrate a total control of your tax life, he or she is going to be reasonable. This means, for example, that the examiner may exercise the authority to accept your word about certain small expenditures and allow you a reasonable deduction even without proof. The IRS allows this because of the precedent established in the George M. Cohan case in 1930 which adopted the rule that, if the evidence indicates that a taxpayer incurred a deductible expense but the exact amount cannot be determined, the court should make an approximation and not disallow the deduction entirely.

A "give and take" session between you and the examiner may involve something like this: You agree to lose a deduction of one item because of lack of substantiation, and the tax examiner will let a second item slip by. In the initial audit, the tax examiner is not supposed to consider the "hazards of litigation," but he will consider the elements of fairness and the pressures of time in trying to close the case.

By using the Cohan Rule, the tax examiner can expedite the audit, and obtain an "agreed" case. An agreed case occurs when you sign the appropriate form agreeing to the proposed assessment and collection of the deficiency.

By now you know what the "proof" requirements are and what rules of law are most likely to be tested. You know, for example, that certain expenses such as travel away from home, and entertainment expenses must meet stringent substantiation requirements. Even so, the tax examiner may be willing to compromise a little if his caseload is backing up. He could be concerned because he has already spent more time on your case than he should have. Or, the case may have a statute problem, and he may want to finish it before the statute of limitations expires.

The IRS realizes that there are always situations in which taxpayers cannot prove every penny of their deduction, even though the deduction may be reasonable under the circumstances. *Internal Revenue Manual Section 4244* allows tax examiners to accept your word, or "oral evidence" as it is called, in these situations provided that the guidelines in Exhibit 5-7 are followed.

Exhibit 5-7

4244 (11–2–81) REASONABLE DETERMINATIONS WHERE ITEMS CANNOT BE FULLY DOCUMENTED

1. Policy statement P-4-39 permits reasonable determinations where deductions (including exemptions for dependents) are based upon a substantial number of small items of expenditure which are not susceptible to complete substantiation by documentary evidence, provided there is a proper basis for allowance under the law and regulations.
2. These instructions are not intended to relieve taxpayers of the burden of proof, nor to sanction failure to comply with the recordkeeping requirements of the law and regulations, but to deal with problems of evidence and its evaluation that are encountered in everyday, practical, administration of the tax laws. Such problems might be involved in determining the amount deductible for church contributions or the total amount expended for support of a dependent.
3. Examiners should exercise sound judgment which will permit reasonable determinations under the law and regulations, if he/she is satisfied that there is a proper basis for some allowance. This involves considering the extent to which detailed documentation is required, the papers or records essential to adequate substantiation, and the weight to be accorded oral statements and explanations. Such elements will necessarily vary according to the nature and relative tax importance of the items involved and the general circumstances surrounding the entire case.
4. Close approximations of items not fully supported by documentary proof can frequently be established through reliable secondary sources and collateral evidence. For example, in questionable exemption cases the fact that the taxpayer cannot furnish documentary evidence in support of some of the amounts he contributed need not be fatal to allowance of the exemption. The taxpayer may be able to demonstrate the total cost of support with reasonable certainty and satisfy the examiner (for example, by third party affidavits) that only nominal amounts were contributed by others.

5. Due consideration should be given to the reasonableness of the taxpayer's stated expenditures for the claimed purposes in relation to his/her reported income, to the reliability and accuracy of his/her records in connection with other items more readily lending themselves to detailed recordkeeping, and to the general credibility of his/her statements in the light of the entire record in the case. The practice of disallowing amounts claimed for such items merely because there is no documentary evidence available which will establish the precise amount beyond any reasonable doubt ignores commonly recognized business practice as well as the fact that proof may be established by credible oral testimony. On the other hand, a percentage or other arbitrarily computed portion of deductions of this character will not be allowed merely for the purpose of closing the case.
6. If a taxpayer cannot document precisely the amounts spent for expenses while away from home for a business purpose, examiners may establish that reasonable amounts were spent for such items if the taxpayer can clearly establish the following:
   a. *Time*—Dates of departure and return for each trip away from home, and number of days away from home;
   b. *Place*—Destinations or locality of travel, e.g., name of city or town;
   c. *Business Purpose*—Business reason for travel or nature of business benefit derived or expected to be derived; and
   d. *Proof that Expenditures were Actually Incurred*—A reasonable showing based upon secondary evidence, including oral testimony, that out-of-pocket expenses were paid.
7. The extent of the allowance in 6 above should be governed by the principles stated in 4 and 5 above. However, allowances should be kept to a minimum consistent with an appraisal of the facts in each case in order to ensure that a taxpayer does not profit from his/her failure to keep required records of all elements of travel expenses.

403(25) (6-8-76) EVALUATION OF ORAL EVIDENCE BY TECHNICAL PERSONNEL

403(25).1 (6-8-76) INSTRUCTIONS FOR EXAMINER

1. *Authority and Responsibility:*
   a. When an examiner conducts an examination, he/she automatically receives authority to recommend the proper disposition of any issues raised by him/her as well as any issues raised by the taxpayer. He/she is expected to arrive at a definite conclusion by a balanced and impartial evaluation of all evidence.

b. The normal responsibility of an examiner is to pursue his/her examination to a point where he/she can conclude that he/she has made a reasonable determination of the correct tax liability. In practical application of this responsibility, he/she must deal with problems of evidence and its evaluation. The evidence which he/she must consider is varied in nature. The examiner usually relies on primary evidence such as invoices, vouchers, bills and receipts, cancelled checks, bank statements and the like. When a business return is involved, he/she also relies on books and records such as journals and ledgers which summarize business transactions. When a nonbusiness return is involved, the examiner relies on primary evidence and collateral information.

c. With the responsibility of coming to a definite conclusion, the examiner cannot stop his/her examination when no single type of evidence is sufficient to make a reasonable determination. He/she must seek whatever type of evidence is available, whether direct or circumstantial, which will assist him/her in arriving at a reasonable finding.

d. Once all available evidence is at hand, the examiner uses his/her professional judgment in arriving at a conclusion. Although his/her findings are subject to review or appeal at higher levels, the examiner should have little concern that someone else might reach a different decision. Other levels may interpret or emphasize facts in a different manner. If the record is complete and the conclusions are based on the record, the judgment of the examiner is valid, whatever different conclusions may be reached at other levels.

2. *Evaluation of Evidence:*

a. *Oral statements*—The principal method of introducing evidence in a court case is through the testimony of a witness. Therefore, oral statements made by taxpayers to examiners represent direct evidence which must be thoroughly considered. Uncontradicted statements which are not improbable or unreasonable cannot be disregarded even if made by an interested party. The degree of reliability placed by an examiner on oral statements must be based on the credibility of the taxpayer as supported by surrounding circumstantial evidence. If the issue involves specific record keeping required by law and regulations, e.g., IRC 274, then of course, oral evidence alone cannot be substituted for necessary written documentation.

b. *Credibility:*

- It is the responsibility of the examiner to establish the degree of credibility of the taxpayer. It is here that the examiner must exercise to the fullest his/her skill and judgment. He/she should take into account the demeanor of the taxpayer, his/her manner of making the statement and the extent of subject knowledge demonstrated. These first impressions should be carefully tested by skillful questioning to bring out all pertinent surrounding circumstances. Corroborative or contradictory details will have an important bearing on determining the reasonableness and probability of the statements.

- If the statements of the taxpayer, although self-serving, are not improbable or unreasonable, self-contradictory, or inconsistent with surrounding facts and circumstances they should be accepted. If the statements of the taxpayer, in the judgment of the examiner, reveal some degree of unreliability, his/her findings should take this into account. Unless the taxpayer's statements have been found to be wholly unreliable, they must be given some weight in the conclusion reached.
- In considering issues susceptible to abuse by taxpayers, the examiner should assess the credibility of the taxpayer with caution. Since oral statements with strained constructions of fact are more likely to be encountered in these cases, the examiner's skill and judgment in developing the surrounding circumstances are especially important, so that the taxpayer does not profit from his/her failure to maintain documentation substantiating his/her income and deductions. Some examples of such issues are personal expenses disguised as business, convention or education expenses and determination of income from tips, prizes, awards, gambling, or miscellaneous independent activities.

3. *Report of Examination*—In preparing a report of examination the examiner is required to present the issues clearly and succinctly with a complete factual record. The report should reflect both his/her position and that of the taxpayer. If oral statements are part of the factual record, the report should include:
   a. The substance of the oral statements. If considered necessary, an affidavit may be secured from the taxpayer for this purpose. When securing such affidavits, examiners should follow instructions in 380 of IRM 4235, *Techniques Handbook for In-Depth Audit Investigations.*
   b. The surrounding facts and circumstances, if any, which corroborate or contradict the oral statements.
   c. An analysis and evaluation of all the evidence at hand.
   d. The conclusions reached and the determinant factors.

One more thing, never use any language that may even remotely be construed as offering a bribe to the tax examiner. Even though there *may be* tax examiners who *may be* susceptible to such an overture, you're best advised not even to attempt to find one. The IRS runs a very tight ship and they are ardent about preserving the integrity of their organization. Their Internal Security Division is a top-notch organization, and they are ever vigilant in weeding out dishonest employees. They do not hesitate to arrest anyone breaching the rules of the system. Offering a bribe is definitely against the law.

POSTAUDIT PROCEDURES

If you agree with the tax examiner's findings you will be asked to sign an agreement form. If you don't agree with the audit findings the tax examiner will explain your appeal rights. If you are in an office audit situation you will have the opportunity to discuss the problem with the examiner's group manager. If you don't reach an agreement with the group manager, or if you are audited in a field audit situation, the tax examiner's next step is to send you a 30-day letter along with a copy of the audit report and an appropriate agreement/waiver form (see Exhibit 5-8 for an explanation of the different forms examiners use). This package is known as the Preliminary Letter and is sent by regular mail.

The Preliminary Letter will give you 30 days to request an administrative hearing within the IRS Appeals Office. Even though the IRS is usually very tough in sticking to the 30-day requirement, it is possible for you to get an extension beyond the 30 days. The *Internal Revenue Manual* states that "as a matter of practice, extensions are granted under certain circumstances," such as:

- The taxpayer retains a representative and demonstrates a need for more time to prepare a meaningful protest.
- The taxpayer retains a *new* representative.
- The taxpayer or his representative is sick or injured.
- The issues are complex, requiring considerable legal research or the need to delve into records of prior years.

Before an extension can be granted, these requirements must be met:

- You must request an extension in writing setting forth the reasons why you need the additional time. If you make a request over the telephone, the tax examiner can verbally grant you the extension, but you will need to follow up in writing. The tax examiner will then confirm the extension to you in writing.
- If the statute of limitations in your case is set to expire within 150 days, you will have to consent to an extension of the statute.
- You will have a very difficult time getting an additional extension on top of the original 30 days unless you can support your request with a "sound, specific reason."

If you sign the form agreeing to the examiner's findings that is included with the 30-day letter, your ordeal is temporarily over and the case will be sent forward for further processing. Temporarily here acknowledges the fact that you will then have to wrestle with the prospect of paying the additional taxes.

If you have not filed a protest with the Appeals Office, but you previously indicated you would do so, the *Internal Revenue Manual* directs the tax examiner to send you form letter 923(C/DO) allowing you an additional 15 days to file your protest.

If you fail to respond to the Preliminary Letter within the required time period, a Notice of Deficiency, called a 90-day letter, will be sent to you by certified mail, or registered mail if you reside outside the US. The Notice of Deficiency will be sent even if the Preliminary Letter cannot be delivered because: (1) You moved and left no forwarding address; or (2) you are temporarily away and not expected to return within a reasonable period of time; or (3) you have not returned after a reasonable extension of time was granted. So leaving town in the middle of the night won't beat the IRS.

If you decide to take your case to the Appeals Office, the tax examiner will promptly refer your case there. For office audit situations conducted by tax auditors a written protest is not required. For field audits conducted by a revenue agent, you must file a written protest if the total amount of proposed tax and penalties exceeds $2,500. Read your Notice of Deficiency for clear instructions.

The Notice of Deficiency gives you 90 days to file an appeal with the Tax Court. It is a legal notice that a tax deficiency exists and it must be prepared and served in compliance with the provisions of the statute. Although the Code authorizes that notices be sent by certified or registered mail to the taxpayer's last known address, it can be hand-served if approved first by IRS's District Counsel.

A Notice of Deficiency consists of a letter stating the amount of the deficiency, and a statement showing how the deficiency was completed. The statement includes paragraphs explaining the nature of the adjustment. These explanatory paragraphs become a part of IRS's basic pleadings in the Tax Court proceeding. They set the pattern upon which IRS's case will be tried.

A Notice of Deficiency must be addressed to the proper person and mailed to the correct address or the courts may hold that it is invalid, and the IRS may then be prohibited from assessing or collecting the tax.

For example, if a joint income tax return has been filed and the IRS has been notified by either spouse that they have separate residences, the IRS must send separate originals of the joint notice by certified mail to each spouse at his or her last known address.

The Notice of Deficiency is a legal and statutory determination which is presumed to be correct. The issuance of the Notice is the beginning of prospective litigation. Tax Court Rule 34(b)(8) requires you to attach a copy of your Notice of Deficiency to your petition.

You must file your petition within the 90-day period or you will lose your chance of appeal. The IRS will then assess the tax and you will have no choice but to pay the tax. Afterward, you can file a claim for a refund, and if denied, you can sue for a refund either in U.S. District Court or in the U.S. Claims Court. (See IRS Publication 556 for more details.)

Protecting Your Refund

If there has been a multi-year audit of your tax returns, it is possible that you will owe additional taxes on one year, and have a refund due for another year. Both situations may be spelled out on the same Notice of Deficiency, and while you may agree to the refund due you for one year, you may not agree to the deficiency proposed for other years.

It's important to know that the Tax Court has no authority to review and redetermine such refund-year overassessments. Therefore, you must protect your claim for refund while you are contesting the proposed deficiency in Tax Court. Remember that there is a statute of limitations on refunds that ends three years from the due date of the return, or 2 years from the date the tax was paid, whichever is later. In order to sufficiently protect yourself from an expiring statute on your refund, you must file either a 1040X, Amended U.S. Individual Income Tax Return, or Form 843, Claim within the statutory period while you are contesting the deficiency.

Exhibit 5-8

IRS Audit Forms

Form 870, Waiver of Restrictions on Assessment and Collection of Deficiency in Tax and Acceptance of Overassessment, is used to secure agreements in certain situations, including those in which a refund may be issued as a result of the audit. Form 870 is usually used when the taxpayer *fully or partially agrees* with the audit report.

Signing Form 870 stops the running of interest 30 days from the date of receipt by the IRS. Signing this form does not constitute a final closing agreement, and does not preclude the IRS from asserting any further deficiencies. Nor does it prevent you from requesting the IRS to further consider other issues on that tax return. Signing Form 870 does permit the IRS to assess the deficiency or start processing for the refund immediately.

Once you sign form 870 the case is closed and the IRS must make the assessment within 60 days. You can, however, pay the deficiency after receiving the 90-day letter, in order to stop the accrual of interest, but still maintain your right to file a petition with the Tax Court. Follow the procedures previously discussed in IRS pub. 556 and *do not sign form 870.* As long as you don't sign the form you do not lose your right to go to Tax Court.

Notice of Deficiency—these are sent on the following forms:

- *Letter 893(RO) or Letter 900(RO)*—for income tax cases where deficiencies for one or more years have been determined and it is believed that the case may be petitioned as a Small Tax Case.
- *Letter 894(RO) or Letter 901(RO)*—for cases where small tax case procedures are not applicable.

Form 4549, Income Tax Examination Changes, is the basic report form for regular agreed cases on individual income tax returns that covers three years. It is used by revenue agents and is primarily designed for cases in which there is an audit adjustment that will result in a tax change. It does not have room for an explanation of the adjustment because tax examiners explain their adjustment at the end of the audit, so the IRS feels a written explanation is not necessary in regular agreed cases. However, they will furnish a written explanation if you request one.

Forms 1902-B and 1902-E, Report of Individual Income Tax Examination Changes, are used by tax auditors for individual agreed cases where an adjustment is proposed. The bottom of the form contains a "Consent to Assessment and Collection." By signing this form, you notify the IRS that you will not appeal the adjustment within the IRS or to the Tax Court.

Exhibit 5-9

Appeal Rights

Because people sometimes disagree on tax matters, the Service has an appeals system. Most differences can be settled within this system without having to go to court. You may not use the appeals system if your reasons for disagreement do not come within the scope of the tax laws. For example, your disagreement cannot be appealed based solely on moral, religious, political, constitutional, conscientious, or similar grounds.

If you do not want to appeal your case within the Service, you can take it to court.

APPEAL WITHIN THE SERVICE

We have a single level of appeal within the Service. Your appeal from the findings of the examiner is to an Appeals Office in the Region. Appeals conferences are conducted as informally as possible.

If you want an appeals conference, address your request to your District Director according to the instructions in our letter to you. Your District Director will forward your request to the Appeals Office, which will arrange for a conference at a convenient time and place. You or your representative should be prepared to discuss all disputed issues and to present your views at this meeting to save the time and expense of additional conferences. Most differences are resolved at this level.

If agreement is not reached at your appeals conference, you may, at any stage of the procedures, take your case to court. See *Appeals to the Courts,* later.

Written Protests

Along with your request for a conference you may need to file a written protest with the District Director.

You do not have to file a written protest if:

1. The proposed increase or decrease in tax, or claimed refund, is not more than $2,500 for any of the tax periods involved; or
2. Your examination was conducted by correspondence or in an IRS office by a tax auditor.

If a written protest is required, you should send it within the period granted in the letter you received with the examination report. Your protest should contain:

1. A statement that you want to appeal the findings of the examiner to the Appeals Office;
2. Your name and address;
3. The date and symbols from the letter showing the proposed adjustments and findings you are protesting;
4. The tax periods or years involved;
5. An itemized schedule of the adjustments with which you do not agree;
6. A statement of facts supporting your position in any issue with which you do not agree; and
7. A statement outlining the law or other authority on which you rely.

The statement of facts under (6) must be declared true under penalties of perjury. This may be done by adding to the protest the following signed declaration:

"Under the penalties of perjury, I declare that I have examined the statement of facts presented in this protest and in any accompanying schedules and, to the best of my knowledge and belief, it is true, correct, and complete."

If your representative submits the protest for you, he or she may substitute a declaration stating:

1. That he or she prepared the protest and accompanying documents; and
2. Whether he or she knows personally that the statement of facts contained in the protest and accompanying documents are true and correct.

Representation

You may represent yourself at your appeals conference, or you may be represented by an attorney, certified public accountant, or a person enrolled to practice before the Internal Revenue Service.

If your representative attends a conference without you, he or she may receive or inspect confidential information only if a power of attorney or a tax information authorization has been filed. Form 2848, *Power of Attorney and Declaration of Representative,* or Form 2848-D, *Tax Information Authorization and Declaration of Representative,* or any other properly written power of attorney or authorization may be used for this purpose.

You may also bring witnesses to support your position.

APPEALS TO THE COURTS

If you and the Service still disagree after your conference, or if you skipped our appeals system, you may take your case to the United States Tax Court, the United States Claims Court, or your United States District Court. These courts are independent judicial bodies and have no connection with the Internal Revenue Service.

Tax Court

If your case involves a disagreement over whether you owe additional income tax, estate or gift tax, windfall profit tax on domestic crude oil, or certain excise taxes of private foundations, public charities, qualified pension and other retirement plans, or real estate investment trusts, you may take it to the United States Tax Court. For you to appeal your case to the Tax Court, the Service must first issue a formal letter, called a ***Notice of Deficiency.*** You have 90 days from the date this notice is mailed to you to file a petition with the Tax Court (150 days if mailed to you when you are outside the United States). If you do not file your petition within the 90 or 150 days, you lose your opportunity to appeal to the Tax Court.

Generally, the Tax Court hears cases only if the tax has not been assessed and paid; however, you may pay the tax after the notice of deficiency has been issued and still petition the Tax Court for review. Therefore, you must be sure that your petition to the Court is filed on time. If it is not, the proposed liability will be automatically assessed against you. Once the tax is assessed, a notice of tax due (a bill) will be sent to you and you may no longer take your case to the Tax Court. You are then required by law to make payment within 10 days. If the tax remains unpaid after the 10-day period, the amount due will be subject to immediate collection. Once the assessment has been made collection of the full amount due may proceed even if you believe that the assessment was excessive. Publication 586A, *The Collection Process (Income Tax Accounts),* explains our collection procedures.

If you filed your petition on time, the Court will schedule your case for trial at a location convenient to you. You may represent yourself before the Tax Court or you may be represented by anyone admitted to practice before that Court.

If your case involves a dispute of not more than $10,000 for any one tax year, the Tax Court provides a simple alternative for resolving disputes. At your request, and with the approval of the Tax Court, your case may be handled under the "small tax case procedures," whereby you can present your own case to the Tax Court for a binding decision. If your case is handled under this procedure, the decision of the Tax Court is final and cannot be appealed. You can get more information regarding the small tax case procedures and other Tax Court matters from the United States Tax Court, 400 Second Street, N.W., Washington, DC 20217.

District Court and Claims Court

Generally, the District Court and the Claims Court hear tax cases only after you have paid the tax and have filed a claim for a credit or refund. As explained later under *Claims for Refund,* you may file a claim for a credit or refund if, after you pay your tax, you believe the tax is incorrect or too much. If your claim is rejected, you will receive a notice of disallowance of the claim unless you signed a Form 2297, *Waiver of Statutory Notification of Claim Disallowance.* If the Internal Revenue has not acted on your claim within 6 months from the date you filed it, you may then file suit for refund. You must file a suit for a credit or refund no later than 2 years after the Internal Revenue Service has disallowed your claim or a Form 2297 is filed.

You may file your credit or refund suit in your United States District Court or in the United States Claims Court. However, the Claims Court does not have jurisdiction if your claim was filed after July 18, 1984, and is for credit or refund of a penalty that relates to promoting an abusive tax shelter or to aiding and abetting the understatement of tax liability on someone else's return.

For information about procedures for filing suit in either court, contact the Clerk of your District Court or the Clerk of the Claims Court. The addresses of the District Courts and the Claims Court are at the end of this publication.

Income Tax Appeal Procedure

Internal Revenue Service

At any stage of procedure:

You can agree and arrange to pay.

You can ask the Service to issue you a notice of deficiency so you can file a petition with the Tax Court.

You can pay the tax and file a claim for a refund.

Examination of income tax return

Preliminary notice
30-Day Letter

Protest
(when required)

Appeals Office

If you do not respond or the 30-day period expires, then

Notice of Deficiency
90-Day Letter

CHOICE OF ACTION

Pay tax and file claim for refund

Consideration of claim for refund

Preliminary notice
30-Day Letter

Protest
(when required)

Appeals Office

Statutory notice
Claim Disallowance

CHOICE OF ACTION

No tax payment

Petition to Tax Court

Tax Court
No appeal permitted in cases handled under small tax case procedure

Not previously considered by Appeals

Appeals Office

Agreed

Unagreed

Reconsidered by Appeals because of settlement possibility

District Counsel

Trial

District Court

Claims Court

U.S. Court of Appeals for the Federal Circuit

U.S. Supreme Court

Court of Appeals

Internal Revenue Service **Department of the Treasury**

Social Security or Employer Identification Number: 987-65-4321

Date: November 29, 1985

Tax Year Ended and Deficiency: December 31, 1984

CERTIFIED MAIL

Mr. Charles Smith, and
Mrs. Cynthia Smith
33 East One Rd.
Oakton, VA 22124

Person to Contact: Joe Jones

Contact Telephone Number: (703)-566-0880

Dear Mr. & Mrs. Smith,

We have determined that there is a deficiency (increase) in your income tax as shown above. This letter is a NOTICE OF DEFICIENCY sent to you as required by law. The enclosed statement shows how we figured the deficiency.

If you want to contest this deficiency in court before making any payment, you have 90 days from the above mailing date of this letter (150 days if addressed to you outside of the United States) to file a petition with the United States Tax Court for a redetermination of the deficiency. The petition should be filed with the United States Tax Court, 400 Second Street NW., Washington, D.C. 20217, and the copy of this letter should be attached to the petition. The time in which you must file a petition with the Court (90 or 150 days as the case may be) is fixed by law and the Court cannot consider your case if your petition is filed late. If this letter is addressed to both a husband and wife, and both want to petition the Tax Court, both must sign the petition or each must file a separate, signed petition.

If you dispute not more than $10,000 for any one tax year, a simplified procedure is provided by the Tax Court for small tax cases. You can get information about this procedure, as well as a petition form you can use, by writing to the Clerk of the United States Tax Court at 400 Second Street NW., Washington, D.C. 20217. You should do this promptly if you intend to file a petition with the Tax Court.

If you decide not to file a petition with the Tax Court, we would appreciate it if you would sign and return the enclosed waiver form. This will permit us to assess the deficiency quickly and will limit the accumulation of interest. The enclosed envelope is for your convenience. If you decide not to sign and return the waiver and you do not timely petition the Tax Court, we will assess and bill you for the deficiency after 90 days from the above mailing date of this letter (150 days if this letter is addressed to you outside the United States).

If you have any questions, please contact the person whose name and telephone number are shown above.

Sincerely yours,

Roscoe L. Egger, Jr.

Commissioner
By William Towner
William Towner, Associate Chief

Enclosures:
Copy of this letter
Waiver
Statement
Envelope

Letter 893(RO) (Rev. 9–84

Form **870** (Rev. December 1983)	Department of the Treasury – Internal Revenue Service **Waiver of Restrictions on Assessment and Collection of Deficiency in Tax and Acceptance of Overassessment**	Date received by Internal Revenue Service

Names and address of taxpayers *(Number, street, city or town, State, ZIP code)*	Social security or employer identification number
Charles & Cynthia Smith 33 East One Rd. Oakton, VA 22124	987-65-4321

Increase in Tax and Penalties

Tax year ended	Amount of tax	Penalty
December 31, 1984	$	$
	$	$
	$	$

Decrease in Tax and Penalties

Tax year ended	Amount of tax	Penalty
	$	$
	$	$
	$	$

(For any remarks, see back of form)

Instructions

General Information

If you consent to the assessment of the deficiencies shown in this waiver, please sign and return the form in order to limit any interest charge and expedite the adjustment to your account. Your consent will not prevent you from filing a claim for refund *(after you have paid the tax)* if you later believe you are so entitled. It will not prevent us from later determining, if necessary, that you owe additional tax; nor extend the time provided by law for either action.

We have agreements with State tax agencies under which information about Federal tax, including increases or decreases, is exchanged with the States. If this change affects the amount of your State income tax, you should file the required State form.

If you later file a claim and the Service disallows it, you may file suit for refund in a district court or in the United States Claims Court, but you may not file a petition with the United States Tax Court.

We will consider this waiver a valid claim for refund or credit of any overpayment due you resulting from any decrease in tax and penalties shown above, provided you sign and file it within the period established by law for making such a claim.

Who Must Sign

If you filed jointly, both you and your spouse must sign. If this waiver is for a corporation, it should be signed with the corporation name, followed by the signatures and titles of the corporate officers authorized to sign. An attorney or agent may sign this waiver provided such action is specifically authorized by a power of attorney which, if not previously filed, must accompany this form.

If this waiver is signed by a person acting in a fiduciary capacity *(for example, an executor, administrator, or a trustee)* Form 56, Notice Concerning Fiduciary Relationship, should, unless previously filed, accompany this form.

Consent to Assessment and Collection

I consent to the immediate assessment and collection of any deficiencies *(increase in tax and penalties)* and accept any overassessment *(decrease in tax and penalties)* shown above, plus any interest provided by law. I understand that by signing this waiver, I will not be able to contest these years in the United States Tax Court, unless additional deficiencies are determined for these years.

Signatures		Date
X		Date
X		Date
By	Title	Date

★U.S. Government Printing Office: 1984—421-441/3616

Form **870** (Rev. 12-83)

Form **4089-A**
(Rev. April 1982)

Department of the Treasury - Internal Revenue Service

Notice of Deficiency Statement

Symbols

AP:DE:JJ

Mr. Charles Smith, and
Mrs. Cynthia Smith
33 East One Rd.
Oakton, VA 22124

Kind of Tax

Individual Income Taxes

Tax Year Ended	Deficiency (Increase in Tax ~~and Penalties~~)
December 31, 1984	$2,278.00

In making this determination of your income tax liability, careful consideration has been given to your protest dated January 6, 1986, and to the statements made therein. Your comments made at the conference of March 26, 1986 have also been considered.

☐ Copy to Authorized Representative:

★U.S. GOVERNMENT PRINTING OFFICE 1982 522-064/6228

Form **4089-A** (Rev. 4-82)

Form **5278** (Rev. May 1982)	Department of the Treasury — Internal Revenue Service **Statement — Income Tax Changes**	Return Form No. 1040	Schedule No.
Name(s) of Taxpayer(s) Mr. Charles Smith, and Mrs. Cynthia Smith	X Notice of Deficiency ☐ Settlement Computation ☐ Other *(specify)*		
	Tax Years Ended		
1. Adjustments to income	Dec. 31, 1984		
a. Business Loss	6,796.00		
b. Employee Business Expenses	3,015.00		
c. Medical & Dental Expenses	294.33		
d. Interest Expenses	1,487.00		
e. Contributions	733.00		
f. Exemption	1,000.00		
g.			
2. Total adjustments	13,325.33		
3. a. ☐ Taxable income ☐ Adjusted gross income X Tax table income b. As shown in: ☐ Preliminary letter dated ____ ☐ Notice of deficiency dated ____ X Return as filed	8,968.00		
4. ☐ Taxable income as revised ☐ Adjusted gross income as revised X Tax table income as revised	22,293.33		
5. Tax from X Tax tables ☐ Schedule TC ☐ Tax rate schedules	2,954		
6. Alternative tax if applicable *(from page ____)*	--		
7. Corrected tax liability *(lesser of line 5 or 6)*	2,954		
8. Less credits *(specify)* a. Withholding	812		
b.			
c.			
9. Balance *(line 7 less amounts on lines 8a through 8c)*	2,132		
10. Plus a. Tax from recomputing prior year investment credit			
b. Self-employment tax			
c.			
11. Total corrected income tax liability *(line 9 plus amounts on lines 10a through 10c)*	2,954		
12. Total tax shown on return or XXXXXXXXXXX	676		
13. Increase or (decrease) in tax *(difference between lines 11 and 12)*	2,278		
14. Additions to the tax *(listed below)*			

* U.S. GOVERNMENT PRINTING OFFICE: 1983-381-541/5235

Form 886-A (Rev. May 1980)	Department of the Treasury — Internal Revenue Service **Explanation of Items**	Schedule No. or Exhibit
Name of Taxpayer: Mr. Charles Smith & Mrs. Cynthia Smith		Year/Period Ended: December 31, 1984

(a) It is determined that the expenses incurred in 1984 in connection with your art activity were not incurred in a transaction entered into for profit. Therefore, the claimed loss of $6,796 is not allowable. See Section 262 of the Internal Revenue Code. Accordingly, your taxable income is increased by $6,796.

(b) It is determined that the deduction of $4,015 claimed as employee business expenses is not allowable to the extent of $3,015, since it has not been established that any amount in excess of $1,000 represents an ordinary and necessary business expense or was expended for the purpose designated. Accordingly, your taxable income is increased ny $3,015.

(c) It is determined that based on the above adjustments which increased your adjusted gross income and the limitations imposed by Section 213 of the Internal Revenue Code, your medical expense deduction is disallowed in the amount of $294.33.

(d) It is determined that the deduction of $3,487 claimed as interest expenses is not allowable to the extent of $1,487 since it has not been established that any amount in excess of $2,000 was paid or was for a bona fide debt. Consequently, your taxable income is increased by $1,487.

Form 886-A (Rev. 5-80) (4-part snapset)

Page________

Form 886-A (Rev. May 1980)	Department of the Treasury — Internal Revenue Service **Explanation of Items**	Schedule No. or Exhibit
Name of Taxpayer Mr. Charles Smith & Mrs. Cynthia Smith		Year/Period Ended December 31, 1984

(e) It is determined that the deduction of $1,733 claimed as contributions is not allowable to the extent of $733 since it has not been established that any amount in excess of $1,000 was paid and met the requirements of Section 170 of the Internal Revenue Code. Accordingly, your taxable income is increased by $733.

(f) It is determined that the deduction of $1,000 claimed on your return as an exemption for your son Don is not allowable since it has not been established that you furnished more than one-half of his support as required by Section 152 of the Internal Revenue Code. Accordingly, your taxable income is increased by $1,000.

Form 886-A (Rev. 5-80) (4-part snapset)

Page________

Chapter 6 Tax Audits by Mail

Not every IRS audit is a face-to-face showdown with an IRS Revenue Agent or a Tax Auditor. About one-third of all of IRS's audits are actually conducted through the mail from an IRS Service Center. In 1986, 584,028 income tax returns were verified or corrected through correspondence from the Service Centers, resulting in $796 million in recommended penalties and interest.

Using low-cost, computerized methodology, tax returns are identified, monitored and tracked in the Service Centers. In a nutshell, the Service Centers identify tax returns with improper or inconsistent reporting, send adjustment letters to taxpayers, and conduct audits of returns with very simple and easily identifiable criteria.

The Service Center correspondence programs cover a variety of issues which can be readily handled by mail. These programs are:

- Returns Preparer Program.
- Unallowable Items Program.
- Multiple Filer Examination Program.
- DIF Correspondence Program.
- Claims.
- Federal-State Cooperative Audit.
- Social Security Form SSA-7000.
- Married persons filing separately.
- Math/Clerical Error Abatement.
- Information Returns Program (known as IRP).

The Service Center Examination Branch is responsible for conducting these examination programs, including issuances of initial contact letters, 30-day letters, Forms 1902-E, and Statutory notices, when necessary.

Even though the programs are designed to be solely handled in the Service Centers, a return initiated for examination by correspondence will be changed to a district office interview audit if the criteria for selecting the correspondence technique becomes invalid or you request an interview examination. However, this does not preclude using the telephone to resolve problems, or the need for further correspondence to secure the information to resolve an issue.

Internal Revenue Manual Section 4(13)12 states that, "All high score DIF returns selected for the Service Center correspondence examination programs will be screened for other issues." Any return with an apparent examination issue other than the issues being examined in the Service Center correspondence program will be transferred to the appropriate field office for personal contact.

The tax returns examined in most of these Service Center programs are selected during the processing cycle, and any refund that would have otherwise been issued is held up for a short period of time. The IRS then computes how much of the total refund relates to the item under question and freezes that portion of the refund while sending out the remainder of the refund check.

Examination Procedures

Once the return has been selected for a Service Center correspondence program, an initial contact letter is sent out requesting the appropriate information, or explaining the corrections. Enclosed with the letter is a solicitation of agreement. Each letter also includes a telephone number and the name of the contact person you can call for information.

Initial contact letters are supposed to be manually completed instead of being computer generated. All penalties and interest will also be computed in the letter. A self-addressed envelope will be included to ensure return to the correct Service Center Examination Branch.

Your reply to the contact letter is supposed to be sent within 45 days of receipt. Typical unsatisfactory replies include:

- Asking for additional time to resolve the issue.
- Requests to pay in installments.
- Requests for reconsideration of the findings, or assessment.
- Agreements to the deficiency, but no ability to pay.

If your reply is satisfactory to the Service Center examiner, the case is closed as a "No Change Audit". If your reply is not satisfactory, a 30-day letter (Letter #525(SC)) is sent advising you of the proposed tax change and your appeal rights. If feasible they may call you, so it's a good idea to give the IRS your telephone number on all your correspondence. If the IRS needs additional information, a follow-up letter will be sent explaining what is required to resolve the case.

If you request an interview to discuss the matter, or if it becomes apparent that an interview is necessary because the issues have become too involved, or if you cannot effectively communicate in writing, the case will be transferred to your local IRS office. For Unallowable Items Program cases, the refund freeze will be released while the case is being transferred.

Many initial contact letters sent to taxpayers are returned to the IRS by the Postal Service for a number of reasons. If the Service Center examiner cannot locate a new address for you, the IRS Manual gives the examiner two options:

- He can hold the undeliverable correspondence case until after April 15th of the next year to see if you file another return with a new address; or,
- He can proceed with the next stage of the examination process by issuing the 30-day or 90-day letter to your last known address. The next stage involves the issuance of a statutory Notice of Deficiency. If you do not respond to the Notice of Deficiency, the examination is closed by default and the tax is assessed.

If the second option occurs, you may never know you've been audited until the IRS starts to collect the deficiency.

RETURN PREPARERS PROGRAM

Under the Return Preparers Program the IRS monitors the tax returns that have been prepared by tax preparers on their "hit list" whom the IRS feels have engaged in a practice of making material errors which demonstrates intentional misconduct or clear incompetence in preparing income tax returns.

Preparers operate under strict IRS guidelines that monitor the quality of their work. During a Service Center correspondence examination, examiners will flag those cases where there are indications of possible income tax return preparer violations. Some of the criteria to be considered when there are indications of such a violation are:

- Unallowable items which are obviously nondeductible, such as funeral expenses, license plate fees, nondeductible attorney fees, etc.;
- Returns from the same preparer containing repetitious deductions in such areas as casualty losses, uniform deductions, other deductions, etc.;
- Returns of married individuals filing separately or separate returns of divorced individuals where the same exemptions are claimed and the same preparer filed the return; and
- Returns where the taxpayer's responses to IRS's initial correspondence indicates that there was a complete lack of documentation or verification of the items questioned.

Examiners are instructed to be on the alert to any indication of a suspect tax practitioner's return.

UNALLOWABLE ITEMS PROGRAM

The Unallowable Items Program is a correspondence correction program used to identify and correct items on individual returns during initial processing. The items questioned under this program are those which appear to be obviously unallowable by law.

Unallowable items are either manually identified during the code and edit processing routine or computer identified. These items are corrected by the Examination Branch through correspondence with taxpayers. The amount of the refund applicable to the unallowable item will be frozen during the period that the returns are being reviewed by the Service Center Examination Branch. However, refund release procedures will be initiated on partial refund returns that are transferred to a district office for completion of the audit. Exceptions include those cases under the jurisdiction of the criminal investigation function, vow of poverty and protester cases, and those in statutory notice status.

Correction of unallowable items on returns will be initiated by Form 4960 (CP-19) or Form 4961 (CP-20) which will include a computer printed explanation of the unallowable item.

AUDIT-PROOFER'S STRATEGY RULE

- ***The Unallowable Items Program is one of IRS's biggest Service Center Examination programs. Therefore it is important that you know what criteria is used to identify unallowable items on the forms 1040 series returns. See Exhibit 6-1 for a listing of that criteria.***
- ***Use Exhibit 6-2 as a checklist to avoid claiming items on your tax return that are absolutely and clearly unallowable, and that will not only result in a loss of part of your refund, but also unnecessarily delay the release of the remainder of your refund.***

MULTIPLE FILER EXAMINATION PROGRAM

The National Computer Center will analyze returns and check to see if more than one return has been filed under the same Social Security number. If more than one return has been filed and the names on the returns are similar, the returns will be pulled as examination cases. For purposes of this program a case is two tax returns associated by a common Social Security number.

The following types of cases will be forwarded to district offices where normal examination and close-out procedures will be followed:

- A joint return followed by a non-joint return which duplicates exemptions and/or deductions.
- Cases which do not clearly identify the exemptions claimed.
- Cases requiring additional information.

A 30-day letter will be sent when the returns filed are to be combined into one return. The purpose of the letter is to explain the corrections to the taxpayer, transmit Form 1902-E with appropriate explanations, and solicit an agreement. If the returns have different addresses, the examiner is supposed to determine the best address.

DIF CORRESPONDENCE (DIF CORR) PROGRAM

The DIF CORR program is a correspondence examination program that corrects simple itemized deductions on low- and medium-income nonbusiness returns. The items questioned under this program will be those that can be readily handled by mail and with taxpayers who can effectively communicate in writing.

Only simple itemized deductions will be examined. Some examples of correspondence items are interest, taxes, contributions, medical expenses, and simple miscellaneous deductions such as union dues, work clothes, and small tools. The aim of the selection is to have the examinations completed at the Service Center and transfer as few cases as possible to the district offices.

The IRS manual suggests that tax returns containing single simple issues generally will not be examined because such examinations frequently result in insignificant or no tax change.

Enumerated below are considerations which should cause a return to be selected for correspondence examination. Under centralized classification procedures, returns selected with these criteria should be flagged for the Correspondence Unit in the Service Center.

- All the questioned items are susceptible to direct verification from records that could be easily submitted by mail.
- Inspection of the previous or subsequent year return is not necessary.
- Some examples of issues which can be verified by correspondence are:
  - —Simple itemized deductions (exclusive of office-in-the-home, and education expense).
  - —Payments to an IRA/Keough Plan.
  - —Interest penalty on early withdrawal of savings.
  - —Child care credit.
  - —Credit for the elderly.
  - —Residential energy credit.
  - —Self-employment tax.

Certain issues do not lend themselves to a correspondence examination. The following issues are inappropriate for correspondence examination:

- Exemptions.
- Income from tips, pensions and annuities, rents and royalties, and income not subject to tax withholding.
- Determination of whether income reported constitutes capital gain or ordinary income.
- Deductions for travel and entertainment.
- Deductions for bad debt.
- Determinations of basis of property.
- Complex miscellaneous itemized deductions such as casualty and theft losses where determination of a fair market value is required.

- Returns in which the classifier feels an office interview is needed to ensure the taxpayer's rights under the law, or the appearance of the return (writing, grammar, neatness, etc.) indicates that the taxpayer may not be able to communicate effectively in writing.
- Taxpayer's income is low in relation to financial responsibilities as suggested from review of the return (number of dependents, interest expense, etc.).
- Taxpayer's occupation is of the type that requires only a limited formal education.

AUDIT-PROOFER'S STRATEGY RULE

If you receive a DIF CORR inquiry from the Service Center Examination Branch, you will have to submit proper proof, documentation or verification. The tax examiner is more interested in how well you can substantiate your deduction than in how well you understand the rules for deducting the expense. Review Exhibit 6-3, Substantiation Required for a Correspondence Examination.

OTHER TYPES OF SERVICE CENTER AUDITS

Claims Program—This involves the verification of claims for refunds, such as Forms 843, 1040X, and informal claims, with simple issues of the type that can be handled by correspondence.

Federal State Cooperative Audit Program—Copies of examination reports from state tax agencies are referred to the service centers for association with the Federal income tax return and possible examination of that return by correspondence.

Social Security Form SSA-7000—These Notices of Determination of self-employment income are referred to service centers in cases where the Social Security Administration has made a determination of self-employment income. The referrals involve adjustments to returns for self-employment and, possibly, income taxes.

Married Taxpayers' Filing Separately Program—This program identifies married taxpayers who are not consistent in the itemized deductions/zero bracket amount elections on their separate tax returns.

Math/Clerical Error Abatement—The Tax Reform Act of 1976 expanded the term "mathematical error" to include clerical errors which are broader in nature than literal errors of arithmetic. The Tax Reform Act of 1976, Act Sec. 1206 states, "the term 'mathematical or clerical error' means:"

A. an error in addition, subtraction, multiplication, or division shown on any return,
B. an incorrect use of any table provided by the Internal Revenue Service with respect to any return if such incorrect use is apparent from the existence of other information on the return,
C. an entry on a return of an item which is inconsistent with another entry of the same or another item on such return,
D. an omission of information which is required to be supplied on the return to substantiate an entry on the return, and
E. an entry on a return of a deduction or credit in an amount which exceeds a statutory limit imposed by subtitle A or B, or chapter 42 or 43, if such limit expressed:
   i. as a specified monetary amount, or
   ii. as a percentage, ratio, or fraction, and if the items entering into the application of such limit appear on such return.

In accordance with this legislation the Service is permitted to summarily assess the additional tax resulting from these errors. However, the statute provides that a taxpayer who receives a math/clerical notice of an assessment for additional tax has the right to appeal. You must make your appeal within 60 days by filing a request for an abatement of the assessment, and explaining any disagreement with the amount of the assessment.

INFORMATION RETURNS PROGRAM (IRP)

The Information Returns Program (IRP) is a Service-wide effort to identify taxpayers who have filed incorrect returns by underreporting their income or who have not filed legally required income tax returns. This identification process is based on data furnished to the IRS on information returns such as W-2s and 1099s. W-2 forms are first filed with the Social Security Administration, all other forms go directly to the IRS.

In 1986 the IRS notified 3.2 million taxpayers of potential discrepancies between income reported on their tax returns and income reported to the IRS on their information returns. In addition, 3.3 million taxpayers received notices of apparent failure to file income tax returns.

The IRS received 859 million information documents in 1986, including 210 million W-2s originally processed by the Social Security Administration—over 760 million of these documents were submitted on computer tape. Almost all of this computerized information was used in the IRP program, along with 55 percent of the 89 million information returns sent in on paper. To identify the underreporters and the nonfilers, the information returns are compared to the IRS's computerized records to discover the discrepancies. With the installation of additional optical character recognition equipment, the IRS expects to match almost all of the paper information returns starting in 1985.

A "discrepancy" occurs when income listed on a taxpayer's information returns cannot be accounted for on the tax return. When the IRS contacts a taxpayer solely to resolve discrepancies, the IRS is not conducting an examination or an inspection of the taxpayer's books of account within the meaning of IRC 7605(b).

An "examination" occurs when the issue goes beyond resolving a discrepancy, such as when unreported income not covered by an information return is discovered. This may occur when the income on the information return cannot be verified without also looking into other sources of income.

Generally, if the Service Center contact on a return that has already been audited can be limited to verification of amounts reported on the information return, it will not be considered by the IRS to be a subsequent reaudit or a reopening of the previous audit.

If you are contacted about a discrepancy on your tax return, it may be that: (1) you never earned the income, or, (2) you never worked for the employer. If either situation exists, make sure you respond promptly to the IRS with that information. The Service Center will follow up in both situations to determine the true facts, even if it means contacting the payer or employer for verification. Whatever you do, don't pay a tax you don't owe.

Exhibit 6-1

Criteria Used to Identify Unallowable Items on Forms 1040 Series

SPECIFIC ITEMS

- Protest letter—A protest letter, attachment, or any similar indication is present.
- Partial exemption—A taxpayer is claiming a partial exemption for other than birth, death, or community property state.
- Deduction for married couple when both work—If the deduction is claimed and it is not a joint return showing that each spouse had qualified earned income.
- Gambling Winnings—If Form W-2G is attached to return and it appears the winnings are not reflected in adjusted gross income (AGI).
- Amounts Deducted Twice—If any deduction, such as interest or taxes, is claimed in two different places on the return, e.g., page 2 of

1040 and Schedule A. This applies only when the same amount is deducted *twice.* (However, it is possible and allowable for the taxpayer to deduct taxes for different purposes on various schedules.)

- Schedule D Loss—(Loss on Personal Residence or Personal Property)—If Schedule D information or entries on Schedule A or other schedules report losses on the sale of a personal asset not related to business (such as furniture, jewelry, automobile, personal residence, *but not sale of stocks.*)
- Surviving Spouse—When the taxpayer has claimed filing status as qualifying widow(er) with dependent child for more than two years.
- Energy Credits: a. Energy Conservation Costs, if nonrefundable energy credits are claimed on tax returns; the items may be: insulated or exterior siding, new or replacement furnace or boiler, supplemental oil or gas furnace, hot-water heater (tank), wood- or peat-burning stove, coal-fired clean-burning stove, fireplace, energy-saving fireplace, fireplace screens (metal or glass), heat pump, fluorescent lighting, draperies, drapery linings, window shades, window films or coatings, awnings, wall paneling, new roof, roof overhangs, new or replacement walls, extra thick walls, attic fans, skylights, patio enclosures, carpeting, energy-saving clothes dryer, energy-saving cooking stove, swimming pool, greenhouse, personal labor, hydrogen-fueled equipment.
- Energy Credits: b. Residential Energy Conservation Costs, if energy credits for conservation costs are claimed on tax returns and the principal residence was not substantially completed before April 20, 1977.

SCHEDULE A ITEMS

- Medical and Dental Expenses:
  1. Auto Expenses for Medical Care—If there is an amount in the Medical and Dental Expenses for "Auto Mileage for Medical Use" in excess of nine (9) cents per mile; e.g., ten (10) cents per mile. Does not apply if actual cost is used.
  2. Personal Expense for Medical Care—Personal or living expenses (except transportation to obtain medical care) incidental to medical treatment, such as meals and lodging, health club dues, diet foods, funeral expenses, and maternity clothes.
- Taxes:
  1. Federal Taxes—Income, Social Security (FICA), and excise taxes on autos, tires, telephone and air transportation, custom and import duties.
  2. Utility Taxes—Sewer, water, phone, garbage, gas, electric, etc.

3. State and Local Taxes—Hotel, meal, air fare, inheritance, stamp, poll, mortgage transfer taxes, etc. Sales tax on autos is allowable.
4. Auto Licenses and Tags—Personal auto registration, tag and license taxes or fees except for residents of Alabama, California, Colorado, Indiana, Iowa, Maine, Massachusetts, Mississippi, Nevada, New Hampshire, Oklahoma, Virginia, Washington, and Wyoming.

- Contributions:
  1. Auto Expenses Related to Contributions—Auto mileage for contributions in rendering services to charitable organizations in excess of nine (9) cents per mile; e.g., ten (10) cents per mile. Does not apply if actual cost is used.
  2. Contributions—Money value of taxpayer's time and labor, contributions to individuals or nonqualifying organizations, such as foreign charities (except Canadian charities), lobbying organizations, etc.
- Miscellaneous Deductions:
  1. Support for Child or Other Individual—If there is an amount for support of an individual (not to be confused with Child Care) claimed in miscellaneous deductions.
  2. Personal Legal Expenses—Expense for wills, trusts, adoption, divorce, and other items not connected with the production of income.
  3. Educational Expenses—Educational and related expenses for other than taxpayer or spouse (tuition, books, transportation, lodging, etc. for children or other individual).
  4. Auto Expenses for Trade or Business—If there is an amount claimed for trade or business transportation that is other than actual cost and is in excess of:
     a. twenty and one-half (20.5) cents per mile for the *first* 15,000 miles, and/or
     b. eleven (11) cents per mile for the miles *over* 15,000 miles, or all miles claimed, if fully depreciated.
  5. Sale of Personal Residence—Expenses for sale or purchase of personal residence (closing expenses, settlement fees, legal fees, realtor commissions, etc.), unless those items are specifically claimed as a part of moving expenses.
  6. Personal Insurance—Life, auto, home, liability, etc., not claimed as employee business expense.
  7. Adoption Expenses—If taxpayer claims a deduction for adoption expenses for a child with medical needs receiving adoption assistance payments under Section 473 of the Social Security Act the deduction may not be more than $1,500.
  8. Personal Living Expenses—Other personal family living ex-

penses such as commuting to and from work, household expenses, maintenance of personal residence or auto, etc.

9. Household and Dependent Care Services—If taxpayer claims child care expense as both an itemized deduction on Schedule A and as a credit against the tax.

- Casualty Loss:
  1. Casualty—Includes losses which in themselves are unallowable, such as termite losses, lost but not stolen items, etc.

Exhibit 6-2

Unallowable Items Checklist

SPECIFIC ITEMS

- Protest letter: A protest letter to the IRS may satisfy your desire to release your anger and/or hostile frustrations at the government, but serves absolutely no useful or constructive purpose when directed at the IRS. A deduction, credit, omission of income, or other adjustment as an indication of protest cannot be allowed.
- Partial exemptions: Not allowed.
- Deduction For a Married Couple When Both Work: Your deduction will not be allowed if you have not filed a joint return showing that each spouse had qualified earned income.
- Gambling Winnings: Your Form 1040 includes the income shown on the Form W-2G attached to your return.
- Medical Expenses—Automobile: Your medical expenses on Schedule A have the correct automobile mileage rate at 9 cents per mile.
- Medical Expenses—Personal: Your medical expenses on Schedule A do not include items such as health club dues, diet foods, funeral expenses, maternity clothes, and meals or lodging (unless provided by a hospital or similar institution for medical care).
- Federal Taxes: The Federal taxes on Schedule A that cannot be deducted include Federal income tax, social security and railroad retirement taxes, the Social Security tax you paid for a personal or domestic employee, Federal excise taxes on automobiles, tires, telephone service, and air transportation, Federal estate and gift taxes, and customs duties.
- Utility Taxes: Utility taxes for sewers, water, phones, and garbage collection are not charged at the general sales tax rate, so they cannot be deducted.
- State and Local Taxes: State and local taxes, such as those for hotel

rooms, air fares, inheritances, stamps, and mortgage transfers are not charged at the general sales tax rate, so they cannot be deducted.

- Automobile License, Registration, Tag Fees or Taxes: Automobile license, registration, tag fees, or taxes may be shown as personal property taxes only if your state charged them annually and in an amount based on the value of your automobile. If your state does not charge the fees and taxes this way, they are not personal property taxes and cannot be allowed.
- Support of Children or Other Dependents: The expenses for support of children or dependents are not deductible.
- Personal Legal Expenses: Legal expenses cannot be allowed if they are expenses for wills, trusts, adoption, divorce, and other items not connected with the production of income.
- Educational Expenses Other than Taxpayer or Spouse: Educational expenses for someone other than yourself or your spouse cannot be allowed.
- Charitable Contribution—Automobile Expenses: The charitable contributions on Schedule A for your automobile mileage rate is at 9 cents per mile.
- Charitable Contributions: Payments to individuals, lobbying organizations, foreign charities (except Canadian charities), and other nonqualifying recipients are not deductible.
- Business Expenses—Automobile Mileage Rate: Your business automobile expenses is correct if the mileage rate is at 20.5 cents (21 cents for 1985) per mile for the first 15,000 miles and 11 cents per mile for each additional mile.
- Casualty Loss: The casualty loss on Schedule A is not allowed if the damage or destruction of property was not identifiable, sudden, unexpected, or unusual.
- Sale or Purchase of Personal Residence: The expenses incurred in the sale or purchase of your residence are not allowed because closing costs (for example, settlement and legal fees) or realtor commissions are not deductible.
- Personal Insurance Premiums: Personal insurance premiums, other than for medical care, are not deductible.
- Adoption Expenses: The deduction for adoption expenses for a child with special needs receiving adoption assistance payments under Section 473 of the Social Security Act may not be more than $1,500.
- Personal Living Expenses: Personal expenses such as commuting to work, household costs, and maintenance of a personal residence or car, are not deductible.
- Child and Disabled Dependent Care Expenses: Expenses for child and disabled dependent care services can be claimed only as a credit.

- Political Contributions: A political contribution can be claimed only as a credit.
- Taxes on Gasoline and Other Fuels: The state and local sales taxes on gasoline, diesel fuel, and other motor fuels are not deductible.
- Income from a Possession of the United States—Only One Exemption Allowed: Citizens of the U.S. entitled to the benefits of the tax laws regarding income from sources within possessions of the United States can claim only one personal exemption regardless of whether a joint or separate return is filed.
- Foreign Tax: An itemized deduction cannot be allowed for foreign income tax if you also claimed a foreign tax credit for income tax paid or accrued to a foreign country.
- Widows and Widowers Filing Status: The filing status for a qualifying widow(er) can be used only the 2 years after the year of the death of the spouse and, during that time, the widow(er) must be entitled to an exemption for a son, daughter, or stepchild who lived with him or her during the entire tax year in a household the widow(er) maintained.
- Energy Conservation Costs: Your expenditure for energy conservation must qualify for a tax credit.
- Residential Energy Conservation Costs: The energy credit for installing insulation or other energy saving devices in or on your personal residence cannot be allowed if the costs were not for your principal residence that was substantially completed by April 20, 1977.
- Loss on Sale of Personal Residence or Property: The loss on the sale of your residence or other property used for personal purposes is not deductible.
- Duplicate Deduction: Your return will be adjusted if the same deduction was reported more than once.

Exhibit 6-3

Substantiation Required for a Correspondence Examination

Below is a list of the proof, documentation, and verification you will need to substantiate your deduction for a correspondence examination.

MEDICAL EXPENSES

- With regard to health insurance, provide paid receipts or possibly pay stubs. If any doubt exists as to the type of coverage, a statement from the payee should be provided with specifics.

- Provide statements from the health insurance company to show the breakdown of the items covered. You should be alert to the possibility of duplicated payments.
- Expenses incurred for drugs must be substantiated with paid receipts or statements from the pharmacy. Cancelled checks are not acceptable because nondeductible items can be included in the amount paid. (For example: Toiletries or cosmetics.)
- Provide the name of the person for whom the medical expense was incurred.
- Cancelled checks, paid receipts, or other documentation should be provided for all expenses.
- Transportation expense can usually be accepted without verification if the amount seems reasonable. Greater transportation expenses can be analyzed based on the information provided. (For example: Your address, physician's address, and frequency of the trips.) Unusual expenses should be substantiated by a statement from your physician and by receipts. For example: You had to travel 1,500 miles (via plane, train, etc.) for special treatment.

TAXES

- Submit receipts and/or checks showing proof of payment and liability of real estate tax. If the property was sold or purchased, provide a copy of the settlement statement.
- Verification is not necessary for a deduction of sales tax based on the tables. You must furnish receipt for any amount larger than the table amounts. Cancelled checks are not acceptable.
- State and city income can be substantiated with copies of the state and city returns and cancelled checks or receipts showing payment.

INTEREST

- Receipts, cancelled checks, and statements from creditors showing amount of interest paid with the names of payees. If the cancelled checks cover principal and interest payments, the terms of the agreement should be analyzed to determine the interest portion.
- The obligation must be yours. If there is joint liability, the entire amount is deductible by the payor. Care should be taken to determine whether the interest expense is a deduction from gross income or from adjusted gross income. Allocation computation may be necessary. (An example is interest paid on an automobile loan that is used for both business and pleasure.)

- Cancelled checks are not always evidence of liability or payment of interest and generally should be supported by documentation.

CONTRIBUTIONS

- For *religious* contributions, submit cancelled checks, receipts, or statements from the religious organization. Statements are rendered periodically or on request when the contributor uses an envelope system or a pledge basis.
- Submit cancelled checks, receipts, or statements for contributions made to *charitable* organizations.
- If the contribution was other than money, provide the name and address of the recipient organization and show:
  1. What was contributed,
  2. Its fair market value,
  3. How it was used by the organization. (For example: You donated bakery items valued at $4.50 to the Boy Scouts for a cake sale.)

- Any unrecognizable name will be checked against the list of exempt organizations to determine if it is qualified. You may be questioned as to the nature and purpose of certain donations.
- Consideration will be given to unsubstantiated contributions, such as:
  1. Are the contributions claimed reasonable in relation to income after other deductions and personal living expense?
  2. Has care been taken in preparing the return?
  3. Is the documentation submitted for other items in question?
  4. What are the overall practices of you and your spouse? (For example: Are you active in voluntary organizations?)
  5. How many children are in the family?

- Substantiation will be analyzed as to the purpose of the contribution. If a cancelled check includes payment for tuition, dinner, or raffle tickets, you should submit a statement from the organization.

CASUALTY AND THEFT LOSS

Once a determination has been made as to the qualifications of the deduction, you may have to provide:

- Fire or police department reports, when applicable.
- Photographs showing the extent of the damage.
- The date the property was acquired.

- The cost or fair market value of the property before and after the casualty. Cancelled checks or receipts can be used as a measure of loss.
- If the property is insured, a statement from the Insuror showing:
  1. Date and nature of loss.
  2. Amount of damage claimed.
  3. Amount of coverage carried.
  4. Date and amount of the claim paid by insurance.

UNION DUES

Union dues and initiation fees paid for union membership are deductible. A statement from the union should be submitted showing a breakdown of the purpose of fees paid. Careful inspection will be made because insurance or other nonqualifying items could be included in the payment.

TAX PREPARER FEES

Expenses incurred for preparation of the tax return are deductible only in the year they are paid. You must submit cancelled checks or receipts to prove this expense.

EDUCATION EXPENSE

- A letter from the employer should be submitted showing:
  1. Whether the education was necessary for you to retain employment, salary or status.
  2. How the education helped maintain or improve your skills needed in employment. You must prove that you have already met the minimum requirements. (For example: You are an accountant. You take several courses in new accounting methods. These courses would improve your skills. Therefore they are allowable.)
  3. If you were reimbursed and how much. You must show the types of expenses incurred.

- You must provide the examiner with:
  1. A list of subjects studied.
  2. A description and number of credits per course.
  3. Information with regard to the period of enrollment.
  4. The number of hours of instruction per week.

- Provide cancelled checks or receipts to verify the amount spent and any information regarding a scholarship or fellowship grant received during the year.

- Provide a brief description of your work during the year.

UNIFORMS, EQUIPMENT AND TOOLS

- Provide an explanation and a statement from your employer showing the requirements for this expense.
- Provide cancelled checks (when applicable) and receipts to verify payment.

GAMBLING LOSS

A gambling loss is deductible on Schedule A only to the extent of reported gambling winnings. You must submit raffle stubs, wagering tickets or any other documentation to substantiate the expense and purpose. The tax examiner will inspect the stubs for possible nondeductible items. (For example: Purchase of dinner raffle tickets.)

UNMARRIED HEAD OF HOUSEHOLD FILING STATUS

Using cancelled checks, receipts, and any other substantiation, you must prove your qualifications under this filing status.

EXEMPTION FOR CHILDREN

- If you are divorced or legally separated, one of the following should be submitted:
  1. A copy of the divorce or separate maintenance decree.
  2. A copy of the written agreement showing which parent will claim the dependency exemption.

- If the dependent does not live with you, the following should be submitted:
  1. Cancelled checks, receipts, and any other documentation to verify the amount spent, from all sources.
  2. The name, the address, and a signed statement from each person the dependent lived with confirming that such person did not claim this dependent.

- If the dependent does live with you, you should submit:
  1. A record of income received by or for the dependent. (For example: Social Security or Trust Fund and how these funds were used.)

2. A record of amount contributed to the household expense by each person living in the same household as the dependent.
3. A record of funds spent for the dependent's support from all sources.

- With regard to general support, such as food, and lodging, the examiner will consider your total income and the number of household occupants.

EXEMPTIONS OTHER THAN TAXPAYER'S CHILDREN

- You must show the total amount of support to the dependent. Each expense may be accepted without verification, if it is deemed reasonable. The number of members in the household, the amount of income and the geographical area the dependent resides in will also be considered.
- You must be specific about any other types of support provided to the dependent and show how the funds were used. The amount, name, and address of the person or public agency that provided aid should be included.
- If the dependent does not live with you, you should provide cancelled checks and receipts to verify amount spent. Also, a statement from each person the dependent lived with indicating that:
  1. You provided more than half of the support.
  2. This person did not claim the dependent on his/her return.

- You and your spouse can claim an additional exemption for age 65 or over. A copy of the birth certificate, social security documents, or employment records are acceptable proof of age.
- An additional exemption for blindness can be substantiated by submitting a statement from a physician or registered optometrist. The statement should indicate the degree of blindness and the probability of future improved vision.

MOVING EXPENSES

- You should provide a complete analysis of all expenses, both reimbursed and unreimbursed. This will include the comparative direct route mileage from the residence to both former employer and the new employer.
- A statement from the employer giving a breakdown of the reimbursed expenses.

- The name, address, and period of employment with the employer.
- The names and relationships of all the members of the household who moved with you. Cancelled checks and receipts for all the expenses.

INDIVIDUAL RETIREMENT ACCOUNTS

- You must be eligible to make qualified contributions to an Individual Retirement Account before a tax-exempt deduction can be allowed. This income adjustment is subject to tax law that has changed in recent years.
- You must submit *specific* information with regard to this deduction. It must show when the contribution was made and the amount. Acceptable substantiation would be Form 1099R and W-2P, along with a bank book or bank statement.

INTEREST PENALTY ON EARLY WITHDRAWAL

A payment of interest penalty on early savings withdrawal is allowable as an adjustment to income. You must submit copies of Form 1099 or a statement from the bank substantiating this expense. A bank book is not specific enough to show the purpose of the charge.

ALIMONY AND SEPARATE MAINTENANCE

- Provide a copy of the decree of divorce, decree of separate maintenance or other written instrument which specifies the basis for alimony payments.
- Submit cancelled checks or receipts to verify the payments made. If alimony payments were not made directly by you, you should furnish documents showing the source such as insurance policies, endowment, or annuity contracts, etc. Also, if the payments are for support under a decree of a domestic relations court, they can be verified from statements rendered to you by the court. In some localities it is the practice of the court to collect and transmit payments. Whenever necessary, the former spouse's name, address, and any other information should be obtained.

CONTRIBUTIONS TO PUBLIC OFFICE

Although subject to limitations and specifications, contributions to public office are allowable. You should submit cancelled checks, receipts, and/or statements from the recipient for proof.

CREDIT FOR THE ELDERLY

- Credit for the elderly is based on a formula subject to your income for the tax year in question. Your age will determine whether he/she should attach Schedule R or Schedule RP to your return to claim the credit.
- When a return is classified for this credit it is usually based on information received from the Social Security Administration (SSA). To substantiate this claim, you must submit a copy of your birth certificate and/or clarification of your income from the payer.

CHILD AND DEPENDENT CARE CREDIT

- A determination must be made as to whether you qualify for the credit. Variables must be considered. Careful consideration should be given to:
  1. Who may claim the credit?
  2. The employment related expenses.
  3. Qualifying expenses.

- You should submit a letter of explanation along with cancelled checks and receipts.

RESIDENTIAL ENERGY CREDIT

- Paid receipts showing what was purchased are the only acceptable substantiation. Cancelled checks must be accompanied by the receipts.

FOREIGN TAX CREDIT

- A determination must be made as to whether you qualify for the foreign tax credit. Form 1116, Computation of Foreign Tax Credit, should be attached to the return.
- You must submit the original, duplicate original, duly certified or authenticated copy of the receipt or return to verify this tax.

Chapter 7 How a Tax Audit Can Turn into a Fraud Investigation

You filed your tax return and got your refund, then the IRS notified you that you are about to be audited and you're scared to death. You know you cheated a little on your tax return and you're worried that IRS might really throw the book at you. First thing that comes to your mind is fraud, and jail. A sense of panic immediately comes over you and you break out into a cold sweat. What will you do?

First, let's set your mind at ease by giving you some figures on what your chances are of getting into real serious trouble with the IRS.

In 1986, out of 102 million individual income tax returns that were filed, the IRS only audited 1.3 million taxpayers. Of those, the IRS initiated only 5,861 criminal investigations for tax fraud. For the year, only 3,524 recommendations were made for prosecution. In 1986, there were 2,954 indictments, and 1,992 pleas of guilty and *nolo contendere*. There were

2,460 convictions after trial. Of 2,418 taxpayers who were sentenced, only 61% actually received prison sentences. So you can see that not many people get into real serious trouble with the IRS.

However, IRS's options are not limited to criminal prosecution. The IRS also has the option of imposing a civil fraud penalty against any taxpayer whom they feel is guilty of civil fraud. Civil fraud and criminal fraud are quite different, with two separate sets of standards that must be met and with two kinds of penalties.

In 1986 there were 11,841 civil fraud assessments made against taxpayers. While civil fraud does not necessarily result in a prison sentence, criminal fraud may, and criminal fraud may also result in the imposition of a civil fraud penalty.

The differences between civil fraud and criminal fraud are in the penalties provided by law and the degree of proof required. Criminal fraud is a felony offense under Internal Revenue Code *Section 7201*. Criminal penalties such as fines up to $100,000 and imprisonment up to 5 years are imposed after a trial by the judge of a criminal court. Civil fraud is provided by Internal Revenue Code *Section 6653(b)*, and involves a monetary fine imposed and collected by the IRS, in an amount equal to 75 percent of the additional tax.

WHAT IS FRAUD?

Actual fraud is defined in Corpus Juris as follows: "Actual fraud is intentional fraud; it consists of deception intentionally practiced to induce another to part with property or surrender some legal right and which accomplishes the end designed." More simply, it is obtaining something of value from someone else through deceit. Tax fraud results in an illegal reduction of taxes through deception. It sometimes involves false documents, returns, or statements, and includes attempted evasion, conspiracy to defraud, aiding, abetting or counseling fraud, and willful failure to file tax returns.

Tax *avoidance* is not a criminal offense. All taxpayers have the right to reduce, avoid or minimize their taxes by legitimate means. The distinction between avoidance and evasion is fine, yet definite. A tax avoider does not conceal or misrepresent. He actually shapes and preplans his financial affairs to reduce or eliminate his tax liability, but reports his transactions by making a complete disclosure on his tax return.

Evasion on the other hand, involves deceit, subterfuge, camouflage, concealment, an attempt to color or obscure events—or generally make things seem other than what they are. For example, suppose you bought 100 shares of stock on January 2, 1986 and decided to sell them on May 2,

1986, just a mere four months later, a sale which would have resulted in a substantial short-term capital gain. But upon realizing the benefits to be derived from the long-term capital gain provisions of the Code, you decide you are going to wait until July 4, 1986 to sell the stock, giving you a holding period in excess of six months, and a long-term capital gain. (The advantage of a long-term capital gain is a much smaller tax on the gain.) This is tax avoidance and is perfectly legal.

However, suppose you realize after the fact that you could have held the stock a little longer and realized the long-term capital gain. Suppose you actually sold the stock on May 2, creating a short-term capital gain. But, because you wanted to exploit the long-term capital gain provisions, you decide to *alter* the date on your purchase statement from your stockbroker to show that you held the stock longer than six months. This is actual *tax fraud*. It's a misrepresentation, a deceit, and it is also an illegal act.

Under *Section 7201* of the Internal Revenue Code: "Any person who *willfully attempts in any manner* to evade or defeat any tax imposed by this title or the payment thereof shall, in addition to other penalties provided by law, be guilty of a felony and, upon conviction thereof, shall be fined not more than $100,000 ($500,000 in the case of a corporation), or imprisoned not more than five years, or both, together with the cost of prosecution."

Civil fraud penalties are provided by Code *Section 6653(b),* which states: "If any part of an underpayment (as defined in Subsection (C)) of tax required to be shown on a return is due to fraud, there shall be added to the tax, an amount equal to 75 percent of the underpayment."

Both civil and criminal penalties may be imposed for the same offense. Although criminal sanctions provide punishment for the wrongdoings, the civil fraud penalty is really a remedial civil sanction to safeguard and protect the revenue for the Government, and to reimburse the Government for the heavy expenses of investigation and the loss resulting from the taxpayers fraud. Even though you may be acquitted in a criminal case you may still be charged with a civil fraud penalty. A criminal conviction for income tax evasion usually decides the fraud issue and you may be prohibited from contesting the civil fraud penalty in any civil proceeding.

The measure of proof differs in civil and criminal cases. In criminal cases the government must prove every facet of the offense and show guilt beyond a reasonable doubt. In civil cases, the IRS's determination of what you owe is presumed to be correct and the burden is placed on you to overcome this presumption. When fraud is alleged, the Government has the burden of establishing such fraud by clear and convincing evidence. (See Chapter 9 for a good explanation of what constitutes evidence.)

Even the tax computations in a case may be different for civil and criminal purposes. For example, the amount the IRS says you owe for civil fraud may be much more than what they compute you owe for criminal fraud. This is because the evidence relating to some of the income adjustments in a criminal case may not meet the necessary criteria of proof, even though it may be perfectly adequate for a civil case.

For criminal or civil fraud to be proven, evidence of willfulness must be found. Even though willfulness is not defined in the Internal Revenue Code, its definition has evolved from many court decisions. Willfulness is a state of mind usually established by circumstantial evidence because direct evidence of willfulness can only be obtained by admission or a confession. An admission includes all statements of the taxpayer as well as his books and records.

To prove a charge of willful fraud, the IRS must establish three elements: knowledge, intent, and purpose. It must be shown that all three elements existed at the time the return was prepared or, in a failure to file case, when the return was not filed. To be guilty of willfulness, you must know the result of your act. That is, you must believe that the omission of income or the gross deductibility of the item in question will result in an illegal understatement of your tax liability. You must intend to commit the act in question and your purpose must be to understate your tax liability. There must also be a definite understatement of the tax liability.

The fraud penalty is an actual percentage of the deficiency or the tax unreported. If there is no tax there cannot be a penalty.

ELEMENTS OF THE OFFENSES

The elements of the offense of "willfully attempting in any manner to evade or defeat any tax" are:

- Additional tax due and owing;
- An *attempt in any manner* to evade or defeat any tax; and,
- Willfulness.

Additional Tax Due and Owing

The Government must establish at the time the offense was committed that an additional tax was due and owing: that the taxpayer actually owed more tax than reported. However, it is not necessary to prove evasion of the full amount alleged in the indictment. The government only needs to show that a *substantial* amount of the tax was evaded; this amount need not be measured in terms of gross or net income or by any particular percentage of the tax due and payable.

Attempt to Evade or Defeat Any Tax

The substance of the offense under Code *Section 7201* is the term, "attempt in any manner." This does not mean that an unsuccessful attempt will not be considered a crime of willful attempt. In fact, the crime is complete when the attempt is made, without regard to the ultimate success of the attempted action. The courts have stated that, "The real character of the offense lies not in the failure to file a return, or in the filing of a false return, but rather in the *attempt*" to evade any tax. The statute does not define "attempt," nor does it limit or define the means or method by which the attempt to evade or defeat any tax may be accomplished.

However, it has been determined by the courts that the term, "attempt" implies some affirmative action or the commission of some overt act. The actual filing of a false or fraudulent return is not a requisite for the commission of the offense, though the filing of a false return is the most common form of tax evasion. A false statement of any kind made to IRS agents for the purpose of concealing unreported income has also been judicially determined to be an attempt to evade or defeat the tax.

The willful omission of a duty, or the willful failure to perform a duty imposed by the statutes (such as a deliberate failure to file a tax return) does not in itself constitute an attempt to evade or defeat. However, a willful omission or willful failure when done with an affirmative act or conduct from which an attempt may be inferred, would constitute an attempt. In the case of *Spies vs. U.S.*, the Supreme Court gave certain illustrations of acts or conduct from which the attempt to evade or defeat any tax, may be inferred. For example, keeping a double set of books, making false entries, alterations, invoices or documents, destruction of books or records, concealment of assets or covering up sources of income, the handling of one's affairs to avoid making the records usual in transactions of that kind, and any conduct the likely effect of which would be to mislead or to conceal. In other words, "in any manner."

Willfulness

Willfulness has been defined as, "an act or conduct done with a bad or evil purpose." The mere understatement of your income in the filing of an incorrect return does not in itself mean that you have willfully attempted tax evasion. The offense is made when there has been conduct as has been specified previously in the Spies case.

Willfulness is an essential element of proof with respect to most criminal violations investigated by the IRS. Because willfulness is not defined by statute, but by various judicial and court decisions, it may mean one thing in civil cases and quite another in criminal prosecutions. Usually, where civil penalties are involved, willfulness means actions that are "knowingly," "consciously," or "intentionally" taken. A voluntary course of action, as distinguished from an accidental course of action, would seem to satisfy the civil requirements. When used in criminal revenue statutes, willful generally means an act done with a bad purpose; without a justifiable excuse; or one that is done stubbornly, obstinately, or perversely.

The Supreme Court once stated, "an evil motive is a constituent element of the crime." Knowledge, specific intent and bad purpose are necessary elements of criminal willfulness. They are distinguished from motive, which is the reason or the inducement for committing an act or a crime. The most laudable motive is no defense when the other elements are present. For example, a taxpayer may deliberately understate his income in order to have sufficient funds to support his invalid parents. While his motive may be admirable, he has demonstrated *specific intent* to evade payment of his income taxes.

AUDIT-PROOFER'S STRATEGY RULE

***Willfulness is a state of mind and is rarely susceptible to direct proof. It is a mental process that is usually only proven through circumstantial evidence. Direct evidence of willfulness occurs when you either admit or confess your wrongdoing.* Don't ever do this without first contacting a tax attorney skilled in handling criminal investigations.**

Frequently, circumstantial evidence of willfulness will consist of acts *after* the filing of a false income tax return. For example, trying to bribe an Internal Revenue agent during a tax investigation, or going to your safe deposit box after having been questioned about your assets, or making false statements, or withholding records during an investigation, or trying to influence the testimony of prospective witnesses. Even though these acts are not evidence to prove the particular element of willfulness, they do show a "continuity of unlawful intent." This is an exception to the general rule that evidence of another crime unconnected with the one on trial is inadmissible. Ambiguous legal points like this almost require that you obtain a skilled tax attorney to help you at the earliest practical moment.

The determination of willfulness of a criminal act is the responsibility of a jury. Usually the jury will be told that direct proof of willful or wrongful intent or knowledge is not necessary; that it is not possible to look into a person's mind to see what went on; that intent can only be determined from all the facts and circumstances; and that *intent and knowledge may be inferred* from various acts. Instructions may also include the comment that the jury may consider the taxpayer's refusal to produce books and records for inspection by the Internal Revenue Service.

Defenses of Willfulness

Relying on the Advice of Counsel, Accountant, or Government Agent: This may be a valid defense to a willful violation. However, if the Government can show that you did not act in good faith upon such advice, by not following it; that you did not fully inform the advisor of all of the facts; that you sought advice from an advisor who was not qualified to give it; or, if you had reason to believe that the advisor was not qualified, then you may have a weak defense.

Disclosures, Amended Returns, and Payments of Tax: Believe it or not, if you make a voluntary disclosure, file an amended return, or make a payment of tax after you have filed a fraudulent return, the IRS may try and use this to establish your state of mind at the time that you committed the alleged criminal act. The IRS will contend that such disclosure and/or delinquent payments were prompted by the fraud investigation and that such acts are an incriminating admission of your culpability. However, most courts have regarded the prompt filing of an amended return or payment of delinquent tax as admissible evidence to show *lack of willfulness*.

Cooperation with the Investigation: This defense is frequently used by taxpayers at the start of investigations to indicate their innocence. The contention is that if the taxpayer willfully defrauded the Government then he will continue to conceal the truth from the IRS investigators. By cooperating with the IRS, the taxpayer is attempting to show that he has nothing to hide. But this defense is rarely persuasive, if the facts and circumstances around the alleged defense create an inference of willfulness. Subsequent cooperation during the investigation may only serve to mitigate the penalty.

Lack of Education and Business Experience: These are frequently used as defenses for criminal intent. Ignorance of Internal Revenue requirements and unfamiliarity with business practices are often cited as mitigating reasons for alleged violations. Taxpayers faced with conclusive evidence of substantial amounts of unreported income will frequently claim that it resulted from mistakes caused by their lowly educational background or inexperience in financial affairs. For example, a successful builder may claim that he is an expert contractor but that he can barely read or write, while a prominent doctor may contend he was never good at figures and was too busy caring for ill people to keep accurate records of his earnings. These defenses may be argued to the jury but their effect will depend, as in the case of cooperation, on all the facts and circumstances surrounding the commission of the offense.

Poor Health, Good Character and Integrity: With this defense, the jury must decide whether the mental and/or physical condition of the taxpayer at the time of the alleged offense was such that he was deprived of his sense of reason. The point of this defense is that a willful act of fraud cannot have occurred if the defendant did not know what he was doing, or was so incapacitated that he was unable to attend to his financial affairs properly. Closely connected with this defense is the claim that the defendant is a person with good character and integrity and could not reasonably have intended to defraud the United States. The courts have held that the jury may consider good reputation to raise a reasonable doubt of the defendant's guilt.

Entrapment: If a government agent induces a person to commit a crime he would not otherwise have committed the taxpayer is a victim of entrapment. To prove entrapment it must be shown that the agent originated and implanted the intent in the mind of the taxpayer. If the agent merely offers the *opportunity* for the person to commit a crime the person already intended to commit, there is no entrapment. For example, IRS agents are permitted to pose as taxpayers pretending to buy businesses, as long as their scam does not motivate an otherwise innocent person to commit a crime. The IRS uses such poses to discover business owners who have been keeping a double set of books, and deliberately underreporting their income to the IRS.

DETECTING FRAUD

Tax fraud is not ordinarily discovered by a routine surface examination. Fraud is usually discovered through an in-depth examination, the techniques of which are discussed in Chapter 9. An in-depth examination is a thorough examination with the objective of determining your current taxable income, and ascertaining if you have complied with all the Internal Revenue laws. An in-depth audit consists of:

- Reconciling your books to your tax return.
- Analyzing your income by source, nature and amounts.
- Determining the reasons for your book entries.
- Understanding all of your transactions.
- Initiating third-party contacts and investigations.
- Reconstructing your income, if necessary.

The *Internal Revenue Manual* states that:

> The first symptom alerting the tax examiner to the possibility of fraud will frequently be provided by the taxpayer. Conduct during the examination and method of doing business may be indicative of the filing of improper returns. The examiner should be alert to the following actions:
>
> - Repeated procrastination on the part of the taxpayer in making and keeping appointments for the examination.
> - Uncooperative attitude displayed by not complying with requests for records and not furnishing adequate explanations for discrepancies or questionable items.
> - Failing to keep proper books and records, especially if previously advised to do so.
> - Disregard for books and records.
> - Destroying books and records without a plausible explanation.
> - Making false, misleading, and inconsistent statements.
> - Submitting false documents or affidavits to substantiate items on the return.
> - Altering records.
> - Using currency instead of bank accounts.
> - Engaging in illegal activities.
> - Failing to deposit all receipts.
> - Quick agreement to adjustments and undue concern about immediate closing of the case may indicate a more thorough examination is needed. (Take particular note of this one, but don't overdo it either way.)

IRS training materials also state that certain suspicious circumstances relating to items on the return can raise pertinent questions. For example:

- Your address may indicate a life-style that cannot be supported by the income you reported on your tax return.
- If your reported income is low and you have large interest or dividend income, it may raise a question of how you got that money in the first place. If you borrowed the money, how are you repaying the loans?
- If you have recently acquired assets listed on your depreciation schedule and you have no increase in your interest expense, the IRS may question the source of your funds used to acquire the assets.
- High real-estate taxes and little mortgage interest expense might also raise a question of your source of funds to acquire the real estate.
- Fluctuations in your income reported from year to year may indicate omissions of income or overstated deductions in your low income years.

Revenue agents are also taught that your actions and manner could indicate possible fraud. Excessive nervousness and an uncooperative attitude may lead the examiner to believe that an in-depth examination is in order. During the initial interview they may ask you about your living expenses, assets, and liabilities. Unreported and unrecorded income is sometimes spent to cover living expenses, to acquire assets or to pay debts. IRS agents are supposed to be alert for assets you have acquired or debts you have paid that you have failed to mention. The Internal Revenue training courses also suggest visiting your home or place of business so that the agent can see if you have new assets that were neither mentioned by you nor recorded in your books.

While examining your books of account and bank records, they may note inconsistencies or irregularities that indicate potential fraud. For example, there are a number of ways in which *income may be understated* that they will be looking for:

- Sales, fees, or other income entered in the books may be offset by fictitious returns, allowances, or refunds.
- Income recorded in the cash receipts or cash journal may be understated.
- Income such as interest, dividends, rents or commissions may be omitted entirely from the tax return.
- Invoices may not all be recorded in sales through irregular numbering, no numbering, alterations, or void invoices.
- Income may be recorded by different taxpayers. An example, corporate receipts may be reported as miscellaneous income on an officer's Form 1040.

- Income might be credited to an officer's account receivable, a partner's capital account, or a proprietor's drawing account instead of to sales. (Even though the books still balance.)
- Income from one or more specific customers may be omitted, or an irregular sale may be omitted for one week, one month, etc.
- Sales or exchanges of assets may be omitted from the return. As an example, business assets can be sold and the proceeds diverted to an individual.
- Inventory or products of a business may be removed and sold, and the income diverted to a corporate officer, partner, or proprietor.
- Checks may be substituted for currency receipts, the checks deposited, and the currency not reported.

The IRS will also be looking for ways in which *overstated expenses* indicate potential fraud. For example:

- Checks drawn to cash may be deducted but not supported by receipts or paid invoices.
- Checks may be drawn to third parties which may be endorsed back to the taxpayer, exchanged with the third party for a check to the taxpayer, or cashed by the taxpayer in amounts expensed on the return.
- The amount of a check, book entry, or journal page total may be raised.
- Purchases or other expenses may be deducted twice, for example, by posting from both the original and the copy of an invoice.
- Deductions may be taken for salary payments to fictitious employees, or for fictitious bonuses to actual employees.
- Substantial amounts of personal expenses may be paid and deducted as business expenses.
- There may be discrepancies between the amount of the check and the book entry, or the cancelled check may be altered.

Basically, the tax examiner is going to be looking for "badges of fraud," indicators of potential fraudulent activity. See Exhibit 7-1 for a list of the badges of fraud. During the examination the tax examiner is going to be mindful of two primary factors involving any indication of fraud—there has been a substantial understatement of taxable income, and you cannot reasonably explain the understatement.

ESTABLISHING FRAUD

In order to establish fraud, two basic facts must be proven: First, that the tax liability was understated (due either to underreporting of income or overstating deductions); second, that the understatement was due to a deliberate attempt to evade the tax.

Understatement of Tax Liability

First it must be proven that you failed to report your correct tax liability; that is, that there was taxable income which was understated, or that you had income subject to tax but failed to file a return and report this tax liability. Proof may be obtained by direct evidence of specific items not properly reported on the return or indirectly by use of income reconstruction methods to show that the tax on your return was an understatement of your actual tax liability. In specific item cases, tax examiners will attempt to show that certain items were not completely or accurately reflected on the return resulting in an understatement of income. For example, failure to report interest income or taking improper deductions of personal living expenses.

By contrast, the examiner may also resort to indirect measures to prove the inaccuracy of the return. These measures include but are not limited to the net worth, source and application of funds, and bank deposit methods of reconstruction of income. With these methods tax examiners can also show that the income reported on the return was understated. The courts have approved the use of these methods in both civil and criminal tax cases. For a complete understanding of these methods see Chapter 9.

Intent to Evade Tax

The government must also prove that the understatement of tax liability was due to a deliberate and intentional effort to evade the tax. The fact that income was understated does not in itself prove that an understatement was intentional. Failure to report the correct income may be due to a mistake, inadvertence, reliance on financial or professional advice, an honest difference of opinion, negligence, or carelessness—none of which constitutes deliberate intent to defraud.

Other Violations

Most of the fraud situations which a tax examiner will encounter concern omitting income and understating taxable income. But there are other violations of the Internal Revenue Code which may or may not be fraudulent and with which the IRS must contend. These violations are:

- Failure to file a tax return.
- Failure to collect and pay over the tax.
- Failure to supply information.
- Failure to pay the tax.
- Issuance of fraudulent withholding statements to employees or failure to issue withholding statements.
- Fraudulent withholding exemption certificates submitted by employees for fictitious or nonallowable exemptions.
- Failure to supply information to employer.
- Making and subscribing to a false and fraudulent return, document, or other statement, or aiding and assisting in such action.
- Submission of false and fraudulent offers in compromise or closing agreements.
- Failure to obey summons.
- Attempts to interfere with the administration of Internal Revenue laws.

The *Internal Revenue Manual* states: "Knowledge of the obligation to file should be assumed if the taxpayer is engaged in an occupation the nature of which can be constituted to be *prima facie* evidence of such knowledge. Examples include the accounting and legal fields, real estate, insurance and stock brokerage, teachers, and business executives. Factors to be considered are:

- The taxpayers refusal or apparent inability to explain the delinquency.
- Statements made by a taxpayer which are contrary to the facts known by the examiner.
- Repeated delinquencies in the past, especially when coupled with an apparent ability to pay.

CONFIRMING SUSPECTED FRAUD

If the tax examiner finds inconsistencies or irregularities in your books or inconsistencies between your reported income and living expenses, accumulation of assets, or reduction of debt, the tax examiner may show you what he has found and ask for an explanation. If no adequate explanation is received, unresolved irregularities or inconsistencies may be the basis for concluding that your books and records are not reliable in determining your correct taxable income. At this point in the examination, the tax examiner may discuss the situation with his group manager.

In most cases the tax examiner must expand his investigation either to resolve the discrepancies and/or to determine your correct taxable income. This may involve an examination of either your subsequent or prior year tax returns in order to determine the existence of a pattern of fraudulent activity.

When an examiner has determined that your books and records are not adequate, a *direct examination* of those records will not enable him to determine your correct taxable income. Therefore, use of an *indirect method* and/or third party contacts is required.

In an indirect method contact, the tax examiner must examine all your financial transactions. Indirect methods include those discussed previously such as the bank analysis, bank deposit analysis, source and application of funds statement, and the net worth and expenditures method. An indirect method is also recommended when examining the return of a taxpayer who uses a single entry system of accounting records.

Two factors are given special emphasis during a reconstruction of income by indirect methods. Each factor will be given top priority during initial phases of an indirect method examination. The factors are: cash on hand, and personal living expenses.

Cash on Hand

Generally, cash on hand is currency that a taxpayer has available that is not on deposit with a financial institution. The accuracy of all indirect methods depends on establishing the amount of cash on hand at the beginning and at the end of each taxable year under examination. Should the examiner fail to establish this factor the taxpayer might claim that an unexplained increase in net worth or unexplained bank deposits are from accumulated cash or currency that was on hand at the beginning of the first taxable year under examination. This is known as the "cash hoard" argument.

IRS agents are taught that the best source of information concerning cash on hand is the taxpayer himself. The IRS may ask you how much money you had available as of December 31st of the year *preceding* the year under examination, and all the years covered under your examination. This statement can be easily corroborated later with financial statements on file at banks or credit and financial institutions.

IRS training materials point out that taxpayers often claim the Fifth Amendment right to remain silent when contacted by a special agent who later steps into the case to conduct the fraud investigation. The instructions are: "The only cash on hand admission then made by the taxpayer will have been made to you during the examination process." You should be aware that if you give the tax examiner information about your cash on hand during the examination, it won't do you any good to refuse to give the information later by pleading the Fifth Amendment. It will then be too late. In order that they will not have to confront a later Fifth Amendment defense, tax examiners are taught to obtain the information early in the examination. The IRS instructs their examiners to question the credibility of sources of large amounts of currency by asking such questions as:

- Who else knows about this?
- Who witnessed and can verify how much money was there?
- What were the denominations?
- How much currency do you have right now?
- Can I count and verify it?
- What was the source of the savings?
- Why was it not deposited into a bank account?

If the answer is that the source was loans from friends and relatives, the IRS examiner will ask their names. Where did they get the money? Was it repaid? How was it repaid? Was the note recorded or interest paid? They may even contact other third parties to verify information supplied by you.

Personal Living Expenses

The accuracy of indirect methods computations also depends heavily on an accounting of personal living expenses. One method for determining the amount of personal living expenses is the checkspread of all disbursements. This is where the IRS will review all your checks by listing them on spreadsheets. Afterward, they will ask you to initial and date each page.

When the examiner discovers a firm indication of fraud, the tax examination will be immediately suspended without disclosing to you or your representative the reason for the actions. The tax examiner will then report his findings in writing through his group manager to the chief of his division. The purpose of this referral is to enable the Criminal Investigations Division to evaluate the criminal potential of the case and decide whether or not a joint investigation should be undertaken.

The Next Step

At this point in the investigation, the tax examiner comes under certain restrictions. For example:

- The examiner can not advise you or your representative of possible defenses or explanations for understatements, acts of concealment, omissions or other possible acts of fraud. The examiner is advised to avoid making statements or remarks, or acting in any way that might be misinterpreted as an attempt to aid you.
- If you or your representative question why the return is being examined or why the audit is so thorough, the examiner will refer to the examination as "routine." He is instructed to state that under selection procedures, it was selected for examination, or that it is his responsibility to determine the accuracy of the return.
- Contemporaneous notes will be kept of all contacts and conversations with you, your employees, or third parties showing the date, time, place, and exactly what was said.
- The examiner will not accuse you of cheating or failing to comply with the income tax laws. Nor should the examiner indicate conclusions in this regard during the audit.
- When suspending the examination, the examiner will not do so in an abrupt manner so as to alarm or embarrass you.
- The tax examiner will not contact you or your representative after the case has been referred to criminal investigations unless he has been authorized to do so.

After receiving the referral report from the tax examiner's division, the Chief of the Criminal Investigations Division must decide whether or not to accept the case. This decision is based upon an evaluation of the criminal potential of the case. Cases will be selected in which it appears that sufficient evidence can be gathered to prove beyond a reasonable doubt a willful violation as required in a criminal case. They will consider such factors as size, flagrancy, significance, public interest, or possible deterrent effect.

If there appears to be potential for a successful prosecution, a special agent will be assigned to the case. The tax examiner and the special agent will work together as a team. While they may have overlapping duties, the tax examiner's primary function is to examine the accounting records, verify their accuracy, and determine the taxpayer's correct tax liability. The special agent has the responsibility of developing and presenting admissible evidence required to prove criminal violations in court. This special agent will determine:

- The method of proof to be used for determining the correct tax liability.
- The identification of those adjustments used in a criminal prosecution case or those which will constitute the basis for a recommendation for the fraud penalty.
- Preparation and issuance of a summons.
- Timing and priority of the investigative actions in the case.

The Crucial Moment

If you are visited by a Special Agent of the Criminal Investigations Division who reads you the following paragraph explaining your constitutional rights, you will know that your deepest fears have been confirmed.

> As a special agent, one of my functions is to investigate the possibility of criminal violations of the internal revenue laws, and related offenses. In connection with my investigation of your tax liability (or other matter) I would like to ask you some questions. However, first I advise you that under the Fifth Amendment to the Constitution of the United States I cannot compel you to answer any questions or to submit any information if such answers or information might tend to incriminate you in any way. I also advise you that anything which you say and any documents which you submit may be used against you in any criminal proceeding which may be undertaken.
>
> I advise you further that you may, if you wish, seek the assistance of an attorney before responding.

AUDIT-PROOFER'S STRATEGY RULE

Once you have been read your rights you should say nothing further, and* immediately *obtain the assistance of a skilled tax attorney. To find one, call your local bar association.

AFTER THE INVESTIGATION

If Prosecution Is Recommended

If the evidence warrants prosecution, the case may go to trial. This trial does not determine the tax liability, but determines if you are guilty of a crime such as income tax evasion or some other charge under the Internal

Revenue Code. The final determination of your income tax liability and the assessment of the civil tax and penalties are deferred until the criminal case is concluded. The case is then returned to the tax examiner for settlement of the civil liability in the usual manner, either agreed or unagreed, and you will be afforded your normal appeal rights. Once criminal prosecution has been recommended to the Department of Justice, the tax examiner cannot remove the civil fraud penalty without a written recommendation or concurrence of IRS District Counsel.

If Prosecution Is Not Recommended

The Criminal Investigation Division may close the case if it is not suitable for prosecution. Even if the Criminal Investigations Division withdraws from a case, it may reenter the investigation if the tax examiner later discovers additional facts to indicate fraud. Once a decision has been made not to proceed with the investigation or the prosecution, the tax examiner will then develop all aspects of the case including the possible application of the civil fraud penalty. At this point if civil fraud is charged the burden of proof is still on the government. If the charge cannot be supported by clear and convincing evidence, the civil fraud penalty will not be asserted. Factors that are considered include:

- Conviction or a plea of guilty concerning a felony violation. In such a case the tax examiner *will recommend* the civil fraud penalty.
- The plea of *nolo contendere* to a felony charge. Nolo contendere means "I will not contest it." In these cases the government must still sustain the burden of proof for civil fraud purposes.
- An evaluation of the documented facts by the examiner indicates that intent to defraud can be proved by clear and convincing evidence.

An analysis of many decisions rendered by the tax court indicates that the Service's assertion of the civil fraud penalty will be sustained if it can be proved that you:

- Intentionally understated income of a substantial amount or an amount which is substantial in relation to the income reported on the return.
- Intentionally overstated your other deductions at a substantial amount or at an amount which is substantial in relation to the unreported income.
- Understated income or overstated expenses over a period of several years thus exhibiting a pattern from which willfulness could be inferred.

- Maintain secret bank accounts in your name or in the names of nominees or dummies.
- Had an undisclosed source of income from other than your regular business activity.
- Failed to maintain adequate books and records which could be expected based on your business experience, education, knowledge of accounting, etc.
- Had unreported income from an illegal business or from illegal transactions especially if the income is earned regularly (such as in the distribution and sales of narcotics).
- Made false entries in your books of account, falsified records furnished to the government, or made false statements to the examining agent.
- Failed to maintain a plausible explanation to the investigating agent or the court regarding why a return was falsely prepared.
- Had been convicted or had pled guilty to criminal charges of tax evasion in prior periods.

Of course, the existence of any of these cited circumstances is not in itself evidence or proof of civil fraud. The IRS must fully develop its case, and examine your return for each tax year to show your actions stem from an attempt to evade payment of income taxes due.

NEGLIGENCE

In many cases where fraud was initially suspected, the tax examiner realizes that the government can not sustain the burden of proof by a showing of clear and convincing evidence. In such cases, the tax examiner will consider asserting a negligence penalty. Imposed by Internal Revenue Code *Section 6653(a)*, the penalty is 5 percent of the additional amount owed plus an addition of 50 percent of the interest payable on the portion of the underpayment attributed to negligence.

In the legal sense, negligence is when one neglects to do something which a reasonable person would do, or does something which a prudent and reasonable person would not ordinarily do. The IRS Manual says that:

> The negligence penalty should be invoked if there has been negligence or an intentional disregard of published rulings and regulations in the preparation of returns, as distinguished from a mere error or a difference of opinion or some controversial question and a willful intent to evade is not present or cannot be substantiated.

The following are examples of situations in which the IRS may hit you with the negligence penalty:

- You have continued to make *substantial errors* in reporting your income or in claiming personal deductions year after year, even though these mistakes have been brought to your attention in previous audits.
- You have failed to maintain proper records after being advised to do so, and have subsequently filed tax returns containing substantial errors.
- You have made careless and exaggerated claims of deductions that are clearly unsubstantiated by the facts.
- You have failed to offer any explanation for understating your income, or for failing to keep books and records.
- You failed to include all your interest and dividend income on your tax return.

The *IRS Manual* points out that the negligence penalty may be asserted even though the return was prepared by a tax preparer. Unlike the fraud penalty, the IRS's assertion of the negligence penalty is presumed to be correct and the burden of proof is on you to prove otherwise, just as in a straight deficiency.

The Tax Reform Act of 1986 expanded the scope and definition of the negligence penalty. It can now be assessed on *all* taxes rather than just the income tax as formerly. The definition of negligence now includes "any failure to make a reasonable attempt to comply with the provisions" of the Code as well as any "careless, reckless, or intentional disregard" of rules and regulations.

The Act also expands the scope of the special negligence penalty to include failure to properly show on your tax return any amount that is shown on an information return, such as a Form 1099. A failure to report will be treated as negligence "in the absence of clear and convincing evidence to the contrary."

Exhibit 7-1

Badges of Fraud

UNDERSTATEMENT OF INCOME

- An understatement of income attributable to specific transactions, and denial by the taxpayer of the receipt of the income or inability to provide a satisfactory explanation for its omission.
    1. Omissions of specific items where similar items are included. Example: Not reporting $1,000 dividend from Company A, while reporting $50 dividend from Company B.
    2. Omissions of entire sources of income. Example: not reporting tip income.
- An unexplained failure to report substantial amount of income determined to have been received. This differs from the omission of specific items in that the understatement is determined by use of an income reconstruction method (net worth, bank deposits, personal expenditures, etc.)
    1. Substantial unexplained increases in net worth, especially over a period of years.
    2. Substantial excess of personal expenditures over available resources.
    3. Bank deposits from unexplained sources substantially exceeding reported income.
- Concealment of bank accounts, brokerage accounts, and other property.
- Inadequate explanation for dealing in large sums of currency, or the unexplained expenditure of currency.
- Consistent concealment of unexplained currency, especially when in a business not calling for large amounts of cash.
- Failure to deposit receipts to business account, contrary to normal practices.
- Failure to file a return, especially for a period of several years although substantial amounts of taxable income were received.
- Covering up sources of receipts of income by false description of source of disclosed income.

Claiming Fictitious or Improper Deductions

- Substantial overstatement of deductions. For example, deducting $5,000 as travel expense when actually the expense was only $1,000.

- Substantial amounts of personal expenditure deducted as business expenses. For example, deducting rent paid for personal residence as business rent.
- Inclusion of obviously unallowable items in unrelated accounts. For example, including political contributions in Purchases.
- Claiming completely fictitious deductions. For example, claiming a deduction for interest when no interest was paid or incurred.
- Dependency exemption claimed for nonexistent, deceased, or self-supporting persons.

Accounting Irregularities

- Keeping two sets of books, or no books.
- False entries or alterations made on the books and records, back-dated or post-dated documents, false invoices or statements, other false documents.
- Failure to keep adequate records, especially if put on notice by the Service as a result of a prior examination, concealment of records, or refusal to make certain records available.
- Variance between treatment of questionable items on the return as compared with books.
- Intentional under or over footing of columns in journal or ledger.
- Amounts on return not in agreement with amounts in books.
- Amounts posted to ledger accounts not in agreement with source books or records.
- Journalizing of questionable items out of correct account. For example: From the Drawing Account to an expense account.

Allocation of Income

- Distribution of profits to fictitious partners.
- Inclusion of income or deductions in the return of a related taxpayer, when difference in tax rates is a factor.

Acts and Conduct of the Taxpayer

- False statement, especially if made under oath, about a material fact involved in the examination. For example: Taxpayer submits an affidavit stating that a claimed dependent lived in his household when in fact the individual did not.

- Attempts to hinder the examination. For example: Failure to answer pertinent questions, or repeated cancellations of appointments.
- The taxpayer's knowledge of taxes and business practice where numerous questionable items appear on the returns.
- Testimony of employees concerning irregular business practices by the taxpayer.
- Destruction of books and records, especially if just after examination was started.
- Transfer of assets for purposes of concealment.

Other Items

- Pattern of consistent failure over several years to report income fully.
- Proof that the return was incorrect to such an extent and in respect to items of such character and magnitude as to compel the conclusion that the falsity was known and deliberate.

The following actions by the taxpayer, standing alone, are usually not sufficient to establish fraud. However, these actions with some of the "badges" listed above, may be indicative of a willful intent to evade tax:

1. Refusal to make specific records available. (Examiner will note time and place records were requested.)
2. Diversion of portion of business income into personal bank account.
3. File return in different district. (This is weak but will be noted.)
4. Lack of cooperation by taxpayer. (Examiner will record specific episodes, threats, etc.)

The presence of one or more of these "badges" of fraud does not necessarily mean that the return is fraudulent. However, it will alert the examiner to this possibility and invite further and more probing inquiry.

Part III

THE IRS AUDIT GUIDELINES (ANNOTATED)

Chapter 8 Official Guidelines for IRS Examiners

The following pages comprise sections 200 through 600 of *Section 4231* of the *Internal Revenue Manual*, titled, "Tax Audit Guidelines for Internal Revenue Examiners." This handbook provides tax examiners with specific pointers and auditing techniques that are to be used in routine examinations of individual income tax returns. It is structured to follow the flow of the tax return—name and address, filing status, exemptions, income, itemized deductions, etc.

To help you understand the instructions I have added annotations that point out current tax law provisions that relate to the corresponding IRM instructions. These annotations do not explain all the rules pertaining to the deductions or expenses, but generally, do cover the basics.

By now you have learned the four steps to audit-proofing your tax return, valuable information you need before you prepare your return. In the following pages you will find valuable information about how the IRS conducts an audit, the questions the examiner will ask you during the audit, and what determinations and tests need to be made.

Study this material very carefully *before* you meet with the IRS. Find the section that corresponds to the items that are being questioned on your tax return, and go over the instructions with your representative during your audit-planning strategy session. Use this material as your guide in planning how you will prepare for and respond to the examiner's scrutiny. Look for specific instructions that tell the examiner to "verify," "determine," "ascertain," "analyze," "ask," "be alert to," "look for," "trace," etc. Make sure that you can withstand the scrutiny of each instruction.

If you are a small business owner, pay special attention to *Section 600*, "Examination Techniques Peculiar to Certain Small Businesses." These guidelines point out peculiarities of certain business activities and outline various procedures that tax examiners follow when verifying income and expense items reported by these businesses. Even if you pay someone else to keep your books and records and prepare your tax return, you should review the section that pertains to your type of business. This will prepare you for the auditing techniques that are described in *Section 600*. Proper preparation is the key to a successful "no-change audit."

Table of Contents

Planning the Examination

210 *(4-23-81)* 4231
Introduction

(1) This chapter discusses preliminary planning of the examination, scope of the examination and workpaper preparation.

(2) The scope of Tax Auditor non-business returns is normally set by Classification unless the return is subject to pre-contact analysis. The auditor will not routinely extend the examination to other issues without the consent of his/her manager. Therefore, preliminary planning of these returns is customarily restricted.

(3) However, on pre-contact analysis cases for Tax Auditors and for Revenue Agent returns, preliminary planning is essential. This planning does not pre-empt an employee from expanding or contracting the scope of the audit based on his/her judgment after the examination has begun.

(4) Workpapers should conform to the standards set forth in Chapter 300 for their preparation. Pro-forma audit aids are included for use by Office Auditors in the examination of the most often examined issues.

220 *(4-23-81)* 4231
Approach to the Assignment

221 *(4-23-81)* 4231
Introduction

Because of variations in operational methods employed in various offices, all or part of this discussion may be inappropriate to some examiners. However, to the extent possible, this section should be given close scrutiny and application.

222 *(4-23-81)* 4231
Prior Examination Record

(1) Form 5546, Examination Return Charge-Out, may indicate the results of a prior examination and if it was a no-change, the issue(s) involved.

(2) In other instances, you may discover during the examination, that a prior audit occurred which may affect the current examination. You should give consideration to the possible existence of recurring issues and ensure that the taxpayer has had an opportunity to take the necessary corrective action determined in the prior examination.

223 *(4-23-81)* 4231
Time

In planning your examination, care must be exercised to spend no more time than is necessary to decide upon a proper course of action.

◀ Some returns selected for examination may require planning by the IRS or contain issues requiring research or analysis prior to contacting the taxpayer. All such returns are identified for *Pre-contact Analysis,* which involves:

- To see whether it is a complete return within the meaning of the law. For example, is it signed, and on the proper form?
- To become familiar with the case, ascertain the problem, and decide a course of action.
- To find any obvious errors or inconsistencies.
- To look for obviously questionable items.
- To scrutinize associated and related documents.
- To research unfamiliar issues and detect factual problems.

◀ Classification is the reviewing of tax returns for audit potential.

◀ Tax Auditors must restrict their exams to issues pre-announced to the taxpayer unless permission is obtained first.

224 *(4-23-81)* 4231

Scrutiny of Associated Documents

(1) Documents which may relate to the income tax liability may be attached to the income tax return or be included in the case file when the tax return is assigned to the examiner.

(2) Examples of these documents are:

(a) Information Returns Program (IRP) Reports.

1 An IRP transcript or IRP listing may be associated with the tax return. The document may contain information regarding wages, pensions, dividends, interest, gambling winnings, and other items that should be reported on the income tax return.

2 The examiner should determine whether or not the items shown on the IRP transcript or listing are properly reflected on the income tax return. Where it is not possible to make a determination based on information contained in the tax return alone, as when only total dividends or interest are shown, the examiner should secure the information from the taxpayer;

(b) Examination Information Reports (Form 5346);

(c) Notice of Examination of Fiduciary, Partnership, or Small Business Corporation Return, Form 918-A;

(d) Claim, Form 843;

(e) Tentative Carryback, Form 1045;

(f) Notice of Determination of Self-Employment Income, Form SSA-1000;

(g) Currency Transaction Reports, Form 4789; and,

(h) Informant Communications.

◀ Through the Information Returns Program (IRP) the IRS tries to identify taxpayers who have filed incorrect returns or no return at all—by matching the information on W-2s, 1099s, etc. with the universe of returns filed. Discrepancies reveal underreporters, those who haven't reported all their income; and underfilers, those who haven't filed even though the records indicate they made enough money to do so. IRP is covered in more detail in Chapter 6.

(3) All information contained in any attachment to the income tax return should be thoroughly and completely scrutinized to ascertain whether or not all of the information contained in the document is adequately reflected on the tax return.

◀ Note that the associated documents to the case may include an informant's communication precipitating the audit.

225 *(4-23-81)* 4231

Research of Unfamiliar Items

(1) On pre-contact Tax Auditor cases and Revenue Agent cases, when an examiner has completed his/her scrutiny of the return, prior examination reports, related documents, informers' letters, and other attachments, problems will often arise because of unfamiliarity with the subject.

(2) A brief period of time spent in research of these problems will in many cases avoid considerable wasted effort later. For example, if a return contains income from mineral royalties and certain deductions therefrom which are not clear to the examiner, a research into the general peculiarities of reporting such income and deductions may resolve the examiner's questions without the necessity of any further verification.

(3) The income tax law is far too complex for each agent to immediately perceive its ramifications and provisions in all returns assigned him/her from a scrutiny of the return. An examiner cannot perform adequately unless he/she is familiar with the issues on the return which scrutiny raises. In addition to these issues, additional ones will be raised during the examination which will require similar research. The tax law, regulations, Treasury decisions, rulings, court cases, the published services, and a myriad of other sources of information are the tools of the trade. No one can work without tools, and no one can improvise substitutes for such tools.

(4) The work of an income tax examiner is professional and should be viewed in that light. Nothing detracts from professional performance as much as lack of preparation for the immediate job at hand.

226 *(5-7-82)* 4231

Scope of the Examination

(1) For Tax Auditors, the scope of the examination on non-business returns not requiring pre-contact analysis will be set by Classification. However, the Tax Auditor may expand the examination when significant issues arise as a result of information secured during the examination. Also, instances may arise where, in the judgment of the Auditor a significant item was not identified during classification. In the latter instance approval of the group manager is necessary, when possible, before the scope may be expanded.

(2) For Revenue Agent returns and for Tax Auditor returns requiring pre-contact analysis, the scope of the examination will ordinarily be set by the examiner. Judgment should be exercised in determining what issues should be pursued. However, gross receipts must be probed in most of these examinations. For minimum tests, see IRM 4253.2 and IRM 4261.4. See also, Chapter 300 of this handbook.

◀ Examiners are required to research the issues before beginning. If the examiner indicates he has not really looked at the case, it could be to your advantage.

◀ This is a very interesting point: If the income tax law is far too complex for each IRS agent to immediately perceive its ramifications and provisions, then it's obviously far too complex for those preparing the returns to perceive its ramifications and provisions.

◀ Another interesting point: "A myriad of other sources of information are the tools of the trade." While the IRS examiner has a library of reference material at his or her disposal, few taxpayers have such access. Few public libraries have much in the way of reference sources on taxes. It is this complexity that almost assures you've made an honest mistake on your return and almost assures the IRS that things will work more in their favor. These reference materials are supposed to keep examiners from using poor subjective judgment and analysis.

◀ *Section 226* sets the parameters for the scope of the exam.

◀ Note the special instructions for widows in *section 226*, paragraphs (3) and (4), on the following page.

◀ A new rule requires tax auditors to carefully screen "no show/no response" examinations to "ensure that all appropriate issues have been raised and penalties applied."

◀ With only minor exceptions, the examiner is required to "probe" for gross receipts. This means checking to determine if you in fact reported all your income. The extent of the probe is up to the judgment of the examiner. However, these minimum tests will be followed:

- On nonbusiness returns, the taxpayer will be questioned about possible sources of income other than those reported.

(3) In a case involving payments to a widow, examination of the returns of the corporation and the widow should be coordinated and, if possible, conducted concurrently.

(4) Each case should be factually developed to include:

(a) the relationship of the widow, or deceased, to stockholders or directors of the corporation;

(b) the extent to which the widow, the deceased, or relatives of either hold, or held stock in the corporation;

(c) a determination, through interviews with responsible parties, as to why the payment was made;

(d) information as to whether consideration was given to the needs of the widow; and

(e) a determination as to whether the payor-corporation has a plan, practice or policy of making payments.

(5) For all Revenue Agent returns using field techniques the pre-contact and/or examination plan should preclude the inclusion of timing issues except those with long term, flagrant short term, indefinite or permanent deferral features. For additional scope limitations involving timing issues refer to IRM 4261.4:(12), Income Tax Examinations.

227 *(4-23-81)* 4231

Workpapers—Definition and Purpose

(1) An examiner's workpapers are the connecting link between the tax return and the examiner's report. Workpapers include all the evidence gathered by the examiner to show the work performed, methods and procedures followed and conclusions reached. They should also include all notes made before, during and after the examination.

(2) Perhaps the most important quality of workpapers is that they are the best evidence of the scope of the examination and the diligence with which it was completed. These papers further constitute the background for the determination of the tax liability.

(3) Workpapers prepared by an examiner may be utilized in the preparation of the report and its review as reference in cases where the determination is to be litigated, and as a source of more detailed information which may be requested later in writing.

- On nonbusiness returns containing a Schedule C or F, the examiner will follow the minimum tests applied to business returns, if the gross receipts have been targeted for examination, or if the return has been identified for precontact analysis.
- On business returns, the examiner will question the taxpayer about sources of income, his or her standard of living, purchases of assets, balances of cash on hand and in the bank, payments on loans, and receipt of borrowed funds.

◀ Based on the answer to the tests, if the examiner has reason to believe that the taxpayer may not have reported all his income, then alternative methods of discovery will be used, such as a Cash Transaction (T) Account, Source and Application of Funds or Bank Deposits Analysis method, to verify receipt of such income.

◀ Workpapers are extensive notes related to the exam.

(4) Each of the workpapers should be headed up clearly, showing the name of the taxpayer, tax year examined, date workpapers prepared, the name or initials of the examiner, and the issues or items being examined. The pages should be indexed, numbered, and securely stapled together.

(5) See Chapter 300 for discussion of the standards for workpaper preparation.

228 *(2–14–83)* 4231

Pro-Forma Audit Aids—Office Examination

(1) Pro forma audit aids have been developed for use by tax auditors on the following frequently examined items:

(a) Miscellaneous
(b) Taxes
(c) Medical
(d) Interest
(e) Casualty Loss
(f) Moving Expense
(g) Contributions
(h) Rental Income and Expenses

◀ See page 185 for the types of questions that will be asked during an audit of these items.

(2) The use of these forms is mandatory on all Office Examination cases where one or more of these items are examined. The aids were designed to assist the Tax Auditor and to provide some degree of uniformity in examination techniques and workpaper documentation.

(3) Examples of pro-forma aids are in Exhibit 200–1. The reminders listed on the pro-forma are to ensure that the Tax Auditor, at a minimum, considers these features. They are not designed to include all possible audit procedures. The pro-formas are not all inclusive as to potential issues, scope and depth of examination, or applicable audit techniques. The examiner must exercise judgment as to what additional audit techniques are necessary based on the circumstances in each case.

229 *(4–23–81)* 4231

Comparison of Audits by Public Accountants with Audits by Internal Revenue Agents

(1) Application of this section is limited to Revenue Agents due to the scope of Tax Auditor Examinations.

◀ Tax auditors do not normally audit business returns, so they will rarely review an audit report by a public accountant. In any event because the end product of a tax examination is the determination of "taxable income," the examiner cannot rely on a previously prepared audit opinion by a public accountant.

(2) The objective of the ordinary examination of financial statements by an independent auditor is the expression of an opinion on the fairness with which they present financial position and results of operations. The auditor's report is the medium through which he/she expresses

his/her opinion or, if circumstances require, disclaims an opinion. In either case, he/she states whether his/her examination has been made in accordance with generally accepted auditing standards. These standards require him/her to state whether, in his/her opinion, the financial statements are presented in conformity with generally accepted principles of accounting and whether such principles have been consistently applied in the preparation of the financial statements of the current period in relation to those of the preceding period.

◀ This section continues the discussion of why the IRS does *not* rely on or use audits by CPAs.

(3) In an audit, the independent accountant is responsible to many persons or organizations, such as the client, creditors, bank, investors, courts, and Government agencies. In accepting an engagement, an accountant often plans the scope of an audit according to the terms of the arrangements made with the client. The limitations of the audit may require qualifying statements in his/her report. The overall work performed, of course, is governed by established accounting principles and professional conduct standards.

(4) By comparison, the end product of an income tax examination is the determination of the correct taxable income, as defined by the Internal Revenue Code, and the determination of the correct income tax liability of the person or entity under examination. In making an examination, the agent has a twofold responsibility: To the taxpayer and to the Government of the United States. The responsibility to both parties is the same in that the agent is required to make a proper determination of the tax liability.

(5) In making the audit the agent is expected to pursue his/her examination to a point where he/she can, with reasonable certainty, conclude that all items necessary for a substantially proper determination of the tax liability have been considered. He/she is expected to extend his/her audit to include all unusual and questionable items. In some cases, it will be necessary to conduct an extensive audit to properly determine the tax liability; in other cases, the examination can be completed after inquiry into only one or two items on the return.

(6) A tax examination frequently will be extended beyond the scope originally intended because of situations not apparent at the outset. The amount of verification work to be done in any single tax examination is a matter of individual judgment for which no rigid rule can be established.

(7) There are differences between net income for general accounting purposes and taxable income for Federal income tax purposes. However, such differences become insignificant when compared with the vast number of transactions which are treated identically for both purposes. It should not be forgotten that the determination of taxable income and the resultant tax liability is contingent upon the net income determined for general accounting purposes.

230 *(11–2–86)* 4231

Initial Interview

(1) The initial interview is the most important part of the examination process. The first few minutes should be spent making the taxpayer comfortable and explaining the examination process and appeal rights. This would also be a good time to ask the taxpayer if he/she has any questions.

(2) Sufficient information should be developed to reach informed judgments as to:

(a) financial history and standard of living;

(b) the nature of employment to determine relationship with other entities and the existence of expense allowances, etc.; this could include the exchange of merchandise or services (bartering);

(c) any money or property received which was determined to be tax exempt and/or nontaxable income; and

(d) the potential for moonlighting income.

(3) If warranted by issues on the return or responses to previous questions, the following information should be developed:

(a) the real and personal property owned, including bank accounts, stocks and bonds, real estate, automobiles, etc., in this country and abroad.

(b) any purchases, sales, transfers, contributions or exchanges of personal assets during the period; and

(c) the correctness of exemptions and dependents claimed;

(4) Remember, the taxpayer is being examined and not just the return. Therefore, develop all information to the fullest extent possible. If the appearance of the return and response to initial questions lead the examiner to believe that indirect methods to determine income may be necessary, the factors in Chapter 500 should also be covered at this time.

(5) In Office Examination, the taxpayer's presence may be necessary at the initial interview, even if an authorized representative is present. Some examinations require information only the taxpayer would have. These include the examination of returns with:

(a) expenses in excess of reported income;

(b) gross receipts classified on a Schedule C or F;

(c) indications of possible additional income; and

(d) indications of fraud.

(6) On these examinations, if a joint return was filed, the spouse(s) who conducted the business, incurred the expenses, or maintained the books and records, should be requested to appear at the initial interview. An authorized representative may be present and participate at the interview, but the taxpayer is expected to answer questions the examiner specifically indicates.

(7) If a representative is present at the initial interview and it is not possible for the taxpayer to appear, the interview should include a telephone call to the taxpayer to secure his/her personal knowledge applicable to the return.

(8) Section 7602 of the Internal Revenue Code authorizes examiners to require taxpayer presence at the interview. However, examiners should be cautioned not to by-pass authorized representatives unless permission is granted.

▲ This section points out why you must *not* go into the audit unprepared. You *must plan in advance* what you will and will not tell the auditor.

Audit Standards for Examiners

310 *(4-23-81)* 4231

Introduction

(1) As previously stated in Chapter 100, the purpose of auditing a tax return is to determine the taxpayer's correct tax liability—no more or no less. A quality audit is the examination of a taxpayer's books and records in sufficient depth to fully develop relevant facts concerning issues of merit; ascertaining the true meaning of applicable tax laws; and correctly applying such laws to the relevant facts.

(2) One responsibility of Examination is to conduct on a timely basis quality audits of selected tax returns to determine the correct tax liability. Examination standards were developed as the level of achievement required for you to discharge this responsibility. Examination procedures necessary to achieve the standards are explained in the sections of the Manual indicated. Efforts have been made to define all standards as fully as possible; however, certain terms in the standards are intangible or subjective, and, as such, do not lend themselves to explicit definition. These include terms such as reasonable and professional judgment. Although the explanations have been written in a manner to show you the intended meaning of the terms, you must use your technical knowledge, training, and experience to correctly apply these concepts to the examination process.

320 *(4-23-81)* 4231

General Standards

(1) The examiner has a responsibility both to the taxpayer and to the government to determine the correct tax liability and to maintain a fair and impartial attitude in all matters relating to the examination.

◀ A discussion of the IRS's purpose in auditing a tax return.

(a) *Explanation*— The Service's goal of achieving the highest degree of voluntary compliance depends entirely on the cooperation and confidence of the taxpaying public. The fair and impartial attitude of an examiner aids in increasing voluntary compliance. An examiner must approach each examination with an objective point of view.

◀ Examiners must be objective and maintain the highest level of integrity.

(2) Employees must maintain the highest level of integrity and avoid circumstances that might impair or give the appearance of impairing their independence.

(a) *Explanation*

1 Examiners will disqualify themselves from the examination or survey of any return

◀ This section lists circumstances under which examiners must disqualify themselves from the case. If you have reason to believe that your examiner should disqualify himself, you should so advise the examiner, or discuss it with his manager. Failing that, notify IRS's Internal Security Division.

assigned to them when either of the following circumstances apply:

a The examiner's personal transactions with the taxpayer have been or are significant in relation to the examiner's or taxpayer's financial position; or

b The examiner's business, social, or other relationships with the taxpayer are of a nature that might impair, or give the appearance of impairing, the examiner's impartiality and independence. (See policy statement P–4–6.)

2 The circumstances in a and b apply equally to examinations of Internal Revenue Service employees and officials.

3 When the assignment of a return to an examiner meets the circumstances above, it will be the responsibility of the examiner to return the case to the examiner's manager with an appropriate explanation. In situations where the examiner is doubtful whether this policy applies, the case in question will always be returned to the examiner's manager.

4 Additional information can be found in IRM 4036, 4042, and 0735.1, Handbook of Employee Responsibilities and Conduct.

(3) The classification, examination, and review of returns will be performed by persons who have adequate technical training and experience.

(4) Professional judgment should be exercised in the identification of significant items, pre-audit planning, performance of the audit, preparation of the report, and subsequent quality review.

(a) *Explanation*

1 An important aspect of a quality examination is the use of professional judgment during various phases of the examination process. It starts with a classifier using judgment to identify significant items, continues with an examiner determing scope and depth, and ends with a reviewer ensuring that sound professional judgment was used during the entire process.

2 Professional judgment is developed through knowledge, training, and experience.

(5) Management personnel will be responsible for the effective use of all allocated resources.

330 *(4-23-81)* 4231

Standards For Examining Returns

(1) The scope of the examination should be limited or expanded to the point that the significant items necessary for a correct determination of tax liability have been considered.

(a) *Explanation—Tax Auditors*

1 The scope of the examination on non-business returns not requiring pre-contact analysis will be set by classification. The classification checksheet should list significant items that warrant examination. However, the Tax Auditor may expand the examination when significant issues arise as a result of information secured during the examination. Also, instances may arise where, in the judgment of the Auditor a significant item was not identified during classification. In the latter instance approval of the group manager is necessary, when possible, before the scope may be expanded.

(b) *Explanation—Revenue Agent*

1 The scope of the examination will be set by the revenue agent. For non-DIF returns, significant items will be identified by the classifier on the classification checksheet. However, the examiner is not precluded from extending the scope of the examination beyond the identified items or from eliminating certain items if circumstances warrant. For DIF returns, classification will not identify significant items, and the revenue agent will have sole responsibility for determining the scope of the examination.

◀ DIF returns are tax returns scored for their audit potential under IRS's Discriminant Function Computer program.

(2) Adequate evidence should be obtained through inspection, inquiry, and analysis of supporting documents to ensure full development of relevant facts concerning issues of merit.

(a) *Explanation*

1 Evidence is the sum total of all information presented by the taxpayer, representative, or third parties regarding an issue. Evidence can include the taxpayer's books and records, the taxpayer's oral statements, statements of the taxpayer's representative, statements of third parties, or documentation submitted by or obtained from third parties. If the issue involves specific recordkeeping required by law, then documentation should be presented as evidence. However, where the issue does not normally involve formal documentation, oral statements may be adequate evidence. Adequate evidence, therefore, does not require complete documentation.

◀ Your oral statement can sometimes be sufficient evidence, depending on the examiner's attitude. For certain items, however, the law requires specific bookkeeping.

Important Note: "Adequate evidence, therefore, does not require complete documentation."

2 Inspection is the critical examination of evidence presented to determine its applicability to the issue questioned and whether it is adequate substantiation for the issue under examination. Based upon the professional judgment of the examiner, it may be necessary not only to inspect the taxpayer's documents or books and records, but also to inspect the taxpayer's place of business, review his/her standard of living, and evaluate third party information.

3 Inquiry is the technique of asking a question or a logical sequence of questions, written or oral, that will secure information regarding the issue being examined or that will determine the relevance of evidence presented. The examiner may pose questions to the taxpayer(s), their representative, and, when appropriate, third parties.

4 Analysis refers to the process of arranging, sorting or scheduling the evidence presented in a logical manner to facilitate reaching conclusions regarding the issue under examination.

(3) Examination results will reflect technically correct conclusions based on consideration of all relevant facts and the proper application and interpretation of the tax laws.

(a) *Explanation*

1 When an examination is pursued to the proper depth, all relevant facts will have been accumulated. To reach technically correct conclusions, the examiner must apply the appropriate tax laws to the facts. The conclusions reached should be based on an objective interpretation of the law, whether it is in the taxpayer's or government's favor.

2 An examiner has various research materials available that will aid in arriving at technically correct conclusions:

a IRC;
b Regulations;
c Commercial Tax Services;
d Published decisions;
e Rulings; and
f Actions on decisions

3 If the examiner is still unable to reach a conclusion, the group manager should be consulted. Formal requests for technical advice should be made if appropriate (see IRM 4550). The examiner should also be aware of formal suspense issues (IRM 4559).

(4) Workpapers will fully disclose the scope, depth, and techniques used in the examination and will support all conclusions.

◀ The examiner may want to visit your business and examine your standard of living. This does not mean that you must allow the examiner in your home, or in the private portions of your business. You are required to allow an IRS agent in your home only if he has a court order.

(a) *Explanation*—The examiner's workpapers are the connecting link between the tax return and the examination report. The workpapers summarize all the evidence gathered by the examiner to indicate the depth and scope of the audit, the techniques used, and the conclusions reached. In addition to being used to prepare the examination report, workpapers are used:

1 In reviewing the case to determine if a quality audit was performed;

2 As a source of information for examiners of subsequent year returns or claims;

3 By Appeals in unagreed cases; and

4 As part of the administrative file for litigation cases.

◀ The examiner's workpapers are also used to determine how well he did his job.

(b) *Workpaper Requirements*

1 The workpapers should contain all notes made before, during, and after the examination, including a history sheet which shows all contacts made with the taxpayer(s), representative(s), third parties, etc., during the course of the audit.

2 The workpapers must be legible.

3 All significant items, whether or not changed, should be commented on in the workpapers.

(c) *Pro Forma Audit Aids*

1 Pro forma audit aids have been developed for frequently examined items. They are designed to assist the examiner and to provide uniform examination techniques and workpaper documentation. The use of these aids is mandatory.

2 The reminders listed on the pro forma aids ensure that those features are considered, but they are not all inclusive. Therefore, the examiner must determine which features are applicable in each case and whether other aspects should also be considered.

◀ Pro-Forma audit aids are designed to help the examiner with minimum considerations. They are the basic questions the examiner will ask when inquiring about taxes, medical, interest, and miscellaneous expenses.

340 *(4-23-81)* 4231

Definition of Significant

(1) Invariably, the definition of significant will depend on your perception of the return as a whole and the separate items that comprise the return. There are several factors, however, that you must consider when determining whether an item is significant. These factors are:

(a) Comparative size of the item—A questionable expense item of $6,000 with total expenses of $30,000 would be significant; however, if total expenses are $300,000, ordinarily the item would not be significant.

◀ Pay particular attention to the six factors [list (a) through (f) under point (1)] that must be considered when the examiner determines that an item is "significant."

(b) Absolute size of the item—Despite the comparability factor, size by itself may be significant. For example, a $50,000 item may be significant even though it represents a small percentage of taxable income.

(c) Inherent character of the item—Although the amount of an item may be insignificant, the nature of the item may be significant. For example, airplane expenses claimed on a plumber's schedule C may be significant.

(d) Evidence of intent to mislead—This may include missing, misleading or incomplete schedules or incorrectly showing an item on the return.

(e) Beneficial effect of the manner in which an item is reported—Expenses claimed on a business schedule rather than claimed as an itemized deduction may be significant.

(f) Relationship to/with other item(s) on a return—No deduction for interest expense when real estate taxes are claimed may be significant. Similarily, the lack of dividends reported when Schedule D shows sales of stock may be significant.

(2) Generally, automatic adjustments (obvious errors or omissions on the return) in excess of the 241 LEM IV tolerance will be considered significant items.

◄ LEM IV is a reference to part four of IRS's *Law Enforcement Manual* that is not available to the public.

(3) During classification, all significant items will be identified for examination on the classification checksheet for those returns requiring checksheets.

(4) Consideration should be given to items that are not shown on the return, but would normally appear on returns of the same examination class. This applies not only to unreported income items, but also for deductions, credits, etc. that would result in tax changes favorable to the taxpayer.

(5) The examiner's report will be clear, concise, and legible, accurately computing the tax, taking into account all automatic adjustments and using the method most beneficial to the taxpayer.

(a) *Explanation (Office Examination)*

1 IRM 428(10), Report Writing Guide for Income Tax Examiners, contains detailed instructions and procedures which should be followed in preparing examination reports.

2 Automated report writing equipment will be used where available.

3 The report should include all necessary information so that both the taxpayer and reviewers will have a clear understanding of the

adjustments made to the return and the reason(s) for those adjustments. If a standard paragraph exists for an adjustment, it must be used as the explanation.

4 Automatic adjustments are those changes to items on the return necessitated by the adjustment of other items. For example, a change to the medical expense deduction based on a change to adjusted gross income is an automatic adjustment. Another example is a change from itemized deductions to the zero bracket amount when, as a result of another adjustment, the zero bracket amount becomes more beneficial.

5 If it appears that a more beneficial method of tax computation is available to the taxpayer, the examiner should secure any information necessary to make such computation, and that method should be used to determine the correct tax liability. The tax change tolerances in 241 of LEM IV will be adhered to in all examinations.

(b) *Explanation (Field Examination)*

1 IRM 428(10), Report Writing Guide, contains detailed instructions and procedures which should be followed in preparing examination reports.

2 The report should include all necessary information so that both the taxpayer and reviewers will have a clear understanding of the adjustments made to the return and the reason(s) for those adjustments.

3 Automatic adjustments are those changes to items on the return necessitated by the adjustment of other items. For example, a change to the medical expense deduction based on a change to adjusted gross income is an automatic adjustment. Another example is an adjustment to allowable investment credit due to a change in the tax liability limitation which is caused by another adjustment.

4 If it appears that a more beneficial method of tax computation is available to the taxpayer, the examiner should secure any information necessary to make such computation, and the method should be used to determine the correct tax liability. The tax change tolerances in 241 of LEM IV will be adhered to in all examinations.

▲ Examiners are also required to make changes in your favor should they be warranted. If you omitted a deduction or expense when preparing the return, you are allowed to bring it up during the audit and the examiner is required to allow it if it passes all the requirements.

Important Note!
Chapter 500 of IRM *(Internal Revenue Manual)* (IRM) Section 4231 includes all of the IRS's audit instructions by individual line items of income, expenses, deductions, and credits. This section can be very valuable to you in audit-proofing your tax return. By knowing what particular questions, information, and documentation you will be asked to furnish the IRS, you can better prepare yourself for an audit early on.

Audit Techniques

510 *(4-23-81)* 4231

Individual Returns

511 *(4-23-81)* 4231

Introduction

The examiner should become familiar with the name(s), address, occupation(s), and filing status shown on the return. Reference to this information will be important as the examination progresses.

512 *(4-23-81)* 4231

Filing Status

(1) If the return indicates that a joint return, head of household, or surviving spouse status has been claimed, determine the validity of the status.

(2) If separate returns have been filed by persons entitled to file jointly, ascertain the similarity of treatment with respect to standard or itemized deductions.

(3) Examiners should pursue filing status when other features indicate that the status is questionable.

513 *(4-23-81)* 4231

Dependency Exemption Cases

513.1 *(4-23-81)* 4231

Proof of Dependency

(1) Taxpayers have the burden of proof when claiming an exemption deduction. However, in certain situations they may not have the information to complete this requirement. One such situation occurs when the dependent does not live in the household of the taxpayer, or lives there only a part of the year.

(2) In cases of the foregoing type, taxpayers will be furnished questionnaires to secure the necessary information from the head(s) of household in which the dependent resided. The questionnaire will be accompanied by the district's preaddressed envelope for direct mailing by the other taxpayer if he/she so desires. The questionnaire provided is Form 2038 (Questionnaire—Exemption Claimed For Dependent).

(3) If the examiner is satisfied that the taxpayer has furnished the major support, the exemption for the dependent(s) will be allowed. Conversely, if the examiner is satisfied that the taxpayer has not furnished major support, the exemption for the dependent(s) will be disal-

Filing Status. Your filing status determines which column in the tax table or which tax rate schedule you should use to arrive at your correct tax. Married taxpayers may be able to file a joint return or they may file separate returns. Some taxpayers may qualify as head of household. You must file single if on the last day of your tax year you are not married or are separated from your spouse by divorce or separate maintenance decree and you do not qualify for another filing status. State law governs whether you are married, divorced or legally separated under a decree of separate maintenance.

Dependency Tests. The following *five* tests must be met for a person to be your dependent:

- Member of Household or Relationship Test.
- Citizenship Test.
- Joint Return Test.
- Gross Income Test.
- Support Test.

Member of Household or Relationship Test. To meet this test, an unrelated person must live with you for the entire year as a member of your household.

◂ A person related to you in any of the following ways need not live with you or be a member of your household to meet this test.

- Your child, grandchild, great grandchild, a legally adopted child, or stepchild.
- Your brother, sister, half brother, half sister, stepbrother, or stepsister.
- Your parent, grandparent, or other direct ancestor, but not foster parent.
- Your stepfather or stepmother.
- A brother or sister of your father or mother.
- A son or daughter of your brother or sister.
- Your father-in-law, mother-in-law, son-in-law, daughter-in-law, brother-in-law, or sister-in-law.

lowed. These determinations may be possible even though total support amounts are not available. In these situations, the inquiry procedure in (4) below will not be necessary unless the case is unagreed. However, Form 5346 (Examination Information Report) should be prepared when it appears that the same dependent may have been claimed by another taxpayer. If the examination originating from the Form 5346 results in allowing the dependents and the return is otherwise acceptable as filed, the regular no-change procedure may be followed. In such cases, the originating district will be advised of the findings by use of Form 5346.

(4) When the taxpayer is unable to furnish sufficient information to show major support of dependent(s) residing in another household, even though he/she did attempt to secure the information by use of the questionnaire, districts may request the information direct from the taxpayer. For this purpose, Letter 977(C/DO) (Third Party Inquiry—Questionable Exemption) will be used when appropriate and necessary. Requests will be limited to cases in which the taxpayer has shown that substantial support payments were made, but additional facts are necessary to determine who furnished the major support for the dependent(s). Letter 977(C/DO) advises the taxpayer that his/her return is not being examined.

(5) When the inquiry procedure does not result in obtaining sufficient facts to resolve the exemption issue, the other taxpayer's return, if filed in the same district, will be inspected for duplicate exemption(s) and, if necessary, will be examined. However, when the dependent resides with a taxpayer in another district, Form 4217 (Duplicate Exemption and Alimony Inquiry) will be used to request a collateral examination. This request will first be reviewed as prescribed in IRM 4416:(1).

(6) If the receiving district determines that a duplicate exemption is not involved, a reply to that effect will be sufficient; however, collateral examination procedures will apply to all other cases.

(7) The related case procedure in IRM 4224.1 will apply only in unagreed cases involving more than one taxpayer, both under examination, and claiming the same dependent(s). This does not include cases in which it is not

Citizenship Test. A person must be a U.S. citizen, resident, or national, or a resident of Canada or Mexico for some part of the calendar in which your tax year begins.

Joint Return Test. You are not allowed an exemption for your married dependent if he or she files a joint return; except if neither your dependent nor the dependent's spouse is legally required to file a return but they do so only to claim a refund of taxes withheld.

Gross Income Test. Generally, you may not take an exemption for a dependent if that person had $1,080 or more gross income for the year (1986).

◀ Gross income is all income in the form of money, property, and services that is not exempt from tax.

◀ If your child is under 19 at the end of the year, this test does not apply, and he or she may have any amount of income and still be your dependent, if the other four dependency tests are met.

◀ If your child is a student, the gross income test does *not* apply. The child's age does not matter. You may claim your child as a dependent if the other four dependency tests are met.

Support Test. You must provide more than half of a person's total support during the calendar year. You figure this by comparing the amount you contributed to the person's support with the entire support received from all sources, including the person's own funds used for support. You may not include in your contribution any part of the support that is paid for by your child with the child's own wages, even if you pay the wages.

known whether or not the other taxpayer is under examination.

513.2 *(4-29-86)* 4231

Children of Divorced or Separated Parents

(1) Special rules apply to determine which parent (divorced, legally separated, or separated under a written agreement, or who lived apart at all times during the last six months of the calendar year) is entitled to the dependency exemption for a child.

(2) Generally, the parent having custody for the longer period of time during the year is entitled to the exemption if;

(a) the parents together furnished more than one-half of the child's support without regard to any multiple support agreements, and

(b) the child is in the custody of either or both of the parents for more than one-half of the year.

(3) The custodial parent may waive the right to the exemption in favor of the noncustodial parent by signing a written declaration that he or she will not claim the exemption. This waiver must be attached to the return of the noncustodial parent on which the exemption is claimed.

(4) A special exception exists if a pre-1985 instrument (decree of divorce, separate maintenance or written agreement) provided the noncustodial parent with the dependency exemption. The noncustodial parent can claim the exemption if he or she provided at least $600 for the support of the dependent child during the calendar year.

513.3 *(4-23-81)* 4231

Disclosure of Dependency Information

(1) An officer or employee of the Service is prohibited from disclosing to a taxpayer information furnished by the taxpayer's former spouse about amounts claimed for support of their child. The taxpayer may be informed only that the amount expended by him/her is not

Support Test for Divorced or Separated Parents. The support test for a child of divorced or separated parents is based on special rules that apply only if:

- The parents are divorced, legally separated under a decree of divorce or separate maintenance, separated under a written separation agreement, or lived apart at all times during the last six months of the calendar year; and
- One or both parents provide more than half the child's total support for the calendar year; and
- One or both parents have custody of the child for more than half the calendar year.

◀ *Exceptions.* This discussion does not apply in any of the following situations:

- A third party, such as a relative or a friend, provides half or more of the child's support;
- The child is in the custody of a person other than the parents for half the year or more;
- The support of the child is determined under a multiple support agreement;
- The parents are separated under a written separation agreement, but they file a joint return for the tax year;
- The parents live apart without a written separation agreement or decree of divorce or separate maintenance; or
- The child is not the child of the divorced or separated parents.

◀ Note: For tax years beginning after 1984, the rules have changed for the support test for a child of divorced or separated parents. See IRS Publication 504.

Child Support. In figuring the support each parent provides, for the purpose of these exceptions, all child support payments actually received from the parent who does not have custody are considered used for the support of the child. For example, the total support of a child is $1,500, and the parent not having custody provides $1,200 for the child's support. This amount is considered as support provided by the parent who does not have custody even if the $1,200 was actually spent on things other than support.

sufficient to establish his/her right to the claimed dependency deduction.

(2) An exception to the disclosure of dependency information is provided for taxable years beginning after December 31, 1966. The exception applies when the parent not having custody claims to have furnished more than $1,200 of support and the parent having custody claims that such amount was not furnished, or claims to have furnished the greater amount of support. In such a case, each parent is entitled to receive an itemized statement of the expenditures upon which the other's claim of support is based. This itemized statement will be limited to the information in Form 2038. A request for such information need not be in writing, nor must a request be made before an examiner is permitted to disclose such information. Disclosure of such information may be informal and not necessarily in writing except when so requested.

Property Transfers Pursuant to a Divorce

(1) Transfers of property before July 19, 1984, and transfers of property after July 18, 1984, made under instruments in effect before July 19, 1984, from one spouse to another incident to a divorce property settlement can result in the recognition of gain or loss.

(2) The Tax Reform Act of 1984 amended the law relative to these provisions. The new rules apply to transfers of property after July 18, 1984. However, these rules will not apply to transfers after July 18, 1984, made under instruments in effect before July 19, 1984, unless both parties elect to have the new rules apply. Also, these new rules can apply to all transfers made after December 31, 1983, if both parties elect to have the new rules apply. Under these new rules:

(a) No gain or loss will be recognized to the transferor in the case of transfers of property between spouses (except where the transferee is determined to be a non resident alien) or between former spouses incident to divorce;

(b) The basis of the transferred property in the hands of the transferor will carry over and become the basis of the property in the hands of the transferee; and

(c) The transfer is treated as a gift for income tax purposes and is therefore excludable from the transferee's income.

◀ *Itemized statement.* In cases involving the exception under *Section 513.2:(3)* on the previous page, either parent can request an itemized statement of support provided by the other parent for the child. The parent requesting the statement must notify the other parent in writing of the intent to take the exemption and must provide an itemized statement on which the claim is based. A failure to make the request will not affect the right to take the exemption. Upon receiving the request and itemized statement, the second parent must inform the first parent of any intent to take the child's exemption and, if requested, send the first parent a copy of the itemized statement on which the second parent is basing a claim for the child's exemption.

◀ The custodial parent should use IRS Form 8332, Release of Claim to Exemption for Child of Divorced or Separated Parents, or a similar statement, to make the written declaration to release the exemption to the noncustodial parent. The statement should include the following information:

- The name of the child being claimed, names of both parents, and, if known, the addresses and social security numbers of both parents;
- The number of months during the calendar year the child lived in the home of each parent or person other than the parents, the amount of income of the child, and the total amount of support for the child, including amounts provided by persons other than the parents;
- An itemized listing of the amounts spent during the year by the parent making the statement for medical and dental care, food, lodging, clothing, education, recreation, and transportation;
- Amounts actually paid by the parent making the statement for the support of the child that were required by a divorce decree or written separation agreement; and
- Other amounts paid for support of the child during the year by the person making the statement.

◀ *Attaching statement to return.* If you claim a child as a dependent and you have either made or received a request for an itemized statement, you must attach to your return a copy of your itemized statement and a copy of the other parent's itemized statement, if available, when you file your return. If you are reasonably sure that the other parent will not claim the child as a dependent, you do not have to attach the statement to your return.

◀ The exemption may be released for a single year, for a number of specified years, alternate years, or for all future years, as specified in the declaration. If the exemption is released for more than one year, the original release must be attached to the return of the noncustodial parent for the first year of such release, and a copy of the release must be attached to the return for each succeeding taxable year for which the noncustodial parent claims the exemption.

520 *(4-23-81)* 4231

Income

521 *(4-23-81)* 4231

Introduction

Examiners must be alert to detect the possibilities of omitted income. Some indications of possible unreported income may be apparent on the face of the return. If income reported appears insufficient to meet the cost of living and other disbursements including those claimed on the return and substantiated during the examination, examiners should ask questions designed to uncover potential sources of income not reported on the return. Two sources are moonlighting income and income from bartering. The reasons for failure to report the income should be developed and the file documented accordingly. Minimum probes are located at IRM 4241.5 and 4253.2.

522 *(4-23-81)* 4231

Income—Wages and Salaries, Unemployment Benefits, etc.

(1) Review compensation arrangement to determine special privileges (paid vacations, use of company car, etc.).

(2) Particular consideration should be given to the source of taxpayer's income as certain occupations and trades are more susceptible than others to omitted income. Some examples are:

◀ Examiners are instructed to be on the lookout for signs of unreported income. *Section 61* of the Internal Revenue Code defines gross income to mean *all income from whatever source derived,* including but not limited to the following items:

- Compensation for services including fees, commissions, fringe benefits and similar items.
- Gross income derived from business.
- Gains derived from dealings in property.
- Interest.
- Rents.
- Royalties.
- Dividends.
- Alimony and separate maintenance payments.
- Annuities.
- Income from life insurance and endowment contracts.
- Pensions.
- Income from discharge of indebtedness.
- Distributive share of partnership gross income.
- Income in respect of a decedent.
- Income from an interest in an estate or trust.

◀ IRS regulations expound on the gross income definition by providing that gross income includes income realized in any form, whether in money, property, or services. It also means all income from whatever source derived, unless specifically excluded by law. Income may be realized, there-

(a) Members of certain trades usually work for contractors from whom they receive a W-2. Due to the nature of their work, they may do part-time work for homeowners and others who may not file W-2's. They should be directly questioned as to the possible existence of such income.

(b) Itinerants, such as fruit-pickers and seasonal workers, may have income from other sources during the off-season.

(c) Practical nurses may be employed by individuals, as well as by hospitals or rest homes and the wages received from individuals may not be covered by a Form W-2.

(d) Returns of taxpayers reporting income from occupations where tips are commonly received should be carefully reviewed to determine if this income was reported. Taxpayers who receive tip income may not maintain complete and accurate records. The examiner should test check to determine the accuracy of the amounts reported.

1 If an adjustment to FICA tax on tip income is made, Form 885-T will be prepared in a minimum of an original and one copy. A copy of only the Schedule T-A will be attached to the front of the case file. The Schedule T-A will serve as a flag to the self-employment control clerk and will be sent to Social Security Administration. The top portion of the form will constitute the employment tax report going to the taxpayer.

2 The following special instructions will be followed in preparing Schedule T-A (Form 885-T).

a *Section A*—Include increase or decrease in tip income not reported to employer. Decreases should be shown in brackets. The total adjustment should be distributed equally to the four quarters unless the taxpayer submits information which establishes that the tips were not earned every month.

b *Section B*—Enter the taxpayer's occupation that accounts for the tip income. Enter the social security number of the taxpayer whose tip income is being adjusted.

c *Section C*—The taxpayer's name and address *must* be correct. This information and the social security number should be verified with the taxpayer.

d *Section D*—This block should always be answered. Social Security Administration needs this information to determine the proper adjustment of taxpayer's earnings record.

fore, in the form of services, meals, accommodations, stock or other property as well as in cash. The Supreme Court first defined income in Eisner vs. Macomber as "the gain derived from capital, from labor, or from both combined; provided, it be understood to include profit gain through a sale or conversion of capital assets." In addition the Supreme Court has repeatedly held that Congress' broad definition of what constitutes gross income was intended to tax all gain unless specifically exempted.

◀ The following representative list shows the range of taxable income items.

Alimony
Annuities
Awards
Babysitting Income
Back Pay
Barter Income
Bonuses
Breach of Contract Damages
Business Income
Commissions
Compensation for Personal Services
Debts Forgiven
Directors' Fees
Dividends
Election Precinct Officials' Fees
Employees' Awards
Employees' Bonuses
Estate and Trust Income
Executors' Fees
Fees
Gain from Sale of Property
Gambling Winnings
Hobby Income
Illegal Income
Interest
Jury Duty Fees
Lottery Winnings
Mileage Allowance
Military Pay
Notary Fees
Partnership Income
Pensions
Per Diem Allowance
Prizes
Rents
Retirement Pay
Rewards
Royalties
Salaries
Severance Pay
Supplemental Unemployment Benefits
Tips and Gratuities
Travel Allowance
Wages

◀ You must include in your gross income *everything* you receive in payment for personal services, including many so-called "fringe-benefits," as well as wages, salaries, commissions, tips, and fees. You must report income you receive in the form of goods or services at their *fair market value*.

e *Section E*—Refile number will be entered by the service center.

(3) Low income of one spouse may indicate the other spouse received income and possibly did not receive a Form W-2 or 1099. The possibility of unreported income is increased if the amount of income reported seems inadequate in view of the reported exemptions and deductions. In these circumstances, the examiner should ask specific questions to determine if additional income was received.

(4) For taxable years beginning after December 31, 1978, unemployment compensation may be taxable. Examiners should be alert to unemployment benefits which may not have been reported.

(5) Be alert to outside employment, prizes, tips, etc.

(6) Development of information verifying reported deductions or income may reveal facts indicating the taxpayer is the beneficiary of an estate or trust and should have reported distributable income from that source.

523 *(4-23-81)* 4231

Income from Bartering

(1) When verifying income, the examiner should be alert to the possibility of "bartering" or "swapping" techniques or schemes. Such noncash exchanges may be done directly; however, the greater volume of these exchanges is handled through reciprocal trade agencies. Both services and inventory may be exchanged for "credits." These "credits" can then be used to obtain other goods or services. Bartering does result in taxable income and should be reported as such.

(2) Some areas of possible tax abuse are as follows:

(a) Nonrecognition of current income.

(b) The trading of services or inventory for capital assets (which would convert ordinary income to capital gain) or for fixed assets (which should be depreciated over the useful life of the assets).

(c) The exchange of inventory or services for personal goods and services, such as vacations, houseboats, luxury cars, use of vacation home or condominium, or payment of personal or stockholder debts.

(3) In addition, examiners should be alert for the following:

◀ *Recordkeeping*. You must keep accurate records of all your earnings that are not subject to withholding.

◀ *Constructive Receipt*. You constructively receive income when it is credited to your account, or otherwise made available to you, even if you do not take physical possession of it.

◀ *Advance commissions and other earnings*. If you receive advance commissions or other amounts for services to be performed in the future, and you are a cash method taxpayer, you must include these amounts in income in the year received. If you repay unearned commissions or other amounts later in the same year in which you received them, you reduce the amount includable in your income by the repayment. However, if you repay the unearned commissions or other amounts in a later tax year, you may deduct the repayment only as an itemized deduction on Schedule A (Form 1040).

◀ *Bartering* is an exchange of property or services for your property or services. You must include in income the fair market value, at the time received, of property or services you receive in bartering. If you receive the services of another in return for your services and you both have agreed ahead of time as to the value of the services, that value will be accepted as fair market value unless the value can be shown to be otherwise.

◀ If you exchanged property or services through a barter exchange during the year, you should have received from the barter exchange, Form 1099-B, "Statement for Recipients of Proceeds from Broker and Barter Exchange Transactions," or a similar statement by January 31 of the following year. The statement should have shown the value of cash, property, services, credits, or scrip you received from exchanges during the year. The IRS should also have a copy of the statement.

◀ *Example:* You are a member of a barter club. The club uses "credit units" as a means of exchange. It adds credit units to your account for goods or services you provide to other members, and it subtracts credit units from your account for goods or services you receive from other members. You must include in your income the value of credit units that are added to your account, even though you do not actually receive goods or services from other members until a later tax year.

(a) Deductions and/or payments for credit liability insurance or insurance guaranteeing lines of credit.

(b) Deductions and/or payments for membership fees, annual dues, or service charges to specialized reciprocal trading companies.

(c) The write-off or mark-down of inventory, especially for excess or supposedly obsolete inventory.

(d) The factoring or sale of accounts or notes receivable to specialized reciprocal trading firms.

524 *(4-23-81)* 4231

Dividend Income

(1) The examination of dividend income reported by the taxpayer should not be limited to the information documents attached to the return. If more than $100 is excluded, the ownership of securities by both husband and wife should be ascertained.

(2) The method used by the taxpayer in determing dividend income should be secured. Understanding the method used may suggest the most appropriate way to check for accuracy. A list of securities owned at the beginning of the taxable year, used in conjunction with subsequent sales and acquisitions, will afford the most exact results.

(3) If the taxpayer merely records dividends when received and also keeps some securities in the broker's custody, the broker's monthly statements should be checked for dividends credited to the account. Most taxpayers who have security trades during the year retain their monthly statements. These statements should be checked when verifying dividend income.

(4) The examiner should verify the accuracy of claims that dividend income is either fully or partially tax-exempt, or nontaxable, such as distributions representing partial return of capital.

(5) Be aware of duplication of credits such as foreign dividends received and recorded net of foreign tax paid, and a further credit being taken on the return.

(6) Be alert for stock splits which increase the number of shares upon which the taxpayer would receive dividend income.

525 *(5-26-82)* 4231

Interest Income

(1) Be alert to income from interest on income tax refunds and savings accounts which may not appear on the tax return or taxpayer's records.

(2) Interest earned on "qualified tax-exempt savings certificates" may be excluded from a taxpayer's return. Verify that certificates qualify and that the amount of the exclusion claimed is proper.

◄ *Dividends* are distributions of money, stock, or other property paid to you by a corporation. You also may receive dividends through a partnership, an estate, a trust, or an association that is taxed as a corporation.

◄ *Form 1099-DIV.* Most corporations use Form 1099-DIV, "Statement for Recipients of Dividends and Distributions," or a similar statement, to report to you and the IRS the distributions you receive from the corporation. Keep this form with your records. You do not have to attach it to your tax return.

◄ Before 1987 you could exclude up to $100 of the total qualifying dividends you received. If you filed a joint return, you could exclude up to $200, no matter which spouse received the dividend.

◄ The Form 1099-DIV you receive will show you whether the dividends you received qualify for the exclusion.

◄ In general, interest that you receive or that is credited to your account so that you can withdraw it is taxable.

◄ As an important part of your records, you should keep a list showing sources and amounts of interest received during the year.

◄ *Form 1099-INT,* "Statement for Recipients of Interest Income," is used by banks, savings and loans, and other payers of interest to report to you and the IRS the interest you received. Keep this form for your records. You do not have to attach it to your tax return.

(3) Verify claims that interest from state or municipal bonds is either fully or partially tax-exempt.

(4) Taxpayers should be asked whether they have cashed or transferred any Government bonds, held any matured Government bonds, or had any savings accounts during the taxable year. When ownership of Series E Bonds is transferred, interest income earned must be reported in the year of transfer.

(5) The verification of interest income should also be made in conjunction with the examination of capital transactions. Interest bearing securities sold during the year should be compared to interest reported. The interest accrued to date of sale is sometimes reported as part of the proceeds, rather than as interest income.

(6) Verify that savings and loan interest, as well as credit union interest, through commonly called dividends, has been treated as interest income for tax purposes.

(7) Verify that other interest income items such as interest on paid up insurance policies, interest on prior year tax refunds, interest on G.I. insurance dividends on deposit with the Veterans Administration, and interest on insurance dividends on deposit with an insurance company which are withdrawable upon demand have been reported.

(8) If property was sold in prior or current years and a purchase money mortgage or second mortgage constituted part payment, interest income should be reflected in the return. Verify that mortgage collections have been allocated to principal and interest.

(9) Verify that interest received on a condemnation award has been included as ordinary income.

526 *(4-23-81)* 4231

State Tax Refunds

Verify that state income tax refunds which caused a decrease in tax in prior years have been included in income in the year refunded. In some instances, taxpayers include in income only the actual amount of state income tax refund received and not the refund figure per the state tax return. Taxpayers may take the position that the difference, credited to state estimated taxes, is not included in income since expenses of equivalent amount would also have to be included and, therefore, a wash results. This is not true in cases where a taxpayer is subject to the minimum tax due to excess itemized deductions. In these situations, any increase in AGI or itemized deductions results in an increase in the tax preference item subject to the minimum tax computation. Similarly, in the maximum tax computation, any increase in AGI will reduce the percentage of income subject to the maximum tax.

◀ Interest you receive from bank accounts, loans you make to others, and from most other sources is taxable.

◀ Certain distributions commonly referred to as dividends are actually interest. You must report as interest the so-called "dividends" on deposits or on share accounts in:

- Cooperative Banks
- Credit Unions
- Domestic Building and Loan Associations
- Domestic Savings and Loan Associations
- Federal Savings and Loan Associations
- Mutual Savings Banks

◀ Interest on U.S. obligations, such as U.S. Treasury bills, notes, and bonds, issued by an agency or instrumentality of the United States, is subject to federal income tax, but exempt from all state and local income taxes.

◀ You may earn interest on U.S. Savings bonds in one of two ways. Some bonds are issued at a discount and the interest is the increase in their value, over stated periods of time. On others, interest is paid at stated intervals by check or coupon.

◀ When you cash a bond, the bank or other payer that redeems it must give you a Form 1099-INT if the interest part of the payment you receive is $10 or more. Your Form 1099-INT should show the difference between the amount received and the amount paid for the bond.

Refunds of State and Local Income Taxes. If you received a refund (or credit or offset) of state or local income taxes this year that you paid last year, you may receive Form 1099-G, "Statement for Recipients of Certain Government Payments," showing the refund. Do not overlook the fact that you may have to report all or part of this amount as income, if the deduction for state and local income taxes in the year you paid the taxes resulted in a tax benefit.

Tax Benefit Rule. If you recover amounts from an item you deducted in a prior year, such as a state income tax refund, you generally must include the recovered amount in income in the year the amount is recovered. You do not include a recovery in income, however, if the prior year deduction did not reduce that year's tax liability. This rule affects individuals who had no taxable income in the year of the deduction, who were subject to the alternative minimum tax, or who had unused tax credits in the year of the deduction. This tax benefit rule is retroactive to 1984. See IRS Pub. 525.

527 *(11-2-86)* 4231

Alimony Income

(1) If the initial interview discloses the taxpayer is divorced or separated, explore the possible receipt of alimony.

(2) Combination alimony and child support payment agreements should be scrutinized for the portion reportable as alimony.

(3) For divorce or separation instruments executed after 1984, there are new rules for payments to qualify as alimony.

528 *(4-23-81)* 4231

Pensions and Annuities

528.1 *(4-23-81)* 4231

Basic Elements and Verification

(1) The four basic elements used in determining the taxable portion of amounts received as a pension or annuity are:

(a) the investment in the contract or the cost of the annuity;

(b) tax-free cost recovery in the past;

(c) the expected return; and

(d) payments received during the taxable year.

(2) The examiner should verify the source of the payments, verify investment in the contract, expected return, and amounts received with proper allowance for refund features.

(3) If employer-employee annuity, determine whether proper reporting has been made.

(4) Military retirement pay, based upon age or length of service, is taxable. However, the amount of reduction in retirement or retainer pay to provide a survivor annuity for a spouse or children is not included in income.

(5) Veterans' disability compensation paid either to the veteran or the family is exempt from tax.

(6) Old age pensions granted for consideration for other than past services are taxable as compensation and are not treated as annuities.

(7) Old age pensions received under the Social Security Act or under the Railroad Retirement Act are entirely exempt from tax.

528.2 *(4-23-81)* 4231

Employer-Employee Financed Plans

The Code distinguishes between employer-employee financed annuities where the em-

◀ *Alimony is income.* Alimony, separate maintenance, or similar periodic payments that you receive are taxable as income to you. You must use Form 1040, not Form 1040EZ or Form 1040A, to report your alimony income. *Note:* For divorce or separation instruments executed after 1984, the requirements have been changed for payments to qualify as alimony. For information, see Publication 504.

Employee Pensions or Annuities. Generally, if you did not pay part of the cost of your employee pension or annuity, or your employer did not withhold part of the cost of the contract from your pay while you worked, the amounts you receive each year are fully taxable and must be reported on your income tax return.

◀ If both you and your employer pay part of the cost of your pension or annuity, you will not pay tax on the part of the pension or annuity you receive that represents a return of your cost. Any additional amount you receive will be taxable. You use either the Three-Year Rule or the General Rule to determine the taxable and nontaxable parts of your pension or annuity.

◀ Your employer or the organization that pays you the benefits should be able to tell you exactly how much you have paid into the plan, what your investment in the contract (your cost) is, and how many months it will take you to recover this amount starting from the date of the first benefit payment.

Three-Year Rule. You must use the Three-Year Rule for any amounts you receive under an employer sponsored pension or annuity plan if:

- Your employer paid part of the cost; and
- You will get back your cost, or what is considered your cost, within three years from the time you get the first payment.

◀ *Taxable amount.* If you will recover the full amount of your cost within three years from the time you receive your first payment, no amounts you receive are taxed until you recover your cost. Thereafter, all amounts you receive are included in your income.

◀ *Note:* The Three-Year Rule has been repealed for any individual whose annuity starting date, as defined next, is after July 1, 1986. The General Rule remains in effect.

The *annuity starting date* is the later of the first day of the first period that you receive a payment from the plan, or the date on which the plan's obligation became fixed.

ployee's cost will be recovered within 3 years, and between other so-called general rule annuities. If the taxpayer claims the cost is recoverable within 3 years, the examiner should verify this fact.

528.3 *(4-23-81)* 4231
Purchased Annuities

(1) Some purchased annuity contracts contain a life insurance feature. If the life insurance remains in effect after payments are received by the annuitant under the contract, that portion of the amount paid which is attributable to the insurance feature should be eliminated from the cost of the annuity. It may be necessary for the taxpayer to secure this information from the insurance company.

(2) Most insurance companies furnish annuitants with a statement showing the exact amount to be entered on Form 1040. The amounts are keyed directly to the annuity schedules on that form. Where the taxpayer produces such a statement, it may usually be accepted without further verification.

529 *(4-23-81)* 4231
Capital Gains and Losses

(1) The technique to be used in the examination of the gains and losses reported on a return will vary depending on the nature of the asset. The two broad classifications of assets, both under the law and for purposes of audit approach, are capital assets and all other assets.

(2) The verification of gains and losses involves several elements; the selling price, expenses of sale, the adjusted basis of the property, and the holding period.

529.1 *(4-23-81)* 4231
Selling Price

(1) The settlement statement is the best approach to verify the transaction. The taxpayer should be requested to submit the settlement statements.

(2) Sales of securities, options, and commodity market transactions are normally effected through brokers. When such is the case, the brokerage "bought" and "sold" slips and the broker's monthly statements are the best ap-

General Rule. If you are not required to recover your cost using the Three-Year Rule, you must use the General Rule. First, divide your cost (contribution) by the amount you expect to receive (your expected return) to derive the *exclusion percentage*. The first regular periodic payment you receive is then multiplied by the exclusion percentage to figure the part *not* taxed. This tax-free part always remains the same, even if the total payment increases or you outlive the life expectancy factor used to figure your expected return. The remaining part of each payment is fully taxable as income.

◀ For more information on the General Rule, see IRS Pub. 575, which not only tells you how to figure your expected return and exclusion percentage, but also contains certain actuarial tables you will need.

◀ For tax years beginning after 1986, the 60% long-term capital gains deduction is repealed. Thus, beginning in 1987, you must treat all capital gains, whether long-term or short-term, as ordinary income. However, the income tax rate for individuals on net capital gains (net long-term capital gains over net short-term capital loss) occurring during the 1987 calendar year will not exceed 28%.

Be aware that the Tax Reform Act of 1986 did not eliminate the Code provisions that distinguished between ordinary or capital income, or between long-term and short-term gains and losses. Those distinctions were retained should Congress reinstate the capital gains rate differential in the event of a future tax rate increase.

◀ A *gain* is the excess of the amount you realize from a sale or exchange over the adjusted basis of the property. A *loss* is the excess of the adjusted basis of the property over the amount you realize from the sale or exchange. Capital losses are still allowed in full against capital gains plus up to $3,000 of ordinary income. The excess of net long-term capital loss over net short-term capital gain will be allowed in full. You no longer have to reduce long-term capital losses by 50% before applying them against ordinary income. You may still carry forward to future years those capital losses not fully deducted in the current tax year.

◀ *Basis* is a way of measuring your investment in property for tax purposes. You must know the basis of your property to figure depreciation, amortization, depletion, casualty losses, or whether you have a gain or loss on its sale or

proach to this phase of an examination. The transaction slips state the purchase price or sales price, the commissions, the transfer taxes (Federal and local), and accrued interest where appropriate. In addition, the dates of the transaction are clearly set forth.

(3) If the transactions reported were not made through a broker, the proceeds and expenses of sale should receive closer scrutiny. Disposition of securities in a closely held corporation should be checked as to the valuation of property received, when in a form other than cash. This valuation should be based on fair market value. A common error is the reporting of gain or loss based on the retained earnings.

529.2 *(4-23-81)* 4231
Expense of Sale

Capital transactions are rarely reported in which there is no appropriate expense of sale. These expenses include legal, accounting, and brokerage fees. When gains or losses appear on a return and no such expenses are set out, the examiner should determine that they have not been claimed as ordinary deductions.

529.3 *(4-23-81)* 4231
Adjusted Basis of the Property

(1) Particular attention should be given the adjusted basis. The examiner should determine whether the adjusted basis properly reflects any nonrecognized gain realized from a prior sale.

(2) In computing capital improvements, an analysis should be made to determine that the value of the taxpayer's labor is not included. In addition, casualty losses previously allowed are a reduction of the basis whereas appropriate reconstruction after the casualty is an addition to the cost.

(3) Appraisal statements are usually acceptable for verifying the basis of property, especially where personal property or portions thereof, have been converted to rental use. These statements should be made by a qualified appraiser and show a logical and acceptable basis for fixing the probable value at the date the property was received or converted. Such appraisals are sometimes a basis for making an FHA loan.

(4) Where the property was inherited, determination of the correct basis may be done by an inspection of copies of the estate tax return or

exchange. Property you buy usually has an original basis that is equal to its cost. However, if you get property in some other way, such as by gift or inheritance, you normally must use a basis other than cost.

Cost as Basis. The basis of property you buy is usually its cost—the amount of cash you pay for it, and the fair market value of other property or services you provide in the transaction.

◀ There are many times when you cannot use cost as a basis. In these cases fair market value may be important.

◀ If you receive property for services, you must include the property's fair market value in income. The amount that you include in income becomes your basis.

◀ *Settlement fees or closing costs*. Purchase commissions and legal and recording fees are includable in the basis of property. Some others are: abstract fees; charges for installing utility services; surveys; transfer taxes; title insurance; and any amounts owed by the seller but which you agree to pay, such as back taxes or interest, recording or mortgage fees, charges for improvements or repairs, and sales commissions.

Adjusted Basis. Examiners are instructed to pay particular attention to adjusted basis, because there's room here for error on your part. Before you can figure any gain or loss on a sale, exchange, or other disposition of property, or figure allowable depreciation, depletion, or amortization, you usually must make certain adjustments (increases and decreases) to the basis of the property. The result of these adjustments to the basis is the *adjusted basis*.

◀ Basis must be increased by the cost of any permanent improvements, by purchase commissions, by legal fees and other charges you choose to capitalize, and by all other capital expenditures, including amounts spent after a casualty to restore the damaged property. Basis must be decreased by amounts you receive that are a return of capital, and by all other amounts that should be charged to a capital account.

◀ You must decrease the basis of your property by the amount of depreciation that you claimed each year on your return, or you could have claimed, whichever is more, and by any amounts of additional first-year depreciation, amortization, obsolescence, and depletion claimed.

appraisal statements. Where it was received as a gift, inspection may be made of the gift tax return.

529.4 *(4-23-81)* 4231
Holding Period

(1) Because the Code varies its treatment of gains or losses depending upon the holding period of the capital asset, the dates of acquisition and disposal are important. They are also important in connection with losses arising out of wash sales and in cases of property acquired in a tax free exchange.

(2) The general rule for determining the holding period is that such period begins the day after contractual purchase (regardless of later delivery or payment date) and ends on the day of contractual sale. Therefore, in verifying sales on a security exchange, the contract date, not the settlement date, is governing.

(3) Further refinements have been made by the Service. In the case of a cash basis taxpayer, the loss on a transaction is deemed to have been realized upon the date of sale despite the fact that the proceeds were received in a subsequent taxable year. Conversely, the gain on a transaction is realized upon receipt of the proceeds. These rules are important since there is usually a flurry of so-called "tax-selling" near the close of a calendar year.

529.5 *(4-23-81)* 4231
Personal Residence

(1) The Code provides unique treatment with respect to gains on the sale or exchange of a residence.

(2) When information is not available from the return and taxpayers are claiming nonrecognition of all or part of the gain, they should be asked to complete Form 2119, Sale or Exchange of Personal Residence. In many cases, it will be necessary to use facts stemming from years other than the one under examination. The is true because of the latitude of time provided in the Code for replacement or reinvestment. It is important for the examiner to realize that completion of the form by the taxpayer is not the equivalent of an examination of the transaction. The amounts entered on the form should be verified.

◀ Although the Tax Reform Act of 1986 eliminated the preferential tax treatment of capital gains, Congress decided to retain the prior statutory structure for capital gains. Therefore, a distinction is still made between ordinary and capital income, and long-term and short-term capital gains.

◀ It is important to be able to substantiate the dates on which you bought and sold property. If you determine that the asset you sold or exchanged is a capital asset, you must then figure whether the gain or loss is short-term or long-term. If you held it more than six months (or more than one year if acquired before June 23, 1984), its sale or exchange results in a long-term capital gain or loss. If you held the asset six months or less (or one year or less if acquired before June 23, 1984), its sale or exchange results in a short-term capital gain or loss, except in the sale of an invention. For regulated commodity futures transactions, see Publication 550.

◀ To figure if you held property more than six months, start counting on the day after the day you acquired the property. The same date of each following month is the beginning of a new month regardless of the number of days in the preceding month. The day you disposed of the property is part of your holding period.

◀ For securities traded on an established securities market, the holding period is measured by the trading date, not the settlement date. However, a gain is not realized by a cash-basis taxpayer until the settlement date. A loss, on the other hand, is sustained on the trading date.

◀ Tax on part or all of the gain from the sale of your principal home (residence) may be postponed. If you didn't, you will probably be asked to file Form 2119, "Sale or Exchange of Personal Residence."

◀ Your entire gain on the sale or exchange of your home is not taxed at the time of the sale if, within two years before or two years after the sale, you buy and live in another home that costs at least as much as the adjusted sales price of the old home. If you are on active duty in the armed forces, or if your tax home is outside the United States, the two-year period may be suspended.

◀ The repeal of the capital gains deduction does not affect the rule that allows you to postpone gain on the sale or exchange of your principal residence.

(3) In addition to the purchase price, the taxpayer usually claims capital additions in the adjusted basis. Unlike the case of rental property, no deductions are allowable for repairs to a residence. To verify the taxpayer's claim for improvements during the holding period, the examiner must clearly understand the distinction between expense and capital items.

(4) Receipted bills of contractors who perform the work would be useful. Comparison of the amount shown on such a bill should be made with the amount of disbursement. The inspection of a cancelled check, for instance, may reveal that the amount of the bill was reduced because of protest by the taxpayer.

529.6 *(4-23-81)* 4231
Multiple Dwellings

(1) Frequently property is sold which consists in part of the taxpayer's residence. The approach to verifying such transactions should take the form of dividing the sale into two parts, one for the residence, the other for the rental property. Treating the sale in two parts may result in a nonallowable loss on the residence portion and a taxable gain on the rental portion.

(2) In dividing the sale transaction, proper allocation must be made for original cost and capital additions between the personal and rental portions of the asset. All depreciation allowed or allowable is an adjustment to the basis of the rental portion only. Similarly, the selling price and expenses of sale must also be allocated between the two segments. The separate gain and loss is measured for each segment, personal and rental, and proper tax treatment applied to each. Regarding the sale as a single transaction allows the taxpayer to offset a nondeductible loss against a taxable gain.

(3) Various methods are available for allocating costs and selling prices between the personal and rental portions. One acceptable method is the ratio of rental value of the two segments. The allocation of capital additions between the personal and rental parts must be tempered by taxpayers' normal inclination to spend more money on their own residence. This should be taken into account absent reasonable substantiation for prorating the costs.

(4) The sale of property that is part personal and part rental, if held the statutory number of months, will be treated as an IRC 1231 transaction for the rental portion. This portion should be verified in the same manner as though it were

◀ If the purchase price of your new home is less than the adjusted sales price of your old home, and you buy and live in the new home within the time period given above, the gain taxed in the year of the sale is the lesser of:

- The gain on the sale of the old home; or
- The amount by which the adjusted sales price of the old home is more than the purchase price of the new home.

◀ The tax on the gain is postponed, not forgiven. You subtract any gain that is not taxed in the year you sell your old home from the cost of your new home. This gives you a lower basis in the new home. If you sell the new home in a later year and again replace it, you may continue to postpone any tax on your gain.

◀ *Renting part of your property.* If you rent part of your property, you must divide certain expenses between the part of the property used for rental purposes and the part of the property used for personal purposes as though you actually had two separate pieces of property.

◀ You may deduct a part of some expenses, such as mortgage interest and property taxes, as a rental expense (applied against the rental income). You may deduct the other part only if you itemize your deductions. You also may deduct as a rental expense a part of other expenses that normally are nondeductible personal expenses, such as expenses for electricity or painting the outside of your house. You may deduct depreciation on the part of the property used for rental purposes as well as on the furniture and equipment you use for these purposes.

◀ Expenses only for the rental part of your property do not have to be divided. If you paint a room that you rent, or if you pay premiums for liability insurance in connection with renting a room in your home, your entire cost is a rental expense.

an independent sale of property held solely for rental income.

(5) IRC 1231 specifies capital gain treatment for sales of certain ordinary assets. Where gains from such sales are reported, look for any casualty losses in the business schedule or among the itemized deductions; gains or losses on similar depreciable property arising from the distribution of partnership assets; and, for gains or losses from involuntary conversions. The Code relief provision requires consideration of these items in the aggregate, prior to classification between ordinary and capital gain.

(6) Often in the sale of depreciable assets or land, the agreement includes the sale of other items such as goodwill and inventories. These extraneous assets must be handled separately and the selling price allocated on the basis of their respective fair market value.

529.7 *(4-23-81)* 4231

Ordinary Income vs. Capital Gains

(1) In determining whether income from the sale of assets should be taxed as ordinary income rather than as capital gains, the examiner should look for:

(a) sales of depreciable property to related taxpayers;

(b) dealings in a manner which would constitute a trade or business, i.e., subdivision of a tract of land and sale of its lots upon which substantial improvements have been made;

(c) redemption of stock by a closely held corporation; and

(d) dealings with related individuals (substance vs. form).

529.8 *(4-23-81)* 4231

Nonbusiness Bad Debts

(1) Ascertain whether there was a valid, existing debt or whether the amount may be a gift as between family members.

(2) Determine that the debt is worthless and that the deduction is claimed in the year during which the debt became worthless.

(3) Ascertain whether the amount claimed exceeds the adjusted basis of the debt.

(4) Ascertain whether the loss has been correctly reported as a short-term capital loss.

◀ *Dividing expenses.* If an expense is for both rental use and personal use, such as heat for the entire house or interest on your mortgage, make sure to divide it between the rental use and the personal use. You may use any reasonable method for dividing the expenses. The two most common methods are one based on the number of rooms in your home and one based on area.

◀ The number of people involved may be the proper method to use to divide certain expenses—for example, a food expense apportioned among tenants and family. Or, if you rent an apartment and your tenants have unrestricted use of your telephone, the number of people using it may be the best method for dividing the monthly charge for the telephone.

◀ In the case of a recognized gain on the sale or exchange of property, including a leasehold that is depreciable property in the hands of the party who receives it, the capital gains provisions do not apply and the gain will be treated as ordinary income if the transaction is either directly or indirectly between: husband and wife, or a person and that person's controlled entity, and between similar arrangements.

Nonbusiness Bad Debts. Bad debts that you did not get in the course of operating your trade or business are nonbusiness bad debts. To be deductible, nonbusiness bad debts must be totally worthless. You cannot deduct a partially worthless nonbusiness bad debt.

◀ Nonbusiness bad debts are deducted only as short-term capital losses on Schedule D (Form 1040), "Capital Gains and Losses." There are limits on how capital losses may be deducted.

529.9 *(4-23-81)* 4231
Installment Sales

(1) The examiner must be thoroughly familiar with the installment sales provision of the Code and regulations and be certain that all requirements are met. Verify that taxpayers have properly computed the amount realized in the year of sale.

(2) When examining installment sales, determine whether the taxpayer has properly included:

(a) payments in the taxable year other than the initial payment;

(b) earnest money deposit or option payments;

(c) any accrued interest, taxes or other liabilities of the taxpayer paid by the purchaser;

(d) any mortgage paid off for the taxpayer by the buyer;

(e) any mortgage assumed by the purchase over the taxpayer's adjusted basis in the property;

(f) any notes receivable from third parties or other property given the taxpayer; and

(g) noncash down payments, i.e., a trailer, house, car, etc., turned over to the seller.

(3) When a case involves installment sales of real estate parcels or subdivisions, the cost of the realty may contain an amount to cover estimated costs for future improvements. In such event, the taxpayer will be asked to sign Form 921 or 921A (Consent Fixing Period of Limitation Upon Assessment of Income and Profits Tax) as appropriate, extending the time in which a deficiency in tax may be assessed.

529.(10) *(12-2-83)* 4231
Capital Losses

(1) Ascertain whether *capital losses* are reflected as ordinary losses in such cases as:

(a) nonbusiness bad debts;

(b) certain casualty and theft losses which may be required to be offset against capital gains.

(2) Ascertain whether sales which reflected no gain or loss are bona fide. Sales to related individuals below fair market value could result in a gift tax liability to the taxpayer.

◀ *Installment sales* are made under a plan that provides for part or all of the sales price to be paid in a later year. If you yourself finance the buyer's purchase of your property, instead of having the buyer get a loan or mortgage from a bank, you probably have an installment sale.

◀ You report your gain on an installment sale only as you actually receive the payment. You are taxed only on the part of each payment that represents your profit on the sale. In this way, the installment method of reporting income relieves you of paying tax on income that you have not yet collected.

◀ Each year, including the year of sale, you must report your income from an installment sale on Form 6252, "Computation of Installment Sale Income." Attach this form to your tax return.

◀ The gain you have from an installment sale will be treated as capital gain if the property you sold was a capital asset, discussed later. However, if you took depreciation deductions on the asset, part of your gain may be treated as ordinary income. See Publication 544 for more information.

◀ For more information on installment sales, see Publication 537, "Installment Sales."

◀ The Tax Reform Act of 1986 denies the use of the installment method in three circumstances:

- Its use for sales pursuant to a revolving credit plan is prohibited.
- For the years after 1986, the installment method may not be used to report income from the sale of stocks or securities traded on an established securities exchange.
- For tax years after 1986, a part of the installment obligation is treated as a payment received at the end of the tax year even though it was not paid at the end of that tax year.

For a more complete explanation of this provision, see IRS Pubs. 553 and 537 (for use in preparing 1987 tax returns).

◀ *Nonbusiness bad debts,* except those evidenced by corporate securities, are short-term capital losses.

If you receive an insurance payment that exceeds your adjusted basis in the destroyed, damaged, or stolen property, you have a gain from the casualty or theft. These type gains are reported on Schedule D if they were for property that was not used in a trade or business or for income-producing purposes. You will also need to use IRS Form 4684, Casualties and Thefts. See IRS Pub. 547 for proper instructions.

529.(11) *(4-23-81)* 4231
Capital Loss Carryover

When a taxpayer has a capital loss carryover; the computation of the loss in the year in which it arose and the computation of income for any other year to which the loss should have been carried is subject to verification. Where the loss year and/or the intervening years have not been examined, the taxpayer's retained copies of the returns should be inspected. The examiner should make any adjustment necessary in the intervening year.

◀ If your deductible capital loss is more than the yearly limit, you may carry over the unused part to the next tax year and treat it as if it occurred in that year. This provision is unaffected by the Tax Reform Act of 1986.

530 *(4-23-81)* 4231
Exclusions From Income

531 *(4-23-81)* 4231
Introduction

When a taxpayer reports that the payment is excludable from income, the examiner should verify the source of the payment and in addition verify the following.

◀ If you are a U.S. citizen or a resident alien of the United States and living abroad, you are, in general, taxed on your worldwide income. However, you may qualify to exclude up to $70,000 of earned income and, in addition, exclude or deduct certain foreign housing amounts. (Before 1987 the amount excluded was $80,000.)

◀ You may also be entitled to exclude from income the value of meals and lodging provided to you by your employer.

532 *(4-23-81)* 4231
Earned Income From Sources Without the United States

(1) There are four basic elements which should be verified for this issue:

(a) determine if the exclusion is claimed as a bona fide resident or for physical presence in a foreign country;

(b) ascertain that the time requirements have been met;

(c) ascertain that no deductions are claimed which are attributable to the excluded income.

(d) ascertain that the excluded income qualifies as earned income.

(2) Residence abroad—In order to determine item (1)(a) above, the examiner should secure such information as the name of the foreign country, the employer's name, and the time period involved. If the taxpayer returned to the United States, find out the reason; e.g., vacation, resignation, completion of work abroad, or temporary assignment in the United States in connection with the job in the foreign country.

◀ To claim either the foreign earned income exclusion or the foreign housing exclusion or deduction, you must have foreign earned income, your tax home must be in a foreign country, and you must be:

- A U.S. citizen who is a bona fide resident of a foreign country or countries for an uninterrupted period that includes an entire tax year; or
- A U.S. citizen or a U.S. resident alien who is physically present in a foreign country or countries for at least 330 full days during any period of 12 consecutive months.

◀ Most U.S. citizens and resident aliens abroad must file U.S. income tax returns, even if their earned income is exempt from tax. You must file Form 2555, "Foreign Earned Income," on which you show the exclusion of foreign earned income and the foreign housing exclusion or deduction, with your Form 1040.

◀ To qualify for the exclusion or the deduction, you must meet either the bona fide residence test or the physical presence test and your tax home must be in a foreign country or countries throughout your period of residence or presence.

(3) Activity in domestic life of foreign country—To further determine item (1)(a) above, ascertain: the type of visa secured for entry into the foreign country; whether the taxpayer has applied for foreign citizenship; whether the taxpayer is required to pay foreign income taxes; address in foreign country; type of dwelling resided in (i.e., purchased home, hotel or other rented quarters, company furnished quarters); address where family resided; local foreign schools attended by taxpayer's children; and citizenship of children and spouse.

(4) Employment abroad—In connection with Item (1)(b) above, the following information would be helpful: name of employer; nature of work performed; and basis of employment, i.e., permanent, for an indefinite period, length of contract; whether or not there is an option to extend the term; and, whether or not taxpayer will return to the United States at the completion of a project. When determining item (1)(d) above, ascertain types of income received by taxpayer, such as salary or wages, commissions or fees, etc.

(5) For further guidance in this area, refer to latest edition of Publication 54, Tax Guide for United States Citizens Abroad.

533 *(6-6-84)* 4231
(Reserved)

534 *(4-23-81)* 4231
Scholarship and Fellowship Grants

(1) When examining this issue, the following questions should be answered:

(a) Is the grantor a tax-exempt organization, or a government unit or agency?

(b) What is the purpose of the grant, the period of the grant, and for whose primary benefit is the grant?

(c) What portion, if any, of the reported grant, constitutes compensation for services rendered or to be rendered?

(d) Is reimbursement for travel and other expenses specifically stated in the grant?

(e) Has the limitation been applied to the amount excludable from income where the recipient is not a candidate for a degree?

(2) A letter from the grantor specifically answering the above questions is usually necessary to verify the issue. Some grantors issue their own publications wherein they indicate the tax consequence to the recipients. Such state-

◀ If you pay foreign income taxes, you may be able to claim a credit for those taxes. You may take the foreign tax credit alone or in connection with the foreign earned income exclusion or the foreign housing exclusion or deduction. However, you may not take a foreign tax credit for taxes paid on exempt foreign income.

◀ Under the Tax Reform Act of 1986, you will be required to submit a tax statement with your U.S. passport application, either original or renewal. This statement must include your Social Security number, any foreign country in which you are residing, and any other information required by regulations. The penalty for not providing this information, if required, is $500, unless you can show that the failure to provide the statement was due to reasonable cause and not willful neglect.

◀ Under new rules, beginning in 1987 only amounts received as a qualifying scholarship by a *candidate for a degree* may be excluded from gross income. The new rules generally apply to scholarships or fellowships granted after August 16, 1986. To be excluded from income, the amounts must meet the definition of a qualified scholarship.

A *qualified scholarship* is any amount received that, in accordance with the conditions of the grant, is used for tuition and course-related expenses. Qualified tuition and related expenses are those used for:

- Tuition and fees required for the enrollment or attendance at an educational organization.
- Fees, books, supplies, and equipment required for courses of instruction at such educational organization.

Any amounts received in excess of the qualified tuition and related expenses (such as room and board) are *not* eligible for the exclusion. Also, any amount received that represents payment for teaching, research, or other services required as a condition of receiving the qualified scholarship may not be excluded from gross income.

For grants made after August 16, 1986, but before 1987, the old rules apply to amounts received before 1987. For more informaton, see IRS Pub. 520.

ments by the grantor should be viewed only as their opinion.

535 *(4-23-81)* 4231
Prizes and Awards

Verify that salespersons have reported expense-paid trips which they have received for exceeding sales quotas. By obtaining a statement from the employer, or determining percentage of time devoted to various activities and reviewing the trip brochure, the examiner should be able to ascertain the purpose and value of the trip.

540 *(4-23-81)* 4231
Adjustments to Income

541 *(4-23-81)* 4231
Moving Expenses

(1) Where a moving expense deduction is claimed and Form 3903 (Moving Expense Adjustment) is not attached to the return, the examiner should secure an analysis of an expense, both reimbursed and unreimbursed. Particular attention should be given to the nature of the expense incurred in connection with the move. Indirect or unrelated expenses such as the cost of refitting rugs or draperies, and penalties for breaking leases, are not deductible moving expenses. Reimbursement of nonqualifying expense constitutes gross income.

(2) In some situations, a statement from the employer, if one is involved, may be desirable. Such a statement should include:

(a) circumstances of the employee's move;

(b) specific expenses and the amount for each type of expense for which reimbursement was made;

(c) amount of reimbursement or allowance included in wages on the Form W-2 Statement;

(d) period of employment in the new location; and

(e) the existence of an agreement between the employer and the taxpayer with reference to arrangements for reimbursing the taxpayer on the sale of a personal residence or an agreement whereby the company purchases the residence that would otherwise be sold at a loss.

◀ If you win a prize in a lucky number drawing, television or radio quiz program, beauty contest, or other event, you must include it in income. For example, if you win a $50 prize in a photography contest, you must report this income as other income on Form 1040.

◀ Beginning in 1987, you may exclude from gross income all or part of the value of employee achievement awards you receive. The award must be tangible personal property for length of service or safety achievements. The excludable value of an award is generally $400. Any value over $400 generally must be included in income.

◀ If you changed job locations last year or started a new job, you may be able to deduct a limited amount of your moving expenses even if you do not itemize your deductions. You may qualify for a deduction whether you are self-employed or an employee. Take care to meet the requirements and to deduct only allowable expenses.

◀ You may deduct a limited amount of your moving expenses if you meet the distance test and the time test, discussed later. Your move must also be closely related, both in time and place, to the start of work at your new job location.

◀ In general, moving expenses incurred within one year from the date you first reported to work are considered closely related in time to the start of work at the new location.

◀ Your move will meet the *distance test* if your new main job location is at least 35 miles farther from your former home than your old main job location was.

◀ Your main job location is usually the place where you spend most of your working time. A new job location is a new place where you will work permanently or indefinitely rather than temporarily.

◀ To deduct your moving expenses, you also must meet one of the *time tests:*

- If you are an employee, you must work full time for at least 39 weeks during the first 12 months after you arrive in the general area of your new job location.

(3) Verify expenses from original documents, if possible. Examples include bill of lading, lodging receipts, escrow statements. Verify that expenses used in the computation of this deduction are not included in the computation of the sale of the residence.

542 *(4-23-81)* 4231
Rents, Royalties

542.1 *(4-23-81)* 4231
Rental Income

(1) Scrutinize transactions with related taxpayers and controlled entities. Look for such features as: shifting income, renting for an inadequate consideration to owner, etc.

(a) Verify the net loss from rentals is not attributable to the fact that the property was rented to a relative or friend for an amount less than the fair market rental value of the property.

(b) Determine if the rental loss involves a vacation home used part of the time by the taxpayer.

(2) Determine whether there may have been income from sources for which no corresponding asset is recorded.

(3) Be alert to possible rental contracts which may be conditional sales.

(4) Depreciation, repairs, and other expenses should be analyzed.

(5) Be alert to prepaid rent or lease deposit items that may not be included in income.

(a) Question the taxpayer directly about the weekly or monthly rent received for each unit and periods of vacancy, if any.

(b) Where rents are received in advance on either the cash or the accrual basis and there is no substantial limitation on disposition, they constitute taxable income when received (constructive receipt). Verify these amounts have been included in income.

(c) A bonus paid by the lessee to the lessor upon execution of the lease constitutes income, as does a lump sum amount paid by the lessee in consideration for the cancellation of a lease. Verify that these amounts have been included in income.

(d) Question the taxpayer about tenants providing services in lieu of rental payments. Verify that the taxpayer has reported the value of the services as income if a deduction has been taken for the value of such services.

- If you are self-employed, you must work full time for at least 39 weeks during the first 12 months and for a total of at least 78 weeks during the 24 months right after you arrive in the area of your new job location.

◄ For tax years beginning after 1986, your moving expenses will be deductible only as an itemized deduction and *not* as an adjustment to gross income as in prior years. Moving expenses are *not* subject to the 2% of adjusted gross income limitation that applies to certain other miscellaneous deductions.

◄ You are allowed a deduction for any passive activity loss or the deduction equivalent of the passive activity credit for any tax year from rental real estate activities in which you actively participated. The amount allowed under this rule, however, cannot be more than $25,000 ($12,500 for a married individual filing separately), and is reduced by 50% of the amount by which your adjusted gross income is more than $100,000 ($50,000 for married filing separately).

◄ You must include in your gross income amounts you receive as rent—not only normal rent payments, but also advance rent in the year you receive it, regardless of the period covered or your method of accounting. You may not reduce advance rent by expected expenses.

◄ Do not include a security deposit in your income when you receive it, if you plan to return it to your tenant at the end of the lease. However, if during any year, you keep part or all of the security deposit because your tenant does not live up to the terms of the lease, you must include the amount you keep in your income for that year.

◄ If an amount called a security deposit is to be used as a final payment of rent, it is advance rent. You must include it in your income when you receive it.

◄ If your tenant pays you to cancel a lease, the amount you receive is includable in rental income for the year you receive it, whether you use the cash or accrual method of accounting.

◄ If your tenant pays any of your expenses, these payments are rental income to you. You may then deduct the expenses that are otherwise deductible.

◄ A lease with an option to buy may be a purchase contract. If it is, payments you receive under the contract are payments of the purchase price and are not includable in your income as rental income.

(6) Determine whether the taxpayer has coin-operated laundry machines located at the rental units and has reported the income.

(7) Look for fictitious rental income for taxpayer's occupancy. Taxpayer may be attempting to make all expenses deductible without apportionment.

◂ If you rent a dwelling unit that you also use as a residence and you rent it for less than 15 days during the tax year, do not include the rent you receive in your gross income. But you may not deduct expenses other than interest, taxes, and casualty and theft losses.

542.2 *(4-23-81)* 4231

Royalties

(1) The royalty contract should be scrutinized to determine that the taxpayer has an economic interest, not an economic advantage.

(2) If the taxpayer has given up all rights in the property from which income is derived, verify the amounts received are reported as the sale or exchange of the property rather than royalty income.

(3) The terms of the contract must be scrutinized to determine whether the taxpayer has sold the property, i.e., divested rights, title and interest, or granted a franchise or right for use only, resulting in ordinary income. Verify the income has been properly reported.

(4) Royalties received from copyrights or patents are usually paid on a unit basis, such as, number of books, machines, tickets sold, etc. Determine the number of units printed and sold.

(5) Copyrights and patents have useful lives. Examiners should determine when the work was created as this fact will affect the useful life for depreciation purposes.

◂ Royalties from copyrights, patents, oil, gas, and mineral properties are taxable as ordinary income.

◂ You generally report royalties on Part I, Schedule E (Form 1040). However, if you hold an operating oil, gas, or mineral interest, or are in business as a self-employed writer, inventor, or artist, report gross income and expenses on Schedule C (Form 1040).

◂ Royalties from copyrights on literary, musical, or artistic works, and similar property, or from patents on inventions, are amounts paid to you for the right to use your work over a specified period of time. You may recover your cost or other basis through depreciation deductions over the life of the copyright or patent. If a patent or copyright becomes worthless in any year before it expires, you may deduct your unrecovered cost or other basis in the year it becomes worthless.

◂ If you give up all your rights in the property from which you derive your income, the amounts you receive are considered payments for the sale or exchange of your property, and not royalty income. Under certain circumstances, the sale may be subject to capital gain or loss treatment on Schedule D (Form 1040).

543 *(4-23-81)* 4231

Alimony

(1) Request a copy of the document under which payments are made such as, court decree and amendments thereto, written separation agreement, or decree of support. Analyze terms and dates that are material in determining deductibility.

(2) Determine that the amount claimed is an allowable deduction under the applicable provisions of the law.

(3) Verify the amounts paid from cancelled checks or other evidence of payment.

◂ You may deduct alimony or separate maintenance payments that you are required to make to your spouse or former spouse. You may not deduct payments for child support. To find out if you may claim your child as a dependent, see either IRS Pub. 17 or Pub. 504. Property settlements are not alimony. You do not have to itemize deductions to claim your alimony payments. You deduct alimony from gross income to find your adjusted gross income.

◂ If you deduct alimony or separate maintenance payments, you must include in your return for the year payment is made your spouse's or former

(4) Verify that payment of premiums on an insurance policy irrevocably assigned to a former spouse are reported as alimony income.

(5) Determine the disposition of the marital residence. Transfer of the jointly owned residence may be a taxable event. Payments on a home mortgage, as well as interest and real estate taxes, are not alimony payments if the nonresident spouse is making the payments and has retained an interest of ownership in the property. The payments, in part, however, may constitute an allowable deduction as interest and taxes.

(6) Where possible, check the return of the recipient to see that the amount is included as income or file an Information Report, Form 5346, if the return is out of the immediate jurisdiction.

544 *(4-23-81)* 4231

Individual Retirement Accounts (IRA's)

(1) Examiner should determine that the taxpayer meets the qualifications for an IRA. Check to see that contributions do not exceed the maximum amount allowed. Such excess may be subject to an excise tax.

(2) Ascertain whether the taxpayer ever withdrew retirement money prior to age 59½ (usually not permitted). If the taxpayer is over age 70½, ascertain if taxpayer began drawing out these accumulated funds. The institution holding the funds may be able to provide this information to the taxpayer.

(3) Taxpayers should be questioned as to whether they have "rolled-over" their investment. "Roll-overs" are permitted only once in a specified time period.

(4) Ascertain that the funds received are taxed as ordinary income.

545 *(4-23-81)* 4231

Keogh (H.R. 10) Plans

Self-employed persons are entitled to set up qualified pension plans for themselves and full-time employees. These are sometimes called Keogh or H.R. 10 Plans, the amount contributable depends on the amount of earned (personal service) income. Verify that the taxpayer is not an inactive owner or partner receiving investment income.

spouse's last name, if different than yours, and Social Security number. Your spouse or former spouse must give you his/her Social Security number. If you do not include the SSN on your return, you may have to pay a $50 penalty, and your spouse or former spouse may also have to pay a $50 penalty for not giving you the SSN.

◀ New rules apply to alimony payments made under a divorce or separate maintenance instrument executed after 1986. Basically, these rules apply if you are required to make payments of $15,000 or more a year. They ensure that the deductions you take for alimony paid remain fairly level by requiring you to include in income (recapture), in later years, certain excess payments. For information on the recapture rule, see IRS Pub. 504.

◀ An Individual Retirement Account (IRA) is a savings plan that lets you set aside money for your retirement. Payments to it are tax deductible and earnings of your IRA are not taxed until they are distributed to you.

◀ The Tax Reform Act of 1986 made significant changes to the IRA rules, effective for tax years beginning after 1986. Whether you can take an IRS deduction depends on:

- The amount of your adjusted gross income (agi); and
- If you are an active participant in an employer-maintained retirement plan. See IRS Pub. 590 for full particulars.

◀ You may be entitled to a limited deduction for payments to a Keogh (HR-10) plan to provide retirement benefits for yourself either as a sole proprietor or as a partner of a partnership, if you have earned income from personal services that you performed for the trade or business. You generally may pay and deduct the lesser of $30,000 or 15 percent of your net earnings.

546 *(4-23-81)* 4231
Tax-Deferred Annuity Plans

These plans are prevalent among the teaching profession and usually, but not always, the annuity has already been excluded from the amount on the W-2. When this adjustment to income is claimed on a return, determine whether or not the item is included in the W-2 Form.

547 *(4-23-81)* 4231
Employee Business Expenses

547.1 *(4-23-81)* 4231
General

(1) Examiners should obtain an analysis of all expenses both reimbursed and unreimbursed. Discuss with the taxpayer the employer's reimbursement policy. If these is any question as to the amount of the reimbursement or as to the fact that the taxpayer was obligated to incur expenses, the examiner should ask the taxpayer to secure a letter from the employer. The letter should contain a positive statement as to whether the employer was reimbursed and if so, how much and whether the amount is included in the Form W-2. The examiner should consider the employees' position in the company in evaluating the letter from the employer.

(2) Once the question of reimbursement has been determined, the taxpayer's deduction must be substantiated. The expenses should be broken down into the broad categories of transportation, meals, and lodging, etc.

(a) Examine selected items within each of the broad categories.

1 Expenses for cash and credit cards should be verified.

2 If a diary is kept, ascertain the manner and method used in maintaining it. Test a sufficient number of entries to determine the reliability and credibility of the diary. The examiner does not have to accept the diary as being correct even though it conforms with the recordkeeping requirements of Reg. 1.274-5.

3 If the amount of expenses claimed in the diary is disproportionate when compared with the business activities and income of the taxpayer, or if the examiner has reasonable grounds for questioning the credibility of the taxpayer's entries, the taxpayer should be requested to submit further substantiation.

◀ Under certain IRC provisions, employees of public schools or certain tax-exempt organizations may qualify for a tax-sheltered annuity treatment that allows them to postpone taxation of their employer's contributions until after they retire.

◀ Effective for tax years beginning after December 31, 1986, the maximum amount that an employee can elect to defer for any tax year under all-sheltered annuity plans in which the employee participates is $9,500.

◀ Beginning in 1987, in general, you may deduct only 80% of your business-related meal and entertainment expenses, including those incurred while traveling away from home.

◀ If you are an employee and have travel, transportation, entertainment, and gift expenses related to your work, you may be able to deduct these expenses on your income tax return.

◀ Travel expenses are your ordinary and necessary expenses while traveling away from home for your business, profession, or job. You may deduct these expenses if you prove them.

◀ Transportation expenses are the ordinary and necessary expenses of getting from one work place to another in the course of your business, profession, or job when you are *not* traveling away from home.

◀ You may be able to deduct entertainment expenses you have for your trade or business. You may take the deduction if the amounts spent are directly related to or associated with your trade or business or if certain exceptions apply. You must meet requirements for proving the amount spent and the business nature of the expense.

◀ You may deduct the cost of business gifts. However, you cannot deduct more than $25 for business gifts you give, directly or indirectly, to any one individual during your tax year.

◀ You should keep the proof you need for travel, transportation, entertainment, and business gift expenses in an account book, diary, statement of expense, or similar record, supported by adequate documentary evidence, that together will support each element of an expense. For example, entries on a desk calendar, not supported by evidence, are not proper proof.

◀ Deductions are not allowed for approximations or estimates, or for expenses that are lavish or extravagant.

(b) The examiner should review documentary evidence such as receipts, paid bills, or similar evidence to support the expenditures. Where the taxpayer generally has good records, the lack of occasional receipts or other element will not prevent the records from being adequate.

(c) The examiner should determine if the taxpayer is in substantial compliance with the law and regulations. The term "substantial compliance" is not defined in the regulations and is a question of degree. It is an area where the examiner must exercise judgment depending on the facts and circumstances in each case. In exercising judgment, the examiner should consider and document in the workpapers such factors as the number of missing elements, the nature of the missing documentation, the reason why the element was not substantiated in accordance with the adequate records requirements, and the availability of other information to substantiate the expenditure.

(d) Examiners can accept taxpayer's statements, if the statements are not improbable or unreasonable, self-contradictory, or inconsistent with surrounding facts and circumstances. If oral statements are part of the factual record, the workpapers should include:

1 The substance of the oral statement. If considered necessary, an affidavit may be secured from the taxpayer for this purpose.

2 The surrounding facts and circumstances, if any, which collaborate or contradict the oral statement.

3 The conclusion reached and the determinant factors. If the issue involves specific recordkeeping required by law and regulations (e.g., IRC 274), then oral evidence alone *cannot* be substituted for necessary written documentation.

547.2 *(4–23–81)* 4231

Unreimbursed Expenditures of State Department Employees

(1) Authorized Certifying Officers of the State Department at overseas posts certify certain unreimbursed expenditures considered necessary in carrying out the duties of a Foreign Service employee's official position abroad. The certification covers two types of expenditures:

(a) those which would have been reimbursed under Title IX of the Foreign Service Act

◀ *Travel*. You must substantiate:

- Each separate amount you spent for travel away from home, such as the cost of your transportation or lodging. You may total the daily cost of your breakfast, lunch, dinner, and other incidental elements of such travel if they are listed in reasonable categories, such as meals, gas and oil, and taxi fares.

- The dates you left and returned home for each trip, and the number of days spent on business away from home.

- The destination or locality of your travel, described by name of city, town, or similar designation.

- The business reason for your travel or the business benefit gained or expected to be gained from your travel.

◀ *Entertainment*. You must substantiate:

- The amount of each separate expense for entertaining, except for incidental items, such as taxi fares and telephone calls, which may be totaled on a daily basis.
- The date the entertainment took place.
- The name, address or location, and the type of entertainment, such as dinner or theater, if the information is not apparent from the name or designation of the place.
- The reason for the entertainment or the business benefit gained or expected to be gained from entertaining and, except for business meals, the nature of any business discussion or activity that took place.
- The occupation or other information about the person or persons entertained, including name, title, or other designation sufficient to establish the business relationship to you.

◀ If you are an employee of a U.S. government agency overseas, you may deduct representation and official residence expenses. To be deductible, your expenses must be more than the allowances or other payments received under appropriate legislation as representation allowances or official residence expenses, provided:

had sufficient funds been available (representation and official residence expenses); and

(b) expenditures which would have been reimbursed from general purpose allocations had sufficient funds been available (restricted almost exclusively to authorized use of the employee's personal car on official business).

(2) The Authorized Certifying Officers also certify similar expenditures by personnel of the United States Information Agency abroad.

(3) The State Department does not certify representation expenses of its Foreign Service officers and employees while they are stationed in the United States, since there is no accounting to the Department by the employee for such expenses. However, the Department has a procedure by which an employee furnishes his/her immediate supervisor with information concerning expenditures for which he/she wishes to claim tax deductions. If the supervisor believes the expenses were ordinary and necessary and were in the interest of the United States Government, he/she furnishes the employee with an endorsement to that effect which the employee may file with his/her tax return.

(4) Even though a Department of State or United States Information Agency employee submits a certification or endorsement, such as described in (1) or (3) above, the examiner may, when appropriate, require additional substantiation.

- These excess expenses are supported by a certificate from the Secretary of State attesting that they were incurred for the benefit of the United States; and
- These expenses would be reimbursable under appropriate legislation if the agency had sufficient funds for these reimbursements.

◀ You should request the certificate from the certifying officer at the post for which the expenses are being claimed. The request must be made in accordance with 4 FAM 824, dated March 4, 1970. In addition, the expenses must be of the types authorized by Chapters 300 and 400 of *Standardized Regulations* (Government Civilian, Foreign Area).

◀ These regulations state what are and what are not allowable official residence expenses. Among the items not allowable are the amounts a principal representative must pay personally for the wages and maintenance of household servants.

◀ Certificates must be signed by authorized certifying officers to be acceptable.

◀ If the excess expenses are not supported by a certificate from the Secretary of State, you can still deduct them on Schedule A (Form 1040) if they are ordinary and necessary in performing your official duties.

◀ To be deductible, excess expenses for travel, entertainment, and gifts, including those certified by the Secretary of State, must comply with the rules for recordkeeping and accounting to your employer.

550 *(4-23-81)* 4231

Computation of Tax

551 *(4-27-83)* 4231

Minimum Tax

(1) Examiners should scrutinize returns and ask taxpayer if they had any transactions involving the items of tax preference applicable to the years under examination.

(2) Examiners should verify that each member of a partnership has taken into account the distributive share of the partnership's items of income and deductions that are items of tax preference.

◀ The tax laws give special treatment to some kinds of income, and allow special deductions for some kinds of expenses. So that taxpayers who benefit from these laws will pay at least a minimum amount of tax, the alternative minimum tax has been enacted.

◀ The alternative minimum tax is figured on benefits received in the form of deductions, lower tax rates, and exclusions from tax. These benefits are known as "tax preference items" because they result from the preferential treatment given in the tax law.

(a) For beneficiaries of estates and trusts, the total items of tax preference for the year are apportioned between the estate or trust and the beneficiaries on the basis of the income of the estate or trust allocable to each.

(b) Tax preference items on forms 1120S (U.S. Small Business Corporation) are apportioned pro rata among the shareholders in the same way any corporate losses would be apportioned. If capital gains are taxed to both the corporation and the shareholder, the capital gains can be an item of tax preference at both the corporate and individual level.

(3) Form 4625, Computation of Minimum Tax—Individuals, should be used to compute the add-on minimum tax. Form 6251, Alternative Minimum Tax Computation, should be used to compute the alternative minimum tax.

552 *(4-23-81)* 4231
Maximum Tax

(1) Examiners should verify whether the earned income on Form 4726, Maximum Tax on Personal Service Income, is limited to wages, professional fees, and other amounts received as compensation for personal services actually rendered. Passive income such as interest and dividends should not be included in earned income.

(2) Where the taxpayer is an officer-stockholder of a closely-held corporation, a determination will be made as to the reasonableness of the taxpayer's compensation for personal services. Only that portion of income received which is deemed reasonable for the services rendered qualifies as earned income.

(3) Examiners should:

(a) Be aware of the effect of capital investment. Where a taxpayer is engaged in an unincorporated trade or business in which both personal services and capital are material income-producing factors, earned income is limited to a reasonable allowance for personal services.

(b) Be alert for situations where the taxpayers include 100 percent of their profits from a trade or business as earned income.

(c) Recognize that "inactive"or "limited" partners, or those receiving distributions from "out of district partnerships," usually contribute little or no personal services to the business.

(4) Verification should be made of the taxpayer's allocation of IRC 62 deductions between earned and unearned income.

(5) Determine if the taxpayer has actually rendered the services for which he/she has

◀ Some itemized deductions can also result in a liability for the alternative minimum tax even though they are not tax preference items. Therefore, you may have to pay this tax even if you have no tax preference items.

◀ Under the Tax Reform Act of 1986, the alternative minimum tax for individuals has been broadened and strengthened. The new rules are effective for tax years beginning after 1986. Under the new rules, the rate at which the alternative minimum tax is computed is increased to 21%, exemption amounts will be phased out for high-income taxpayers, and alternative minimum taxable income will be computed in a different way. See IRS Pub. 909 for more information.

◀ The maximum tax of 50 percent on *personal service income* was repealed by the Economic Recovery Tax Act of 1981. The maximum tax rate on *all taxable income* was then set at 50 percent.

◀ The tax rates for individuals have been reduced for tax years beginning after 1986. For 1987, the rates are a mixture of the old rates and the new rates. The top rate for 1987 is 38.5% (down from 50%). For tax years beginning in 1987, there are five rates imposed on the taxable incomes of individuals.

For tax years beginning in 1988, there will be two tax rates of 15% and 28%.

For tax years beginning after 1988, the amount of taxable income in each bracket will be adjusted, if necessary, so that taxes will not increase due to inflation.

Beginning *in 1988*, the benefit of the 15% bracket is phased out for taxpayers having taxable incomes exceeding certain dollar amounts. Taxable income above the applicable dollar amounts will be subject to an additional 5% tax (subject to limitations). The applicable dollar amounts of taxable income above which the additional tax will apply are shown in the following table:

Filing Status	*Applicable Dollar Amount*
Single	$43,150
Married filing jointly and Qualifying Widow(er)	71,900
Married filing separately	35,950
Head of Household	61,650

The applicable dollar amounts will be adjusted for inflation beginning in 1989.

been compensated. If the income is for future services, it does not qualify as earned income.

553 *(4-23-81)* 4231
Income Averaging

(1) Examiners should consider this option which is available to taxpayers, especially when large adjustments are being proposed.

(2) The examiner should ask the taxpayer to provide copies of prior year returns which are needed to make this computation. Examiners should question taxpayers about prior audits which may have increased base year taxable income.

◀ For tax years beginning after 1986, you can no longer figure your tax under the income averaging method. For information on income averaging for tax years beginning before 1987, see IRS Pub. 506.

560 *(4-23-81)* 4231
Credits

561 *(4-23-81)* 4231
Introduction

This section discusses the most common credits. Although several of these credits will be found only on business returns, they are all listed in this section. The examiner should question the taxpayer as to any allowable credits which may not have been claimed on the return.

562 *(6-6-84)* 4231
Credit for the Elderly

(1) Examiners should determine the taxpayer's age, filing status and Adjusted Gross Income (AGI) since these items directly effect the computation of the credit.

(2) Examiners should also determine whether the taxpayer retired on disability before the close of the taxable year and was permanently and totally disabled at the time of retirement.

(3) Taxpayers should be asked whether they are receiving Social Security, Railroad Retirement, or other excludible pensions. Verify that these items have been used to reduce the amounts on which the credit was determined.

◀ *Credit for the Elderly:* You may claim this credit if you are 65 or older, or if you are under 65 and retired on disability and were permanently and totally disabled when you retired. Generally, if you were eligible for the disability income exclusion and are still retired on permanent and total disability, you are eligible for this credit. You figure the credit on Schedule R (Form 1040), "Credit for the Elderly and the Permanently and Totally Disabled," and claim the credit on Form 1040. You may not take the credit if you file Form 1040A or Form 1040EZ.

◀ For 1984 and later years, if you are under age 65, you can claim the credit for the elderly and the permanently and totally disabled only if you retired with a permanent and total disability.

563 *(4-23-81)* 4231
Investment Credit

(1) The investment credit is a mandatory credit. Taxpayers claiming this credit should attach Form 3468 (Computation of Investment Credit) to the return.

◀ *The Investment Credit:* The Tax Reform Act of 1986 made extensive changes to the tax law covering the investment credit for 1986 and later tax years. The most significant of these changes is the repeal of the regular investment credit. With certain limited exceptions, you cannot take the regular investment credit for property you place in service after December 31, 1985.

(2) In verifying the credit, the examiner should ascertain that the allowable credit does not exceed the total of the correct income tax and the correct statutory credits for retirement income and foreign tax. Adjustment of one or more of these items may affect the investment credit.

◄ However, there are exceptions to the general rule. For example, the rules for the rehabilitation credit were unchanged in 1986. The rehabilitation credit for property placed in service after December 31, 1986, will be changed to a two-tier credit. The credit percentages will be 20% for certified historic structures and 10% for other buildings placed in service before 1936.

(3) The general rules for determining basis are applicable in the verification of the basis of new section 38 property.

◄ The energy credit, which had expired for most property at the end of 1985, has been extended for certain kinds of property. The credit has been extended for three years for solar, geothermal, and ocean thermal property, and for two years for biomass property.

(4) The examiner should verify that the basis of used section 38 property or the basis of new section 38 property acquired as a replacement for property which was destroyed by casualty, etc., has been properly computed.

(5) Schedule D, Gains and Losses from Sales or Exchanges of Property, and Form 4797, Supplemental Schedule of Gains and Losses, should be reviewed for disposition of property which qualified for the investment credit. If appropriate, the examiner should consider recapture provisions. The recapture rule is also applicable if the property ceases to qualify as section 38 property.

◄ The energy credit is for your investment in certain new energy property. It can be 10, 11, or 15 percent of your qualified investment in the property, depending on the type of property. Beginning in 1986, the energy investment credit is no longer available; thus you cannot claim the credit for items or property you install after 1985.

564 *(4-23-81)* 4231

Foreign Tax Credit

(1) Ascertain that the foreign tax has been paid or accrued and is an income, war profits, or excess profits tax and has been imposed on the taxpayer.

(2) A foreign tax credit or deduction claimed is an immediate flag to the examiner that income from foreign sources should also be reflected on the return. Where all foreign income is exempt from gross income, no credit or deduction for foreign taxes is allowable.

◄ The foreign tax credit is intended to relieve U.S. taxpayers of the double tax burden when their foreign source income is taxed both by the United States and the foreign country from which the income comes. Generally, if the foreign tax rate is higher than the U.S. rate there will be no U.S. tax on the foreign income. If the foreign tax rate is lower than the U.S. rate, U.S. tax on the foreign income will be limited to the difference between the rates. Since the foreign tax credit applies only with respect to foreign source income, however, it does not affect U.S. taxes attributable to U.S. source income.

(3) Verify a credit has not been taken for excess tax payments which would be refunded by a foreign country with which the U.S. has a tax treaty if a claim were filed.

◄ You may choose either to take the foreign tax credit on all qualified foreign taxes or to deduct them.

(4) Form 1116, Computation of Foreign Tax Credit, should be used as a worksheet to compute this credit.

565 *(4-23-81)* 4231

Energy Credit

(1) This credit is allowed for energy saving items installed in a taxpayer's principal residence.

◄ The law provided tax credits for the purchase and installation before 1986, of certain energy-saving items and renewable energy source property. Beginning in 1986, the residential energy credit is no longer available.

(2) Examiners should verify:

(a) the item qualifies for the credit

(b) the cost of the item from source documents

(c) the taxpayer has reduced the basis of the residence by the credit claimed.

(3) Form 5695, Energy Credits, is useful to compute this credit.

(4) In connection with the verification of credits for energy conservation property or the examination of producers or distributors of insulation, examiners should refer apparent violations of flame resistance and corrosiveness safety standards set by the Consumer Product Safety Commission to the Director, Examination Division, Attention CP:E:G:E.

566 *(4-23-81)* 4231
Earned Income Credit

(1) Verify the taxpayer's income and dependents.

(2) Determine if others in the household may be claiming the credit for the same exemption.

(3) Ask the taxpayer if they have filed Form W-5, Earned Income Credit Advance Payment Certificate, with their employer.

(4) Inspect Form W-2, Wage and Tax Statement, for amount of advance EIC payment.

(5) Adjust the Earned Income Credit whenever a change is made to adjusted gross income.

◀ You may be entitled to a refundable credit of up to $851.20 (only for 1987) if your earned income and your adjusted gross income are each less than $15,432 (only for 1987). If the credit is larger than your tax, the difference will be refunded to you. To be eligible for the credit:

- You must have a child living with you for more than half the year (prior to 1986, your child must have lived with you for the entire year);
- Your principal home must be in the United States;
- You must not have excluded from your gross income an amount of income that is earned in foreign countries or U.S. possessions, or claimed a deduction for a foreign housing amount;
- You must have a full 12-month tax year; and
- You must file a joint return if you are married.

567 *(11-2-86)* 4231
Child Care Credit

(1) The examiner should verify the amounts claimed and determine that the credit is taken in the proper year. Also, the dependency status should be verified to ensure that it is in accord with the tax law in effect.

(2) The examiner should determine the reasonableness of payments, the relationship of the payee, and whether the services were provided to a qualifying individual.

(3) For taxable years beginning after December 31, 1978, examiners should be alert to changes in the law regarding payments to relatives.

◀ If you pay someone to care for your dependent who is under 15, your disabled dependent, or your disabled spouse so that you can work or look for work, you may be able to take a tax credit of up to 30 percent of the amount you pay. You may use up to $2,400 of these expenses to figure your credit if you have one qualifying dependent and up to $4,800 if you have two or more qualifying dependents. Your credit can be as much as $720 if you have one qualifying dependent, or as much as $1,440 if you have two or more qualifying dependents.

(4) Since some child care expenses can also qualify as medical expenses, examiners should check for double deductions.

(5) Form 2441, Credit for Child and Dependent Care Expenses, is a useful worksheet in computing child care expenses.

(6) When cash wages of $50 or more have been paid in a calendar quarter for domestic services, the examiner should verify that Form 942, Employer's Quarterly Tax Return for Household Employees, has been filed.

(7) If the wages paid were $1,000 or more in a calendar quarter, the examiner should verify that Form 940, Employer's Annual Federal Unemployment Tax Return, has also been filed.

◀ To qualify for the child-care credit:

- You must file Form 1040, or Form 1040A;
- Your child and dependent care expenses must be to allow you to work or look for work;
- You must have income from work during the year;
- You must keep up a home that you live in with one or more qualifying persons;
- You must file a joint return if you are married, unless certain exceptions apply to you; and
- You must pay someone other than your child under 19 or a person you can claim as your dependent.

568 *(4-23-81)* 4231

Work Incentive (WIN) Credit

(1) Verify that the wages were paid —
  (a) Under a qualified program, and
  (b) to eligible employees

(2) Verify that the deduction for wages has been reduced by the amount of the credit.

(3) Verify that the taxpayer has not claimed the Targeted Jobs Credit if WIN credit has been claimed.

(4) Form 4874, Credit for Work Incentive (WIN) Program Expenses, should be used as a worksheet to compute this credit.

◀ The Work Incentive Credit, as provided by IRC 50A and 50B expired at the end of 1981. It was a credit available to employers for hiring certain disadvantaged individuals, and has now been merged into the targeted jobs credit.

569 *(4-23-81)* 4231

Jobs Credit

(1) Verify the wages were —
  (a) subject to FUTA
  (b) paid to a qualified individual
  (c) within the maximum limitation

(2) Verify all employees have been certified by a local designated agency (generally the State Employment Security Agency).

(3) Verify that the deduction for wages has been reduced by the amount of the Jobs Credit.

(4) Form 5884, Jobs Credit, should be used as a worksheet to compute this credit.

◀ As an employer, you can take a targeted jobs credit for qualified wages you pay to members of targeted groups who work for you. The amount of the credit was reduced for eligible employees hired after December 31, 1985. For more information, see IRS Pub. 906.

56(10) *(9-3-81)* 4231

Royalty Owners Credit

(1) This credit is allowed for individuals that have paid or had withholding of Windfall Profit Tax on domestic crude oil production.

(2) Examiners should verify whether:
  (a) taxpayer qualifies for the credit,
  (b) taxpayer does not have to share the credit with another member of taxpayer's family,
  (c) the credit equals the amount of withholding for Windfall Profit Tax,
  (d) royalty owner credit not previously claimed,
  (e) taxpayer is claiming any other credit or refund for overpaid Windfall Profit Tax, and
  (f) taxpayer has reduced amount of Windfall Profit Tax deduction by credit claimed.

◀ There is a windfall profit tax on the domestic production of crude oil, paid by the producers, or those who have an economic interest in the oil underground. For 1981 only, certain taxpayers who held royalty interests in crude oil production were entitled to a $2,500 credit against the windfall profit tax. For 1982 and thereafter, the credit has been replaced by an exemption of 2 to 3 barrels of oil per day.

570 *(4-23-81)* 4231

Schedule A—Deductions

(See Pro-forma Aids in Exhibits 200-1 through 200-1 cont.(7))

In verifying deductions claimed by a taxpayer, examiners should also be alert to the possibility of unclaimed deductions. If one examination reveals such unclaimed items, they should be allowed in the examination report.

571 *(4-23-81)* 4231

Medical Expense

(1) Verify amounts claimed and determine that the deduction is claimed in the proper year.

(a) Determine whether medical expenditures of a capital nature increase the value of the property.

(b) Determine that costs of transportation do not include amounts spent for board and lodging.

(2) Ascertain whether any insurance reimbursement has been made or is expected.

(3) Determine that the expense was incurred primarily for the diagnosis, cure, mitigation, treatment of prevention of disease, or for the purpose of affecting any structure or function of the body (including transportation and medical insurance).

(4) Medicines should be separated so that the proper limitation can be applied.

(5) Determine that the percentage limitation, the maximum amount limitation and the dependency qualification have been correctly applied.

(6) Be aware that amounts allowed as child care expense cannot also be claimed as medical expense.

572 *(4-23-81)* 4231

Taxes

(1) Verify amounts claimed and determine that the deduction has been taken in the proper year.

(2) Determine whether the tax is of the type deductible in accordance with the rules and regulations.

(3) Ascertain that no foreign income taxes have been claimed as a deduction where election has been made to claim the foreign tax credit.

(4) Examiners should verify that the taxpayer has not claimed duplicate deductions for taxes, i.e., itemized deduction and rental expense.

573 *(4-23-81)* 4231

Interest

(1) Verify amount claimed and determine that the deduction has been taken in the proper year.

(2) Determine whether the payments are for interest or for other items, such as discounts,

◀ You may deduct certain medical and dental expenses—for yourself, your wife or husband, and your dependents—if you itemize your deductions on Schedule A (Form 1040).

◀ Medical expenses are payments you make for the diagnosis, cure, relief, treatment, or prevention of disease, affecting any part or function of the body. You may deduct the cost of transportation for needed medical care, and payments for medical insurance for yourself, your spouse, and your dependents.

◀ There are limits on amounts you may deduct. You may deduct only the part of your medical and dental expenses, and medical insurance that is more than 7½ percent of your adjusted gross income shown on Form 1040, for tax years beginning after 1986.

◀ For tax years beginning after December 31, 1984, the law has changed with regard to expenses for a child of divorced or separated parents or of parents who live apart during the last six months of the calendar year.

◀ Your medicine and drug expenses are also subject to the 7½ percent limit. As of 1984, amounts paid for medicines or drugs are deductible only if they are for prescribed drugs or insulin.

◀ You must reduce your medical expenses by reimbursements received for those expenses.

◀ To be deductible, the tax must be one of the following:

- Income tax (state, local, or foreign).
- Real property tax (state, local, or foreign).
- Personal property tax (state or local).
- State and local sales taxes are not deductible after 1986.

◀ Generally, you may only deduct taxes that have been imposed on you, and those that were paid during the tax year.

◀ Interest is an amount paid for the use of borrowed money. Most creditors will give you a statement showing the amount of interest you paid during the year. Where you deduct interest on your return depends on whether you borrowed the money for personal use, for rental or royalty property or for your business.

finance charges or principal. Finance charges on revolving charge accounts are considered to be interest and are deductible.

(3) Ascertain whether the interest payments are made on a valid, existing debt owed by the taxpayer. If there is a joint and several liability, the entire amount of interest is deductible by the payor. Interest paid as a guarantor does not constitute an interest deduction.

(4) Ascertain whether the debt was incurred to carry or purchase the income from which is tax-exempt, or was incurred to purchase a single premium life insurance, endowment or annuity contact after March 1, 1954.

(5) Loans from related individuals should be analyzed to determine that the interest rate paid does not exceed the normal rate for available money.

(6) When verifying an interest deduction, the examiner should inspect the instruments of indebtedness, such as mortgage statements, loan contract, etc. Cancelled checks are not usually evidence of the liability or payment of interest, and generally, should be supported by documentation.

(7) If the taxpayer maintains brokerage accounts, the statements should be analyzed. Interest charged on margin accounts should not be netted against interest or dividend income. It must be claimed as an itemized deduction.

(8) Examiners should verify that the same interest deduction is not claimed twice, i.e., Itemized Deductions and Rental Expense.

(9) Examiners should be alert for situations where taxpayers have claimed deductions for accrued interest on existing liabilities and foreclosure proceedings have subsequently occurred. Verify the taxpayer has included the difference between the liability per the books and the liability which was relieved by the foreclosure as income.

(10) If the taxpayer moved during the year under examination, the examiner should check the allocation of interest on the closing statement.

(11) If the taxpayer assumed a mortgage during the year under examination, the examiner must make a proper allocation between the buyer and the seller since the lender will normally issue a statement on total interest paid during the year for that mortgage.

◀ *Beginning in 1987 and continuing through 1990*, the amount of your personal interest expense allowed as an itemized deduction on Schedule A, Form 1040, will generally be *limited* to only a portion of the interest you paid. Except for a limited amount of mortgage interest, after 1990 no deduction will be allowed for personal interest accrued or paid during the year. Personal interest generally includes interest you pay on car loans, credit cards, and personal loans. The percentage of personal interest you may deduct for 1987 through 1990 is as follows:

1987	65%
1988	40%
1989	20%
1990	10%

Items you may deduct:

- Interest on a personal loan (limited).
- Interest on a business loan.
- Mortgage interest (restricted).
- "Points," if you are a borrower.
- Mortgage prepayment penalty.
- Redeemable ground rents.
- Installment plan interest (limited).
- Bank credit card plan interest (limited).
- Finance charges separately stated (limited).
- Revolving charge account interest (limited).
- Unstated interest.

Items you may *not* deduct:

- "Points," if you are a seller.
- Nonredeemable ground rents.
- Service charges.
- Loan fees.
- Credit investigation fees.
- Interest relating to tax-exempt securities.
- Certain expenses treated as interest in connection with the short sales of tax-exempt securities.
- Interest paid to carry single-premium life insurance.
- Penalties.
- Premium on a convertible bond.
- Interest to purchase or carry certain straddle positions.

◀ To deduct interest on a debt, you must be legally liable for that debt. You may not deduct payments you make for someone else if you were not legally liable to make them. Both the lender and the borrower must intend that the loan be repaid.

574 *(4-23-81)* 4231

Contributions

(1) Verify amounts claimed and determine that the deduction has been taken in the proper year.

(2) Determine whether the payments were made to qualified organizations. An individual may claim a charitable contribution deduction to a church that has not been recognized by the Service as tax exempt. Such deduction is not barred merely because the church has never applied for recognition of exempt status. Similarly, when an organization has applied but has not provided the Service with sufficient information upon which to make a favorable determination of exempt status, a charitable deduction is not automatically barred.

(3) Determine that percentage limitation is correctly computed, has not been exceeded, and that any contribution carryover is correct.

(4) Determine if contributions claimed are nondeductible personal expenses and ascertain if donor received benefits or consideration in return.

(5) Where a taxpayer claims out of pocket expenses in rendering donated services to a qualified organization, the examiner should determine whether there was reimbursement by the organization.

(6) In a case where property is contributed, ascertain:

(a) whether ordinary income property, capital gain property, or a combination are involved,

(b) cost and fair market value at time of gift, and

(c) whether donor retains any control over the property. If inventory or stock in trade is involved, be alert to double deductions.

(7) When examining unsubstantiated cash contributions, examiners should ask themselves this question: Is the total amount of contributions claimed reasonable in relation to the amount available out of which contributions could have been made? Such available cash must take into consideration the amount of gross income less the other deductions claimed on the return, personal living expenses, income tax withheld and any estimated tax payments.

◀ Generally, you may deduct your contributions of money or property to, or for the use of, qualified organizations. If you give property, you generally may deduct its fair market value at the time of the contribution. Your deduction for charitable contributions is limited to 50 percent of your adjusted gross income, but in some cases, 20 percent and 30 percent limits may apply.

◀ You may deduct a contribution only if the value of the contribution is more than the value of any benefit or privilege you may receive. If you pay more than fair market value to a qualified organization for merchandise, goods, or services, the amount you paid that is in excess of the value may be a charitable contribution.

◀ When donating services to a charitable organization, you may deduct amounts you pay for transportation from your home to the place where you serve, and reasonable payments for necessary meals and lodging while you are away from home overnight, but *not* the value of your time or services.

◀ Deduct unreimbursed out-of-pocket expenses directly related to services you give to a charitable organization, such as expenses for gas and oil for your car. You may not deduct general repair and maintenance expenses. If you do not want to deduct your actual expenses, you may use a standard rate of 9 cents a mile to figure your contribution for years before 1985—12 cents a mile beginning in 1985.

◀ If you donate property to a qualified organization, you generally may deduct fair market value of the property at the time of the contribution. However, if the property has increased in value, you may have to make some adjustments.

◀ Fair market value (FMV) is the price at which property would change hands between a willing buyer and a willing seller, neither being required to buy or sell, and both having reasonable knowledge of all the necessary facts. Generally, the value of used clothing or furniture is far less than its original cost.

◀ You must keep records for all your contributions. If the claimed value of your noncash charitable contributions is more than $500, you must attach Form 8283, Noncash Charitable Contributions, to your return.

575 *(4-23-81)* 4231

Casualty and Theft Losses

(1) Ascertain that a loss has actually been incurred. Property may have been fully depreciated, nonexistent, sold, previously expensed, lost, etc. It may be necessary to verify the adjusted basis of the property. In such a case, the taxpayer should be required to submit evidence as to the original cost, subsequent improvements, and the amount of depreciation claimed in prior years.

(2) Be alert to the possibility that cash stolen may not have been included in income.

(3) Trace handling of losses involving inventory or stock in trade to ascertain that a double deduction is not claimed.

(4) Ascertain that the loss is claimed in the proper year—casualty losses generally in the year incurred—theft or embezzlement in the year discovered.

(5) Determine if gains from involuntary conversion are reported which would change the tax treatment of the casualty and theft losses.

(6) Determine that the amount claimed is equal to the difference in value before and after the loss (limited by cost or other basis), and that the taxpayer was the owner of the property. If a personal residence is involved in the loss deduction, the examiner should ensure that the basis of the property has been reduced for all gains previously unrecognized.

(7) Ascertain that insurance proceeds or claims, salvage proceeds, or salvage value have been properly taken into account.

(8) Casualty losses affecting items, incidental to real property, such as trees or shubbery, must be verified as a loss of a minor portion of the asset. The shrinkage in market value, limited to adjusted basis, which forms the allowable deduction, must be determined by reference to the property as a whole, both as to FMV and adjusted basis.

(9) Be alert to the possibility that the taxpayer may be engaged in arson-for-profit activities.

(a) Indicators of possible arson schemes with potential tax consequences are:

1 Failure to report insurance proceeds which exceed the basis of the property destroyed by fire.

2 Failure to report the correct adjusted basis of the property destroyed.

3 Failure to reduce a casualty loss claimed on a return by the insurance proceeds received.

◀ As a result of hurricanes, earthquakes, tornadoes, fires, vandalism, car accidents, floods, and similar events, many people suffer damage to their property. When property is damaged or destroyed by an event like this, it is called a "casualty." The loss you have because of a casualty may be deductible on your federal income tax return. If your property is stolen, you may also have a deductible theft loss. You must itemize your deductions on Schedule A (Form 1040) to be able to claim a casualty or theft loss to nonbusiness property.

◀ A casualty is the damage, destruction, or loss of property resulting from an identifiable event that is sudden, unexpected, or unusual. *Sudden* means swift, not gradual or progressive. *Unexpected* means ordinarily unanticipated and unintended. *Unusual* means not day-to-day and not typical of the activity in which you were engaged.

◀ A theft is the unlawful taking and removing of money or property with the intent to deprive the owner of it. It includes, but is not limited to, larceny, robbery, and embezzlement. If money or property is taken as the result of extortion, kidnapping, threats, or blackmail, it may also be a theft. You need only to show that the taking of your property was illegal under the law of the state where it occurred, and that it was done with criminal intent.

◀ To take a deduction for a casualty or theft loss, you must be able to show that there was actually a casualty or theft, and you must be able to support the amount you take as a deduction.

◀ For a *casualty* loss, you should be able to show:

- The type of casualty (car accident, fire, storm) and when it occurred;
- That your loss was the direct result of the casualty; and
- That you were the owner of the property, or, if you leased the property from someone else, that you were contractually liable to the owner for the damage.

◀ For a *theft,* you should be able to show:

- When you found that your property was missing;
- That your property was actually stolen; and
- That you were the owner of the property.

4 Reducing insurance proceeds by payoffs to "torches"—individuals starting the fires.

(b) Examiners should consider using in-depth examination techniques in cases where the taxpayer is suspected of being engaged in arson-for-profit activities.

◀ For tax years beginning after 1986, if you have a nonbusiness casualty loss that is covered by insurance, you cannot take the casualty loss deduction unless you file a timely insurance claim for that loss.

576 *(4-23-81)* 4231

Educational Expenses

(1) Determine if the expenses were primarily incurred for the purpose of maintaining or improving skills or meeting express requirements for retention of status.

(2) Examiners should be alert to the special situation of school teachers. Often the requirement of a local board are different than those of a State Board of Education. A teacher may be incurring educational expenses in order to meet the minimum requirements of one of the boards.

(3) If the educational expense involves overseas travel, the tour folio, registration receipt, and transcript of studies from the overseas educational institution should be reviewed. Consideration should be given to the amount of time devoted to educational pursuits.

(4) Verify amounts claimed and determine that the deduction is claimed in the proper year.

(5) Ascertain whether any reimbursement has been received from an employer, governmental agency, or other third party.

◀ You may deduct your ordinary and necessary expenses for education, even though the education may lead to a degree, if the education:

- Is required by your employer, or by law or regulations, for keeping your salary, status, or job (if the requirements are for a business purpose); or
- Maintains or improves skills required in doing your present work.

◀ You may not deduct expenses you have for education, even though the above requirements are met, if the education is:

- Required in order to meet the minimum educational requirements to qualify you in your work or business; or
- Part of a program of study that will lead to qualifying you in a new trade or business.

◀ You may not deduct the expenses for education that qualifies you for a new trade or business even if you did not intend to enter that trade or business.

577 *(4-23-81)* 4231

Union Dues

Verify the amount claimed includes only Labor Union dues and initiation fees and does not include payment for sickness, accident or death benefits.

◀ You may deduct union dues and initiation fees you pay for union membership, subject to the excess above 2% of your miscellaneous itemized deductions, beginning in 1987.

578 *(4-23-81)* 4231

Return Preparer Penalties

(1) Examiners should ascertain whether a return was prepared for compensation by someone other than the taxpayer.

(2) If the taxpayer has utilized the services of a preparer, and preparer penalties may be applicable, the examiner should refer to IRM 426(27).5 for Return Preparer Penalties.

◀ In order to monitor *return preparers*, IRS examiners must ascertain whether the return preparer has violated any part of the IRC. Return preparers have civil liability for no less than 13 different infractions with penalties of fines and/or imprisonment.

580 *(4-23-81)* 4231

Business Returns

581 *(4-23-81)* 4231
General

581.1 *(4-23-81)* 4231
Introduction

Before beginning an examination, examiners must have a knowledge of the type of service performed or merchandise sold. They should also know the approximate volume of business, the expected gross profit ratio or markup practices, and the method of accounting. In addition, the taxpayer should be questioned about banking methods used and whether all receipts are deposited.

581.2 *(4-23-81)* 4231
Basis of Accounting

(1) Examiners must determine at the beginning of an examination the basis of accounting, that is, whether cash or accrual, and in the course of the examination must see that whatever basis is used is consistently maintained as to all accounts.

(2) Unusual items of income and deductions which tend to distort a taxpayer's income should in every case receive special attention and comment.

(3) Items of income and expense deductions which occur in each taxable period should be scrutinized for any inconsistency in the manner of handling.

581.3 *(4-23-81)* 4231
Examination of Employer's Accounting Procedures for Employees' Expenses

(1) Examination of an employer's return may disclose allowances or reimbursements made by the employer for travel, entertainment, and other such business expenses incurred by employees, including officers of a corporation. Unless the total amount of allowances or reimbursements is insignificant, the examiner will ascertain during each such examination whether the taxpayer uses acceptable accounting procedures in requiring an accounting of business expenses incurred by employees.

(2) If the examiner determines that the accounting required by the employer from the employees adequately reflects the correctness of travel, entertainment, and other such business expenses incurred by officers and employees, he/she will include a statement re-

◀ You must choose an accounting method—cash or accrual—for income and expenses of the business. If you do not have the right to choose, such as when inventories are an income-producing factor, you must decide which method you are required to use.

◀ In addition to the cash and accrual methods, there are special accounting methods such as the installment and deferred-payment methods. If you meet certain requirements, you may choose a special method of reporting income from long-term contracts.

◀ You may deduct as business expenses any *reimbursements* and *allowances* you give to your employees for travel and transportation expenses they have in the conduct of your business.

Keeping records. If you require that your employees account to you, you must keep the records and supporting documents given to you by your employees to prove the deductions on your return for the allowances and reimbursements you paid them. Do not include these amounts on your employees' Forms W-2, "Wage and Tax Statement." If you do not require proof from your employees, you must include the amount you paid them as a reimbursement in the amount shown in box 10 on Form W-2.

garding his/her finding in his/her report transmittal or workpapers.

582 *(4-23-81)* 4231

Gross Receipts or Sales

(1) In the initial testing of the sales account the following techniques may be considered:

(a) Test methods of handling cash to see if all receipts are included in income. Scan daily cash reconciliations and related book entries and bank deposits. Note any undeposited cash receipts on hand at the end of the year.

(b) Test reported gross receipts by the gross profit ratio method. (See gross profit ratio test, Text 584)

(c) Note items unusual in origin, nature, or amount in the books of original entry and test them by reference to original sales slips, contracts, job record book, bank deposits, etc. Also, check selected entries made at different times of the year, including some at the beginning of the year. Test check footings and postings to the general ledger.

(d) Review bank statements and deposit slips for unusual items. Test check deposits by comparing selected items to cash receipts and income entries on the books. Determine the net increase or decrease in the bank balances at the beginning and end of the year. If a taxpayer has not reconciled the bank statements, the examiner must do so for this analysis. Compare the ending balance to the balance per books.

(e) Scan the sales account in the ledger for unusual entries. Test entries from the general journal and sales journal. Compare total receipts to total business income bank deposits and reconcile any differences.

(f) Be alert to the possibility of income which may be taxable even though not appearing on the books (dealer reserve income, constructive, receipt, income from foreign sources etc.)

(2) If the results of these initial tests compare favorably with gross receipts reported, further verification would generally be based on the particular circumstances of the case. For example, a high percentage of cash receipts which are not regularly deposited or properly accounted for would be a basis for further testing.

(3) If further verification is necessary, the following techniques should be considered.

◀ Accounting to you means that employees are required to submit to you an account book, diary, statement of expenses, or similar record in which the information as to each element of an expense is recorded at or near the time of the expense. There must also be supporting documentary evidence.

◀ You must report on your tax return any income you receive from your trade or business or any other source unless it is excluded by law. The income may be in the form of cash, property, or services. Some types of income are:

- Interest, dividends, rents, royalties;
- Payment for services, including fees, commissions, and similar items;
- Gains from dealings in property;
- Income from the discharge of indebtedness; and
- Distributive shares of partnership gross income.

◀ This section is only concerned with income from a trade or a business.

◀ Business income is income that you receive when you sell your product or services. Interest is business income to a lending company. Fees are business income to a professional person. Rents are business income to a person in the real estate business. Dividends generally are business income to a dealer in securities.

◀ All income that you earn is taxable to you. You cannot avoid the tax by having the income paid to a third party.

◀ *Property or services bartering.* An exchange of property or services for your property or services is sometimes called bartering. Income received in the form of property or services must be included in income at its fair market value on the date received. If you receive the goods or services of another in return for your goods or services and you both have definitely agreed ahead of time as to the value of the goods or services, that value will be accepted as fair market value unless the value can be shown to be otherwise.

(a) If original receipts and records are not too numerous, match up invoices, contracts or similar documents with any records kept by job or contract and reconcile any differences. If receipts and records are numerous, test check at various intervals and also look for unusual items. If possible, make test of quantities of the principal product sold in comparison with production or purchases (automobile dealers, builders, etc.)

(b) Check the receipts to the sales or general journal and reconcile any differences.

(c) Question any unusual sales discounts or allowances.

(d) Determine the extent to which receipts were used to pay operating expenses, liabilities, personal expenses, etc. At this phase of the examination, consideration should be given to test checking cash register tapes or other records of receipts to see that all are included in income.

(e) Determine the method and adequacy of accounting for merchandise withdrawn for personal use. Withdrawals should be accounted for as the merchandise is withdrawn and not on an estimated basis. Normally, purchases will be reduced by the cost of such merchandise; however, the amount may be credited to sales.

(f) If the taxpayer reports on the accrual basis, determine if all receiveables are included in income.

(g) Scan sales agreements, contracts, and related correspondence for leads to unrecorded bonuses, awards, kickbacks, etc.

(h) If the records indicate that contracts or sales may have been completed but corresponding income not reported, further inquiry should be made about the sales. If practicable, check journal entries and bank deposits for the first few weeks of the following year to see if the amounts were taken into income at that time.

(i) Review workpapers made for tax return purposes and make sure that adjustments are appropriate. Reconcile receipts per books with receipts reported. Resolve any differences.

(j) It may be necessary during the examination to secure additional records, documents, or other clarifying evidence. If such additional data will resolve matters, advise taxpayers of what is in question and the information needed. They should then be given an opportunity to furnish the information.

(k) Be alert to indications of:

1 Capital gains treatment of items which may constitute ordinary income. For example, capital gain on the sale of lots held for resale by

◀ Accounting for your income tax purposes differs at times from accounting for financial purposes.

◀ The income from your business is figured on the basis of a tax year and according to your regular method of accounting. If the sale of a product is an income-producing factor in your business, the use of inventories usually is required to clearly show your income.

◀ *Installment method*. For tax years ending after 1986 a part of the installment obligation is treated as a payment received at the end of the tax year even though it was not paid at the end of that tax year. The new rule applies to:

- Sales after February 28, 1986, by dealers in real and personal property; and
- Sales after August 16, 1986, of business or rental real property if the selling price exceeds $150,000.

Exceptions: These rules do not apply to the sale of:

- Property that is not used substantially in a trade or business or in the production of income.
- Property used or produced on a farm.
- Real property for $150,000 or less, if the property was used as business or rental property.

For more information see Section 453C of the Internal Revenue Code, or IRS Pub. 537.

◀ *Cash discounts*. These are amounts that the seller permits you to deduct from the invoice price for prompt payment. For income tax purposes you may use either of two methods to account for cash discounts. You may:

- Deduct the cash discount from purchases; or
- Credit the cash discount to a discount income account.

◀ You must use the method you select every year for all your purchase discounts.

◀ *Constructive receipt*. Income is constructively received when it is credited to your account or set apart in a way that makes it available to you. You do not need to have physical possession of it. The income must be reported in the year it is constructively received.

a real estate dealer in the regular course of business.

2 Sales made or services rendered in exchange for other goods and services which were not included in income.

3 Unreported commissions or rentals from activities operated on the taxpayer's business premises. In some cases, there may be arrangement for operating concessions or businesses such as cafes, bars, candy counters, vending machines, and newsstands.

583 *(4–23–81)* 4231

Cases Involving Contractual Obligations Treated as Amounts Realized

(1) Examiners should determine the following:

(a) The date on which the contract was discounted or sold.

(b) The name of the purchaser of the contract and the amount of the discount.

(c) Information as to whether the purchaser of the contract previously engaged in the purchase of similar contracts and evidence as to the extent of such trading.

(d) Whether the purchaser of the property was willing to pay the entire price at the time of the sale.

(e) Information as to whether any banks in the area have the right to discount similar contracts supported by documentary evidence, such as bylaws, charters, or regulations, etc.

(f) Information to establish the fair market value of the contract when received. Usually, the best evidence would be the prices at which similar contracts were sold.

(g) Name and addresses of people in the vicinity who have purchased contracts of this type.

584 *(4–23–81)* 4231

Gross Profit Ratio Test

(1) In cases where inventories are a material income producing factor the gross profit test serves as a guide for the reasonableness of gross receipts, inventories, purchases, and business net profit.

(2) The term, gross profit ratio, refers to the ratio of gross profit realized on sales to gross receipts from the sales. It is expressed as a percentage of the selling price.

◂ *Checks*. A valid check received before the close of the tax year is constructive receipt of income in that year, even though you do not cash or deposit the check until the following year.

◂ Some sales are made under arrangements that provide for part or all of the selling price to be paid in a later year. These sales are called "installment sales." If you finance the buyer's purchase of your property yourself, instead of having the buyer get a loan or mortgage from a bank, you probably have an installment sale.

◂ The buyer's "installment obligation" to make future payments to you might be in the form of a deed of trust, a note, a land contract, a mortgage, or some other evidence of the buyer's indebtedness to you.

◂ If you sell or discount the buyer's installment obligation, you will be considered to have collected all of what you owed on the installment debt. If this takes place during the year of sale, report your entire gain on your return for that year. You do not have an installment sale. If it takes place in a later year, you may have a disposition of an installment obligation.

◂ After you have figured the gross receipts from your business and figured the cost of goods sold, you are ready to figure your gross profit. Gross profit is the amount you must arrive at before you may take any deductions for business operations.

(3) Expressed in another manner it is the margin between the cost of sales and gross receipts expressed in terms of a percentage or sales.

(4) The selling price is always 100 percent because it is the total amount of money expected from the sale.

(5) *Margin* is always figured on the selling price. It is a *percentage of sales*. Example: Suppose an article is purchased for $1.20 and sold for $1.60. The margin would be 40 cents, which is ¼ or 25 percent of the selling price. Therefore, the margin or gross profit ratio on this article would be 25 percent.

(6) A related term sometimes used is *markup*. Markup can be computed either as a *percentage of cost or of selling price.* Although many consider markup a percentage of the selling price, figuring markup on the cost price is easier and less confusing. The examiner may wish to compute markup on the cost of goods to determine the correct sales. Bear in mind that the percentages of margin and markup on cost are not the same. Margin and markup in dollars are identical, however, the percentages are different. Both represent the differences between cost of merchandise and selling price.

(7) The table in Exhibit 500–1 shows what the markup on cost must be to give the desired margin in a number of more common cases to use this table, find your margin or gross profit percentage in the left column. Multiply the cost of the article by the corresponding percentage in the right or markup column. The result added to the cost gives the correct selling price.

(8) The important thing to keep in mind is that when markup is figured on the selling price, a different markup percentage must be used than when figuring the markup on the cost price. Otherwise, the anticipated margin will not be attained. Example: Suppose an article is purchased for $1.20 by the seller who then marks it up 25 percent. What must the selling price be? The markup of 25 percent times the cost, $1.20, equals 30 cents. Add 30 cents to the cost price of $1.20 and we have a selling price of $1.50 with a margin of 30 cents, or 20 percent gross profit ratio. However, if we want to markup the article so that we have a 25 percent margin, we must first determine the percentage that will yield the desired margin when applied to the cost price. Looking at the markup table in Exhibit 500–1, we see that a 25 percent margin is equivalent to a 33⅓ percent markup on cost.

◀ To figure gross profit, first figure your net receipts. Do this by subtracting any "returns and allowances" from gross receipts. Returns and allowances include cash or credit refunds you make to customers, rebates, and other allowances off the actual sales price.

◀ Next, subtract the cost of goods sold from net receipts. The result is the gross profit from your business.

◀ However, if the sale of inventory items is not a major source of income for your business, you will not have to figure the cost of goods sold. Your gross profit will be the same as your net receipts—gross receipts minus any refunds, rebates, or other allowances. Most professions and businesses that sell services rather than products are able to figure gross profit directly from net receipts in this way.

◀ *Illustration:* This shows how gross profit is figured in the income statement of a business.

Income Statement
Year Ended December 31, 1984

Gross receipts	$400.000
Minus: Returns and allowances	14.940
Net receipts	$385.060
Minus: Cost of goods sold	288.140
Gross profit	$ 96.920

The cost of goods sold for this business is figured as follows:

Inventory at beginning of year		$ 37.845
Plus: Purchases	$285.900	
Minus: Items withdrawn for personal use	2.650	283.250
Goods available for sale		$321.095
Minus: Inventory at end of year		32.955
Cost of goods sold		$288.140

Items	Cost	Market	Whichever is lower
R	$300	$500	$300
S	200	100	100
T	450	200	200
Totals	$950	$800	$600

Multiplying 33⅓ percent times the cost, $1.20, equals 40 cents. Adding 40 cents to the cost price gives us a selling price of $1.60, and a margin of 40 cents, or 25 percent.

(9) But, a *markup on cost* of 25 percent gives a selling price of $1.50. Therefore, if it were necessary to have a margin of 25 percent to cover the cost of operation and net profit, the taxpayer would be losing money by pricing merchandise on the basis of a 25 percent markup on cost. To realize a 25 percent margin, the taxpayer would have to use a markup of 33⅓ percent on the cost price.

(10) The following example illustrates the application of the gross profit ratio as a percentage of sales:

Example:

Gross Sales	$50,000
Cost of Sales	40,000
Gross Profit (Margin)	$10,000

(a) Here, the gross profit ratio is 20 percent. In other words, 20 percent of $50,000 sales gives the margin of $10,000.

(b) From the markup table it is found that a 20 percent gross profit ratio (margin) is the equivalent of a 25 percent markup based on cost. In other words the cost of sales in the amount of $40,000 must be increased by 25 percent or $10,000, to give the $50,000 gross sales.

(11) A change in the gross sales results in a change in the gross profit ratio and the markup:

Example:

Gross Sales	$60,000
Cost of Sales	40,000
Gross Profit (Margin)	$20,000

(12) There has been an increase in gross sales of $10,000 ($50,000 to $60,000) or a 20 percent increase in gross sales. This has resulted in a gross profit ratio now of 33⅓ percent. The markup (on cost) formerly 25 percent is now 50 percent.

(13) After the ratio for the business under examination has been determined, compare it with prior years ratios of the same business and with the ratio for businesses engaged in similar activities. In making the comparison with the ratio of similar businesses, remember that the ratio will vary according to the size, sales volume, and location. For example, a neighborhood gorcery and market with sales of $10,000 to $50,000 would have a different gross profit ratio than a supermarket in a shopping center with sales in excess of $100,000.

Points to Check

◀ *Gross receipts*. Even very small businesses will find it helpful to use cash registers to keep track of receipts. You should also use a proper invoicing system and keep a separate bank account for your business. At the end of each business day, make sure your records balance with your actual cash and credit receipts for the day.

◀ *Inventory at beginning of year.* Compare this figure with last year's ending inventory. The two amounts should be the same.

◀ *Purchases*. If you have taken any inventory items for your personal use—used them yourself, provided them to your family, or given them as personal gifts, etc.—be sure to remove them from the cost of goods sold. Subtract the amount from your purchases for the year.

◀ *Inventory at end of year.* Check to make sure that your procedures for taking inventory are adequate. These procedures should provide you with a way of making sure that all items have been included in the inventory, and that proper pricing techniques have been used.

◀ Avoid using adding machine tapes as the only evidence for your inventory. Inventory forms are available at office supply stores. These forms have columns for recording a description, the quantity, the unit price, and the value of each inventory item. Each page has space to record who made the physical count, who priced the items, who made the extensions, and who proofed the calculations. These forms will help satisfy you that the total inventory is accurate. They will also provide you with a permanent record to support its validity.

(14) Average figures on gross profit ratios for different sizes and types of businesses are available in various publications prepared by private concerns. These may be suitable for testing purposes.

(15) If the comparison indicates that there is a probable error in the reported gross profit figure, consider the items included in the following list as possible reasons for the error.

(a) *Gross Receipts*

1 Possible inclusion of extraneous items not subject to the gross profit ratio, such as (rents, interest, dividends, etc.).

2 All accounts receivable not reported when accrual basis of accounting is used.

3 All collections of accounts receivable not reported when cash basis or accounting is used.

4 Income constructively received not reported.

5 Installment sales incorrectly reported.

6 Sale of ending inventory not included in gross receipts, when business is sold.

7 Theft of inventory items by employees.

8 Unreported gross receipts from bartering.

(b) *Inventory*

1 Inventory improperly valued or incorrect amount carried over from the prior year.

2 Figures are estimated.

3 Inventories not used even though they are a material income producing factor.

4 Ending inventory understated.

(c) *Purchases*

1 Items included which are not properly a part of cost of sales.

2 Personal withdrawals not properly accounted for.

3 Purchases not reduced for returned merchandise.

4 Purchase discounts not properly reflected.

590 *(4-23-81)* 4231

(Reserved)

5(10)0 *(4-23-81)* 4231

Business Expenses

5(10)1 *(4-23-81)* 4231

Introduction

(1) Many expenses claimed on business returns can be verified utilizing the following general techniques:

(a) Verify payment against cancelled checks and/or receipts.

(b) Determine validity of deduction by analyzing contracts, and/or original source documents such as invoices.

(2) The following common business expenses utilize the above techniques as well as specific techniques applicable to a particular expense.

Testing Gross Profit Accuracy

◀ If you are in a retail or wholesale business, you can check the accuracy of your gross profit figure. First, divide gross profit by net receipts. The resulting percentage measures the average spread between the merchandise cost of goods sold and the selling price.

◀ Next, compare this percentage to your markup policy.

◀ Little or no difference between these two percentages shows that your gross profit figure is accurate. A large difference between these percentages may show that sales, purchases, inventory, or other items of cost have not been figured accurately. The reason for the difference should be determined.

◀ *Example*. Joe Able operates a retail business. On the average, he marks up his merchandise so that he will realize a gross profit of 33⅓ percent on its sales. The net receipts (gross receipts minus returns and allowances) shown on his income statement for 1984 is $300,000. His cost of goods sold is $200,000. This results in a gross profit of $100,000 ($300,000 minus $200,000). To test the accuracy of this year's results, Joe divides gross profit ($100,000) by the net receipts ($300,000). The resulting 33⅓ percent confirms his markup policy of 33⅓ percent.

5(10)2 *(4-23-81)* 4231
Cost of Goods Sold

5(10)2.1 *(4-23-81)* 4231
Purchases

(1) Review the cutoff date. Determine if year-end purchases have been recorded in the proper accounting period.

(2) Determine if the owners consume or withdraw merchandise for personal use, such as food, clothing, appliances, building material, boats, motors, etc. If so, proper reductions should be made to purchases or cost of sales. Also consider possible tax effect of such withdrawals to the recipients.

(3) Scan purchases column in the cash disbursements journal, voucher register, etc., and look for items unusual in amount and to payee or vendors not generally associated with the products or services handled by the taxpayer.

(4) Review entries in the general ledger control account. Note and verify entries which originate from other than usual sources (general journal entries, debit and credit memos, etc.).

(5) Test check the recorded purchases for a representative period with vendor's invoices and cancelled checks, etc. Be alert to such items as:

(a) personal expenses (clothing, boats, motors, furniture, etc.);

(b) capital expenditures;

(c) fictitious or duplicate invoices, etc.

(6) If purchases are made from related taxpayers or controlled foreign entities, review a representative number of such transactions to determine if the following are present:

(a) prices in excess of fair market value;

(b) excessive rebates and allowances;

(c) goods or services not received (this would be a good device to improperly withdraw funds and receive a resultant tax deduction).

(7) Ascertain if merchandise, prizes, trips, etc., were received from suppliers as a result of volume purchases.

5(10)2.2 *(5-26-82)* 4231
Inventories

(1) To the extent necessary, examiners will verify inventories reported. In each case involving inventories, the examiner will make an affirmative statement in the report transmittal or the workpapers regarding the examination steps taken to verify that inventories are correct as reported. This statement should also describe the taxpayers method of pricing inventories. If inventories are not examined, the examiner will comment in the workpapers as to why this issue was unworthy of examination.

(2) In all cases wherein inventories are worthy of examination, the following minimum checks will be made:

◀ If you make or buy goods to sell, you are entitled to deduct the cost of goods sold on your tax return.

◀ Inventories are factors in figuring the cost of goods sold and are required at the beginning and end of each tax year for manufacturers, wholesalers, retailers, and every other business that makes, buys, or sells goods to produce income. Inventories include goods held for sale in the normal course of business as well as raw materials and supplies that will physically become a part of merchandise intended for sale.

◀ Inventories must be used whenever they are necessary to clearly show income. The inventory methods described apply to sole proprietorships, partnerships, and corporations.

◀ If you must use inventories, only the accrual method of accounting will correctly show your gross income.

◀ Add to your inventory at the beginning of your tax year the cost of merchandise and materials purchased during the year for sale or manufacture and all other items entering into the cost of obtaining or producing the goods held for sale. From this total subtract your inventory at the end of the year. The remainder represents the cost of goods sold during the tax period. It should not include selling expenses or any other expenses that are not directly related to obtaining or producing the goods sold.

◀ The most common kinds of inventories are:

- Merchandise or stock in trade.
- Raw materials.
- Work in process.
- Finished products.
- Supplies (that will become part of the item intended for sale).

◀ To arrive at a dollar amount for your inventory you need a method for *identifying*, and a basis for *valuing* the items in your inventory.

(a) verify that any method of inventory valuation conforms to the "prescribed methods" as indicated in Regs. 1.471;

(b) compare inventory balances in the return under examination with the balances for the prior and subsequent years' returns, and verify these with the taxpayer's records;

(c) check for unauthorized changes from cost to cost or market;

(d) check for gross profit percentage variations;

(e) determine meaning and significance of any notes or qualifying statements on financial reports prepared by independent accounting firms;

(f) determine that all direct and indirect overhead and burden expenses are in the overhead pool that is used in the computation of overhead rates where applicable;

(g) analyze unusual entries to cost of sales account for labor, material, and burden charges not directly related to sales or transfers of finished goods, if applicable;

(h) determine that year-end purchases were included in closing inventory;

(i) determine if there have been write-downs for "excess" inventory to below cost. Verify that the method of inventory valuation for "excess" inventory is in accordance with Rev. Rul. 80–60; and

(j) determine that inventory costing conforms to Regs. 1.471–11 for taxpayers engaged in manufacturing or production activities. Examiners should be aware that while the Regulations do not specifically define "manufacturing operations or processes", there are court cases, Revenue Rulings, etc. outlining activities which constitute manufacturing activities. Such activities include the conversion, transformation, or processing of raw materials into a finished, marketable product; purchasing a product and sub-contracting the work which will complete the item into a finished product; or, purchasing the individual parts of an item, e.g., a toy, and assembling these parts into a final product.

(3) The above minimum checks should not deter an examiner from making a more detailed audit when the situation warrants. If the elective method of inventorying provided by IRC 472 is used, the examiner will ascertain whether the requirements in Regs. 1.472–1 to 1.472–6, inclusive, have been complied with.

◀ Inventory valuation rules cannot be the same for all kinds of businesses but the method you use must be within the scope of the best accounting practice used for similar businesses and clearly show income. To clearly show income, you must use the same inventory practice from year to year.

◀ To value your inventory you must know what items to include and what items to exclude from the inventory.

◀ Inventories include all your finished or partly finished goods and raw materials and supplies that will become a part of the merchandise you intend to sell.

◀ Merchandise should be included in your inventory only if you have title to it.

◀ Exclude from your inventory all goods you have sold, but be sure that the title to them has passed to the buyer. Also exclude goods in your possession that are consigned to you and goods you ordered for future delivery if you do not yet have title to them.

◀ *Cost identification*. The specific identification method is a method used to identify items in an inventory with their costs by matching the goods with their invoices (less appropriate discounts) to find the cost of each inventoried item.

◀ The first-in first-out (FIFO) method assumes that the items you purchased or produced first are the first items you sold, consumed, or otherwise disposed of.

◀ The last-in first-out (LIFO) method assumes that the items of inventory that you purchased last are treated as if you sold or removed them from inventory first.

◀ *Cost or market method*. Lower of cost or market means that you compare the market value of each item on hand at the inventory date with its cost and use the lower value as its inventory value. Thus, if at the end of your tax year you had the following items on hand, the value of your closing inventory would be $600.

5(10)2.21 *(5-26-82)* 4231
Examples of Inventory Adjustments

(1) Any changes to the inventory as reported will be effected either by changing the taxpayer's method of accounting or by correcting errors within the method used. Because of the unsettled status of the precise distinction between the terms, the following specific examples are presented to show the Service position as to the applicability and nonapplicability of IRC 481.

(2) Examples of inventory adjustments which are to be treated as changes in methods of accounting are:

(a) changes from cost to lower of cost or market, and vice versa;

(b) changes resulting from failure to use inventories where required;

(c) changes to or from specialized methods of accounting for inventory, such as the farm-price method, unit-livestock-price method and retail method; and

(d) a taxpayer who regularly charges all overhead, or specific items of overhead, directly to cost of sales for both book and tax purposes is considered to be following a method of accounting, although this method is not an acceptable method under the Regulations. Correction of a taxpayer's inventory for the improper omission of overhead is a change in method of accounting.

(3) If any of the changes listed in (2) above occurred for the first time during a series of taxable years beginning with the calendar year 1954 or the first fiscal year subject to the 1954 Code, IRC 481 would, of course, apply to prevent amounts from being duplicated or omitted. On the other hand, where the use of any of the following inventory practices occurred for the first time during a series of open 1954 Code taxable years, a correction in the *first year* in which use of the practice occurred would not involve an adjustment subject to IRC 481:

(a) the use of arbitrary reserves to reduce the inventory value;

(b) the reduction of cost to an alleged market value by the use of arbitrary rates or amounts, resulting in a valuation other than market;

(c) the omission of items of stock from inventory;

(d) the valuation of inventory items at a nominal price or at price obviously incorrect;

Items	Cost	Market	Whichever is lower
R	$300	$500	$300
S	200	100	100
T	450	200	200
Totals	$950	$800	$600

◀ If you use this method, you must value each item in the inventory. You may not value the entire inventory at cost ($950) and at market ($800) and use the lower figure. If you use the cost method, the value of your closing inventory would be $950.

◀ *Market value,* under ordinary circumstances and for normal goods, means the usual bid price at the date of your inventory. This price is based on the volume of merchandise you usually buy. Thus, if you buy items in small lots at $10 an item and a competitor buys identical items in larger lots at $8.50 an item, your usual market price will be higher than your competitor's.

◀ The lower of cost or market rule applies to goods purchased and on hand, and to basic elements of cost (materials, labor, and overhead) of goods in process of manufacture and finished goods on hand. It does not apply to goods on hand or in process of manufacture for delivery at fixed prices on a firm sales contract (that is, not legally subject to cancellation by either you or the buyer). These goods must be inventoried at cost.

◀ *Lower than market.* When, in the regular course of business, you have offered merchandise for sale at prices lower than market (as defined earlier), the inventory may be valued at these prices, less the direct costs of disposition. Figure these prices from the actual sales for a reasonable period before and after the date of your inventory. Prices significantly different from the actual prices determined are not acceptable.

(e) the classification of stock as unsalable which was disposed of at normal prices during the subsequent year;

(f) the use of arbitrary overhead rates; and

(g) failure to apply to the inventory the proper proportion of the differences between actual and standard costs.

(4) With respect to taxpayers who have changed to the full absorption method of inventory costing under Regs. 1.471–11, inventory records and cost analysis should be carefully examined even for those taxpayers who received a letter from the National Office regarding the change or the use of this method. Examiners should be aware of any change to the full absorption method made by taxpayers by increasing their opening inventory in the year of change without a corresponding pick up of the IRC 481 adjustment. Taxpayers should be questioned as to how they made the change and how they reported the resulting adjustment. Schedule M should also be examined as inventory adjustments may be reflected therein.

◀ Perpetual or book inventories that are kept by following sound accounting practices are acceptable for figuring the cost of goods on hand. Inventory accounts, however, must be charged with the actual cost of goods purchased or produced, and credited with the value of goods used, transferred, or sold. Credits must be figured on the basis of the actual cost of goods acquired during the year and the inventory value at the beginning of the year.

◀ Physical inventories must be taken at reasonable intervals and the book figure for inventory must be adjusted to agree with the actual inventory.

5(10)2.22 *(4–23–81)* 4231
Year of Change Initiated by the Service

(1) If the proposed adjustment to inventory, or any other account, is a change in method of accounting, generally the change will be made in the earliest open year so that it is reflected for the entire series of open years.

(2) In the case of a partnership, or any other case involving more than one taxpayer, the year of the change should normally not be earlier than the earliest open year for all affected taxpayers.

(3) In determining the year of the adjustment, the provisions of IRM 4023, regarding reopening examined cases, must be observed.

5(10)3 *(4–23–81)* 4231
Abandonment and Demolition Losses

(1) Determine if an abandonment or demolition has actually occurred. Property may have been fully depreciated, previously expensed, nonexistent, sold or held for resale, transferred to owner, etc.

(2) Verify the basis of the asset and the related reserves.

(3) Ascertain the period to which such loss is applicable.

(4) Determine if salvage value has been taken into account in computing net loss.

(5) Ascertain if the abandonment or demolition has related to the acquisition or construction of new property, incurred for the purpose of securing a lease, etc. If so, consideration should be given to capitalizing the remaining basis and cost of removal.

◀ *Abandoned property.* If you physically abandon property, you may deduct as a loss the adjusted basis of the asset at the time of its abandonment. Your intent must be to discard the asset so that you will not use it again or retrieve it for sale, exchange, or other disposition.

(a) Where a building was demolished as a condition to selling the land, any loss should be reflected in the disposition of the land.

(b) Where a demolition loss was made in connection with a contract to lease land, the loss must be amortized over the life of the lease.

(c) Intention is always difficult to determine. Some help may be obtained by determining the time interval between acquisition and demolition, scanning the minute book, if any, and questioning the taxpayer. Sometimes the dates on architectural plans or construction contracts for a replacement building or paving job (if used as a parking lot) will be indicative of intention.

(6) Determine if the retirement or abandonment loss is specifically allowable under the taxpayer's method of accounting for depreciable property.

(7) If the property was used in or relates to the operation of a mineral property where percentage depletion is claimed, determine if such loss has been included as an operating cost.

5(10)4 *(4-23-81)* 4231

Advertising

(1) Examiners should verify that:

(a) Items of a capital nature are not being charged off as a current expense. In general, however, the intangible benefits to be received in the future from present advertising are not capitalizable.

(b) Expenditures are not being claimed in connection with campaigns of political candidates or for the indirect promotion or defeat of legislation.

(c) Advertising in publications of charitable and other organizations has been allocated between its value to the taxpayer as pure advertising and the remainder as a contribution or personal expense. As an example, Mr. Birch, a retail automobile dealer in an Eastern State, purchases a full page ad in a fraternity paper sold at a university on the West Coast, where he graduated. Mr. Birch would be required to show what particular business benefits he expected to derive from the ad, before it could be considered allowable as advertising expense for income tax purposes.

(d) If the expenditure is of a type generally considered to constitute entertainment, amusement or recreation, it is classed as entertainment even though it may have some advertising or public relations value. If such an expenditure would not qualify as a deduction for entertainment, it should not be allowed as an advertising expense.

◀ *Demolition of buildings.* For tax years beginning after December 31, 1983, you cannot deduct any amount paid or incurred to demolish any structure, or any loss pertaining to the undepreciated basis of a structure. Instead, you must add these costs to the basis of the land on which the demolished structure was located.

◀ *Advertising expenses.* You may deduct advertising expenses if they are reasonable and they bear a reasonable relationship to your business activities. You cannot deduct the cost of advertising if its purpose is to promote or defeat legislation.

◀ Expenditures for institutional or goodwill advertising to keep your name before the public are usually deductible as an ordinary and necessary business expense if they are related to the amount of business you may reasonably expect in the future. For example, the cost of advertising that keeps your name before the public by encouraging people to contribute to organizations such as the Red Cross, to buy U.S. Savings Bonds, or to participate in similar causes usually will be deductible.

5(10)5 *(4-23-81)* 4231
Bad Debts

(1) Determine if the method of deducting bad debts is acceptable and consistent with the preceding year.

(2) Obtain list of accounts charged off. Review to determine if any of the following are present:

(a) Chargeoff of accounts due from owner, related taxpayers, or controlled foreign entities, etc.

(b) Chargeoff of accounts due from police, politicians, etc.

(c) Large and unusual items. These should be fully verified.

(d) Premature chargeoffs.

(3) Consider business vs. nonbusiness nature of the debt and any statutory limitations.

(4) Verify that the amounts being charged off were previously reported as income.

(5) Where a reserve method of deducting bad debts is used, these additional techniques should be followed:

(a) independently compute the additions to the reserve;

(b) verify correctness of rate used;

(c) determine if the additions to and the balance of the reserve are reasonable.

(6) If accounts charged off were created through installment sales, determine if repossessions, if any, have been properly handled, and if the amount charged off represents only unrecovered cost.

(7) Determine if recoveries are properly handled. Absence of bad debt recoveries may indicate diversion of funds, etc.

5(10)6 *(4-23-81)* 4231
Commissions

(1) Examiners should verify that payments made are actually commissions and not employee salaries misclassified to avoid employment taxes.

(2) Verify that Forms 1099-NEC, Nonemployee Compensation were issued where required.

(3) Reconcile Forms 1099 issued to Form 1096, Annual Summary and transmittal of U.S. Information Returns.

5(10)7 *(4-23-81)* 4231
Depletion

◀ *Business bad debts*. A business deducts its bad debts directly from gross income. Unlike nonbusiness bad debts, business bad debts are not deducted as short-term capital losses, but are deducted directly from gross income.

◀ To be deductible as a business bad debt, a debt must be closely related to the activity of your business. There must have been a dominant business reason for you to have entered into the transaction as the creditor.

◀ You may deduct business bad debts using one of two methods:

- The specific chargeoff method, which allows you to deduct specific business bad debts that become totally or partially worthless in your tax year.
- The reserve method, which permits you to deduct a reasonable addition to your reserve for bad debts.

◀ You may take a bad debt deduction on your accounts and notes receivable only if you have included the amount you are owed in your gross income for the current or an earlier tax year.

◀ For a business bad debt, you must attach a statement to your return that contains:

- A description of the debt, including the amount and the date it became due;
- The name of the debtor, and the business relationship between you and the debtor;
- The efforts you made to collect the debt; and
- Why you decided that the debt was worthless.

◀ Form 1099-MISC is now used for payments of $600 or more for fees, commissions, or other forms of compensation paid to persons not treated as your employees for services rendered in your trade or business.

5(10)7.1 *(4-23-81)* 4231
General

(1) Utilize special depletion Form T (timber) where applicable and available. If such forms have not been filed currently, or filed in prior years and not brought up to date currently, and if considered essential in the case, the taxpayer should be requested to submit the form or equivalent information.

(2) If considered necessary, request engineering advice or assistance in the case.

5(10)7.2 *(4-23-81)* 4231
Cost Depletion

(1) Determine that any prior elections binding on subsequent years have been complied with.

(2) Determine that any aggregation or separation of mineral interests are proper. Insure that taxpayer has an economic interest not an economic advantage.

(3) Determine that recoverable units are based on the latest geological or engineering surveys applicable to the property and that recoverable units with respect to all mineral interests included in each aggregation are taken into account.

(4) Be aware of the various types of expenditures which are recoverable only through depletion. Ascertain that no expenditures paid or incurred in the period under review have been expensed, or capitalized as a depreciable or amortizable item.

(5) Ascertain that the adjusted basis of the property has been properly computed, giving particular attention to prior percentage or discovery depletion taken which may not be recorded on the books. (Review retained copies of prior year returns and examination reports where available.) Also, consider allocation of lump-sum purchases between land, mineral, timber, etc.

(6) In regard to timber depletion, determine whether growth of timber has been properly taken into account in determining recoverable units.

5(10)7.3 *(4-23-81)* 4231
Percentage Depletion

(1) Ascertain that the taxpayer has an economic interest in the mineral in place.

(2) Determine that any aggregation of mineral interests are proper.

◀ *Depletion* permits the owner of an economic interest in mineral deposits, oil wells, gas wells, geothermal deposits, or standing timber to deduct the cost over the economic life of the property.

◀ The depletion deduction may be available to you as an owner and an operator if you have an economic interest in mineral deposits or standing timber.

◀ You have an economic interest if you have a legal interest in minerals in place or standing timber and you have the right to income from the extraction and sale of the mineral or the cutting of the timber, to which you must look for a return of your capital.

◀ There are two ways of figuring depletion: cost depletion and percentage depletion. Percentage depletion does not apply to timber.

◀ *Cost depletion* is usually figured by dividing the adjusted basis of the mineral property by the total number of recoverable units in the deposit, and multiplying the resulting rate per unit:

- By the number of units sold and for which you receive payment during your tax year if you use the cash method; or
- By the number of units sold if you use the accrual method of accounting.

◀ The adjusted basis is your original cost or other basis of the mineral property, plus any capitalized costs, minus all the depletion allowed or allowable on the property. Depletion allowed or allowable each year is the greater of percentage depletion or cost depletion. However, the adjusted basis can never be less than zero.

◀ The number of units in place in a natural deposit is mainly an engineering problem. It is your responsibility to prove, by using accepted methods, the number of recoverable units.

(3) Ascertain that the sales reported in regard to each property do not include sales applicable to another property, sales of purchased minerals, nonmineral sales, or other income items.

(4) Ascertain, where applicable, that mineral sales have been adjusted to "gross income from the property" by reduction for such factors as unallowable treatment costs; unallowable transportation costs; rents and royalties; including a proportionate part of lease bonuses; amounts paid to others in contract mining or similar operations where the other party has acquired an economic interest and is entitled to depletion; certain ad valorem property taxes, trade discounts allowed, etc.

(5) In situations in which the basis for percentage depletion is not the actual sales price of a finished product, but a value of the mineral at the point at which it has passed through the last allowable treatment process, determine if the value used is the correct representative market or field price.

(6) Ascertain that mineral sales made to a business controlled by the taxpayer are not inflated to gain a tax advantage through depletion.

(7) Ascertain that all expenses applicable to a property have been charged to that property, including a proper allocation of general, administrative, and overhead expenses. Be alert to shifting of expenses from a profit year to a loss year by overaccruals, underaccruals, or prepayments. Also casualty, demolition, or abandonment losses applicable to the property should be included in cost of operations.

(8) Be alert to possible reduction of expenses by improper offsets such as income from scrap sales, cash discounts earned, sales of assets, etc.

(9) Consider whether nonproductive activities involving the furnishing of goods or services to employees at prices or amounts which consistently result in losses on that activity should be held to constitute a cost of operating the mineral property (housing furnished employees, merchandise sold at or below cost, etc.).

(10) Ascertain that the proper rates of depletion and the statutory limitations have been complied with.

5(10)8 *(4-23-81)* 4231

Depreciation and Amortization of Assets and/or Improvements

◀ *Percentage depletion* is a certain percentage, specified for each mineral, of your gross income from the property during the tax year, but the deduction for depletion under this method cannot be more than 50 percent of your taxable income from the property, figured without the deduction for depletion.

◀ The use of percentage depletion for oil and gas is not allowed except for certain domestic production (production from certain domestic gas wells and that of independent producers and royalty owners of oil and gas wells). If you are a qualified independent producer or royalty owner of oil and gas the deduction for depletion may not be more than 65 percent of your taxable income (reduced for an individual by the zero bracket amount) from all sources, figured without the depletion allowance, any net operating loss carryback, and any capital loss carryback.

◀ Rents and royalties (which are depletable income to the payee) you pay or incur for the property must be excluded from your gross income from the property when figuring your percentage depletion.

◀ *Fifty-percent limit*. In figuring the percentage depletion deduction and the 50 percent limit for percentage depletion, you reduce your gross income from the property by the allocable part of any bonus you paid for a mineral lease or an oil and gas lease on the property. You figure that part of the bonus by multiplying the total bonus that you paid by a fraction, the numerator (top number) of which is the number of units that you sold in the tax year, and the denominator (bottom number) of which is the number of total estimated recoverable units from the property.

5(10)8.1 *(4-27-83)* 4231

Depreciation and Amortization

(1) Compare total depreciation as shown by the depreciation schedule with the deduction claimed on the return. Reconcile any differences. Be alert for duplication of deductions.

(2) Determine whether assets shown on the depreciation schedule, which have a prior year acquisition date, are the same as shown on the tax return for the prior year. If not, this indicates depreciation claimed on the assets which have previously been expensed, fully depreciated, etc.

(3) Determine if costs, such as freight-in, installation costs, title costs, back taxes and legal and brokerage fees relating to the acquisition of assets have been capitalized.

(4) For property acquired after 12-31-82, determine if the basis has been reduced by the appropriate amount of investment credit.

(5) Ascertain if assets include items of a personal nature.

(6) If the taxpayer is a building contractor or in a business related to the building trades, give particular attention to the basis of any building owned by the taxpayer. The taxpayer may have built the property and may be depreciating market value rather than cost.

(7) Determine if the taxpayer furnished goods or services to others in return for the depreciable asset (bartering).

(8) Determine if the methods used for computing depreciation or amortization are acceptable and applied in accordance with applicable laws, rulings, and regulations.

(9) Review the rates to determine if they are reasonable.

(10) Determine if an appropriate amount of salvage value has been taken into account.

(11) In the case of items on which amortization is claimed or applicable, review leases, franchises, certificates of necessity, etc., to verify if the period and amount used is correct. Also determine if accelerated depreciation is being claimed on items which should be amortized.

(12) Test check a representative number of items listed on the depreciation schedule, to determine if the depreciation reserve at the end of the accounting period exceeds the depreciable basis of the asset, taking into account salvage value where applicable.

◀ If you buy business property that has a useful life of more than one year, you may be able to deduct a limited amount of the cost as an expense when you figure your business income for tax purposes. You must spread the remainder of the cost of this property and the cost of most other business property over more than one year and deduct it a part at a time. This is called *depreciation*. You may only take depreciation deductions on property that is called depreciable property.

◀ *Amortization* is a method that permits you to deduct certain capital expenditures in a way similar to depreciation.

◀ Property is depreciable if it meets these requirements:

- It must be used in business or held for the production of income.
- It must have a determinable life and that life must be longer than one year.
- It must be something that wears out, decays, gets used up, becomes obsolete, or loses value from natural causes.

  In general, if property does not meet all three of these conditions, it is not depreciable.

◀ You may only deduct depreciation on property that you use in your trade or business or hold for the production of income. You may not deduct depreciation on nonbusiness property.

◀ To figure depreciation, you generally must first determine three things about the property you intend to depreciate. They are: 1. its basis, 2. the date it was placed in service, and 3. the method of depreciation you are permitted to use.

◀ You *must* use the accelerated cost recovery system (ACRS) for *tangible property* that you place in service after 1980, unless you are specifically prevented from using ACRS. If you cannot use ACRS, you must use one of the other methods, such as:

- Straight line method.
- Declining balance method.
- Sum-of-the Years' Digits.

◀ Examiners must determine "if start-up expenses as defined in Internal Revenue Code Section 195 have been properly amortized over at least a 60-month period."

(13) Test check some extensions and prove footings to determine if current depreciation has been correctly computed.

(14) Ascertain if proper allocation has been made on bulk purchase of depreciable assets.

(15) Determine that proper election has been made for accelerated first-year allowances and that the amount claimed does not exceed the limitation.

(16) For property placed in service after December 31, 1980, ascertain that taxpayer has complied with the requirements of the Accelerated Cost Recovery System (ACRS).

5(10)8.2 *(4-23-81)* 4231

Component Depreciation of Real Property Improvements

(1) Examiners should be alert to the possibility of improper allocation of component costs and the use of improper lives on building components.

(2) In order to determine whether a detailed examination of component costs is required, the examiner should compare depreciation claimed under the component method with depreciation that would be allowable under the composite method.

(a) If the amount claimed by taxpayer is significantly higher, the examiner should make a detailed review of the records on which the component costs are based. The term "significantly higher" in this context means approximately 15 percent above the amount allowable under the composite method.

(b) This rule of thumb should not be overriding if the facts indicate the existence of excessive depreciation.

(3) When component costs are analyzed, contractor's invoices should be reviewed to determine if charges for short-lived elements, such as air conditioning systems, plumbing, and electrical wiring, contain amounts for elements which will last the life of the buildings.

(4) If it is not possible to obtain a sufficiently detailed breakdown of costs from the taxpayer or there are problems which require specialized knowledge of construction, the examiner should seek advice or assistance from a Service engineer.

(5) If component cost records have been examined in detail (whether or not an adjustment is proposed to depreciation), the examiner should clearly state in the report transmittal or workpapers that this was done so that it need not be repeated in future audits.

◂ Property that you use in your trade or business is generally referred to as an asset of that business. The cost or other basis of every asset that can be depreciated is recorded in an asset account. You may set up as many accounts for depreciable property as you wish. You may either list each asset separately, or combine two or more assets into one account.

◂ Amendments to the law since original enactment have changed the life for certain real property depending on when the structure was placed in service. Examiners are instructed "to be alert to those changes when ascertaining taxpayer compliance with the ACRS rules."

◂ *Components of real property.* Under ACRS, the components of a building (plumbing, wiring, storm windows, etc.) are depreciated in the same way as the building itself. If the building is 18-year real property, the components are also 18-year real property. The recovery period for a component begins when the building is placed in service or, if later, the date the component is placed in service.

◂ *Component accounts.* You may account for depreciable property (other than ACRS recovery property) by treating each component or part of the property as a separate account.

◂ Generally, you cannot allocate the basis of used property into separate components. However, you may use the component method to figure depreciation for a used building. To qualify, the cost of the property must be properly allocated to the various components. Also, the useful life that is assigned to each component must be based on the condition of that component when you acquired it and based on a competent appraisal. You cannot use this method if you use the CLADR (Class Life Asset Depreciation Range) method or for ACRS recovery property.

◂ *Composite* accounts include assets without regard to their character or useful lives.

5(10)9 *(4-23-81)* 4231
Employee Benefits

5(10)9.1 *(4-23-81)* 4231
Medical Insurance

When medical insurance is claimed as a business deduction, ascertain it covers employees, rather than the personal cost for taxpayer's family.

5(10)9.2 *(4-23-81)* 4231
Life Insurance

(1) Verify that group life insurance policy premiums cover the lives of employees who designate their beneficiaries. The policy premiums are usually deductible as being in the nature of additional salary, provided the total compensation, including the premiums, is reasonable. In such cases the amount of the premium is taxable to the individual employee. However, in the ordinary group life insurance policies, where the employee's rights in the insurance or benefits are subject to forfeiture by subsequent separation from service, the payment of the premium is not income to the employee.

(2) Verify that a deduction has not been taken for life insurance premiums paid by the employer where the employer is a direct or indirect beneficiary.

5(10)(10)0 *(4-23-81)* 4231
Insurance

(1) Examiners should ask taxpayers for a breakdown of insurance payments. Verify that personal life insurance and medical insurance have not been deducted.

(2) Review insurance premiums and relate coverage to specific business asset or risk.

(3) Check for the expensing of premiums covering periods subsequent to the year under review.

(4) If there has been a fire or other casualty, ascertain that insurance proceeds received, or claims pending, have been properly accounted for including use and occupancy, business interruption, and similar types of insurance. If a fire or other casualty occurred in a prior period, inquire as to proper handling in the prior and current period.

(5) Be alert to policies cancelled and ascertain that any rebates of premiums are properly accounted for.

(6) Be alert to the possibility that the taxpayer may be engaged in arson-for-profit activities.

◀ *Health insurance premiums.* Group hospitalization and medical care premiums you pay for the benefit of your employees are deductible expenses, as long as the group health plan provides continuation coverage to employees and their beneficiaries when "qualifying events" occur. See IRS Pub. 535.

◀ *Life insurance premiums.* Life insurance premiums are not deductible if paid on any policy covering the life of an officer of a corporation, an employee, or any other person who has a financial interest in the employer's business if the employer is either directly or indirectly a beneficiary under the policy. In other words, if the employer rather than the employee is to get or have a right to the proceeds, the premiums are not deductible.

◀ *Group life insurance premiums* paid or incurred by you on policies covering the lives of your officers and employees who designate their own beneficiaries are deductible if you do not retain any incidents of ownership, and if you are not directly or indirectly the beneficiary.

◀ You may deduct the costs of the following kinds of insurance premiums that are related to your business: fire, theft, flood, or other casualty; merchandise and inventory; credit; employee's group hospitalization and medical plans; employer's liability; public liability; malpractice; worker's compensation; state unemployment; use and occupancy and business interruption; overhead insurance; employee performance bonds or other bonds required by law; and car and other vehicle insurance.

5(10)(11)0 *(4-23-81)* 4231

Legal and Professional Fees

(1) The broad classification of "legal and professional" embraces many types of services. In considering such expenses, it should be kept in mind that account classifications vary widely among taxpayers, and may be grouped in a single account, or separate accounts. Typical account classifications are: legal, accounting, engineering, appraisals, surveys, etc.

(2) There is a tendency to assume that all such expenses are deductible. To the contrary, these charges are subject to a variety of tax treatments and accordingly each charge should be considered on its individual merits.

(3) Where the taxpayer has been billed for professional services rendered, without a detailed description of the exact services involved, the examiner should seek clarification if the amount is material.

(4) Verify expenses claimed in regard to the acquisition or sale of property, lease arrangement, etc. Such items may be capital expenditures.

(5) Determine if any expenses relate to exempt or partially exempt income.

(6) Insure that legal fees are not applicable to the personal affairs of the taxpayer.

(7) If the expense deductions are based on retainer fees, determine whether the professional services received cover items of a capital or nondeductible nature. Consider the propriety of allocating an appropriate share to such items.

(8) Be alert for political contributions being deducted as legal or professional fees. The examiner should analyze the services performed in relation to the payments made.

◀ *Legal and professional fees.* Legal and professional fees, such as fees charged by lawyers and accountants, that are ordinary and necessary expenses of operating your business are deductible as business expenses. However, legal fees you pay to acquire business assets usually cannot be deducted. They are added to the basis of the property.

◀ If the fees you are charged for legal or professional services include payments for work of a personal nature (such as making out a will or preparing your personal income tax return), you may deduct only the part of the fee that has to do with your business as a business expense. Some of the other fees may be deductible on Schedule A (Form 1040) if you itemize deductions.

5(10)(12)0 *(4-23-81)* 4231

Pension, Annuity and Profit Sharing Plans

(1) Where pensions are paid directly to close relatives, ascertain that the recipient was an employee and the pension paid is reasonable in relation to prior service, etc.

(2) Ascertain whether the employee trust or plan giving rise to a deduction is a qualified trust or plan. In this connection, consideration must be given to the provisions of the original trust instrument or plan, whether exemption or approval of the trust or plan has been secured, subsequent changes if any, and actual operation of the plan or trust.

◀ *Pension plan.* A pension plan is a plan set up to provide systematically for the payment of definitely determinable retirement benefits.

◀ *Annuity plan.* An annuity plan can also be set up to provide systematically for the payment of definitely determinable retirement benefits. However, a qualified annuity plan does not need to operate through an exempt trust. Under an annuity plan, you purchase annuity or insurance contracts covering your employees directly from an insurance company.

(3) Consider the requirements and limitations applicable to the type plan or trust in question and to related deductions. Determine if the deductions claimed are allowable in the light of the requirements and limitations. Verify payments to determine if they were paid within the prescribed time and are correct in amount.

◀ *Profit-sharing plan.* A profit-sharing plan is a plan that enables your employees or their beneficiaries to share in the profits of your business. You make payments to the plan from current or accumulated earnings. The plan must have a definite predetermined formula for allocating the payments to the plan among the participating employees and for distributing the funds accumulated under the plan.

5(10)(13)0 *(4–23–81)* 4231

Rent Expense

(1) Rent expenses can usually be verified as to amount from leases and contracts as well as receipts or cancelled checks. The examiner should determine whether the expense constitutes an allowable business deduction, and if so, to what extent. In making this determination, the examiner must be aware of the following.

(a) Payments covering a period extending beyond the taxable year are not deductible, regardless of whether the taxpayer is on the cash or accrual basis of accounting.

(b) Where the lessor is related directly or indirectly to the taxpayer, as where a corporation rents property from a principal stockholder, consideration should be given to whether the rentals paid are reasonable. This is particularly true where there is no lease and the rents fluctuate from year to year.

(c) Capital expenditures are not deductible as a current expense even though improvements are made to the lessor's property. When such expenditures are capitalized, the depreciation or amortization deduction should be adjusted accordingly.

(d) Sometimes lease contracts are in actuality purchase contracts. If by the terms of the lease the lessee may, for nothing or for a nominal sum, acquire title to the property at a time when there is substantial value remaining, the transaction may actually be a purchase. In this case, the rental should be disallowed and depreciation allowed.

(2) Examiners should verify that Forms 1099, Miscellaneous, have been filed, if applicable.

◀ Rent is the amount that you have to pay for the use of property that you do not own. In general, you may deduct rent as an expense only if the rent is for property that you use in your trade or business. If you have or will receive equity in or title to the property, the rent is not deductible.

◀ *Rent on a personal residence.* If you use part of your home as your place of business, you may be able to deduct the rent you pay for that part. For more information, see Publication 587, "Business Use of Your Home."

◀ *Rent paid in advance.* If you pay rent in advance, you may deduct only the amount that applies to your use of the rented property during that tax year. The rest may be deducted only over the period to which it applies.

◀ *Lease or purchase.* To determine if you may deduct payments as rent, you must first determine if your agreement is a lease or a conditional sales contract. If under the agreement you acquired, or will acquire, title to or equity in the property, the agreement should be treated as a conditional sales contract. Payments made under a conditional sales contract are not deductible as rent, unless your lease is a "finance lease."

5(10)(14)0 *(4–23–81)* 4231

Salaries and Wages

(1) Verification of this deduction can be made from the payroll account, cancelled checks, and retained copies of Forms 941 and W-2. These documents will assist in determining if salaries are being paid to the taxpayer, spouse, children, relatives, or domestic ser-

◀ Salaries, wages, and other forms of pay you make to employees may be deductible business expenses if they meet these tests:

- You must be able to show that the payments are ordinary and necessary expenditures divants. Form W-3, Transmittal of Income and Tax Statements, should be reconciled to the payroll account and Forms W-2, Wage and Tax Statement.

(2) Examiners should be alert to situations where business employees may perform non-business services for the benefit of the owners of the business.

(3) During the examination of a business tax return, examiners should refer to IRM 4034 for package audit requirements.

(4) When Jobs Credit or WIN Credit has been claimed, the examiner should verify that the salary and wage account has been reduced by the amount of the credit.

(5) Examiners should be alert to the tax protestors who claim tax-exempt status or fictitious exemptions on the Form W-4, Employee's Withholding Allowance Certificate.

(6) Examiners should be alert to the use of helpers by employee-drivers for unloading trucks and verify that the helpers salary expenses are supported by payroll records showing names and social security numbers.

5(10)(15)0 *(4-23-81)* 4231

Taxes

(1) Determine that taxes paid or accrued relate to the business of the taxpayer. Be alert to such items as Federal and State income taxes improperly claimed, taxes on domestic employees, taxes on personal property owned by taxpayer, relatives, etc.

(2) Determine if deductions include any items of an unsettled or contested nature.

(3) Check year-end accruals of significant items to determine if they are proper.

(4) Determine if there are any taxes on the purchase of capital assets that should be capitalized.

(5) Determine if any taxes deducted relate to the acquisition or disposition of real property. If so, a proration may be required.

(6) Ascertain that no foreign income taxes have been claimed as a deduction where election has been made to claim the foreign tax credit.

(7) Verify that there are no double deductions for social security taxes paid. A deduction for such taxes paid on an employee's salary should not include the employee's share of the tax if this amount is included in the salary and wage expense deduction.

rectly connected with or pertaining to your trade or business.

- You must be able to prove that the pay is reasonable.
- You must be able to prove that the payments were made for services actually rendered.
- You must have actually made the payments or incurred the expense during the year.

◀ Any deduction taken for salaries and wages must be reduced by the dollar amount of any targeted jobs credit allowable for the tax year.

◀ You may deduct various taxes imposed by federal, state, local, and foreign governments if you incur them in the ordinary course of your trade or business and if they are directly attributable to that trade or business. Certain other taxes not attributable to your trade or business are deductible only if you itemize deductions on Schedule A (Form 1040).

◀ Real estate taxes are the taxes you pay on real property that you own. Ordinarily, you may deduct them, but sometimes you may elect to capitalize expenditures for taxes as part of the cost of property. Sometimes you must capitalize expenditures for real property taxes.

◀ You can choose to capitalize property tax, mortgage interest, and other carrying charges on real property you own, as long as the property remains unimproved and unproductive.

◀ During the time you are either constructing improvements on or developing real property, you can choose to capitalize taxes on the wages of your employees doing the construction work, and sales and use taxes on materials used in the construction work.

(8) Verify that the Federal and State income taxes and FICA tax withheld have not been claimed as a business expense and also included in the gross wage figure. However, some small businesses deduct all amounts paid to IRS as tax expense, but then show as wages only the net amounts actually paid to the employees. In this case the total expenses will be correct, only the allocation is improper.

◀ If real estate is sold, the deduction for real estate taxes must be divided between the buyer and the seller according to the number of days in the real property tax year (the period to which the tax relates) that each held the property.

5(10)(16)0 *(4-23-81)* 4231

Travel and Entertainment

(1) Many T and E items are not identified as such on returns filed by taxpayers, being earmarked instead under the functional activities which generage the expense, for example, "advertising," "promotion," "selling," "miscellaneous," etc., expense.

(2) Examiners should be alert for such items as company-owned or rented automobiles, hunting lodges, fishing camps, resort property, pleasure boats or yachts, airplanes, apartments and hotel suites; families at conventions or business meetings; and expense-paid vacations of owners and employees, or members of their families, not reported on Form W-2.

(3) Cash expenditures and checks payable to owners and employees closely related by blood or marriage to the owners, should be closely examined as to the actual payment of the expenditures and the business purpose.

(4) Examiners should verify whether prize of awards in money or any other form have been made to an individual.

(a) If the recipient of the prize or award is an individual other than an employee of the corporation making the award, the examiner should ascertain whether proper Forms 1099 have been filed reporting the amount of money or fair market value of the prize or award given to each recipient.

(b) If Forms 1099 required to be filed have not been filed, the procedures in IRM 4562.5 should be followed.

◀ You must keep records to show when you started using your car for business and the cost or other basis of the car. Your records must also show the business miles you drove your car during the year and the total miles you drove your car during the year. If you use actual expenses, you must keep records of the costs of operating the car, such as car insurance, interest, taxes, licenses, maintenance, repairs, depreciation, gas, and oil. If you lease a car, you must keep records of this cost. To the extent the car expenses reflect travel away from home, you will be considered to have met the proof requirement for that expense if you can prove the actual business miles you drove.

◀ A receipt is ordinarily the best evidence to prove the amount of an expense. Documentary evidence will be considered adequate if it shows the amount, date, place, and essential character of the expense. A cancelled check, together with a bill from the payee, ordinarily establishes the cost. However, a cancelled check does not by itself support a business expense without other evidence to show that it was for a business purpose. A written statement of the business purpose of an expense generally is required.

5(10)(17)0 *(4-23-81)* 4231

Lobbying Expense Deductions

(1) During the preplanning and the examination of business returns, examiners should be alert for deductions which may be related to "grassroots" lobbying activity. Allowable direct lobbying deductions are expenses incurred in connection with:

◀ You may deduct expenses you have for appearing before, submitting statements to, or sending communications to the U.S. Congress, its committees, or its individual members, or to any legislative body of a state or political subdivision in

(a) appearances before, submission of statements to, or sending communications to members of legislative bodies with respect to legislation or proposed legislation of direct interest to the taxpayer; and

(b) communication of information between the taxpayer and an organization of which the taxpayer is a member with respect to their proposing, supporting, or opposing legislation of direct interest to the organization and the taxpayer.

(2) No deduction is allowed for expenditures for participation or intervention in a political campaign on behalf of any candidate for public office, or in connection with any attempt to influence the general public or segments thereof with respect to legislative matters (otherwise known as "grassroots" lobbying), elections, or referendums. Also, deductions are not allowable for expenses in connection with attempts to influence legislation that is not of a direct business interest to the taxpayer.

(3) The following examples extracted from the Basic Revenue Agent Training, illustrate some basic principles of deductibility. While these examples discuss lobbying by business taxpayers, the same rationale in each example would be applied to any lobbying by trade associations, labor unions, or similar organizations.

(a) Example 1—The Ways and Means Committee of the House of Representatives is considering proposed legislation to increase social security benefits. Mr. Adder owns a small manufacturing plant in Ohio employing 100 people. He appears before the Committee in Washington, D.C. to give information opposing the bill. He incurs expenses of $500 in gathering information and $150 air fare to Washington and return in connection with his appearance. The expenditures are deductible by Mr. Adder under the provisions of Code section 162(e)(1)(A). The legislation is of direct interest to Mr. Adder. It is reasonable to assume that the increases in benefits would increase Mr. Adder's portion of FICA taxes.

(b) Example 2—Mr. Cliffrose owns a number of retail stores in a Midwest city. The city government is considering imposing a retail sales tax on the types of merchandise sold in Mr. Cliffrose's stores. The tax would be passed on to the consumer, but collected and remitted by the retailer. Mr. Cliffrose expends $400 in gathering data to present his view that the tax should not be imposed. The amount is deductible under Code section 162(e)(1)(A). The legislation is of direct interest to Mr. Cliffrose be-

connection with legislation or proposed legislation of direct interest to you in carrying on your trade or business. Expenses of communications between you and an organization of which you are a member about such legislative matters of direct interest to you and to the organization may also be deducted.

◀ You also may deduct the part of the dues you pay to an organization of which you are a member that is for the expenses of communicating information between the organization and the U.S. Congress, its committees, or its individual members, or to any legislative body of a state or political subdivision in connection with legislation of direct interest to that organization.

◀ You may not deduct expenses paid or incurred to influence public opinion on any legislation, election, or referendum. The cost to a corporation of preparing, printing, and distributing a pamphlet to its stockholders urging action on their part to influence legislation is not deductible.

cause the collection of the tax will impose additional administrative burdens of collection and recordkeeping upon him. In addition, the tax will increase the cost of Mr. Cliffrose's merchandise to the consumer and may reduce the demand for it.

(c) Example 3—Mr. Gallwind, a retail merchant, met with a House subcommittee which was considering proposed legislation relating to presidential succession. Mr. Gallwind's expenses are not deductible. The legislation has only a remote potential effect on Mr. Gallwind's business and does not meet the direct interest test of Code section 162(e)(1)(A).

(d) Example 4—Mr. Juniper was very concerned about the contents of a proposed foreign aid bill providing for the sale of Widgits to a foreign country. He took out a full page ad in the local newspaper, at a cost of $1,000, stating reasons why the public should object to the bill. The amount paid would not be deductible under the provisions of Code section 162(e)(2)(B).

(4) Accounts which may contain lobbying expense amounts include but are not limited to advertising, professional and association dues, and legal and professional fees. When verifying deductions for media advertising, the examiner should read and analyze the source documents-the media ads or transcripts. In addition, the examiner should discuss with company officials their criteria for separating nondeductible "grassroots" advertising from other categories of advertising. When verifying professional and association dues, the examiner should be alert for special assessments to support lobbying campaigns or activities. When verifying legal and professional fees, correspondence as well as source documents should be reviewed.

5(10)(18)0 *(4-23-81)* 4231
Verification of Self-Employment Tax Liability

(1) The tax on self-employment income will be treated as part of the income tax and will be included in determining any deficiency or overassessment. The determination and verification of self-employment income and self-employment tax liability, except mathematical verification, will generally be made only in those cases in which the income tax returns have been selected for examination.

◀ The **self-employment tax** is a social security tax for individuals who work for themselves. It is similar to the social security tax withheld from the pay of wage earners.

◀ Social security benefits are available to individuals who are self-employed just as they are to wage earners. Your payments of self-employment tax contribute to your coverage under the social security system.

(2) The following items will be verified during an examination involving self-employment features.

(a) Name, social security number, and business or profession of self-employed person.

(b) Total net earnings from self-employment.

(c) Wages subject to withholding tax for old-age and survivors insurance.

(d) Self-employment income.

(e) Self-employment tax.

(3) If consideration of the above features results in an adjustment of the self-employment tax or discloses information of a nature which should be transmitted to the Social Security Administration, the examiner will prepare Form 885-F (Self-Employment Tax Adjustment). (See (14)11, IRM 428(10), Report Writing Guide for Income Tax Examiners, for instructions relating to the preparation and use of Form 885–F.)

◀ You may be liable for self-employment tax even if you are now fully insured under social security and are now receiving benefits.

◀ *Income limits.* You must pay self-employment tax if you have net earnings from self-employment of $400 or more. (Beginning in 1984, you must also pay self-employment tax if you are paid $100 or more in a year as an employee of a church or qualified church-controlled organization exempt from social security taxes.) The maximum amount of 1987 earnings subject to self-employment tax is $43,800. (In 1986 the maximum amount was $42,000 and in 1985 it was $39,600.) However, no self-employment tax is due on your self-employment income if the wages you received in 1987 as an employee were $43,800 or more, and were subject to social security tax or railroad retirement tax or both.

◀ The self-employment tax rate for 1987 is 14.3% of your net earnings from self-employment. However, you paid at a tax rate of only 12.3% in 1987 because a credit of 2.0% was applied against the amount of your self-employment tax. In 1988 the rate will be 15.02% with a 2.0% credit.

◀ Schedule SE (Form 1040) is used to compute self-employment tax. This form is illustrated in Publication 533, "Self-Employment Tax."

Examination Techniques Peculiar to Certain Small Businesses

610 *(4-23-81)* 4231
Introduction

(1) The following examination technique guidelines have been prepared to assist examiners in the examination of specific types of small business returns. The guidelines point out peculiarities of certain business activities and outline various procedures which can be followed in the verification of income and expense items reported by these businesses.

(2) It should be emphasized that the guidelines are not all inclusive, nor are they minimum requirements for an examination. Examiners must use judgment in determining the depth and scope of the examination and the extent to which they wish to follow the guidelines.

(3) During every examination of an individual or other business entity, examiners should be alert to the possibility of "bartering" or "swapping" techniques of exchanging services for merchandise or exchanging merchandise for personal services.

620 *(4-23-81)* 4231
Appliance Service and Sales

621 *(4-23-81)* 4231
Records

The records maintained by these businesses may range from the simplest form of single entry bookkeeping to double entry books with accounts receivable and payable. The taxpayer may use the cash, accrual, or hybrid method of accounting depending upon the size of the business.

622 *(4-23-81)* 4231
Gross Receipts

(1) Determine taxpayer's method of reporting gross receipts. Ensure (that all cash removed from the cash register to purchase merchandise or pay expenses has been recorded in daily receipts. Where net income is low check source of funds for personal expenditures. This test check may indicate the need for an indirect method of determining income.

(2) If the taxpayer performs the services personally, the gross profit ratio should be relatively high, because of reduced labor costs.

(3) If invoices are used as customer receipts, any break in numerical sequence should be explored thoroughly, since this could indicate unreported income. Also, any abnormal lapse of time between invoices should be investigated.

623 *(4-23-81)* 4231
Expenses

(1) Review depreciation schedule for proper basis, normal life and salvage value of assets.

(2) Review purchase invoices for any unusual purchases not related to taxpayer's business. This could reveal personal items included in merchandise purchase.

(3) Reconcile any at normal decrease in closing inventory over opening inventory.

(4) Review expenses which require allocation for personal and business use. This is an area where inadequate recordkeeping can, and does, result in abuse of the business use allocation.

(5) Question taxpayer regarding exchange of services for merchandise, or exchange of merchandise for personal services.

630 *(4-23-81)* 4231
Auto Repair Shops

631 *(4-23-81)* 4231
Records

(1) Persons engaged in the auto repair business generally use the cash receipts and disbursements method of accounting even though they maintain a small inventory of parts. Records will usually consist of a journal type book showing receipts and disbursements. Some small operators may maintain nothing more than a file of customer repair orders, purchase invoices, and paid bills.

(2) More than likely the taxpayer will either do the repair work personally or retain the services of a helper. This type of business may be carried on at the taxpayer's personal residence in a garage or similar type building, but for the most part the shop will be located in the commercially zoned districts.

(3) The business can range in size from the "alley garage" to a fairly large establishment with several mechanics and helpers on the payroll. Common practice is to have an auto repair facility as part of a gasoline service station or a new or used car dealership. Repair shops under

these conditions usually handle all phases of auto maintenance and repair, whereas individually operated repair shops usually specialize in specific types of auto maintenance and repair, such as, transmissions, electrical circuits, bodywork, radiators, etc. The following techniques are aimed toward the small operator and can be used whether the taxpayer engages in general auto repair or in one of the aforementioned specialites. For auto dealers, refer to Techniques Handbook 4232.2, Techniques Handbook for Specialized Industries—Auto Dealers.

632 *(4-23-81)* 4231
Gross Receipts

(1) One method for determining whether gross receipts are substantially correct is to compare the purchases and cost of labor to the total sales reported. Recognizing that auto parts are purchased at a discount of as much as 40% below the price which the customer is charged, and that the garage operator will bill the customer for labor at least equivalent to the wages paid to mechanics or helpers, and that the customer will also be charged at the prevailing rate for any labor or services performed by the operator personally, a rough, quick calculation can be made to determine if the gross receipts are proportionate to the labor and parts.

(2) If the mechanics are paid a commission based on a percentage of the total labor and parts charged to the customer, a quick calculation of the ratio of the cost of labor or commissions paid to the mechanics compared to gross receipts reported may be indicative of the accuracy of the receipts.

(3) The verification of income (sales) and gross profit will generally be the key to a good examination. Some specifics that can affect income are:

(a) sale of rebuilt automobiles;

(b) trading of services, e.g., auto repair for paint job on home;

(c) insurance appraisal fees;

(d) sale of junk.

633 *(4-23-81)* 4231
Expenses

(1) The cost of labor and auto parts may be charged to expense where it was actually incurred for the taxpayer's personal auto. The same may be true if the taxpayer has a gasoline pump. The use of a service truck for personal use may be the source of a tax adjustment.

(2) Where inventories appear, ascertain that opening inventory in the year under examination is the same as closing inventory reported the preceding year.

640 *(4-23-81)* 4231
Barber Shops

641 *(4-23-81)* 4231
General

(1) Due to the similarity of operations, some audit techniques for examining barber shops are the same as those for beauty shops.

(2) In the majority of cases the cash-basis method of accounting is used since inventories are not a significant income producing factor.

(3) Where barber shops are located in department stores, customer charge accounts may be used. Charges made for services will vary according to the location and clientele of the barbershop.

642 *(4-23-81)* 4231
Records

(1) Some of the more common records found include:

(a) cash register tapes;

(b) single entry books;

(c) inoices for purchases—these could be indicative of the number of customers;

(d) cash box receipts;

(e) copies of cash service slips, used mostly in larger shops (The original slip is given to the customer to present to the cashier when paying for services. The duplicate slip is turned over to the shop owner by the receptionist or barber who prepared the slips.); and

(f) copies of Forms 941.

643 *(4-23-81)* 4231
Gross Income

(1) The verification of a barber's income is a technique which calls for skill and judgment. The numerous cash transactions can increase the possibility of unreported receipts.

(2) The owner may rent barber chairs instead of hiring employees. It should be determined whether the taxpayer is self-employed. A check should be made to find out whether the supplies of the employee barbers were purchased from the proprietor and still included in expenses.

(3) In some cases, however, a barber will employ other barbers on a salary and a percentage of sales or a commission. Where this is done, an approximation of gross receipts may be made from employee's services. Examination of the payroll records is a good starting point. A reasonable portion of receipts should be applicable to the barber-owner's services. Note that each employee may have a different commission rate.

(4) Cash register tapes as well as service sales slips, will show daily cash intake.

(5) Tip income should not be overlooked.

(6) A check should be made of bank deposits (comparison should be made with the Cash Receipts Book).

(7) Questions should be asked about revenue derived from shoeshine stands and manicurists. Both may be working for a salary or a percentage of service sales. The same technique described in paragraph (2) above could be employed here.

(8) Inquiry should be made concerning the possible sale of used equipment or other disposition of assets used in the business. In many instances the cost will have been fully recovered through depreciation.

(9) Where the amount of income reported is less than normal requirements or standards of living, inquiry should be made as to other jobs, part-time or otherwise which would have increased their income.

(10) Many barber shops also sell a variety of toiletries. The examiner should check for income from this source.

644 *(4-23-81)* 4231
Expenses

(1) Barbers using the cash basis of accounting would deduct expenses as they are paid. Exceptions to this are depreciation, prepaid rent, insurance, and other items of this type which should be deducted ratably as they expire.

(2) Specific attention should be paid to the charges for supplies. Large amounts of supplies could indicate a large column of business, or possibly the resale to customers. Check to determine if personal items are included in purchases.

(3) Taxes, insurance and license fees to operate are normal expenses. The expenses should be verified by receipted bills, cancelled checks, etc.

(4) Invoices for equipment purchases should be examined to determine if any capital items have been included with repairs or ordinary expense items.

(5) Salary expense should be checked to determine if the owner has charged off a salary for personal services.

(6) Laundry expense, in such terms as the number of towels used during the year, is sometimes an indication of the number of customers visiting the shop for services.

(7) Where the amount charged for "Other expense" is relatively large, examine the schedule for unauthorized deductions.

650 *(4-23-81)* 4231
Beauty Shops

651 *(4-23-81)* 4231
General

(1) Beauty shop operators (hereinafter referred to as stylists) have numerous cash transactions.

(2) In the majority of cases the cash-basis method of accounting is used since inventories are not a significant income-producing factor. However, where beauty shops are located in department stores, the customer may charge rather than pay for the services. Prices will vary according to location and clientele.

652 *(4-23-81)* 4231
Records

(1) Although stylists may use a variety of methods to record their income and expenses the examiner should find in one form or another the following records:

(a) appointment book,
(b) disbursement journal and ledger, and
(c) schedules or worksheets.

(2) *Appointment Book*—The appointment book is the most commonly used record to cash receipts and in many cases is the only record of income kept by the stylist. This record contains customer appointments listed in chronological order, with the specific charges usually entered by cash customer's name.

(3) *Disbursement Journal and Ledger*—Disbursement records may consist of nothing more than cancelled checks. Occasionally, a disbursement journal and ledger may be used.

(4) *Schedules or Worksheets*—Occasionally, the stylist prepares a schedule of fees re-

ceived each month. The receipts are totaled and posted weekly to the schedule which is then used at year's end to assist in preparing the return. The examiner is cautioned to make audit tests of the appointment book or daily log rather than to rely solely on the monthly summary figures. If only the summaries are furnished during the examination, the examiner should make every effort to obtain the original record to determine the actual fees charged.

(5) The following additional records can be expected to exist.

(a) Cash register tapes.

(b) Invoices for purchases. These could be indicative of the number of customers.

(c) Cash box receipts.

(d) Copies of cash service slips, used mostly by larger shops. The original slip is given to the customer to present to the cashier when paying for services. The duplicate slip is turned over to the shop owner by the receptionist or operator who prepared the slips.

(e) Copies of Forms 941.

653 *(4-23-81)* 4231

Gross Receipts

(1) When stylists fail to keep complete records of gross income, it should alert the examiner to the fact that other than the usual examination procedures will apply.

(2) If a stylist's return shows low gross receipts, the examiner should question the taxpayer. This may be attributable to the taxpayer having recently started to practice, an elderly or semiretired person, or, in some cases, the person may be operating the shop on a part-time basis. The reason for low gross receipts should be determined as early in the examination as possible before time-consuming examination procedures are undertaken.

(3) The examiner should take into consideration the particular area in which the shop is located.

(4) Most stylists have a specific rate for different services. If possible, this should be determined during the initial interview. With this information, tests can be made to determine the gross receipts. Fees may be received from regular or drop-in customers. However, most fees are from scheduled appointments, and are recorded upon receipt. If the appointment book does not show gross receipts, the length of time allocated per customer will usually indicate the type and cost of the service rendered. For example. A one-hour appointment may indicate a shampoo and set with cost established by the shop owner. A two or three-hour appointment may indicate a permanent or other long-lasting service with a higher cost.

(5) If a cash receipts book is maintained, a test check of cash receipts against the appointment book is a good crosscheck to determine the accuracy of records. A check of the bank deposits should also be made.

(6) Examiners should verify that the stylist has included tip income on the return.

(7) In some cases, beauty shop owners employ other stylists. Usually the employee is paid a salary and a percentage of sales or a commission. If salary and commission are paid, an approximation of gross receipts may be made from employees' services. Examination of the payroll records is a good starting point. A reasonable portion of receipts should be applicable to the stylist-owner's services. Note that each employee may have a different commission rate.

(8) At times the stylist may also sell cosmetics and toiletries to customers. The cost of the articles sold usually is included in purchases. The examiner should verify that these sales have been included in income.

(9) A good check on gross receipts is the ratio of supplies expense to gross receipts. If the ratio is out of line with the known ratio of similar businesses in the area, this would indicate that perhaps gross receipts may be understated, and a more comprehensive examination is necessary.

(10) Inquiry should be made as to the possible sale of used equipment or other disposition of business assets.

(11) Where the amount of income reported is less than normal requirements or standards of living, inquiry should be made as to other jobs, part-time or otherwise which would have increased their income.

(12) Inquiry should be made about special jobs outside of the shop such as weddings, pageants, funerals, house calls, etc.

654 *(4-23-81)* 4231

Expenses

(1) Specific attention should be paid to the charges for supplies. Large amounts of supplies could indicate a large volume of business, or possibly the resale or customers. Check to determine if personal items are included in purchases.

(2) Taxes, insurance and license fees to operate are normal expenses. The expenses should be verified by receipted bills, cancelled checks, etc.

(3) Verify the cost of transportation. In most cases, supplies are delivered.

(4) Invoices for equipment purchases should be examined to ascertain if capital items are included with repairs or ordinary expense items.

(5) Salary expense should be checked to determine if the owner has charged off a salary for personal services. An inspection should be made of employment tax returns and/or information returns.

(6) Laundry expense in such terms as the number of towels used during the year, is sometimes an indication of the number of customers visiting the shops for services.

(7) Where the amount charged for "Other Expense" is relatively large, examine the schedule for possible personal expenses.

(8) Occasionally, stylists work in their homes, and it will be necessary to apportion the personal and business expenses.

660 *(4–23–81)* 4231

Bowling Alleys

(1) Modern bowling establishments are automatic pin spotting equipment. Many of them follow the practice of leasing the equipment rather than buying it.

(2) The lease is usually based on a fixed charge for each game bowled. The machines have meters which record the games as they are played. These meters are read monthly or as otherwise agreed upon and a report is submitted to the lessor along with the amount due.

(3) These reports provide a good basis for verifying gross receipts from bowling. The number of games reported multiplied by the normal charge per game would equal the approximate income to be derived from bowling.

(4) In those instances where the books and records are adequate, this provides a test of the amounts reported. Where the books and records are inadequate, this would provide a reasonable method of determining gross income from bowling.

(5) Determine the existence of vending machines, pinball machines or other electronic games which would provide additional income.

670 *(4–23–81)* 4231

Building Contractors

671 *(4–23–81)* 4231

Records

(1) The activities of small building contractors range from home improvement work to construction of homes and small commercial buildings. The books and records may range from almost none to formal double entry books. The contractor's record of income may be nothing more than a notebook. Methods of accounting will vary depending on the nature of the activities performed. Businesses which concentrate on short term jobs may use the cash receipts and disbursements method of accounting because they do not maintain inventories, while businesses which have long-term contracts may use the accrual method because inventories are a factor in determining income.

(2) In some instances building permits may be secured and in other instances, such as, in rural areas and within cities on small home improvements, such permits will not be secured.

(3) Contractors generally buy their own materials and do the job on a completed contract basis with items, such as, electrical and plumbing work, subcontracted. In some cases, contracts will specify labor and materials cost plus a percentage of gross cost for the contractor's services and overhead expenses.

Also see IRM 4232.7, Techniques Handbook for Specialized Industries—Construction.

672 *(4–23–81)* 4231

Gross Receipts

(1) Verification of the income of the small "home improvement" contractor may be difficult. A general idea of income can be obtained by an analysis of labor and material costs. For these small contractors, bank accounts may give much information.

(2) The larger "small contractors" income may be verified to some extent through building permits and an analysis of information concerning subcontracts for plumbing and electrical work. The number of subcontracts may indicate the total general contracts. The income from each account should be checked against the books.

(3) Match invoices, contracts, and similar documents with records kept by job and reconcile any differences.

(4) Establish to what extent the taxpayer participates in performance of services. This will

assist you in determining the correct gross profit.

(5) Be alert for completed or partially completed homes for which cost of materials has been included in the cost, but no consideration given for the closing inventory value of these assets, etc.

(6) Some contractors make loans to customers in order to get the job. Many have income from interest.

(7) Some contractors sell sand, cement mix, concrete blocks, etc. in the ordinary course of their business.

(8) Other sources of income may be:

(a) kickbacks on purchases;

(b) architect's referral fees;

(c) sale of old brick and other salvage material from demolished buildings;

(d) sale of dirt, sod. etc.,

(e) rent from leased equipment.

(9) Some home improvement firms will help a customer finance the job by taking back a second trust note. The examiner should be alert for interest income as well as an occasional repossession where the customer defaults on the note.

673 *(4-23-81)* 4231

Expenses

(1) Some contractors attempt to subcontract as many things as possible in order to minimize unemployment taxes and withholding taxes. Verify that these subcontractors are not actually employees. Verify that information returns have been issued for payments to subcontractors.

(2) Methods of reporting income and expenses should be scrutinized to be certain that expenses are not being duplicated. If the taxpayer is using a completed-contract method, expenses might be claimed in the year paid or incurred and claimed again in the year the contract is completed. If taxpayers are using a cost-plus method, purchases, etc., should be scrutinized to be certain that they are not claiming expenses paid by another.

(3) Forms 940, 941 and W-2 must be checked to verify labor costs and their reasonableness.

(4) Expenses should be checked to be certain that taxpayer is not deducting the cost of major repairs on heavy equipment, such as engine and transmission overhauling. Frequently the small contractor leases equipment. Make certain that depreciation is not being claimed on the leased equipment.

(5) When checking invoices note where the materials were deliverd. If preliminary test check indicate materials were delivered to the site or subdivision where the taxpayer's residence is located, the line of inquiry should be directed toward verifying whether or not such material and related labor costs were for the taxpayers personal residence.

(6) Written agreements with subcontractor may indicate location or address of the job site and may help in determing whether they worked on the taxpayer's personal residence.

(7) A casualty loss or interest paid on a home improvement loan claimed as an itemized deduction may indicate repairs on the personal residence of the contractor.

(8) If the residence was sold, the appropriateness of the nonrecognition provision should be determined. There is the possibility that the so-called personal residence was built with the express purpose of selling it after relatively short period of occupancy.

(9) Ascertain correct allocation of home expenses, if business is operated from taxpayer residence.

680 *(4-23-81)* 4231

Delicatessens

681 *(4-23-81)* 4231

General

Delicatessens are retail outlets for specialty food items, including frozen and health foods as well as a variety of imported foodstuffs. In some instances, delicatessens have expanded operations to include restaurants. This type of business should not, however, be confused with the small grocery and/or meat store, confectionery store, and/or candy store, which are separate types of concerns.

682 *(4-23-81)* 4231

Records

The recording of the sales in a cash register and using the register tape total as the results of the daily operations, is generally the primary source of the total sales figures. Verification of gross sales becomes a problem of generally analyzing other factors to arrive at whether or not the sales appear substantially correct as reported. Taxpayers will generally present, in support of these sales, register tapes. State sales tax returns, or some form of accouting record. It becomes then, a case of working with the information at hand to substantially verify the sales reported or to question the documentation presented for reasons evolving from other than the documentation itself.

683 *(4-23-81)* 4231

Gross Receipts

(1) The simplest approach to verifying sales is determining the gross profit margin and comparing it with the margins of similar business. The method is rapid but not fool-proof. For example, a taxpayer could understate purchases as well as gross sales and still show a relatively normal gross profit margin. However, if purchases are accurately reported, and gross sales are understated, then an abnormally low gross profit margin will result. Bear in mind that a gross profit margin that is out of line with margins of similar businesses is not always the result of an understatement of gross sales. It may be the result of an extraordinary though legitimate, ajdustment to cost of goods sold, such as spoilage, theft, etc. The important thing for the examiner to remember is that an out-of-line profit margin necessitates further inquiry.

(2) Some delicatessen operators may report as gross receipts only the cash on hand at the end of the day and fail to include cash received but withdrawn for personal use. Some may fail to reduce purchases by the cost of merchandise withdrawn for personal use.

(3) The second approach to determine the correctness of gross sales is to use one or more of the indirect methods of reconstructing income.

684 *(4-23-81)* 4231

Expenses

(1) Scrutinize "bad debts" to be certain these accounts were included originally in sales reported. The cost of spoiled merchandise should not be allowed as a separate deduction since this is reflected in closing inventory.

(2) Retained copies of Forms 941 and W-2 are helpful in verifying deductions claimed for salaries and wages. Ascertain that a deduction is not being claimed for salaries or wages paid to domestic employees, or to children, parents, or other relatives who are not performing adequate services in the business.

(3) In some cases the taxpayer and family will live in part of the building that houses the delicatessen. Therefore, check rent, depreciation, insurance and utilities for any personal use. Check for capital items. Also, portions of the building or premises may be rented to others.

(4) Some delicatessen stores have vending machines, juke boxes, game machines, etc. from which they receive a percentage of profit. Verify that this income has been reported.

(5) Consideration should be given to transportation or delivery expense to determine that personal transportation costs are excluded. Check pickup and delivery points. Any adjustment here should be followed with an adjustment to depreciation of the delivery vehicle.

690 *(4-23-81)* 4231

Farmers

691 *(4-23-81)* 4231

Introduction

(1) The examination of returns filed by farmers requires ingenuity, and generally should not be solely confined to the available records. Examiners should judge items of income in their proper relation to other items of income or expense as well as the visible financial condition of the taxpayer.

(2) A return reflecting a loss from "farming" operations can raise the question: Is the loss due to expenditures personal in nature (personal consumption, hobby, etc.) or capital expenditures (certain preparatory or conservation expenditures, etc.), or is it in fact a transaction entered into for profit? Sometimes a portion of the operation will qualify but certain expenditures will not be deductible. Determining whether a "farming" loss is deductible should be considered in light of IRC 165 and 183.

692 *(4-23-81)* 4231

Records

Where records are absent or inadequate, it will be necessary to approach the examination from the viewpoint of an indirect method. The problem is to determine that all income has been reported and that all deductions are allowable. This determination may involve special auditing techniques, some of which are mentioned below.

693 *(4-23-81)* 4231

Income

693.1 *(4-23-81)* 4231

Gross Receipts

(1) The problems involved in determining the correct income to be reported on returns of farmers may vary greatly due to the type of farming conducted in different areas of the

country. It has been found that observing the percentage of gross profit or net profit from farming is misleading. This results when a farmer, in one year, markets the current crop and part of last year's crop, or holds back the current year's crop giving a distorted picture of receipts. There will often be no general income pattern among individual farmers in the same areas due to variation in the size of farms, methods of marketing, etc.

(2) Determine and verify that all income from sales of livestock and produce raised and held primarily for sale is being reported.

(3) Scrutinize sales of livestock reported as capital gains, and verify that they are eligible for capital gain treatment.

(4) Ascertain if anything of value, such as goods or services, is received in exchange for livestock, produce, or other items, and verify that the market value of the goods or services is included in income.

(5) Establish if any receipts are being "netted." Sales and purchases between the same parties often occur and sales income may be offset by personal purchase costs with only the net amounts being reflected in income.

(6) Determine if an election has been made with respect to Commodity Credit Corporation loans as to the inclusion of the amount of the loan in income at time of receipt. If so, ascertain that the election is being consistently followed.

(7) If inventories are used in determining income, ascertain the valuation method, and determine that it is properly applied and consistently followed.

(8) Compare patronage dividends reported with gross cooperative sales. Farmers' cooperative dividends may be reported in one of two ways on a return: as dividend income or as a reduction of purchases. Reportable dividends include capital stock, revolving fund and retained certificates, etc.

(9) Ascertain if common packaging material is used in marketing produce, and determine quantities used. Sales may be approximated by multiplying unit selling price and quantities used.

(10) Review depreciation schedule and ascertain if equipment is included therein, that may be used for hauling, harvesting, plowing, etc., for others, of if the equipment investment is out of proportion with the farm acreage.

(11) Compare income from sale of wool or fleece with shearing expenses, as shearing is usually charged on a per-head basis.

(12) Analyze freight expenses and compare dates of shipment with dates of sale of livestock, produce, etc.

(13) Ascertain various grain acreage plantings, average crop yield, average unit crop price, and grain inventories, and make comparision of approximated and reported sales. Check for grain sales in the name of empioyees.

(14) Determine inventory of sows at beginning and end of period. Each sow usually produces an average of five pigs per litter, with two litters a year. Compute the number of pigs available for sale, and compare with actual reported sales.

(15) Check deductions for purchases of baby chicks. If such purchases are present, comensurate income from sale of eggs should be expected.

(16) Ascertain that all gin statements have been included, both for long and short staple cotton. Income can be computed from picking expense.

(17) In checking sources of income, the examiner may wish to also consider:

(a) soil bank income,

(b) soil conservation payments;

(c) capital gains—(livestock);

(d) supplementary crops, and roadside sales;

(e) transactions between farmers (custom work and machine hire);

(f) sales of wool or fleece;

(g) sales of crops not reported in succeeding year;

(h) insurance proceeds;

(i) sale of timber and wood, soil, sod, or gravel;

(j) pasture rental;

(k) auction sales

(l) outstanding loans where production credit or banks apply sales checks directly to the loan as a normal practice.

693.2 *(4-23-81)* 4231

Hedging

(1) When used by farmers, hedging can be recognized for income tax purposes as a legitimate form of business insurance, used to reduce speculative risks due to commodity price fluctuations. As such, any losses sustained or profits realized will be includible in gross income as ordinary gain or loss.

(2) Gains or losses on commodity future contracts may be found in various schedules on the tax return, such as Schedule D or Schedule F as part of the cost of grain or livestock sold. If reflected as part of the cost of grain or livestock, such transactions will not be apparent on the face of the return.

(3) Since gains or losses on speculative transactions, as opposed to hedging transactions, are capital gains or losses, a problem could result if hedging gains are reported as capital gains and speculative losses are reported as an ordinary loss.

(4) In order to determine the intent of the farmer, it is necessary to match up the various positions held by the taxpayer on the future transactions with the off-setting positions.

694 *(4-23-81)* 4231

Expenses

(1) Determine and verify that expenses are proper under the method of accounting and represent ordinary business expenses.

(2) If the farmer has minor children, ascertain if they receive wages for work performed. If so, determine if the wages are reasonable, and whether there is a bona fide employer-employee relationship.

(3) Check to see if premiums have been received in connection with any major purchases that should be either treated as reductions of purchases or taken into income.

(4) If election with respect to soil and water conservation expenses has been exercised, determine whether gross income limitation on amount of deduction applies and whether any capital items are included in expenses.

(5) Payments received under certain Federal-State cost-sharing conservation programs are excludable from gross income to the extent that the Secretary of Agriculture determines the payment is used for conservation purposes and to the extent that the Secretary of Treasury determines that the annual income derived from the property is not increased substantially by reason of such payment.

(6) Verify methods and basis of determining depreciation.

(7) Determine amount consumed for personal use of livestock, chickens, eggs, etc.

(8) The following list of the more common expense items is intended merely as a check list. Each expense item is followed by suggested leads:

(a) interest, taxes utilities, etc.—personal element, state taxes on farm schedule rather than Sechedule A;

(b) insurance—life, medical, and personal fire insurance included;

(c) death or other livestock losses—double deduction if inventories are used; basis (zero if raised);

(d) chicks purchased—egg and poultry sales;

(e) livestock purchased—livestock sales;

(f) depreciation of equipment (gas, oil, twine, supplies)—custom work;

(g) wages and salaries—commensurate with receipts from operations;

(h) repairs and supplies—personal, capital, or soil conservation;

(i) feed—livestock and poultry sales; dairy product sales;

(j) equipment—lease vs. purchase

(k) depreciation—assets disposed of or fully depreciated, or of a personal nature; investment credit recapture or allowance.

(l) depreciation (livestock)—qualifying for depreciation and capital gains; salvage value; livestock raised;

(m) diary farmers—net milk receipts; sales of calves; personal consumption of milk and calves;

(n) seed—premiums received; not delivered in year puchased and cancelled in following year; market value of raised seed taken as expense;

(o) storage, warehousing, and transportation; double deduction (Net sales reported);

(p) fuel tax credit—part of package audit requirement.

695 *(4-2-84)* 4231

Farms Filing IRC Section 2032A Elections

(1) Under the provisions of IRC Section 2032A, an estate may value qualified farm property or real property of a closely-held business at a "special use value" rather than its fair market value. This special use value is determined by a formula set forth in the statute. This can result in substantial tax savings for the estate.

(2) In order for the estate to qualify for this election, two important conditions must be maintained:

(a) the qualified beneficiaries of the property cannot sell the property for 10 years from the date of death; and

(b) during this period, the beneficiaries must continue to use the property as a farm.

(3) To protect its interest, the government can file a special use value lien under IRC Section 6324. If the property is sold, or its qualified use ceases, within the 10 year period, the estate tax which was saved by the estate is subject to recapture.

(4) In order to ensure that farm property is not sold and is being used as a farm, during the examination of the Forms 1040, 1041, 1120, 1120S, and 1065, which contain a farm operation, the examiner should:

(a) make inquiries as to whether the farm was received from an estate; and

(b) determine whether an IRC Section 2032A election was made.

(5) If there are indications the farm was recently sold or an active farming operation was discontinued, examiners should make every effort to determine if a IRC Section 2032A election was filed. If an election was filed, appropriate information reports (Form 5346) should be completed for use by the district Estate Tax personnel. If there are any questions relating to a possible IRC Section 2032A election, the examiner should consult with the local Estate Tax Manager.

(6) The above provisions also apply to the examination of returns of closely held businesses (corporations, trusts, partnerships or sole proprietorships).

6(10)0 *(4-23-81)* 4231
Funeral Directors or Morticians

(1) The charges made by undertaking establishments to the account of a funeral are for the following items:

(a) sale of caskets and vaults;
(b) sale of clothing;
(c) compensation for services rendered;
(d) reimbursement for cash outlay.

(2) One basis of charges is for specific items of service rendered, such as the price of the casket, the use of the chapel, limousines, casket bearers, etc. But a more prevalent basis of charges now in use is the setting of an all-inclusive price covering every essential detail, based on the cost of the selected casket plus other articles supplied and the value of various services rendered. The style of the casket is used as the basis for unit prices charged. The style and cost of a casket can be used as an indication of the amount being charged for the funeral services. The profit on the casket is the chief source of income, even though billing is usually made as a flat price for the complete service.

(3) Cash outlays are made for certain items, and are charged to the account receivable for reimbursement. Items such as newspaper advertising, cemetery fees, burial clothing, hiring of pallbearers, rental of vehicles, transporation of decedent by air or rail, and honorariums to ministers represent typical items for which cash outlays are made.

(4) Often the undertaking establishment is paid by the survivors of the deceased by tendering an insurance check for the proceeds of a life insurance policy. This may be in excess of the total funeral charges, and the excess is refunded to the beneficiary of the policy by the issue of a check by the undertaker. A test of the refunds should be made by the examiner to verify that such check issued is not entered as a deduction. A reconciliation of cash receipts with bank deposits and with income recorded may reveal that cash receipts include the insurance checks, but the recorded income is not in balance with the receipts by the amount of the excess of the insurance checks over the funeral charges. Yet the refunds may be deducted as an expense item. This method results in a double deduction of the amount refunded. In some areas funeral directors sell funeral services much like life insurance, i.e., ten cents a week for life. These amounts constitute income in the year of receipt, not the year of death of the policyholder.

(5) The inventories of an undertaker include caskets, casket materials and supplies, embalming supplies, and miscellaneous supplies. The most significant item in the inventory is the caskets.

(6) In examining the returns of morticians, the examiner should be aware that there may be death certificates filed without corresponding burial permits, and vice versa. This comes about through deaths of visitors or of residents who are buried in other places than the city where the mortician is located. Where items such as advertising, cemetery fees, pallbearers, etc., are being deducted as expenses of the undertaking establishment instead, of being charged to accounts receivable, the examiner should make sufficient inquiry to determine that reimbursement was not made to the undertaker for those items in addition to the charges for services. Normally such items are charged to accounts receivable and not to expense.

(7) Examiners should ask the taxpayer if limousines are rented out for other occasions.

6(11)0 *(4-23-81)* 4231
Grocery Stores

6(11)1 *(4-23-81)* 4231
General

(1) In the preliminary analysis of a return the examiner should look for indications of omitted income. The indications may vary by a disproportionate gross profit and/or net profit percentage.

(2) Since inventories are a factor in determining the gross profit of a grocery store, the accrual method should be used for sales and purchases. The cash method may be used for other expenses. Regardless of the method used, the examiner must determine if it properly reflects income.

6(11)2 *(4-23-81)* 4231
Records

(1) The single entry method of bookkeeping is often used by small retail grocers. These records usually consist of a journal, cash book, and ledger.

(2) Frequently, the cash book is the only formal record maintained by a grocer. In these cases, the examiner must refer extensively to invoices, vouchers, bills, receipts and cash register tapes.

(3) Where the records are found to be inadequate, the taxable income of the business may be determined by an indirect method such as the net worth method of application of funds method.

6(11)3 *(4-23-81)* 4231

Gross Receipts

(1) The examiner must keep in mind that the gross profit ratio will vary according to the size, sales volume, and location of the business.

(2) If gross receipts are determined by cash on hand, examiners should verify that amounts paid for cash purchases or cash withdrawn for personal use has been added to the total. Verify that income reported includes the amounts received in the form of premiums obtained by redeeming incentive coupons packed with certain merchandise. Verify that premiums, prizes, etc., given to the taxpayer by vendors for promoting the sale of the vendor's merchandise, have been included in income.

(3) Copies of State sales tax returns may be helpful, but not conclusive, in determining if the taxpayer reported the correct amount of sales.

(4) Grocers who give trading stamps will generally have records of the number or amount of trading stamps purchased. Since ten stamps are usually given for each dollar sale, a good indication of total sales can be easily determined. However, oftentimes grocery stores will offer stamp specials and may or may not keep a record of the number of stamps issued during these specials.

(5) A check should be made for income from sales of scrap to rendering companies and other scrap dealers.

(6) Consideration should be given to other income, such as fees from sale of money orders, charges for cashing checks, etc.

(7) If the grocer sells money orders, determine that this income is properly reflected in the return.

6(11)4 *(4-23-81)* 4231

Expenses

(1) Scrutinize "bad debts" to be certain these amounts were previously included in sales reported. A deduction for spoilage should be traced to assure that a double deduction is not claimed. In most cases a loss due to spoilage will be reflected in closing inventory.

(2) Retained copies of Forms 941 and W-2 can be helpful in verifying deductions claimed for salaries and wages. Ascertain that a deduction is not being claimed for salaries or wages paid to domesitc employees, or to children, parents, or other relatives who are not performing adequate services in the business.

(3) In some cases the taxpayer and family will live in part of the building that houses the grocery. Therefore, check rent, depreciation, insurance and utilities for any personal use. Also, portions of the building or premises may be rented to others.

(4) Some grocery stores have vending machines, juke boxes, game machines, etc., from which they receive a percentage of profit. Verify that this income has been included on the return.

(5) If a deduction is claimed for sales tax remitted to the State, ascertain that the taxes collected have been included in gross receipts.

(6) When verifying tax deductions, consideration should be given to such items as Federal or State income taxes, tax on domestic employees, and taxes on personal residence or property.

(7) Special attention should be given to transportation and delivery expense to determine that personal transportation costs are not included. Any adjustment here (for personal usage) should be followed by adjustment to depreciation claimed.

(8) Purchase invoices sometimes reveal items which generally are not sold in this business. This may indicate that the taxpayer, through a wholesaler, has purchased personal items for self, family or friends.

6(12)0 *(4-23-81)* 4231

Laundromats

(1) When examining coin operated laundromats the examiner can reconstruct gross receipts by the use of the following method. Divide the total gallons of water consumed, as shown by taxpayer's water bills or by correspondence with the local water company, by the number of gallons required for each wash load. Multiply this result by the rate per load to arrive at gross income from washing machines.

(2) The receipts from dryers can be estimated by assuming that one or more wash loads were dried at the same time in one dryer. This assumption should be made only after careful analysis of taxpayer's supplied information concerning the make and capacity of the machines. Multiply the dryer loads by the rate per load to arrive at gross income from dryers.

(3) Miscellaneous sales of soft drinks, candy, soap, and bleaches can be arrived at by applying the appropriate markup to costs.

6(13)0 *(4-23-81)* 4231
Motels

6(13)1 *(4-23-81)* 4231
Records

(1) Motels usually vary in size according to location. The highway motel depends entirely on the overnight guest, and may do a cash business in addition to credit card sales. This type motel usually is on a cash basis and their receipts and cash expenditures are probably recorded in a simple cash receipts and disbursements journal.

(2) The city motel would, in all probability, have overnight guests as well as guests for extended periods such as a week or even several weeks. It appears reasonable to assume that this type motel would have accounts receivable. Conversely, since they extend credit they find themselves in the position of asking for credit. They also will generally report on a cash basis. The books of record usually consist of a cash receipts and disbursements journal and a multicolumn check register in lieu of an accounts payable journal.

6(13)2 *(4-23-81)* 4231
Gross Receipts

(1) Gross receipts may be tested by determining the cost of laundering a change of linens and dividing this into the total laundry cost for the year to arrive at an estimated number of guests for the year.

(2) If a guest register is available, the number of names appearing thereon should be multiplied by the charge per room, taking into account single and double occupancy and possibly seasonal rates. The possibility of owner-occupancy should also be checked.

(3) The motel located near towns and cities may be examined in much the same way as described in paragraphs (1) and (2) above.

(4) An analysis of registration cards and the total number of units available is often a good lead to unreported receipts.

(5) A check should be made for rental income received from space leased to outside business concerns, such as, restaurants, souvenir shops, etc.

(6) A determination should be made as to whether vending machine income has been included in income.

(7) Some motels operate their own coin operated laundry machines. The income derived from such source should be checked to determine whether it has been included on the return.

6(13)3 *(4-23-81)* 4231
Expenses

(1) Examine the check register for unusual items and personal expenditures. The more common expenses for this type operation would be utilities, laundry costs and wages.

(2) Specific adjustments might arise from:

(a) depreciation—improper basis and useful life;

(b) personal expenses of the owner charged to business expenses, i.e., meals for the family and depreciation of living quarters;

(c) capital expenditures charged to operating expenses.

6(14)0 *(4-23-81)* 4231
Professional Persons

6(14)1 *(4-23-81)* 4231
Introduction

(1) Professional persons use many different systems for recording income and expense. Many professional persons practice their professions as sole proprietors, maintain single entry systems of accounting and use the cash basis method of reporting income on their returns. In other instances where partnerships, joint ventures, and associate arrangements exist, the systems tend to be more formal.

(2) The income of professional persons is derived from fees for personal services. Usually there are no inventories nor direct costs of sales involved in earning fees. Consequently, it is seldom that reliable ratios will be available as a rule-of-thumb test in estimating receipts.

(3) Generally, the professional person will employ one or two persons such as a secretary, receptionist or nurse. In small offices where one person is responsible for the receipt and disbursement of funds, examiners should assure themselves that adequate records are maintained and that income is properly reported.

(4) As a general rule, it is important in the examination of a professional person's return to check for omitted income. Of course, expenses should be given appropriate attention, considering the manner of payment and whether substantial in amount.

(5) Techniques suggested herein are not intended to be all-inclusive, but are mentioned to point out features which are found in most professions. It would be impractical to apply all techniques in each case. The facts and circumstances in each instance should guide the examiner.

(6) Precontact analysis techniques for a professional person's return and similiar, in many ways, to those used for other types of returns. When possible, computations should be made to determine significant financial information in regard to investments, capital assets purchased, and the type and size of the taxpayer's practice. A source and application of funds computation prepared quickly from the return itself will frequently reveal useful information.

(7) Some of the inquiries appropriate to the examination of a professional person's return are:

(a) What is the accounting system and manner of recording fee income?

(b) What records were used to account for income?

(c) What records were used, and by whom, to prepare the return?

(d) Who handles receipts in the office, who deposits same, and are they all deposited?

(e) Length of time in practice and speciality, if any.

(f) Did the taxpayer engage in teaching, writing, or lecturing?

(g) Number of offices, interoffices or chairs.

(h) Investment data.

(i) Names of all bank accounts, account numbers, and nature (business and personal).

(j) What method is used for billing accounts? (If billings are made on a specific date during the month, some response in the form of collections should be apparent in the subsequent days.)

(k) Are delinquent accounts turned over to collection agencies? If so, how are ultimate collections from this agency reported?

(l) Is the taxpayer associated with universities, governmental agencies, schools, industrial concerns, life insurance companies, etc? If so, how is such income reported?

(m) Were any services rendered without cash remuneration but in exchange for some other asset or service performed by the patient or client? (See text 523 bartering income)

(8) Securing the above information in the initial interview will usually save many hours of examination time.

(9) The remainder of this section will cover specific information dealing with certain professions, the type of records generally found in these professions, and examination techniques which can be effectively used to test these records and to verify the reported income.

6(14)2 *(4-23-81)* 4231
Medical Practitioners

6(14)2.1 *(4-23-81)* 4231
General

6(14)2.11 *(4-23-81)* 4231
Records

(1) Regardless of the system used by doctors to record income and expenses, the examiner should find in one form or another the following records:

(a) appointment book;

(b) daily log showing dates, patients and payments;

(c) receipt book;

(d) bank records;

(e) disbursement journal or ledger (active and inactive);

(f) recapitulation schedules or worksheets.

6(14)2.12 *(4-23-81)* 4231
Appointment Book

The appointment book is not ordinarily used for recording bookkeeping entries, however, it may contain informal notations. This record contains the chronological listing of appointments with patients whose names are recorded in advance usually by the doctor's nurse or secretary. This book is a control device for the doctor's time, and thus is a good indicator of business volume. If doctors state the appointment book has been lost or destroyed, the examiner may be able to use the patients cards and other records for current and prior years to determine if income has been properly reported.

6(14)2.13 *(4-23-81)* 4231
Daily Log

When the patient appears for an appointment, the visit may be recorded in a "Daily Log." A payment or charge may also be recorded after the visit. This log identifies the patient treated on the indicated date, and it is here that the charges for services are usually recorded.

Receipts by mail are also usually recorded in the log.

6(14)2.14 *(4-23-81)* 4231
Receipt Book

If a patient makes a payment in cash, there should be a receipt issued. If the receipts are serially numbered, they can be checked to the record containing cash payments received. If the receipts are not numbered, examiners should make tests to satisfy themselves that all fees are consistently recorded as income.

6(14)2.15 *(4-23-81)* 4231
Bank Records

(1) An important step in examining a doctor's return is to analyze the following:

(a) check stubs and canceled checks;

(b) bank statements—business and personal;

(c) deposit slips (or duplicates);

(d) deposit books (savings accounts).

6(14)2.16 *(4-23-81)* 4231
Disbursement Journal or Ledger

This record may be in any form and, if disbursements are made by check, will not differ from other taxpayers' records.

6(14)2.17 *(4-23-81)* 4231
Patient Cards

It is customary to prepare a card for each patient. The information will vary, but essentially it will be used by the doctor for identification of the patient, and to record charges and payments (including those by mail).

6(14)2.18 *(4-23-81)* 4231
Recapitulation Schedules or Worksheets

(1) Weekly or monthly totals are usually posted to a schedule used for preparing the income tax return. If only the summaries are furnished during the audit, the examiner should make every effort to obtain the original records.

(2) The examiner should make tests of the patient cards and/or daily log to verify fee income.

6(14)2.2 *(4-23-81)* 4231
Determining Gross Income

6(14)2.21 *(4-23-81)* 4231
General

Low gross receipts may be due to starting a new practice, illness, age or semiretirement. It also may be that the doctor simply does not have a large or profitable clientele. Whatever the reason, the examiner should attempt to establish the true facts before time-consuming audit procedures are undertaken.

6(14)2.22 *(4-23-81)* 4231
Fees

(1) Every doctor has a fee scale. If possible, this should be determined during the initial interview. This information facilitates test checks for receipts, charges, and fee income reported. Fees may be received from regular or referred patients, drop-in or emergency patients, insurance companies, and health and accident companies.

(2) Ask how payments from health insurance companies, are recorded. If any doubts arise, examiners, after consulting, may have to utilize the paying agencies to verify those receipts.

(3) Examiners should verify that fees from after hours office or house calls are included in income.

6(14)2.23 *(4-23-81)* 4231
Other Income

(1) Some doctors will teach or lecture at medical schools. Sometimes doctors write articles or books and some are professional lecturers. The examiner should question the doctor on these activities to determine if income was received and if it was reported correctly.

(2) At times the doctor may testify as an expert witness. Ask how fees from this activity are recorded.

(3) Many doctors are active investors in securities, bonds, rental properties, oil properties, and real estate. The examiner must not only audit the professional records but must also investigate the investment features in these returns.

(4) Doctors who enjoy a profitable practice, yet report little or no investment income, should be questioned about these areas.

(5) Occasionally a doctor has income producing arrangements with other doctors or professional people. Some of these have been kickback arrangements with druggists on prescriptions, with opticians on prescriptions for glasses and frames, or with specialists on referrals. The examiner should be alert to indications that any of the above practices may exist, and are properly recorded.

6(14)2.3 *(4-23-81)* 4231
Verification of Income

(1) To test the records, the examiner should assemble the appointment book, patient cards, daily log, and deposit slips if available, for a selected period. Some techniques would be:

(a) Test the footings in the daily log to the monthly recapitulation schedule, and then to the annual total gross receipts as reported on the return. Check receipts from daily log to deposit slips. Compare patient card financial records with daily log.

(b) Analyze or reconcile the total deposits to gross funds available to the taxpayer.

(2) If some of the records are not available or all receipts are not deposited, the examiner may wish to ascertain if there has been a substantial increase in net worth in the years under review. If the informal net worth computation indicates an unexplained source of funds the examiner should bring this to the attention of the group manager.

6(14)2.4 *(4-23-81)* 4231
Expenses

6(14)2.41 *(4-23-81)* 4231
General

(1) Since most doctors are on the cash basis of accounting, the expenses must be paid to be deductible. Exceptions to this are depreciation, prepaid rent and insurance and other items of this type which should be deducted ratably as they expire.

(2) If the doctor maintains a home office, it will be necessary to check the apportionment of personal and business expenses. The examiner must be alert to personal expenses claimed under the guise of business deductions.

(3) Although no specific comparison can be made between a physicians' gross income and the amount of drugs and supplies purchased, large expenditures for drugs and supplies would normally indicate either a large volume of business or that they are physician-pharmacists who administer and sell preventive vaccines and drugs. An examiner should be aware that physicians do receive many free samples of drugs and supplies.

6(14)2.42 *(4-23-81)* 4231
Salaries and Wages

In some cases, a doctor will employ other doctors as assistants. Also, there may be a participation or bonus arrangement with them. In this event, the disbursement should be verified from the cash records. These persons are usually paid as independent contractors not subject to withholding tax. Examiners should verify that information returns (1099-NEC) have been issued. Referral fees or fee splitting payments are deductible when they are customary in the profession and in the community and are not prohibited by law.

6(14)2.43 *(4-23-81)* 4231
Domestic Labor

The examiner should compare the payroll records to Form 941 and W-2's to determine the number of employees involved and inquire as to the duties of each, for the purpose of eliminating the cost of domestic help. If the doctor maintains an office in the home, an apportionment of expenses for domestic labor must be made.

6(14)2.44 *(4-23-81)* 4231
Taxes

If the doctor owns any property, other than his/her home, and claims real estate taxes, the tax bills should be examined to eliminate any personal taxes from the business schedule. See text 526 of this Handbook for method of deducting state income taxes.

6(14)2.45 *(4-23-81)* 4231
Bad Debts

As has been stated, most doctors report on the cash basis, which usually precludes their claiming losses from bad debts. Occasionally a fee is paid by a check which is not honored by the bank. If the check was reported when received, the taxpayer would then be entitled to a deduction when the check proves bad. If doctors report gross fees as billed, they would be entitled to a bad debt deduction for fees not actually received. If delinquent accounts are turned over to a collection agency, it should be determined how recoveries are handled.

6(14)2.46 *(4-23-81)* 4231
Depreciation

The year and manner of the acquisition of assets should be checked, noting the financial arrangements and whether the funds used came from a properly identified source.

6(14)2.47 *(4-23-81)* 4231
Repairs

The cancelled checks should be examined in conjunction with the invoice to determine the nature of the expenditure as well as to verify the actual cost.

6(14)2.48 *(4-23-81)* 4231
Insurance

Obtain a breakdown of payment and verify that personal items such as life, health, and auto insurance have not been deducted.

6(14)2.49 *(4-23-81)* 4231
Travel and Entertainment

(1) The examiner should pay particular attention to amounts claimed for entertainment and similar expense.

(2) Travel expenses paid in connection with attending a medical convention are generally deductible, (but not the family portion).

(3) The entertainment of other doctors and patients which is of a reciprocal nature should not be allowed. An example of this would be a group of doctors who customarily refer patients to one another and who also attend social events together for which they take turns purchasing the tickets. Another example would be the reciprocal cost of meals by doctors who are associated with the same hospital or who share a medical suite and lunch together.

6(14)2.5 *(4-23-81)* 4231
Automobile

Examiner should ascertain that the expenses for commuting between a doctor's residence and the office were not claimed. The examiner should apportion auto expense as to business and personal. The facts in each case should govern.

6(14)2.6 *(4-23-81)* 4231
Education

(1) The cost of refresher courses may be allowed only to the extent they are necessary to keep doctors advised as to new developments in their field. The cost of instruction in a field in which they have not previously engaged is not allowable. Prolonged courses may indicate new skills were being acquired.

(2) Psychoanalysis and psychiatrists frequently incur expenses for personal analyses which may be required in their profession. Such expenses usually arise near the close of their training or just prior to the start of their practice. Such expenditures are not deductible as medical or business expenses.

6(14)2.7 *(4-23-81)* 4231
Physician and Patient—Privileged Communications

The Federal courts have assumed the communications made by a patient to a physician, while seeking professional advice, are privileged. This privilege has not been extended to financial matters, such as the amount of fees paid for professional services.

6(14)3 *(4-23-81)* 4231
Dentists

(1) The accounting system and records of dentists are very similar to that of other doctors. A dentist usually keeps an appointment and daily log book designed especially for dentists.

(2) In contrast to the examination of other doctors, the costs of supplies in a dentist's work will be higher, due to the use of gold, silver, etc.

(3) In determining correct income, the examiner should verify that the sale of used precious metals has been included in gross income.

(4) The procedures for verification of income of a doctor should be followed in the examination of a dentist's tax return.

6(14)4 *(4-23-81)* 4231
Attorneys

6(14)4.1 *(4-23-81)* 4231
Privileged Communications

(1) The important issue of "privileged communications" between an attorney and clients, as related to an examination of the attorney's return must be understood by the examiner. This is particularly so if the examiner is to secure pertinent financial information when dealing with an attorney.

(2) The mere relationship of attorney and client does not render confidential every communication made by the client to the attorney. If the attorney is just a conduit for handling funds, or the transaction involves a simple transfer of title to real estate, and there is no consultation for legal advice, communications made by the client are not privileged.

(3) Communications made in the course of seeking business advice rather than legal advice are likewise not privileged.

(4) It has been held that the privilege is inapplicable to communications made to a person who is both an attorney and accountant, if they have been made solely to enable him to audit the client's books, prepare a Federal income tax return, or otherwise act solely as an accountant.

(5) Examiners should be able to secure from attorneys any records or information in their possession, except those containing the privileged communications, which will aid in the examination of personal returns.

6(14)4.2 *(4-23-81)* 4231
Records

(1) The accounting and financial records of an attorney will vary, according to the business arrangements of those involved. In a partnership, or office where there is an associate arrangement, there will usually be complete and adequate records, consisting of all or some of the following:

(a) appointment book;
(b) client's card index;
(c) a daily log or receipts book;
(d) a disbursement book or ledger, showing breakdown of regular expenses paid, as well as disbursements made from trust funds;
(e) individual client's accounts showing description of service, charges and credits;
(f) case time record per client;
(g) register of cases in progress, by client's name; and
(h) time report per attorney and per client, showing time, dates of work, and billings or charges.

(2) The records that may be found in the office of a single attorney are:

(a) an appointment book;
(b) diary or day book;
(c) a recording of fees received (many times this is kept by the attorney personally);
(d) a running account of expenses paid;
(e) costs relating to a case which may be maintained on the inside page of the folder containing the case file;
(f) single entry disbursement book, ledger or sheet;
(g) monthly recapitulation schedule of fees and expenses; and/or
(h) duplicate deposit slips, bank statements and canceled checks.

6(14)4.3 *(4-23-81)* 4231
Trust Fund or Escrow Account

(1) An accounting feature, peculiar to practicing attorneys, is the trust fund or escrow account. Some States prescribe responsibility for the accounting of client's funds, or funds held in suspense by the attorney.

(2) Usually the attorney will deposit into this account funds received from the client which will be subject to disbursement for various reasons. Some will apply to the attorney's fee, some will be disbursed to other attorneys and/or other parties to a suit or business transactions, and some to expenses. Good practice dictates that attorneys clearly identify funds withdrawn, and record them in another part of their records, but this is not always done.

(3) The examiner should be alert to determine that the attorney has disclosed all special accounts, all accounts with associates, all trust fund accounts (since there may be more than one), and all partnership accounts.

6(14)4.4 *(4-23-81)* 4231
Source of Fees

(1) A practicing attorney's principal source of income is from fees received for representing clients in any number of situations.

(2) Types of fee arrangement include single retainer fees, annual retainer fees, contingent fees, and referral fees. The single retainer fee may be received in advance, in full or in part. The annual retainer fee may be received monthly or at other intervals. Contingent fees are based upon a percentage of amounts collected or recovered. Referral fees are received from other attorneys to whom clients are referred for services.

6(14)4.5 *(4-23-81)* 4231
Expenses

(1) The expenses of attorneys, such as rent, utilities and automobile, are similar to those of

other professional persons. In addition to the ordinary expenses of the profession, an attorney has expenses on behalf of clients. Generally, advances in cash for expenses incurred by an attorney on behalf of a client are not deductible where the attorney is entitled to reimbursement and in fact is to be reimbursed. The usual practice in regard to a client's cost on a case is to charge for the costs and deduct them from the settlement received. In personal injury claim cases taken on a contingent fee basis, the attorney may not be entitled to reimbursement; therefore, the expense would be deductible in the year expended. If claimed as current expenses, the examiner should determine that the proper amount is included in income when settlement is received. If these expenditures are made through the trust fund, an analysis of that account will reveal whether the disbursements were properly recorded.

(2) Many attorneys contribute to election campaign funds of State, county, and local officials. Examiners should satisfy themselves that these contributions have not been claimed as business expenses by the attorney.

6(14)5 *(4–23–81)* 4231

Engineers

(1) Engineers are usually subject to registration in the various States in order to operate on a professional basis. The work of the engineer is divided into several highly specialized fields and includes designing, estimating, supervising construction, consulting and related activities.

(2) The income of professional engineers consists of fees which are usually received in accordance with the terms of a contract. A written contract should exist between the engineer and the principal for each job undertaken. The contract should include a description of the services to be rendered, an estimate of the time required to perform the work, and the terms for the settlement of the fee.

(3) Fees may be received upon the completion of work or when it is delivered and accepted, or progressively as the work is completed. It is not unusual to find that the engineering services on long-term contracts are paid for in accordance with the percentage of completion of the job, or in installments over the period of the project.

(4) The contracts should be available for the verification of income, and the specific job costs can usually be related directly to the income items. Estimates of the percentage of completion of the jobs in progress at the end of the period are usually available for the verification of reportable income.

6(14)6 *(4–23–81)* 4231

Architects

(1) The profession of the architect is in some respects similar to that of the engineer. The architect is employed to design buildings and to supervise their construction to see that it conforms to specifications. Income is derived from fees.

(2) The compensation of the architect is sometimes a fixed percentage of costs of construction. It is also based on direct labor costs plus an allowance for overhead, fees for consultants, etc. The compensation is usually paid in installments, the first payment being made when the contract is signed. Other installments may be received as the work progresses, with full settlement when the completed structure is accepted.

(3) There are occasions when architects are issued stocks or securities in the corporation for which they have performed services. The examiner should be aware of the possibility that this type of transaction has been negotiated.

(4) When contractors bid on the construction designed by the architect they are usually required to deposit performance guarantees with the architect as security for the building plans and specifications used in making their estimates. The deposits are returnable to the contractor when the performance is completed. Until such time, the architect reports the deposit as a liability. The return of the deposit is not an expense.

(5) The architect may be called upon to make advances on behalf of the client, such as for the purchase of certain equipment which the client is obligated to furnish. This type of transaction is an account receivable until satisfied. It should not be charged as an expense.

(6) A large item of expenditure by architects is for blue prints and supplies. The costs of blue prints are usually charged to the cost of specific jobs.

(7) Usually contracts are signed with clients for the specific jobs, wherein the basis of compensation is defined. The examiner should examine these contracts in connection with the verification of the fees recorded.

(8) The accounts peculiar to architects are: advances for clients, fees to engineers and consultants, and blue prints. These items are usually charged to the specific costs of jobs for which the expenditures were made or to accounts receivable.

(9) The examination of the return of an architect does not generally present any features not found in other types of business. The examiner should be alert to any indication that reported income does not include all fees received. The examination of the expenses deducted follows the general procedures of other types of examination.

6(15)0 *(4–23–81)* 4231
Real Estate Brokers

(1) Real estate brokers engage in the management of properties for landlords and in the sales of real estate for owners. A percentage of the rents received or of the selling price of the property is received by the broker for services.

(2) A real estate agency often is licensed by one or more insurance companies to write fire, automobile, and casualty insurance.

(3) Some real estate brokers, in addition to the above activities, buy real estate for resale on their own account or for investment purposes. Under these circumstances the examiner will often have to determine whether the real estate sold was purchased by the broker for resale, or whether it was originally purchased for investment. Where the sale is claimed as a capital transaction, the examiner should require the submission of proof by the taxpayer that the property was not purchased primarily for resale. Very often the properties are purchased to be held until a satisfactory sale can be effected. In the meantime, the property is rented to a tenant and depreciation is claimed. The deduction of depreciation is not necessarily determinative of intent.

(4) The examiner should be alert to situations which would in fact be rentals with options to purchase. Examination of contracts will usually reveal the true intent of the parties.

(5) An examination of the broker's copies of sales agreements and settlement sheets will assist in determining when sales were consummated, thus indicating when commissions should be included in income.

(6) Sources of information on real estate dealer's transactions are records of deed transfers, mortgages, title company records, banks, mortgage companies, and savings and loan associations. Where brokers deal on their own accounts, the financial establishments usually have statements of their net worth in the files. These statements may be useful in verifying that the broker's activities are properly reflected in their records.

(7) Where brokers also sell insurance, additional accounts will appear in their records reflecting accounts receivable from policy holders and accounts payable to insurance companies.

(8) The insurance companies require their agents to render monthly "Accounts Current" reflecting the issue and the cancellation of policies. The premium charged, commissions earned, cash received, and balance due are recorded for each policy issued. A carbon copy of the "Account Current" is retained by the broker, and is often referred to as the policy register. This register provides a means of verifying the insurance transactions. There should be a monthly policy register for each insurance company represented.

6(16)0 *(4–23–81)* 4231
Restaurants or Cafés

6(16)1 *(4–23–81)* 4231
Records

The average small cafe or restaurant is usually on a cash basis. Their recordkeeping may consist of a simple "cash receipts and disbursements journal" in which are recorded the cash sales (from cash register tapes, meal checks, or both) and cash disbursements (from paid receipts and/or checks).

6(16)2 *(4–23–81)* 4231
Gross Income

(1) Generally, successful cafes should have an appreciable gross profit percentage. The examiner should determine the applicable gross profit percentage by reference to commercial publications. Such factors as location, gross profit percentages of similar businesses, etc., should be considered.

(2) Inquiry should be made as to the number of hours worked and the number of meals eaten at the cafe by the taxpayer, the spouse, and other family members to determine the cost of personal food consumption.

(3) Bank statements and paid receipts should be scrutinized. If records are inade-

quate, it may be necessary to determine income by indirect methods.

(4) It is common practice for vending or pinball machines to be owned by vendors and placed in a cafe or restaurant under an arrangement whereby the proceeds from the machines are divided between the vendor and the cafe owner. In the usual situation there will be no machines listed on the depreciation schedules to tip you off to this source of income. Where it is established that machines are located in this business under this type of arrangement, the vendor will have records to substantiate the receipts received by the cafe owner.

(5) Another source of information regarding gross receipts from sales would be copies of sales tax reports submitted by the taxpayer to the State tax authorities.

(6) Examiners should verify that cafe owners or restauranteurs have not erroneously reported as gross receipts only the cash on hand at the end of the day, failing to include in gross receipts that cash received but withdrawn for personal use or used to pay daily business expenses. There is also the possibility that purchases may not have been reduced by the cost of merchandise withdrawn for personal use.

6(16)3 *(4–23–81)* 4231

Expenses

(1) Retained copies of Forms 941 and W-2 are useful in verifying deductions claimed for salaries and wages. Ascertain that a deduction is not being claimed for salaries or wages paid to children, parents, or other relatives who are not performing adequate services in the business.

(2) In some cases the taxpayer and family live in part of the building that houses the cafe or restaurant. Therefore, the examiner should check rent, depreciation, insurance and utilities for any personal use. Also, portions of the building or premises may be rented to others.

(3) If a deduction is claimed for sales tax remitted to the state, ascertain that the taxes collected have been included in gross receipts.

(4) Verify tax deductions, including Federal or State taxes, tax on domestic employees, and taxes on personal residence or property.

(5) Special attention should be given to transportation or delivery expense to determine that it is a true business expense and that personal transportation costs are not included. Any adjustment here should be followed by adjustment (for personal usage) to depreciation claimed.

(6) Purchase invoices sometimes reveal items which generally are not sold in this business, which may indicate that the taxpayer, through a wholesaler, has purchased personal items for self, family or friends.

(7) Spoilage or theft is usually reflected in inventory, and is not to be considered under operating expenses.

6(17)0 *(4–23–81)* 4231

Service Stations

6(17)1 *(4–23–81)* 4231

General

(1) Service stations are operated under a variety of arrangements. Examples of the types of arrangements follow:

(a) the building, land, and equipment is owned by the operator;

(b) the building and equipment is owned by the operator but the land is leased;

(c) the equipment is owned by the operator and the premises are leased from the oil company;

(d) the premises and equipment, except small tools are leased from one of the major oil companies.

(2) Since inventories are an income producing factor, the accrual or hybrid method of accounting should be used. However, if a different method of accounting is used, the examiner must determine whether income is properly reflected.

6(17)2 *(4–23–81)* 4231

Records

Service station operators, may use single or double entry bookkeeping systems. In some cases the only records available may be cash register tapes of daily sales and folders containing invoices of purchases and operating expenses.

6(17)3 *(4–23–81)* 4231

Gross Receipts

(1) The first test for accuracy of reported receipts is the gross profit ratio. See the section in this chapter for determining this ratio.

(2) Oil companies which lease newly constructed service station facilities to independent operators, frequently provide the initial inventory and sell merchandise to operators on consignment. Since title to consigned goods remains with the consignor until sold, examiners should satisfy themselves that inventories do not include merchandise held on consignment.

(3) Examiners should check to see that credit card sales are included in gross income. Many independent service station operators use the credit card sales to satisfy liabilities for purchases from the oil companies.

(4) Check the following sources of income for possible omitted receipts:

(a) Commissions earned from vending machine sales.

(b) Sales of used tires, batteries, and oil.

(c) Fees for towing charges, minor auto repairs, and auto washes.

(d) Income from rental of tools.

(e) Recovery of state gas taxes due to evaporation of gas.

(f) Income from parking charges.

(g) Repayment of loans to distributors often included in purchases. Verify that installment payments on equipment are not deducted.

(h) Specialized service income, such as lawn mower repairs.

(i) Income from trailer rentals.

(j) Income from sales of autos, for themselves and others, including finder fees.

(k) The total gasoline gallonage sold is readily determinable from the gas purchase vouchers. Station operators have a prescribed markup per gallon. In addition, if they own the building or facility they usually receive a monthly lease payment from the oil company which is based on gallons purchased and is paid in a separate check. Verify that the rental payments have been included in receipts.

(5) Purchase invoices should reflect gas and oil purchases, replacement of parts used in performing services, and other merchandise, such as by-products from suppliers.

(6) A review should be made of the sales tax return to compare it with reported gross receipts.

6(17)4 *(4-23-81)* 4231
Expenses

(1) Check to see if merchandise, such as gas and oil, is being withdrawn for personal use. If it is, purchases should be reduced by the amounts withdrawn.

(2) In some cases you may find that lease payments are included on gas purchase invoices. When this occurs, the taxpayer may be including the lease payment in purchases and also deducting them as rent.

(3) Where the taxpayer lives in the same building, be certain that a pro rata determination has been made for depreciation and other applicable expenses, such as, taxes, interest, etc.

(4) A review should be made of any bad debt deductions to ensure that a proper inclusion in income has been made.

6(18)0 *(4-23-81)* 4231
Truckers

6(18)1 *(4-23-81)* 4231
Records

Truckers may own and operate a tractor and trailer for themselves or may lease the tractor to a large trucking company. Where the trucker owns the tractor and pulls company owned trailers, companies usually issue a commission sheet showing trips made, gross commissions less advances, state fees paid, gas and oil purchases made on the company account, and any other charges.

6(18)2 *(4-23-81)* 4231
Gross Receipts

(1) Determine if gasoline or diesel oil charges have been deducted from truck rental income by the leaseholder, and if Form 1099 reports net payments after expenses have been deducted. If the charges were deducted by the leaseholder, be sure that the trucker does not report the net rental income and then duplicate the fuel deduction.

(2) After delivering their cargoes, drivers frequently solicit "cash hauling" for the return trips to the terminals. Check to determine that any income from this source is reported.

(3) Occasionally the operator will hire other drivers. Where the trucking company has issued a Form 1099, the examiner should be satisfied that the Form 1099 is for the gross commissions paid and not the net. Occasionally some Forms 1099 are issued for the net difference due the trucker. Verify that Forms 940, 941, and W-2 have been filed.

(4) In situations where the operator does not have regular runs, the line of inquiry should pertain to the use of the truck, keeping in mind the type of trailer and type cargo carried.

6(18)3 *(4-23-81)* 4231
Expenses

(1) In verifying expenses, the examiner should be alert for discounts applicable to fuel oil and gasoline and to repair parts. Repair invoices should be scrutinized to eliminate personal items.

(2) Where a trucking company has issued commission sheets, the tractor owner will generally have receipts to cover the expense items included therein. Verify that the tractor owner has not claimed these expenses again as separate deductions.

(3) Review depreciation schedules to determine that proper basis has been used. Determine the useful life of the asset. In many instances depreciation is being accelerated and the salvage value is understated or not taken into consideration in determining the basis for depreciation.

(4) Away from home expenses must be substantiated. Many companies pay for lodgings. Log books and diaries may be utilized.

(5) Scrutinize repairs; the segregate major improvements which extended the useful life of the asset, such as the cost of a new or used motor.

(6) In most instances itemized invoices for gasoline, tires, lubrications, etc., are issued by the leaseholder. Toll charges may be verified with receipts. Ascertain whether other expenses are attributable to the operation of the truck; and if so, request verification.

(7) Check to make sure that highway use tax returns have been filed and are substantially correct.

(8) It is common practice for employee-drivers in the trucking industry to use hired help at in-between points to unload. The employee-driver pays the helpers and is later reimbursed by the company. Under these conditions, such helpers are considered employees of the company for Federal employment taxes and income tax withholding purposes.

(a) Examiners will determine that helpers' salary expenses are supported by payroll records showing names and social security numbers. These salary expenses are sometimes reported in other accounts.

(b) The fact that names and social security numbers were not obtained by the employer will not, by itself, be considered sufficient reason for disallowing the salary deduction. However, this fact will be considered in determining whether or not the deduction should be disallowed where there is any question of proper substantiation.

(c) When it is found that the taxpayer has not shown such hired helpers as employees, the examiner will explain the position of the Service and advise steps for compliance in future years.

(9) The situations cited in (8) above would also be applicable to owner/drivers who use hired help to unload their trucks. In this instance, the helpers are employees of the owner/driver for Federal employment taxes.

6(19)0 *(4-23-81)* 4231
Television & Radio Repair Shops

6(19)1 *(4-23-81)* 4231
Records

(1) Usually small radio-TV repair shops keep very simple business records. Generally, a record of cash receipts and disbursements is kept with few if any records of accounts receivable and payable. Some taxpayers maintain a more complete set of books and may be on the accrual or hybrid method of accounting. In this type of business it has been found that inventories are not necessarily large and may not have a material effect on profit because supplies are purchased as needed from the wholesalers.

(2) Quite frequently, an operation such as this will be carried on in the taxpayer's garage or basement, either as a full-time business or as a "side line." In a full-time operation, repairs and services are normally performed by someone other than the taxpayer, and in the larger TV repair shops you may find several repairment on the payroll.

(3) Bank statements, canceled checks and paid invoices will be needed for the examination.

6(19)2 *(4-23-81)* 4231
Gross Receipts

(1) The sales records should be totaled and compared with the bank deposits. If there is a substantial difference between deposits and reported income, the discrepancy should be analyzed. Verify that the owner's "time" or services have not been included in the payroll account.

(2) One method which may be employed by the examiner to test purchases would be to use a random verification, taking one month out of each quarter, verifying the additions, and matching invoices against checks. At this point an annualization of the four months might indicate whether it would be necessary to check out each and every item during the interview.

6(19)3 *(4-23-81)* 4231
Expenses

(1) Unusually large costs should be analyzed since the wholesale cost of supplies is extremely low in this type business. Sometimes dealers take advantage of their wholesale license to purchase TV sets and radios, etc., to resell. Trace a sample of such purchases through to the sales register.

(2) Suppliers occasionally give points or coupons with the purchase of tubes and parts which are redeemable for prizes.

Chapter 9

In-Depth Audits—The IRS Handbook

The following pages comprise sections 100 through 700 of *Section 4235* of the *Internal Revenue Manual*, titled, "Techniques Handbook for In-Depth Examinations." This handbook teaches examiners how to extend an examination beyond the scope originally intended when indications of tax fraud have been discovered or suspected.

The manual states "where a regular or normal tax examination ends, an in-depth examination should begin." Whereas the focus of a routine examination is mainly to test the validity of deductions and expenses, the focus of an in-depth examination shifts to testing the validity of reported income, with the main objectives of ferreting out unreported and untaxed income, and locating hidden interests and assets. According to the manual, the purpose is to bring to justice "those who have blatantly deprived the Government of revenue, properly due."

If you've read Chapter 7 you already know how a tax audit can turn into a fraud investigation. You also know how the IRS detects fraud, and what points of law must be established by the Government to prove fraud. In the following section you will learn IRS's step-by-step procedures for conducting an audit examination of such depth and scrutiny as to prove the elements of fraud beyond a reasonable doubt.

There are two reasons for including this material. First, to alert you to audit techniques that go beyond the normal, routine audit. By knowing the difference between routine audit techniques and those used in in-depth examinations, you will be able to know when the IRS suspects that you have violated a criminal statute.

Secondly, reading these sections taken from the manual will dispel many false, but commonly held notions about what the IRS can do, and about the ways in which the IRS can be beat. For example, many taxpayers who skim cash from their businesses erroneously believe that the IRS has no way to catch them as long as there is no paper trail involved in the cash transaction. Also, some taxpayers believe that if they are caught they can invent some crazy, illogical story to justify their actions, and the IRS agents will have no choice but to accept their story without question.

A full reading of the *Internal Revenue Manual* instructions should reveal two facts: first, that the IRS is fully prepared to handle almost any situation; and secondly, that unlike other types of federal crimes where third party informants and witnesses are essential ingredients to proving a case beyond a reasonable doubt, when it come to a tax fraud trial, *you* are your own worst enemy. For example, the IRS can use an analysis of your lifestyle and spending habits to show that you have lived beyond your reported means.

It is hoped that the in-depth substance of this information will dispell any erroneous notions you may have about tax fraud, and impress you sufficiently to serve as a deterrent to violating any tax laws.

Table of Contents

700
Examination Investigative Techniques

Introduction

110 *(4-11-80)* 4235
Purpose of Handbook

This Handbook is issued to Internal Revenue Agents to assist them in examination of income tax returns and in any in-depth fraud examinations or investigations. Its contents do not alter any existing technical or procedural issuances of the Service. Although some agents may have had considerable experience in examining income tax returns and may be already using many of the techniques described, this Handbook will be valuable for reference purposes, especially for seldom encountered situations. Newer employees will be aided materially by becoming acquainted with the audit techniques in this Handbook. A knowledge of these techniques will provide the newer agent greater self-confidence when beginning an examination.

120 *(4-11-80)* 4235
Suggestions Required to Improve Handbook

Revenue agents, supervisors, and managers are put on notice that this Handbook is not, we repeat not, to be considered a stagnant document. We expect suggestions from districts and regions for improvements, additions and deletions. Tax fraud is an ever-changing arena and those of us making investigations must change and, in fact, try to stay one step ahead if we are to achieve our program. Therefore, your suggestions are solicited and should be submitted to the Director, Examination Division, National Office, Attention: CP:E:S:S, as frequently as thoughts arise.

130 *(4-11-80)* 4235
Comparison of Normal Tax Examinations with In-Depth Examinations

131 *(4-11-80)* 4235
Normal Tax Examinations

(1) The usual end product of an income tax examination is to establish the correct taxable income, as defined by the Internal Revenue Code and regulations, and thence the correct income tax liability of the person or entity under examination. In making an examination, the agent has a twofold responsibility: to the taxpayer and to the Government of the United States.

(2) In making their examination agents are expected to pursue the examination to a point where they can, with reasonable certainty, conclude that they have considered all items necessary for a substantially proper determination of the tax liability. Agents are expected to extend the examination to include all unusual and questionable items. In some cases, it will be necessary to conduct an extensive examination to properly determine the tax liability; while in other cases, the examination can be completed after inquiry into only one or two items on the return.

(3) A tax examination frequently will be extended beyond the scope originally intended because of situations not apparent at the outset. The amount of verification work to be done in any single tax examination is a matter of individual judgment for which no rigid rule can be established.

132 *(4-11-80)* 4235
In-Depth Examinations

(1) It has been indicated that, where a regular or normal tax examination ends, an in-depth examination should begin.

(2) This undertaking calls for maximum effort, imagination, and thoughtfulness on the part of investigative revenue agents and supervisory personnel. We need to be more penetrating in every respect, more discerning, more comprehensive in the collection and presentation of information. We must recognize that normal standards for examination are not applicable, if we are to meet our objectives of ferreting out the sources and amounts of untaxed income; locating hidden interests and assets, and bringing to justice those who have blatantly deprived the Government of revenue, properly due.

(3) Maximum effort, initiative, energy, and skill must be applied by revenue agents and supervisors in planning, directing and conducting in-depth examinations if we are to fulfill our obligations. By establishing and assessing a true liability, it will even be possible to slash into organized crime's profit margin and some of its ill-gotten gains.

(4) The commitment we seek from revenue agents assigned to these in-depth investigations is an extremely important and difficult one. The revenue agent in many cases will be oper-

ating independently without a witness, and will be confronted with adverse conditions and deal with the best taxpayer representation available; books and records will not be readily available as in other cases and innumerable other difficulties may be anticipated. The agent must be bold, follow every suspicious transaction to its conclusion and obtain definitive answers wherever possible.

140 *(4-11-80)* 4235

Contents of Handbook

This Handbook is organized so that the first chapters deal with general information and a revenue agent's authority. Then it progresses through pre-examination procedures, initial contact, special examination and investigation procedures, and ends with comments regarding violations of other Federal agency statutes. Each chapter is presented to assist examiners in determining facts and applying audit techniques rather than in presenting governing statutes, court decisions, or procedures.

141 *(4-11-80)* 4235

Safeguarding of IRS Files

141.1 *(4-11-80)* 4235

Documents

(1) All employees are responsible for providing reasonable security for all information, documents and property with which they are entrusted and for complying with all security requirements.

(2) Sections 226.1 and 226.2 of IRM 0735.1, *Handbook of Employee Responsibilities and Conduct,* addresses the care of official documents and accountability for money and property.

(3) IRM 1(16)41, *Physical and Document Security Handbook,* provides minimum requirements for safeguarding all tax returns and information protected under the Privacy Act of 1974.

(a) All tax returns, information, reports, communications, workpapers and case files shall be secured in accordance with Chapter 500 of IRM 1(16)41.

(b) When returns or return information is carried outside of the office no labels or taxpayer identifying information should be visible on the outside of folders, envelopes or other containers. Material carried outside the office must be kept with the individual. If it becomes necessary to leave the material in an automobile, it must be locked in the trunk with the rest of the car locked and then left for only a short period. Hotels and motels are usually not good locations to secure tax information.

(c) Access to the documents shall be on a "need to know" basis by authorized personnel only.

(d) Waste or unnecessary documents containing protected information should be destroyed in accordance with Section 345, IRM 1(16)41.

(4) Agents should discuss with their supervisor the need for special security requirements for Fraud, Strike Force or Grand Jury information.

141.2 *(4-11-80)* 4235

Personnel

(1) Revenue Agents should be alert to improper or unusual contacts, attacks upon their integrity, indications of bribes, or threats emanating from the taxpayers or their representatives. Never do anything that could be interpreted as an invitation to a bribe. Bribe attempts will be reported directly to Inspection as set forth in IRM 403(12).

(2) The security and safety of IRS personnel are considered uppermost. Consideration should be given as to whether, in a particular case, all contacts with the taxpayer should be conducted in the presence of an accompanying agent.

(3) Taxpayer matters should be discussed with authorized personnel only, and then on a "need to know" basis.

150 *(4-11-80)* 4235

Use of Handbook

(1) This Handbook is to be used as a guide to good methods in determining facts and in recognizing schemes of tax avoidance or evasion. It is designed for use as a reference volume which may be carried by agents at all times. It may be used both before and during an examination. It will assist in adequate planning prior to approaching the taxpayer as well as in pointing out audit and investigative techniques to use during an examination. It is not all-inclusive nor is it intended to replace or limit individual initiative in developing audit techniques.

(2) Agents with little experience should study carefully the contents of this Handbook. It will answer many questions raised by new agents who are encountering difficult problems for the first time and wonder "what to do" and "how to do it" once a tax return has been assigned to them for an in-depth examination.

(3) The guidelines in this Handbook are permissive; therefore, any provisions herein which have a mandatory tone should not be considered as specific instructions which must be followed. However, the permissive nature of these guidelines should not be construed as preventing supervisors or Strike Force Representatives from requiring that any appropriate part be followed in a particular situation. In the event of a conflict with a specific provision of the Internal Revenue Manual, the Manual provisions will prevail.

160 *(4-11-80)* 4235

Distribution of Handbook

The Handbook is distributed to all Internal Revenue Agents and appropriate supervisory and management personnel, and to all offices of the Assistant Regional Commissioners (Examination) and (Criminal Investigation) and to Chiefs and Assistant Chiefs, Criminal Investigation Division.

Definitions

210 *(4-11-80)* 4235

Terms and Words Defined

211 *(4-11-80)* 4235

Independent In-Depth Audit

A thorough investigation by the Examination function. Its primary objective, including the determination of correct taxable income, is to ascertain whether the taxpayer being audited has fully complied with the applicable Internal Revenue laws. It is to be expected that the books will be in agreement with the tax return. The agent should reconcile the books to the tax return, then commence the investigation. All income will be analyzed as to source, nature, and amount. All peculiar or unusual items of income, irrespective of amount, should be analyzed and clarified. The agent must look behind the book entries and determine the reasons for the entries. The agent must look for leads to unrecorded receipts. The agent should check with all parties to a transaction to fully understand the item. Third party contacts and investigations will be required in most cases. Many times books and records will be nonexistent, nonavailable, or inadequate, necessitating reconstruction of income by indirect methods. Audit procedures and techniques as suggested in the following pages should be utilized.

◀ An *in-depth audit* is a *thorough* examination by the IRS with the objective of determining your current taxable income and ascertaining if you have complied with all the Internal Revenue laws.

◀ An in-depth audit involves:

- Reconciling books (business records) to the tax return
- Analyzing income by source, nature and amount
- Determining reasons for book entries
- Understanding all transactions
- Initiating third party contacts and investigations
- Reconstructing income, if necessary

212 *(4-11-80)* 4235

Joint Investigation

A thorough, comprehensive and complete investigation conducted jointly by Criminal Investigation and Examination functions to determine if criminal tax fraud is involved and whether criminal prosecution should be recommended.

◀ The Criminal Investigation Division has the responsibility to investigate all alleged criminal violations arising under the Internal Revenue laws. These investigators are called "Special Agents."

213 *(4-11-80)* 4235

Joint Examination-Criminal Investigation Projects

This program encompasses enforcement of tax law violations against those involved in illegal activities whether it be In-Service racketeer, organized crime, Strike Force or cases in which the Department of Justice has formally expressed an interest.

◀ IRS *Policy Statement P-9-46* requires the IRS to identify taxpayers who derive substantial income from illegal activities and requires their continued scrutiny. The policy statement also requires an annual review of the latest tax returns filed by persons identified as major special enforcement subjects.

214 *(4-11-80)* 4235

Organized Crime

The wide spread, large scale and profitable criminal activities operated as a continuing business or criminal activities organized and controlled by a syndicate.

215 *(4–11–80)* 4235
Strike Force

A Strike Force is a project in a selected area (referred to as a site) in which various Federal enforcement and regulatory agencies concentrate their efforts on designated organized crime subjects. IRS has assigned representatives to each Strike Force.

216 *(4–11–80)* 4235
Joint Strike Force

A Joint Strike Force is a Strike Force which includes State and local enforcement agencies.

217 *(4–11–80)* 4235
Strike Force Representative

The IRS representative to a Strike Force will be known as the Strike Force Representative. The individual coordinates the local district organized crime activities with Department of Justice attorneys and other enforcement agencies. The individual acts as liaison between Department of Justice Strike Force and IRS field management. The individual provides guidance and assistance to district personnel.

218 *(4–11–80)* 4235
Strike Force Subject

The organized crime figure to be examined.

219 *(4–11–80)* 4235
Related Cases

An examination or investigation of another person or taxable entity which is conducted because of the relationship to a principal subject and to ensure a complete, full investigation of the subject.

21(10) *(4–11–80)* 4235
Strike Force Case

A Strike Force Case is an investigation of an organized crime figure listed in a Strike Force Work Program. It includes a taxpayer or taxable entity which is investigated as a part of the investigation of the organized crime target. The investigation of the subject and related cases

The Strike Force/Racketeer Project was established to monitor Criminal Investigation's information gathering and investigative activities or those taxpayers who are involved in organized criminal activities.

Definition of Organized Crime

◀ "Organized Crime" refers to those self-perpetuating, structured, and disciplined associations of individuals, or groups, combined together for the purpose of obtaining monetary or commercial gains or profits, wholly or in part by illegal means, while protecting their activities through a pattern of graft and corruption.

◀ Organized crime groups possess certain characteristics which include, but are not limited to the following:

- Their illegal activities are conspiratorial;
- In at least part of their activities, they commit or threaten to commit acts of violence or other acts which are likely to intimidate;
- They conduct their activities in a methodical, systematic, or highly disciplined and secret fashion;
- They insulate their leadership from direct involvement in illegal activities by their intricate organizational structure;
- They attempt to gain influence in government, politics, and commerce through corruption, graft, and illigitimate means; and
- They engage in patently illegal enterprises such as drugs, gambling, and loansharking, and also such activities as laundering illegal money through an investment in legitimate business.

should be conducted as one package using the team examination concept.

21(11) *(4-11-80)* 4235
Slush fund

Corporate slush funds are accounts or groups of accounts generally created through intricate schemes outside of normal corporate internal controls for the purpose of making political contributions, bribes, kickbacks, personal expenditures by corporate officials, and other illegal activities. Top level corporate officers are generally involved and the schemes are carried out by various transactions through the use of both domestic and foreign subsidiaries.

21(12) *(4-11-80)* 4235
High-level Drug Leaders Tax Enforcement Project

This project is aimed at high-level drug leaders and financiers engaged in organized criminal activities; as being notorious or powerful with respect to local criminal activities; or as receiving substantial income from illicit dealings in narcotics as a principal, major subordinate, or important aider or abettor.

◀ The Strike Forces are directed toward the identification and investigation of taxpayers who derive substantial income from organized criminal activities. Coordination of enforcement efforts and close cooperation and liaison with other federal, state, and local enforcement agencies are necessary for effective Strike Force operations.

◀ As a major participant in the Strike Force, the IRS has two objectives:

- To enforce criminal sanctions by appropriate recommendations for prosecution of taxpayers investigated by the Strike Force for criminal violations of the Internal Revenue Code or other related statutes when committed in contravention of the Internal Revenue laws.
- To assess and collect the proper taxes due, and to enforce civil sanctions by assessing and collecting applicable penalties.

◀ Investigations undertaken by the IRS in participation with a Strike Force are solely IRS operations. At all times control of the investigation is under the authority of the Commissioner of Internal Revenue or his/her delegate.

Procedures—Examination

310 *(4-11-80)* 4235
Introduction

(1) The authority of a revenue agent to conduct an examination or investigation is spelled out under IRC 7801, 7601 and 7602 which are respectively quoted herewith.

(a) IRC 7801(a)—"Powers and Duties of Secretary—Except as otherwise expressly provided by law, the administration and enforcement of this title shall be performed by or under the supervision of the Secretary of the Treasury."

(b) IRC 7601(a)—"General Rule—The Secretary or his delegate shall, to the extent he deems it practicable, cause officers or employees of the Treasury Department to proceed, from time to time, through each internal revenue district and inquire after and concerning all persons therein who may be liable to pay any internal revenue tax, and all persons owning or having the care and management of any objects with respect to which any tax is imposed."

(c) IRC 7602—"For the purpose of ascertaining the correctness of any return, making a return where none has been made, determining the liability of any person for any internal revenue tax or the liability at law or in equity of any transferee or fiduciary of any person in respect of any internal revenue tax, or collecting any such liability, the Secretary or his delegate is authorized—

"1 To examine any books, papers, records, or other data which may be relevant or material to such inquiry;

"2 To summon the person liable for tax or required to perform the act, or any officer or employee of such person, or any person having possession, custody, or care of books of account containing entries relating to the business of the person liable for tax or required to perform the act, or any other person the Secretary or his delegate may deem proper, to appear before the Secretary or his delegate at a time and place named in the summons and to produce such books, papers, records, or other data, and to give such testimony, under oath, as may be relevant or material to such inquiry; and

"3 To take such testimony of the person concerned, under oath, as may be relevant or material to such inquiry."

(2) In some instances agents are reluctant to assert their authority and thereby may impede their effectiveness.

◀ The investigation of criminal cases may stem from information discovered by IRS agents in the course of their audits and examinations; by special agents who may learn of indications of tax noncompliance and, when authorized, develop such cases; by Chiefs, Criminal Investigation Divisions, through making authorized surveys of selected individuals, groups, or activities; by Regional Commissioners, through Assistant Regional Commissioners from surveys conducted for the purpose of identifying areas of evasion; by the Assistant Commissioner (Criminal Investigation), through analyses of cases, special studies, and authorized surveys; and by revenue officers or other employees of the IRS in the performance of their duties.

Information of multiple address changes and identical names involved in income tax refunds may be received from a service center. This information may indicate false claims for refund. Information returns may furnish a basis for referrals.

◀ Investigations may also stem from information received from other government agencies; from application for the redemption of mutilated currency; from newspapers, magazines, and other publications; and from the general public. Chiefs of Criminal Investigation Divisions in districts where local customs officers are maintained may, when authorized, request from such officers information relating to importers who are suspected of substantially underevaluating merchandise. This may be a lead to attempted tax evasion.

(3) Historically, individuals subject to in-depth audits may not cooperate and may attempt to create obstacles to prevent an agent from making a complete and thorough investigation. This atmosphere, coupled with the reluctance of agents to insist that all records, etc. be made available, can prove harmful to an examination or investigation.

(4) In addition to having outstanding technical and investigative skills the assigned revenue agents should be bold, tenacious, inquisitive, and imaginative in their examinations and investigations and dedicated to the aims of the Service.

(5) The internal revenue agent has authority to perform all duties conferred upon such officers under all laws and regulations administered by the Internal Revenue Service, including the authority to investigate, and to require and receive information, as to all matters relating to such laws and regulations.

(6) Regardless of individuals or organizations under investigation, under no circumstances should a subject be denied any of the rights afforded him/her by our judicial system. To do less would compromise the program and cause the Service's efforts to be futile.

(7) Several problem areas have been identified and are elaborated upon in this Chapter. These areas are as follows:

(a) the determination of the place of examination;

(b) the right to request books, records and accountants' workpapers;

(c) the recognition of a power of attorney;

(d) inadequate records;

(e) Procrastination;

(f) utilization of third party information;

(g) securing affidavits;

(h) the use of the summons procedures;

(i) reopening of closed cases;

(j) jeopardy, quick, and transferee assessments.

◀ Listed here are major problem areas for IRS agents in carrying out in-depth examinations.

320 *(4-11-80)* 4235

Place of Examination

(1) It is imperative that the tone of the examination or investigation be established immediately; therefore, after allowing ample time for the taxpayer or his/her representatives to assemble necessary books and records, the time

◀ Note that the revenue agent reserves the right to set the time and place of the audit.

and place of the examination will be established by the revenue agent.

(2) With few exceptions, the examination of the records should be made at the taxpayer's place of business. If the place of business does not provide the necessary security, privacy, or minimal comforts necessary for the examination or if the taxpayer does not have any place of business, the agent should ask that the records be brought up to the taxpayer's representative's office or the local IRS office for examination.

(3) If the examination is not to be conducted at the taxpayer's place of business, the agent should inform the taxpayer that all pertinent records must be made available to him/her and that he/she will visit the place of business as often as necessary to fully understand the method of operation or to assist him/her in gathering visual information about the taxpayer's business interest.

(4) The agent must always extend the normal courtesies regarding all phases of the examination.

◀ The audit will normally occur at your place of business.

330 *(4-11-80)* 4235

Authority to Request Books, Records and Accountants' Workpapers

(1) The Internal Revenue Code, IRS Regulations, the Internal Revenue Manual, and the Revenue Agent's Pocket Commission, cover the authority to request and receive books, records, etc. necessary to properly examine an individual's tax affairs.

(2) An agent must never lose sight of the fact that an individual might deny him/her access to his/her books and records.

(3) When a taxpayer indicates a reluctance to produce the necessary records, the revenue agent must be insistent, yet courteous in his/her request. The following suggestions can be adopted in dealing with this situation.

(a) Apprise the taxpayer of the appropriate requirements to produce individual books and records. Further, to deny access to the records will only prolong the examination or investigation since a third party inquiry will, by necessity, be initiated.

(b) Do not attempt to create an atmosphere of complacency on the part of the taxpayer by indicating that this is a normal tax audit.

◀ You must keep good records that will enable you to prepare a tax return. Good recordkeeping is to your benefit so that you do not pay more tax than what you are legally required to pay. Good records will also expedite an IRS audit.

◀ The law does not require that you keep any particular kinds of records, but you should keep all sales slips, invoices, receipts, canceled checks, stock brokerage statements, Forms W-2, W-2P, and 1099, and other documents that substantiate the amounts you show on your return as income, deductions, and credits.

◀ The revenue agent may want you to think that the audit could lead to a criminal investigation, to keep you on your toes.

(c) Do not mislead or misrepresent the scope of the examination or investigation or your assignment to a special group.

(d) Do not assert your authority in a manner that could be interpreted as a threat.

(e) Do not summons the records unless the action is first approved by the group manager and, if Strike Force subject, the Strike Force Representative advised.

(4) When records are to be made available, the agent must specify at the earliest possible time the specific records he/she will need; however, he/she should alert the taxpayer that he/she will probably request additional records as the examination progresses. There follows some additional suggestions:

(a) Never indicate the length of time an examination or investigation will take, but only that the time can be minimized by the taxpayer's unrestricted cooperation and prompt accessibility of the records.

(b) If the question of time or inconvenience is raised, it would be appropriate to suggest that the records be removed to the Internal Revenue Service office where they would be more accessible to the agent and in all probability will reduce the required examination time.

(c) Another suggestion, for the sake of convenience, is that the agent photograph the records. To do so should avoid the inconvenience to the taxpayer by having an agent in his/her place of business for a prolonged period of time. (The photography can be accomplished by use of a portable microfilmer.)

(d) If records are removed from the taxpayer's premises or his/her representative's office, the provisions of IRM 403(13), requiring the use of document receipt Form 2725 will be followed.

(5) As long as an agent demonstrates sound professional judgment and adjusts his/her examination or examination plan as he/she progresses, he/she should never be accused of prolonging an examination or investigation regardless of the time element.

(6) Agents should remember that accountant's workpapers used in the audit of tax records or in preparation of a tax return are not the property of the taxpayer and are not privileged information. Therefore, the workpapers can be summoned.

(7) Guidelines for requesting workpapers are in IRM 4024 which provides, in part, that:

◀ Paragraph (6) is not a new provision, but has always been the services position, recently confirmed by the Supreme Court in *U.S. v. Arthur Young & Co.*

(a) The term "audit workpapers" as defined in IRM 4024 means workpapers compiled for creditors, stockholders, and other third parties and not for compiling data preparatory to placing it on a tax return.

(b) The provisions of IRM 4024 do not apply to cases under joint investigation with the Criminal Investigation function.

(c) Revenue agents will not request workpapers as a matter of standard investigative procedures, and they should request only the workpapers believed to be materially relevant to the investigation. The agent should bear in mind that the primary source of information is the taxpayer's records, and the accountant's workpapers should normally be used only as a collateral source of information.

(d) If it is necessary to issue a summons to secure workpapers, IRC 7603 provides that the records should be described with reasonable certainty. This requirement can be satisfied if the description of the records is specific and unambiguous and the summoned party can reasonably identify the exact records sought.

(e) The fact that the accounting firm whose workpapers are needed did not prepare the tax return in no way diminishes the authority granted by IRC 7602.

◀ There is no such thing as a "privileged communication" between an accountant and his client, under common law or federal law. The accountant's work papers belong to the accountant, are not privileged, and must be produced when summoned by the IRS.

◀ However, an accountant employed by an attorney, or retained by you at your attorney's request to perform services essential to the attorney-client relationship may be covered by the attorney-client privilege.

◀ The term "audit work papers" means work papers retained by the independent accountant as to the procedures followed, the tests performed, the information obtained, and the conclusions reached pertinent to his examination. Work papers may include work programs, analyses, memorandums, letters of confirmation and representation, abstracts of company documents, and schedules or commentaries prepared by the auditor.

340 *(4-11-80)* 4235

Power of Attorney

(1) The recognition guidelines in IRM 4055 spell out rules, regulations, and the mechanics of recognizing and dealing with persons authorized to represent a taxpayer. Exhibit 300-1 further assists the agent in dealing with recognized representatives.

(2) When dealing with someone other than the taxpayer, the agent has two things to bear in mind:

(a) Service personnel are prohibited from disclosing tax information of a confidential nature to any unauthorized person; and

(b) practice before the Service is restricted to persons recognized or qualified under provisions of Circular No. 230.

(3) Historically, cooperation received from taxpayers and their representatives in in-depth examinations is minimal; also there is a tendency on the part of some practitioners with powers of attorney to procrastinate.

(4) Many agents neglect to take a positive approach to this problem, therefore they lose the impetus that is usually generated on a significant examination or investigation. By so do-

◀ A *power of attorney* can be given to anyone, but only attorneys, CPAs, and enrolled agents can "practice" before the IRS.

◀ It's important to mention here that a privileged communication only exists between an attorney and his client, and not between accountants or enrolled agents and their clients.

◀ A mere attorney-client relationship does not make every communication confidential. To be confidential your communications must be made to your attorney in his capacity as such—employed to give legal advice, represent you in litigation, or perform some other function strictly as your attorney.

ing, an agent may inadvertently permit the taxpayer's representative to lead the examination.

(5) IRM 4055.22 provides means for the agent to bypass a recognized representative and deal directly with the taxpayer. When a recognized representative has unreasonably delayed an examination by failing to honor requests for nonprivileged information, the agent may report the situation through channels to Chief, Examination Division, by memorandum and request permission to contact the taxpayer directly for such information. If the Chief, Examination Division, grants such permission, the case file will be documented citing the circumstances that justified his/her action.

(6) Permission to by-pass a representative and to contact a taxpayer directly does not constitute suspension or disbarment of the practitioner; therefore, he/she may continue to represent his/her client.

(7) Unreasonable delay or hindrance of an investigation by a representative may be referred to the Director of Practice for possible disciplinary proceedings under Section 10.23 of Circular 230 if the district director deems it advisable.

350 *(4-11-80)* 4235

Inadequate Records

(1) Inadequate records is defined as the lack of records, or records so incomplete that correctness of taxable income cannot be determined.

(2) Chapter 900 of IRM 4231, Audit Technique Handbook for Internal Revenue Agents, covers the subject of inadequate records in detail.

(3) The approach to this problem must start with the preexamination plan in which the agent recognizes the probability that any records presented will not lend themselves to proper examination. Furthermore, since illegal income is generally not fully recorded, the indirect method of construction of income will probably have to be employed.

(4) In addition, the preparation of a net worth statement will probably be required in all cases; therefore, planning must be directed accordingly.

(5) Emphasis is placed on preexamination planning since it is highly possible that the most important phase of the investigation will revolve around the initial interivew. This is the time the

◀ Note that the revenue agent has procedures to bypass your tax practitioner and essentially nullify your power of attorney, if your tax practitioner creates lengthy delays and thereby frustrates the Revenue Agent in his quest for information.

◀ *Circular 230* governs rules of practice before the IRS. The Director of Practice will not hesitate to suspend or disbar a practitioner from practicing before the IRS when there has been a violation of the *Circular 230* provisions.

◀ *IRC 6001* and accompanying IRS regulations require that every person liable for any tax keep adequate records so that taxable income can be correctly determined. Except for farmers and wage-earners, any person subject to income tax or required to file an information return of income (such as a W-2), must keep permanent books of account or records, including inventories, to establish their gross income, deductions, credits, or other matters for tax or information return purposes. Farmers and wage-earners are not required to keep permanent books of account, but if their gross income includes wages, salaries, or similar compensation, they are required to keep records that will enable the IRS to determine the correct amount of taxable income.

agent is afforded the opportunity to obtain information that may not be forthcoming at a later date.

(6) Since the interview should be developed to its utmost, it is advisable when an inadequate record situation is anticipated to have a witness to help document all answers and to attest to their accuracy. The interrogation must be preplanned and well conceived. Details for developing the initial interview are covered under heading of Initial Contact.

◀ The required records and books should be available at all times for inspection by the IRS and should be retained for as long as their contents may become material in administering any Internal Revenue law.

360 *(4-11-80)* 4235

Procrastination

(1) Agents should be aware that time always gives the taxpayer an advantage. To permit a taxpayer or his/her representative to procrastinate will eventually permit them to dictate the conduct of the examination or investigation.

(2) An agent must be courteous but firm in requesting the cooperation of all parties concerned. In every in-depth examination he/she, should document all contacts, cancellations of appointments, and unanswered telephone calls or letters.

(3) When an agent encounters delays he/she, should alert his/her manager of the situation and if appropriate, the manager should attempt to contact the parties involved and attempt to resolve any problems. At this time consideration should be given to the issuance of a summons.

◀ A summons may be issued under authority of *IRC 7602* either to require you to produce your books and records, or to compel you to give certain testimony. If you refuse to submit requested information, the IRS will weigh the importance of the information against the time and expense of obtaining it through court action.

(4) If the unreasonable delay is generated by a representative, who has a power of attorney, the agent should consider making direct contact with the taxpayer. The procedure to accomplish this is covered in 340:(5) and IRM 4055.22.

(5) If direct contact is unsuccessful, third party contacts should be initiated.

370 *(4-11-80)* 4235

Third Party Contacts

(1) In in-depth examinations, the fact that a taxpayer cooperates will not in itself remove the need for third party information. If at any time an agent is not satisfied with the documentation of a transaction or a series of transactions, he/she should pursue any developed leads to their conclusion.

◀ A summons may be issued not only to the person liable for the tax, but to any person having possession, custody, or care of books of account containing entries relating to the business of the taxpayer, and also to "any other person" the IRS deems proper.

(2) Experience has shown that an intensive third party investigation may be the only method available to an agent to arrive at an accurate conclusion.

(3) In the case of inadequate records (as broadly defined earlier) the third party method will be the only avenue available to an agent. The agent must observe the rules governing disclosure of information.

(4) The use of discretion in making third party contacts must be exercised in all cases. There have been occasions, however, when a bold approach by the agent has made reluctant taxpayers reconsider their earlier decision not to cooperate and they have presented the agent with all the information required.

(5) The importance of third party contacts cannot be overemphasized. This is evidenced by the recommendation that probable third parties be identified as early as possible and included in the examination plan.

(6) In making a third party inquiry, the agent must apprise the contacted party that he/she is making an investigation on another party and requests full cooperation to resolve an issue. He/she should then obtain the history of the relationship or transaction, paying particular attention to such details as origin of the association, whether the association still exists, availability of any contracts or correspondence, and the subject's association (business or social) with the third party. The agent should also make every effort to obtain copies of all documents available.

(7) The initial contact with a third party should be developed the fullest, and, when applicable, the agent should obtain an affidavit attesting to the accuracy of the information received.

(8) In essence, the contact with a third party must be minutely planned, covered in detail, supported by documentation, and it should be completed on one contact. A friendly summons could be prepared prior to the contact and be ready for service.

(9) In the event a third party refuses to produce necessary records unless a formal summons is presented, the procedure in IRM 4022 and 390 of this Handbook on the issuance of a summons will be followed.

380 *(4-11-80)* *4235*

Securing Affidavits

(1) Among the principal responsibilities of a revenue agent is the continuing need to obtain early and accurate information.

◀ A third party witness need not produce a summoned document unless it is in his possession and relevant to the tax liability of the person named, or material to the inquiry. Also, a third party witness may plead the Fifth Amendment against self-incrimination. The IRS demand for records must not be unreasonable or oppressive.

◀ A taxpayer cannot prohibit the production of a third party's records, since the privilege is personal to the owner of the records, and the third party cannot assert the privilege of self-incrimination on behalf of the taxpayer, since such a defense is personal to the one making the claim.

◀ The Supreme Court has held that an individual has no right to intervene in a summons proceeding where the summons was directed to a third party and had to do with records in which the taxpayer has no proprietary interest, which are owned and possessed by the third party, and which are related to the third party's business transactions with the taxpayer.

(2) Revenue agents making in-depth examinations must initiate and proceed with investigations on the assumption that cases will eventually be resolved in formal litigation. It is, therefore, incumbent upon the agent to obtain as much documentation as possible.

(3) One source of documentation that is frequently overlooked is the securing of affidavits or statements.

(4) During an examination or investigation, an agent will obtain many verbal statements which may significantly affect the outcome of the case. The agent should have the individual attest to the accuracy of his/her statements by preparing and signing an affidavit or statement.

(5) While the average individual cannot quote the "law," he/she generally knows that the preparation of or giving a false statement is a criminal offense. Therefore, an attested statement has great validity when properly prepared and voluntarily given.

(6) Some statements which may be used by a revenue agent are as follows:

(a) Affidavits—Use Form 2311(Affidavit).

(b) Summarized Narrative—A summary of a conversation or statement made by a taxpayer or witness who should be requested to sign the document. It should always be signed by the agent or agents who are a party to the interview.

(c) Question and Answer—Available forms should be used and, when appropriate, have the witness attest to its accuracy.

(d) Reports of Interview—A summary of an interview which is not signed by the witness but attested to by the agents.

(7) The purposes and uses of a statement are outlined below:

(a) to record the testimony of a witness.

(b) to refresh the memory of a witness.

(c) to deter a witness from becoming hostile and changing his/her testimony.

(d) to impeach a hostile witness.

(e) to be used as evidence.

(f) to help accumulate complete and accurate information.

(8) The statements may be handwritten, dictated to an authorized stenographer, by the witness or the revenue agent, or summarized statement prepared by the agent and signed by the witness, or a question and answer type statement.

(9) The type of statement primarily used by revenue agents is the narrative type which should contain the following:

(a) heading

(b) introduction

◀ The authority of an IRS agent to administer oaths and affirmations, whether pursuant to the issuance of a summons or a request for information, is in *IRC 7622*.

(c) body
(d) concluding paragraph
(e) signature
(f) witnesses
(g) certifications

(10) Exhibit 300–2 has been prepared as a format for the preparation of a narrative affidavit or statement. Variations are acceptable so long as they contain the basic elements as indicated in the exhibit. If feasible, the subject should be requested to examine and sign the document. If he/she refuses to sign, the following legend should be inserted at the end of the statement:

"This statement was read by (subject's name) on (date), who stated that it is true and correct, but refused to sign it."

(11) A form of question and answer statement should contain the following:

(a) heading.

1 name and address of witness.

2 place and date of statement.

3 names of others present, including questioner, witnesses, attorneys and stenographer.

4 name of questioner and respondent unless otherwise shown.

(b) introduction

(c) statement by questioner as to the purpose of the interview.

(d) identification questions.

(e) direct questions or fact producing questions.

(f) develop full testimony chronologically.

(g) questions to develop details.

(h) questions as to further information.

(i) questions to show interest of witness in the case.

(j) questions as to truthfulness of answers.

(k) further remarks by the witness.

(l) closing remarks by questioner.

(m) read and corrected clause (if read and corrected).

(n) signature of witness.

(12) The securing of affidavits or statements minimizes the number of contacts an agent will be required to make and thereby avoid unfounded accusations of harrassment, etc.

(13) Every agent must learn the technique of preparing and obtaining affidavits and/or statements.

390 *(4-11-80)* 4235
Summonses

(1) An effective tool which an agent may use in pursuing his/her investigation is the issuance

◀ A summons may be used to compel relevant and material testimony, and/or the production of relevant or material books, papers, records, or other data for any of the following purposes:

of a "Summons to Appear to Testify and to Produce Books and Records." The authority to issue a summons is covered in IRC 7602. A summons may only be used for the administration of the Internal Revenue Code.

(2) Before a revenue agent prepares a summons he/she should be completely familiar with IRM 4022 and the general instructions included herein.

(3) The need for issuing the summons must be carefully weighed, since once issued the revenue agent must be prepared to see the matter to its final conclusion. Abandonment of enforcement of a summons may adversely affect voluntary compliance.

(4) There are two situations where the issuance of a summons may be advisable.

(a) To the taxpayer and/or his/her representative as a last resort after prolonged procrastination, or refusal to produce books and records.

(b) To third parties when they refuse to produce the required information and after exhausting all other means to obtain compliance.

(5) When an agent has exhausted all other means to obtain needed information he/she will apprise his/her manager of the situation and determine if the issuance of a summons will contribute to the success of the investigation. At this time, technical assistance in the preparation of the summons will be solicited from District Counsel.

(6) If it is agreed that a summons should be issued it will be typed and prepared in accordance with existing instructions. A sample is shown as Exhibit 300–3 and instructions for summons preparation are shown as Exhibit 300–4.

(7) The completed summons should be reviewed for accuracy by all who concurred in its issuance to be certain that the document will be legally enforceable.

(8) The service of a summons, enforcement of a summons, special procedures for third-party summonses, and failure to obey a summons are covered by IRC 7603, 7604, 7609, 7210 and IRM 4022.9.

(9) If a summons is not honored on the date prescribed, the issuing agent must prepare a statement attesting to that fact and follow established procedures. A sample statement is shown as Exhibit 300–5.

(10) There has been considerable interest expressed by taxpayers, Congress, and prac-

- Ascertaining the correctness of any return;
- Making a return when the taxpayer has not;
- Determining the liability of any person for any internal revenue tax;
- Determining the liability of any transferee or fiduciary of any person;
- Collecting any tax liability;
- Inquiring into any offense connected with the administration or enforcement of the tax laws, including criminal investigations.

◀ Before issuing a summons, the revenue agent must consider these factors:

- Whether the desired information could be obtained through other means, such as from the taxpayer's tax return, or from other parties, such as banks or an employer;
- The importance or necessity of the information being sought, weighed against the action required to enforce compliance with the summons and the adverse effect on voluntary compliance if enforcement is abandoned;
- The tax liability involved compared with the importance of the information sought. A case important to voluntary compliance may necessitate issuance of a summons without regard for the amount of the liability.

◀ The U.S. District Court where the summoned person resides or is found has jurisdiction for enforcement of a summons. You could be arrested for not complying with a court order requiring you to comply with the summons.

A fine, or imprisonment, or both, are provided by *IRC 7210*, upon conviction for willfully failing to comply with an IRS summons properly issued in accordance with the tax laws.

tioners in the Service's authority relating to the issuance of Administrative Summonses. The Administrative Summons Reporting System NO–PR–1, has been revised to include statistics on compliance with summonses, as well as issuances. It encompasses the number, purpose, and to whom summonses have been issued. Accordingly, the agent will complete Form 5535 (Administrative Summons Control Form) and forward the transcription copy to his/her group manager.

◀ Form 5535 is for IRS internal use.

3(10)0 *(4–11–80)* 4235

Reopening of Closed Cases

(1) The established Service policy is not to reopen or reexamine previously examined returns except when there are compelling reasons. (See policy statement P–4–3 and IRM 4023.)

(2) The three principal conditions which would support a reopening if there are adjustments unfavorable to the taxpayer follow:

(a) a substantial error.

(b) a serious administrative omission.

(c) evidence of fraud, malfeasance, collusion, concealment, or misrepresentation of a material fact.

(3) The third reason quoted is probably the most prevalent with Strike Force cases.

(4) When an agent has reason to believe that a reopening is warranted, he/she should apprise his/her supervisor of the facts; and, if it involves a Strike Force subject, the case should be discussed with the Examination Strike Force Representative.

(5) When it is agreed that the reopening is proper, a Form 4505, Reopening Memorandum, should be prepared and routed as prescribed in existing instructions.

(6) The responsibility to recognize the conditions spelled out in IRM 4023 (restated in part below) rests with the agent, IRC 7605(b) provides that "No taxpayer shall be subjected to unnecessary examination or investigations, and only one inspection of a taxpayer's books of account shall be made for each taxable year unless the taxpayer requests otherwise or unless the Secretary or his delegate, after investigation, notifies the taxpayer in writing that an additional inspection is necessary."

◀ *IRC 7605(b)* provides that, "No taxpayer shall be subjected to unnecessary examination or investigations, and only one *inspection* of a taxpayer's books of account shall be made for each taxable year unless the taxpayer requests otherwise, or unless the Secretary after investigation, notifies the taxpayer in writing that an additional inspection is necessary." *Policy Statement P-4-3* lists the same three principal conditions for reopening a case that are given here.

◀ If a reexamination of your books and records are necessary, you will receive IRS *Letter #939* signed either by the Chief, Examination Division, or the Chief, Compliance Division of the IRS District in which you live.

(7) When a reopening or reexamination is approved, Letter 939(DO/IO), signed by the District Director or by the Director of International Operations for cases under his/her jurisdiction will be delivered to the taxpayer by the examiner at the time the reexamination is begun.

(8) Cases may be reopened to make adjustments favorable to the taxpayer without regard to the procedures in IRM 4023.

(9) The types of cases that may be reopened without approval and without issuance of Letter 939(DO/IO) are identified in IRM 4023.3.

◀ The following types of cases may be reopened without approval and without the issuance of IRS *Letter #939:*

- Cases involving *IRC 1311* relating to a correction of an error;
- Cases involving the year of deduction of a net operating loss carryback or similar type of carryback under other provisions of the code;
- Cases in which there have been involuntary conversions and the taxpayer has not recomputed his tax liability because he did not replace the property within the time provided by law *(IRC 1033);*
- Cases involving an overpayment in excess of $200,000, subject to consideration by the Joint Committee on Taxation under *IRC 6405*.

(10) For the purpose of the reopening procedures, closed cases are defined:

(a) *Agreed Cases*—Considered closed by the district office when the taxpayer has been notified in writing at the district level of the final proposal of adjustments to the tax liability or acceptance of the return as filed.

(b) *Unagreed Cases*—Cases referred to Appeals are not considered closed for purposes of reopening procedures. Unagreed excise or employment tax cases are considered closed when the period for filing a protest and requesting consideration by Appeals expires and no protest or request for consideration by Appeals is filed.

(11) Detailed definition of the reopening criteria is covered in IRM 4023.5. Close analysis of the subject matter will enable the agent to make a proper determination when contemplating utilizing this effective tool.

3(11)0 *(4-11-80)* 4235

Jeopardy, Quick Termination, and Transferee Assessments

3(11)1 *(4-11-80)* 4235

General

It is incumbent upon revenue agents to be alert to the attempted concealment or transfer of any assets to evade payment of tax or collection of any tax deficiency or taxes properly due. Sometimes jeopardy or some other type of immediate assessment becomes necessary. There are a number of circumstances which will give rise to such assessments each of which is discussed below.

◀ All jeopardy assessments have a common characteristic: It is always determined, before assessment, that collection of the tax will be endangered if the regular assessment and collection procedures are followed. Under jeopardy procedures a tax liability can be assessed not only after a tax return has been filed, but also when no tax return has been filed.

3(11)2 *(4-11-80)* 4235

Jeopardy Assessments

(1) IRC 6861 and 6862 authorize jeopardy assessments where collection of tax is endangered. These sections further provide that the

◀ According to *IRC 6861*, if the IRS believes the assessment or collection of a deficiency relating to income, estate or gift taxes, will be jeopardized by delay, it may assess such deficiency immediately. *IRC 6862* is the authority for immediate assessment and collection of other types of taxes.

usual rights of a taxpayer to protest and appeal will be temporarily set aside in order that an assessment may be made. Subsequent to the jeopardy assessment the taxpayer's usual rights of appeal may be resumed. Although this procedure should be used discreetly, the jeopardy assessment procedure is an effective tool to ensure protection of the revenue.

(2) IRM 4584 contains definitions, limitations, and the mechanics of jeopardy assessments which are related, in part, in succeeding paragraphs.

(3) Jeopardy assessment action should be used when it appears that, if normal assessment and collection procedures are followed, collection would be endangered. To recommend a jeopardy assessment, one of the three following conditions must exist:

(a) the taxpayer is or appears to be designing quickly to depart from the United States or to conceal himself/herself.

(b) the taxpayer is or appears to be designing quickly to place property beyond the reach of the Government either by removing it from the United States, or by concealing it by dissipating it, or by transferring it to other persons.

(c) the taxpayer's financial solvency is or appears to be imperiled. (This does not include cases where the taxpayers become insolvent by virture of the accrual of the proposed assessment of tax, penalty, and interest.)

(4) Because of the sensitivity of the use of jeopardy assessments, IRM 4584 should be carefully studied prior to making such a recommendation. A jeopardy assessment must be personally approved by the District Director or the Director International Operations.

◀ These three conditions are stipulated in IRS *Policy Statement P-4-88*.

Specific types of cases where jeopardy assessments may be used include:

- Narcotic cases.
- Organized crime cases.
- Wagering cases.
- Strike Force cases.
- Cases where taxpayers receive income from an illegal activity.
- Cases involving taxpayers known or suspected of having plans for leaving the U.S. without making provisions for paying their taxes.
- Cases involving over $10,000 in cash and its ownership is disputed by the person in possession.

3(11)3 *(4-11-80)* 4235
Quick Assessments

(1) Another assessment procedure is the "quick" assessment. It is used to assess additional taxes and agreed deficiencies when the statutory period for assessment would otherwise expire before these assessments could be made under normal procedures. (IRM 4584.2.)

(2) Deficiencies involving bankruptcy and receivership cases under IRC 6871 and additional and delinquent taxes in bankruptcy and receivership cases are also assessed as "quick" assessments (IRM 4583). Here, the "quick" assessment procedure is permitted without the necessity of the case being agreed. This is

◀ Quick assessments apply to any type of tax return filed. Under the Internal Revenue Code, you are not entitled to any delay in the assessment of your taxes after you have voluntarily filed your tax return. However, a quick assessment does not give the Service the authority to make immediate demand for payment. Notice and demand will be made, but you are entitled to the normal ten days allowed for payment of the assessment. Collection action must wait until the eleventh day.

evidenced by IRM 4583.5, relating to bankruptcy cases, where a waiver Form 870 (Waiver of Restrictions on Assessment and Collection of Deficiency Tax and Acceptance of Overassessment) consenting to the assessment of the tax, should not be secured.

3(11)4 *(4-11-80)* 4235
Termination Assessments

(1) A third type of immediate assessment action is the termination assessment of income tax under IRC 6851. When the District Director finds that due to certain acts of the taxpayer (including in the case of a corporation distributing all or a part of its assets in liquidation or otherwise) tending to prejudice or to render wholly or partially ineffectual proceedings to collect the income tax for the current or immediately preceding taxable year unless collection is begun without delay, he/she shall make a determination of tax for the current taxable year, or for the preceding taxable year, or both. In the case of a preceding taxable year, a termination assessment may not be made once the due date (determined with regard to extensions) for filing the full year return has passed. Such tax shall become immediately due and payable. For details of procedures see IRM 4585.4.

(2) Termination assessments of income tax must be used sparingly and care taken to avoid excessive and unreasonable assessments. They should be limited to amounts which reasonably can be expected to equal the ultimate tax liability for the terminated period. Therefore, a termination of taxable year and assessment must be personally approved by the District Director. A termination assessment will not be made without the existence of at least one of the three following conditions.

(a) The taxpayer is or appears to be designing quickly to depart from the United States or to conceal himself/herself.

(b) The taxpayer is or appears to be designing quickly to place his/her property beyond the reach of the Government either by removing it from the United States, or by concealing it, by dissipating it, or by transferring it to other persons.

(c) The taxpayer's financial solvency is or appears to be imperiled. (This does not include cases where the taxpayer becomes insolvent

◀ *Termination assessments* effectively terminate a taxpayer's taxable year at some point and make the taxpayer's tax liability immediately due and payable. A characteristic of a termination assessment is that the taxpayer has not filed a tax return, and collection of the tax is in jeopardy, for the same reasons discussed for jeopardy assessments. Unlike jeopardy assessments though, a termination assessment normally occurs *during* the taxable year, *before* the taxable year ends. They can be made after the end of the taxable year, but only before the due date of the return for that year. For example, a termination assessment for income earned during the calendar year 1986 can be made at any time during 1986 and up to April 15, 1987. If collection of the tax is in jeopardy after April 15 for a tax return for the year ended previously then a jeopardy assessment will have to be made.

◀ Termination assessments are only for income tax returns and cannot be made for any other type of tax. Even though revenue agents will assess the tax, revenue officers do the collecting.

◀ These three conditions are stipulated by IRS *Policy Statement P-4-89*.

by virtue of the accrual of the proposed assessment of tax, penalty and interest.)

(3) Frequently persons arrested by the local police, Secret Service, Drug Enforcement Administration, Immigration and Naturalization Service, etc., have sizeable amounts of cash in their possession. A liaison should be developed whereby the arresting agency holds the seized money and immediately notifies Internal Revenue Service, the routing being to the Examination function through the Criminal Investigation function so that an assessment if warranted can be made against which the seized money will be applied. It is obvious that the person arrested will do his/her utmost to repossess his/her money, therefore, it is imperative that this type of activity be handled expeditiously.

(4) It is recognized that due to the many conditions and factors having a bearing upon recommendations for termination of taxable year and assessments no specific rules can be established for preparing reports in support thereof in every case. However, sufficient information must be furnished and should include the following to the extent practicable.

(a) name, address, and SSN or EIN of taxpayer;

(b) a complete computation of taxable income;

(c) tax and penalty to be assessed by periods;

(d) nature of the taxpayer's business or activity;

(e) taxpayer's present financial condition;

(f) information regarding the taxpayer's activity giving rise to the recommendation, such as transfer of assets without consideration;

(g) record with respect to continuing business or personal losses;

(h) filing record of taxpayer;

(i) the taxpayer's record for resisting payment of taxes in the past; (Collection delays and unpaid taxes.)

1 open Collection and "53" files can be checked, and, if there is an outstanding balance due from the taxpayer, the money should be applied against that balance;

(j) the nature and location of the taxpayer's assets and the source of his/her income;

(k) any other information having a bearing upon the taxpayer's financial condition, future prospects for losses, etc.

◀ Most potential subjects for possible income tax violations come to the attention of the IRS after arrests or criminal charges are placed against them. Gains or profits from their activities may be a principal source of income and such income is usually not reported on income tax returns. Some tax violators are identified through a routine audit of their tax returns, some by other law enforcement agencies, some by informants, and some through other sources.

(5) An assessment made as a result of termination assessments must be based on a reasonable computation of tax liability. An assessment equal to the amount of money or other valuable property held by a person at the time of arrest is not considered a reasonable computation unless supported by other facts.

(6) The basis on which the adjusted gross income is computed will be stated. This will be an acceptable legal basis (for example, a source and application of funds statement or net worth computation). All known assets, liabilities, income and expenses will be considered. A reasonable estimate will be made of expenses, if appropriate, as for example in connection with a net worth computation.

(a) Cost of living expenses should include professional estimates by a narcotics agent (or other expert) as to the "Cost of Habit" for a narcotics addict.

(b) Estimates of income from the sale of narcotics should be supported, if possible, by testimony from a narcotics agent (or other expert) who may have knowledge of the subject's activities. (See IRM 4585.4:(4)(c).)

(c) Estimates of income from illegal gambling, including "gross take" and "payoffs" may be supported by testimony of the law enforcement officers who are familiar with the gambler's operations. Efforts should be made to obtain similar testimony in cases involving other illegal activities.

(d) The taxpayer should be interviewed, if feasible, preferably before assessment is made, in order to afford him/her an opportunity to explain questioned assets, liabilities, income or expenses, filing history, etc. Such an interview may also be of value in revealing previously unknown assets, liabilities, incomes, or expenses.

(e) Efforts should be made to locate and examine books and records, if any, of the taxpayer to the extent possible in the available time.

(7) Because of peculiar circumstances in cases involving suspected narcotics traffickers, several examples of income computation by different methods, for possible use in termination assessments, are provided in Exhibit 300–6. In said exhibit, exemptions and standard deductions are allowed on the basis of a married person filing separately.

(8) Of the methods in Exhibit 300–6, it is suggested that (1), (2), or (3) be used whenever possible and (4) and (5) be used only as a last resort.

◀ *IRC 7429(a)(1)* requires the IRS to provide the taxpayer with a written statement of the information relied on in making the assessment within five days of making the assessment. The taxpayer may then request an administrative review of the action taken within thirty days. The appeals officer will determine whether the termination assessment action was reasonable under the circumstances and whether the amount assessed was appropriate.

◀ The taxpayer also has certain judicial appeal rights. He can bring action in U.S. District Court. The IRS has the burden of proving whether the termination assessment was reasonable under the circumstances, but the taxpayer has the burden to prove the reasonableness of the amount assessed. The court can order the IRS to abate the assessment or to redetermine the amount assessed in whole or in part.

◀ If the revenue agent interviews the taxpayer while in custody, a criminal investigator will accompany the interviewer to advise the taxpayer of his rights.

◀ In the interesting case of *Albert Lee Simpson* v. *IRS*, the U.S. District Court said: "The plaintiff's alleged involvement in a profitable criminal enterprise, his possession of large amounts of cash, and his failure to file tax returns in the past made it reasonable for the Government to conclude that the plaintiff had and would continue to conceal his assets. The plaintiff's alleged removal of his belongings from his dwelling, furthermore, made it reasonable to presume he was concealing himself and his assets. Finally, plaintiff is dissipating his assets by paying his attorneys for defending him against his criminal charges and pursuing this review . . . Thus, not one but all of the factors which make a termination assessment are present in this case."

(9) A recommendation that the 25 percent penalty provided by IRC 6658 be added to the tax must be based on the fact that the taxpayer performed, or attempted to perform, an act or acts tending to prejudice or to render wholly or partially ineffectual proceedings to collect income tax made due and payable by virtue of IRC 6851. (See Rev. Rul. 68–96, 1968–1 C.B. 566.)

3(11)5 *(4–11–80)* 4235

Transferee Assessments

(1) The use of nominees or straw parties to divert income or secrete assets is a method used to either avoid or evade the payment of taxes.

(2) Revenue agents should be constantly alert to such tactics and cognizant of the use of the transferee-transferor procedure. The mechanics for recommending transferee assessments are covered under IRM 4582.

(3) The same form prepared in triplicate is used for each taxpayer involved in a transferee liability, or assessment of 100 percent penalty, as provided in IRC 6672. A further requirement is the preparation of Form 2645, List of Property Belonging to the Taxpayer.

◂ Property is considered to have been fraudulently transferred or conveyed to another party if the object, intent, or result of such transfer was to remove the property beyond the reach of the government. The party disposing of the property is the "transferor" and the recipient of the property is the "transferee." One of the IRS's collection techniques involves making the transferee liable for the transferor's back taxes up to the amount of the value of the transferred property.

◂ A 100 percent penalty is another collection technique where the IRS can make a corporate officer personally liable for 100 percent of the unpaid employee withholding taxes. (See Chapter 9 in my book, *When You Owe The IRS*.)

3(12)0 *(4–11–80)* 4235

Pursuit of Civil Processes

3(12)1 *(4–11–80)* 4235

Introduction

The Service is committed to aggressively pursuing all civil tax processes in order to ensure total and complete compliance with the Revenue Code and Regulations and to ensure that tax revenue is properly reported by all segments of society.

3(12)2 *(4–11–80)* 4235

Definition

Civil process may be defined as all appropriate civil enforcement action to be taken to protect the tax revenue in a prompt and positive manner as demanded by the situation.

3(12)3 *(4–11–80)* 4235

Action on Cases in District Offices

(1) Upon the initiation of a joint investigation by the Examination and Criminal Investigation functions, or upon notification from the Criminal

Investigation function to the Collection function, consideration shall be given by the Criminal Investigation, Examination and Collection functions as to what civil action can be taken or continued against the taxpayer or a related taxpayer, without adversely affecting the contemplated criminal case.

(2) Following referral of a case for joint investigation, it shall be the continued responsibility of both the Examination and Collection functions to make periodic examinations of the circumstances involved to ensure that the Government's interests are adequately protected.

(3) The criteria to consider in determining whether examination or collection activity should be delayed should consist of, but not be limited to, the following factors.

(a) The nature of the proposed criminal offense and the effect of disclosure of the civil aspects upon such prosecution.

(b) The factual relationship of related taxpayers or transactions involved and other circumstances bearing upon whether examination or collection activity for the related taxpayer will adversely affect successful criminal prosecution of the taxpayer.

(c) The ultimate tax liabilities that may accrue pending investigation, trial, and ultimate disposition of the proposed criminal case.

(d) The extent that collection and examination action should be deferred, i.e., for what years, what type of tax, and what entities.

(e) The risk to assessment and ultimate collection.

(4) If it is concluded by the Collection or Examination functions, or jointly by them, that collection or examination activities should proceed, after considering the criteria in 3(12)3:(3) above, a memorandum will be prepared to the Chief, Criminal Investigation Division, in quadruplicate, furnishing all pertinent facts concerning any recommended action with respect to the case of the taxpayer or a related taxpayer.

(5) Where the Chief, Criminal Investigation Division, does not concur in the recommended action and mutual agreement as to the proper course cannot be reached at divisional level, the District Director should be advised of the facts and circumstances in the case. The District Director shall decide the course of action in cases under his/her jurisdiction, pursuant to policy statement P–4–84. The District Director in such cases may request the advice of the Regional Counsel.

3(12)4 *(4–11–80)* 4235
Action on Cases Pending in Office of Chief Counsel or Department of Justice

(1) After a determination has been made by a District Director's office that specific collection or examination action should be taken, a recommendation similar to the one mentioned in 3(12)3:(4) above will be made to Regional Counsel.

(2) In cases where a prosecutive recommendation is still under consideration by Regional Counsel, he/she will notify the District Director of his/her concurrence or nonconcurrence in the recommended civil action.

(3) Regional Counsel will, where appropriate, coordinate any proposed action by him/her with the Office of the Chief Counsel.

(4) The Office of the Chief Counsel will conduct, where appropriate, any necessary liaison on cases which have been referred to, or are under the jurisdiction of, the Department of Justice.

3(12)5 *(4–11–80)* 4235
Other Actions

(1) To protect the Government's interest, timely civil enforcement action must be considered during all stages of a tax investigation, and shall be initiated when appropriate. Some additional actions required are listed below:

(a) verification of the filing of all required returns and their scrutiny to determine the need for examination;

(b) recommendation for assertion of jeopardy and quick assessments when appropriate;

(c) request for waivers and consents from taxpayers should be consistent with established policies, particularly when joint investigations are involved;

(d) issuance of statutory notice of deficiency;

(e) recommendation of civil fraud, trust fund, negligence, and 100 percent penalties when appropriate;

(f) recommendation for transferee assessment;

(g) issuance of summons when required;

(h) resolution of civil issues consistent with the facts and evidence presented, in an expeditious manner;

(i) In the event of the death of a subject, an information report should be prepared for the attention of the Estate and Gift Tax Group(s) alerting them of any potential liability and furnishing any further information which may be beneficial to any subsequent investigation.

Initial Contact

510 *(4-11-80)* 4235
Introduction

During the initial contact, the taxpayer must be allowed to discuss himself/herself, family, business, successes, failures, hobbies, financial history and sources of income, including that of members of his/her family. The agent should guide the interview to enable him/her to secure as much information as possible. Complete information regarding interviewing techniques is included in this chapter for this purpose.

520 *(4-11-80)* 4235
Techniques of Interviewing

521 *(4-11-80)* 4235
Introduction

(1) During the interview the agent should attempt to secure sufficient facts to enable him/her to survey the taxpayer's entire financial picture, such as his/her mode of living, insurance program, unusual expenditures, and sources of income including the receipt of any nontaxable income.

(2) If the casual conversation method is not effective, the agent may use a memorandum of interview similar to the one in Exhibit 500-1. This sample memorandum is designed to enable the agent to ask pertinent questions and record the answers immediately. If during the interview the taxpayer becomes uncooperative or adamant regarding a particular question the agent should request that the taxpayer submit an affidavit of any statements to which he/she is willing to attest. This should go a long way in resolving pertinent issues at an early date.

(3) The agent should not hesitate to request any information bearing on the determination of the correct tax liability. This includes requesting permission to inspect the taxpayer's safety deposit box. If the request is granted, the agent must be accompanied by another Service employee as a witness and the inspection should be accomplished at the earliest possible moment after permission is received.

522 *(4-11-80)* 4235
Definition and Purpose of Interviewing

(1) An interview is defined as a meeting between two persons and usually includes holding

◄ All persons called as witnesses before the IRS, whether they are prospective defendants for a criminal prosecution or not, are entitled to certain rights and obligations defined by the U.S. Constitution, statutes, and numerous court decisions. During an in-depth examination, you will be glad these rights are there for your benefit. Also, they exist for corporate entities and for all situations whether it be in response to a court or grand jury subpoena, an IRS summons, or a simple request to appear for an interview.

◄ An individual taxpayer may refuse to exhibit his books and records for examination on the ground that compelling him to do so might violate his right against self-incrimination under the Fifth Amendment and constitutes an illegal search and seizure under the Fourth Amendment. However, in the absence of such a claim, a court may instruct a jury that it may consider the refusal to produce books and records when determining "willfulness."

◄ The privilege against self-incrimination does not permit a taxpayer to refuse to obey a summons issued by the IRS or a court order directing his appearance. He is required to appear and cannot use the Fifth Amendment as an excuse for failure to do so, although the Fifth Amendment may be invoked in connection with specific questions.

◄ A taxpayer *cannot* refuse to bring his records as specified by a summons or a court order, but he may decline to submit them for inspection on constitutional grounds. However, where records are

a formal consultation for the purpose of resolving or exploring issues.

(2) Interviews are used to obtain leads, develop information, and establish evidence. The testimony of witnesses and the confessions or admissions of alleged violators are major factors in resolving tax cases. Cases are presented to a jury through the testimony of witnesses. Therefore, it is the agent's duty to interview the taxpayer and every witness connected with the case. The record of such interviews will usually take one of the following forms: Transcript of interview or question-and-answer statement, affidavit, memorandum of interview, and recording (wire, tape, wax, etc.).

523 *(4-11-80)* 4235

Authority for Interviewing

(1) IRC 7602.—Authorized the Secretary or his/her delegate to examine books and records and to take testimony under oath.

(2) Before a revenue agent prepares a summons he/she should be completely familiar with IRM 4022.

524 *(4-11-80)* 4235

Preparation and Planning for Interviewing

(1) Timing—Proper timing of the interview is essential in obtaining information that is material in resolving a case.

(2) Review Available Information—Prior to any interview the agent should review all the information and data he/she possesses relating to the case. Such information may then be divided into three general categories:

(a) information which can be documented, and need not be discussed;

(b) information which may be documented, but needs to be discussed and;

(c) information that must be developed by testimony.

The interview file should contain only data or information arranged in the order it is to be discussed or covered in the interview. The less data the agent has to cope with during the interview, the easier it will be for him/her to vary his/her line of questioning. It is very distracting, and may even cause some confusion, for the agent to delay the interrogation to find a document or an item in a voluminous file. However, the files should contain sufficient data to cover

required to be kept as an aid to enforcement of certain regulatory functions enacted by Congress, such records have been held to be public records, and their production may be compelled without violating the Fifth Amendment. This reasoning has also been applied in some income tax evasion cases, but other cases have stated the opposite. There has not yet been any Supreme Court decision holding the public records doctrine applicable in income tax cases.

◀ When an examiner conducts an examination, he automatically receives authority to recommend the proper disposition of any issues raised by him as well as any issues raised by the taxpayer. The normal responsibility of an examiner is to pursue his examination to a point where he can conclude that he has made a reasonable determination of the correct tax liability. In practical application he must deal with problems of evidence and its evaluation.

◀ For evidence the examiner usually relies on primary evidence such as invoices, vouchers, bills and receipts, canceled checks, bank statements and the like. For businesses, he also relies on books and records such as journals and ledgers.

◀ The principal method of introducing evidence in a court case is through the testimony of witnesses. Therefore, oral statements made by taxpayers to tax examiners represent direct evidence which must be thoroughly considered. The degree of reliability placed by a tax examiner on statements must be based on the credibility of the taxpayer as supported by surrounding circumstantial evidence.

all the matters under discussion, provided it isn't unwieldy.

(3) Prepare Outline—Before the interview, the agent should determine the goal of, or purpose for questioning the subject. The topics that will enable the agent to accomplish this goal should be outlined in more or less detail, depending upon his/her experience and the complexity of the case. The outline should contain only information which is relevant and material (including hearsay). Extraneous matter should be excluded because it may be confusing and may adversely affect the end desired. Important topics should be set off or underscored and related topics listed in their proper sequence. A suggested outline is shown in Exhibit 500–1. Specific questions should be kept to a minimum, since they tend to reduce the flexibility of the questioner. In addition to the topics to be discussed, the outline should include the following, if applicable:

(a) identification of the subject,

(b) information to be given the subject about his/her constitutional rights,

(c) the administration of the oath,

(d) the purpose of the interview, and

(e) questions showing that the subject was not threatened or intimidated in any manner, and that his/her statements were made freely and voluntarily without duress or any promises whatsoever.

(4) Provide Suitable Surroundings.

530 *(4–11–80)* 4235

Conduct of Interview

(1) Be Adaptable and Flexible—The agent should keep an open mind that is receptive to all information regardless of the nature, and be prepared to develop it. If he/she is not flexible, he/she may waste a great deal of time and ask unnecessary questions, resulting in a voluminous statement of little or no value. Although the agent may find it easier to adhere to a fixed pattern of interviewing, or to rely upon a series of questions or topics, rigid adherence to any notes or outline will seriously handicap his/her flexibility. The outline and data should serve only as aids and not as substitutes for original and spontaneous questioning. A carefully planned outline will provide enough leeway to allow the agent to better cope with any situation that may occur and permit him/her to develop leads that may arise.

◀ It is the responsibility of the tax examiner to establish the degree of credibility of the taxpayer, calling into play the examiner's skill and judgment. The examiner is to take into account the demeanor of the taxpayer, his manner of making the statement and the extent of subject knowledge demonstrated. Examiners will test their first impressions by skillful questioning to bring out all pertinent surrounding circumstances.

(2) Follow Through—Incomplete and irresponsive answers have little or no probative value. Any answer, apparently relative to a pertinent matter, that is not complete and to the point should be followed up by questioning the subject about all knowledge he/she has concerning every facet of the topic. The agent should follow through on every pertinent lead and incomplete answer. He/she should continue asking questions until all information which can reasonably be expected has been secured.

(3) The following suggestions will help the agent to follow through, and to obtain answers that are complete and accurate:

(a) Use short questions confined to one topic which can be clearly and easily understood.

(b) Ask questions that require narrative answers; avoid "yes" and "no" answers, whenever possible.

(c) Whenever possible avoid questions that suggest part of the answer, i.e., "leading questions."

(d) Question the subject about how he/she learned what he/she states to be fact. The subject should also be required to give the factual basis for any conclusions he/she states.

(e) Be alert so as to prevent the subject from aimlessly wandering. Where possible, require a direct response.

(f) Prevent the subject from leading the agent far afield. He/she should not be allowed to confuse the issue and leave basic questions unanswered.

(g) Concentrate more on the answers of the witness than on the next question.

(h) To avoid an unrelated and incomplete chronology, the agent should clearly understand each answer and ensure that any lack of clarity is eliminated before continuing.

(i) When all important points have been resolved, terminate the interview; if possible, leave the door open for further meetings with the subject.

(4) The subject should completely answer the following basic questions:

◀ Examiners are required to accept statements of taxpayers, even though they may be self-serving as long as they are not improbable or unreasonable, self-contradictory, or inconsistent with surrounding facts and circumstances.

◀ Unless the taxpayer's statements are totally unreliable, they must be given some weight in the final analysis and conclusions reached in the case.

◀ Examiners are told to assess the credibility of the taxpayer with caution. Other guidelines state:

> Since oral statements with constrained constructions of fact are more likely to be encountered in these cases, the examiner's skill and judgment in developing the surrounding circumstances are especially important so that the taxpayer does not profit from his/her failure to maintain documentation substantiating his/her income and deduction. Some examples of such issues are personal expenses disguised as business, convention, or education expenses, and determination of income from tips, prizes, awards, gambling, or miscellaneous independent activities.

(a) Who?—Complete identification should be made of all persons referred to. This includes: Description, address, alias, "trading as," "also known as," citizenship, reputation, and associates. If the person cannot be identified by name, a physical description should be requested and should include: Age, height, weight, color of eyes, hair, skin, description of build, clothing, unusual markings, scars, mental or physical defects. Questions should also cover any aids worn by the individual, such as glasses, hearing aid, wig or toupee, cane, braces and other items.

(b) What?—Complete details as to what happened. Questions should relate to events, methods, and systems. A complete answer should be developed. Trace the event from its inception to its ultimate termination. For example, a sale starts with a customer placing an order, either orally or in writing, and terminates when the cash receipt is ultimately placed in some depository. Every detail concerning what happened to that sale and what happened to every book, record, document, or person connected with it should be determined.

(c) Where?—Complete details regarding the location of books, records, assets, bank and brokerage accounts, witnesses, clients, customers, safe deposit boxes, safes, and the like. A description of the location should include the general area, as well as the identification of the person who has custody and control of the item. A complete description of the place should include the size, shape, color, and location.

(d) When?—The time can be established by direct questioning, by relating the incident to some known event to some person, place, or thing.

(e) How?—Complete details about how the event occurred, or how the operation was conducted. How did the subject acquire knowledge? Was it through seeing, hearing, feeling, or smelling, or performing duties? How were transactions recorded: written, typed, matching entries, others?

(f) Why?—Everything is done for a reason. Determine the motive by questioning the subject about his/her actions. What caused him/her to act? Who caused him/her to act? How was he/she motivated? Since these are the most important questions, they should receive special consideration.

(5) Maintain Control

(a) The agent should maintain full control of the interview. He/she usually can accom-

◀ When responding to an examiner's questions, the taxpayer always has the right to invoke his constitutional privilege against self-incrimination. Notwithstanding the privilege, information or evidence furnished voluntarily by a person summoned may be used even though it may be incriminatory.

Even if the testimony is given under a summons, the taxpayer will have no luck in pleading that the testimony or evidence given was done so under compulsion and therefore should be inadmissible. Although a summoned person is required to appear, the question is whether it can be shown that he was or was not thereafter compelled to testify as to incriminatory matters. A witness who contends in court that information or evidence was not given voluntarily has the burden of sustaining that contention. Tax examiners are prohibited from giving assurances that use of any information given to them will be restricted in any way.

◀ If the taxpayer or witness appears as directed or summoned, but claims either the Fifth Amendment privilege against self-incrimination or the attorney-client privilege, the examiner will continue with the examination even though it is clear the questions will not be answered. All questions necessary to develop the required information will be asked anyway, as well as requests for the production of documents. If the person refuses to submit to questioning or to produce the documents, the tax examiner cannot compel him or her to remain and continue with the examination.

plish this by limiting each participant to the rights, duties, and privileges he/she is entitled to at the interview. Any deviation should be corrected immediately by informing the individual of his/her roll and by not allowing him/her to go beyond it. If the agent cannot maintain complete control of the interview, he/she should end it and arrange to correct the individual's improper conduct, as well as the agent's reason for terminating the interview before it is completed.

(b) After all persons are informed of why they are present at the interview, the agent should confine their activities to the roles indicated:

1 Principal—The principal is called upon to answer questions, and he/she should be permitted to make any explanations in any reasonable manner he/she may desire. He/she should be encouraged to tell his/her side of the case, without interruption. He/she has a right to refuse to answer any question that he/she feels will incriminate him/her. This is a personal right and can be invoked only by the subject.

2 Witness—The witness must comply with every request made by the agent that is both legal and reasonable. However, the witness has a right to refuse the request, if he/she feels that the information may be incriminating. This right cannot be invoked on the ground that the information will incriminate the defendant or someone else.

3 Agent—The agent should question the taxpayer about any matters he/she deems relevant to the tax case, unless the agent feels that it would be to the government's disadvantage to ask questions that would reveal particular information. Since the agent is responsible for the development of evidence, it is his/her obligation to conduct the interview in any manner he/she deems appropriate.

4 Accountant representative—The accountant's duty is to assist his/her client in all bookkeeping and accounting matters.

5 Legal representative—The attorney has a duty to furnish legal advice to his/her client relating to any matter discussed. This is the attorney's principal function at an interview.

6 Recorder—The recorder's function is to prepare a permanent record of the interview. A mechanical recording device may be used in conjunction with the recorder or in lieu of a recorder, where necessary, provided all parties to the proceeding consent thereto.

◀ IRS *Revenue Procedure 68-29* provides that a taxpayer has the right to use the services of any person he or she may elect as a witness for the purpose of explaining his books, records, or returns to the examiner during the examination process. The fact that the elected person is not enrolled to practice before the IRS and not eligible for limited practice under other procedures, does not disqualify him or her from recognition as a witness. Witnesses, though, are not permitted to represent the taxpayer as an advocate when controversies arise out of the development of the case.

◀ Taxpayers are allowed by IRS policy to make their own tape, stenographic or other verbatim recording of any examination proceeding, except when the IRS believes that the taxpayer's behavior is clearly disruptive of the normal examination process or investigative proceeding.

(6) The aforementioned rights, duties, and privileges are subject to changes by the courts, legislatures, and the policy of the Service.

540 *(4-11-80)* 4235

Record of Interview

541 *(4-11-80)* 4235

Introduction

(1) The principal purpose of interviews is to obtain all the facts helpful in resolving the case. Therefore, it is necessary to prepare a permanent record of every interview to be preserved for future use. It is usually prepared using the following:

Format	Exhibit No.
(a) Affidavit	500–2
(b) Statement	500–3
(c) Question and answer statement	500–4
(d) Memorandum of interview	500–5
(e) Informal notes or diary entries	500–6 and 500–7

542 *(4-11-80)* 4235

Affidavit

An affidavit is a written or printed declaration or statement of facts made voluntarily, and confirmed by the oath or affirmation of the party making it before an officer having authority to administer such oath. No particular form of affidavit is required at common law. It is customary that affidavits have a caption or title, the judicial district in which given, the signature of the affiant, and the jurat, which properly includes authentication. Exhibit 500–2 is a suggested format containing all these characteristics which add to the dignity and usefulness of the affidavit.

543 *(4-11-80)* 4235

Statement

A statement in a general sense is a declaration of matters of fact. Although the term has come to be used for a variety of formal narratives of facts required by law, it is in a limited sense, a formal, exact, detailed presentation of the facts. The statement may be prepared in any form and should be signed and dated by the person preparing it. If possible, the subject should also sign the statement and signify that he/she read and understand it or that it was read to him/her. A statement (Exhibit 500–3) generally contains the comments and remarks of the subject, and is used whenever it is not feasible to place the subject under oath e.g., a so-called "affidavit," without the affiant's oath is in effect a statement.

544 *(4-11-80)* 4235
Question and Answer Statement

544.1 *(4-11-80)* 4235
Elements

(1) A question and answer statement is a transcript of the questions, answers, and statements made by each participant at an interview. It may be prepared from the recorder's notes or from a mechanical recording device. A mechanical recording device may be used to record statements when no stenographer is readily available for that purpose, with the express advance consent of all parties to the conversation. The source used to prepare the transcript should be preserved and associated with the case file because it may be needed in court to establish what was said. The transcript (suggested format shown in Exhibit 500–4) should be prepared on standard size (8" × 10½") plain bond paper with each question consecutively numbered and should contain the following:

(a) the time and place where the testimony is obtained;

(b) name and address of person giving testimony;

(c) the matter the testimony relates to;

(d) name and title of person asking questions and person giving answers;

(e) the names and titles of all persons present, including attorney or accountant present to assist the subject. Also the reason for each person being present, if not self-evident;

(f) generally, the purpose for the interview should be stated;

(g) administration of oath;

(h) questions and answers establishing that the statement was made freely and voluntarily, without duress, and that no promises or commitments were made by the agents;

(i) offer to allow subject to make any statement for the record, and, if advisable, an opportunity to examine and to sign the transcript;

(j) Jurat: the officer who administers the oath should complete the jurat. It is preferable, but not essential, to have the same officer who interviewed the taxpayer complete the jurat;

(k) signatures of any Government witnesses present;

(l) signature and certificate of person preparing the statement, showing the source of the original information used to prepare it.

◀ Courts have ruled that the privilege against self-incrimination must be specifically claimed or it will be considered to have been waived. *(Lisansky* v. *U.S.)* In *Nicola* v. *U.S.* the taxpayer permitted a revenue agent to examine his books and records. The taxpayer was then indicted for income tax evasion and invoked his constitutional rights under the Fifth Amendment for the first time at the trial, by objecting to the revenue agent's testimony concerning his findings. The court ruled that "It was necessary for him to claim immunity before the Government agent and refuse to produce his books. After the Government had gotten possession of the information with his consent, it was too late for him then to claim constitutional immunity."

◀ A taxpayer who makes verbal statements or gives testimony to IRS agents during an investigation, or at a Tax Court trial may still rely upon his constitutional privilege and refuse to testify at his trial for income tax evasion. However, any statements, inconsistent with his innocence, may be used against him as admissions of guilt.

544.2 *(4-11-80)* 4235
Off-Record Discussions

Off-record discussions should not be permitted during a recorded interview of a taxpayer, and kept to a minimum during a recorded interview of a witness.

545 *(4-11-80)* 4235
Memorandum of Interview

A memorandum of interview is an informal note of instrument embodying something that the person desires to fix in memory by the aid of written record. It is a record of what occurred at the interview and usually is in the format shown in Exhibit 500-5. The memorandum shows the date, time, place, and persons present as well as what transpired. It should be promptly signed and dated by the agent(s) present.

546 *(4-11-80)* 4235
Informal Notes or Diary Entries of Interview

Informal notes should contain sufficient details to permit the agent to refresh his/her memory as to what transpired at the interview. Any method of recording the entries is sufficient, if it shows the time, place, persons present, and what occurred. Details of interviews should not be entered in the diary, but rather a memorandum should be made and kept in the case file (see Exhibit 500-6). A note should be made in the diary of the time, place, and persons interviewed (see Exhibit 500-7).

550 *(4-11-80)* 4235
Procedure

(1) Review and corrections—Every record of an interview should be carefully reviewed for any typographical errors, and for accuracy of context. If the statement is to be examined by the subject, he/she may be permitted to correct typographical errors or to make minor modifications of his testimony. The subject should never be permitted to alter the record, or to delete any of his/her testimony. He/she may, however, submit an affidavit or give testimony modifying his/her original statements.

(2) Execution—Every document made under oath should have a simple certificate evidencing the fact that it was properly executed before a duly authorized officer. The usual and proper form, referred to as the "jurat," is "Subscribed and sworn to before me at (address)," followed by the date, signature and title of the officer. If the jurat shows an affirmation, the word "affirmed" will be sufficient. The agent usually administers the oath by having the subject stand, raise his right hand, and make a declaration to God, that the document is true and correct.

(3) Persons entitled to copies—Upon request, a copy of an affidavit or transcript of a question and answer statement will be furnished a witness.

(4) Subsequent use by the agent—The record of interview generally is not admissible as evidence at the trial, but may be used to refresh the memory of a witness or to discourage a witness from changing his/her testimony. It may also be used to impeach a witness on the stand when previous statements are inconsistent with his/her testimony, or to furnish a basis for prosecution of a witness who testifies falsely at the trial. If the statement constitutes a confession or an admission against interest, the pertinent parts may be used as such in evidence at the trial. The record also serves as a valuable source of information for subsequent examinations if it contains the personal and financial history of the taxpayer. It may be used to establish a starting point of "cut-off" for a subsequent net worth case, or to provide leads to other violations by the subject or other individuals.

560 *(4-11-80)* 4235
Availability of Books for Civil Purposes Only

(1) When requesting books and records the examiner should be courteous, tactful, and considerate of any problems in producing records which may be several years old. A reasonable but firm approach may enable the examiner to gain the taxpayer's confidence and cooperation, and may expedite disposition of the case.

(2) Examiners shall not assure taxpayers that their books and records will be used solely for civil purposes. If a taxpayer insists upon such assurances, or asks the examiner to sign a statement that the books and records are only being made available for limited purposes, the examiner should refuse to grant any assurances and further discuss the matter with the taxpayer to determine the taxpayer's reasons for refusing to furnish his/her records without restriction. The agent will discontinue the examination at this point and report the matter to his/her manager. The group manager and the ex-

aminer should then discuss the matter with the Criminal Investigation function (IRM 4241.2:(5)). That office will study any available information concerning the taxpayer and will advise on further steps to be taken. Criminal Investigation may decide that, in view of all known factors including taxpayer's refusal to furnish records unconditionally, there is a possible indication that fraud exists. When appropriate, a referral to Criminal Investigation will be made in accord with procedures in IRM 4565.21. Advice should be sought from the District Counsel whenever necessary.

Exhibit 500–1

Sample Memorandum of Interview With Taxpayer ◊

This memorandum is designed to enable the agent to ask pertinent questions and record the answers immediately. It is not all inclusive and is not intended to be used in total as presented. The agent should be selective on a case-by-case basis as to the questions to be asked.

The heading of the memorandum should include the following information:

1. name of taxpayer
2. name of interviewer
3. date of interview
4. place of interview
5. names of other persons present
6. information as to whether taxpayer was sworn.

Questions which the agent may wish to ask the taxpayer are:

1. What is your full name?

1a. What is your Social Security number?

2. Have you ever used any other name(s)?
3. What is your current address?
4. What is the date and place of your birth?
5. Are you a citizen of the U.S.?
6. What is the date, place, and name of court, if naturalized?
7. What is your marital status (single, married, divorced or separated)?
8. What is your wife's maiden name, date and place of marriage?
9. What are the names and dates of birth of your children?
10. What is the extent of your education? (State year of graduation from High School and College)
11. What is your occupation and the estimated amount of your income for each of the years 19 , to 19 inclusive?
12. Did you file Federal income tax returns for each of the years 19 to 19 inclusive?
    (a) If so, where?
    (b) If not, explain.
13. Did your husband/wife file separate returns for any of the years 19 to 19 , inclusive?
    (a) If so, what are the years for which filed, name and address shown on return, and place of filing?
14. Did you file any Federal income tax returns for any partnership, joint venture, corporation or fiduciary for the years 19 to 19 inclusive? If so, what type of returns, names, etc., did you file?
15. Can you identify the following Federal income tax returns?

Form No.	Period Covered	Serial No.	Name of Taxpayer	Answer (Yes or No)

(a) Did you sign each of these returns?
(b) Are these the returns you filed?
(c) Who prepared these returns?
(d) Is all the information contained in these returns true and correct?
(e) Do these returns (if joint returns) show all the income received by you and your husband/wife during the years 19 to 19 , inclusive?
(f) Do you know of any business costs or expenses or deductible personal expenses which you paid or incurred which are not shown on these returns?

16. Give the following information regarding the person who prepared the Federal income tax returns filed by you:

(a) Name:
(b) Address:
(c) His/her business profession:
(d) Nature and extent of the services performed by him/her:
(e) Did he/she prepare the returns solely from information obtained by from books and records? If not, explain:

Sample Memorandum of Interview With Taxpayer ◊

17. Have you ever engaged in business as a sole proprietor?
If so, state:
(a) Name under which operated;
(b) Employer's identification number;
(c) Principal place of business;
(d) Kind of business;
(e) Date commenced; and
(f) Is business active?

18. Have you ever owned any interest in any partnership?
If so, give the following information with respect thereto:
(a) Trade name;
(b) Employer's identification number;
(c) Principal place of business;
(d) Kind of business;
(e) Date partnership was formed;
(f) Is partnership active?
(g) Name and addresses of all partners;
(h) Terms of partnership agreement;
(i) Where are the books and records of the partnership?
(j) Where were the partnership Federal income tax returns filed for the years 19 to 19 , inclusive?

19. Have you ever owned any interest in any corporation?
If so, give the following information with respect thereto:
(a) Name of corporation;
(b) Employer's identification number;
(c) Principal place of business;
(d) When and where incorporated;
(e) Kind of business;
(f) Names and addresses of all officers;
(g) Total number shares of each class of stock issued and outstanding;
(h) Does corporation file Form 1120?
(i) What consideration did you give for the shares of capital stock owned by you?
(j) Where are the corporate books and records?
(k) Where were Federal income tax returns of the corporation filed for the years 19 to 19 , inclusive?

20. Have you engaged in any other business or in any joint venture since January 1, 19 ?

21. What books and records were kept with respect to each business in which you owned an interest during the years 19 to 19 , inclusive?

22. What are the names and addresses of the principal bookkeepers employed by (Name of Firm) during the years 19 to 19 , inclusive?

23. What are the names and addresses of all public accountants who performed any services for you and (Name of Firm) during the years 19 to 19 , inclusive?

24. At what banks were business accounts maintained by you and (Name of Firm) during the years 19 to 19 , inclusive?

25. Were all business receipts deposited in these accounts?
If not, explain.

26. Do all deposits in these accounts represent receipts from sales?
If not, explain.

27. Do any deposits in your business banking account(s) during the years 19 to 19 inclusive, represent loans or exchanges?
If so, explain.

28. Were all business expenses paid by check?
If not, explain.

29. Were all receipts from sales, commissions, fees, and any other sources recorded on the books and records of (Name of Firm)?

30. How were cash sales handled?

Sample Memorandum of Interview With Taxpayer ◊

31. Give the following information with respect to all bank, savings and loan, and credit union accounts maintained by you, your spouse, and dependent children since January 1, 19 (in addition to accounts listed under Question No. 24).

Name of Bank	Name of Account	Type of Account

32. What was the source of the funds deposited in the bank accounts in the names of your spouse and dependent children?

33. Did your spouse or dependent children receive any income during the years 19 to 19 , inclusive?
If so, from whom and how much?

34. Have you or your spouse ever maintained any bank accounts or held any property for your children or for any other persons?

35. Have you or your spouse ever maintained any bank accounts or held any property as attorney or agent for anyone?

36. Have you or your spouse rented or had access to any safe deposit box since January 1, 19 ?
If so, give particulars:

37. What do you have in any safe deposit box or boxes now?

38. Have you, at any time, kept any currency in a safe deposit box?

39. What is the largest amount of cash or currency which you have had at any time at your home, in a safe deposit box, or at any place other than on deposit in a bank?

40. How much cash or currency did you and your spouse have, other than monies on deposit, as of:

Jan. 1, 19 ? Jan. 1, 19 ?

Jan. 1, 19 ? Jan. 1, 19 ?

Jan. 1, 19 ? Jan. 1, 19 ?

41. Did anyone else ever keep or hold for you, cash, currency, or any money belonging to you?

42. Will you consent to an immediate inventory of your safe deposit box in the presence of representatives of the Internal Revenue Service?

43. Have you or your spouse purchased securities through a bank?

44. Have you or your spouse purchased or sold or redeemed any stocks or bonds (including U.S. Government bonds) since Jan. 1, 19 ?
If so, give details:

Description	Date Acquired	Cost	Date Sold	Selling Price

45. Have you or your spouse ever owned any real estate?
If so, state:

Description	Date Acquired	Cost	Date Sold	Selling Price

46. Did you or your spouse receive any income from rents or royalties during the years 19 to 19 , inclusive?

Sample Memorandum of Interview With Taxpayer ◊

47. Have you ever given any mortgages on any real estate or chattels owned by you? If so, state:

Property Mortgaged	Mortgagee	Date Given	Original Amount	Present Balance	Rate of Interest

48. Have you or your spouse borrowed any money from any bank, individual or firm since Jan. 1, 19 ?

49. Have you ever submitted a statement of your assets and liabilities to any bank, concern or individual?
If so, to whom and when?

50. Have you or your spouse loaned any money to any person or firm since Jan. 1, 19 ?
If so, give details.

51. Give the following information regarding all annuity contracts and life insurance policies issued at any time in the name of, or on the lives of, yourself, your spouse, and your dependent children:

Name of Company	Insured	Face Value	Annual Premium	Type Policy	Date Issued

52. Have you, your spouse, or children ever received any gifts or inheritance?
If so, give details.

53. Have you, your spouse, or dependent children ever received any monies from any trust fund?

54. Did your spouse or any other person supply, lend, or make any contribution to the funds used to purchase any of the assets acquired by you or acquired jointly by you and your spouse during the period from January 1, 19 , to January 1, 19 , inclusively?
If so, give full details.

55. Have you ever purchased any cashier's or treasurer's checks from any bank?

56. Have you or your spouse made any investments or acquired any assets since January 1, 19 , which have not been discussed during this interview?

57. Have you or your spouse received any income from any source during the years 19 to 19 , inclusive, which have not been discussed during this interview?

58. Has anyone as a straw party or nominee or as a favor to you, or in any way, held for you any real property, personal property, cash currency, or anything of value?

59. Do you or your spouse maintain any charge accounts?
If so, give names of firms.

60. Will your personal books and records and the books and records of (Name of Firm) be made available for examination by representatives of the Internal Revenue Service?

61. Will all cancelled checks pertaining to all banking accounts maintained by you, your spouse, and (Name of Firm) be made available for examination by representatives of the Internal Revenue Service?

62. Will you agree to submit a statement of your assets and liabilities as of (Date)?

63. Will you agree to submit a statement of your estimated personal and family living expenditures for the year(s) ?

64. Do you wish to make any further statement regarding any of the matters discussed during this interview?

The interviewer should sign and date the memorandum.

Exhibit 500–2

Narrative Affidavit

Statement of: John Doe
1417 Water St.
Deepwater, Colorado

Made: September 20, 19 , at Room 1415, Post Office Building, Deepwater, Colorado

In Presence of: Jim R. Long and Ralph M. Short, Internal Revenue Agents, Deepwater, Colorado

OR

Statement of John Doe, 1417 Water St., Deepwater, Colorado, made September 20, 19___, at Room 1415, Post Office Building, Deepwater, Colorado, in the presence of Jim R. Long and Ralph M. Short, Internal Revenue Agents, Deepwater, Colorado.

INTRODUCTION

The introduction to the narrative statement will chiefly identify the taxpayer or the witness.

BODY

The body of the narrative statement will constitute the testimony presented. It may be one paragraph or several pages long and should be arranged chronologically.

The concluding paragraph should contain a "read and corrected" clause. Following is a suggested paragraph:

I have read the foregoing statement consisting of this page only. I fully understand this statement and it is true, accurate, and complete to the best of my knowledge and belief. I made the correction shown and placed my initials opposite each.

I made this statement freely and voluntarily, without any threats or rewards, or promises of reward having been made to me in return for it.

AFFIANT

Witness Date

Witness Date

Internal Revenue Agent Date

Exhibit 500–3

Suggested Format for Statement

In re: Name and address of subject

Time: Date and hour if interview

Place: Location of Interview

On 19 , I, Internal Revenue Agent,

questioned (Subject) about (Subject)

stated

Note: If feasible, the subject should be requested to examine and sign it. If he/she refuses, the following legend will be inserted at the end of the statement when applicable. "This statement was read by (the subject), on 19 who stated that it was true and correct, but refused to be placed under oath or to sign it.

Date and Time — Internal Revenue Agent, Internal Revenue Service

Date and Time — Witness

Date and Time — Witness

Exhibit 500–4

Suggested Format for Question and Answer Statement

Testimony of John J. Jones, 115 South Street, Chester, Pennsylvania 19013, given in the office of the Internal Revenue Service Room_______, United States Courthouse, 401 N. Broad Street, Philadelphia, Pennsylvania, at 9:30 am. on Tuesday, September 7, 19____, about his Federal income tax.

Present: John J. Jones, Taxpayer
Adam Adams, Attorney
Alexander White, Revenue Agent
Evelyn Green, Reporter

(Questions were asked by Internal Revenue Agent White and answers were given by Mr. Jones unless otherwise specified).

(John Jones, this interview is being recorded, as we agreed, by means of the tape recorder on your left).

Q. John Jones, you were requested to appear at this office to answer questions concerning your Federal income tax for the years 19____to 19____, inclusive.

Q. Please stand and raise your hand. Do you, John J. Jones, solemnly swear that the answers you are about to give to the questions asked will be the truth, so help you God? (The Agent will stand while administering the oath).

(Note: After the questioning is concluded the meeting is brought to a close with the following questions.)

Q. Mr. Jones, have I, or has any other Federal agent, threatened or intimidated you in any manner?

Q. Have I, or any other Federal agent, offered you any reward or promises of reward or immunity, in return for this statement?

Q. Have you given this statement freely and voluntarily?

Q. Is there anything further you care to add for the record?

(After this statement has been transcribed, you will be given an opportunity to read it, correct any typographical errors, and sign it.)

United States of America
Eastern Judicial District of Pennsylvania } SS

I have carefully read the foregoing statement consisting of pages 1 to____, inclusive, which is a correct transcript of my answers to the questions asked me on the _____day of____________19____, at the offices of the Internal Revenue Service, Philadelphia, relative to my Federal income tax. I hereby certify that the foregoing answers are true and correct, that I have made the corrections shown and have placed my initials opposite each correction, and that I have initialed each page of the statement.

Subscribed and sworn to before me at _____________, this __________day of _________ 19 ____, at ____

____

____

Internal Revenue Agent

I. _______________________, Reporter, do hereby certify that I took the foregoing statement of _______________________in shorthand, personally transcribed it from my shorthand pages, and initialed each page.

Reporter

Exhibit 500–5

Example of Memorandum of Interview

In re: Name and address of subject (s) being investigated

Date and time of interview: Tuesday, July 19

a.m. to p.m.

Place: Location of interview

Present: (Taxpayer, witness, etc.)

Internal Revenue Agent

Witness

Interview conducted by Internal Revenue Agent

Date and Time

Internal Revenue Agent

Place

If pertinent the following may be included:

I (prepared) (dictated) this memorandum on , 19 , after refreshing my memory from notes made during and immediately after the interview with the taxpayer.

Internal Revenue Agent

I certify that this memorandum has recorded in it a summary of all pertinent matters discussed with the taxpayer on , 19

Witness

Exhibit 500–6

Example of Informal Notes ◇

On Wednesday July ________, 19 ________ at 10:00 a.m., I questioned Tom Brown of 1124 Euclid Street N.W. Washington, D.C., 20017 in his office 117 Elm Street, Washington, D.C., about his purchase of a 19 ________ station wagon from Smith Motors Inc. He stated that he purchased the station wagon, bearing serial number 1173945, for $3,250.00 from Joseph Smith, President, of Smith Motors, and that he gave Mr. Smith his personal check number 117, dated ________ 19 ________ for $3,250.00. He agreed to submit an affidavit relating to his purchase. Internal Revenue Agent King, of Baltimore, Maryland, witnessed the interview which was concluded at 10:47 a.m.

Exhibit 500–7

Suggested Diary Entry ◇

WEDNESDAY, JULY 9, 19–

Re: Brown Company

Interviewed Tom Brown, President of the Brown Company, (telephone no.) on this date between 10:00 a.m. and 10:47 a.m. Internal Revenue Agent Edward King was present during the interview. Memorandum of interview in case file.

Special Examination Procedures

610 *(4-11-80)* 4235

Introduction

In-depth examinations will generally require, in addition to the usually prescribed techniques, some specialized investigative procedures. These procedures go to the core of the in-depth examination theory in that they depart from the books and records and look to information about the taxpayer from other sources. Examination of bank records, including not only cancelled checks and the bank statements, but also records maintained by the bank (such as the teller's daily record sheets) which the taxpayer does not have available to him/her, should be carefully examined where appropriate. Indirect methods of determining income, net worth, cost of living, cash availability, are the order of the day in in-depth examinations. Any of such methods should be pursued diligently in an attempt to ascertain the taxpayer's true and correct income.

620 *(4-11-80)* 4235

Financial Institutions

621 *(4-11-80)* 4235

Introduction

(1) Some of the most important information and evidence that an agent can obtain during his/her investigation will usually be found in financial institutions. A list of all the various types of financial institutions that the agent might encounter is contained in this section.

(2) The basic functions of banks are to receive deposits, pay checks drawn thereon, transfer funds, make loans, rent safe deposit boxes; sell money orders, bank drafts, certified checks, traveler's checks, and cashier's checks; handle and administer property of others, and transmit funds to foreign countries.

(3) The investigating agent can also find other helpful information in banks such as deposit tickets, signature cards, teller's daily record sheets, transmit deposit items, ledger cards, daily transaction journals, depositors' detailed statements, withdrawal tickets, details of auto loans, details of property loans, personal loans, type and amount of collateral posted against loans, interest payments, transactions regarding foreign exchanges, and borrower's financial statements. The correspondence files on a particular taxpayer can be especially helpful.

(4) Requests for information from any financial institution should be limited to that neces-

◀ The key sentence for this section: "Indirect methods of determining income, net worth, cost of living, cash availability, are the order of the day in in-depth examinations." From this point on, the central focus will be on how the IRS goes about discovering unreported sources of income.

◀ Income may be established by a direct or an indirect approach. The former consists of the specific item method which involves proof of transactions (sales, expenses, etc.) affecting income. The latter approach relies upon circumstantial proof of income by use of such methods as net worth, expenditures, and bank deposits. Usually income can be more easily established by the direct approach.

◀ Almost without exception, individuals determine their income by the *specific items* or *specific transactions method:* Their computations are based on the sum total of the transactions they engaged in during the period. Most individuals engaged in legitimate pursuits maintain books and records in which these various transactions are recorded as they occur.

◀ In numerous cases the courts have approved the use of the following indirect methods of determining income: net worth, expenditures, and bank deposits. Although these methods are considered circumstantial proof of income, the courts have approved them for use in determining income for criminal prosecution on the theory that proof of unexpended funds or property in the hands of a subject may establish a prima facie understatement of income requiring the subject to overcome the logical inference drawn from the provable facts.

sary to establish a particular taxpayer's liability. Agents should offer to do as much of the research themselves as the bank will permit. They should not be deterred by the reluctance of bank employees to retrieve vital information, especially from ADP systems.

622 *(4-11-80)* 4235

Listing of Accounts

A listing of accounts in any financial institution the taxpayer has transacted business with should be compiled by name, number, and location of each account. Accounts in names of others, such as those of a spouse, parent, child, other relatives, mistress, close associates, partners, or accounts of others which might lead to the taxpayer should also be listed.

623 *(4-11-80)* 4235

Analysis of Signature Cards

(1) Whenever a depositor opens an account, the financial institution requires him/her to sign a signature card. By signing the card, the depositor accepts the rules of the institution and authorizes it to honor orders for withdrawing funds. For a corporation or partnership account, the signature cards will be accompanied by copies of resolutions of the board of directors or partnership agreements naming the authorized signatories.

(2) The signature card is a source of valuable information. It usually shows the date the account was opened, the amount of the opening deposit, the mother's maiden name of the customer, the name of the person who introduced the customer, prior banking references, the names of other institutions where accounts may be located, the account number, the designation of the type of account, and the name of the person in whose presence the signature was executed.

◀ The bank signature card shows the signature of the person or persons authorized to sign checks, make withdrawals, or initiate transactions through or against the account of the customer. The signature is usually executed in the presence of an officer of the bank or a teller or a clerk, and by comparison can be used to prove authenticity of the customer's alleged signature on other papers. Even a bank teller who has frequently handled a customer's checks would be a competent witness to identify the taxpayer's signature not only on documents normally passing through the teller's hands but also on other papers.

624 *(4-11-80)* 4235

Bank Deposits

(1) The agent's careful analysis of the taxpayer's bank deposits could well constitute the most important phase of his/her investigation. The agent should accomplish as much of this analysis as possible at the taxpayer's office in order to save time. He/she should examine the duplicate copies of deposit slips and determine all items making up the deposits. The deposits

◀ The *bank deposits method* is another means of proving income by indirect or circumstantial evidence. By this method, taxable income is proved through analysis of deposits in all bank accounts. The IRS expects to find cash payments that were made from undeposited currency receipts. Such cash receipts or cash expenditures must be taken into account in computing additional gross income. The usual formula by the bank deposits then should be reconciled to the books of original entry. Where significant, the sources of the deposits should be ascertained. The agent should be especially alert for transfer of funds from another bank by the taxpayer. This could uncover an account that was not previously known. A separate schedule of currency deposits should be prepared by dates, amounts, and sources wherever possible. Any particularly large coin deposits, where these are not normal to the business under examination, should be noted.

(2) The investigating agent should be alert to bank symbols appearing on bank statements, especially "EC" and "ICD". EC indicates an Exchange charge for converting foreign currency into US dollars, or a charge for cable or transmittal costs. The source of such foreign monies should be identified to determine their taxability. ICD indicates an application to customer loans which source should be verified. (See 625.2 below).

(3) The thorough agent will examine all personal and business as well as nonbusiness deposits, including deposits to trust accounts, loan accounts, special accounts, savings accounts, and any other accounts, both domestic and foreign.

(4) Repeated deposits of the same amounts may indicate rental income, dividend income, interest, or other types of recurring income.

(5) If the agent cannot obtain the information he/she needs about a taxpayer's deposits from the taxpayer, he/she should not hesitate to go to the bank to obtain it. The bank's copies of deposit slips for currency deposits should be examined. Many bank tellers list the denominations of deposited currency on the back of the deposit slips (particularly the large bills) and they add up the sums of the denominations to arrive at the total deposit. This information could prove to be very helpful; therefore, currency deposit slips should be examined on both front and back. The deposit slip itself should be examined, if possible, as the account ledger card will reflect only the net deposit and cash withdrawls from checks deposited will not be reflected.

(6) Where feasible, the agent should look at the teller's cash sheets, in connection with the investigation of a certain taxpayer, since any large or unusual currency transactions are noted there so that the bank will know who received the cash in the event there is an error.

method for determining the taxable income of a taxpayer whose only source of income is from a business operation is as follows:

1.	Total deposits	$______
2.	Add: Payments made in cash	+______
3.	Subtotal	=______
4.	Less: Nonincome deposits & items	−______
5.	Total receipts	=______
6.	Less: Business expenses & costs	−______
7.	Net income from business	=______
8.	Less: Deductions and exemptions	−______
9.	Taxable income	=______

◀ Bank deposits have been a factor in the determination of the additional taxable income involved in many criminal tax cases and may be used:

- If no books or records of the taxpayer are available;
- If the taxpayer invokes constitutional privilege and will not allow an examination of his books and records;
- If the taxpayer's records are not complete and do not adequately reflect his current taxable income; or
- If the taxpayer uses the bank deposits method in preparing his tax return.

However, the courts have held that there is no necessity to disprove the accuracy of the taxpayer's books and records as a prerequisite to the use of the bank deposits method. And although the bank deposits method has been used in numerous criminal cases, there is no statutory provision defining the methodology to be used, or specifically authorizing its use by the IRS.

The teller's cash sheets will also disclose transactions where the customer cashed checks to obtain currency for a deposit or for himself/herself. This type activity would be contrary to normal business practice and may indicate that such checks were not reported as income.

(7) Most banks have now converted to automatic data processing systems and may no longer maintain customer ledger sheets. Some of the banks send their depositors a shortened statement, which contains an opening balance, the number of deposits and amount, the number of disbursements and amount, and the closing balance. The majority of such banks make printouts of their transaction journals which will show the details of any activity. Many of these banks will microfilm all items, including daily deposits and microfilm the depositor's checks for the statement period at the statement date.

(8) The agent should be alert to possible substantial currency deposits in Time Deposit Accounts, where they are left for greater lengths of time at higher rates of interest. Applications for withdrawals from these accounts, at other than the end of the specified time, must usually be accompanied by financial statements which may be helpful to establish evidence of net worth.

(9) The examiner should be alert for deposits and withdrawls of like amounts on or around the same date. This is sometimes done with a single large deposit and several smaller checks written to equal the total deposits. This, generally, is an indication of laundering of funds.

625 *(4-11-80)* 4235

Analysis of Safe Deposit Box Records

(1) Safe deposit boxes have long been used to secrete funds. Contracts for rentals of safe deposit boxes should be analyzed carefully. Such contracts will usually show the following information:

(a) the name and address of the person renting the box;

(b) the date the rental began, the fee, and renewals, if any;

(c) the mother's maiden name of the renter;

(d) the names and signatures of persons with authorized entry to the box;

(e) the names of those who were issued keys;

(f) access code or password.

◀ The bank deposits theory assumes that under certain circumstances proof of deposits is substantial evidence of taxable receipts. The circumstances are the existence of a business or calling of a lucrative nature and proof that during the prosecution years the taxpayer made periodic deposits to accounts in his or her own name or accounts over which he or she exercised dominion and control. The government must establish that the deposits reflect *income* that is *current*. This may be accomplished by showing (1) that the taxpayer was engaged in an income-producing business, (2) that he or she made periodic deposits to the bank account, and (3) that the deposits have been analyzed to eliminate nonincome items such as loans or gifts as well as income items which may be duplications of amounts actually accounted for and reported or amounts earned in prior years. The analysis may indicate that certain withdrawals from the bank account represent business expenditures. If these were not claimed by the taxpayer as deductions, they will nevertheless be allowed for prosecution purposes.

(2) Safe deposit box access records will show dates and times of entry along with the signature of the person entering the box. The dates and frequency of entries may be significant and may coincide with the dates of deposits to or withdrawals from various accounts.

(3) The examining agent should ask the taxpayer at the earliest possible opportunity if he/she will consent to an inventory of the safe deposit box contents. If the taxpayer agrees, this should be done immediately, before he/she has a chance to empty the box and before he/she changes his/her mind. The inventory of the contents should be taken in the presence of the taxpayer and another Service representative. The taxpayer should be asked to initial all pages and to sign the last page of the inventory, as acknowledgement of the contents of the box. If the taxpayer refuses to permit the inventory, this fact should be noted by the agent in a memorandum of the conversation to that effect.

625.1 *(4-11-80)* 4235

Analysis of Cancelled Checks Procedure

(1) The agent should examine the checks which have been cancelled to determine where they were cashed and to observe unusual endorsements. The examination may uncover transactions which could have a material effect on the ultimate findings of the case.

(2) The agent should compare the amounts entered on the cancelled checks by the payer with the amounts printed on the lower right hand side of the check during the processing of the check. This procedure should be followed to determine if the checks have been altered.

(3) The agent should make a comparison of the total amount claimed to be expended by the taxpayer with the checks written to cover the expenditures. The comparison should be made even though the taxpayer has receipts or invoices to substantiate all claimed expenditures. The comparison may indicate that some of the payments may have been made by third parties or may have been made with receipts that were not deposited and that the taxpayer may have received, either directly or indirectly, unreported income.

625.2 *(4-11-80)* 4235

Analysis of Loans Procedure

(1) The agent should examine all loan accounts to determine the amount of funds made

◀ In *Gleckman* v. *U.S.* the government proved that in each of the indictment years, the taxpayer had gross deposits exceeding $90,000. There was evidence that he was involved in illegal liquor transactions, and testimony that he had expended substantial amounts of money. Gleckman claimed that his bank deposit slips were erroneously admitted in evidence because the government did not prove that they reflected specific amounts of taxable income. Gleckman argued that it was improper for the government's expert witnesses to testify that there was additional tax owing, based on consideration of the deposits as income. The Court of Appeals overruled this contention stating that the testimony proved there was taxable income, and that the bank deposits did not stand entirely alone as the sole proof of the existence of a tax due from him, but they were identified with business carried on by him, and therefore were sufficiently shown to be of a taxable nature.

available by the loans. He should consider whether the loans were new loans or renewal of outstanding loans.

(2) Where applicable, a description of assets used to secure the loan should be obtained. The value of the security may indicate that the taxpayer has received income in excess of that reported, and the nature of the security may furnish leads to additional sources of income.

(3) The agent should determine the purpose of the loans and determine where the funds were actually applied.

(4) The agent should determine who repaid the loans and the source of funds used to repay the loans.

626 *(4-11-80)* 4235

(Reserved)

627 *(4-11-80)* 4235

Investigative Techniques

(1) Examine all pertinent bank accounts, commercial and savings for any large withdrawals of currency. Endorsements on cancelled checks for large withdrawals by check may produce additional examination leads.

(2) Inspect teller's cash sheets for any large currency deposits or withdrawals.

(3) Analyze large currency transactions reported to the currency supervisory teller.

(4) Note any coincidental dates of entries into safety deposit boxes.

(5) Scan list of cashier's checks purchased, and examine endorsements of cancelled ones. They will show the payee and their locations by the banks, where the checks were cashed, or deposited.

(6) Determine if any sizable amounts of currency were received from sales of property, from theft, by extortion, by gift or otherwise.

(7) Analyze bank drafts, sight drafts, money orders, letters of credit, and certified checks, to see if they were negotiated at the bank for cash.

(8) Determine if any certificates of deposit, or bonds redeemed for cash.

(9) Be alert for other violations such as smuggling, dope peddling, fencing, etc.

(10) If no specific items are found, prepare a rough net worth.

(11) Verify items collected by the bank to see if proceeds were remitted to the customer in currency.

◀ In *Stinnett* v. *U.S.* the defendant argued that under the Gleckman case, the bank deposit theory required not only a showing of periodic bank deposits but some further corroboration (in Gleckman there was a corroborative net worth analysis). Although the court believed that there was corroborative evidence in the Stinnett case, the court stated that "a gross discrepancy between bank deposits and gross receipts without any adequate explanation by the taxpayer is . . . sufficient in itself to take the case to the jury." This would appear to indicate that corroboration of bank deposits proof is not a legal requirement in a tax evasion prosecution.

◀ The chief defense contentions in bank deposits cases (other than lack of criminal intent) are:

- That the sporadic nature or unconventional amounts of the deposits indicate the involvement of prior accumulated funds, and not current receipts.
- That the deposits reflect, in whole or in substantial part, nonincome items, income items attributable to other years, or duplication of current income items already accounted for by the taxpayer.

(12) Prepare cash flow and cash availability statements.

(13) Go through Criminal Investigation files to see if there are any other leads from information reports or other TCR's.

(14) Examine stock brokers daily sheets. They list incoming and outgoing items along with the names of purchasers and sellers. Unregistered bearer bonds, which are most difficult to trace, have been found and identified in this manner. Usually these are purchased and sold for currency.

(15) Examine bank records for purchase and disposition of U.S. Treasury Bills Notes and Bonds, state and local government bonds and other types of commercial paper.

◀ In *Kirsch* v. *U.S.* a conviction based chiefly on bank deposits evidence was reversed because the government's own testimony showed that the deposits could not be identified as income. The court stated "that the bare fact standing alone that a man had deposited a sum of money in a bank would not prove that he owed income tax on the amount."

630 *(4-11-80)* 4235
Analyze Financial Accounts

631 *(4-11-80)* 4235
Analysis of Income

(1) Of primary importance in any in-depth audit is making a detailed analysis of all income taxable and nontaxable, regarding source, nature and amount of funds received.

◀ In *Buttermore* v. *U.S.* the court held that what facts and circumstances constitute a proper foundation for an assumption that bank deposits represent income must be left to a considerable extent to the discretion of the trial court.

(2) Some of the more common areas or situations which would involve an in depth analysis are as follows:

(a) The acquisition of substantial assets may be indicated by an analysis of deductions for depreciation, real estate taxes, mortgage interest or casualty losses. Funds used to acquire these assets should be traced to the source.

(b) Sizable increases in the capital account and in loans payable to officers should be noted for investigation to determine source of funds.

(c) Substantial amounts of interest and dividend income earned by a taxpayer reporting nominal income should raise the question of the source of funds used to acquire the investments.

(d) The taxpayer may report a sizable income, but show no income from investments. The agent should make the disposition of the income. This may lead to the identification of unreported income, such as dividends from securities.

(e) Deductions for contributions and medical expenses, if not commensurate with the income reported, should create doubt as to whether the taxpayer has additional income not disclosed or has overstated his/her deductions.

(f) A casualty loss may lead to the discovery of undisclosed assets acquired with income previously unreported.

(g) A bank deposit analysis of personal or nonbusiness bank accounts may reveal unusual deposits having little or no direct relationship to the taxpayer's business. These deposits may disclose that the taxpayer is in the gambling or loan shark business or possibly is borrowing funds from a loan shark.

(h) Agents should be aware of the importance of identifying the source of all nontaxable items of income deposited in the taxpayers bank accounts. The analysis may reveal the acquisition of nontaxable securities with "illegal funds."

(i) Agents should always determine the amount of funds on hand at the beginning of the period covered by the investigation. This is a very important feature to be considered in cases where income is being reconstructed by the net worth method, bank deposit method or cash expenditures method. He/she should also determine the amounts and sources of nontaxable income during the period. The most common sources of nontaxable income are:

1 Inheritance
2 Nontaxable capital gains
3 Excludable sick pay
4 Gift
5 Tax exempt interest
6 Insurance proceeds

(3) Revenue agents should always be alert when examining the books and records of manufacturers and processors to the potential for income from the sale of scrap material or by-products. Investigations have uncovered sources of unreported income from the sale of eggs and poults by a turkey grower, sales of hides by a meat processor, sale of meat scraps by a supermarket chain, and sale of scrap metals by a manufacturer.

(4) An excellent source of information to identify likely by-products is a document called Census of Manufacturers issued by the Bureau of the Census. This publication is available at public libraries and contains a breakdown, by industry groupings, of primary and secondary products of each industry.

(5) Third party contacts with processors of by-products and scrap materials may develop leads to taxpayers not reporting income from this source.

(6) Examiners will make use of proxy statements and annual reports in their determination of ordinary and necessary executive remuneration to ascertain whether or not corporate officers included perquisites ("perks") with their compensation.

(7) A comparison will be made between information in the current year and that in the years under examination.

(8) "Perks" information is not contained in the Securities and Exchange Commission (SEC) Form 8-K, Current Report but is required to be included in the proxy statements or annual reports submitted to the SEC.

(9) All proxy statements and annual reports are available to the general public.

632 *(4-11-80)* 4235

Loans and Exchange Accounts

(1) One of the most commonly used schemes for reducing income for tax purposes is through the use of loans and exchange accounts.

(2) In in-depth audits, the revenue agent should analyze thoroughly all unusual entries in loan and exchange accounts to determine the purpose, effect on income, source and disposition of funds, and motive behind any unusual transactions.

(3) The agent should be alert to the possibility that one or more of the following methods may be used by the taxpayer under examination.

(a) A sole proprietorship or partnership understating cash sales by making credits to a loan account in the exact amount as the unreported sales. This is usually accomplished by extracting the original sales records and replacing them with rewritten sales records showing the reduced sales figures. This method can be used to obtain cash to be used for kickback purposes or for repaying loans borrowed from loan sharks.

(b) Fictitious expenses may be claimed and credits in the exact amounts made to the loan account. Examination may provide leads to third parties.

(c) A corporation upon direction of its president and sole stockholder may deliberately omit sales receipts from income by crediting the receipts to a loan account to obtain cash for payment of gambling losses.

(d) Non-interest bearing loans made by a taxpayer to outside parties should be scrutinized closely for the possibility of payoffs or kickbacks. The tax return of the recipients of these funds should also be investigated for possible unreported income.

633 *(4-11-80)* 4235
Other Transactions

(1) The examination of any account with the headings capital contributions, officer's drawing accounts, or investments should be performed with this thought in mind; transactions in any of these accounts, traced to their final disposition, could lead the agent to a possible transaction whose effect the taxpayer would prefer to keep from being known.

(2) The principal and more common transactions which may be considered are: acquisition and disposition of assets, and funds loaned and/or borrowed.

633.1 *(4-11-80)* 4235
Asset Sales or Acquisitions

(1) Suspicious transactions, in the form of asset sales or acquisitions, should be investigated because the transaction could have been used to accomplish any of the following:

(a) To pass on to some purchaser, even two or more transactions removed from the original seller, an increase in value of the property sold in excess of the selling price, the increment in value having occurred while the asset was in the possession of the original seller.

(b) To create a deductible loss while still transferring a greater monetary value than the one represented by the selling price to the final owner.

(2) In an in-depth audit, any substantial asset acquisition should, in addition to the normal auditing procedure, be investigated; as to its true value, based on the trend of the economic conditions between time asset was acquired and time of disposition in question; as to the legitimacy of the transaction; and as to the ownership of the asset after its final disposition. Transactions of this type could easily be used to pay off gambling losses, extortionary demands, or for other illegal purposes.

(3) Very often transactions of this nature are not handled between the original seller and the final purchaser. Therefore, an agent should look for intervening owners who may have held the asset for only a short period of time.

(4) If the asset sold or acquired is real estate, the asset's history from date of transaction to present date should be ascertained by an examination of property records maintained by the local office having custody of such records. This can be determined by inspecting each recorded transaction beginning with the last transaction and working chronologically back to the original transaction. While inspecting the instruments, the names of notaries and witnesses should be noted.

(5) If the assets in question are other than real estate, tracing them may take longer. However, if the circumstances warrant, the follow through should be made.

633.2 *(4-11-80)* 4235
Funds Borrowed

(1) If taxpayer's records indicate that funds have been borrowed, the source of the loan should be investigated and documented. If the lender is an individual, evidence should be obtained to ascertain that a true lender-borrower relationship existed, funds were really loaned; a customary rate of interest is being charged, an enforceable contract has been executed, and the terms of the contract are being met. Why were funds not borrowed from a financial institution? Could the source of funds be unreported sales? Could the funds be from an illegal operation?

(2) If the funds were borrowed from a financial institution, in addition to the steps mentioned above, the agent should obtain certain other information ex., type of loan. Was the borrower required to meet the normal conditions customarily demanded by the lender? Was normal collateral demanded? If so, obtain description of collateral and its ownership. If owned by someone else, what is the connection? Were the borrowed funds used personally by the borrower or were they in turn loaned to another party? If funds were reloaned, could the taxpayer be involved in a loan sharking operation? Was a financial statement submitted? If so, were the mails used to submit it? Also determine sources of income reflected in the loan records. Why did taxpayer select this particular institution?

633.3 *(4-11-80)* 4235
Funds Loaned

If funds are loaned, the identity of the borrower should be determined. What is the relationship between the lender and the borrower? Is the taxpayer in the habit of loaning money? If not, why is he loaning it at this time? Could the exchange of funds represent a transaction other than a true loan? Such as pay-off, bribe or other illegal activity? What document did lender receive for security? Was loan made with check or by cash? If by cash, how was cash obtained?

633.4 *(4-11-80)* 4235
Contributed Funds

The contributing stockholder or partner should be asked the source of the contributed funds. If contributor cannot answer, a thorough attempt should be made to determine the source. As mentioned previously, this could be an attempt to legitimatize "illegal funds."

633.5 *(4-11-80)* 4235
Drawing Accounts

(1) The drawing accounts should be thoroughly analyzed. The debit entries in the drawing accounts normally represent payments made for officer's personal expenses. The expenses may reveal his/her mode of living, liabilities, restaurants frequented, charge cards, stock broker, and stores where the officer and his family shop. In addition the debit entries may sometime include abnormal and unusual payments the destination of which may lead to a completely new trail.

(2) The credit entries in a drawing account normally represent the amount of the officer's net salary. However, occasionally, when the account has a substantial debit balance, the officer may contribute funds, from outside the corporate structure, to either eliminate or reduce the debit balance. When this happens, the source of the funds and the factual conditions should be determined.

633.6 *(4-11-80)* 4235
Acquisitions of Investments

(1) When an examination of the records discloses acquisitions of investments, whether of securities, real estate or other assets, careful scrutiny should be made. If the investment represents commonly traded securities and the investment was made through a brokerage firm then the source of the funds invested should be determined.

(2) If the investment represents real estate, other various assets, or securities acquired directly from the seller then the investigation should be more thorough. In such cases the investigation should determine if there is a relationship between the buyer and seller; if the purchase price reflects the true fair market value of the asset; what brought the two parties together; had the asset sold been owned by the seller for a long period of time, or was the seller merely used as a channel to transfer the asset to the buyer?

(3) The same procedure in reverse should be followed in case of disposition of investments. When the transaction represents the sale of an investment an attempt should also be made to determine if the buyer of record is really the purchaser of the asset or if the asset has been retained by the buyer. The following transaction will illustrate the type of occurance which could be discovered:

(a) One stockholder, of two who owned all the stock of a certain corporation, sold 19 of his 20 shares to an individual for $1,900, which was the par value and the stockholder's basis. On the same day the other stockholder sold all of his/her 120 shares back to the corporation for $156,000, or $1,300 per share. There is an indication that market value was considerably higher than par value and the new stockholder was getting a considerable break for some reason. Question for the agent, what reason? Pay-off gambling debt, loan sharking, etc? Additional facts, a few years later, the new stockholder sold all of the 19 shares back to the corporation for $760,000 or $40,000 per share. Question for the agent, what sort of enterprise has the corporation been involved in to have such meteoric rise in value? Black market, sale of hot merchandise, front for some illegal operation, etc.?

634 *(4-11-80)* 4235
Investigative Techniques

(1) In the performance of a normal type audit, some cancelled checks may be examined as to payees, amounts, date of issuance, and numerical sequence. In an in-depth examination the agent should be much more observant and investigate other data.

(2) Before an in-depth examination is started the agent normally is already acquainted with names of certain individuals and other entities that may belong, be related to, or are owned by organized crime elements. Any checks issued to these individuals or entities should be closely

scrutinized and useful information recorded for future reference.

(3) The scrutiny should cover, but not be limited to, the following items:

(a) Name of payee on checks to determine that it is the same as on cash disbursement book.

(b) Endorsement and reendorsement to determine all the parties that took part in the check negotiation.

(c) Checks issued to businesses are normally endorsed by stamp; when hand endorsed a closer scrutiny is warranted. Taxpayers may be forging checks.

(d) Note bank teller stamp. It may reveal dispositon of funds by indicating the department through which the check was negotiated. A trust department stamp may indicate an investment; or note teller stamp, a loan payment; a bond teller, purchase of bonds.

(e) Location of bank where check was negotiated. If the negotiating bank is from out of town this information may be helpful to other Federal agencies to prove whereabouts of payee on a certain date.

(f) Both date check was issued and date it was negotiated. If the time spread is great and the physical appearance of the check is good, it may indicate a pre-dated check. On the other hand, if the physical condition of the check is old (sometimes indicated by the crease on a check which has been folded) and the spread between issuance and negotiation date is short, this could indicate a post-dated check.

(g) Missing checks. In such instances it should be determined to whom the missing checks were issued, verify amount based on invoice, determine if check cleared bank, and follow through for other necessary information available from the payee of the check.

(h) Checks issued out of numerical sequence may lead to payments for gambling losses or loan shark payments. Such checks may have been omitted from the check register.

(i) Periodically reoccurring checks issued for the same amounts could disclose payments for illegal loans, expense payments for friends, or other payments which could lead to unreported income.

635 *(4-11-80)* 4235

Cash Transactions

(1) Cash transactions may occur both in personnal and business sales and acquisitions. In personal dealings a cash transaction could indicate lack of faith in financial institutions, or tax evasion by either party involved in the transaction. In a business operation, cash transactions could be the result of the same condition; however, especially in cases in the Strike Force Program, they could indicate more intricate reasons. Therefore, various possibilities should be considered.

(2) If the transaction is personal and substantial, determine if funds can be accounted for by the income previously reported. Also did purchaser receive adequate value for the amount of cash involved?

(3) If the transaction is related to a business transaction, a different approach should be taken based on whether the transaction is a sale or a purchase.

(4) If the transaction represents a purchase, the agent should ascertain the legitimacy of the seller and the relationship of his product to the purchaser's operation. This may disclose that the purchaser received nothing for the cash, received something of a much lesser value than the cash paid, or some nominal product completely unrelated to his business operation. Agent should also document the source of the funds used for the purchase. If purchaser's business is an operation where most of the sales are in cash, then a comparative analysis between cash sales and amounts deposited should be made to detérmine whether undeposited revenue from sales is the source of the cash. If the business sales are paid for mostly by checks, which were deposited, consideration should be given as to whether purchaser can show how the cash was accumulated.

(5) If the transaction represents a sale, the relationship of the item sold to the purchaser's operation should also be ascertained. Did taxpayer really consummate a sale or is he/she manufacturing a phony transaction only to legitimatize "illegal funds"?

640 *(4-11-80)* 4235

Indirect Method of Computing Income

641 *(4-11-80)* 4235
Request Financial or Net Worth Statement

641.1 *(4-11-80)* 4235
Introduction

A computation of net worth should be considered on every in-depth examination. Subjects selected for IRS Strike Force work programs usually have backgrounds indicating less than accurate voluntary compliance with Internal Revenue laws. Their income may be from illegal sources. Records are usually nonexistent or not available. Income from legal sources may be understated as this is the nature of racketeering. A subject's standard of living and/or net worth is a measure of income received by him/her.

◀ The *net worth method* is probably the best known of the weapons for detecting income from an illegal source. Historically it has been used primarily in tax fraud cases. Courts have recognized the net worth method probably because it is presented in the familiar balance sheet format readily recognized in the business world. The net worth method is based on a complete financial picture of the taxpayer and on the theory that increases or decreases in a person's net worth during a period, adjusted for living expenses, results in a determination of income. Funds from unknown or illegal sources can be discovered by subtracting total funds from known sources, such as salaries, wages, loans, and dividends.

641.2 *(4-11-80)* 4235
Authority

IRC 446(b) states that if no method of accounting has been regularly used by taxpayer, or if the method used does not clearly reflect income, the computation of taxable income shall be made under such method as, in the opinion of the Secretary, does clearly reflect income.

641.3 *(4-11-80)* 4235
The Method

(1) Next to the specific items method of proof, the net worth method is probably the most frequently used way of proving income in both civil and criminal income tax cases. In an indirect method of proof, income is determined by circumstantial evidence; that is, by showing what happened to the taxpayer's funds. The net worth method is based upon the theory that increases in a taxpayer's net worth during a taxable year, adjusted for nondeductible expenditures and nontaxable income, must result from taxable income. Exhibits 600-1 through 600-4 are suggested formats for the computation of understatement of taxable income by the net worth method.

(2) The theory of the net worth method is based upon the fact that for any given year, a taxpayer's income is applied or expended on items which are either:

(a) Deductible; or

(b) Nondeductible—including increases to his/her net worth through the purchase of assets and/or reduction of liabilities.

◀ In this type of examination, a person's net worth, that is the difference between his assets and his liabilities, must be determined at the beginning and end of a period, usually a calendar year. The difference between these two amounts is the increase or decrease in net worth. Adjustments are then made for living expenses to arrive at income. Income, therefore, would be funds derived from any source.

◀ The net worth method is an excellent one to use on taxpayers whose books appear to be false, incomplete, or missing. The IRS will also use it when two or more years are under examination and when a taxpayer has several assets and liabilities which changed during the year.

(3) The taxable portion of the income can thus be reconstructed by calculating the increase in net worth during the year, adding the nondeductible items and subtracting that portion of the income which is partially or wholly tax-exempt.

641.4 *(4-11-80)* 4235

When to Use

(1) The net worth method is most often used when one or more of the following conditions prevail:

(a) The taxpayer maintains no books and records

(b) The taxpayer's books and records are not available

(c) The taxpayer's books and records are inadequate

(d) The taxpayer withholds books and records.

(2) The fact that the taxpayer's books and records accurately reflect the figures on his/her return does not prevent the use of the net worth method of proof. The Government can still look beyond the "self-serving declarations" in a taxpayer's books and records and use any evidence available to contravene their accuracy.

(3) While the method was originally used against taxpayers whose principal source of income was some kind of illegal activity, it is now regularly recommended in general fraud cases, especially where significant changes in net worth have occurred and other methods of proof are insufficient.

(4) In addition to being used as a primary means of proving taxable income, the net worth is relied upon to corroborate other methods of proof and to test-check the accuracy of reported taxable income.

641.5 *(4-11-80)* 4235

Indications of Unreported Income

(1) In an in-depth audit investigation the agent should suspect unreported income when any of the following conditions exist.

(a) books and records are inadequate for audit purposes.

(b) reported income is not commensurate with taxpayer's standard of living.

(c) reported income is low for the type of business.

(d) taxpayer consistently reports low income.

(e) pre-contact analysis reveals limited cash availability. Exhibit 600-5 is a suggested

◂ There is no statutory provision defining the net worth method and specifically authorizing its use by the IRS. However, courts have approved the use of this method in numerous cases. Perhaps the leading case in this respect is the 1954 Supreme Court decision of *Holland* v. *U.S.* and three companion cases. Those cases outlined the broad principles governing the trial and review of cases based on the net worth method of proving income.

◂ The formula for computing income by this method is:

(a) Assets less liabilities = Net worth

(b) Net worth at end of year .... $_______
    Less: Net worth at beginning of the year .... − _______
    Increase or decrease in net worth .... $_______
    Add: Nondeductible expenditures .... + _______
    Total $_______
    Less: Nontaxable income . − _______
    Adjusted gross income .... $_______

(c) Less: Funds from known sources .... − _______

(d) Result: Funds from unknown or illegal sources .... $ _______

format which should be helpful in disclosing available cash.

641.6 *(4-11-80)* 4235
Procedure

As soon as possible after the agent determines that he will conduct an in-depth examination, he/she should request a statement of net worth as of the beginning and the end of the period under investigation. The more complete the statement the better, but even a rough approximation would be helpful. If possible, the agent should prepare a rough net worth statement during this initial interview. Keep in mind that the taxpayer may withdraw his/her cooperation at any time. Suggested questions to ask the taxpayer appear in 920 of IRM 4231, Audit Technique Handbook for Internal Revenue Agents. This net worth statement, as part of the file on the taxpayer, would then be available as a starting point for any future income verification.

641.7 *(4-11-80)* 4235
Opening Cash on Hand

(1) The determination of the approximate amount of cash on hand at the beginning of the period under investigation is crucial in every case in which the income is reconstructed by the net worth, bank deposit, or cash expenditures methods. Cash on hand is intended to cover cash:

(a) on his/her person,
(b) in a safe deposit box,
(c) in a safe, or
(d) any other place for safe keeping.

If taxpayer does not provide the net worth statement, the agent should try to obtain an affidavit as to cash on hand at the beginning of the period.

(2) Of all categories of beginning assets, cash-on-hand item is the most difficult to prove and is, therefore, almost universally claimed by defendants to exist as a secret hoard of sufficient size to account for the increase in net worth. This allegation is sometimes called a "cash hoard story." The taxpayer may claim, for example, that the cash hoard was accumulated from savings out of earnings in prior years; or

◀ In the Holland case the Supreme Court said that an essential condition in a net worth determination of income is the establishment "with reasonable certainty" of an *opening net worth* to serve as a starting point from which to calculate future increases in the taxpayer's net worth. This is important because an inaccurate beginning net worth will affect the accuracy of the determination of income subsequent to the base point. For instance, if a taxpayer's beginning net worth is understated, taxable income for the period under consideration will be overstated.

◀ In order for income to be taxable, it must come from a taxable source. The government must either prove a likely source of taxable income, or negate all nontaxable sources of income. If the government resorts to the latter type of proof, it is even more important for the IRS to establish a firm starting point, particularly of cash on hand. Proof of a likely taxable source of income has been found sufficient in a number of criminal income tax cases by:

- Showing that the defendant did not report certain income on his tax returns.

that the cash is the result of gifts and bequests; or that the money was brought from a foreign country where it was saved. In claiming that the cash hoard is not reflected in the opening net worth, the taxpayer is trying to minimize any increase or discredit the computation. You must anticipate this particular defense and show that the defendant had no large sum of cash, for which he/she was not given credit. Consequently, it is important that you interview the taxpayer early in the investigation to tie down a *maximum cash accumulation.* You should attempt to obtain the following information:

(a) the maximum amount claimed to be on hand at the end of each year from the starting point through the present.

(b) how it was accumulated

(c) where it was kept and in what denominations

(d) who had knowledge of it

(e) who counted it

(f) when and where it was spent

(3) All of the above information is necessary to establish the consistency and reliability of the taxpayer's statements. Usually no direct cash on hand evidence is available but statements made as to the source, amount, and use of funds can be corroborated or refuted with circumstantial evidence. Examples of evidence which may tend to negate the existence of a cash hoard include:

(a) written or oral admissions of the taxpayer to investigation officers concerning a small amount of cash on hand;

(b) financial statements prepared by the taxpayer showing a low net worth;

(c) financial inability of others to make gifts or bequests to the taxpayer.

(d) comprimises of overdue debts by the taxpayer;

(e) foreclosure proceedings against the taxpayer;

(f) collection actions against the taxpayer;

(g) tax returns (or lack of) evidencing little or no income in prior years.

(4) The question as to the existence of cash on hand is a matter to be decided by the jury. Essentially, the Government must prove that the taxpayer could not have had a greater cash on hand than is reflected in the opening net worth. Consequently, while your investigation must prove cash on hand to be reasonably accurate, it does not have to prove it to be

- Showing that the defendant did not report certain income for years prior to the indictment period.
- Comparing the business operations and profits of the defendant for the indictment years with the profits or prior operations for a comparable period.
- Effectively contradicting defendant's assertions as to the nontaxable sources.
- Revealing opportunities of the defendant to receive graft.
- Showing that the character of the business has the capacity to produce income in amounts determined by the net worth method.

◀ During the course of many income tax investigations involving the net worth method of proof, the taxpayer will make admissions that the government will use in evidence against him or her during trial. Admissions may pertain to any facet of the case, although in many instances they pertain to the starting point, items of living expenses, sources of income, and willfulness. Admissions after the commission of the crime must be corroborated, if they embrace an element vital to the government's case.

mathematically precise. It may also be possible to reconstruct the taxpayer's cash on hand from prior earnings records. If cash on hand for an earlier period can be reasonably established, income earned from the period forward to the starting point could be used to establish a maximum available cash on hand.

641.8 *(4-11-80)* 4235
Other Sources

Banks, loan companies, charge accounts, credit agencies, etc. may have been utilized by the taxpayer. Taxpayer may have provided them with a financial statement. The agent should always check with the source of granted credit or loans. Agents should request copies from the taxpayer of any financial statements he/she may have given financial institutions. If the taxpayer is an alien or a naturalized citizen, the Immigration and Naturalization Service would have a sworn statement signed by the taxpayer as a declaration of the value of property brought into the country by him/her. See 462 and 463 for contacting that agency.

641.9 *(4-11-80)* 4235
Verification of Items

Every item on a statement of net worth or financial statement should be verified, if possible. Usually large nontaxable sources derived from related parties should be carefully scrutinized. A statement by the taxpayer or third party serves only as a lead to the agent. Keep in mind that normally the taxpayer's statements are self-serving. Sworn statements should be secured where possible. The agent must reconstruct the net worth or financial condition of the taxpayer through records and other evidence. Examination of related parties books and records may be necessary to verify unrealistic transactions.

642 *(4-11-80)* 4235
Cost of Living

642.1 *(4-11-80)* 4235
Introduction

The standard of living generally is an accurate barometer of a taxpayer's income. Since living costs are assumed to represent taxable income unless shown otherwise, in-depth examinations should include a computation of cost of living.

◀ Living expenses include, but are not limited to: household expenses, auto expenses, insurance, contributions, medical expenses, taxes paid, net gambling losses, entertainment, gifts and loans, losses on the sale of assets, clothing, and food. Living expenses may be determined by statements

642.2 *(4-11-80)* 4235
Addition to Net Worth Statement

The determination of the cost of living is essential in the reconstruction of income by the net worth method. The schedule of living costs is incorporated into the net worth schedule. When the net worth is negligible it may be more feasible to reconstruct income by the expenditures method.

642.3 *(4-11-80)* 4235
Procedure

The agent should request taxpayer to provide a schedule of living costs. This request should be made at the initial interview. The schedule should arrive at an annual cost. To facilitate its preparation and increase its accuracy, the schedule should provide for weekly, monthly or irregular expenditures. Exhibit 600-5 is a suggested format which could be used in scheduling living expenses. However, the taxpayer will not be asked to sign the schedule or any other format serving the same purpose. In addition to the requested schedule, the agent should prepare a rough schedule of living expenses at this initial interview by questioning the taxpayer. The spouse should be drawn into the discussion of living costs. This rough, prepared on the spot, schedule will be available to measure the reliability of the taxpayer prepared schedule or for use if the taxpayer refuses to provide a schedule. The Bureau of Labor statistics should be used where reasonable approximation of living costs cannot be easily ascertained.

642.4 *(4-11-80)* 4235
Observations

Taxpayer's standard of living is subject to observation. The agent should observe the neighborhood, house, furnishings, automobiles, etc. The quality of clothing worn by taxpayer and family, as well as their shopping places and methods, should be noted. Their travel, entertainment and recreation styles are good barometers. The schools attended by the children afford another guide. The observant agent can draw a very good picture of taxpayer's income by evaluating these signs of taxpayer's standard of living.

642.5 *(4-11-80)* 4235
Verification of Items

Items of living expenses must be verified to the extent possible. Obviously, some items will be estimations and not subject to verification.

of the taxpayer or through an analysis of his or her bank account. The IRS may also rely on surveillance or interviews with third parties to determine sources of expenditures. If the net worth statement is being prepared for use at a trial, estimated living expenses will not be used unless the taxpayer agrees to the amount. In some cases courts have allowed minimum estimated living expense figures to be used.

◀ IRS guidelines suggest that the agent study the taxpayer's insurance coverage to help determine the extent of the income. Life insurance and an-

The agent should use sources other than the taxpayer to establish reasonableness of the estimated items. In determining the validity of assets and as a possible lead to unrecorded assets, the insurance policies of the taxpayer should be examined. These policies can sometimes lead to the discovery of furs, jewelry, objects of art, and other personal assets. The Internal Revenue Service has successfully used the Costs of Living as published by the Bureau of Labor Statistics.

643 *(4-11-80)* 4235
Cash Availability

643.1 *(4-11-80)* 4235
Introduction

Cash transactions require a minimum of records. A schedule showing the flow of cash should be helpful and may reveal unreported income. It may disclose the expenditure of cash before cash is available as shown by taxpayer's records, raising the question of the source of the cash. Also individuals prominent in organized crime are known to deal in cash.

643.2 *(4-11-80)* 4235
Cash on Hand, Beginning and Close of Period

It has been previously stated, but bears repeating, that determination of cash on hand at the beginning of the period under investigation is of paramount importance. Amount of cash on hand at the close of the period is also important as it is an asset in the net worth schedule and provides a starting point in any future investigation.

643.3 *(4-11-80)* 4235
Sources of Cash

Determine sources of cash receipts. Checks received or issued are considered cash. Savings accounts are considered accounts receivable for the purpose of studying the availability of cash. Cash may be received from the usual sources such as wages, sales, loans, gifts, etc., but unusual or illegal sources could be the case.

643.4 *(4-11-80)* 4235
Schedule of Receipts and Expenditures

The agent should prepare a schedule showing cash receipts and cash expenditures by

nuity policies are good reflections of a person's own opinion of his or her earning power. Insurance on the stock of merchandise inventory might give a clue to its true value. Burglary and theft insurance could disclose the existence and value of furs, jewelry, antiques, and rare collections.

◀ A common defense against the net worth method is the assertion that the taxpayer had a large amount of cash on hand that the government did not include in the beginning net worth. The taxpayer may also allege that cash balances are wrong for years subsequent to the base year. The IRS will anticipate this defense in all cases where the net worth method is the primary method of proving income, and will attempt to get evidence to negate it.

◀ Note this IRS instruction: "Admissions of the taxpayer are most effective to pin down the cash amount, and should be obtained at the initial interview or early in the investigation." The line of questioning will be directed toward determining:

- The amount of cash on hand (undeposited currency and coins) at the starting point and at the end of the prosecution year.
- The amount of cash on hand at the date of the interview.
- The source of all cash referred to above.
- Where the cash was kept.
- Who knew about the cash.
- Whether anyone ever counted it.
- When and how the cash was spent.
- Whether any records are available with respect to the cash on hand.
- The denominations of the cash on hand.

date, amount and balance of cash available. Obviously, a question of unreported income arises whenever, on any given date, there is a cash expenditure where there is no cash available. This schedule would also show if income is received periodically, irregularly, or at special or unusual times. The schedule may provide the opening to secure information as to unreported income. The single entry, cash bookkeeping record would serve as this schedule.

◀ In most cases, spouses will also be questioned about cash on hand as well as other matters. The IRS thinks this will serve to check the accuracy of the taxpayer's statements about cash on hand.

643.5 *(4–11–80)* 4235

Unusual Receipts or Expenditures

Analyze all unusual receipts or expenditures, not only as to source or destination, but also as to the reason for it. What was the disposition of the unusual receipt of cash? What was the source of cash which was used for the unusual expenditure? These are not the ordinary questions asked in the normal tax audit.

643.6 *(4–11–80)* 4235

Application of Funds

One of the indirect methods of reconstructing income is through the application of funds. It is a comparison of all known expenditures with all known receipts for the period. Only the net increases and decreases in assets and liabilities are taken into account along with nondeductible expenditures and nontaxable receipts. There is no need to carry assets or liabilities which are the same at the end and the beginning of the period. The excess of expenditures over the sum of reported and nontaxable income is unreported income. The agent may find it helpful to make an application of funds to quickly get indications of unreported income. Exhibit 600–6 suggests a format for this purpose. The reconstruction of income by the application of funds method may be the most feasible in a particular case. As in other indirect methods of reconstruction of income, determination of opening cash on hand is very important.

◀ The *source and application of funds method* is probably the most commonly used means of reconstructing income. Actually a variation of the net worth method, it differs only in format. Simply stated, it involves the comparison of all known expenditures with all known receipts. The theory is that if a taxpayer's expenditures during a given year exceed reported income, and the source of funds for such expenditures is unexplained, the excess expenditures represent unreported income. In making the actual computation, increases and decreases in assets and liabilities along with nondeductible expenditures and nontaxable receipts are used.

643.7 *(4-11-80)* 4235
Cash Transactions (T) Account

(1) The cash transactions, or T account, is a method that can accommodate varied situations without becoming overly technical. This method can be used in any examination because of the relatively short time it takes to develop the necessary information. The results are accurate and the information easy to obtain.

(2) The primary method of testing the income reported is an analysis of cash transactions or T account. The theory is to consider all types of income and all types of expenditures as "cash transactions" flowing in and out of the cash account in double entry accounting records. Income items will appear in the "T" acount as "debit" and expenditure items will appear in the "T" account as "credits". If the total credits exceed the total debits, the difference represents an understatement of gross receipts. Exhibit 600–7 suggests a format of the computation.

643.71 *(4-11-80)* 4235
Identification of Understatement

(1) This understatement may result from unreported gross receipts, from overstated expenses, from omitted nontaxable income, or from a combination of these items. Enlist the taxpayer's cooperation in explaining the discrepancy. You may use one of the other indirect methods to reinforce your position. If the understatement is resolved, make any technical adjustments and close the case.

(2) If the cash transactions method indicates that taxpayer had sufficient money to cover the known expenditures, accept the income as reported. Do not try to refine figures to the point of perfection. Time is important and should be kept to a minimum if possible.

(3) If the "debit" column is substantially larger than the "credit" column the situation warrants further investigation. More than likely there are investments or other personal expenses of which you are not aware. You might then assume that these investments would create additional income. Because there are no sure answers to any imbalance, be very careful before concluding that an under or overstatement exists. You will need to be sure of your ground before presenting your findings to the taxpayer.

643.72 *(4-11-80)* 4235
Adjustments

A problem may develop when you recognize personal expenses claimed as business expenses. Do you adjust these items by reducing business expenses and also eliminating such items from the personal living expense computation, or leave them as business expenses and include them as personal living expenses? If the former computation were chosen specific adjustments would be required after determining the correctness of the gross receipts by the "T" account method.

The preferred computation considers all expenses representing cash expenditures on Form 1040, Schedule C as business expenses and includes in the personal living expenses all the personal living expenses you can identify. Therefore, the only difference in the figure used as Schedule C expenses in the "T" account and those reported on the return is noncash expenditures.

Because the gross income test is designed to verify the correctness of gross receipts, any understatement calculated will not require any other adjustments to items representing cash expenditures claimed as business expenses.

As an overstatement of expenses creates an understatement of income, additional adjustments to the business cash expenditure items would duplicate the adjustment considered in the gross receipts.

When the test results in no understatement, indicating that gross receipts are correct as reported, specific adjustments are applicable.

Technical adjustments to depreciation, bad debts, or other items representing noncash expenditures should always be made.

643.73 *(4-11-80)* 4235
Cash on Hand at Beginning of Period

It is important to get complete information about nontaxable income as your efforts may be wasted if the taxpayer later provides information regarding a nontaxable source of funds which explains the understatement. This is especially true of cash on hand or cash hoard. This information is a must in every indirect method. The best adjustment for unreported income will be lost if this item is not determined from the beginning. Once faced with an understatement, the taxpayer will try to explain it. He/she cannot use the defense of "cash hoard" if the amount has already been furnished. See 641.7 for determination of cash.

650 *(4-11-80)* 4235
Undervaluation of Inventories

651 *(4-11-80)* 4235
Introduction

(1) Normal audit procedures tend to generate the concept that errors in inventories would cancel out over the years resulting in a tendency for the agents to avoid the requirements of IRM 424(10). While such a concept is correct in many instances, it ignores the varying tax rates and therefore, the proper tax liability has not been determined for a particular year.

(2) Aware of this concept, some taxpayers continually understate their inventories by using various devices to accomplish this end.

(3) Large profits can be made by stealing marketable commodities. In examinations, inventories may be unusually important when the subject has a history as a fence or is engaged in a legitimate business that would lend itself to the disposition of stolen goods.

(4) Certain court decisions have set a precedent which compelled the Commissioner, when correcting continuing understatements, to adjust the opening and closing inventories in all open years. The resulting increase in the closing inventory in a closed year created a deficiency that could not be collected due to the statute of limitations.

(5) IRC 481, regarding changes in method of accounting, contains a possible remedy to this situation and it should be carefully reviewed by the investigating agent.

652 *(4-11-80)* 4235
Investigative Techniques

(1) under IRM 424(10) the examiner will verify inventories by making the following minimum tests:

(a) compare inventories on the return with prior and subsequent years and verify them with the records.

(b) check for unauthorized changes in reporting inventories.

(c) compare for gross profit percentage variation.

(d) determine significance of any qualifying statements or financial reports prepared by independent accounting firms (an unqualified opinion by a public accountant should not be interpreted as assurance that inventories are correct for income tax purposes).

(e) determine that all direct and indirect overhead and burden costs are properly allocated.

(f) analyze unusual entries to cost of sales and ascertain the proper allocations of labor, material and burden charges not related to sales.

(g) determine that the year end purchases were included in the closing inventory.

(h) determine any unusual fluctuation in the amount of inventories reported.

(i) raise any question that will assist in making a proper determination as to the accuracy of the inventory.

(j) in analyzing the inventory sheets, ascertain whether any items in inventory were not reflected in the purchase invoices.

(k) make a physical inspection of the premises and try to relate the quantity of inventory with the amount reported on the return, also unusual or items of inventory not related to the business.

(l) make test checks and pursue any discrepancy.

(m) insist on the examination of the inventory sheets. If unavailable, make an in-depth audit of the inventory account.

(n) ascertain that inventory does not include items deducted elsewhere on the return, ie., freight, labor, etc.

(2) If it is decided that the inventory requires a thorough check, the agent should consult with his/her team leader or manager and prepare a list of questions pertaining to the item and a list of documents that should be obtained for verification.

660 *(4-11-80)* 4235
Missing Taxpayers

(1) The following represents some of the ways that may be used in attempting to locate a missing taxpayer. In following some of these suggested sources, keep in mind the taxpayer's immediate family, i.e. the taxpayer's spouse and children. All too often, a taxpayer will cover his/her trail, but others in his/her family may not have covered theirs;

(a) In-Service Sources—Check the taxpayer's latest return for a possible new address. If the taxpayer's return indicates his/her employer or type of occupation, this could be followed up by contacting the employer, union, or any third party with whom the taxpayer may have been connected. Always scrutinize the taxpayer's available tax returns for possible leads that could be used to locate him/her through some governmental agency, bank, brokerage house, physician, hospital, union, etc. Contact the Criminal Investigation function and Strike Force Representatives to see if their records reflect a new address or follow-up leads. See if there is any collection activity in regard to the taxpayer. Check to see if there are any delinquent taxes or estimated taxes being paid.

(b) Post Office—Ascertain whether the taxpayer has moved from his/her last known address. If so, check to see if he/she left a forwarding address. If there is a regular postman/postwoman, an interview with him/her might be fruitful. He/she might have some idea where the taxpayer may now be located or the type of mail that the taxpayer had been receiving. Such information could open the door to new leads.

(c) Telephone Company—Where did the telephone company send its last bill for any charges due? Do they have a record of any new installation? Is there any record of an unlisted number? Did the taxpayer make any out of town calls (perhaps a lead as to where he/she might have moved)? In obtaining information from the telephone company, it is especially important that you ask for the same information in the name of the spouse or children inasmuch as it is common practice to use their names when obtaining phone service or listings.

(d) Utility Companies—Here, as with the telephone company, a check should be made to see where the last bill was mailed, or if they are servicing the taxpayer at a new address. Although the taxpayer may not have directly paid a gas or electric company in his/her old residence, it is very possible that he/she may now be making such payments. Again, as with the telephone company, it is important to check out the names of all of his/her immediate family as the new residence could be listed in one of their names.

(e) Neighbors and Schools—The former landlord, superintendent of the building, or the neighbors might be able to tell you where the taxpayer moved. If furniture was professionally moved, contact the movers. Are there any children in the family? Determine where the children's school records were transferred. A check of children's playmates and friends might disclose that the children had mentioned where they were moving.

(f) Credit Agencies and Department Stores—Canvassing the various local or major credit agencies and the credit departments of the major local department stores or shops could reveal the taxpayer's new residence to which bills are being mailed to the taxpayer. Contact local shops to determine if the taxpayer's spouse mentioned the new location to which they are moving. See IRM 4082.4 for restrictions on availability of information from consumer reporting agencies.

(g) Banks—In some areas where there are a number of branch banks, they will have a central filing system at a main office. Where this is so, the main office should be contacted. If such a central filing system is not available, then all banks within the area of the taxpayer's old residence and place of business should be canvassed. When canvassing banks, solicit information on all members of the taxpayers household whether the records are in the open or closed files and accounts. Request to see the signature card(s) as these cards also give information such as address, name of person who introduced the "customer," or other institutions where the taxpayer may have an account. Obtain the correspondence file that the bank maintains as well as any information in regard to loans or mortgages. Scrutinize the microfilmed cancelled checks issued two or three months prior to the time of your inquiry or closing of taxpayer's account. The last check issued to close the account could lead to the opening of a new account.

(h) Last Known Employer—You should visit the last known employer of the taxpayer or members of his/her family. The employer may provide the name of the new employer, a Social Security Number, or whether the employee was a member of a union whose membership rolls could be used to identify the taxpayer's current employer.

(i) Motor Vehicle Bureau—The Motor Vehicle Bureau should be contacted for a possible change of address as reflected on the taxpayer's drivers license or automobile registration. The automobile registration may also give you a lead to the insurance company, last employer, and Social Security Number.

(j) Associates—If any associates of the taxpayer are known, they should be contacted for any possible information.

(k) Hospitalization and Other Insurance Agencies—Any known insurance company that the taxpayer deals with should be contacted. A review of their records might reflect a new address or possibly the issuance of additional coverage which would lead to other possible sources of information. Hospitalization insurance records may lead to family doctors who could then be contacted.

(l) Unions and Associations—Scrutiny of the taxpayer's tax return might indicate a union affiliation that could be used to help locate him/her. It might reveal dues payments or indicate sources of income that would lead you to a union or association with which the taxpayer was directly or indirectly connected.

(m) Social Security Administration—A form questionnaire can be mailed to the Social Security Administration to try to locate a missing taxpayer. Through them you might discover, if not the new address, the latest employer. Once the latest employer is known, the proper follow-up procedures can then be pursued.

(n) Board of Health—It is possible that a taxpayer who is missing may be deceased. A check should be made at the local Board of Health or other appropriate agency to determine if this is the situation.

(o) Department of State (Passports)—You should consider checking with the Department of State to see if a passport has been issued or an application for a passport received. See 453:(1), 462, and 463 for other Government Agency procedures.

(p) Police Department—A visit to the Police Department's Intelligence, Racketeer, or Criminal Investigation unit may result in your obtaining a complete file on the taxpayer. Within the file you may find the taxpayer's complete arrest record. This could lead to a current Parole or Probation Officer. It will also tell if there is any current action pending which could be followed up to locate him/her. There may also be listings of his/her associates or places he/she is known and has been seen to frequent. There could be surveillance reports which will give you current readings on the taxpayer's activities, license plate numbers of cars he/she used, names and addresses he/she has used or visited, present associates, restaurants or clubs he/she goes to, businesses he/she is known or alleged to own, etc. You will also find articles or newspaper clippings dealing with the taxpayer. When visiting the Police Department, it is also a good idea to try to interview a police officer who is knowledgeable about the taxpayer.

670 *(4-11-80)* 4235

Social Security Administration Verification

(1) With the continuing use of the Social Security Number as a means of identifying an individual, the importance of the Social Security Administration as a source of information for the Federal Investigating Agencies cannot be overemphasized. The Armed Forces have discarded the old military serial numbers for the use of the Social Security number as a means of identification. IRM 4083.6, which cites the authority and procedure for obtaining Social Security information, states:

(a) The disclosure of official records and information is covered by Regulations No.1, as amended, under the Social Security Act. This authorizes the Social Security Administration to disclose information to any officer or employee of the Treasury Department lawfully charged with the administration of titles II, VIII, or IX of the Social Security Act, the Federal Insurance Contributions Act, the Self-Employment Act, or the Federal Unemployment Tax Act, or any Federal Income Tax Law, for the purpose of such administration only. The regulations expressly forbid further disclosure of information thus obtained, or its use for any purpose other than administration of the employment and income tax laws.

(b) The Request for Social Security Account information is made by preparing Form 2264 in duplicate for each individual involved.The following information which must be typed or printed legibly on Form 2264:

1 taxpayer's full name.

2 taxpayer's full Social Security Number.

3 address, district number, and location of originating office must be shown in appropriate spaces.

4 form must be manually signed on behalf of the District Director by the requestor.

(c) The Social Security Administration will check its records only for the calendar year for which the Form 2264 (Request for Social Security Account Information) is submitted. If no employee record is found for the requested year, the two preceding calendar years will be checked.

(d) Requests for itemization of quarterly earnings may be made by memorandum prepared in duplicate and signed on behalf of the District Director. In addition to the information required for the preparation of the Form 2264, the requestor will include in the memorandum the period or periods to be covered.

(e) Since the Social Security Administration processes all requests as expeditiously as possible, follow-up inquiries should not be made within sixty days from the date of the original request. In the event a follow-up is necessary, a second request should be prepared in original only and not identified as a follow-up or as a second request. No reference should be made to the original request.

(2) In the investigation of organized crime figures, the agent should be alert to the use of fictitious social security numbers by individuals who also use aliases. Accordingly:

(a) close scrutiny of social security numbers may assist in detecting possible fraud practices in reporting and accounting for individuals deemed subject to payroll deductions or individuals allegedly on the payroll of an employer;

(b) see Exhibit 600–10 of Law Enforcement Manual IV.

(3) Emphasis on enforcement in the employment tax area, which in turn becomes a source of investigative information, is evidenced by the Social Security Administration's efforts in providing their claims manual to the Internal Revenue Service. A copy of this manual is available in each district office.

680 *(4-11-80)* 4235

Data Processing

See text 7(21)0, (Computer Fraud).

690 *(4-11-80)* 4235

Canvassing of Banks

691 *(4-11-80)* 4235

Scope of Bank Canvas

(1) The scope of bank canvassing to be undertaken will depend upon the potential number of banks in the geographic area in which the taxpayer operates and the specific circumstances of the case itself. In major population areas where there are a large number of banks, it would not be feasible to canvass all of them. In situations like this, the canvass might be confined to the immediate area of the taxpayer's place of business and his/her residence. In canvassing a bank that has a number of branches within the metropolitan area, the examiner should determine if the bank uses a central filing system. If it does, it would be much easier to check all the individual branches through the central files than to visit them individually.

(2) When canvassing banks, requests for information should include all possible pertinent information about the taxpayer and all other members of his/her household, and should encompass the bank's open and closed files.

692 *(4-11-80)* 4235

Types of Bank Canvas

(1) There are basically two types of bank canvassing that may be made. These are either by mail or by personal visit to the banks. When canvassing by mail, a letter should state that the information being requested is in connection with an official investigation under the authority granted by IRC 7602. A return addressed envelope, which requires no postage, should be enclosed. The request for information should be specific and complete as discussed in 691 above. When paying a personal visit to the bank, the same type of letter should be prepared and presented to the bank officer with whom you are dealing. This type of canvassing provides the means for examining the files personally.

(2) Certain banks will ask for service of a summons before permitting an examination of the taxpayer's account. An agent should comply with such a request. Carefully follow the proper procedures for preparation of summons, taking into account any and all records that might in any way be available and pertinent to your investigation.

693 *(4-11-80)* 4235

Out-of-State Banks

During an investigation of the taxpayer's records, information might be discovered pertaining to out-of-State banks. In order to facilitate locating such banks, refer to the listing of The Numerical System of The American Bankers Association included as Exhibit 600–9.

6(10)0 *(4-11-80)* 4235

Surveillance

(1) Sometimes the only way to get any information on a particular taxpayer may be through means of surveillance. When an investigation has reached a dead end as to where an individual earns his/her income, or what activities he/she is involved in that lead to income, surveillance of that individual might provide the answer.

(2) Some other reasons for conducting a surveillance might be: to locate hidden assets, to locate persons or interests of a taxpayer by

observing his/her associates, or places they frequent, to verify information from a confidential source to develop leads and information received from other sources, to obtain detailed information about a subject's activities, such as customers, and to obtain information for later use in questioning.

(3) A request for surveillance must be in writing, and must be in connection with an official investigation in progress. It should state all the particulars, including the reasons why surveillance is believed necessary. The request should be cleared with the Field Examination Group Manager before submission to the Chief, Examination Division, for approval. The approved requests will be forwarded to the Chief, Criminal Investigation Division, who will make a determination whether a surveillance will be undertaken. If undertaken, the matter will be formally referred to Intelligence in accordance with IRM 4565.21.

6(11)0 *(4-11-80)* 4235
Percentage Markup

6(11)1 *(4-11-80)* 4235
Introduction

The markup method is considered to be the least maintainable method of determining gross receipts and should be used only as a last resort. However, when properly used and applied to businesses, such as bars, furniture stores, etc., whose purchases can be more readily broken down in groups with approximately the same percentage of markup, this method may be effectively used. This method can be used only if purchases and/or sales can be determined.

◄ The *percentage method* is not a prime method of proof and by itself would be of very little value in criminal cases. However, there have been cases in which taxes and penalties based on this kind of circumstantial evidence have been sustained by the tax court. The percentage method is very useful for test checking; for corroborating the results obtained by some other means of proof such as the specific item, net worth, expenditures, and bank deposits methods; and for evaluating allegations from informants regarding unreported profits or the income of others.

6(11)2 *(4-11-80)* 4235
Records of Purchases Available

(1) If the records of purchases are available, the purchases should be grouped in items with the same percentage of markup. The appropriate percentage of markup should then be applied to each group of items to arrive at the gross receipts.

(2) If the taxpayer cooperates, it is preferable to determine the percentage of markup from selling prices obtained from the taxpayer. However, if cooperation is lacking the information should be obtained from competitive businesses in the same general locality.

(3) Once a gross receipts amount has been determined, the taxpayer should be afforded an opportunity to explain any discrepancies between the reconstructed receipts and the amounts indicated by the records and the income tax return. The taxpayer may argue that the percentage markup should not be applied to merchandise stolen, broken, spoiled or taken for personal usage.

(4) The purchase records may be available and the taxpayer may be cooperative; nevertheless, it behooves the agent to always think of items which have not been recorded. There have been cases where both the purchases and the related sales were not recorded. Therefore, when reconstructing income using the markup method, possible unrecorded purchases should be considered.

6(11)3 *(4-11-80)* 4235

Records of Receipts Available

When the records for gross receipts are available in an examination, but purchases cannot be ascertained, the reverse procedure to a markup case cannot be applied to determine the cost of sales. This approach can only be used if the receipts are the result of sales of merchandise with a fairly uniform percentage of markup. To determine the cost of sales when both the sales and percentage of markup are known the sales are divided by a divisor which represents the sum of the percentage of markup plus 100.

6(12)0 *(4-11-80)* 4235

Bad Debts and Interest Expenses

(1) Even though the tax treatment is different, a bad debt could be the result of either a business or a nonbusiness transaction. The distinguishing feature between a business and non-business bad debt and their respective tax treatment is generally known. Here the discussion is limited to possible transactions created and used for tax purposes and disguised in the form of bad debts.

(2) Before it can become "bad" a debt has to exist. In order for a debt to exist, a transaction, either in the form of a loan or sale, had to occur. The occurrence had to happen with the expectation of receiving payment without any attached contingency, and with expectation of collecting, based on the borrower's financial condition when loan or sale is made. Many

◀ This method of computation involves percentages or ratios considered typical of the business under investigation. By reference to similar businesses or situations, percentage computations are secured to determine sales, cost of sales, gross profit, or even net profit. Likewise, by the use of some known base and the applicable percentage, individual items of income or expense may be determined.

lower echelon members of organized crime never accumulate any tangible wealth or recorded assets; therefore, they may never be sued for collection. A fictitious loan to these individuals could easily be converted into a deductible bad debt. If money is supposedly loaned to one of these individuals when the borrower is in a non-collectible status the resulting bad debt deduction should be thoroughly analyzed. The instrument which created the debt should be scrutinized to determine if the loan calls for the payment of interest at the then normal rate. If the instrument calls for periodic interest payments, it should be determined if these payments are met and, if not, whether they were ever made and how soon after the transaction they ceased to be made.

(3) Interest expenses claimed as deductions in returns examined should be closely scrutinized to determine their validity.

(4) The interest deduction could be a disguise for repayments of a non-existent loan. It could also represent payments to loan sharks. Therefore, the identity of the payment recipient should be ascertained, the existence of a true legal debt ascertained, and, if the amount in question warrants, it should also be established if the recipient is reporting the interest.

6(13)0 *(4-11-80)* 4235

Analysis of Gross Profit and Expense Ratios

(1) Since some individuals, particularly those engaged in illegal activities try to avoid examination of their tax returns, they have endeavored to file better balanced returns. This is accomplished by spreading the falsification of records over many items of expenses as well as sales and purchases.

(2) This is not to imply that cost of goods sold should not be closely analyzed but to emphasize the need for close scrutiny of deductions as well as sales.

(3) Of the many ways of falsifying sales, the three examples that follow have been extremely successful:

(a) the sale of scrap or a by-product of the business in which the owner, corporate officer, etc. will insist that payment will be made to him in cash.

(b) Payment for services will be made in the form of household products, such as furniture, appliances, etc., the cost of which is never reported as income.

(c) Payment for services or a product will be made to a third party ostensibly to repay a debt but in reality the third party is a conduit to divert income.

(4) These schemes and others can only be uncovered by in-depth investigations into the individuals' activities.

(5) This same determination must be generated in examining purchase invoices and expense items. This gives the subject a wider area to manipulate and not create a questionable ratio in any one expense item.

(6) Purchases is usually one of the larger items (by ratio) on the return and is the catch-all for the acquisition of personal assets, including stocks, bonds, mink coats, furniture, household goods, etc. Experience has shown that household food bills have been charged to purchases.

(7) By preparation of fictitious purchase invoices, a taxpayer may divert income to his personal use or create a condition whereby he can receive tax benefit for illegal payoffs and kickbacks. One audit uncovered a scheme in which a corporation was formed that consisted of an address, a phone number, a bank account, and a letter head. The president of this fictitious corporation prepared bills to contractors for materials allegedly supplied. The contractors sent checks which were deposited in the corporate bank account. The corporate president would immediately write a check to cash for 90 percent of the check received, cash the check and with it pay off municipal officials. If it were not for the curiosity of the agent to question the ratio of materials purchased for a particular job and tracing the checks, the scheme might still be in operation.

(8) No item is immune to possible falsification. The agents pre-audit and audit investigation plan should reflect close scrutiny of expense items and look for the following:

(a) missing invoices;

(b) missing checks;

(c) checks to cash;

(d) regular payments of the same amounts for an expense item;

(e) names and aliases of all members of the family on the payroll. In line with that, an unannounced visit to the place of business to inspect the premises and observe the operation may prove fruitful;

(f) careful scrutiny of even the smallest checks for leads.

(g) Any discrepancy should be pursued.

6(14)0 *(4-11-80)* 4235
Clearance Prior to Closing

(1) The closing of an in-depth audit investigation involves several factors not present in the closing of the ordinary audit. As stated in the introduction of this Handbook, the ideal conclusion of any in-depth audit investigation should be to obtain facts to establish the taxpayers' correct tax liability. However, when warranted, in-depth audit cases should be referred to the Criminal Investigation Division in accordance with IRM 4565.21. Because by these highly sophisticated techniques being frequently employed, these cases will serve particularly well the deterrent goal of criminal prosecution.

(2) Prior to closing the examination of a Strike Force case which has not been the subject of a joint investigation, the examiner, through appropriate channels, will contact the Strike Force representative to determine if there is any additional information on the taxpayer. The Strike Force representative may have received information or allegations on the taxpayer which may have not been considered in the examination. There are other Federal agencies cooperating in the Strike Force. The Revenue Agent during his/her examination may discover a violation of laws which are enforced by another Federal agency. The Strike Force representative is responsible for coordination with these agencies. If no additional information is obtained from the Strike Force representative, the examiner and his group manager will make the decision to close the case.

(3) If the in-depth audit of a subject results in a fraud referral to the Criminal Investigation Division the case will follow the usual practice and procedure in IRM 4565 and thereafter resume as a joint investigation.

(4) When the revenue agent completes an investigation of a Strike Force subject, with no fraud referral involved, and he/she feels the case should be closed, he/she will discuss the case with his/her group manager. The report and the administrative file will be reviewed to ensure total fulfillment of Strike Force objectives and consideration of all Strike Force data. An additional purpose of the review will be to determine what information may be of interest to other enforcement agencies cooperating in the Strike Force operations and to ensure maximum use of intelligence made available by oth-

er enforcement agencies. See 442.5 of this Handbook and IRM 4097.

(5) It is anticipated that the transmittal letter on a Strike Force case will be in detail and may contain schedules and exhibits of all items of information or allegations and all items in the investigative plan should be commented upon. Strike Force reports will be prepared on Form 4665 (Report Transmittal) and Form 4549-A (Income Tax Examination Changes) rather than Form 4549 (Income Tax Examination Changes).

(6) After the Strike Force Representative concurs with the RAR, the RAR and administrative file will be reviewed and concurred with by the Criminal Investigation function. Any exceptions taken by the Criminal Investigation function will be resolved through district procedures.

(7) If all exceptions are removed the approved RAR will then be returned to the agent and he/she can attempt to close the case and solicit the agreement in accordance with established procedures. If exceptions cannot be resolved the case should be referred to Criminal Investigation.

Exhibit 600–1

Net Worth Computation

◇

Assets	12-31-76	12-31-77	12-31-78
Cash on Hand	$ 1,000	$ 500	$ 1,500
Cash in Banks	15,000	20,000	22,500
Securities	22,000	18,500	18,500
Inventory	37,500	42,500	55,000
Loans and Accounts Receivable	34,000	35,000	38,000
Furniture and Fixtures	7,500	7,500	9,000
Real Estate	45,000	45,000	70,000
Personal Automobiles	6,000	6,000	7,000
Total Assets	$168,000	$175,000	$221,500
Liabilities			
Accounts Payable	$ 4,000	$ 3,500	$ 3,500
Notes Payable	-0-	10,000	5,000
Mortgage Payable	35,000	22,000	40,000
Accumulated Depreciation	4,000	4,500	5,500
Total Liabilities	$ 43,000	$ 40,000	$ 54,000
Net Worth	$125,000	$135,000	$167,500
Less: Prior Year's Net Worth		125,000	135,000
Increase in Net Worth		$ 10,000	$ 32,500
Adjustments to Increase Net Worth (Exhibit 600–2)		16,600	15,000
		$ 26,600	$ 47,500
Adjustments to Decrease Net Worth (Exhibit 600–3)		5,600	14,900
Corrected Adjusted Gross Income		$ 21,000	$ 32,600
Adjustments to Arrive at Taxable Income (Exhibit 600–4)		1,500	4,550
Corrected Taxable Income		$ 19,500	$ 28,050

Exhibit 600–2

Adjustments to Increase Net Worth (Nondeductible Items)

	12–31–77	12–31–78
Personal Living Expenses (below)	$14,000	$12,300
Federal Income Tax	1,100	1,000
Nondeductible Capital Loss	-0-	500
Nondeductible Personal Loss	-0-	1,200
Gifts Made	1,500	-0-
Total Adjustments	$16,600	$15,000
Personal Living Expenses		
Food	$ 3,000	$ 3,500
Outside Meals	100	100
Home Repairs	1,900	100
Utilities	200	250
Domestic Help	500	-0-
Auto Expenses	1,700	1,750
Department Store Purchases	1,200	100
Recreation and Entertainment	1,100	100
Vacation	2,300	-0-
Contributions	500	500
Interest	-0-	1,000
Taxes	500	1,500
Medical	1,000	400
Alimony	-0-	3,000
Total Personal Living Expenses	$14,000	$12,300

◇

Exhibit 600–3

Adjustments to Decrease Net Worth (Nontaxable Items)

	12–31–77	12–31–78
Nontaxable Capital Gain (Section 1202 Deduction)	$5,000	$ -0-
Tax-exempt Interest	500	500
Social Security	-0-	1,200
Dividend Exclusion	100	100
Life Insurance Proceeds	-0-	8,100
Inheritance	-0-	5,000
Total Adjustments	$5,600	$14,900

◇

Exhibit 600–4

Adjustments to Arrive at Taxable Income ◊

Itemized or Standard Deduction:	12–31–77	12–31–78
Contributions	$ 500	$ 500
Interest	–0–	1,000
Taxes	500	1,500
Medical (net of limitation)	370	–0–
Alimony	–0–	3,000
Total Itemized Deductions	$1,370	$6,000
Excess Itemized Deductions	$ –0–	$3,800
Exemptions	1,500	750
Total Adjustments	$1,500	$4,550

Exhibit 600–5

Statement of Estimated Living Expenses ◊

For ______________________ for year ending ____________

ITEM	MONTHLY By Cash	MONTHLY By Check	YEARLY By Cash	YEARLY By Check
Food (groceries, etc.)				
Outside meals				
Clothing				
Medical & dental expenses				
Rent or mortgage payments				
Repairs (home)				
Improvements (home)				
Home furnishings and appliances				
Utilities (gas, electricity, water, etc.)				
Telephone				
Laundry, dry cleaning				
Domestic help, FICA tax				
Auto expense (repairs, maintenance, etc.)				
Commuting expense				
Recreations—entertainment				
Vacation—travel				
Education				
Insurance (life, medical, auto, home, etc.)				
Dues (club, lodge, union, etc.)				
Taxes (Federal, state, local)				
Contributions				
Gifts and allowances				
Alimony				
Child Support				
Personal (tobacco, liquor, barber, beauty shop, cosmetics, etc.)				
Child care				
Miscellaneous				
Total Cash				
Total Checks				
Total Estimated Living Expenses				

Exhibit 600–6

Example of Application of Funds Method ◊

Funds Applied	19	
Increase in cash on hand	1,000.00	
Increase in cash in banks	5,000.00	
Increase in accounts receivable	1,369.27	
Increase in loans receivable	3,000.00	
Increase in inventory	890.96	
Increase in stocks and bonds	273.28	
Increase in furniture and fixtures	1,100.00	
Increase in real estate	15,000.00	
Increase in personal automobile	1,000.00	
Decrease in accounts payable	500.00	
Decrease in Mortgage payable	13,000.00	
Personal living expenses	7,370.00	
Federal Income Tax Paid	500.00	
Nondeductible loss on bonds	60.00	
Nondeductible capital loss	1,200.00	
Nondeductible personal loss	1,500.00	
Gifts Made	1,100.00	
		$53,863.51
Sources of Funds		
Decrease in cash on hand	1,100.00	
Decrease in bank balance	2,059.07	
Decrease in securities	3,500.00	
Increase in accounts payable	821.17	
Increase in notes payable	2,100.00	
Increase in mortgages payable	7,822.33	
Increase in accrued payroll taxes	95.78	
Increase in accumulated depreciation	920.00	
Nontaxable portion of capital gain	3,035.38	
Tax exempt interest	75.00	
Social Security	1,200.00	
Veteran's pension	380.00	
Dividend exclusion	200.00	
Inheritance	1,000.00	
		$24,308.73
Adjusted gross income as corrected		29,554.78
Less: Excess Itemized deductions	2,600.00	
Personal exemptions	1,500.00	4,100.00
Taxable income as corrected		25,454.78
Taxable income per return		15,161.48
Understatement of taxable income		$10,293.30

Exhibit 600–7

Cash Transactions (T) Account ◊

Computation
After the pre-contact analysis has been made, prepare a "T" account and enter the known items from the return. The remainder are added after the interview and after the books and records have been examined. An example follows:

"T" ACCOUNT

Gross Receipts (Per Return)	Business expenses (less depreciation)
Gross Rents	Rental expenses (less depreciation)
Miscellaneous Income	Personal living expenses
Interest Income and Dividends	Purchase of assets
Cash on hand (at beginning of year)	Cash on hand (at the end of year)
Cash in banks (at beginning of year)	Cash in banks (at the end of year)
Loans	Loan Payments
Accounts receivable (at beginning of year)	Accounts receivable (at the end of year)
Accounts payable (at the end of year)	Accounts payable (at beginning of year)
Nontaxable income	
Wages	

Only items representing cash transactions should be entered.

(A)

Adjustments are needed if the taxpayer is on an accrual basis. Beginning and year-end balances of accounts receivable and accounts payable must be entered. Accounts receivable are the same as cash and are similarly entered, with the beginning balance on the debit side of the "T" Account. Accounts payable are the reverse. The ending balance is a debit, since it represents expenses deducted but not paid and, therefore, does not require cash.

(B)

Only those dividends representing cash payments should be entered. Neither the exclusion nor dividends reinvested appear.

(C)

Cash on hand or cash hoard represents the money which the taxpayer has on his/her person, a safe deposit box or any other place for safekeeping.

(D)

Cash in banks requires several adjustments, as the bank statements do not reflect checks or deposits which have not cleared the bank at beginning and year end. (Reconciled balances)

(E)

Business expenses do not include such items as depreciation, bad debts, spoilage, inventory, etc., as they do not represent cash transactions.

(F)

Loan payments and specific asset purchases should be checked carefully to avoid duplication.

(G)

Personal withdrawals affect the figure entered for purchases. Enter the net figure in business expenses. Personal withdrawals will be picked up later in the personal living expenses figure.

Exhibit 600–8

Computation of Available Cash

INCOME

Gross Receipts—Business Schedules
Gross Receipts—Rental Schedules

Wages

Proceeds from Sale of Assets
Other Income:
—Interest
—Gross Dividends (Gross Distributions)
—Total Pensions and Annuities
—Alimony
—Partnership and 1120–S Income
—Directors Fees
—Prizes and Awards
—Other Receipts

TOTAL RECEIPTS—

DISBURSEMENTS

Expenses Paid—Business Schedules (Purchases and Other Expenses—Depreciation)

Expenses Paid—Rental Schedules (Do not include Depreciation)

Schedule "A" Deductions (Not including casualty losses, depreciation or non-cash contributions)

1% and 3% Medical Expense Limitations to the Extent Applied

Capital Purchases Made During the Year

FICA Taxes Withheld

Investments in Partnerships or Corporations (If determinable)

Other Disbursements per the Return

TOTAL DISBURSEMENTS—

CASH AVAILABLE (Receipts—Disbursements)

Examination Investigative Techniques

710 *(4-11-80)* 4235
Introduction

(1) The audit techniques that an internal revenue agent uses will depend upon the circumstances and alleged enterprises of the specific taxpayer being investigated. Imaginative agents are constantly developing new techniques as their knowledge and awareness of tax avoidance schemes increases.

(2) Within this chapter are techniques which are, or may prove to be, frequently used.

(3) The investigating agent should consider the use of these techniques when applicable but should not consider them all-inclusive. The number of techniques that can be used are endless and grows larger with each examination.

720 *(4-11-80)* 4235
Payroll Padding

721 *(4-11-80)* 4235
Introduction

(1) Payrolls may be padded for numerous reasons; however, the purpose is invariably the same: getting funds out of a business in the form of a deduction without the recipient paying income tax on the income. This method is used mostly where the paying enterprise is in the type of business which does not sell for cash and money can only be taken out by check. This method could be used merely as a tax evasion scheme in order to pay gambling losses or debt to loan sharks or extortion.

(2) Another way to pad the payroll is by having political party workers on the payroll even though the employee performs no services from the payor company.

722 *(4-11-80)* 4235
Investigative Techniques

(1) To detect indications of payroll padding special attention should be focused on payroll records.

(a) If there is a suspicion or knowledge that fictitious employees are being used then the negotiation of the check should be pursued. If checks are cashed in the same bank, payee may be known at the bank. If checks are being cashed through other parties, reendorsers may know the payee.

(b) Forms W-2 returned by the Post Office as being undeliverable. All payroll checks to

◄ The remainder of this section is devoted to various types of tax evasion activities and the IRS techniques for discovering them. While the various scams outlined here make for very interesting reading, there is a certain danger in reproducing this portion of the *Internal Revenue Manual*. While it may certainly give some people ideas of evasive behavior that had never occurred to them before, only those who are so inclined to criminal activity will be so moved to use this material as a guide to such behavior. The purpose in reproducing this material is to demonstrate that there really is "nothing new under the sun," that the IRS has already "seen it all," and that techniques are available for uncovering these scams. The lesson here is simply this: *Don't try it, and don't let others persuade you* that any prospective idea is foolproof.

◄ The scams listed here are the type of activities used by organized crime figures. What is not shown are the myriad of other scams used by people not involved in racketeering, but who are merely trying to evade their full share of taxes. Other portions of the *Internal Revenue Manual* cover the investigative techniques the IRS uses to discover them. Just because you don't see a particular type of evasive activity listed here doesn't mean the IRS doesn't have techniques for uncovering it.

such employees should be thoroughly scrutinized as to their disposition and the route they took back to the bank.

(c) Social security numbers on W-2's and Forms 941 should be checked for their legitimacy. See Exhibit 600-10 and 600-11 for information on social security number structure and validation.

(d) If the company provides or assists in insurance coverage, pension plans, etc., test employee terminations to see if the employee was also withdrawn from the payroll.

(e) A company may continue receiving the check of an employee who has left. Randomly select employees and compare endorsements at different times of the year.

(f) The examining agent should be aware of the possibilities that key employees or officers may be loaned to political parties to perform various services while being paid their salary by their employer. Attempts should be made to determine where the employees' services were performed during the payroll periods in question. Examination of expense reimbursement reports would be of assistance in determining the geographical location of the employee at a particular time. This information may serve as a basis for a follow-up interview of the employee.

730 *(4-11-80)* 4235
Salary Haven

731 *(4-11-80)* 4235
Introduction

There are some prominent figures in organized crime who have no legitimate source of income. Their only means of livelihood is from income realized through illegal activities. Therefore, in order to be able to prove how he/she supports himself/herself and his/her family he/she has to have a source of legitimate income which he/she reports for income tax purposes. He/she accomplishes this by finding a business which is willing to put him/her on the payroll and issue him/her regular payroll checks. These payments are made even though the employee performs no services. The employer normally is a retail outlet owned by or associated with some other member of organized crime. In most cases these payroll

◀ *In-depth examination techniques* involve the uncovering of evidence to prove a violation of the law. This is a good place to discuss the general rules of evidence, and various legal definitions, as espoused in the *Internal Revenue Manual* section for criminal investigations.

◀ *Laws* are rules of conduct which are prescribed or formally recognized as binding, and are enforced by the governing power.

◀ *Common law* comprises the body of principles and rules of action relating to government and the security of persons and property which derive their authority solely from usages and customs or from judgments and decrees of courts recognizing, affirming, and enforcing such usages and customs.

◀ *Statutory law* refers to laws enacted and established by a legislative body. All federal crimes are statutory but common law is frequently resorted to for defining words used in the statutes. For example, statutes provide penalties for attempted evasion of income tax, but they do not define the terms "attempt" and "evasion."

payments are returned to the payer in cash and diverted.

732 *(4-11-80)* 4235
Investigative Techniques

(1) When the entity being examined is suspected of being used as a salary haven by a prominent figure in organized crime, the examining agent should look for certain indications to support the suspicion.

(a) Determine if checks are cashed by the employer.

(b) Establish whether the employee has the qualifications to perform the function for which he/she receives the salary.

(c) If the records indicate that the employee is still on the payroll at time of audit, attempt to establish whether he is actually present on the premises.

(d) If the position held by the employee is that of an outside salesman, determine who supposedly are his/her customers and establish if the employee contacts these customers.

(2) In most salary haven cases the employee's return discloses no other sources of income.

(3) Extend the examination to the suspected prominent figure in organized crime and trace the disposition of his/her payroll checks to determine if any of the money was returned to the corporation.

740 *(4-11-80)* 4235
Shifting of Income and Losses

741 *(4-11-80)* 4235
Introduction

Some taxpayers think nothing of shifting income and losses, to reduce tax or to eliminate tax altogether. They are continually devising new ways of using their businesses as conduits to transfer income to themselves or to their nominees. The criminal element is known to resort to fictitious corporations and to corporations in foreign countries. This is a big aid to them in tax evasion, because the financial transactions there are cloaked by the secrecy afforded by foreign law. Also in certain foreign countries, if the corporation or individual has a bank account, the fruits of the crime are readily hidden, because of the strict bank secrecy rules. The problem is not confined to Switzer-

◀ *Criminal law* is that branch of law which defines crimes and provides punishments.

◀ *Civil law* relates to the establishment, recovery, or redress of private and civil rights.

◀ *An act is a crime* against the United States only if committed or omitted in violation of a statute forbidding or commanding it, or in violation of a regulation having legislative authority. Crimes are classified and defined in *Section 1, Title 18, U.S. Code,* as follows: "Notwithstanding any Act of Congress to the contrary:

(1) Any offense punishable by death or imprisonment for a term exceeding one year is a felony.
(2) Any other offense is a misdemeanor.
(3) Any misdemeanor, the penalty for which does not exceed imprisonment for a period of six months or a fine of not more than $500, or both, is a petty offense."

◀ *A principal* as defined by *Section 2, Title 18,* is one who commits an offense against the United States; aids, abets, counsels, commands, induces, or procures its commission; or willfully causes an act to be done which if directly performed by him or another would be an offense against the United States.

◀ An *aider* or *abettor* may be convicted even if the person who commits the offense has not been indicted, tried, or convicted *(Gray* v. *U.S.; Beauchamp* v. *U.S.).* One who causes a criminal act may be convicted even if the performer of the act is acquitted *(U.S.* v. *Lester).*

land, as similar secrecy prevails in Lichtenstein, Panama, and the Bahamas.

742 *(4-11-80)* 4235
Examples

(1) One of the most common ways to reduce the income tax in a profitable business is to create additional corporations, either foreign or domestic. The one common characteristic of such entities is that they are really shells, which have form on paper only, and have no substance in fact. They may not have an office. They usually will have a post office box. They have one employee or in many cases, none at all. The billing, mailing, planning, correspondence, and all other work will normally be handled out of the parent office. The examining agent should determine where all the paper work is done, whether the entity really exists and is in fact active in a business, and whether or not the entity is acting as a conduit for the flow of funds back to the parent or to some individuals. Generally, the system of internal control the business has established (even if informal or ineffective) will ordinarily prevent the diversion of receipts for a variety of reasons. However, this is not the case with expenditures (purchases, expenses, and payables). The diversion of funds from the business by the employer via the use of seemingly legitimate invoices for goods and services to his/her shell entity is easily accomplished and difficult to discover.

(2) Another method used to shift income has been the use of false or fictitious sales or purchase prices between a parent and its affiliates, or between corporations by a controlling stockholder. As an example, in one instance the parent corporation arranged for an affiliate to purchase its product at cost, plus 10 percent. This price was less than 10 percent of the parent's regular list price for its product. In effect this resulted in a commission of over 90 percent to the affiliate. This was not an arm's-length transaction, and did not clearly reflect true income. Of course, if evidence is found of billing of goods on paper, but where no purchases were actually made and no merchandise delivered, this would constitute out-right fraud. The padding of the Cost of Sales Account by a parent through overpayments or premium payments to an affiliate has the same effect.

◀ Acquittal of one mistakenly charged with commission of a crime does not affect the guilt of one proved to have aided and abetted, so long as it is established that the crime was committed by someone *(Von Patzoll* v. *U.S.; Legatos* v. *U.S.).*

◀ To *aid and abet,* a defendant must associate himself with a venture, whether or not there is a conspiracy, and try to make it succeed. Thus, in *U.S.* v. *Johnson,* where the crime of attempted tax evasion by the main defendant was based on alleged concealment of his interest in, and income from, gambling clubs, his co-defendants were held to be guilty because they consciously were parties to the concealment by pretending to be proprietors even if they did not actually share in the making of false returns. A defendant charged with aiding and abetting in bribery need not have been present when the bribe was paid *(Daniels* v. *U.S.).*

◀ A *principal* is not liable for a crime committed by an agent solely because of the relationship. He will be liable only if the act of the agent is with his knowledge or consent or he otherwise comes within the provisions of *Section 2, Title 18.* The agent, himself, is criminally responsible for his own actions.

◀ A person becomes an *accessory after the fact,* if, with knowledge of the commission of a crime, he or she assists in preventing or hindering the apprehension, trial or punishment of the perpetrator *(18 USC 3).* Suppressing important evidence also comes within this category *(Neal* v. *U.S.).* A person is guilty of *misprision of felony* if he or she has knowledge of the actual commission of a felony, conceals it, and does not make this known to a person in authority as soon as possible *(18 USC 4).*

◀ A corporation can be prosecuted for the criminal acts of its officers concerning corporate affairs, but the only possible punishment is by fine. However, the officers themselves are also criminally liable for these same acts *(Currier Lumber Co.* v. *U.S.).*

(3) Some parent companies do all of the buying of supplies, pay for all of the advertising, insurance, and other expenses of its affiliates, but they fail to allocate the proper shares of the expenses to the affiliates. They thus reduce their taxes by claiming additional expenses which are not really theirs. Of course the affiliate is probably already in a negative taxable position, and the additional expenses would not help it. The examining agent can best spot this condition by inspecting invoices to see where the merchandise was delivered, or where or for whom the services were performed. If the invoices are not made available, the agent can determine this condition by checking with the suppliers or vendors.

(4) Another method of shifting income occurs where materials are delivered to an affiliate, but the entire billing is made to the parent. The parent firm pays the bill, charging its purchases, but does not bill the affiliate, even though the latter received the materials. This situation can best be detected by inspection of invoices, preferably at the taxpayer's office, but if not, at the office of the supplier.

(5) A method used by some firms to reduce their taxes is to pay huge interest expense on sham notes. Was the loan necessary and did it in fact exist? This is pure out and out shifting of income from a profitable entity to one not as profitable. Was the rate of interest comparable to prevailing rates? The examining agent should determine whether loans were actually made, whether they were necessary, and ascertain the source of the funds. He/she should also examine the notes, and verify to see whether payments were actually made, or whether they were merely entries.

(6) Taxpayers have been using yet another method with great success. First they acquire a business in the U.S., which sells products in Europe. Then they obtain a secret bank account, either in their own name, or in the name of the business. After sales are made, they submit two invoices to the customer. They ask the foreign customer to pay the lower amount

Evidence (General Rules)

Definition of Evidence

◀ *Evidence* is all the means by which any alleged matter or fact, the truth of which is submitted to investigation, is established or disproved. Investigators obtain evidentiary facts that by inference tend to prove or disprove the ultimate, main, or principal fact. The latter is a matter for determination by a court or a jury. For example, a special agent obtains, in connection with a net worth case, documents and oral statements showing that a taxpayer's bank balance has increased substantially. That is an evidentiary fact from which an inference may be drawn relative to the ultimate or principal fact, namely, that the taxpayer willfully attempted to evade income tax. Legal evidence is such as is admissible in court under the rules of evidence, because it tends reasonably and substantially to prove a fact. Evidence is distinguished from proof in that the latter is the result or effect of evidence.

◀ *Direct evidence* is that which, if believed, proves the existence of the principal or ultimate fact without any inference or presumption. It is direct when the very facts in dispute are sworn to by those who have actual knowledge of them by means of their senses. It may take the form of admissions or confessions made in or out of court.

◀ *Circumstantial evidence* is that which tends to prove the existence of the principal fact by inference. The use of circumstantial evidence is recognized by the courts as a legitimate means of proof, and involves proving several material facts which, when considered in their relationship to each other, tend to establish the existence of the principal or ultimate fact. In the absence of a confession of a witness to whom the violator has expressed his intent, violations involving willful intent are proved by circumstantial evidence. Indeed, it is the only type of evidence generally available to show such elements of a crime as malice, intent, or motive, which exist only in the mind of the perpetrator of the deed.

The proof of most Internal Revenue violations, therefore, is based on circumstantial evidence. Circumstantial evidence includes direct testimony as to secondary facts which are relied on to establish the main fact in issue. For example, in a tax evasion case, a taxpayer's customer testifies that he or she paid $10,000 for merchandise and a government agent testifies that the payment does not appear on the taxpayer's books and tax re-

directly to the business and the balance to the secret bank account. They thus effectively shift the income from the local business to the foreign depository. This scheme has been used quite well in the opposite direction also. When buying products abroad, the seller is asked to submit an overstated invoice, with the understanding that when it is paid, the difference over the true cost will be transmitted to the secret bank account.

(7) Another method used to shift income was through the creation of a foreign corporation. The officers who controlled the corporation directed that commissions and fees which they earned here, were to be sent to their corporation, on the pretext that the foreign corporation had earned the income. Another variation of this scheme is to direct commissions or fees to a Lichtenstein trust. The trust deposits the funds in the account of the taxpayer. The same results are obtained when a controlling stockholder of a closely held corporation, causes the corporation to pay commissions or amounts said to represent business expenses to a foreign national. The foreign national then forwards the money to a foreign bank account to the credit of the controlling stockholder, or his/her nominee. The investigating agent should examine all foreign payments and invoices in a highly inquisitive and detailed fashion.

(8) An example of shifting a loss occurred where a company that purchased a profitable business, altered the books of the business it bought, to show a loss for the current year. It then absorbed the loss and merged it with its own operations. It thus effectively shifted a "loss" to itself to reduce its tax. How was this accomplished? Who ordered it? The agent's documentation of the alteration of the books and pertinent excerpts from correspondence or memos concerning the alteration, could provide evidence necessary to arrive at correct income and tax.

turns. Those facts constitute direct evidence of the omission of $10,000 in income but not of the main issue, which is, "Did the defendant willfully attempt to evade income tax?"

- In addition to proving intent (a subject covered in greater detail later in the text on willfulness), circumstantial evidence is also frequently used to prove unreported income as shown by increases in net worth, expenditures, or bank deposits.
- Circumstantial evidence may be as cogent and convincing as direct evidence and the jury may properly find that it outweighs conflicting direct evidence. However, the inference must be based on convincing facts and must be a more probable and natural one than other explanations offered. The Supreme Court in the Holland case stated as follows:

> Circumstantial evidence in this respect is intrinsically no different from testimonial evidence. Admittedly, circumstantial evidence may in some cases point to a wholly incorrect result. Yet this is equally true of testimonial evidence. In both instances, a jury is asked to weigh the chances of the evidence's correctly pointing to guilt against the possibility of inaccuracy or ambiguous inference. In both, the jury must use its experience with people and events in weighing the probabilities. If the jury is convinced beyond a reasonable doubt, we can require no more.

(9) Some corporations have been found to shift income and losses by the devices of having officers and stockholders improperly filing partnership returns. The business of the "partnership" is really that of the corporation. The corporate officers or its principal stockholders thus shift the corporate loss to reduce their own income or its profit to evade the corporate tax. An example of this type of income shifting is demonstrated by the following. The stockholders of a corporation engaged in coal mining, formed a partnership to mine coal on the corporation's coal lands. The corporation purchased the partnership's entire production. The corporation also entered into agreements with nonrelated contract miners to mine coal on the corporation's coal lands. The corporation also purchased the entire production of these contractors. The examining agent recognized the close relationship between the corporation and the partnership and decided to examine in detail, all transactions between the two entities. A comparison of cost of contract coal to the cost of partnership coal, disclosed that the corporation was paying the partnership substantially more per ton for its production, than was being paid to the nonrelated contractors. The corporation thereby shifted its profits directly to the stockholders and evaded the corporate tax. This method is frequently resorted to by the criminal element. How can this sort of shifting be uncovered? Was the partnership legal? The examining agent should verify the authenticity of the partnership, its office, its business, its name, its number of years in business, and its actual transactions by tracing them through third parties, if necessary.

(10) The simplest and most expedient method of shifting losses to profitable affiliates is by book entries, usually at the end of a year. Allocations are made of expenses, materials, supplies, or overhead, whether appropriate or not. This can best be spotted by full inspection of all entries, their explanations, the basis for allocation, the reasons for, and at whose instigation were such entries made, and comparison to see if the entries are consistent with prior years' practices and the facts.

◀ *Evidence may be positive or negative*—Evidence is positive when it relates to proof that a fact did or did not happen or exist. Evidence is negative when a witness states that he does not have knowledge of the happening or existence of a fact or circumstance. Examples of the latter are testimony that the records of a District Director show that the taxpayer filed a return and testimony of an agent that he examined records relating to real estate, bank accounts, and other assets in a given area and did not find any additional assets at the starting point. Positive evidence is stronger than negative evidence. In the Holland case the Supreme Court held that proof of a likely source of unreported income was sufficient to convict in a net worth case without negating all possible nontaxable sources of the alleged net worth increases. However, certain facts can be shown only by negative evidence. In the Massei case the Supreme Court held that proof of a likely source of unreported income is not necessary where all possible sources of nontaxable income were negated.

◀ *Evidence also may be classified as oral, documentary, and real.* Evidence may be presented orally through witnesses, or by the introduction of records or other physical objects. Oral testimony consists of statements made by living witnesses under oath or affirmation. Documentary evidence consists of writings such as judicial and official records, contracts, deeds, and less formal writings such as letters, memorandums, and books and records of private persons and organizations. Maps, diagrams, and photographs are classed as documentary evidence. Real or physical, sometimes called demonstrative evidence, relates to tangible objects or property which are admitted in court or inspected by a trier of facts.

(11) The use of loan and exchange accounts to hide various types of illegal activities and unreported income is increasing. Detailed analysis of deposit tickets and follow through of disbursements, particularly checks to cash, will be necessary to uncover such schemes. In certain instances, interviews of individuals at both ends of the transactions may be required. Agents should be alert to use of loans and exchange accounts for:

(a) hiding gross receipts
(b) land sharking
(c) money laundering
(d) slush funds

743 *(4-11-80)* 4235

Investigative Techniques

(1) In addition to the usual audit techniques, the following investigative techniques are suggested:

(a) Analyze bank transfers, both foreign and domestic.

(b) Examine any of the taxpayer's dealings with the U.S. branch of Swiss Banks or with U.S. correspondents of foreign banks.

(c) Examine details of exchange charges, cable or transmission charges, advisory service charges, and telephone toll slips, particularly for overseas calls.

(d) Examine travel vouchers, especially those for foreign trips.

(e) Examine cancelled checks for leads to affiliates, or to foreign entities.

(f) Take affidavits from the responsible officers or employees regarding shifting of income or expense.

(g) Examination Techniques to discover shell entity:

1 Scan check register for unusual payee names, even amounts, frequency, compare to cancelled check and inspect deposit stamp.

2 Select sample based on above and compare to accounts payable debit.

3 Enlarging on the first sample, compare to invoices.

4 Note description of goods/services, address of vendor (is it foreign?), P.O. Box, if in city-check city directory, lack of freight billing for goods, and exchange for foreign goods.

Relevancy and Competency of Evidence

◀ To be admissible, evidence must be relevant and competent. If a fact offered in evidence relates in some logical way to the principal fact, it is *relevant*. The word relevant implies a traceable and significant connection. A fact need not bear directly on the principal fact, but can constitute one link in a chain of evidence or relate to facts which would constitute circumstantial evidence that a fact in issue did or did not exist. One fact is logically relevant to another if, taken by itself or in connection with other facts, it proves or tends to prove the existence of the other fact. If the fact is logically relevant, it is also legally relevant unless it is barred by some rule of evidence. The principal question to be resolved in determining relevancy is: "Would the evidence be helpful to the finder of the fact in resolving the issue?" *(Rule 401, Federal Rules of Evidence)*

◀ The terms relevant and competent are not synonymous. Evidence must not only be logically relevant and sufficiently persuasive but also legally admissible, in other words, *competent*. Relevant evidence may be incompetent and hence inadmissible because it is hearsay, or not the best evidence.

5 Make use of an individually prepared letter under authority of Section 7601. Send it to selected vendors requesting verification. This is quite similar to certified audit procedures on verification of receivables. This is a very efficient method in that it takes little time to accomplish. In particular, follow up on no response, responses without letterhead, and undeliverable responses.

6 Check selected payees for state corporate filings to ascertain incorporators.

7 Test payroll records for nonexistent employees, examine rental arrangements of facilities, determine if the rent is reasonable and if the rental income was reported by the owner.

8 Note the authorized signatures on pertinent documents.

9 Examine the records of quit claims, deeds, judgments, and transfers back of properties.

10 Determine the eventual recipients of funds, assets, or business, etc.,

750 *(4-11-80)* 4235
Nominee Ownerships

751 *(4-11-80)* 4235
Introduction

The real and controlling ownership of funds, deeds, properties, businesses, bank accounts, options, contracts, stocks, or partnership interests, etc., will quite often be someone other than the owner of record. There are many different types of nominee ownerships and reasons for them, some obvious, and some not so obvious, some legitimate, and some illegitimate. Organized crime frequently resorts to nominee ownerships to conceal its interests. For example, convicted felons are prohibited by law from holding a liquor license in most jurisdictions, so they use nominees. This presents a real challenge to investigating agents to be able to ferret out the true owners. There follows below a description of some of the types of nominee ownerships, their purposes, and some suggestions on how to look for them.

752 *(4-11-80)* 4235
Types

(1) There are many different forms the nominee ownership may take. In its most expedient and trusted form the title of property or other assets might be placed in the name of a close relative. Many racketeers have been known to secrete assets in the name of a trusted friend or

◀ The word "irrelevant" usually refers more particularly to the statement sought to be elicited. Although incompetency may relate to documents, in many cases it may go to the person of the witness in that he or she may be under some disability that prevents him or her from testifying in the particular case. For example, a person is not competent to testify if he or she does not understand the nature of an oath or is unable to narrate with understanding the facts he or she has seen.

◀ As applied to evidence such as documents, evidence is competent if it was obtained in a manner, in a form, and from a source proper under the law. Examples of incompetent evidence are a confession involuntarily obtained or an unsigned carbon copy of a document which is offered without any explanation of the failure to produce the original.

◀ Evidence may have limited admissibility. The fact that certain evidence is not admissible for one purpose, does not preclude its use for another. An evidentiary fact may not be admissible as independent proof of the principal fact and yet be admitted to corroborate or impeach. To illustrate, tax returns for years prior to those in an indictment may be used to corroborate the starting point for a net worth computation although they would not be admissible as proof of the charge of attempted evasion.

◀ A special agent will obtain and report all facts that logically relate to the subject under investigation. The agent should not omit any significant facts because of doubt regarding their relevance. There are no absolute and concrete standards for relevance because the facts vary in each case. Therefore, judges have broad discretion in determining what evidence is relevant. Likewise, the special agent will not omit evidence because of doubt as to its materiality or competency.

associate. Others have used the maiden name of their wife or daughter-in-law.

(2) The underworld proprietors frequently set up operations under a fictitious name. Or they may place the business in an employee's name or in the name of a close associate. Many known criminals place their financial operations in the name and address of their attorney. Contractors have been found to use fictitious subcontractors to hide branches of their operations. There have been many fictitious partnerships used to disguise true ownership. A common ploy is to adopt an alias.

(3) Past experience has shown that commercial and savings bank accounts have often been set up under false names, or under someone else's name. However, actual control of the account will be exercised by the true owner, whether by himself/herself, or through the nominee. Bank accounts in fictitious business names, are quite common, as are U.S. citizens' accounts in foreign banks. Of course, some racketeers have used U.S. depositories for transfers of funds from foreign banks, under assumed names.

(4) U.S. taxpayers who deposit in foreign banks frequently have that bank transfer their funds back to this country to buy real estate in the name of the foreign bank. Ownership of the "transferred assets" then appears in the bank's name. In this manner the foreign depositors have recaptured the use of their secret cash, and have sheltered from U.S. taxation the income from the real estate, and any eventual gain on its sale.

(5) Some taxpayers use closely held corporations as nominee. This is particularly true for individuals in the real estate business. Some individuals have both form 1120 corporation and form 1120–S corporation dealing in real estate. The corporation can then act as nominee or seller and if real estate commissions are paid, all income can be shifted to the taxpayer or corporation that would have the least tax consequences.

753 *(4–11–80)* 4235

Purposes

(1) There are in fact many reasons for nominee ownerships. Some of the more obvious are to reduce taxes or eliminate them entirely, to divert funds illegally, to skim cash, to pay off gambling debts, to claim losses, or to deceive

Judicial Notice

◀ To save time and expense, a trial judge may accept certain facts without requiring proof, if they are commonly and generally known, or can be easily discovered (application of *Knapp-Monarch Co.; Porter* v. *Sunshine Packing Co.*). Judicial notice of such facts takes the place of proof and is of equal force. This does not prevent a party from introducing evidence to dispute the matter (application of *Knapp-Monarch Co., 9 Wigmore on Evid. (3rd Ed.) sec. 2567*).

A matter of judicial notice may be said to have three material requisites:

- It must be a matter of common and general knowledge or capable of accurate and ready demonstration (application of *Knapp-Monarch Co.*);
- It must be well-settled and not uncertain; and
- It must be known to be within the limits of the jurisdiction of the court (*20 Am. Jurisprudence*, Evidence, p.81, sec.59).

◀ A federal court must take judicial notice of such matters as the Constitution, statutes of the United States, including legislative history *(Alaska* v. *American Can Co.),* treaties, contents of the Federal Register, in which the IRS and other administrative regulations are published, and the laws of each state *(Lamar* v. *Micou;* application of *Dandridge*). Laws of foreign jurisdictions are not judicially noticed.

◀ A Federal court will judicially notice its record in the same case *(U.S.* v. *Russell).* It is not required to notice prior litigation in the same court *(Benetti* v. *U.S.),* but may do so under certain circumstances where the prior proceedings are closely related, as in a contempt proceeding *(O'Malley* v. *U.S.).*

the public and particularly the tax collector. Thus two or more businesses can be owned by one person but falsely represented as being owned by others. The profits after payment of minimal taxes by the nominee owners will then be turned over to the true owner.

(2) Some other reasons for nominee ownerships might be simply to hide the true owner, to lend an aura of respectability to the business actually operated by an underworld character, or to make it possible for a racketeer to acquire an interest in a legitimate business, which he/she would not have been able to do under his/her true identity.

(3) Nominee ownerships have been known to be set up for bribery, for political payoffs, for kickbacks, to extract a better price, to use a conduit for illegal payments, to conceal the real buyer of a property or a business, or just to have someone else take the rap for illegal acts.

(4) Quite often individuals will secrete their assets in another's name in event of law suits to prevent attachment, in cases of divorce, at times of impending bankruptcy, or just to reduce the real net worth where the subject is under investigation.

(5) Secret foreign bank accounts figured in the takeover of some corporate ownerships through dummy nominees. Criminal elements have used foreign banks to buy stocks in the banks' names. They would then accumulate the stocks prior to a tender offer to avoid the reporting requirements of securities laws. In some of these instances millions of dollars worth of securities were acquired through secret bank accounts and then were used in subsequent corporate takeovers through dummy nominees.

(6) Another reason for nominee ownership is to facilitate the "laundering" of a large amount of income generated from illegal activities. The laundering or hiding of the source may include a scheme whereby the taxable nature of the money is lost.

754 *(4-11-80)* 4235

Investigative Techniques

(1) Ascertain the source of funds involved in acquiring ownership.

(2) Look behind the transaction for possible undisclosed ownership.

(3) Note any relation to the name owner.

(4) Question the name owner.

◂ Federal courts may also judicially notice such matters as scientific and statistical facts, well-established commercial usages and customs, and historical and geographical facts.

Presumptions

◂ A *presumption* is a rule of law which permits the drawing of a particular inference as to the existence of one fact not certainly known from the existence of other particular facts. Although it is not evidence, it may be considered as a substitute for evidence. Any inference is a permissible deduction from the evidence and may be accepted or rejected by the trier of fact whether it be the court or a jury. It differs from a presumption in that the latter is a rule of law affecting the duty of proceeding with the evidence.

For example, there is a presumption in civil cases that the Commissioner's determination of additional income is correct *(Rule 32, Rules of Practice,* Tax Court: *Welch* v. *Helvering, Botany Mills* v. *U.S.*), although he still has the burden of proving intent to evade tax. However, an *inference* of such intent may arise from certain proved facts. Presumptions may be conclusive or rebuttable.

◂ A *conclusive presumption* is binding upon the court and jury, and evidence in rebuttal is not permitted. For example, it is generally recognized that an infant under the age of seven is conclusively presumed to be incapable of committing a felony.

◂ A *rebuttable presumption* is one which prevails until it is overcome by evidence to the contrary. Some rebuttable presumptions are:

- In criminal cases, a defendant is presumed to be innocent until he is proved guilty beyond a reasonable doubt.

(5) Determine who exercises effective control.

(6) Note who benefits or payouts go to.

(7) Note the authorized signatures on pertinent documents.

(8) Examine the records of quit claims, deeds, judgments, and transfers back of properties.

(9) Determine the eventual recipients of funds, or assets, or business, etc.

760 *(4-11-80)* 4235
False Documents and Statements

761 *(4-11-80)* 4235
General

Agents should be constantly alert to the probability of encountering false documents and statements. During the course of an investigation an agent may find that such documents have been submitted as part of the taxpayer's income tax return. Upon discovery of such documents the revenue agent should immediately refer the matter to Criminal Investigation function in accordance with IRM 4565.21.

762 *(4-11-80)* 4235
Applicable IRC Penalties

(1) Criminal penalties are provided for the submission of a false document in connection with tax matters. Some of these provisions are:

(a) IRC 7205—See (10)20:(4)(e).

(b) IRS 7206—See (10)20:(4)(f).

1 Statutory provisions IRC 7206(l)

a The elements of a criminal violation under IRC 7206(l) are: making and subscribing to a return, statement or other document under penalty of perjury; knowledge that it is not true and correct as to every material matter; and willfulness.

b This Code section imposes the penalty upon a person who willfully falsifies a return as to a material matter, whether or not his/her purpose was to evade or defeat the payment of taxes. Prosecution is appropriate when the Government is able to prove falsity of a partnership return, the issue being falsity rather than evasion. The test of materiality is whether the false statement was material to the contents of the return. It is not necessary that the government actually rely on the statement.

- A presumption as to authenticity of signatures on Internal Revenue documents is covered by *IRC 6064,* which provides: "The fact that an individual's name is signed to a return, statement, or other document shall be prima facie evidence for all purposes that the return, statement or other document was actually signed by him." Presumptions as to the authorization for signing corporation and partnership returns are contained in *IRC 6062* and *6063*.
- It is presumed that public officers perform their duties according to law and do not exceed their authority.
- Every person is presumed to know the law, and ignorance of the law is no excuse for its violation. This presumption does not relieve the government from proving willfulness in criminal actions for violation of the Internal Revenue laws. The defendant may show his misconception of the Internal Revenue law as evidence of his lack of willfulness *(Haigler* v. *U.S.).*
- A person signing an instrument is presumed to have knowledge of its contents.
- A person of ordinary intelligence is presumed to intend the natural and probable consequences of his voluntary acts. Although this presumption in itself will not relieve the burden of proving willfulness, it does operate to permit inferences to be drawn from the acts of the defendant which may constitute the circumstantial proof of willfulness *(McKenna* v. *U.S.).*
- The deductions and exclusions appearing on an income tax return are presumed to be all that exist *(U.S.* v. *Bender).*
- Every person is presumed to be sane.
- Proof that a letter, properly stamped and addressed, was mailed and not returned to the return address creates a presumption that it was received.
- The flight of a person accused of a crime or an attempt to evade arrest may create a presumption of guilt.

c It is sufficient that it be made with the intention of inducing such reliance. Prosecutions under this Code section should involve only false returns or statements presented to or filed with the Internal Revenue Service. This sanction is appropriate when it is possible to prove falsity of a return but difficult to establish evasion of an ascertainable amount of tax, or, when the falsification results in a relatively small amount of tax evasion.

d If an individual files a false and fraudulent return, it is possible for him/her to incur criminal liability for attempting to defeat and evade the tax and for making a false and fraudulent statement under penalty of perjury even though both offenses relate to the same return and the making of the false statement is an incidental step in consummation of the completed offense of attempting to defeat and evade taxes.

2 Statutory Provisions IRC 7206(2)

a The elements of a criminal violation under IRC 7206(2) are: aid, assist, counsel, advise, or procure the preparation or presentation of a false or fraudulent document; a matter under, or in connection with any material matter arising under the Internal Revenue Laws; and willfulness.

b Generally, income tax returns or partnership information returns are involved but any document required or authorized to be filed can give rise to this offense.

c If two partners are responsible for a false and fraudulent return, they have each committed a criminal offense, but if there is evidence that only one of the partners is responsible then only he/she could be held liable. The choice of 26 USC 7206(l) or 26 USC 7206(2) depends upon whether the responsible partner signed the return or caused the entries that produced the false return.

d The aiding and assisting in the preparation of a false return and the subscribing of a false return are two separate offenses.

e It is sufficient to establish that the defendant willfully and knowingly prepared or caused to be prepared false and fraudulent income tax returns for another although the fraud involved was without the knowledge and consent of the person required to make the return.

- The destruction, mutilation, or concealment of books and records or other evidence creates a presumption that the production of the records or evidence would be unfavorable to the person destroying them. A fabricator of evidence also creates a presumption against himself. It is proper for a court to charge the jury that it may consider the taxpayers refusal to produce his books and records for Internal Revenue inspection, in determining the question of willfulness. *(Louis C. Smith* v. *U.S.; Beard* v. *U.S.; Olson* v. *U.S.; Myres* v. *U.S.)*

Burden of Proof

◀ *Burden of proof* is the obligation of the party alleging the affirmative of an issue to prove it. This burden remains on the government throughout a criminal trial although the burden of going forward with evidence may shift from one side to the other *(Linsasky* v. *U.S.).* The doctrine of judicial notice and the operation of presumptions are aids in carrying the burden of proof and in proceeding with evidence. When the party having the burden of proof has produced sufficient evidence for the jury to return a verdict in favor of such party, a prima facie case has been established. This does not mean that the jury will render such a verdict, but that they could do so from the standpoint of sufficiency of evidence. At this point the defendant has two choices. He may choose to offer no evidence, relying on the court and jury to decide that the government has not overcome the presumption of innocence, or he may offer evidence in his defense. If he wishes to introduce new matters by way of denial, explanation, or contradiction, the burden of going forward with evidence is his, although the prosecution still has the burden of proof with respect to the entire case. The court pointed this out to a jury in the Littlefield case in the following language:

763 *(4-11-80)* 4235
False, Fictitious, or Fraudulent Claims (18 USC 287)

(1) During third party investigations, agents may examine documents submitted to financial institutions, governmental agencies, customers, suppliers, etc. A false document or statement could constitute a criminal violation of a non-IRS violation. Where such a situation is encountered, the matter should be referred in accordance with 442.5 of this Handbook and IRM 4097. However, when the false claim is a refund return, then it is an IRS violation and should be referred to Criminal Investigation in accordance with the established procedures.

(2) The elements of a criminal violation under 18 USC 287 are:

(a) making or presenting a claim upon or against the United States; and

(b) knowledge that the claim is false, fictitious or fraudulent.

(3) Whether the claim is false, fictitious, or fraudulent must be determined in view of all of the facts and circumstances surrounding it and it is not essential that the bill, voucher, or other things used as the basis for the claim should in and of itself contain fraudulent or fictitious statements or entries.

764 *(4-11-80)* 4235
False Statements Generally (18 USC 1001)

In connection with any matter within the jurisdiction of any department or agency of the United States, it is a criminal offense to willfully falsify, conceal or cover up by trick, scheme, or device a material fact or to make any false, fictitious, or fraudulent statements or representations or to make or use any false writing or document knowing the same to contain any false, fictitious or fraudulent statement or entry.

765 *(4-11-80)* 4235
False Invoices

False invoices are sometimes submitted to a business and paid, with the payment eventually being returned to the owner of the business. This scheme requires at least two participants. The invoice can be prepared by either the owner of the business or the third-party accomplice. He/she will either cash the check and return the cash to the owner of the business, or he/she will deposit the check to his/her personal ac-

The burden of proof is not upon the defendant to prove that he did believe that the way in which he computed and returned his income was correct, but the burden is upon the Government to prove beyond a reasonable doubt that the defendant intended to commit a crime and intended willfully to defraud the Government. If you have a reasonable doubt arising from the evidence as to whether or not in computing and returning his income for the years involved here the defendant acted in good faith according to the best of his knowledge and understanding, even though his method of computation might have been entirely wrong, it is your duty to find him not guilty.

◀ *Proof beyond a reasonable doubt* of every element of the crime charged is necessary for a conviction. In charging a jury as to the meaning of reasonable doubt, the judge in *U.S.* v. *Sunderland* stated:

> A reasonable doubt, is a doubt founded upon a consideration of all the evidence and must be based on reason. Beyond a reasonable doubt does not mean to a moral certainty or beyond a mere possible doubt or an imaginary doubt. It is such a doubt as would deter a reasonably prudent man or woman from acting or deciding in the more important matters involved in his or her own affairs. Doubts which are not based upon a reasonable and careful consideration of all the evidence, but are purely imaginary, or born of sympathy alone, should not be considered and should not influence your verdict. It is only necessary that you should have that certainty with which you transact the more important concerns in life. If you have that certainty, then you are convinced beyond a reasonable doubt.
>
> A defendant may not be convicted upon mere suspicion or conjecture. A defendant should be acquitted if the evidence is equally consistent with innocence as with guilt.

count and issue a personal check to the businessman/businesswoman. The result is that the businessman/businesswoman gets a tax deduction on payment of the invoice and also keeps the payments for personal use. Normally, both participants are using the same schemes to take money out of their business and get a tax deduction for it.

766 *(4-11-80)* 4235
Elements of Offense

(1) The term "jurisdiction" means the power to deal with a subject matter and the term "department" includes the United States Treasury Department.

(2) It is not necessary that the statement be required to be made by some regulation or law.

(3) The weight of authority requires proof of materiality in any prosecution under 18 USC 1001.

(4) The violation may involve formal or informal records, forms and instruments, and even oral statements. It is not essential that the statements be under oath, and the perjury corroboration rule does not apply.

(5) Knowledge cannot be imputed to a corporate officer merely because he/she appears to be active in corporate affairs.

(6) The statute is concerned with false statements which might impede the exercise of Federal authority. Pecuniary loss to the Government is not necessary. Any impairment of administration of its governmental functions is sufficient and the commission of the crime is not dependent upon the success of the fraudulent intent.

767 *(4-11-80)* 4235
Specific Examples of False Documents and Statements

(1) A false statement in a tax return (also a violation of 26 USC 7206(1)).

(2) Concealed part ownership of individuals with felony records, whose ownership of liquor establishments may be prohibited by State law, may be designed to avoid State laws. Therefore, when the Bureau of Alcohol, Tobacco and Firearms requires that the actual owners of liquor establishments be listed on applications for Federal liquor tax stamps, the names of racketeer owners are omitted intentionally (26 USC 7206—Aiding and Abetting).

◀ In civil cases the burden of proof ordinarily is on the plaintiff to prove his case, without any presumption against him at the outset. *In tax cases, however, the burden is upon the plaintiff or petitioner (taxpayer) to overcome the presumption of correctness of the Commissioner's determination of the tax deficiency (Avery* v. *Comm.). Rule 32* of the *Rules of Practice,* Tax Court, provides: "The burden of proof shall be upon the petitioner, except as otherwise provided by statute, and except that in respect of any new matter pleaded in his answer, it shall be upon the respondent."

There are four important exceptions to the above rule, namely, fraud cases *(Paddock* v. *U.S.),* where assessment is asserted within the six-year limitation on account of alleged omission of more than 25 percent of gross income stated in the return, other new matters pleaded by the Commissioner, and transferee proceedings.

◀ The Internal Revenue Code provides that the burden of proof is on the Commissioner where fraud is alleged. *IRC 7454* states: "In any proceeding involving the issue whether the petitioner has been guilty of fraud with intent to evade tax, the burden of proof in respect of such issue shall be upon the Secretary or his delegate." As a matter of general law it has always been held that one who alleges fraud must prove it *(Budd* v. *Comm.).*

(3) Deliberate misrepresentation of material facts at administrative hearings by Federal agencies such as SEC.

(4) False representations in a protest to a proposed income tax determination (18 USC 1001).

(5) Submission of a false net worth statement to a Federal Savings and Loan Association (18 USC 1014).

(6) Falsification of FHA application (18 USC 1010).

(7) False statements relative to highway projects under Federal-Aid Road Act (18 USC 1020).

(8) In addition, violations may occur in connection with applications for credit submitted to any agency disbursing Federal funds such as the Home Loan Bank Board or Small Business Administration. Inaccurate financial statements submitted to a commercial bank may also constitute a "false statement."

768 *(4-11-80)* 4235

Investigative Techniques

(1) Fraudulent claims as well as false document situations often require the preparation and back-dating of documents such as a section 1244 stock election.

(2) Practitioner billings should be scrutinized for high typing services at the time the suspected fraudulent claim or document would have been prepared and inquiry made thereof.

(3) Where the agent has reason to believe such documents are false and timing of the document is of the essence, the agent should make every effort to secure the original document for the purpose of a chemical analysis by the Criminal Investigation function. An analysis of the paper (known as paper-dating), ink, and/or typewriter print will disclose when the subject item was available for sale or transfer.

(4) Unsigned copies of documents submitted should be confirmed with originals or at least with signed copies. Likewise, if a part of a document is submitted for substantion it should always be confirmed with the completed document.

(5) It is a good practice to question the taxpayer or his representative if the examination receives a suspected fraudulent document in order to determine:

(a) if the document was screened by the accountant or attorney;

(b) if the document is complete; and,

◂ Where, under *IRC 6501(e),* the Commissioner makes an assessment after the three-year limitation period, but within six years after the return is filed, because of omission of more than 25 percent of the amount of gross income shown in the return, the burden of proving the required omission is on him *(Reis* v. *Comm.).* This is in line with the general rule that one relying on an exception to the statute of limitations must prove the exception *(Wood* v. *Comm.).*

◂ Tax Court *Rule 32* provides that the Commissioner has the burden of proving new matters pleaded by him in answer to the petition. This is an application of the general rule of law regarding evidence which places the burden on the party alleging the fact at issue.

◂ The Commissioner has the burden of proof to establish transferee liability. *IRC 6902* provides: "In proceedings before the Tax Court the burden of proof shall be upon the Secretary or his delegate to show that a petitioner is liable as a transferee of property of a taxpayer, but not to show that the taxpayer was liable for the tax." The original tax deficiency is presumed to be correct and the transferee has the burden of establishing its incorrectness.

◂ The degree of proof required in civil cases is a *preponderance of evidence,* except where fraud is alleged. In the latter case, "clear and convincing evidence" is necessary in order to prevail on the fraud issue *(Rodd* v. *Fahs).*

◂ *Preponderance of evidence* is evidence that will incline an impartial mind to one side rather than the other so as to remove the cause from the realm of speculation. It does not relate merely to the quantity of evidence. In the Wissler case the court's instruction concerning preponderance of evidence was as follows:

(c) who prepared the document and who typed it.

(6) The following are suggested techniques to assist the examining agent in detecting the existence of false invoices.

(a) Look for business checks that have been cashed.

(b) Compare the checks listed on the business bank statements with deposits on the personal bank statements.

(c) Look for unusual payees or endorsements.

(d) Look for any unusual pattern.

(e) Reconcile any debit balance in accounts payable for a particular vendor.

(f) Match selected check register payments to vendor invoices.

(g) Where appropriate, consider third party contacts to determine if the taxpayer's suppliers are making large payments to other parties at the same time they receive payments from the taxpayer. Trace the suppliers payments to their final destination being alert to the possibility that the funds are being returned to the taxpayer either directly or indirectly.

770 *(4-11-80)* 4235
Kickbacks and Payoffs

771 *(4-11-80)* 4235
Introduction

(1) The receipt of income from "kickbacks" can occur in nearly every segment of business, large or small.

(2) The payment of kickbacks can take the form of cash, goods, or services to or for others for some kind of preferential treatment or to influence another party for such treatment.

(3) Because of the difficulty involved in tracing the receipt or payment of kickbacks, it has become a favorite source of revenue to organized crime. Kickbacks can be difficult to trace through records as they could be hidden in a maze of bookkeeping entries and buried in any number of accounts such as cost of sales, sales returns, advertising, repairs, travel and entertainment, loans and exchanges, promotional expenses, miscellaneous expenses or practically any other account. Additional difficulty occurs where the kickbacks do not appear on the books and records of the business at all, e.g., an individual will pay a kickback from his/her personal account or from personal cash on hand. Further, if such a payment is uncovered, there is the additional problem of determining who actu-

> The terms 'preponderance of evidence' and 'greater weight of evidence' as used in these instructions are terms of practically the same meaning, and when it is said that the burden rests upon either party to establish any particular fact or proposition by a preponderance or greater weight of evidence, it is meant that the evidence offered and introduced in support thereof to entitle said party to a verdict, should when fully and fairly considered produce the stronger impression upon the mind and be more convincing when weighed against the evidence introduced in opposition thereto. Such preponderance is not always to be determined by the number of witnesses on the respective sides, although it may be thus determined all other things being equal.

◀ *Clear and convincing evidence* is that which need not be beyond a reasonable doubt as in a criminal case but must be stronger than a mere preponderance of evidence. In the Gladden case the court instructed the jury on this point as follows:

> A mere preponderance of the evidence, meaning merely the greater weight of the evidence, is not sufficient to prove fraud. This does not mean that you must be convinced of fraud beyond a reasonable doubt, because this is not a criminal case. However, an allegation of fraud does require a greater degree of proof than is required in most civil cases, and a mere preponderance of the evidence, while enough to incline the mind of an impartial juror to one side of the issue rather than the other, is not enough to prove fraud. Fraud must be established by evidence which is clear, cogent and convincing.

ally received the payment as the payor will often refuse to identify the payee.

(4) In an attempt to uncover the existence of kickbacks and/or payoffs, the examining agent should determine the applicability of the provisions of Chapter 900 of this handbook.

772 *(4-11-80)* 4235

Income and Deduction Features

(1) In dealing with kickbacks that are discovered, it is generally agreed that:

(a) kickbacks are always taxable to the recipient;

(b) if the name of recipient is not disclosed, no deduction will be allowed to the payor;

(c) kickbacks are not deductible unless they are both ordinary and necessary business expenses.

773 *(4-11-80)* 4235

Examples of Kickback Areas

(1) The following are illustrative of the types of kickback payments, made or received, and schemes that are used in this area of tax abuse.

(a) Loans are arranged for individuals or corporate entities that would otherwise be difficult for them to obtain. These loans are arranged through financial institutions or other third parties. For this "service" a substantial fee would be paid to the individual(s) arranging the loan, c.g. an individual needing a loan of one million dollars would be given a loan for one million one hundred thousand dollars. The additional one hundred thousand dollars would then be paid to the individual, or representative of the individual, who arranged the loan that could not otherwise have been obtained.

(b) Members of organized crime involved with labor unions will receive extorted funds or payoffs for preventing, or not initiating strike action by the members of the union.

(c) Customers or clients are "steered" to business concerns who in turn will pay kickbacks based on the income received from these customers (popularly called "finders fees").

(d) Business entities owned or operated by members of organized crime will make large purchases which are paid for by check and covered by a bill for the full amount. The supplier would then be required to kickback, in cash, a certain percentage of the payment.

Hearsay (Federal Rules of Evidence Article VIII)

◀ *A statement* is an oral or written assertion or nonverbal conduct of a person, if it is intended by a person as an assertion [*Rule 801(a)*]. Hearsay statements are inadmissible at trial unless an exception is applicable *(Rule 802)*. Lack of opportunity for cross-examination and unreliability are the principal reasons for excluding hearsay testimony.

◀ *Hearsay* is a statement, other than one made by the declarant while testifying at the trial or hearing, offered in evidence to prove the truth of the matter asserted [*Rule 801(c)*]. Evidence that does not come from the personal knowledge of the declarant but from the repetition of what the declarant has heard others say is hearsay. For example, testimony of a special agent that third parties made statements to the agent that checks written by a taxpayer were personal in nature is hearsay and inadmissible. The personal nature of the checks would be proved through the taxpayer's admissions and records, and testimony and records of the third parties.

◀ The following statements are *not* hearsay under the provisions of *Rule 801(d):*

(1) Prior statement by witness. The declarant testifies at the trial or hearing and is subject to cross-examination concerning the statement, and the statement is (A) inconsistent with his testimony, and was given under oath subject to the penalty of perjury at a trial, hearing, or other proceeding, or in a deposition, or (B) consistent with his testimony and is offered to rebut an express or implied charge against him of recent fabrication or improper influence or motive [this could also include identification of a person made after perceiving him], or

(e) The contract price for the acquisition of property could be overstated in a scheme whereby part of the purchase price is kicked back to the purchaser and the money used to set up a slush fund. The contractor/seller will refund the money as a reduction of sales price and the funds are diverted into a slush fund account or to the personal benefit of the purchaser. The examining agent should consider employing the following techniques to detect these transactions.

1 Examine contracts for changes in acquisition price without corresponding changes in contract plans, i.e, excessive purchase price.

2 Examine correspondence between the parties to the contract for indications of diversion of funds.

3 Examine add on costs, such as legal fees, consultant fees, settlement fees, and finders fees to determine the reasonableness of expenditures.

4 When examining contractors, test refunds or reduction of contract price for correctness. Examine refund cancelled checks for areas of deposit by the purchaser. Prepare information reports on the purchaser for unusual or large refunds by the contractor.

(2) These examples are illustrative only and investigation should not be restricted to these areas of business activities.

774 *(4-11-80)* 4235
Investigative Techniques

(1) The audit techniques to be used in identifying income received from kickbacks depends on whether the records being examined are those of the one alleged to be paying the kickback, or receiving it.

(a) Where the records are those of the one alleged to be paying the kickback, the following audit techniques and trails should be considered.

1 If an employer does not remit the applicable union dues and welfare payments for all his/her employees, it may be an indication that these monies are given in cash to union officers to insure labor peace. This could possibly be

(2) Admission by party-opponent. The statement is offered against a party and is (A) his own statement, in either his individual or a representative capacity, or (B) a statement of which he has manifested his adoption or belief in its truth, or (C) a statement by a person authorized by him to make a statement concerning the subject, or (D) a statement by his agent or servant concerning a matter within the scope of his agency or employment, made during the existence of the relationship, or (E) a statement by a coconspirator [sic] of a party during the course and in furtherance of the conspiracy.

◀ *Rule 801(d)(1)(A)* provides that when a witness testifies at a trial or hearing and is subject to cross-examination concerning a prior statement inconsistent with the witness' present testimony, the prior statement may be admitted for its truth if the witness made it under oath in a previous proceeding (excluding grand jury) or deposition. A proceeding is a formal evidentiary hearing where the witness/declarant is subject to cross-examination. Testimony taken by a special agent in an affidavit or question and answer statement does not qualify.

◀ Admissions of a party-opponent (e.g., taxpayer) which are offered against the party are not hearsay [*Rule 801(d)(2)*]. The admissions include statements:

- Made of the party; or
- Shown to have been adopted or believed by the party (adoptive/implied admission); or
- Made by a person authorized by the party to make a statement concerning the subject of the statement; or
- Made by an agent or servant of the party concerning a matter within the scope of the agency/employment, and made during the existence of the relationship; or
- Made by a coconspirator during the course and in furtherance of a conspiracy.

detected by determining the amount required to be paid to the union for each individual employee, computing what it would be for all employees, and matching this figure to the actual amount paid by the employer. Any discrepancy should then be further pursued to determine why there is a difference.

2 Loans made by a corporation, unsecured and interest free, should be scrutinized as to the name of the recipients and business purpose or reasons why such loans were made. Further investigation should be considered to determine if the named recipient might have only been a "middleman" with the proceeds then going to a third party or if the named recipient might have returned the loan in cash and the funds then given as a kickback or payoff.

3 Payments made to individuals or concerns allegedly for consulting fees or commissions should be traced to their final disposition as these could be, in reality, a source of kickback or payoff. As a side point it is interesting to observe how not only does organized crime infiltrate legitimate business or control labor unions but they will also act as a "middleman," on a consulting fee or commission basis, to insure labor peace.

4 All other accounts should be scrutinized for payments being made to possible suspect third parties who may be serving as a conduit for the actual recipient of kickbacks.

(b) Where the taxpayer being examined is the alleged or potential receiver of kickback payments:

1 Careful scrutiny should be made of his/her, and his/her immediate relatives' checking and savings accounts for any possible unexplained deposits. Investment accounts should also be closely analyzed for such remittances.

2 Loans received by a corporation from an outside party should be scrutinized as to its source and disposition.

3 An analysis of the sales account and related documentation may reveal income from sales for which there is no record of merchandise being shipped.

◀ *Rules 803 and 804* specify certain exceptions to the hearsay rule. The exceptions are based on the theory that under appropriate circumstances a hearsay statement is of the type that makes its trustworthiness and truthfulness highly probable and the statement is necessary to prove the fact alleged. In these instances the statements can be introduced by other than the declarant even though the declarant is available to testify. Examples:

- *Rule 803(2), Excited utterance.* "A statement relating to a startling event or condition made while the declarant was under the stress of excitement caused by the event or condition."

  This exception refers to spontaneous declarations and acts committed during the event. The trustworthiness of such statements lies in their spontaneity, for the occurrence must be startling enough to produce a spontaneous and unreflective utterance without time to contrive or misrepresent. Once the excitement passes, statements made are not within this exception. They may be made by participants or bystanders, and a person who made or heard such statements may testify about them in court. The trial judge has wide discretion in deciding the admissibility of unsworn statements. The circumstances involved in a raid on a bookmaking establishment may be used to illustrate the application of this rule. One of the persons in the establishment, upon seeing the raiding officers enter the room says: "Burn the betting slips!" Even though the speaker is never identified and is not available as a witness, an agent who heard the statement may be permitted to testify about it in a trial of John Doe, to prove that betting slips existed.

(2) As can be seen from the above illustrations, the payment or receipt of kickbacks can be hidden very easily, or even not reflected at all, in any books or records. The important thing to remember is that in planning the scope of the examination careful thought should be given to the possibility of kickback payments or receipts. Are kickbacks a practice in the industry? What "angle" or facet of that particular business or industry would lend itself to having to make kickback payments? Once the possible areas are realized then the audit process can be done. The evidencing of kickback payments or receipts requires detailed and imaginative investigation. The audit techniques and examples illustrated above are just a few that can be used in this area.

780 *(4-11-80)* 4235
Payments To or For Public Officials

781 *(4-11-80)* 4235
Introduction

Corruption of public officials has long been a necessary prerequisite to the successful operation of organized criminal activities. It is frequently found in the area of public works and contracting. Over the years such payments have assumed many guises. The suitcase full of cash has now given way to more sophisticated methods. The methods used today will vary to meet the specific circumstances of the individuals who can, or will, be corrupted.

782 *(4-11-80)* 4235
Types of Payments

Payments to public officials will take varied shapes. Public officials involved in the investigative or lower level management strata may receive an offer of cash in hand. Higher level public officials might also be approached with promises of further promotion or higher appointed offices. Elected public officials could be approached through the offer of large political contributions, large blocks of votes at election time or even, for the minor elective official, the offer of loudspeaker sound trucks to broadcast his/her message in the local streets.

783 *(4-11-80)* 4235
Examples of Payments

(1) The above types of payments can be illustrated by the following:

- *Rule 803(5), Recorded recollection.* "A memorandum or record concerning a matter about which a witness once had knowledge but now has insufficient recollection to enable him to testify fully and accurately, shown to have been made or adopted by the witness when the matter was fresh in his memory and to reflect that knowledge correctly. If admitted, the memorandum or record may be read into evidence but may not itself be received as an exhibit unless offered by an adverse party."

  Example: A special agent has taken a question and answer statement from a witness. At trial, the witness no longer recollects the facts in the statement. Even if the witness has not initialed the pages and/or signed the statement, the facts of the statement could be read at trial as a record adopted by the witness. In the case of an unsigned affidavit, if it can be shown that the witness indicated that the facts recorded were true, the facts of the unsigned affidavit could be read as a statement adopted by the witness. Similarly, if a witness had in some way indicated the adoption of a memorandum prepared by a special agent, the memorandum could be read as evidence.

- *Rule 803(6), Records of regularly conducted activity.* "A memorandum, report, record, or data compilation, in any form, of acts, events, conditions, opinions, or diagnoses, made at or near the time by, or from information transmitted by, a person with knowledge, if kept in the course of a regularly conducted business activity, and if it was the regular practice of that business activity to make the memorandum, report, record, or data compilation, all as shown by the testimony of the custodian or other qualified witness, unless the source of information or the method or circumstances of preparation indicate lack of trustworthiness."

a) Taxpayers were high ranking elected state officials instrumental in granting state banking charters. When a charter was granted, the bank directors contacted the officials with a proposition to sell the stock in the bank with the bank carrying a note of the officials large enough to purchase the stock. After one year and one day had lapsed, the bank directors repurchased the stock from the state officials at twice the original cost, taxable as a long term capital gain. From the proceeds of the sale, the officials paid the bank note used to finance the stock purchase.

b) Taxpayer was a friend of an elected U.S. official. Taxpayer leased farm land from the official at a fixed amount per year. The farm land leased was never titled, farmed, or used by taxpayer in any way. The U.S. official intervened on occasion for taxpayer in his dealings with government agencies.

c) Taxpayer was a benefactor and personal friend of a national politician. The politician invested in capital stock of a newly formed corporation in taxpayer's home state which was far removed from his own home state. The newly formed corporation entered into several lucrative contracts with companies owned or controlled by taxpayer. After three month's operations, the newly formed corporation had generated a substantial net profit. At this time, taxpayer and his associates purchased all of the stock owned by the politician. The politician reported the sale as a short term capital gain and offset a capital loss carryover from prior years.

d) Taxpayer corporation was in the public relations and advertising business. Taxpayer contracted with a state politician to handle the public relations and advertising campaign for a statewide election. After several months campaign, the corporation had an account receivable on its books from the politician's campaign committee and the politician was defeated in the primary election. The receivable was not paid and after a few months, taxpayer corporation wrote off the receivable, thereby making an illegal corporate political contribution.

784 *(4-11-80)* 4235

Methods of Payment

(1) Some methods employed to channel currency to public officials are presented below. They are by no means new methods nor do they represent more than a small fraction of meth-

This rule permits showing that an entry was made in a business record maintained in the ordinary course of business without producing the person who made the entry. Where there is an indication that the particular record lacks trustworthiness, this rule does not apply. The rule covers data compilations whether stored in a computer or elsewhere.

- *Rule 803(21), Reputation as to character.* "Reputation of a person's character among his associates or in the community."

- *Rule 803(22), Judgment of previous conviction.* "Evidence of a final judgment, entered after a trial or upon a plea of guilty (but not upon a plea of *nolo contendere*), adjudging a person guilty of a crime punishable by death or imprisonment in excess of one year, to prove any fact essential to sustain the judgment, but not including, when offered by the Government in a criminal prosecution for purposes other than impeachment, judgments against persons other than the accused. The pendency of an appeal may be shown but does not affect admissibility."

ods employed, but are pointed out here to emphasize the need for imaginative investigative techniques to uncover instances of corruption of public officials.

(a) Exchange of funds through a legitimate business—A firm controlled by a member of organized crime pays a large sum of money to an unrelated corporation in return for fictitious invoices for alleged consulting fees. That corporation in turn makes checks payable to one of its corporate officers who then cashes the checks with the aid of a bank official. The cash is returned to the first corporation's officers.

(b) Transfer of funds through a spurious business—A bank account is opened in a fictitious name as a conduit for converting checks to cash. Invoices printed in the fictitious business name are prepared as evidence of purchases. Checks issued to the fictitious business are deposited, and then currency withdrawn.

(c) Payment of campaign expenses—One example of making indirect political contributions is where the campaign committee or candidate provides an unpaid bill for some campaign expense, such as for the hiring of sound trucks or for the printing of handbills, posters, etc.

(d) Indirect payments to public officials—One method of indirect payments to public officials has been found to be by way of making payments to a law firm In this instance, the lawyer acts merely as a conduit to which checks are issued for ostensible legal services rendered. The payments are deposited to the lawyer's trust accounts and disbursements made from those accounts to the public official. This method is also used through public relations, advertising, or accounting firms.

(2) The audit techniques to be employed in this area are substantially the same as those suggested for the investigation of kickbacks. In this instance, the books and records being examined will more than likely be those of the one making the payment to the public official. Careful scrutinization will have to be made of the various accounts to ascertain the validity of the individual expenses. Consider what specific items might lend themselves to subterfuge. Are there really services being performed for certain payments; and, if so, are the services commensurate with the payments being made for them? What is important to remember is that disbursements are not always what they seem to be. Good investigation calls for more through follow-up to determine if the disbursement is a valid one and not just a mere conduit or means through which cash can be filtered through with the ultimate payee being a public official.

(3) Political contributions by corporations—Since it is illegal for corporations to make contributions to federal campaigns, several methods have been devised to conceal the contributions. The following section describes some of the most common methods employed.

a) Corporate Officers' Salaries—under this method of operation an officer of the corporation will get a bonus or an increase in salary and will contribute this bonus or salary increase to a political party or campaign. The examining agent should review corporate minutes to determine if large bonuses or salary increases have been authorized, and if in fact they are justified. Additionally, consideration should be given to the examination of selected corporate officers individual tax returns.

b) Advertising Agencies—corporations frequently make contributions through advertising agencies and take a deduction for advertising costs. This can be accomplished by paying the firm a retainer to be used for the contribution or through payment of invoices for work not performed.

c) Disguised Political Contributions—disguised political contributions can occur in the following manner:

1) The item or service is furnished directly to the candidate or campaign and charged off as a business expense. This type of item can usually be recognized as being out of context with the remainder of the taxpayer's expenses or the product or service is described in such detail that an examiner would inspect the item carefully;

2) The item or service is not *directly* furnished the politician but is billed direct to the taxpayer by the providing third party, or indirectly by another party with whom taxpayer usually does business. These items are usually found in accounts such as Advertising and Rents. This is the most difficult to identify since there will be no lack of context or other description of services or goods to alert the examiner. The only way to "identify" such items is to check with the billing party and ascertain if the billed items are bona fide expenses. The examiner's alertness in ascertaining if the charges are reasonable or if they might lend themselves to political use appear to be the only "flag" on the taxpayer's records.

d) Professional Services—all source documents behind amounts charged to Professional Services should be examined carefully for adequacy of description and explanations of services performed as well as any unusual increases. It has been determined that many firms simply "loaded" fees relative to projects and specific cases over and above the amount the normal billing would have been for the actual work performed. This excess billing was used to recover prearranged political payments by the firms on behalf of the taxpayer.

e) Travel and Entertainment Expenses—examination of expense accounts has disclosed that illegal payments may be deducted under the guise of travel and entertainment. Employee expense accounts and correspondence were used to develop an itinerary of selected employees. Correspondence, as well as Board of Directors' expense vouchers, were carefully examined to determine political events, functions, and travel to make political contributions. All the above sources were used to identify a date, time, and place that the taxpayer was involved in illegal political activity. All travel expense connected with each particular event was picked out from source documents supplied by the taxpayer. The following categories were the prime source of the adjustments.

1) Executive travel expense

2) Charter air travel—whether by the taxpayer's employees or paid directly for travel by a political candidate.

3) Expenses of pilots of taxpayer's private aircraft.

4) Expenses of various selected employees including direct credit card charges.

Index